PRAISE FOR *October S*

"*October Song* is wonderful—a vivid account of the Revolution, moving beyond the merely defensive to thoughtful consideration of not only external challenges but also internal problems among the revolutionaries, critical-minded yet at the same time deeply sympathetic."

—China Miéville, author of *October*

"*October Song* is an important and timely contribution at a moment when large numbers of young people are turning to socialist politics and beginning to grapple with the lessons of the Russian Revolution. Combining a sharp analytical focus with illuminating anecdotes from political practice and daily life, Le Blanc provides a sweeping and engaging account of the revolution, the Bolsheviks, and their strengths and weaknesses. For all those seeking to make sense of this inspiring but ultimately tragic history, *October Song* is an essential read."

—Eric Blanc, author of *Anti-Colonial Marxism:*
Oppression & Revolution in the Tsarist Borderlands

"*October Song* provides an essential primer on the major debates engendered by the Russian revolution. Drawing on the rich intellectual legacy of revolutionaries, eyewitnesses, historians, and theoreticians, the book is a must-read for any activist seeking to understand the heady promises and unanticipated pitfalls of revolutionary change. Analyzing the internal splits and social forces that ultimately defeated the revolutionary-democratic vision, *October Song* offers important lessons for everyone committed to social change today."

—Wendy Z. Goldman, Paul Mellon Distinguished Professor
of History, Carnegie Mellon University

"Excellent in every respect . . . the writing is extraordinarily clear and interesting and the coverage of different interpretations is fair and thoughtful. . . . The use of the commentary by early participants and witnesses of these years makes the text original in many ways. . . . A strikingly effective synthesis of various sources provides a 'richness' that I regard as really extraordinary."

—Jonathan Harris, professor of political science, University of Pittsburgh

"*October Song* provides a gripping retelling of the Russian Revolution, in which long-disputed issues receive close analysis and fresh but balanced judgments. The narrative is enlivened by nuggets from the full range of English-language testimony and historiography. A special bonus: close attention to the much-neglected peasant experience."

— John Riddell, editor of *To the Masses* and *Toward the United Front*

October Song

BOLSHEVIK TRIUMPH, COMMUNIST TRAGEDY, 1917–1924

Paul Le Blanc

Haymarket Books
Chicago, Illinois

Published in 2017 by
Haymarket Books
P.O. Box 180165
Chicago, IL 60618
773-583-7884
www.haymarketbooks.org
info@haymarketbooks.org

ISBN: 978-1-60846-848-5

Trade distribution:
In the US, Consortium Book Sales and Distribution, www.cbsd.com
In Canada, Publishers Group Canada, www.pgcbooks.ca
In the UK, Turnaround Publisher Services, www.turnaround-uk.com
All other countries, Ingram Publisher Services International, IPS_Intlsales@
ingramcontent.com

Cover design by Rachel Cohen. Cover image of *The Bolshevik* by Boris Kustodiev, 1920.

This book was published with the generous support of Lannan Foundation and Wallace Action Fund.

Printed in Canada by union labor.

Library of Congress Cataloging-in-Publication data is available.

10 9 8 7 6 5 4 3 2 1

To the memory of my son
Gabriel Seth Le Blanc
(1971–2016)

CONTENTS

PREFACE

*F*reedom, creative labor, and genuine community for each and every person—the free development of each as the condition for the free development of all, and rule by the people, to the extent possible, over the institutions, activities, and conditions that shape our lives—such are the elements of the socialist or communist society envisioned by Karl Marx and his closest comrades (who included his beloved life-companion, Jenny Marx, and his best friend, Frederick Engels).[1] I have embraced these ideas for most of my life, as well as the belief that we must, as did Marx, use the social sciences to understand the world, while at the same time supporting struggles against oppression and exploitation, struggles waged by humanity's laboring majorities down through the centuries, in present times, and into the future.

The How and Why of This Book

What I said above animated my doctoral dissertation in history of the late 1980s, from which the present book is derived. The dissertation was a comparative analysis of the Russian and Nicaraguan revolutions, examining the conditions leading up to them, the dynamics of the revolutionary overturn, and the early years of struggle and consolidation after each.[2] I have recently summarized and updated what I have to say on Nicaragua's revolution in an essay that is included in a collection of my writings entitled *Revolutionary Studies.*[3]

In preparation for the one hundredth anniversary of the Russian Revolution, however, I have further developed the Russian piece. In the dissertation and in a book written and published at roughly the same time—*Lenin and the Revolutionary Party*—I offered a positive interpretation of Bolshevik theory and practice. There was, at the same time, a critical approach toward this tradition in the book and even more in the dissertation, but this was articulated *within* the broad framework of the tradition itself. What is offered in this revised and updated account is no less critical, but it contrasts with other works advancing criticisms from the standpoint of contempt, hostility, or disillusionment. Even some who disagree with this different slant may find in what is offered here a useful challenge within the realm of scholarship on revolutionary Russia.

At the same time, my hope is that activists who want to confront and overcome the crises of global capitalism facing us today can benefit from positive but also critical-minded engagement with the Bolshevik tradition. We cannot afford to be dismissive of our diverse and vibrant comrades who were part of the Bolshevik experience—we must take them seriously and learn what we can from them, even those with whom, on one or another extremely important issue, we disagree. (Just as many of them disagreed with each other.)

What Is in This Book

This book is an attempt at synthesis as much as a product of research. It is marked by a strong inclination to privilege older things—earlier sources, earlier expressions of opinion, which may seem decades or more past their "shelf date," superseded by newer and more fashionable commodities. But sometimes the newer stuff is not much different from (and when different, sometimes isn't much better than) things offered earlier. Perhaps the fact that I am old is related to this preference for what is older, but there it is. And, of course, far from being a finished product, what is offered here is part of an individual and collective interpretive process.

The subtitle of the book merits at least brief comment. The term *Bolshevik* existed in the Russian revolutionary movement from 1903 onward; it means "member of the majority" because at least for certain moments in the history of the Russian Social Democratic Labor Party (RSDLP), those so named represented a majority faction within that organization. It was seen as an extreme revolutionary wing of the RSDLP. From 1912 onward it constituted itself as an independent party, sometimes tagged "RSDLP (bolsheviks)" up until 1918. It then changed its name to "Russian Communist Party (bolsheviks)." In one respect, the Bolshevik Party and the Communist Party were basically the same group with different names, but there is also a deeper difference. The former was the party that made the October Revolution, while the latter was the party in power after the 1917 revolution. I don't believe "all power corrupts"—although a tragic corruption of the original revolutionary triumph did take place—but one purpose here is to understand what happened, both 1917 triumph and post-1917 tragedy.

The initial chapter in this book is partly celebratory and partly a survey of previous accounts and interpretations—slightly revised from an introduction to a recent and splendid set of texts produced by Ernest Mandel, David Mandel, and others, under the title *October 1917*.[4] The second chapter deals with the destabilizing and crisis-ridden blend of capitalism and tsarism, giving substantial attention to the two laboring classes that made up the majority of the people whose struggles would culminate in revolutionary upsurge: the vast Russian peasantry and the small but incredibly dynamic working class that was being generated by industrial capitalism.

The third chapter highlights the Bolshevik triumph—the ascendancy of Lenin's organization within the cluster of revolutionary organizations that together provided the activist cutting edge of mass struggles and insurgencies culminating in the destruction of the old regime. Chapters 4 and 5 survey the early years of the revolutionary transition, during which Communist activists as well as the proletarian and peasant masses, each in their own ways, struggled to survive and improve their lives within the shifting realities of soviet democracy and bureaucratization: post-1917 mixed economy, followed by "war communism," which gave way to a New Economic Policy—all unfolding amid imperialist intervention, brutalizing civil war, and hopeful revolutionary internationalism. Chapter 6 focuses on how the initial revolutionary ideals were overwhelmed by violence and authoritarianism, with the Bolsheviks losing their balance in a manner carrying them some distance from their initial goals. Contradictions in the Bolshevik understanding of, and policies involving, the majority of the Russian people, the peasantry, constitutes the seventh chapter's focal point. The eighth chapter gives attention to the contradictory mix of positives and negatives in the early Soviet Republic. The consolidation of the new regime is the focus of the ninth chapter, followed by a final chapter of reflections and conclusions.

There is an appendix on the analytical tools that structure our critical explorations drawn from (1) challenges of the group that can be termed "post-Marxists," (2) reflections on the meaning of democracy, and (3) an historical materialist approach involving "uneven and combined development."

What Is Distinctive in This Book

This book presents "objective" realities and at the same time gives a sense of the "subjective" mixture of personalities, hopes, ideas, and experiences of people actually involved in the history we are looking at—as do other accounts. It is hardly the only book demonstrating that the Russian Revolution of 1917 led by Lenin and his comrades was profoundly democratic in its intent, its aspirations, and its potential. Nor is it the only book stressing the democratic qualities of the actual revolutionary process and of the Bolshevik Party that sought to advance the process. Still, a sustained concern with democracy defines much of this book. Democracy—rule by the people—is central to the actuality of socialism, as I understand it, as well as to what is inspiring about the Russian Revolution. The "Defining Democracy" section of the appendix identifies perspectives and concerns that permeate this entire study.

The insistence over the revolution's democratic qualities is linked to three distinctive aspects of what this book does: it (1) focuses on continuities between the events of 1917 and some of what can be found in the "interregnum" of the early 1920s; (2) focuses on qualities of the "mixed economy" experience of late 1917 and early 1918, which was repeated more substantially from 1921 to 1928; and (3) stresses the centrality of the revolutionary internationalist orientation and efforts of the revolutionaries. A failure to give sufficient attention to these aspects, in my opinion, undermines our ability to understand the revolutionary-democratic qualities of what Lenin and his comrades were actually trying to do.

The revolutionary-democratic triumph was overcome by tragic defeat, and this book labors to understand how and why this happened. Historically, some of the revolution's partisans denied that there was any such defeat— they defended the perspectives and practices of the Stalin regime of 1929–53 as being consistent with the intentions and aspirations of the revolutionaries of 1917. (Many critics have done the same—putting minus signs where the partisans put plus signs.)

Among the revolution's more critical-minded partisans, the explanatory focus of why things turned out badly has been on a number of external factors (primarily, assaults and hostility on the part of foreign capitalist powers, and the heritage of backwardness bequeathed by the tsarist system) that blocked, defeated, and overwhelmed the revolutionaries. In this book, attention is given to those external factors. But there is also a need to explore significant internal factors in the theories of the revolutionaries and in the insurgent masses they inspired, and of whom they were a part. Throughout, divergent and contradictory elements can be found. Within the very same element we find a dynamic, if unstable, "unity of opposites." Within insightful perspectives of the revolutionaries we can identify serious blind spots, and within the diverse psychologies and personalities among the masses we can find the bad and the ugly as well as the good.

There are several defining points in the narrative unfolding in these pages. One is the truism that people make their own history but that they do not make it under circumstances of their own choosing—their actions are conditioned, their thoughts are influenced, and the possibilities of what they can and cannot do are limited by the material realities, especially the economic dynamics, in which they are enmeshed. Another defining point is that socio-economic classes, whose "members" do all of the things that make history, encompass multiple dimensions and layers. These include politically more conscious and active layers (sometimes referred to as "vanguard" layers), and organizations rooted in such vanguard layers can make a difference in what happens and fails to happen.

Based on such generalizations, an examination of the Bolshevik organization—an essential and genuinely working-class element in the 1917 revolution and its aftermath—reveals that this was a force animated by radical-democratic aspirations and dynamics, a force with genuine strengths, but also a force that was afflicted with four serious limitations:

1) a failure (perhaps inevitable) to fully anticipate how overwhelming and violent would be the difficulties and hostile forces with which they were forced to contend;

2) a blind spot regarding the dangers of authoritarian "expedients" in dealing with such difficulties and hostile forces;

3) a failure to anticipate the potential of bureaucratic degeneration arising from within their own movement; and

4) a problematical understanding of Russia's peasant majority that would undermine the democratic and revolutionary orientation that had historically been central to their movement.

I advanced all of these points in my 1989 dissertation, but I expand and deepen them here.

The revolutionary regime that consolidated itself in the period following 1917 was increasingly pushed from a radical-democratic to a radical-authoritarian trajectory by the interplay of these internal limitations with the three objective difficulties regularly cited by partisans of the Bolshevik revolution: (1) foreign powers launched military interventions, funding and encouraging a brutal civil war, and attempting to strangle revolutionary Russia with an economic blockade; (2) the aftereffects of World War I, combined with Bolshevik inexperience, had a devastating impact on Russia's economy; and (3) the failure of working-class socialist revolutions in other countries resulted in the isolation of the Bolshevik regime in a hostile capitalist world.

There is much to be learned from the mistakes of the Bolsheviks who embarked on the revolutionary course with such profound insights and worthy intentions. The mistakes can be explained, but some of them assumed destructive forms with inhumane consequences that cannot be defended. And yet, as indicated by the poem "October Song" by my friend Dan Georgakas, the negatives do not invalidate the amazing triumph of 1917. To set aside the revolutionary understanding and revolutionary goals associated with those who made the Bolshevik revolution undermines the possibility of dealing effectively with the crises, oppression, and violence of global capitalism in our own time.

History, Self, Meaning

The late Marshall Berman once characterized Edmund Wilson's *To the Finland Station*—a sweeping account of the crystallizations of socialism, Marxism, and the Russian Revolution—as similar to Tolstoy's *War and Peace*, commenting that "it is equally at home in the philosopher's study, in the prisoner's cell, on the steppes, in the streets, melancholy in great country houses, choking in the fetid industrial slums," presenting "an inexhaustible cast of brilliant, exciting, driven, beautiful, heroic, demonic people, . . . not only great figures, but minor characters as well—dozens of them, wives and children, friends, enemies, lovers, rivals—nearly every one a real individual, drawn with exquisite sensitivity and care."[5]

At the conclusion of Wilson's amazingly panoramic "study in the writing and acting of History," he sees Lenin at the Finland Station in 1917—arriving by train in revolutionary Petrograd—as representing something new: "Western man at this moment can be seen to have made some definite progress in mastering the greeds and the fears, the bewilderments, in which he has lived." The immense creative effort in which the writer had been inspired to engage in the tumultuous and insurgent 1930s soon gave way to bitter disappointments, and as Berman has noted, Wilson "felt a great surge of anger toward the people he most loves, all the passionate, complex, radiant, tragic people who fill his book."[6]

Yet the tragedies cannot be allowed to obliterate the triumphs. Three decades after the publication of Wilson's masterpiece, Berman mused that a central problem of our own time is "to believe that by simply ignoring history we can conjure away its power to shape and define what we do and who we are." He aptly tags the time when the twentieth century was making way for the twenty-first as "an age of historical amnesia," but he insists this "history is alive and open and rich with excitement and promise." He concludes: "It can help us learn to create ourselves."[7]

◆

I have many debts to the scholars, activists, and dear friends who have deepened my understanding and sustained me in multiple ways. There are too many to list here, but regarding this specific volume I would like to thank Tom Twiss, Alex Rabinowitch, and Kevin Murphy for substantial conversations that helped spur me on, and I would especially like to thank Sebastian Budgen, Alexei Gusev, Jonathan Harris, Lars Lih, China Miéville, Tom Twiss, and Eric Blanc for providing helpful feedback as I labored to complete this book. Naturally, I alone bear responsibility for lingering limitations. Thanks must also be extended to the dedicated comrades associated with Haymarket Books who made possible the miraculous transition from manuscript to actual book (with special mention due to the thoughtful and astonishingly thorough copy editor Brian Baughan). And as has been true for more than a decade, the supportive and loving friendship of Nancy Ferrari has helped sustain me in all that I do.

◆

As I was working on this book, my son Gabriel died, not only forcing me to deal with the upside-down agony of losing this beloved, conflicted, wondrous man who was my child, but also to sort through what had happened and why. Elements of that process—comprehending both his triumph and his tragedy—have worked their way into some of what I have written here. I dedicate this book to his memory.

OCTOBER SONG

They who never ruled before
        poured from their factory districts
        across the bridges of Petrograd
to make October.
The moon was so startled
                . all global tides
        shifted.
The lights went on all over Europe.
                Nothing
        can ever be the same.

—Dan Georgakas

1

NOTHING CAN EVER
BE THE SAME

*A*n arduous voyage in 1917 brought four close friends, idealistic
young journalists from the United States, to the shores of Russia.
In the midst of an immensely destructive world war, the centuries-old tyranny of monarchist autocracy had been overthrown. The revolutionary process
was continuing, and the four wanted to understand what was going on.

The revolution began with International Women's Day rallies on March 8
(February 23 according to the old tsarist calendar) that got out of hand. They
sparked momentous insurgencies among the common working people of Petrograd, with the military's rank and file refusing to repress the people's uprising
and instead joining it. Masses of workers and soldiers (the latter mostly peasants
in uniform) organized a growing and increasingly substantial network of democratic councils—the Russian word was *soviety* (or *soviets*)—to coordinate their
efforts. In addition to liberty (indicated by freedom of speech and organization,
equal rights for all, the right of workers to form trade unions, and so forth),
they demanded peace and bread as well as land for the country's impoverished
peasant majority. In the wake of the monarchy's sudden collapse, conservative,
liberal, and moderate socialist politicians scurried to form a provisional government that would contain the revolutionary process and consider how "best"
to address the demands for peace, bread, land. The most militant faction of the
Russian socialist movement—the Bolsheviks (majority-ites) led by Vladimir

1

Ilyich Lenin—insisted that peace, bread, and land would only be achieved by overthrowing the provisional government and giving all political power to the soviets. This, they believed, would spark a world process of workers' revolutions that would end war and imperialism, overturning all tyrannies and bringing a transition from capitalism to socialism. After several months of intensive activity and experience, the Bolsheviks and their allies won majorities in the soviets and went on to make the second revolution of 1917—a popularly supported insurrection on November 7 (October 25 according to the old calendar).

One of the eyewitnesses, John Reed, cabled the news back to the United States: "The rank and file of the Workmen's, Soldiers' and Peasants' Councils are in control, with Lenin and Trotsky leading. Their program is to give the land to the peasants, to socialize natural resources and industry and for an armistice and democratic peace conference. . . . No one is with the Bolsheviki except the proletariat, but that is solidly with them. All the bourgeoisie and appendages are relentlessly hostile."[1]

The first of the four friends to get their books out (in October 1918) were Louise Bryant and Bessie Beatty. After ten decades, the freshness of their astute observations and vibrant impressions continues to reward the reader.

With *Six Months in Red Russia*, Louise Bryant is visibly wrestling toward an understanding of the vast and complex swirl of experience. "I who saw the dawn of a new world can only present my fragmentary and scattered evidence to you with a good deal of awe," she tells us. "I feel as one who went forth to gather pebbles and found pearls." Reaching for generalization, she writes: "The great war could not leave an unchanged world in its wake—certain movements of society were bound to be pushed forward, others retarded. . . . Socialism is here, whether we like it or not—just as woman suffrage is here, and it spreads with the years. In Russia the socialist state is an accomplished fact."[2]

"Revolution is the blind protest of the mass against their own ignorant state," writes her friend Bessie Beatty in *The Red Heart of Russia*. "It is as important to Time as the first awkward struggle of the amoeba. It is man in the act of making himself." Obviously still trying to comprehend what she had seen, she muses: "Time will give to the world war, the political revolution, and the social revolution their true values. We cannot do it. We are too close to the facts to see the truth." But she immediately adds: "To have failed to see the hope in the Russian Revolution is to be a blind man looking at the sun rise."[3]

The last of the books to appear (in 1921), Albert Rhys Williams's *Through the Russian Revolution*, reaches for the interplay of cause and effect, of objective and subjective factors:

It was not the revolutionists who made the Russian Revolution.... For a century gifted men and women of Russia had been agitated over the cruel oppression of the people. So they became agitators.... But the people did not rise.... Then came the supreme agitator—Hunger. Hunger, rising out of economic collapse and war, goaded the sluggish masses into action. Moving out against the old worm-eaten structure they brought it down.... The revolutionists, however, had their part. They did not make the Revolution. But they made the Revolution a success. By their efforts they had prepared a body of men and women with minds trained to see facts, with a program to fit the facts and with fighting energy to drive it thru.[4]

The "middle" book of the four—appearing on January 1919—was the one destined to become the classic eyewitness account, John Reed's magnificent *Ten Days That Shook the World*. A fierce partisan of the Bolsheviks, he quickly joined the world Communist movement that the Bolsheviks established in the same year that his book was published. But no one of any political persuasion can disagree with the generalization that appears in the book's preface: "No matter what one thinks of Bolshevism, it is undeniable that the Russian Revolution is one of the great events of human history, and the rise of the Bolsheviki a phenomenon of worldwide importance."[5]

In more than one sense, these friends continue to reach out to us. Of course, they offer their own lived experience and eyewitness impressions of what happened in one of the great events in human history. But also, while they and all they knew have long since died, the patterns and dynamics and urgent issues of their own time have in multiple ways continued down through history, to our own time. The experience, ideas, and urgent questions they wrestle with continue to have resonance and relevance for many of us today, and this will most likely be the case for others tomorrow.

Corroboration and Contrasts

In the 1930s three particularly significant accounts of the revolution appeared. Leon Trotsky's three-volume *History of the Russian Revolution*, released in 1932–33, was followed by William H. Chamberlin's two-volume *The Russian Revolution, 1917–1921*—both published outside of the Soviet Union. From within the USSR, in 1938, came the most authoritative account, embedded in the seventh chapter of *History of the Communist Party of the Soviet Union (Bolsheviks): Short Course*—composed by a commission of that organization's Central Committee, with the very active participation of Joseph Stalin.

"Trotsky's writing was absorbing, and the translator, Max Eastman . . . did him justice," recalled Carl Marzani, one of many radicalizing intellectuals in the United States during the 1930s. "The details, from the revolutionary insider, were fascinating, but the volume excited me most as a sample of Marxist writing and methodology. Trotsky set the revolution within a historical context, and treated the Tsarist Empire as a whole, a society rich with contradictions." High praise indeed from someone who would soon become a Communist Party organizer in the Age of Stalin. More recently, the decidedly non-Trotskyist scholar Ian Thatcher has chimed in: "Trotsky's summary of the factors he had highlighted to account for 1917 still forms the research agenda. . . . Measured against *The History of the Russian Revolution* most 'modern' research does not seem so modern after all. . . . It is essential reading." Chamberlin, a highly respected correspondent of the *Christian Science Monitor* with twelve years of journalistic experience in Soviet Russia, was evolving from radical supporter to conservative critic of the Soviet regime, but he sought to provide a balanced account that later scholars have viewed—in the recent words of Sheila Fitzpatrick—as "still the best general work on the Revolution and Civil War." Both Trotsky's and Chamberlin's accounts drew from primary source materials and reminiscences of participants, and both were consistent with what John Reed, Louise Bryant, Albert Rhys Williams, and Bessie Beatty had reported years before.[6]

In stark contrast, the account from Stalin and his collaborators contained major elements that were missing from the accounts of the four American friends. While none of them had even mentioned Stalin, the *Short Course* volume reported that in 1917, Lenin was especially reliant on "his close colleagues and disciples in Petrograd: Stalin, Sverdlov, Molotov, Ordjonikidze," and that the Bolshevik Central Committee "elected a Party Centre, headed by Comrade Stalin, to direct the uprising." More than this, it was claimed that people they had seen as among Lenin's closest comrades were in fact his enemies, and that "the Bolsheviks defeated the attempts of the capitulators within the Party—Zinoviev, Kamenev, Rykov, Bukharin, Trotsky and Pyatakov—to deflect that Party from the path of Socialist revolution." In the same period, General Secretary of the Communist International Georgi Dimitrov explained to Communists and others throughout the world the need to "enlighten the masses . . . in a genuinely Marxist, a Leninist-Marxist, a Leninist-Stalinist spirit," mobilizing "international proletarian unity . . . against the Trotskyite agents of fascism," and recognizing that a "historical dividing line" in world politics was represented by one's "attitude to the Soviet Union, which has been carrying on a real existence for twenty years already, with its untiring struggle against enemies, with its dictatorship of the working class and the Stalin Constitution, with the leading role of the Party of Lenin and Stalin." The *Short Course* was designed to facilitate this task.[7]

No less divergent from the early accounts of John Reed and his friends, and similarly inclined to stress the unity of Lenin and Stalin, were a proliferation of works from the late 1940s to the 1960s by Cold War anti-Communist scholars. A bitter ex-Communist working for the US Department of State, Bertram Wolfe, pioneered a distinctive development of the continuity thesis. "When Stalin died in 1953, Bolshevism was fifty years old. Its distinctive views on the significance of organization, of centralization and of the guardianship or dictatorship of a vanguard or elite date from Lenin's programmatic writings of 1902," Wolfe wrote. "His separate machine and his authoritarian control of it dates from . . . 1903." In that half-century, Wolfe insisted, "Bolshevism had had only two authoritative leaders": Lenin and Stalin. There were many who followed this lead. "Stalinism can and must be defined as a pattern of thought and action that flows directly from Leninism," asserted Alfred G. Meyer. "Stalin's way of looking at the contemporary world, his professed aims, the decisions he made at variance with one another, his conceptions of the tasks facing the communist state—these and many specific traits are entirely Leninist." Robert V. Daniels, contrasting "the Trotskyists" with "Stalin and more direct followers of Lenin," elaborated: "Leninism begat Stalinism in two decisive respects: it prepared a group of people ready to use force and authority to overcome any obstacles, and it trained them to accept any practical short-cut in the interest of immediate success and security of the movement." W. W. Rostow agreed: "Lenin decided . . . to rule on the basis of a police-state dictatorship," and "Stalin, having cheerfully accepted the police-state dictatorship as the basis for rule, radically altered the tone of society" in a grimly totalitarian manner.[8]

A sharp contrast both to Stalinist and Cold War anti-Communist interpretations was represented by two outstanding scholars whose attitude toward the Russian Revolution approximated the sympathies of John Reed and his friends and whose understanding of events more or less corresponded to what Trotsky and Chamberlin had presented—E. H. Carr and Isaac Deutscher. A maverick member of the British elite, Carr shifted from a diplomatic career and editorial writing for the *London Times* to the writing of a remarkable number of biographical and historical studies largely focused on Russia. Deutscher, in contrast, was a Polish "non-Jewish Jew" rising from humble beginnings. A militant in the early Communist movement who became a Trotskyist because of his opposition to the Stalinist corruption, he was by the end of the 1930s driven from his native land and had left the revolutionary movement, morphing into a brilliant English-language journalist. Deutscher produced a massive biography of Stalin and a three-volume biography of Trotsky that—in multiple ways and with great erudition—set the historical record straight while advancing challenging interpretations. The first three installments of Carr's monumental fourteen-volume *History of Soviet Russia* provided a meticulous account of the Bolshevik revolution from the standpoint of institutional history, at a high level of intellectual seriousness.[9]

The fact that Carr and Deutscher were each attacked and slandered by partisans of both Cold War power blocs highlights their importance in opening a vital space for scholars dealing with the Russian Revolution. Others—with somewhat divergent perspectives but displaying careful research and intellectual honesty—further opened that space with serious work in the 1970s. Robert C. Tucker ensured that English-language students and scholars would have easy access to reliable collections of writings by Lenin as well as Marx and Engels, but also a clearer comprehension of the actual role and meaning of Stalin.[10] One of his students, Stephen Cohen, played a decisive role in broadening the understanding of Bolshevism with his pathbreaking biography of Nikolai Bukharin. In a similar fashion but with broader scope, Moshe Lewin made fundamental contributions in tracing the history involved in the making of the Soviet Union (where he had lived for a number of years).[11] Strongly influenced by the Marxism associated with the émigré Menshevik current of Russian socialism, Leopold Haimson, Alexander Dallin, Israel Getzler, and Alexander Rabinowitch opened up additional new pathways in Soviet studies,[12] as did Paul Avrich and Teodor Shanin, two other scholars influenced by the rich traditions of, respectively, Russian anarchism and populism.[13]

A radical ferment that developed and spread during the 1960s and 1970s among student-age youth in "the capitalist West" (certainly in the United States, Canada, and Britain) would generate an explosion of exciting new work, highlighted in a seminal essay by Ronald G. Suny, "Toward a Social History of the October Revolution" in the prestigious *American Historical Review.* Younger scholars, fluent in Russian and often accessing new material, gave center stage to in-depth studies of the Russian working class. They included Suny himself, Victoria Bonnell, Laura Engelstein, Rose Glickman, Tsuyoshi Hasegawa, Diane Koenker, David Mandel, Donald J. Raleigh, William Rosenberg, Steven A. Smith, Rex A. Wade, Reginald Zelnik, and others, including the Menshevik-influenced Leopold Haimson and Alexander Rab-inowitch. Such work, judiciously integrated and popularized, found its way into a widely read trilogy by W. Bruce Lincoln (*In War's Dark Shadow*, *Passage through Armageddon*, and *Red Victory*) and in such outstanding collections as the 1997 *Critical Companion to the Russian Revolution, 1914–1921.* Taken together, such impressive work seemed to corroborate the kinds of things that John Reed, Louise Bryant, Albert Rhys Williams, Bessie Beatty, Leon Trotsky, and William H. Chamberlin had conveyed in earlier years.[14]

Not surprisingly, there was a powerful conservative counterattack, given special impetus by the 1989–91 collapse of Communism in Eastern Europe and the USSR, and by the right-wing triumphalism associated with the seem-ingly unstoppable and irreversible neoliberal revolution associated with Ron-ald Reagan and Margaret Thatcher. Old-time Cold War anti-Communists such as Martin Malia and especially Richard Pipes wrote massive, hostile "new" accounts of the Russian Revolution that simply ignored the work of all whose scholarship differed from their conservative interpretations, and these fat books were widely proclaimed to be the "magisterial" and correct exposi-tions of what really happened. They were joined, from the former USSR, by Communist careerists transitioning into anti-Communist careerists (such as Dmitri Volkogonov and Alexander Yakovlev), with supplements from disillu-sioned one-time radicals in the West who produced a *Black Book on Communism.* All of this was accompanied with an avalanche of well-funded promotion and supercharged "now it can be told" hype designed to convey the impression that any other view is now simply unthinkable.[15]

A terrain has been occupied in between by another layer of scholars who combine attitudes reminiscent of Cold War sensibilities (of one side or the other, or in some cases both) with a scholarly inclination to take more serious-ly the newer social history. For example, Sheila Fitzpatrick and J. Arch Getty have pushed hard for a "more objective" appraisal of Stalin and Stalinism, in the process coming up with material and interpretations certainly worth con-sidering. "Stalin did not initiate or control everything that happened in the party and country," Getty argues. "The number of hours in the day, divided by the number of things for which he was responsible, suggests that his role in many areas could have been little more than occasional intervention, prod-ding, threatening or correcting." He could hardly have been the Evil Genius (or Benign Genius) behind every important thing—he can only be under-stood adequately within the context of the complex political and social struc-tures within which he functioned. Getty concludes: "He was an executive, and reality forced him to delegate most authority to his subordinates, each of whom had his own opinions, client groups, and interests."[16]

But one aspect of their approach involves positing an elemental consistency between Lenin and Stalin. According to Getty, Stalin and those associated with his repressive regime were partly animated by "Bolshevik traditions of intolerance, fanatical unity against opponents, and easy recourse to violence." For Fitzpatrick, Stalin's political characteristics (and Lenin's) were part of something by no means restricted to Bolshevism. "All revolutionaries are enthusiasts, zealots," she tells us. "They are intolerant of disagreement, incapable of compromise; mesmerized by big, distant goals, violent, suspicious and destructive."[17]

Variants of this approach can be found in the work of other influential scholars dealing with the Russian Revolution, such as Orlando Figes, who utilizes fragments of social history to deepen his point. Figes presents the struggle for a better world as an "experiment" that went "horribly wrong, not so much because of the malice of its leaders, most of whom had started out with the highest of ideals, but because their ideals were themselves impossible." Bolshevik intellectuals, "with their own idealized vision of what the workers were supposed to be," were destined to be foiled by "the workers' actual tastes—vaudeville and vodka, for the most." The struggle to mobilize the working class to take political power in order to usher in a glowing socialist democracy was, Figes concludes, doomed from the start: "The state, however big, cannot make people equal or better human beings."[18]

There are ample biographies and autobiographies of working-class people that collide with Figes's vodka and vaudeville stereotype: August Bebel from Germany, Louise Michel from France, J. Keir Hardie from Britain, "Mother" Mary Jones from the United States, Alexander Shlyapnikov from Russia, and countless more from these and many other lands.[19] As was evident in the earlier social histories of the Russian Revolution (and also in the lived experience of many of us today), the working class is an immense human group reflecting a broad array of identities, ideologies, inclinations, and tastes. Nor does the suggestion hold up that the Russian Revolution can be explained as impractical intellectuals taking control of the state for the purpose of somehow making everybody "equal or better human beings." Of course, the revolutionaries certainly favored *a society that would provide equal rights and a better life for all*—which is something else altogether, an eminently practical goal, and well worth fighting for.

The present volume provides a contrast to the neoconservative and in-between interpretations, as well as to the older anti-Communist and Stalinist distortions from the Cold War era, instead drawing from and highlighting the more valuable accounts of what happened, not least of which were the eyewitness reports from John Reed, Louise Bryant, and their friends. We see a story in which an oppressive political, economic, and social order generates mass discontent within the population, exacerbated by converging crises, resulting in resistance and rebellion. These revolts are advanced particularly by a small but growing working class—dynamic and strategically placed—which, in turn, is animated by its more conscious and activist elements that organize themselves into trade unions, political parties, soviets (councils), factory committees, workers militias, and more. A decisive role, within this complex mix, comes to be played by a specific revolutionary current steeped in Marxist theory and containing a number of strong personalities that have been shaped by considerable previous experience. The result is the world's first socialist revolution.

There has, of course, been additional work dealing with various facets of the revolutionary experience, and scholars are still wrestling with many questions of fact and interpretation. For those concerned with what actually happened in history, and specifically with how revolutions actually happen (with an eye on the possible need for making revolutions of our own), such further wrestling is important—and it is that to which we will now turn.

Multiple Insurgencies

Rex Wade has summed up complexities of the Russian Revolution in a manner that deserves to be quoted at length:

> The Russian revolution of 1917 was a series of concurrent and overlapping revolutions: the popular revolt against the old regime; the workers' revolution against the hardships of the old industrial and social order; the revolt of the soldiers against the old system of military service and then against the war itself [i.e., against the First World War]; the peasants' revolution for land and for control of their own lives; the striving of middle class elements for civil rights and a constitutional parliamentary system; the revolution of the non-Russian nationalities for rights and self-determination; the revolt of most of the population against the war and its seemingly endless slaughter. People also struggled over differing cultural visions, over women's rights, between nationalities, for domination within ethnic or religious groups and among and within political parties, and for fulfillment of a multitude of aspirations large and small. These various revolutions and group struggles played out within the general context of political realignments and instability, growing social anarchy, economic collapse, and ongoing world war. They contributed to both the revolution's vitality

and the sense of chaos that so often overwhelmed people in 1917. The revolution of 1917 propelled Russia with blinding speed through liberal, moderate socialist and then radical socialist phases, at the end bringing to power the extreme left wing of Russian, even European, politics. An equally sweeping social revolution accompanied the rapid political movement. And all this occurred within a remarkably compressed time period—less than a year.[20]

This poses multiple questions that deserve attention. To narrow this to only a few issues:

1) Given simply the occupational complexity of class, and the multiple facets of consciousness related to this, what were the consciousness and the underlying social reality involved in what Wade refers to as "the workers' revolution against the hardships of the old industrial and social order"?

2) What was the interplay of ethnic/national oppression, gender oppression, and class oppression (what some today might refer to as "intersectionality") in the social reality of 1917 Russia?[21]

3) What was the understanding (or what were the different, perhaps divergent, understandings) of such intersectionality among the Bolsheviks, and how did this play out, or fail to play out, practically?

The key category for Russian Marxists was, of course, *working class*—for practical no less than theoretical reasons. In an early study, published in 1932, Joseph Freeman observed: "The growth of the working class continued so rapidly that between 1897 and 1913 the number of wage-earners in census industries increased 70 percent and in the domestic-craft industries 50 percent." Rex Wade emphasizes that "central to the history of the revolution, key players in all stages of its development, were the urban, especially industrial workers. . . . The revolution began as a demonstration of industrial workers and they never relinquished their leading role in both political and social revolution in 1917. They represented a potent force for further revolutionary upheaval if their aspirations were not met—as they almost certainly would not be, at least not in full."[22]

I have already alluded to the complex nature of the working class, and of working-class consciousness. An aspect of this involves occupational differences—typographical workers were often seen as being more moderate, mine workers were often seen as being more militant, skilled workers (such as metalworkers) were often seen as more politically advanced than unskilled

workers (such as textile workers). In addition, the consciousness and mentality of many workers were permeated by earlier experiences in and continuing
ties with the peasant village, workers fresh from the countryside were often
scorned by seasoned city dwellers, gaps sometimes tended to open between
younger and older generations of workers, and so forth.[23]

Wade tells us that "while their own economic, working and personal
conditions were their most pressing concern, broader political issues also
animated the workers." For the many contingents that made up a thick organizational network—including trade unions, factory committees, local and
district soviets, cultural and self-help groups of various kinds, workers' militia groups, and so on—all were means through which workers sought "to
use their newfound freedom and power to obtain a better life for themselves
and their families." He notes that these and other developments "had the
effect not only of solidifying working-class identity, but also of broadening
the circle of those who identified themselves as workers." Previously unorganized elements outside of the factories—cab drivers, laundry workers, bath-
house workers, restaurant waiters, bakers, barbers, retail clerks, lower-level
white-collar workers such as office clerks and elementary school teachers—
all now identified themselves as part of the working class, worked to organize
unions, and sent representatives to the soviets.[24]

The question of who is or is not part of the working class, *and who self-identifies
as a worker,* was complex in more than one way. The basic Marxist distinction—
a proletarian is someone who sells labor power to an employer in order to make
a living—might, depending on context, be seen as subordinate to whether one
has an education (and can be defined in some sense as part of the intelligentsia)
and whether one works on a factory floor or someplace more "refined." Leopold
Haimson discusses the example of pharmacy workers during the 1905 revolutionary upsurge, who formed a union—as employees in various workplaces
were doing—but then were faced with the issue of whether they, as pharmacists' assistants, should self-identify as "workers" (which would place them with
predominantly working-class socialists of the Russian Social Democratic Labor
Party) or as "intelligentsia" (which would place them with professional groups in
the "bourgeois liberal" Union of Unions). Between 1905 and 1917, he notes, various working-class strata "were alternatively drawn to (or indeed torn between)
the representations of being class-conscious proletarians" or something other
than that, which would have implications for political allegiances.[25]

There was also the matter of how class and class consciousness intersect-
ed with gender and with ethnicity or nationality. The vast empire of tsarist

Russia had been infamous as "a prison-house of nations," and what came to be known as Great Russian chauvinism combined with the ruling elite's ongoing efforts to squeeze wealth out of subject peoples. Ethnic and national divisions in such situations have the capacity to cut across class in multiple ways, with prejudices and "blind spots" and resentments (not to mention linguistic and other cultural differences) dividing workers and having complex impacts on class consciousness and class struggle. Serious mistakes can be made, and were made, in such situations, but also new insights can develop and important corrections can lead to new opportunities. There is much to be learned (and more to be discovered, by scholars no less than activists) about what happened in the revolutionary struggle leading up to 1917, about the role of ethnic and national struggles within the overthrow of Russia's old order, and about the subsequent policies of the new revolutionary regime.[26]

No less complex, and sometimes similarly explosive, was "the woman question." One aspect of the complexity is intersectionality—it is problematical to deal with gender abstracted from multiple other identities: Is one in a rural or urban context, for example? Is one an aristocrat, a peasant, or a bourgeois? An "intellectual" white-collar worker or a factory worker? Part of one ethnic community or another?[27] As with the "national question," there were Marxists—including among the Bolsheviks—who were inclined to take a reductionist and sectarian stand: the future socialist revolution carried out by the working class would bring an end to all bad things, including the oppression of women (or of subjugated nationalities and ethnic groups), and separate struggles against such oppression could divide workers and divert them from the class struggle and the primary task of overthrowing capitalism. This logic could also be convenient for not creating discomfort among male (or Russian-majority) workers and comrades, and keeping women (or other oppressed groups) "in their place."[28]

Despite such debilitating conservatism, even critical historians generally agree that the Bolsheviks were far more engaged in organizing for women's liberation than other groups on the left, and that Lenin was ahead of many of his comrades in supporting this work. A cautiousness and even prudishness prevented him from endorsing some of the more radical perspectives advanced by Alexandra Kollontai and Inessa Armand, however. The fact remains that from the start, the Russian Social Democratic Labor Party, following the examples of Marx, Engels, and August Bebel, had, as Barbara Evans Clements puts it, "a good record on women's issues" (the right to vote; equal civil, educational, and employment rights, among which the right to receive services for the special needs of women in the workplace; including maternity leave and day care for their children). She adds that "publicly renouncing the sexism that was standard among European politicians in the early twentieth century, . . . allowed its female members to achieve considerable prominence and personal freedom." It is essential, in understanding the workers' and peasants' uprising of 1917, and of the Bolshevik role, that we not see *worker* and *peasant* and *Bolshevik* as meaning "male." This essential and obvious fact shaped much of what happened. While the Bolsheviks, as Marxists, "stressed the oppression of class over gender, they also recognized that women suffered a double oppression which they believed had its basis in peasant patriarchy as well as in capitalism," Jane McDermid and Anna Hillyar point out. "In addition, the Bolsheviks were forced to pay attention to the woman question, not only by the circumstances of greatly increased numbers of women entering the labor force, especially during the First World War, but also under pressure from some of the female members of their own party."[29]

While Bolshevik women went out of their way to denounce "bourgeois feminism," they nonetheless needed to push their own comrades (many male, but some female) to support special efforts to agitate, educate, and organize among working-class women. In the course of 1917, the political forces in the struggle for power, according to Richard Stites, "were led by and overwhelmingly composed of men: government, parties, soviets, peasant associations, national organizations, cooperatives, industrial enterprises, and trade unions," yet he also cites a pamphlet in which Alexandra Kollontai insists that "in our revolution women workers and peasants played . . . an active and important role." Aspects of the truth can be found in both statements. The deep patriarchal patterns and male dominance of Russian (and European) culture naturally were manifest at all levels, but as Rex Wade observes, "women entered public and political life in unprecedented numbers and ways," reflecting the fact that during the First World War the number of women in the factories rose from 25 percent to 43 percent of the nationwide industrial labor force, and in the Moscow region, for example, they constituted 60 percent of all textile workers. "Military defeats, economic breakdown, and soaring prices drew large numbers of women into sporadic strikes against deteriorating conditions," according to Gail Warshofsky Lapidus, and—Wade points out—women "voted in general elections and participated in selection of factory committees, soviets and trade union leadership. Some served as deputies in these and in city councils. Thousands became involved in the enormous variety of economic, social and cultural organizations that sprang up across Russia in the revolutionary year." There is also the well-known point stressed by Lapidus: "It was a massive strike touched off by women textile workers on International Women's Day that culminated in the February Revolution of 1917."[30]

Revolutionary Party

Essential for the making of the Russian Revolution was interplay between the broad masses of workers and peasants, in all their variety, and an organization of revolutionary intellectuals and activists having a predominantly working-class base and a Marxist ideology. This was the Bolshevik Party, whose central leader was Vladimir Ilyich Ulyanov—known to the world as Lenin.

In the 1919 volume *Lenin: The Man and His Work,* a sympathetic Albert Rhys Williams suggested that "one of the secrets of Lenin's power is his terrible sincerity," elaborating: "This stamp of sincerity is on all his public utterances. Lenin is lacking in the usual outfit of the statesman-politician—bluff, glittering verbiage and success-psychology. One felt that he could not fool others even if he desired to. And for the same reasons that he could not fool himself: His scientific attitude of mind, his passion for the facts." In his 1924 study *The Man Lenin,* a more critical observer, Isaac Don Levine, commented that "his mentality . . . may have been extraordinarily agile and pliant as to methods, his erudition may have been vast and his capacity to back up his contentions brilliant, his character may have been such as to readily acknowledge tactical mistakes and defeats, but these he never would have ascribed to the possible invalidity of his great idea [that is, Marxism]." Levine added that Lenin "combined this unshakeable, almost fanatic, faith with a total absence of personal ambition, arrogance or pride. Unselfish and irreproachable in his character, of a retiring disposition, almost ascetic in his habits, extremely modest and gentle in his direct contact with people, although peremptory and derisive in his treatment of political enemies, Lenin could be daring and provocative in his policies, inflexible in the execution of his principles."[31]

Both the Stalinist and Cold War anti-Communist versions of Lenin have him developing a tightly organized, elitist, authoritarian "party of a new type" with a personality to match (Stalinists presented him as flawless; anti-Communists presented him as deeply flawed)—an image, in its negative variant, captured after Communism's collapse in Robert Service's *Lenin: A Biography*. Inconsistent with portrayals provided by John Reed and his friends, by Trotsky and Chamberlin, and by a variety of later scholars (Carr, Deutscher, Lewin, Cohen), it has been definitively demolished by the recent work of Lars Lih, in an exhaustive examination of the activity and thinking of Lenin and his comrades in Bolshevism's earliest incarnation—a massive volume entitled *Lenin Rediscovered*—as well as in his succinct and rich biography, *Lenin*.[32]

Lih's portrayal finds additional corroboration in my own *Lenin and the Revolutionary Party*, which presents Lenin's party as an essentially democratic collectivity rather than a one-man organizational dictatorship. Indeed, it is difficult to see anything but the kind of organization described in these studies, given the complex multiple insurgencies we have noted, as capable of bringing about what happened in October 1917. This comes through, as well, in the eyewitness and partially eyewitness accounts, respectively, of Bolshevik dissidents Eduard M. Dune (*Notes of a Red Guard*) and Victor Serge (*Year One of the Russian Revolution*). Lih has also emphasized the fact that Lenin did not see himself building a "party of a new type," that his model had been the massive German Social Democratic Party whose central theoretician, Karl Kautsky, saw socialism and democracy as inseparable. Lih has suggested that Lenin's outlook was basically indistinguishable from Kautsky's prior to 1914 (after which Lenin denounced him for betraying their common revolutionary perspective). While there was certainly much overlap between Lenin and Kautsky, recent work by Tamás Krausz, Alan Shandro, and others compellingly present Lenin's perspectives as having their own quite distinctive quality.[33]

Lih's insistence on the Bolshevik Party as a "collectivity" rather than a one-man show has been a particularly important corrective, and in the process he has advocated rehabilitation and respect for some of Lenin's comrades— such as Lev Kamenev and Gregory Zinoviev—who have been dismissed not only by Stalinists but also Trotskyists. Lih even suggests (quite controversially) that Kamenev was more right than wrong in the debate over Lenin's *April Theses* of 1917, and that he essentially won the debate. While Nadezhda Krupskaya remembers the *April Theses* debate differently (as do many others from the time, of various persuasions), she also conveys in her important reminiscences a vivid sense, with considerable detail, of the collective nature of the Bolshevik Party: in her view, it was by no means simply Lenin calling the shots. This comes through as well in the attentive contemporary portraits one finds in Bolshevik Anatoly Lunacharsky's *Revolutionary Silhouettes* and in the more substantial collection of contemporary biographies supplemented with the scholarship of Georges Haupt and Jean-Jacques Marie, in *Makers of the Russian Revolution*.[34]

There is need for more research—following along the lines of Ralph Carter Elwood's rich account *Russian Social Democracy in the Underground* and August Nimtz's revealing exposition of the centrality of electoral work in Bolshevik strategy—to add new dimensions and detail to our understanding of the Bolshevik Party. But it also makes sense to reach for the kind of historical overview provided in Gregory Zinoviev's still valuable *History of the Bolshevik Party,* despite its brevity and other limitations. In this regard, the work of Vladimir Nevsky, a long-time Bolshevik activist, calls out to be made available. "Like so many others in his generation, he was arrested in the mid-thirties and executed in 1937," reports Lars Lih. "After the revolution, Nevsky became a pioneering party historian whose magnum opus, published in 1925, was entitled *Istoriia RKP(b): Kratkii ocherk* [*History of the Russian Communist Party (Bolsheviks): A Short Essay*]. Despite the modest subtitle, this massive 500-page study constitutes the first history of the Bolshevik party to be fully documented and based on a full range of sources."[35]

While more research remains to be done, the fact remains that Moshe Lewin's characterization appears to describe what actually was: under tsarism, the Bolshevik Party was "small, illegal, frequently decimated by the police," but it also was "a network of very active committees, with well-maintained contacts in the factories, and with little experience, historically, of the rural world. It had some influence among students and those circles of the intelligentsia who were open to the appeal of Marxism." Especially important was the fact that "it adapted easily to the fluctuation of political mobilization, especially in the working class." While decimated and marginalized by severe repression during the First World War, in 1917 it "underwent a rather astonishing change in structure and nature: the number of its cadres, which had not gone beyond 20,000, increased toward the end of the year to 300,000 or more, so that it became an authentic party of the urban masses, a legal democratic party made up from diverse social strata and heterogeneous ideological horizons."[36]

What Went Wrong?

John Reed, in *Ten Days That Shook the World,* recounts the conclusion of Lenin's speech after the Soviet seizure of power, that now "the labor movement, in the name of peace and socialism, shall win and fulfill its destiny." Reed adds: "There was something quiet and powerful in all of this, which stirred the souls of men. It was understandable why people believed when Lenin spoke."[37] Yet within four years, Reed's friend Albert Rhys Williams, would write:

"Repressions, tyranny, violence," cry the enemies. "They have abolished free speech, free press, free assembly. They have imposed drastic military conscription and compulsory labor. They have been incompetent in government, inefficient in industry. They have subordinated the Soviets to the Communist Party. They have lowered their Communist ideals, changed and shifted their program and compromised with the capitalists."

Some of these charges are exaggerated. Many can be explained. But they cannot all be explained away. Friends of the Soviet grieve over them. Their enemies have summoned the world to shudder and protest against them. . . .

While abroad hatred against the Bolsheviks as the new "enemies of civilization" mounted from day to day, these selfsame Bolsheviks were straining to rescue civilization in Russia from total collapse.[38]

Rosa Luxemburg saw problems as the Russian Civil War unfolded in 1918: "Whatever a party could offer of courage, revolutionary far-sightedness and consistency in a historic hour, Lenin, Trotsky and the other comrades have given in good measure," but, Luxemburg warned, "socialist democracy begins . . . at the very moment of the seizure of power by the socialist party," and "with the repression of political life in the land as a whole, life in the soviets must also become more and more crippled," leading not to socialist democracy but "the dictatorship of a handful of politicians."[39]

There were fluctuations in the people's fortunes after the brutalizing Civil War. Important accounts—both contemporary and later—indicate improvements in material life and cultural freedom in the 1920s. Nor does it seem a foregone conclusion that the new Soviet Republic would have necessarily devolved into a bureaucratic tyranny destined for eventual collapse. "There is no doubt that Lenin suffered his greatest defeat when, at the outbreak of the civil war, the supreme power that he originally planned to concentrate in the Soviets definitely passed into the hands of the party bureaucracy," Hannah Arendt noted in *Origins of Totalitarianism,* but she insisted that "even this development, tragic as it was for the course of the revolution, would not necessarily have led to totalitarianism." Her elaboration, for which there is substantial and reliable corroboration, is worth pondering:

At the moment of Lenin's death [in 1924] the roads were still open. The formation of workers, peasants, and [in the wake of the New Economic Policy] middle classes need not necessarily have led to the class struggle which had been characteristic of European capitalism. Agriculture could still be developed on a collective, cooperative, or private basis, and the national economy was still free to follow a socialist, state-capitalist, or free-enterprise pattern. None of these alternatives would have automatically destroyed the new structure of the country.[40]

The fact remains that by the 1930s, claiming to be "Lenin's faithful disciple and the prolonger of his work," Joseph Stalin consolidated control over party and state.[41] This came after winning a set of factional conflicts, preceded in the mid-1920s by the crystallization around Stalin of a tight clique of top functionaries (thanks to his key position in the party apparatus as general secretary), and decisively drawing on support within the lower levels of the party and state apparatus. Sincere Communists throughout the world, and many others as well, took Stalin's claims for good coin, seeing the consequent destruction of millions of lives—direct and indirect consequences of his modernizing "revolution from above"—as representing the necessary defense of revolutionary goals and principles. An avalanche of material, against which no serious scholar can contend, has long since demolished this line of reasoning (although a US professor of medieval English literature, Grover Furr, continues to lead a crusade in Stalin's defense).[42]

Overviews of Soviet and Russian history can be utilized to help sort through the meaning of matters dealt with in this book.[43] But those inclined to take seriously the approach animating the men and women who made the Russian Revolution will be especially concerned with how well Marxism can explain what happened, and Dutch historian Marcel van der Linden has provided a detailed survey of critical (but incredibly diverse) Marxist analyses. Among the most incisive of these is the analysis developed by Leon Trotsky in *The Revolution Betrayed*.[44]

Key elements in this analysis flow from an understanding that economic democracy (socialism), which would allow the free development of each person as the condition for the free development of all people (as Marx and Engels had posited in the *Communist Manifesto*), depends on the immense economic surplus and productivity, plus the complex of socioeconomic and global relationships among people and resources, built up by the modern world capitalist economy. An attempt to build socialism in a single country with a low level of economic development cannot be successful. As Marx stressed in *The German Ideology*, "a development of the productive forces [generated by the Industrial Revolution] is the absolutely necessary practical premise [of Communism], because without it want is generalized, and with want the struggle for necessities begins again, and that means all the old crap will revive" the exploitation and oppression of laboring majorities by powerful minorities that has characterized civilization for thousands of years.[45]

Stalin's commitment to building "socialism in one country" was a recipe for bureaucratic tyranny. This is why Marx and Engels concluded with the appeal: "Workers of all countries unite!" It is also why Lenin, Trotsky, and the other leaders of the new Soviet regime utilized precious time and resources to build up a Communist International that might be able to facilitate victories of workers' revolutions in other countries. "The contradictory social structure of the Soviet Union, and the ultra-bureaucratic character of its state," Trotsky argued, are the "direct consequence" of the unforeseen "pause" in the process of world revolution.[46]

Despite remarkable progress in "modernization," and despite (but also because of) the fierce and murderous repressiveness of the Stalin regime, the socialist goals of the October Revolution could not be reached, and the bureaucratic tyranny that crystallized in the place of those goals proved incapable of being sustained beyond 1990, even with desperate but doomed attempts at bureaucratic self-reform.

Just as many people who are unsympathetic to the Bolshevik revolution, all too glibly insist that Leninism naturally and necessarily led to Stalinism, it is also the case that many revolutionary socialists succumb to the temptation of exonerating Lenin, Trotsky, and like-minded comrades from any responsibility for bad-to-horrific developments following the 1917 revolution.

In the realm of human psychology, of course, we know that it makes no sense to insist on one's own purity, or to reject the possibility of responsibility for negative consequences to one's more or less well-intentioned actions. We also know that it makes no sense to blame ourselves (or specified others) for all the terrible things that go on around us. Reality is more complicated—a fact that serious historians and social scientists must also acknowledge as they try to make sense of such immense realities as the Russian Revolution and its aftermath. No less is that the case for activists who want to understand the world in ways that enable us to be more effective in our efforts to change it for the better—to expand and enhance freedom, creative labor, and genuine community for each person and for all people (as Marx and Engels urged in the *Communist Manifesto*).[47]

If we want to bring about necessary changes in our society, we would do well to be able to learn from both the positive and the negative actions and experiences of people like ourselves in such earlier contexts (so different from ours, but not completely different from ours) as revolutionary Russia.

Framing Questions

The Methodological Appendix features a discussion of the approach guiding the composition of this study: a sympathetic engagement with the analytical conceptualizations imparted by Marxist theory (with special reference to Marx and Trotsky) and democratic theory (including perspectives of such diverse figures as Peter Bachrach, Robert A. Dahl, John Dewey, Harold Laski, Henry Mayo, C. B. Macpherson, and George Novack). There is a serious engagement as well with sharp challenges to Marxist and/or democratic theory posed by a number of post-Marxist theorists who were prominent in US political and social thought in the twentieth century, especially from the 1940s through the 1970s. (This includes labor historian Selig Perlman, maverick publicist Max Nomad, political philosophers Sidney Hook and James Burnham, sociologist Daniel Bell, and economic historian W. W. Rostow.) It could be argued that such methodological elaborations belong right up front, though that might get in the way of the narrative flow. Readers wanting to examine notions framing this study, however, are encouraged to turn to that appendix.

In what follows, I will critically explore Russia's revolutionary experience, informed by democratic and Marxist theory, but I also sometimes will use a post-Marxist "Greek chorus" to prod us into honoring Marx's injunction to "doubt everything." Perhaps it would be helpful to list some of the questions with which we will deal in the course of this study:

1) What is the relationship of the proletariat, the peasantry, and the bourgeoisie to the revolutionary process?

2) How are we to understand the reality of that key category *the proletariat* (its structure, its internal dynamics, its relation to other classes, even its definition)?

3) What is the meaning of the concept *revolutionary vanguard,* and what was the process through which the revolutionary vanguard was formed, and through which it evolved, won out against competitors, and acquired hegemony in the revolutionary struggle?

4) What was the process through which the revolutionary struggle triumphed?

5) In what way is the concept *dictatorship of the proletariat* (defined as working-class rule) relevant in the period under examination, and how does the historical experience clarify the meaning of that term?

6) What is the balance (and what explains the balance) between democracy and authoritarianism in the first years after the revolution?

7) What are the economic policies that followed the revolutionary overturn, and how can these policies best be understood?

8) What are the international ramifications of this revolutionary experience, particularly the impact of international realities on the revolution?

In the Russia of 1917–24 we find a pyramid of soviets (ostensibly democratically representative councils) as the basis for the government, as well as trade unions and factory committees (all of which were soon controlled by the Communist Party, which soon repressed most active opposition groups, formally outlawing all of them in 1921–22). All of this can be expanded upon in considerable detail without necessarily giving a clear answer to the question of who rules.

The question of democracy is a focal point of this study. A simple question: Who rules? The simple answers—"the working people" or "the revolutionary elite"—are, each in their own way, true and false and inadequate. The development of an answer is, of course, shaped by one's own particular ideological orientation. Such inevitable biases don't prevent any serious work of history from helping to advance the collective understanding. Used in an honest and relatively disciplined manner, they may shed light on what is being studied.

2

PREREVOLUTIONARY RUSSIA

*P*rerevolutionary Russia has been a subject of many controversies between (and also among) non-Marxists and Marxists—one of the most interesting being over whether socioeconomic development could have been advanced more efficiently without a revolutionary upheaval.

In what economic historian and modernization theorist W. W. Rostow once praised as "a great work," *The Great Retreat: The Growth and Decline of Communism in Russia* (1946), the Russian émigré scholar N. S. Timasheff conducted a "mental experiment" by projecting Russia's major socioeconomic trends of the 1890s to 1913 forward in time. He concluded from this that Russia would have reached the same or even higher levels of industrialization, income, and education by the 1940s without the Bolshevik revolution and Communist dictatorship as were achieved with them. Rostow, utilizing more recent data, agreed: Russia's period of economic "take-off" (to use Rostow's term) began in the 1890s, was hindered by a period of industrial stagnation in the early years of the twentieth century, but then was followed by "a second surge down to 1914, firmly launched by 1908. The latter saw a more diversified industrial expansion, marking the beginnings of the Russian drive to technological maturity. It also saw a definitive completion of the freeing of the serfs, an accelerated increase in agricultural output, greatly enlarged allocations to education, and a diminished role for foreign capital and entrepreneurship."[1]

On the basis of such considerations, a sophisticated post-Marxist social democrat like George Lichtheim could write with assurance that even without the Bolshevik revolution "Russia would surely have become a great industrial and military power (it was already a sizeable one in 1914)," going on to ask—in light of the destruction of millions of people under Stalin's version of "socialism"—whether it would "not have been better to let the industrialization of Russia go forward under bourgeois auspices." He added: "In that case Russia in all probability would—after an interval of military rule [that would have followed the overthrow of tsarism and the inept Provisional Government]—have become a democracy in the Western sense of the term. Well, not quite Western, perhaps, but near enough."[2]

In contrast to this general approach was an influential line of Marxist analysis developed in the 1950s and '60s by such theorists as Paul Baran and André Gunder Frank. They suggested that "underdeveloped societies" were blocked from making a transition to modernity, freedom, and rational economic growth because the advanced capitalist countries dominating the world market have a stake in keeping them underdeveloped.

Operating within this general framework while drawing on more recent studies, Teodor Shanin argued, "Russia was a country with a massive peasant population, a per capita annual income of less than 100 dollars, a major presence of foreign capital and a government pursuing industrialization policies in a world increasingly dominated by 'the West,' that is, the main capitalist industrial societies." Of course there are important differences between Russia and many other countries matching this description, but Shanin explains that "the 'developing' or 'peripheral' societies should be treated as a diverse form of social organization" within the global capitalist economy. Making positive reference to analyses by Paul Sweezy and E. J. Hobsbawm about "the plausibility of different capitalisms" and the need to reject "the universality of the feudalism-to-capitalism road to transition," Shanin goes on to reject "evolutionist solutions by which societal forms are essentially different steps along the necessary-capitalist road (into socialism, for those who are socialists)." He concludes: "The 'uneven' and combined development of different societies would mean . . . not only different speeds and 'clocks' but also different 'roads,' each with its own consistencies, potentials and logic."[3]

Stimulating challenges to Shanin's "populist" interpretation have been advanced by such scholars as Peter Gatrell, John Bushnell, and S. A. Smith. Gatrell lends support to a more "mainstream" Marxist analysis in his stress on the tendency of Russian capitalism to become increasingly dominant in the economy agriculturally as well as industrially, insisting that Shanin under-estimates growing stratification and the increasing importance of wage-labor within the peasantry. Bushnell argues that the "steadily rising agricultural productivity" revealed by recent scholarship "does not readily accord with Shanin's bleak picture of deepening agrarian crisis." He adds (although notes that Shanin also acknowledges) that "millions of peasants worked seasonally in cities, mines, or railway construction. Others worked for a year or two in the cities, almost always sending money home in the meantime. More mil-lions produced non-agricultural goods in their villages (toys, trays, and icons in some famous villages near Moscow, for instance)." From this, Bushnell concludes: "If agricultural productivity rose rather than fell, if peasants ben-efitted in any appreciable measure from the growth of the urban economy and urban markets, then Russia was not, economically speaking, suffering from cumulating weaknesses." Smith also notes that "the balance of scholar-ly opinion has increasingly challenged the view that the agrarian economy was in crisis," and that "capitalist agriculture was making rapid headway, especially on the steppes of southern Ukraine and south-eastern Russia, and where they had access to railways, the Volga river or the Black Sea, peasants were not slow to seize new market opportunities." He adds that in "the region of Ukraine north of the Black and Azov seas, peasants replaced oxen with horses, rye with barley, adopted steel instead of wooden implements, and the size of peasant harvest expanded by 25% from the 1870s to the 1880s and by a further 36% in the following 10 years." However, Smith then inclines toward acknowledging that, in fact, there *was* something of an agrarian crisis, since "even at the end of the century the average harvest was insufficient to sustain most households, which were now working substantially less land than a generation earlier."[4]

Such critiques and analyses highlight contradictory and countervailing tendencies of Russian socioeconomic development, but hardly constitute an obliteration of the peasant cultural and economic realities—not to mention blockages to "capitalist progress"—that are documented by Shanin and oth-er scholars, and discussed by contemporary eyewitnesses as well. "To reject Shanin's view of the Russian peasantry's economic situation is not to reject his analysis of the operation of the peasant economy," Bushnell acknowledges. There was most certainly a "crisis of modernization" that not only was "deep-ly threatening to the autocracy," as Smith has emphasized, but also very neg-atively affecting the peasantry, particularly given population increases that meant intensification of pressure on land resources, with the average peasant allotment shrinking by one-third between 1861 and 1900. While there was clearly "progress" in the commercialization of agriculture, Smith comments, "the agrarian system as a whole remained backward and the peasant deeply alienated," particularly given the fact that "the average peasant still lived a life of poverty, deprivation, and oppression, one index of which was that infant mortality was the highest in Europe."[5]

Added to this are realities highlighted in the account of Russian historian Alexander Polunov, who notes: "Beginning in the mid-1890s, social, political, ethnic and religious tensions began to snowball, producing a full-scale crisis" that would destroy the monarchy. This was largely generated, he argues, by the quintessential peculiarity of Russian capitalism—the tsarist system itself, which drew from "the most reactionary segments of Russian society" in an effort to "turn back the clock." The imperious Tsar Alexander III labored to push back earlier modernizing reforms to "assert a much greater degree of control over society," and his son Tsar Nicholas II vowed to continue this good work. Determined to repress "any protest by workers, peasants, students, and ethnic minorities," the regime was attracted to the temptation—voiced by Minister of the Interior Viacheslav Plehve—that Russia's "own distinct history and social structure" would allow it to "avoid the yoke of capital, the bourgeoisie, and class struggle." Even when such blockages were partly overcome through the efforts of such tsarist policy modernizers as Sergei Witte and Pyotr Stolypin, the results often added to the problems. "Witte's policy of taxing the peasant hard, and Stolypin's policy of helping the strong peasant squeeze out the weak," as J. N. Westwood comments, while carried out in the interests of overcoming backwardness, to be sure, and also yielding modernizing results, "intensified rural discontents and rural hatred. Moreover, when the taxed-out or squeezed-out peasant moved to the unsalubrious factory barracks, he became part of an ill-paid, unhealthy, unskilled and uneducated proletariat which was a social problem in itself."[6]

The overall situation is aptly characterized in the summary analysis of Stephen Wheatcroft, who frames the analysis with reference to the interplay of tsarist policy and capitalist economy: "The government was intent on a policy of rapid industrialization, which was to be paid for by large grain exports," setting up an equation involving the changing level of international grain prices, weather-induced fluctuations in grain yields, and the effectiveness of the tsarist administrative machinery. Wheatcroft makes an important distinction between three types of crises: (1) agricultural crisis, involving a decline in agricultural production; (2) crisis in peasant living standards, which is influenced not only by agricultural production, but also by the role of the market and government policy; and (3) agrarian crisis, which "is a crisis in the sociopolitical system and is manifested by the peasantry threatening to disrupt the social and political order." These three forms of crisis are obviously interrelated, but each has its own dynamics and may even unfold with a certain relative autonomy. Wheatcroft also makes the point that generalizations for all of Russia can be problematical, given the specifics of its different vast regions—what is decisive in the Central Black Earth Region and the Volga, for example, may be less important in the Eastern region comprising the Urals, Siberia, and the Steppe. There are also fluctuations within broad time spans. For example, "grain-production data indicate a general trend toward increased production per capita but with a large concentration of unfavorable years in 1889–1892 and 1904–1908 (which were to a very large extent a direct result of the weather)." More than this, "grain exports had been rising over this period, but the growth in grain production was sufficient to maintain a long-term per-capita production even net of exports," except that "in the short term grain exports undoubtedly added to the severity of the crisis" in the unfavorable years of declining production. Furthermore, optimal conditions in the Eastern and Southern regions "masked the very serious stagnation in per-capita production" in the central and northern regions. "Distress in the countryside" is suggested by tax data, and the crisis associated with the devastating famine of 1891 is matched by a "gentler but longer crisis of 1896–1908," adding up to a "crisis in living standards . . . less severe but of much longer duration." The accumulation of such experiences, combined with aftershocks when temporary relief policies were terminated—despite statistical long-term trends militating against "overall peasant destitution"—profoundly contributed to "the growth in peasant unrest" and a genuine agrarian crisis marked by "the apparent loss of government authority" and "large-scale disorders which were aimed largely at the landowners," generating "mass repression . . . applied to the peasantry in martial-law circumstances."[7]

Careful examination, then, suggests that essential points in Shanin's sweeping analysis hold true. Against the sanguine assumptions of Timasheff, Rostow, and Lichtheim, it can be argued that the peculiarities of capitalist development in Russia were destined to block the progressive unfolding of abundance and democracy that those scholars envisioned. The optimistic statistical scenario tends to "conjure out of existence" (to use Alec Nove's phrase) not only the disastrous explosion of the First World War, but also the peculiarities of Russian capitalism—the dominating and intractable conservatism of the nobility and the tsarist bureaucracy, the inherent weakness of their capitalist "junior partners," the severe social instabilities and crises that industrial capitalist "progress" was itself helping to generate and deepen, which brought damage and radicalization to the vast peasantry and growing working class.[8]

Historian John Marot has recently advanced a sweeping theorization of "tsarist Russia's independent, *non-capitalist* economic development," but the two suppositions he presents usefully highlight the *peculiarity* of what we will identify as *Russian capitalism*, even though Marot would not term it as such: (1) the strengthening of the tsarist state "was the prime mover of industrial development and agricultural under-development in tsarist Russia," and (2) the agricultural surplus utilized by the state to advance its industrial modernization was "appropriated from a landowning peasantry," laboring "largely under non-capitalist conditions," by means of heavy taxation (i.e., "essentially extra-economic, non-market mechanisms") by the tsarist state.[9]

The Crisis of Russian Capitalism

The conflicting perspectives we have reviewed find partial reflection in a major controversy of Marxist historiography that has centered on the question of when capitalism became dominant in Russia. One of the most eminent Soviet Marxist historians of the 1920s, M. N. Pokrovskii, argued that the rise of tsarist absolutism over Russia—and the subordination of the landed nobility to it—in the seventeenth and eighteenth centuries was a manifestation of the predominance of commercial capitalism in that part of the world. Pokrovskii was proceeding from a generalization that the rise of absolutist monarchs in Europe, involving the formation of the nation-state (and coherent national economies), represented the passage beyond feudal economic forms under the pressure of merchant and financial capitalists.[10]

Pokrovskii's analysis contains elements worth considering and has a pleasing "Marxist" neatness. At the time Trotsky argued what has also been asserted by more recent scholars, both from the East and West—that it grossly overstates the capitalist nature of tsarism, gives a false impression of the extent of capitalist development in Russia, and glosses over historical peculiarities that must be grasped in order to comprehend the crisis of Russian capitalism and of the society as a whole.[11]

In what follows we will first examine the realities experienced by the most numerous sector of Russian society, the peasantry. Then we will examine the interplay of the tsarist autocracy and capitalist development. Finally we will turn our attention to the experience of the Russian proletariat, whose roots were in the peasantry and whose character was shaped by the interpenetration of tsarism and capitalism.

The Peasantry

At the end of the nineteenth century, over 86 percent of the 108.8 million population of the Russian empire (and roughly the same percentage of those living in European Russia) was rural. The differentiation within the rural population has been a matter of controversy.

Earlier analysts operating within a Marxist framework were inclined to stress supposed "proletarian" layers that later research (also by Marxists) found to be relatively marginal. There was also a tendency to overestimate the number of "poor peasants," as opposed to "middle" and "rich" peasants.[12] Teodor Shanin, on the basis of the most reliable studies, has offered a view of the peasantry summarized in table 1. These bare statistics require further comment, particularly on the question of the extent of capitalist development in the countryside.

Table 1: Rural Stratification in Prerevolutionary Russia

European Russia, 1897–1905	Population (%)	Peasant households (%)
Capitalist farmers	0.8	1.2–1.8
Peasant family farmers		
Rich	2.6	
Well-to-do	12.4	
Middling	51.8	94.2–95.8
Poor	24.4	
Rural proletarians	8.0	3.0–4.0

Source: Shanin, *Russia as a "Developing Society,"* 101.

Some historical background may be useful. The seventh through twelfth centuries had seen the rise of a feudal-type economy in much of what became Russia, with princes at the top of the social hierarchy providing military protection and internal "order" with the assistance of a council of boyars (independent landowners evolving into a landed aristocracy). Beneath the princes there existed a mass of peasants working their own land but paying tribute to their "protectors," plus landless peasants (legally free) laboring on the domains of the landowners. This general structure endured throughout the various transformations wrought by invasions, internal strife, and economic and political developments, up through the rise of the expanding Russian nation-state under Ivan the Great and Ivan the Terrible in the fifteenth and sixteenth centuries.

In this period, however, a process of enserfment crystallized, tying the peasants to the land where they could be subject to increasing domination and exploitation. As Sir John Maynard put it: "The land is wide: eastwards almost boundless: and empty. Hands, whether for weapons or the plough, are precious. There is a struggle to keep the laborer in his place: and, on the other side, to find more freedom or a larger life by flight. . . . The 'Time of Troubles' [a crisis arising after the death of Ivan the Terrible] gave special opportunities and motives for flight, and the new dynasty's needs made it inevitable to bring the elusive peasant under control." And yet the peasantry did not remain simply a passive victim in the face of gradual enserfment, the mounting demands of the state (which "swelled up [while] the people grew lean" in the words of the historian Klyuckevskii), and the ravages of famine and war. A series of massive peasant rebellions shook Russia in the seventeenth and eighteenth centuries as "the old rights" were defended against state and boyar incursions. "Increasingly," writes Shanin, "these were class wars in which the state, its officers and its squires faced rebels consisting of the lowly social orders only. . . . The totality of the defeat of all those attempts and the disappearance of massive popular revolt in the late eighteenth and nineteenth centuries, on par with the vanquishing of all neighboring states of Muscovy, were paramount to the making of tsardom."[13] By the end of the eighteenth century, more than 50 percent of the rural population existed in serf bondage, slightly more than half belonging to individual squires, the rest belonging to the state.

Yet serfdom was not an economic success, particularly by standards of the rising capitalist market: it was a relatively inefficient means for exploiting labor, resulting in low productivity. Economic considerations, combined with fear of peasant restiveness and potential rebellion, led Tsar Alexander II—after much consultation with intellectual experts and the landed nobility—to abolish serfdom in 1861. The conditions of emancipation, however, gave the best lands to the big landowners, leaving the ex-serfs with relatively paltry plots and compelling them to pay redemption fees to their former masters (to the tune of 1 billion rubles between 1861 and 1901). The disappointment, resentment, and smoldering expectation that followed was captured by a contemporary observer: "It is evident that in the people, obscurely, but down to a great depth, a tradition has survived, a memory of a time when landed property was not yet, or not to any great extent, in the hands of the nobles, when nearly all the meadow lands and the forest lands in particular were used indiscriminately and in an undefined way by all." The emancipation of the serfs, although seen by liberal reformers as a way of easing peasant distress and discontent, also generated hopes that such "old ways" would once more come to the fore.[14] The fact that this was, in fact, not to be would greatly add to rural discontent.

Even two decades after emancipation, however, a frustrated revolutionary intellectual, Sergei Mikhailovich Stepniak-Kravchinsky (commonly known as Stepniak), noted that the peasants were not inclined to draw the fundamental revolutionary conclusion: "The tillers of the soil, who form the bulk of the nation, still profess devotion to an ideal Tsar—the creature of their own imagination—believe that the day is at hand when he will drive all landowners out of the country, and bestow their possessions on his faithful peasants."[15]

The fact remains that much of the old way of life had been maintained by the peasants, in the midst of all of Russia's changes, repressions, and disappointments down through the years. "By a strange inconsistency," wrote Stepniak, "the peasantry of that despotic country enjoy—save for some abuses—almost as great a measure of self-government as the rural communes of Switzerland and Norway." He was referring to the ancient commune (*mir* or *obschina*) that was more or less central to Russian peasant life, a relatively democratic decision-making body that provided a minimum of social security and economic equality among its members; the lands of the peasants were often seen as belonging to the commune, although distributed (and sometimes redistributed) to be worked individually by peasant families. "On the one hand, the peasant saw before him his *mir*," wrote Stepniak, "the embodiment of justice and brotherly love; on the other, official Russia, represented by the *tchinovniks* [minor functionaries] of the Tsar, his magistrates, gendarmes, and administrators—through all the centuries . . . the embodiment of rapacity, venality, and violence." The commune was for many years ignored by the powers that be, which gave rise to the saying: "Live and enjoy yourselves, children, while Moscow takes no notice of you."[16]

Yet Moscow did, in fact, take notice. Attempts were made first to integrate village communes into the polity of tsarist Russia, later to undermine and displace them. Particularly with the stratification and differentiation taking place among the peasantry after emancipation (and the direct impact of the marketplace on the peasants), the commune was weakened by defections from the more well-to-do, or in some cases from domination by the more well-to-do. Alexander

Kerensky was hardly the only left-wing intellectual in the early twentieth century to argue that "the authorities turned the commune into a bulwark of economic backwardness and gradually drained it of all vitality." His future adversary Vladimir Ilyich Lenin explained to readers of *The Development of Capitalism in Russia* (1899) that "the system of economic relations in the 'community' village does not at all constitute a special economic form ('people's production,' etc.), but is an ordinary petty-bourgeois one." Challenging precisely the notions of Stepniak and other revolutionary populists, he insisted: "Despite the theories that have prevailed here during the past half-century, the Russian community peasantry are not antagonists of capitalism, but, on the contrary, are its deepest and most durable foundation." However, in seeming contradiction to this, in the same work he describes in one very long sentence the precapitalist peasantry as being at loggerheads with capitalist progress: "One has only to picture to oneself the amazing fragmentation of the small producers, an inevitable consequence of patriarchal agriculture, to become convinced of this progressiveness of capitalism, which is shattering to the very foundations the ancient forms of economy and life, with their age-old immobility and routine, destroying the settled life of the peasants who vegetated behind their medieval partitions, and creating new social classes striving of necessity towards contact, unification, and active participation in the whole of the economic (and not only economic) life of the country, and of the whole world."[17] (We will see that within a few years Lenin's thinking on "the peasant question" underwent at least a partial evolution.)

Despite the perceptions of Kerensky and the young Lenin, the commune seems to have endured as a relatively vital precapitalist, indeed pre-class, influence among the peasantry. "It is not a little strange that this primitive system of land tenure should have succeeded in living into the twentieth century," wrote Sir Donald MacKenzie Wallace in 1912, "and still more remarkable that the institution of which it forms an essential part should be regarded by many intelligent people as one of the great institutions of the future, and almost as a panacea for social and political evils." Panacea or not, Teodor Shanin has noted that in European Russia, which contained 75 percent of the population, there were "about 110,000 rural communes in existence, divided into roughly 500,000 settlements. . . . That made for an average of twenty-one households per settlement, or 745 per commune."[18] One informed observer described their functioning in this manner:

> There were no written laws governing the conduct of the affairs of the mir, and nothing could have been more informal than their assemblies. But habit created a body of precedents which were rigorously enforced. Times of seeding, har-

vesting, and mowing were as inflexible as the laws of the Medes and Persians. Each village had its own inviolable methods of dividing the land. The assemblies themselves were usually held out of doors because there was no other place to contain the crowd. Each family might have a representative at the meeting, and if there were no man living to represent the house, even a woman might come and be heard with the attention due any householder. The village elder seems to have never sought the office, because it always carried more responsibility than reward. Parliamentary rules in the meeting were simple. Everybody talked on the subject in hand, and often two at once, until there seemed to be nothing more to be said. The elder would then appear from some place in the crowd and state the summary result of the discussion as the decision of the mir. If there was a close division, upraised hands were counted.

It must be remembered that these assemblies were not political in any wide sense. They were concerned merely with the division and cultivation of their own lands, the repair of a bridge, the building of a public bath house and other such practical problems.... Courts, taxes, police, and so on, continued to be the exclusive machinery of the central government. But the village had learned to think of itself as an economic unit ... [through] ancient practice ... [19]

To a very large extent, then, the culture, worldview, and way of life of the Russian peasantry did not mesh with the "possessive individualism" characteristic of capitalism as such, undercutting tendencies to make peasants a "commercial petty bourgeoisie." This was structured not only into the rural commune, but into the peasant household that was the basic unit of Russian agriculture. (The household is essential: in the Legal Code of the Russian empire, family property took the place, among peasants, of private property among non-peasants; "the life of a family is the life of a farm," one observer commented.) This peasant economy—in which small producers on the land, "with the help of simple equipment and the labor of their families, produce mainly for their own consumption and for meeting obligations to the holders of political and economic power" (as Shanin puts it)—generates attitudes and decision-making that are irrational and "backward" from the standpoint of those operating in other frameworks (capitalist, tsarist, some Marxists, and so forth), but that make good sense within the framework of traditional peasant life.[20]

One writer who grew up in a peasant village, Maurice Hindus, pushes against romanticizing this way of life. On the one hand he argues the while "the peasant is ignorant—more than half can neither read nor write—ignorance does not imply stupidity, not more than college training implies intelligence. On the contrary, in his own way the peasant is highly intelligent." On the other hand, "to this day the Russian peasant follows very largely the same methods of cultivation his ancestors practiced before him. He inherits these just as he sometimes inherits his father's boots or sheepskin coat." More than this, the rural commune—the *mir*—helps to perpetuate the backwardness by perpetually redistributing the strips of land to be individually farmed, thereby giving the peasant "no incentive to improve his land." Hindus concludes that "in the vast majority of cases he is ignorant of the contributions of science, is enslaved to the deadening traditions of the *mir*, has little land, lacks machinery, lacks horses. No wonder that year after year in Russia, perhaps the richest agricultural country in the world, millions of industrious farmers have had to face starvation."[21]

Four decades later, however, Hindus seems to have rethought his severe judgments:

> The muzhik [peasant] had never heard of planning. Yet as I view him in retrospect I am bound to say that he was a magnificent planner. He had to be to survive. He planned crops in proper proportion: so much land for cereals, including millet and buckwheat for soup and *kasha,* so much for flax, so much for potatoes, cabbage, cucumbers, beets other vegetables. . . . He planned principally for his own needs, for the number of mouths of his family. His system was infallible. . . . He did the best he could with what tools he could afford, some of which—like the wooden pitchfork, the wooden flail, and sometimes even the wooden harrow—he fashioned with his own hands. But he and his wife and children sweated on the land in rain or shine, wind or storm, performed their work on time, gathering every spear of hay, every stalk of grain and flax, every potato however small or green. Waste even of a small green potato which a pig would eat was an unpardonable sin.[22]

This way of life, however, was up against terrible assaults—from the state and landlords (taxes and rents ate up 18 percent of the total peasant income by 1913), from the necessity of producing for the market in order to obtain the means for meeting financial obligations (which caused them to overwork themselves and to consume less than they needed—as growing amounts of grain and other agricultural produce were exported). "We shall under-eat, but we will export," one tsarist finance minister had vowed. As Shanin comments, "under the Russian conditions that meant, of course, under-eating by peasants and exporting by profiteers." Official reports from the early twentieth century described peasant conditions as involving the most abject poverty—diseases of all kinds, overcrowded and unclean living conditions, undernourishment and hunger in bad times. Even in "good times" the peasants' diet was poor. "The normal fare consists of bread, kvas (a kind of weak beer brewed from rye) and often cabbage and onions, to which vegetables may be added in autumn," Maynard wrote. Rural poverty and desperation increased over the years as the average land unit (measured in *dessiatins*) per peasant male dropped from 4.8 in 1861 to 3.5 in 1880, then again to 2.6 in 1900 and 1.8 in 1917.[23]

One's ability to connect with and comprehend the dynamics of the larger world—beyond one's insular local reality—is often, and aptly, seen as being related to the ability to read and write. As the nineteenth century made way for the twentieth, the literacy rate in Russia was among the lowest in Europe—overall, 72 percent of the people (61 percent of all males, 83 percent of all females) were illiterate. The situation was worst among the masses living in the countryside (cities such Moscow and St. Petersburg suffered only 40–43 percent illiteracy).[24]

Quality of Life in the Countryside

Let us first examine more closely the qualities that distinguished Russia's peasant communities and then give attention to the quality of life within these communities.

The totality of peasant life—incredibly complex and contradictory and in some ways fluid—has posed a challenge to social scientists, Marxists included, that has generated confusion, controversy, and contending interpretations. Among the Marxist theorists within the Russian Social Democratic Labor Party in the early twentieth century, Lenin made perhaps the boldest shift from an inadequate "orthodoxy" to an insightful appreciation of the complications and possibilities inherent in "the peasant question"—and even he proved unable to fully comprehend the seemingly chaotic dynamism of the reality.[25] A comment from Trotsky seems to capture one element of the reality: "The peasantry . . . contains in itself in a rudimentary form all the classes of bourgeois society. . . . [It] constitutes that protoplasm out of which new classes have been differentiated in the past, and continue to be differentiated in the present." The fecundity of this vast social layer is narrowed, however, in Trotsky's next comment: "The peasantry always has two faces, one turned towards the proletariat, the other toward the bourgeoisie."[26]

Trotsky's comments capture an important aspect of the Russian reality and are consistent with other efforts to develop a Marxist understanding of what constitutes "the peasantry"—among the more important of which was by another Russian Bolshevik theorist, Leonid Kritsman: "Peasant farming is the farming of petty producers. A characteristic of them is the presence in their enterprise of their own means of production and its use by their own labor." In fact, as T. J. Byres has pointed out, "peasantries with such character-istics"—constituting the great majority of humanity, historically, since the rise of civilizations in agricultural societies throughout the world—"have existed within a variety of modes of production since the dawn of recorded history."[27] This recognition of the peasantry existing as an essential element in "a variety of modes of production," however, transcends the capitalist focus characterizing Trotsky's second comment, suggesting the possibility of qualities that transcend the two options he identifies.

Teodor Shanin adds important dimensions: "Peasants can be defined as small producers on land who, with the help of simple equipment and the labor of their families, produce mainly for their own consumption *and for meeting obligations to the holders of political and economic power*" (emphasis add-ed). As this suggests, the very possibility of civilization—and of the various civilizations that arose—is based on the expropriation and utilization of the agricultural surplus produced by the peasantry. This surplus has made possible the growth of social classes (powerful minorities living on the sur-plus wealth produced by the labor of the many), the rise of towns and cit-ies, the crystallization of elaborate governmental and religious structures, occupational specialization, and all of the cultural developments related to such things. Such civilizations, in considerable variety, have come into being in different parts of the world (in distinctive regions, on almost all continents) at different periods in human history, taking unique form in dif-ferent "modes of production" (types of economic systems) which Marxists have identified as ancient slave civilizations, feudalism, the so-called Asiatic mode of production (a term masking still more diverse realities) in China and India and elsewhere, and the early capitalism of Western Europe. In all of these and more, it is the peasantry that has constituted the bulk of the population—making each form of society possible, helping to shape those societies while also experiencing the changes generated by these various modes of production. "Peasantries change constantly and ever interact with non-peasants," as Shanin puts it.[28]

While this is consistent with Trotsky's insight regarding the dynamical-ly mixed "proletarian" and "bourgeois" elements that one could find in the peasantry, Shanin (in part following the idiosyncratic analysis developed by a maverick Marxist theorist, Alexander Chayanov, and the later analysis of historian Viktor Danilov) offers a more complex understanding. Inherent in Russian peasant life were qualities that were far removed from capitalist dy-namics. The "functioning of the family production unit" and "the life of small rural communities" could best be understood as "specific social relations and political economy attached to the underdog position in society," with distinctive cultural traits naturally tending toward a perpetuation of the traditional peasant economy.[29]

The complexity of these realities has already been stressed, but it is worth emphasizing it further. Moshe Lewin tells us that "in populist literature, the peasant appears as the salt of the earth, the ultimate repository of all the highest moral qualities; the village community was the embryo of a future socialist society which would even be able to assist the West to free itself from a 'decaying' regime." He elaborates that the "populists regarded the peasant as 'good and thoughtful, a tireless seeker after truth and justice,'" but then offers the sharp challenge articulated by left-wing writer Maxim Gorky, who drew from his own considerable experience in rural Russia: "In my youth, I assiduously sought such a man in the villages of Russia, and no where did I find him."[30]

It is worth consulting more of what Gorky has to say: "I met there instead a tough, cunning realist who, when it was favorable to him, knew quite well how to make himself out as a simpleton." He adds: "By nature the peasant is not stupid and knows it well. He has composed a multitude of wistful songs and rough, cruel stories, created thousands of proverbs embodying the experience of his difficult life." He cites a number of the proverbs to bolster his case. "The peasant is not stupid, it is the world which is the fool," one tells us, and there is a follow-up: "A truthful man is like a fool, both are harmful." Related to this: "Truth will not feed you." Insular and wedded to the "old ways" one is used to, resistant to the so-called "truths" of science and modernization, the peasant showed a deep and natural inclination to embrace traditional forms of agriculture with low productivity. This would, therefore, feed into the perpetuation of peasant misery. Gorky saw the peasantry as "the fundamental obstacle in the way of Russian progress," thanks to "the deadweight of illiterate village life which stifles the town, the animal-like individualism of the peasantry, and the peasants' almost total lack of social consciousness."[31]

Lewin comments that "there is a great deal of truth in this verdict, despite the obviously exaggerated terms in which it is expressed." He elaborates that a peasant's life involved "total dependence on a natural environment which was both harsh and unpredictable, his spells of intense hard work alternating with periods of enforced idleness, and a life lived in villages far removed from any center of civilization," all combining to forge "a type that was both superstitious and mistrustful, unsure of himself except when treading the well-worn paths of tradition and already predisposed to submit to overmastering forces, whether these forces be supernatural, or the political forces of law and order, or simply the power of a richer neighbor."[32]

In 1917, Gorky wrote:

> Our peasantry lives in horrible conditions, lacking properly organized medical care. Half of all peasant children die of various diseases before the age of five. Almost all the women in the village suffer from women's diseases. The villages are rotting with syphilis; the villages have sunk into destitution, ignorance, and savagery. The Russian peasant is unable to cultivate his land so that it will yield the greatest possible amount of food. . . . Our country is large and abounds in natural resources, but we live like beggars in filth and unhappiness.[33]

Such brutalizing conditions often helped generate terrible cycles of brutalization within the very dynamics of some peasant families. "Peasant children on winter evenings when they are bored and not yet sleepy, catch cockroaches and tear off their legs one by one," wrote Gorky. "This pleasant pastime reminds one very much of the general significance of our attitude toward our neighbor . . ." Lewin tells us that "any infraction of paternal discipline was severely punished, usually by physical cruelty in the shape of beatings of sometimes maniacal violence. This element of cruelty was a general feature of peasant life." He adds: "Gorky has many descriptions of the forms which it took. Women and children pitilessly beaten with sadistic delight, bloody fights with knife and hatchet, murder for vengeance and fire-raising—these were all commonplaces of village life."[34]

One might argue that the degradation described by Gorky is precisely that—*degradation* of the traditional peasant economy under the combined impacts of tsarist autocracy, aristocratic oppression, and capitalist development. That is certainly the way many critical-minded observers explained the problems of rural Russia that they perceived. As we linger over accounts of prerevolutionary Russia, we see graphic descriptions linked with pointed comments on the oppressive system. As part of his indictment of tsarism, Moissaye Olgin describes the peasant village by sharing a lengthy quotation from a 1905 account written by M. Menshikov, a supporter of the old regime:

> Let us enter a village and look upon it with the eyes of modern, cultivated people. The roads are deep in mud, often rendering them impassable. Near the houses there are no trees, no bushes to rest your eyes on. The horse-pond is close to the well, and the dung oozes into it. In the courtyards everything is filthy, the odor quite intolerable. The cattle in their enclosure stand knee-deep in excrement. The entrance room and the living-room are black from neglect, and the floors are

strewn with the excrements of poultry. In winter, the living-room is shared with pigs, sheep, geese; sometimes the cow is also placed here to get warm (an English traveler wondered at the low standards of a Russian cow, that it was able to endure such a room). Still, where there are cattle the lowest pitch of poverty has not been reached. In the same room, a baby crawls on the floor with a potato in its hands. Cockroaches, bedbugs, fleas infest the rooms in legions, and the heads, beards, mustaches and even eyebrows of grown-up men are filled with the most hideous insects. "Well, 'tis nothing." . . . Everything is so utterly foul, there is not a spot where you can lie down. The mark of evil taste and barbarism is stamped on everything, on the household, on the devastated natural surroundings.[35]

It is worth considering, for another moment, the interior of the peasant home, in which "large families are the rule and not the exception" according to Maurice Hindus. "And then there are the grandparents and perhaps some non-relative, an adopted orphan or an illegitimate child, all living in the same room which is kitchen, bedroom, dining hall, reception parlor and during the cold month also calf-pen, pig-sty and lamb stall!"[36]

"Do not convict the peasant too hastily of uncleanliness," urges William English Walling, a sharp-eyed and well-informed US socialist who studied Russia first-hand in 1905–07. "There is no doubt that he lives in contaminating proximity with his calves, chickens, and sometimes pigs. The reason for this is not far to seek. In the long and severe winters the animals would often freeze if it were not that they got a little heat of the living room." He adds: "Furthermore, it is true the peasant does not often change his clothes. An answer to this charge is, he has not the clothes to change." Walling reflects on the causes:

> The terribly low productivity of the peasant's agriculture and the small size of his income are of course at the bottom of his suffering. . . . To discuss a remedy for this condition leads at once to the whole social problem, the whole economic and political situation of the country. . . .
>
> Let us remember that the Government and the landlords, and all the innumerable writers and journalists in their pay all over the world, blame the peasants themselves for their tragic condition . . . [L]et us realize to the full the criminal character of a monarch and nobility that can sustain their self-respect before the modern world only by this most infamous campaign of lies against the people to whose exploitation and misery they owe their very existence.[37]

Walling adds other details—for example, "the shoe is not of leather, but is of woven bark," and "even in winter one sees more boots of felt than of leather." The pathetic "housekeeping" recorded by Menshikov and Gorky is suggested in other observations by Walling: "Of course, it is impossible for any woman that must work like a man in the fields to give any attention to cooking; occasionally, with a great effort and at sacrifice of her already exhausted strength, a peasant women will be able to cook a little potato or cabbage soup in the evening. Ordinarily she leaves a few pieces of bread at home for the children, takes more with her to the fields and returns only after an absence of twelve to fifteen hours—for we must remember that the Russian system forces the peasants to work at great distances from the villages." He adds that "nearly every peasant woman of middle age is sick in some way or another." And he continually emphasizes the systemic nature of the peasants' plight. "We must remember that not only do famines occur occasionally, but that in the larger part of the country they occur with the greatest regularity every two or three years." His indignation comes through again and again: "Considering the many millions of persons that have died in Russia in the last decade from direct starvation or diseases that are derived from it, the amount borrowed and spent on such an absolutely prime national necessity as the relief of famine has been trivial—a total of few million rubles in all these years."[38]

Some observers attributed the plight of the peasantry to more than the tsarist system. "The 'primitive accumulation' of capital thrived wonderfully in Russia from [the regime's] promotion of all manner of state subsidies, guarantees, premiums, and orders placed by the government, and reaped profits that would become legend in the West at the time," wrote Rosa Luxemburg in her 1913 study *The Accumulation of Capital*. "As a result, internal conditions in Russia offered nothing less than an attractive and promising picture at the time. In the countryside, the decline and disintegration of the peasant economy under the pressures of heavy taxation and the monetary economy yielded terrible conditions, periodic famines, and peasant unrest."[39]

More recent scholarship has added important detail. "The vast mass of the peasantry was marked, above all, by its remoteness, which greatly complicated economic development, political education and cultural enlightenment in the countryside," according to Viktor Danilov. He goes on to emphasize the importance of considering the differences between one region and another. Speaking of innumerable tiny villages in the country's northwest, he comments: "These were truly God-forsaken places—cut off, without roads, from the matrix of economic life and culture. Patriarchalism and the disenfranchisement of the poorer peasant masses were ever present." On the other hand, "the size and the character of villages changed fundamentally from the wood zones of the north to the steppe-and-wood and steppe zones of Russia's main agricultural regions (the Black-Earth center, the middle and lower

Volga regions, the northern Caucasus and the Ukraine)." With vast areas of fertile soil, and extensive grain farming, "peasant settlements, stretched along rivers, were larger and more sparsely spread." He adds: "The concentration of the rural population facilitated political and cultural work. Village life in these regions was less remote. Hamlets and *khutora* [farmsteads and villages] were connected with their neighboring village. Class differentiation was more clearly marked." The Siberian and Asian hinterlands involved yet more different patterns and smaller settlements, as well as "more remote, nomadic and semi-nomadic peoples."[40]

A stark generalization in 1913, however, was articulated by Gregor Alexinsky (a left-wing Bolshevik before being de-radicalized by the First World War), who wrote that "the economic and social life of the Russian village . . . is not life: it is the slow death of creatures incessantly hungry, whose starvation can only be compared with that of the more poverty-stricken masses of the East—of Persia, India, and China," regions penetrated by Western capitalism. Just as the prevalence of famine in those areas had increased, "the death-rate in Russia, instead of diminishing, is continually increasing. At the end of the eighteenth century it was 20 per 1,000. At the end of the nineteenth century this figure had risen to 35 per 1,000, and in some parts to 50. Between 1891 and 1892 a large number of entire villages were literally extinguished." In the same study, he emphasized the dramatically uneven impacts of capitalist development within Russia: "Being based upon the poverty of the State and the retrograde condition of the wretched and innumerable Russian villages, the oasis of economy and capitalist culture attained a considerable development." He goes on to quote the prominent economist Mikhail Tugan-Baranovsky: "The great capitalists, having already led the way in our industrial life, assumed a greater importance than ever, profiting by the ruin of smaller competitors. Social contrasts thus became more marked than ever at a time when the country was generally impoverished."[41] The key to the worsening plight of the peasantry, as well as to the coming of the Russian Revolution, was precisely this interplay between the tsarist autocracy and capitalist development.

The Tsarist Autocracy and Capitalist Development

At the very apex of the tsarist autocracy, of course, stood the Tsar. Nicholas II—buttressed by officious support from Tsarina Alexandra—was quite clear on what he should do with the immense power he had inherited. "His only duty was to keep Russia great, and to maintain intact the powers that God had entrusted him," emphasizes Marc Ferro, and the tsar was particularly good at what he knew how to do—such as "ceremonies and festivals, first nights at the opera, the life of high society generally," and all things "identified with the intangible grandeur of the autocracy." At the same time, "he avoided all serious talk, especially talk about the situation in the country: ministers were appointed to see to all that." Not even the most capable of ministers, however, were sufficiently capable of overcoming the unraveling of the old regime. (Those most sophisticated and effective—such as Sergei Witte and Pyotr Stolypin—ultimately ran afoul of powerful traditionalists dominant within the tsar's court.) Sometimes he was called "Nicholas the Unlucky," because "he was always at the receiving end of events, never their initiator," but he did his best to maintain order amid the subsequent popular discontent, thereby (especially during the uprising of 1905) earning his other appellation—"Nicholas the Bloody." In the words of Grand Duchess Maria Pavlovna: "In every fold of this little man's royal mantle there is the autocrat." As Ferro also emphasizes, however, Nicholas—who "looked with tender kindness on those he loved"— was most definitely *not* bloodthirsty. The "cruel consequences of measures he decreed" flowed from his belief "that he had a duty to oppose change," which meant that, strengthened by loyal advisors who saw to such things and considerable forces of repression at the regime's disposal, he conscientiously oversaw "shooting people as a matter of scruple."[42]

A key weakness of the Tsar is identified in Dominic Lieven's analysis of Russia's arrogant stumble into the disastrous 1904 Russo-Japanese War, which paved the way for the revolutionary explosion of 1905. "He listened far too much to unofficial aristocratic advisors with mostly military backgrounds who fueled his dreams about Russia's glorious future in the east," Lievin tells us. "They also encouraged his distrust for the cautious policies urged by his ministers of foreign affairs, war, and finance, whom they despised as 'mere bureaucrats.'" Consequently, Nicholas "undermined the whole regular system of decision making, in the process sowing uncertainty, paralysis, and confusion." Lieven concludes: "If Nicholas himself had been competent to realistically judge priorities and risks and then to impose his decisions, all might have been well. As it was, he created a hole in the center of decision making that he was unable himself to fill."[43]

Just as the tides of history had placed him in the position in which he felt compelled to become "Nicholas the Bloody," so would they pitilessly lead his dynasty and all associated with it to final ruin and destruction. Surveying the long trends in Russian history, we can see how unlucky Nicholas truly was. "He held on to his throne as if in a delirium and with a fanatical obstinacy," wrote a Russian correspondent shortly after the revolution that overthrew him, "as if trembling for his life, with which he identified his authority. His system was the complicated system of distrust of all. . . . The sphere of his mental activity was, of course, very limited. He knew that it was necessary to command. He knew that in no case must one make concessions unless absolutely forced by circumstances. His obduracy during the last days was, however, equivalent to sheer insanity."[44]

Russia's early history is not a simple replication (with "time lags") of Western European feudalism evolving into capitalism. There were also powerful influences from the East, particularly with the Mongol invasion of the thirteenth century. Lionel Kochan has summarized: "What Mongol rule did contribute to Russian life was a certain absolutist and autocratic framework. By far the most important effect of the Mongols was to further the creation of the Muscovite type of autocracy that emerged at the end of the fifteenth century. What the Russians at first dreaded they later imitated as a measure of self-defense." This conflicts with the notion put forward by Pokrovskii that tsarism was a form of monarchist-absolutism similar to the reigns of England's Henry VIII and France's Louis XIV, tied to the rise of commercial capitalism and the modern nation-state. Indeed, some more recent Soviet historians, such as M. Ia. Volkov, argued that the tsarist autocracy "should not be likened to the European absolute monarchies for it was closer to what Marx called 'the Asiatic mode of rule.'"[45]

The impact of "Asiatic despotism" had similarly affected the evolution of the landed nobility in Russia, which had provided tsarism's immediate base, and the upper reaches of which blended with the tsarist court. Observers such as Sir Donald MacKenzie Wallace have stressed that this aristocracy was not comparable—in historical experience or latter-day mind-set—to that which arose under Western European feudalism. While in earlier times boyars and knights had enjoyed considerable power, making the central monarch little more than the first among equals, "under the Mongol domination this political equilibrium was destroyed. When the country had been conquered, the princes had become servile vassals of the Khan, and arbitrary rulers toward their own subjects." When Mongol rule finally disintegrated and an indigenous tsarism arose to rule over "all the Russias," Wallace notes that "the Tsars had adopted . . . a good deal of the Mongol system of government." Addressing the question of why a landed nobility, "which had formerly shown a proud spirit of independence," would submit to the new despotism of the tsar, he wrote: "But we must remember that the nobles, as well as the princes, had passed in the meantime through the school of Mongol domination. In the course of two centuries they had gradually become accustomed to despotic rule in the Oriental sense." And yet, there continued to be an undercurrent of pull and tug between tsar and nobility: Peter the Great sought total authority and demanded that nobles serve the state; Catherine the Great owed her throne to a Court conspiracy and support of the nobles, and therefore sought to win their voluntary service through flattery, honors, and rewards.[46]

The pendulum swung back and forth from the nineteenth to the twentieth century. "During the time of darkest reaction, under Alexander III, the nobility was only one of our estates, even if first among them," wrote Trotsky. "The autocracy, vigilantly protecting its own independence, never for a moment allowed the nobility to escape from the grip of police supervision, putting the muzzle of state control on the maw of its natural greed." Indeed, in that period strong liberal and radical currents arose among the nobility (generating even such deities of anarchism as Bakunin, Tolstoy, and Kropotkin). In the twentieth century, Trotsky continued, the pendulum swung the other way: "The nobility is the commanding estate in the fullest sense of the word: it makes the provincial governors dance to its tune, threatens the ministers and openly dismisses them, puts ultimata to the government and makes sure that these ultimata are observed. Its slogan is: not a square inch of our land, not a particle of our privileges." Roberta Manning has corroborated: "Faced with the unprecedented loss of their landholdings and a corresponding decline in the role they played in government service, growing numbers of Russia's traditional governing elite came to eschew the service careers of their ancestors in order to live full time on their country estates, involving themselves with agriculture and local affairs in the newly founded zemstvos and the more than century-old noble assemblies." From this newly shored-up political base they moved "in an increasingly conscious fashion to regain their lost influence in national affairs from the hands of a new, alien, professionalized bureaucracy, drawn ever more heavily from the nongentry."[47] And yet this resurgent aristocratic stratum did not see itself in conflict with tsarism itself—quite the contrary. Describing the outlook of one conservative landowner, Wallace has commented:

> He maintains that the only firm foundation for the Russian Empire, and the only solid guarantee of its future prosperity, is the autocratic power, which is the sole genuine representative of the national spirit. Looking at the past from this point of view, he perceives that the Tsars have ever identified themselves with the

nation, and have always understood, in part instinctively and in part by reflection, what the nation really required. Whenever the infiltration of Western ideas threatened to swamp the national individuality, the autocratic power intervened and averted the danger by timely precautions.[48]

And yet the massive state bureaucracy—increasingly composed of nonaristocratic careerists, and in some ways generating Western-influenced changes throughout Russia—was essential to tsarism's power, policy, and *raison d'être*. One of its primary purposes was to maintain "order" and counteract "subversion," to be sure, but another was to make Russia competitive in the struggle for wealth and power on a world scale, and often this meant "modernization" policies distasteful to aristocratic traditionalists. Particularly from the time of Peter the Great in the late seventeenth century, the tsars perceived the necessity of fostering the country's industrial development, which was especially important for the military protection of Russia in the face of a technologically superior West. "New branches of handicraft, machinery, factories, big industry, capital, were, so to say, artificially grafted on the national economic stem," Trotsky commented. "Capitalism seemed to be an offspring of the state." This was a reversal of Pokrovskii's schema: the tsarist state generated Russian capitalism, rather than capitalism generating tsarism. The earlier existence of merchants, who were needed to facilitate trade over the vast expanse of Russian territory (similar to the need for trade in many precapitalist societies), created a different dynamic than that of wage-labor and capital accumulation; this came from other sources. After the free labor created by the 1861 abolition of serfdom, the industrial revolution was ready to come to Russia. Especially under the impact of government policies in the 1890s—extensive railway construction, protectionist tariffs, government orders to manufacturers, the adoption of the gold standard—there was a rapid expansion of heavy industry. If Russian capitalist development was largely imposed from above, it was also largely imported from abroad. Western European firms supplied both technology and capital in the form of loans to the tsarist state. By the end of the nineteenth century, especially with the pool of free labor created after 1861, European capital began to pour across the border to invest directly in Russian industry. Entrepreneurs were "attracted by the untouched natural wealth of the country, and especially by the unorganized labor-power, which so far had not been accustomed to put up any resistance," Trotsky recounted. Contrary to W. W. Rostow's assertion about the diminished role of foreign capital and entrepreneurship in the first decade and a half of the twentieth century, conservative estimates indicate that between 1900 and 1913 foreign capital—largely French and British—in private companies rose from 28.5 percent to 33 percent (with some sources placing the figure at about 50 percent). Foreign capital increased in these years by more than 85 percent (as opposed to a less than 60 percent increase from Russian capital), dominating the oil industry but also providing 42 percent of the capital in metal goods, 28 percent in textiles, 50 percent in chemicals, and 37 percent in woodworking. "Russian banks formed close links with foreign banks," writes Alec Nove, "and were effective in the cartelization of Russian industry, through the creation of so-called Syndicates, which followed the depression of 1900–3." As Soviet economic historian Peter I. Lyashchenko noted, while "in terms of absolute size Russian capital was far more important than foreign capital in the capitalist system of Russia, the system as a whole was nevertheless falling more and more under the influence of foreign capital." (Lyashchenko also noted that, by World War I, capital from England, France, and Belgium accounted for 69.5 percent of total foreign capital engaged in Russia's industrialization, while German capital investments accounted for only 20 percent, suggesting that this helps explain why Russia would join the former, and not the latter, as an ally in the global conflict.)[49]

By the early twentieth century, Wallace reported that an indigenous "wealthy, enlightened bourgeoisie" (not more than 100,000 people, according to Shanin) was being formed in Russia, resulting from the fact that "the old spirit of caste and routine which long animated the merchant class is rapidly disappearing." Wallace added that "not a few nobles are now exchanging country life and the service of the State for industrial and commercial enterprises." On the other hand, according to Trotsky, "the tremendous part played . . . by foreign capital has had a fatal influence on the Russian bourgeoisie's power of political influence." Trotsky went on to explain: "As a result of state indebtedness, a considerable share of the national product went abroad year by year, enriching and strengthening the European bourgeoisie. But the aristocracy of the stock exchange, which holds the hegemony in European countries and which, without effort, turned the tsarist government into its financial vassal, neither wished nor was able to become part of the bourgeois opposition within Russia, if only because no other form of national government would have guaranteed it the usurer's rates of interest it exacted under Tsarism." In his study of Moscow businessmen covering over half a century, Thomas Owen has argued that it was not until 1905 that they had made the shift from a parochial and subservient merchant ideology to a more confident, class-conscious bourgeois ideology, a point corroborated by Jo Ann Ruckman's study—although Ruckman argues that even then they were "not entirely . . . reborn as a modern bourgeoisie," and Owen suggests that many Russian industrialists were drawn less to a forward-looking bourgeois liberalism than to perspectives providing common ground with tsarism: "In the difficult transition from a traditional agricultural society to a modern industrial one, Russian nationalism, articulated persuasively by the prophets of Slavophilism and Official Nationality, outweighed the desire for economic and political freedom." Trotsky suggested that the capitalist sector that was engaged in heavy industry—being "everywhere dependent on state activities and, principally, on militarism"— proved more conservative, while the employers in the textile industry, being less dependent on the state and more interested in reforms that could raise the purchasing power of the masses, proved to be more liberal (up to a point). He denied, however, that the Russian capitalist class could "take up a position at the head of the national struggle with Tsarism, since, from the first, it was antagonistic to the popular masses—the proletariat, which it exploits directly, and the peasantry, which it robs indirectly through the state [i.e., taxes on the peasantry utilized to bolster industrial development]."[50]

We might be well served, in considering the nature of the Russian bourgeoisie, to give attention to the story of one of the most powerful capitalist families native to Russian soil—the Morozovs. Arising from peasants who were Old Believers (dissident Christian purists who did not accept the Russian Orthodox Church), through pluck and luck and intensive labors, and under the lead of Savva Vasilevich Morozov, they rose out of serfdom in the late eighteenth century, built businesses that survived the Napoleonic Wars, with dye and ribbon and then textile factories that helped pave the way for the expansion of industrial capitalist enterprise in tsarist Russia throughout the nineteenth century. Old Savva died a multimillionaire at the age of ninety in 1860, and the growing business empire was taken over by his tough-minded youngest son, Timofei Savvich Morozov. "Success never softened [Timofei], and he remained always a despot in the fullest sense of the term," according to W. Bruce Lincoln, ruling "his workers and his family with an iron hand." This devout Old Believer exploited his workers so brutally, Lincoln tells us, that "he spent tearful hours before his icon, asking for forgiveness." His industrial despotism turned his laborers into working-class heroes who organized the powerful Morozov Strike of 1885, which became a beacon of labor resistance that inspired militant workers and Russian Marxists for years to come. Although the strike initially won all of its demands, the regime of Tsar Alexander III intervened to overturn the results, arrest the strike leaders, and send hundreds of the temporarily victorious strikers back to their peasant villages.[51]

The crucial affiliation between the capitalist and the tsar that we see above hardly gave support to the notion that capitalists would lead that "bourgeois revolution" seen by Marxists as the next big step of Russia's historical agenda. What followed, in the saga of the Morozovs, complicates the picture even further.

When Timofei Savicch Morozov died four years later, he left four sons who may have loved him but also hated him, and a shrewd if cold-hearted wife, Maria Fedorovna Morozova—a devout Old Believer with powerful business sense, just like him, and who consequently inherited a controlling interest in the family's industrial empire. She chose the most innovative of her sons, Savva Timofeivich Morozov, to run the business. On the one hand, he was the perfect choice; on the other hand, he was a disaster. A hard-working modernizer applying to the Russian context advanced technology and new production techniques (with which he became familiar as a young man through an immersion in the British industrial scene), young Morozov sought to ensure industrial peace by improving wages, hours, and working conditions in his factories. His mind was stirred by the natural sciences and by the heady intellectual-cultural currents of the Enlightenment, Romanticism, and Social Realism. His heart was more engaged with the arts than with business; he was enamored with the theater through his contact with the likes of Anton Chekov and Konstantin Stanislavsky, and he was the leading patron of the new Moscow Art Theater. He also became a fast friend and supporter of the left-wing writer Maxim Gorky. Through Gorky, he connected with the Russian Social Democratic Labor Party, and began funneling thousands of rubles to the Bolsheviks. As if treating his workers fairly was not enough, he began exploring how workers' self-management and profit-sharing might be implemented in the factories of the Morozov empire. Far from becoming a force for the triumph of capitalism over tsarism, he was reaching for a transition from both to socialism. By 1905 his horrified mother made use of her controlling interest to throw him unceremoniously out, turning the Morozov enterprises over to those dedicated to maintaining capitalist profits and tsarist order—with her deposed son suffering a nervous breakdown and then (after funneling more money to the revolutionaries) committing suicide.[52]

Savva Morozov may not have represented a majority of Russian capitalists, but he was part of a significant trend that Carter Elwood has termed "repentant capitalists" who were drawn to the revolutionary movement. "What kind of bourgeoisie was this?" a revolutionary activist, George Denike, reminisced in wonder. "To the extent that they became politically involved and actually revolutionary they joined a party that was antagonistic to the bourgeoisie." Bertram Wolfe would later tag it a capitalist "death wish."[53]

Those who didn't have such a "death wish" veered away from anti-tsarist revolution (despite frustrations with tsarism). Consider the testimony of someone who was especially active in Russian business circles of this period, Simon Liberman. Liberman had been active in the socialist movement up to the 1905–07 period, as a Menshevik; then, like many others, he drifted away to "make a life" for himself—though he maintained some of his old radical sympathies and contacts. His Menshevik ideology as well as his new life situation made him sensitive to possibilities of the Russian capitalists playing a role in the "bourgeois-democratic" struggle against the tsarist autocracy. He was destined to be disappointed. One of "the most progressive industrialists of Russia," Alexis Meschersky, Liberman observed, "would often wax indignant over the stupidity of the tsarist regime" in private conversation; yet he also made the following remarks to Liberman in regard to the tsarist troops the two of them saw battling workers in early 1917: "It's too bad the authorities are acting with such caution, afraid to shed blood. We need a real blood-letting to put an end to these disorders." Liberman went on to offer a description of the outlook of the Russian capitalists that is so revealing it merits quotation in full:

> In tsarist times I was a frequent participant in the conferences of sundry councils of Russian industrialists. Some of the latter had come up the hard way, beginning as poor and radically inclined university students and attaining their commanding posts after many years of intellectual and physical sweat. A majority of them were opposed to the tsarist regime, seeing in it as they did a feudalistic encumbrance. They felt that industrial capital was the lawful heir of this regime and should take over. But it was the working class that represented the only real and fighting force of the revolution against tsarism and its feudalism. The industrialists were afraid of the workers and also of the peasants.
>
> They declared openly that they were ready and willing to make their peace with the tsarist regime in order to withstand the desires and demands of the working class and, in part, of the peasantry, too. In the more progressive strata of Russian society we could discern awareness that the revolution against tsarism could triumph only if Russia's most active classes—the workers and the peasants—received some social boons in the process. Some Russian capitalists would not have minded seeing the workers and the peasants overthrow tsarism—but they would not allow for one moment the unpleasant thought that capital, too, would have to make concessions to those very classes which might make this revolution a success.[54]

Contrary to common sense expectations of many Marxists (who assumed that the bourgeoisie would naturally lead the "bourgeois-democratic revolution"), the Russian variant of capitalism seemed unable to produce a bourgeoisie capable of struggling for power, or of leading the way in overcoming the crisis afflicting the combined tsarist-capitalist order.

The crisis that arose in this peculiarly Russian variant of capitalism had several dimensions. Of particular interest is the analysis of Tim McDaniel's study *Autocracy, Capitalism and Revolution in Russia,* which argues that, with Russia's distinctive *autocratic capitalism,* "the beliefs, practices, and institutions of derivative capitalist modernization combined with the traditional political model to give rise to a new and insoluble set of social and political challenges"—a form of uneven and combined development leading (as did a similarly peculiar variant in the Southern portion of the United States of America, with its blend of capitalism and slavery) to an "irrepressible conflict."[55]

It is especially interesting to see how the dynamics of this played in the experience and thinking in regard to the thorny question of the peasant *mir* or *obschina,* as viewed by conservative and liberal supporters of the Old Regime:

> One of the main sources of the government's impotence was administrative incoherence aggravated by the project of autocratic capitalism. Governmental disarray was evident on the ideological as well as organizational levels. Throughout the last decades of tsarist rule everything was in flux. Western ideas and institutions had been imported but not assimilated. The traditional models had decayed but not entirely so, and many conservatives hoped to revive them. These conflicting views of the future of Russia could be seen not just on the labor question but also in the debate over the peasant commune. On one hand conservatives favored traditional institutions because they were presumed to maintain patriarchal relations and prevented the emergence of a landless peasantry. Reformers criticized their economic inefficiency and wanted to stimulate the creation of a prosperous peasantry as a bulwark for the autocracy.[56]

There were, of course, additional complications. On the eve of the First World War, Russia was "a country half-industrialized, living on foreign capital and managerial personnel, lacking the discipline of modern industrial methods," according to Maurice Dobb. Investments by foreign capitalists in railway building and industrial development, and also successive governmental loans from such governments as France, created a mounting pressure on the Ministry of Finance to see that there was a sufficient trade surplus to make possible the required repayments, profit remittances, and meeting of interest charges. "One consequence was the constant concern of the government to increase the export surplus of agricultural produce; this led to an effort to restrict consumption by the peasants and to increase sales by levying taxes on the peasants," Alec Nove comments. "Yet Russian industry, particularly in consumer goods, depended to a considerable extent on the purchasing power of the peasants for its market." On the other hand, as Shanin observes, "the powerful and highly centralized Russian state was able to mobilize considerable resources and, to an extent, check foreign political and economic pressures." What's more, a worldwide rise in the price of foodstuffs created a positive balance of payments (generating especially high income from Russian grain) and contributed greatly "towards the national 'capital formation.'" While an extrapolation from this situation would seem to create grounds for optimism, one should note that following World War I terms of trade for such primary products as foodstuffs on the world market were to become extremely unfavorable. "The basic determinant of Russia's positive balance of payments and a 'booster' of its internal market," Shanin concludes, "was on the point of an extended downward turn."[57]

The crisis of Russian capitalism, then, was also the crisis of the tsarist order, which was multiplied and intensified by the overwhelming pressures of the First World War. At this point we are brought back to the "mental experiment" of N. S. Timasheff and others considered earlier—extrapolation from earlier economic trends indicating that the socioeconomic progress made after the Bolshevik revolution would have been realized even if the revolution had never taken place. Nove addresses this succinctly: "If the growth rates characteristic of the period 1890–1913 for industry and agriculture were simply projected over the succeeding fifty years, no doubt citizens would have been spared many dreadful convulsions. However, this assumes not only that the tendencies toward military conflict which existed in Europe had been conjured out of existence, but also that the Imperial authorities would have successfully made the adjustment necessary to govern in an orderly manner a rapidly developing and changing society."[58] Given the aspects of the crisis indicated by Nove, Dobb, and Shanin, there are certainly grounds for skepticism regarding adjustments that the tsarist order might have been capable of.

Of course, the Imperial authorities were not the only actors on the scene. We have already surveyed some of the others—the bourgeoisie, such as it was, and the massive peasantry. And of course there was the working class, small but militant, on which we will focus our attention shortly. Here it is worth noting the perception of Russia's incredibly knowledgeable police chiefs who had been closely monitoring the situation for decades and played, of course, an intimate and bloody role in helping to crush the revolutionary upsurge of 1905. "They knew that although the 1905 revolution had been defeated, the revolutionary socialist movement had not been destroyed and could appeal to deeply rooted collectivist traditions among the masses," Dominic Lieven tells us, "not to mention outrage about aspects of capitalist modernization and the failure of the tsarist authorities to agree upon a coherent industrial relations policy."[59]

Yet another key to the puzzle of early twentieth century Russia was the fact that the Russian empire was the product of the tsarist order's military expansion—not a cohesive Russian nation-state, but instead what was denounced by critics as a "prison-house of nations." As the historian Pokrovskii wrote: "It was a collection of several dozen peoples, among whom the Russians constituted a clear minority (about 47 percent), peoples who were united only by the general exploitation on the part of the ruling clique of landowners and united moreover through the help of the most brutal oppression." There were 146 ethnic-linguistic groups recognized by the official 1897 census. Sir John Maynard (although convinced that some cultures are superior to others) felt domination could not be equated with superiority, commenting that many of the subject peoples "were inheritors of cultures superior to that of the Great-Russians, and materially richer than the latter." Ronald Suny points out that the authoritarianism of the tsarist order was inseparable from the need to enforce unity and domination over this diverse and potentially explosive mix of subject peoples. As he puts it, "The very longevity of the autocracy and its accompanying ideological rationalizations were connected to the political imperative of maintaining state unity and hierarchical social and ethnic structure in the face of the ethnic heterogeneity of the Russian empire." Nineteenth-century radical Alexander Herzen noted the historic roots of this principle when he commented that "Moscow saved Russia by stifling everything that was free in Russian life," and tsarist intellectual Sergei Urvarov reflected the same reality (including a stress on the ideological glue provided by the Russian Orthodox Church) in stressing Russia's "firm foundations" as "Orthodoxy, Autocracy, Nationality." While the manner in which domination was enforced varied over the span of geography and centuries, under the strident administration of Tsar Alexander III beginning in the 1880s, there was a powerful uptick in "anti-national and anti-semitic policies that threatened a forced cultural homogenization," as Suny puts it. A policy of forcible "Russification" (linguistic, religious, cultural) was combined with discriminatory policies against the non-Russian peoples. "It goes without saying that official efforts to Russianize the population were not crowned with success," according to Avrahm Yarmolinsky.

"Here and there the upper classes were won over, but the masses resisted assimilation. In fact, all through the second half of the nineteenth century a nationalist movement was steadily gaining ground among the lesser peoples of the empire."[60]

Yet Yarmolinsky's stirring generalization is far too sweeping. As Maynard emphasizes, "It was the Ukrainian Gogol, who penned at the end of his story of Cossack life, the famous patriotic description of Russia as a swift troika rushing ever onward." Indeed, such major revolutionary figures as Trotsky (Ukrainian and Jewish) and Stalin (Georgian) were, in fact, more or less successful examples of "Russification." Lenin had insisted on a unified *Russian* Social Democratic Labor Party that was not fragmented into separate, distinctive ethnic organizations, a position that caused an early famous split with the Jewish Bund. Yet as Liliana Riga stresses in *The Bolsheviks and the Russian Empire,* the Bolsheviks were themselves composed largely of ethnic minorities within Russia's prison-house of nations: "Ethnic Russians were a significant minority, but Jews, Latvians, Ukrainians, Georgians, Armenians, Poles, and others composed two thirds of the revolutionary elite."[61]

Great Russian oppression of the ethnic minorities was an integral part of the tsarist order. It was also an essential element in the socioeconomic formation (capitalism mixed with precapitalist forms) that existed in prerevolutionary Russia. It became a source of instability as well: in the periods of revolutionary upheaval, it was in the ethnic peripheries where unrest tended to be greatest. Not surprisingly, "the peripheries were the testing ground for repressive techniques," according to Shanin, "with an extra dash of cruelty thrown in where 'they' were concerned." This helped foster order in the short run and an explosive situation in the long run. The two divergent elements we have identified—a subversive anti-Russian nationalism, and a multiethnic subversion of "Russianism"—each made themselves felt. The response to national oppression varied dramatically—in some contexts oppressed-nationalist sentiment was "largely centered among the ethnic intelligentsia, students and the lower middle classes of the towns," according to Suny, while other contexts caused the oppressed to respond through a "shared social and religious communality." While specific situations might generate mobilizations of "an inclusive, all-class nationalism," in other situations "class-based socialist movements were far more potent than political nationalism." This last point is emphasized in Riga's study of the Bolsheviks: "Ethnicity was strongly aligned with class, suggesting that class and ethnicity were intersectional experiences of varying significance in the political radicalism of the Bolshevik revolutionaries."[62]

As this indicates, it was the spread of industrial capitalism throughout the Russian empire that created a new force subversive to the maintenance of the old order. What became decisive in determining the fate of the tsarist autocracy and Russian capitalism—combining with the peasant and ethnic insurgencies and assuming predominance (or hegemony) in the revolutionary upsurge—was, in fact, the Russian proletariat.

The Russian Working Class

There has been considerable controversy over how to define the terms *working class* or *proletariat*. Sometimes a distinction has been made between the two terms, the latter being reserved for factory workers or those actually producing goods as opposed to services, or—according to some theorists—*productive* workers (producing surplus value) and *unproductive* workers (not producing surplus value). Sometimes many or all categories of service workers are excluded from the working class altogether. Often the term *middle class* (or *petty bourgeoisie* or *new middle class* or *mixed-class location*) is employed to distinguish those who are not genuine proletarians. Indeed, over the past half-century this "class-locations" debate has at times flourished among Marxist scholars. Fortunately, there has been what some consider a more "simplistic" tradition within Marxism, which will be employed here: the *working class* means the same thing as the proletariat and refers to that social layer (families included) whose livelihood is secured primarily through income derived from the sale of labor-power.[63] (Additional complexities can be factored in, particularly in "developing countries" where within single families—or even within the life of single individuals—there is an occupational mixture that blends experience as a peasant, a sometime rural and sometime urban wage worker, an independent petty merchant or vendor, and so on.)

In a study of Russian workers from 1900 to 1914, Victoria Bonnell takes a similar approach: "The composition of the working class, as defined here, includes a multiplicity of groups in manufacturing, sales-clerical, construction, transportation, communication, and service occupations who belonged to the hired labor force and were engaged in manual [i.e., blue-collar] or low-level white-collar jobs." Such an approach, she insists, is necessary to capture the realities from which the abstract categories are derived, taking into account "both the shared characteristics of this group and the common experiences that induced highly diverse segments of the Petersburg and Moscow labor force to 'feel and articulate the identity of their interests as between themselves, and as against other men whose interests [were] different from (and usually opposed to) theirs.'"[64] A somewhat similar approach, as we shall see, was adopted by Lenin.

Size and Shape

In the period leading up to the Russian revolution, there was a spectacular increase in urbanization and capitalist industry in Russia. This was a focal point of Lenin's *The Development of Capitalism in Russia* (1898). He noted that from 1863 to 1897, the total population increased 53.5 percent, but in the rural areas the increase was only 48.5 percent while in the urban areas it was 97 percent. The influx of rural inhabitants into the towns and cities averaged more than 200,000 per year. As Lenin commented, "The diversion of the population from agriculture is expressed, in Russia, in the growth of towns, suburbs, factory and commercial and industrial villages and townships, as well as in non-agricultural migration." The development of capitalism could be gauged by the extent to which wage-labor was employed, given that "capitalism is that stage of development of commodity production in which labor-power, too, becomes a commodity." It was estimated that by the mid-1890s there were ten million wage workers in European Russia, out of a total population of about ninety-two million. Lenin, like other Marxists, believed that capitalism was "historically progressive" because it brought about an "increase in the productive forces of social labor, and the socialization of labor." The development of technology and of socially organized labor vastly increased the quantity and quality of goods that could be produced, at the same time drawing all of society together in new ways: "The very growth of commodity production destroys the scattered condition of small economic units that is characteristic of natural economy and draws together the small local markets into an enormous national (and then world) market. Production for oneself is transformed into production for the whole of society; and the greater the development of capitalism, the stronger becomes the contradiction between the collective character of production and the individual character of appropriation." This last point, involving the tyranny of a capitalist minority over the economy and over the great majority of people who contribute to and are dependent on it, underlay much of what Lenin saw as "the negative and dark sides of capitalism, . . . the profound and all-round social contradictions which are inevitably inherent in capitalism, and which reveal the historically transient character of this economic regime." The changes brought about by capitalist development "inevitably lead also to a change in the mentality of the population" and "cannot but lead to a profound change in the very character of the producers."[65]

Lenin recognized that these producers, the growing working class, did not constitute simply an undifferentiated proletarian mass. In *The Development of Capitalism in Russia*, he sketched out the following five distinctions: "1) Agricultural wage-workers. These number about 3 million. . . . 2) Factory, mining and railway workers—about 1 1/2 million. . . . 3) Building workers—about 1 million. 4) Lumber workers (tree-fellers, log trimmers, rafters, etc.), navvies, railway builders, goods loaders and unloaders, and in general all kinds of 'unskilled' laborers in industrial centers. These number about 2 million. 5) Workers occupied at home for capitalists, and also those working for wages in manufacturing industries not included in 'factory industry.' These number about 2 million." Of these ten million wage workers in all, Lenin estimated that approximately one-fourth were women and children.[66]

This all roughly corresponds to the findings offered in more recent studies. Shanin counts 3.2 million workers in manufacturing, mines, and railways as the Russian proletariat's "hard core"—the second, third, and fourth categories cited by Lenin—in 1897, with a "fringe" of 5.9 million (including 2.7 million in agriculture, 1.1 million day-laborers, and 2.8 million servants). Roughly 15 percent of the Russian labor force was composed of wage workers, then, one-third of this being the industrial, railway, and mining "hard core." Women constituted 13.9 percent of the working class, according to his calculations. (Rose Glickman offers figures indicating that women were 26.8 percent of factory workers in 1901 and 31.7 percent in 1914.) There were a number of fascinating contrasts within the Russian working class. Nove writes that small-scale (workshop and artisan) industry as late as 1915 accounted for 67 percent of "those engaged in industry or 5.2 million persons." Victoria Bonnell notes that even in Petersburg and Moscow at the turn of the century artisanal workers made up 48 percent and 52 percent of the working class, respectively. On the other hand, of the industrial workforce (two million, more or less) more than half were employed in factories with five hundred or more employees—a concentration much greater than in more industrialized countries, whether Germany, Belgium, or the United States. Nor was industrial growth (which doubled between 1890 and 1900) concentrated exclusively in the urban areas. The tsarist regime encouraged factories to locate in rural areas, which resulted in only 41 percent of Russia's factory workers recorded as living in cities. Trotsky noted: "Hence the appearance in Russia of modern capitalist industry in a completely primitive economic environment: for instance, a huge Belgian or American industrial plant surrounded by dirt roads and villages built of straw and wood, which burn down every year, etc. The most primitive beginnings and the most modern European endings." In both urban and rural areas, the process of proletarianization continued in the first decades of the century. "The growth of the working class continued so rapidly," according to Joseph Freeman, "that between 1897 and 1913 the number of wage-earners in census industries increased 70 percent and in the domestic craft industries—50 percent."[67]

James Bater makes the important point that although only a small percentage of Russia's labor force was engaged in factory work, "in absolute terms the numbers involved were still huge, and given the transient nature of at least a part of the factory labor force, many more people than the 2.6 million operatives counted in manufacturing establishments in 1913 could have had firsthand acquaintance with factory production." Within the urban population (about 14 percent of the total at the turn of the century), it is estimated that 30.9 percent made their living in industry, 5.9 percent in transport, 17 percent in commerce. (It should be noted that two-thirds of these urbanites lived in "small" or "medium" towns with less than 100,000 inhabitants, predominantly wooden dwellings, unpaved streets, no sewage system, etc.) According to Shanin, between the bourgeoisie and the manual laborers of Russia "stretched a much larger group of middle and poor tradesmen, publicans, small craftsmen and so on, then the shop and bar assistants all the way down to what in contemporary 'developing societies' came to be called the 'lumpen bourgeoisie,' the petty 'go-betweens,' peddlers, etc. with an income that could be lower than that of manual workers," making up perhaps five million people. As such, in more ways than one, elements of this plebian mass sometimes blended into the working class (in terms of living conditions, community life, family membership, and consciousness). Many scholars have also stressed, as Glickman puts it, "the degree to which the path between agrarian life and factory life was traversed in both directions at once." A major part of the urban wage workers were the predominantly female house servants of peasant background and peasant-oriented factory hands who returned seasonally to the village to help with the harvesting.[68]

Glickman comments:

Even workers who eventually abandoned the land to live year round within the factory radius, who married in the factory or brought their families with them from the village, often returned to the village for the important rituals of their lives—births, deaths, christenings, and the numerous holidays in the Russian religious calendar. The larger portion of their work lives and incomes may have derived from the factory rather than the land, but their identity, their emotional commitments, and an important part of their social lives remained in the countryside. By the early years of the twentieth century, the number of second- or third-generation workers with no ties to the peasantry—known as hereditary workers—increased. But the rapid growth of the industrial labor force from the 1890s to 1914 could not have occurred through the utilization of only the labor of hereditary workers, and new peasant recruits were constantly nourishing the factory's growing appetite for working hands.[69]

Conditions of Work and Life

Up to 1897, the workday in Russian industry generally ranged from twelve to eighteen hours, Monday through Saturday. The tsarist state then decreed a workday of eleven and one-half hours in order to "establish peace between capital and labor," as Manya Gordon commented, but this was not achieved because "the reduction in hours brought a corresponding decrease in wages. In other words, the workers and not the industrialists were paying for the reform." More than this, the employers commonly devised ways to increase the workday—forcing workers to clean their machinery after the shift had formally ended, sometimes also demanding compulsory overtime (in some cases unpaid). "In the formal sense, overtime was a voluntary option," writes Glickman, "but few workers could refuse without risking their jobs." Workers, largely through militant struggles, were able to decrease the average length of the workday to 10.7 hours by 1904 and 9.87 hours by 1913. The employers sought another method for saving money through the implementation of fines for a variety of infractions by workers—for tardiness, absences, failure to meet production quotas, "rudeness" and "disobedience," and so on. Between three and five day's pay was often the fine for one day's absence, according to Freeman, and "fines, as high as one-third of the workers' wages, could be imposed for 'disorderly conduct,' such as smoking on the premises, making noise, or disobedience."[70]

Russian factories, from the most primitive to the most modern, were generally notorious in their neglect of workers' health and safety. There was a steady increase in accidents from 4.2 per 100 workers in 1904 to 4.6 per 100 in 1912, according to official statistics. Such figures as these—drawn up for an exposition in Paris—understated the reality. For example, for 1910, while the official report claimed a total of 593 killed and 3,307 injured, government medical statistics for the same year showed 702 killed and 81,145 injured. Medical aid and accident insurance was meager or nonexistent for most workers. After 1903, and even more after 1905, gains were made—an accident insurance law for industrial workers was enacted, and expanding numbers of enterprises provided medical aid (required by law and increasingly brought into being through workers' pressure). Nor were accidents the only problem. Tugan-Baranovsky observed what many scholars have repeated: "The sanitary and hygienic conditions of the Russian factory are horrible."[71] In fact, simply the normal workday routine— day in and day out, week after week, months accumulating into years—had a devastating impact on the lives shaped by factory labor. One militant worker in 1902 compared the workers' plight to the earlier years of serfdom:

> The same old oppression, the same old misery, and although they no longer beat us with birch rods, no longer murder us with their sticks, they don't make things any easier. . . . The economic situation of the toiling masses is equally gloomy. Living all over Russia—whether in Moscow or Baku—I have seen how the workers are cooped up in cellars and kennels. I have seen workers when, exhausted after a hard day's work, they returned to their living quarters. Apathetic, lifeless, they grew duller with each passing day and looked like old men at the age of fifty. Their health, their spirits, the suppleness of their muscles and their minds—all disappeared. Everything was destroyed by the long workday, everything evaporated in their gray, monotonous lives. Nothing was left of their humanity; they were nothing now but walking labor power, capable of doing nothing but work.[72]

This bleak description is at least partially contradicted by the vitality of the worker who is articulating it. He was one of many vibrant individuals who refused to be simply a downtrodden victim. In fact, the struggles of workers like him brought improvements, yet these were often eroded by the ongoing dynamics of the system that he was judging so severely.

In 1900–1901, average earnings of adult males were 242 rubles a year. By 1910 they had improved: the lowest-paying industry, food processing, paid an average of 268 rubles; one of the highest-paying sectors of the labor force, metal working, paid an average wage of 516 rubles per year. Unfortunately, budget studies indicated that a family in Petersburg required 600–700 rubles per year to purchase basic necessities. One result was that workers—particularly those with families—were generally in debt. Another result was that many women and children worked. Of course, by the early 1900s an earlier child labor law, forbidding children under the age of twelve to work, was finally being enforced, but children over the age of twelve continued to be employed: minors between twelve and fifteen were permitted to work eight or nine hours a day, and adolescents fifteen and over worked without restriction. On the other hand, especially as child labor declined, the employment of women increased, as it was the remaining source of cheap labor (women were paid only one-half to two-thirds of men's wages in the same occupation). Female and child labor tended to be vital supplements to family incomes. Between 1880 and 1908 the proportion of female factory workers who were married increased from two-fifths to about one-half. ("After 1912," reported Joseph Freeman, "women were forbidden to work four weeks before child birth, but for this period they received no pay unless they belonged to sick benefit societies where they paid dues.")[73]

Another major consequence of meager proletarian incomes, obviously, was low living standards. Workers who utilized the barracks-like housing provided by some factories spent an average of 15 percent of their earnings on lodgings if married, 3 percent if single—generally in abysmal conditions offering minimal comfort and privacy. Petersburg workers living outside of factory or shop accommodations, on the other hand, paid an average of 21 percent of their income on rent if married, 15 percent if single. Sometimes rents could consume as much as 50 percent of one's income. At the turn of the century, municipal authorities in Moscow found that 174,622 persons were living in 15,922 flats in industrial sections of the city, an average of 11 persons per flat (of which four-fifths consisted of one room). Later estimates indicate an average of 8 to 10 persons per apartment (as opposed to 3.6 in Berlin, 4.2 in Vienna, and 2.7 in Paris during the same period). Many rented "stalls," sections of a room separated by a partition not reaching the ceiling, or corners or hallways, for five or six rubles a month. In 1908, 70 percent of Petersburg's unmarried workers lived in such "stalls" or corners, and only 28.5 percent of working-class families occupied separate apartments (and even 75 percent of these took in boarders to help pay the rent). It wasn't uncommon for six people to occupy a single room and for five or more people to share a bed, often sleeping in shifts. Reports of investigators were invariably negative: "The sight of the flat is horrifying. The plaster has crumbled down, the walls are full of holes which are stuffed with rags. . . . All the flats in the house are in a similar condition." "The air is suffocating. The exhalations of the people, the evaporations of wet clothes and filthy linen fill the air." "In these dwellings there is dampness, filth, darkness, foul air. Frequently there is no running water or flush toilets, which constitute an essential part of any comfortable dwelling. In the vast majority of cases, tenants use the primitive outhouses which contaminate the ground and spread stench in backyards and apartments." This accounts for the housing not simply of factory workers, but of the urban-plebian strata generally—in Freeman's words, "the families of factory workers, artisans and their apprentices, cabmen, laborers, petty merchants, store clerks, domestic servants, and railway workers."[74]

In addition to shelter, food, of course, is key to one's standard of living. For single workers, expenditures for food consumed 31 to 48 percent of total earnings; for married workers, 38 to 52 percent. Starch accounted for as much as 50 percent of the food budget; meat, between 9 and 19 percent. The major meal of the day typically consisted of soup with potatoes or kasha; along with bread, these were the staples of the Russian worker's diet. Medical care was also something workers could ill afford—but there wasn't much available for them in any case: there was a ratio of perhaps 150 doctors per 100,000 residents in Petersburg and Moscow (which was better, though, than the 1 to 33,000 ratio in the countryside). Not surprisingly, one-fifth of all military conscripts called up at the turn of the century were rejected as physically unfit. The average life expectancy was thirty-two years in European Russia, which had the highest death rate in Europe—28.6 per 1,000 from 1911 to 1913. The general infant mortality rate was 270 per 1,000.[75]

Those who survived, however, did not live by bread alone. Alcohol consumption was quite high, both on the job and at various social occasions. The tavern or saloon was an important leisure-time gathering place, and sometimes a center for experiencing the relaxation of card games and exhilaration of gambling. The church was yet another important social and cultural center for large (though declining) numbers of Russian workers, who were also drawn to dances and picnics, particularly during holiday celebrations. Some also took advantage of theaters and museums, and for a growing number of workers reading and education became important activities. In 1897, only 21.1 percent of the entire population was literate, but among workers 50.3 percent were literate; in Petersburg, 74 percent of the male workers and 40 percent of the females were so classified. Over the next twenty years, workers' literacy rates continued to climb. Many saw education as an important means and outlet for the development of their own humanity. As the working-class militant whom I cited above argued, "We workers must have the eight-hour day if we are to become human beings; if we are to have time not only for work, but for self-education and the education of our children; if we are to stop becoming so exhausted at work that we turn dimwitted."[76]

Working-Class Consciousness

The industrial workforce increased nearly fourfold from 1860 to 1913. It would be a profound error to see all of the members of this workforce as people who thought of themselves as members of a distinctive working class. Many had recently arrived from the countryside and maintained strong ties with the peasant culture from which they came. Characteristics of the peasantry and of these transitional worker-peasants were "servility, individualism, and indifference to public life" (according to Soviet historian Iu. I. Kir'ianov), a strong attachment to relatively narrow religious beliefs, a worshipful attitude toward "our little Father the Tsar," often a serf-like deference to all authority figures, a general tendency to turn to prayer and vodka instead of rebellion in response to oppressive conditions (although periodically there might be an elemental, violent lashing out), an inclination to place whatever hopes one had for improving one's condition in acquiring and working a little piece of land.[77]

Yet many also began to make an important transition, described in the memoirs of S. I. Kanatchikov:

> Two feelings were struggling in my soul. I longed for the village, for the meadows, the brook, the bright country sun, the free clear air of the fields, and for the people who were near and dear to me. Here, in the hostile world of Moscow, I felt lonely, abandoned, needed by no one. While at work in the painting shop, . . . which smelled of paint and turpentine, I would remember pictures of our village life, tears would come to my eyes, and it was only with great effort that I could keep from crying. But there was another, more powerful feeling that gave me courage and steadfastness: my awareness of my independence, my longing to make contact with people, to become independent and proud, to live in accordance with my own wishes, and not by the caprice and will of my father.

Kanatchikov goes on to give us a sense of an even profounder shift that was taking place within him, one that caused him to self-consciously embrace the identity of "worker," which is an important first step in the development of class consciousness:

> I began to be gripped by the poetry of the large metal factory, with its mighty metallic roar, the puffing of its steam-driven machines, its columns of high pipes, its rising clouds of black smoke, which sullied the clear blue sky. Unconsciously, I was being drawn to the factory, to the people who worked there, who were becoming my near ones, my family. I had the feeling that I was merging with the factory, with its stern poetry of labor, a poetry that was growing dearer and closer to me than the quiet, peaceful, lazy poetry of our drowsy village life.[78]

The elementary working-class consciousness was even stronger among second- and third-generation workers (about 40 percent of Russia's factory labor force at the end of the nineteenth century), as was an inclination to develop new interests, new values, to become literate and read, to grapple with ideas and seek answers to a broad range of questions regarding society, the world, and the universe. "In the first decades after the Reform of 1861 [i.e., the abolition of serfdom], a tormented search for truth on the part of many progressive workers was accompanied . . . by a sincere enthusiasm for religion, which had taken a monopoly on justice," notes the historian Kir'ianov. Yet gradually "their feelings of helplessness and loneliness were supplanted by a sense of collectivism and mutual support and assistance. The proportion increased of second and third generation workers who had lost their ties to the village, where secularization occurred much more slowly than in the cities." As early as the 1870s, growing numbers of urban workers in their "tormented search for truth" turned to the study of science and history and the ideas of liberal, radical, and revolutionary intellectuals, spontaneously forming small study circles to read and discuss literature that might provide them with answers. In the 1880s, according to a participant, "workers' circles were growing more and more. . . . Progressive workers . . . were looking for books and buying them from second hand dealers." They would generally find a radical student or intellectual to help guide them through the new realms of knowledge. Another participant gave a sense of their range of interests: "A good propagandist [or educator] must be able to answer such questions as why there is day and night, seasons of the year, eclipses of the sun. He must be able to explain the origin of the universe and the origin of the species, and must therefore know the theories of Kant, Laplace, Darwin, and Lyell. In the program must be included history and the history of culture, political economy, and the history of the working class." They naturally began to gravitate to the works of Marx. "I myself," recalled a worker active in the circles of the 1880s, "had to tear up *Das Kapital* into parts, into chapters, so that it could be read simultaneously in three or four circles."[79]

Participants in these circles then shared their knowledge with fellow workers, often becoming influential figures within the workplace. Historian Reginald Zelnik vividly describes one of the "conscious workers" of the 1890s who worked in a metal shop: "The stranger's bench soon became the center of jocular chatter, interwoven with serious political and religious discussion, marked by the near absence of the heavy cursing that normally salted workshop banter."[80] Zelnik indicates one of the first challenges to authority commonly expressed in such contexts: "A worker should recognize that his hell was here on earth, which was the paradise of the rich. The pains of hell were nothing more than the stratagem of priests whose function it was to obscure the truth from the common people." Inquisitive young workers not frightened off by such ideas were "exposed to quasi-scientific explanations of such phenomena as the origins of the earth and the evolution of man, none the less effective for the simplicity with which they were presented." It was a short step from the natural sciences to the social sciences, and from there to revolutionary theory.

Over time, different revolutionary currents cohered within Russia. One of the most significant currents consisted of the populists who looked to "the people" (especially the peasant majority, which they blurred together with the working class) to liberate Russia from tsarist oppression; they believed that a particularly Russian form of socialism could be achieved through bypassing capitalism altogether, and they were inclined to use individual terrorism against representatives of the autocracy. Adherents of this perspective formed the Socialist Revolutionary Party in 1901.

While this attracted some workers (especially among those maintaining ties with the countryside), a majority of "conscious workers" were drawn to the Marxist program of the Russian Social Democratic Labor Party. Zelnik comments: "Although they were familiar with many of the works of Marx and Engels (and, indeed, Lassalle, whom they did not distinguish very sharply from Marx), their sense of what constituted their 'Marxism'—beyond their solidarity with the German [workers'] movement—was vague but in essence contained two major points: 1) factory workers, rather than peasants, must lead the way to the radical transformation of existing society; and 2) mass organization, rather than acts of individual heroism, . . . must be the primary means of effecting that transformation."[81]

A more significant division, however, was that between radicalized "conscious workers" and those who were not inclined to share the view that "real life" meant combating human injustice and defending one's ideals. Some of these "nonconscious" workers, while not adverse to "mouthing some heretical ideas on the shop floor or in the tavern," were inclined to stay out of trouble and spend their nonworking lives in "the enjoyment of the distractions of city life" or in the quest for personal advancement out of the ranks of the working class.[82]

Such "distracted" workers as these, however, shared with the bulk of the "conscious workers" the status of skilled workers in the metal shops and semi-artisan crafts. Perhaps the greatest division within the working class was between skilled and unskilled workers. One reason for this was that a far greater number of unskilled workers were newly arrived to the ranks of the working class, maintaining many more psychological and cultural and even economic ties to peasant life. The literacy rate among them was substantially lower as well, and a much higher percentage of them were women, whose status and self-image were particularly low in patriarchal Russia. Alexandra Kollantai writes:

> The life of Russia's six million proletarian women was, in those early years of the twentieth-century, one long round of hunger, deprivation and humiliation. The working day lasted twelve hours, or at the very least eleven. The wom-

en worked for starvation wages of twelve to thirteen rubles a month and they lived in overcrowded barracks. . . . Even much later, when Marxism had firmly established itself in the Russian workers' movement it was only the occasional proletarian woman who took part in political life. . . . It was only rarely that a factory girl could be persuaded to attend an illegal meeting. Neither did working women visit the Sunday evening classes held on the outskirts of St. Petersburg which were the only 'legal possibilities' in those times, the only way the broad masses could make contact with the ideas of Marxism and revolutionary socialism, presented under the guise of harmless lessons in geography and arithmetic. The working women were still avoiding life and struggle, believing that their destiny was the cooking pot, the washtub and the cradle.[83]

Actually, at least by the late 1890s there were "conscious" female workers participating in socialist study circles—but this was a rare occurrence, and they came largely from the small percentage of women employed in the skilled trades. No less decisive than gender or the village background of many unskilled workers was the very nature of their work. One contemporary observer noted that skilled workers were generally able to earn enough to secure moderately decent living standards (compared to unskilled workers), but that in addition the nature of the work itself "must develop in a man the urge toward individuality. Here there must be room for creativity. The worker must think a great deal, reason in the very process of work. And, therefore, the very essence of his work gives him a push toward self-determination." Compare that with the following description of unskilled textile workers: "The weaver and spinner are of a totally different type [than the skilled metalworkers]. They are the slaves of the machine. The machine has devoured them with all their essence. It is stubbornly mechanical work. . . . Here the people are numbers. Here, on the faces is written that which is most terrible in a work atmosphere: the hopelessness of labor. People grow dull and go to seed. . . . [There is a total] absence of demand for individual creativity." Another account of women textile workers asserted: "Exhausted, sick from unhealthy, endless mill work, knowing no peace at home, from morning to night, day in and day out, month after month, the worker mother drudges and knows only need, only worry and grief. Her life passes in gloom, without light."[84]

Not only did such conditions inhibit the intellectual and political development of unskilled workers, but the differences between unskilled and skilled workers created barriers between these two strata of the working class. As one worker recalled: "At that time, the difference between metal and textile workers was like the difference between the city and the countryside. . . . Metalworkers considered themselves aristocrats among other workers. Their occupations demanded more training and skill, and therefore they looked down on other workers, such as weavers and the like, as an inferior category, as country bumpkins: today he will be at the mill, but tomorrow he will be poking at the earth with his wooden plough." Yet there were also expansive countertendencies among the politicized skilled workers. As one said: "Only a conscious working person can truly respect a human individual, women, cherish a tender child's soul. We will not learn from anyone but ourselves. We, the conscious working people, have no right to be like the bourgeois." Noting the impulse of many "conscious workers" to reach out to their less fortunate class brothers and sisters, one observer wrote that "the spiritual process is an active one. Once the voice of the individual has begun to speak in the worker, he can neither sit under a bush . . . nor limit himself to words. . . . The strength of this process is in its dynamism: the upper strata of the proletariat raise up the backward strata to their own level."[85] This process took years before coming to fruition. But even at the turn of the century, networks of Marxist intellectuals and "conscious workers" (some of whom were themselves being transformed into worker-intellectuals well-grounded in Marxist theory) were able to envision expanding working-class solidarity as a goal toward which progress was slowly but surely being made.

It's worth noting that the very concepts of "class" and "class society" constituted a different worldview than the statuses assigned by the tsarist regime (see table 2).

Table 2: The "Social Estates" of Russia in 1897 (% of population)

The Social Estate	Russian Empire	European Russia
Nobles (hereditary)	0.97	0.95
Nobles (of service)	0.50	0.52
Clergy	0.47	0.54
Merchants and "honored citizens"	0.49	0.58
Urbanites	10.66	10.65
Peasants	77.12	84.16
Cossacks	2.3	1.54
Aliens ("uncivilized") ethnic groups)	6.61	0.45
Foreigners	0.48	0.27

Source: Shanin, Russia as a "Developing Society," 62.

The collective experience of a particular occupational sector—and the individual experiences of various members of that sector—determined the extent to which individuals would embrace the traditional tsarist or the Marxist labels, and which class or social identity they would see as best describing the reality of their existence. Thus, during the 1905 revolutionary upsurge in Moscow, pharmacists' assistants formed a union—as had other members of the city's higher and lower professions, various trades, factory workforces, etc. The union of pharmacists' assistants then had to decide whether it was an organization of "workers" or of the "intelligentsia" in order to determine what course it should follow—whether to join the predominantly working-class Social Democrats or to join with other professional groups in the "bourgeois liberal" Union of Unions. Even among socialist-minded workers there could be significant differences in self-perceptions. "Consider, for example," writes Leopold Haimson, "the changing attitudes displayed by various strata of industrial workers who at different moments in the course of the Revolution of 1905 and indeed during much of 1917 were alternatively drawn to (or indeed torn between) the representations of being 'class conscious proletarians,' *trudiashchikhsia* (i.e., laboring people just like other members of the *narod*) or members of a workers' (*rabochaia*) intelligentsia and wavered accordingly in their political allegiances between the various factions of social democracy and of the Socialist Revolutionaries."[86] There were many fascinating complexities.

Mass membership of workers in the working-class parties would not take place until 1905. Suspicions and resentments existed among workers toward the revolutionary students and intellectuals, whose class origins were so different. This was heightened by the tactlessness and insensitivity that sometimes cropped up among upper-class and petty bourgeois radicals ("the examples range from patronizing praise to the flaunting of material and cultural advantages," writes Zelnik), but also the suspicion on the part of workers that revolution was "an amusement, a sport" for the youthful radicals who were able to "live off their papas and mamas.... You make a lot of noise, yell, mouth radical phrases when you're young, but then you finish your educational institutions, obtain nice little positions, get married, and become the same kind of exploiters and hard-driving masters as your papas."[87]

Also, in a related vein, some of the "conscious workers" who had transformed themselves into worker-intellectuals were irritated by something else: they perceived from many nonworker revolutionaries a resistance to allowing the workers themselves to have sufficient voice within the underground movement. Lenin and others who were gathered around the underground newspaper *Iskra* argued that repressive conditions under the tsar necessarily limited the amount of democracy and openness possible at that time, but they also had a commitment to drawing increasing numbers of workers into central positions within the movement. Despite some impatience with nonworker revolutionaries, a number of workers found these arguments to be reasonable and rallied around *Iskra*. As one later commented, the relative isolation of a single "conscious worker" is a difficult thing and "is why for the workers a comradely milieu, an organization, and eventually a party become his family home and hearth, and his comrades in struggle take the place of his brothers, sisters, father and mother. And it is then that the distinctions between him and those who came from another class, but have burned all their bridges behind them, are effaced."[88]

Other workers did not immediately see things this way, and finally drew away from the Social Democratic milieu for a time. Some continued to carry on educational activity of their own while engaging, in some cases, in trade union efforts. The tsarist police were particularly anxious to encourage this development and, through the initiative of the imaginative police agent Sergei Zubatov, actually sponsored the establishment of legal nonpolitical trade unions in order to divide workers from revolutionaries in the early 1900s. Thousands of workers flooded into these organizations, but soon they became too militant for the tsarist authorities and a source of extreme tension between the regime and the business community. The consequent restrictions and repression drove the workers in a radical direction. Many of the "conscious workers" involved in these ventures, as well as many who had dropped out of all organized activity, were later drawn into the revolutionary upheaval of 1905, and afterward assumed prominent roles in the labor and socialist movements.[89]

Presently we will consider more closely the development and fortunes of these movements.

3

REVOLUTIONARY
TRIUMPH

*T*here is a common perception of the interaction between revolutionary vanguard and insurgent masses: the former tricks the latter into
making a revolution. Before we examine the Russian revolution, we should
critically examine this influential notion.

"Lenin argued that only a professional revolutionary, only a conspirator,
could be a party member," according to sociologist Daniel Bell, adding that
"it was the will of Lenin alone which altered the [Bolshevik] party's politics,"
and that "the Bolshevik party, more than any party in history, has demonstrated the nature of will." In the Bolshevik Party "individuals may join from
a variety of motives, but all must be stamped in the [Leninist] mold or driven
out." Just as he molded the party, Bell indicates, Lenin was convinced of "the
necessity for tutelage of the proletariat" by an elite infused with the principles
of "vanguard party, dictatorship of the proletariat, Bolshevik ideology." At the
same time, according to Selig Perlman, "Lenin's engineering feat in Russia,
far from being one of the wonders of human achievement, was in reality a mediocre accomplishment. In Russia, for historic reasons, the communist social
engineer found himself in an ultra-passive community." The nonrevolutionary scholar presumed that a revolutionary intellectual could have an easier
time if "the masses" were pliant. In particular, the peasantry "was impelled
by its land hunger to side with Lenin," and as for the working class, Perlman

offered this characterization: "Russia's industrial working class, deprived of the protection of trade unionism and effective labor legislation, was a veritable tailor-made proletariat in the Marxian sense, as contrasted with Germany's working class, which, in the critical years of 1918–20, arrayed itself under its trade union leadership on the side of conservatism. In brief, Lenin, while he operated upon Russia, dealt with ultra-plastic stuff." This naturally contributed to the later rise of Stalinism and would, as Bell suggests, "take one through a period of the Stalinist type even without a Stalin"—although it is recognized that aspects of Leninism were developed by Stalin in a "grosser" form than Lenin would have liked.[1]

Aspects of the post-Marxists' perspective on Russia are relevant to, and will be discussed in, the portion of this study dealing with the period of transition and consolidation following the revolutionary overthrow of the old regime. One striking feature of this component of their analysis is the tendency to focus exclusively on the (real or presumed) "conscious will" of the revolutionary vanguard to explain (real or alleged) negative and repressive developments in those countries. Minimized or conjured away altogether are such things as inherited economic problems, the immediate disruptive effects of revolutionary change (in *every* revolution), and the "conscious will" and active policies of former ruling classes and other opponents of the revolution inside and outside the country. All disasters are attributed to the blueprint or the incompetence of the revolutionary vanguard.

A similar distortion affects the view of the revolutionary overthrow itself, and of the process leading up to that overthrow, especially in regard to the masses of people necessarily involved in a revolution. Diane Koenker has aptly criticized the resulting historiography on the Russian Revolution because it generates "an image among Western historians of these masses as irrational, easily swayed, and prey to the machinations of political leaders. They are acted upon, they do not act." In fact, this is intimately related to the manner in which Bell has developed the concept of ideology—which is central to post-Marxist thought and helps to shed considerable light on different ways of interpreting revolutions. He defines ideology as "an all-inclusive system of comprehending reality, . . . a set of beliefs infused with passion . . . [which] seeks to transform the whole way of life." He also asserts that it "is the conversion of ideas into social levers," and he describes its function in the following terms: "A social movement can rouse people when it can do three things: simplify ideas, establish a claim to truth, and in the union of the two, demand a commitment to action. Thus, not only does ideology transform ideas, it transforms people as well." Elsewhere he has expressed the same idea with more of an emotional edge: "Ideologies . . . [are] organized systems of belief with ready formulas for the manipulation of the masses." The elitism inherent in this definition is made explicit when Bell explains: "The analysis of ideology belongs properly in the discussion of the intelligentsia. One can say that what the priest is to religion, the intellectual is to ideology."[2]

Neither religion nor ideology nor revolution can be properly understood with this approach. A broader definition of ideology is essential. Thus the anthropologist Clifford Geertz speaks of "extrapersonal mechanisms for the perception, understanding, judgment and manipulation of the world." Political scientist William Delaney speaks of "symbol systems that vary widely in such properties as dogmatism, probability of realization, rationality, integration, and rhetorical passion." Historian George Rudé (drawing particularly from Antonio Gramsci) insists on the inclusion of more than simply the products of intellectual elites, encompassing also "those less structured forms of thought that circulate among the common people, often contradictory and confused and compounded of folklore, myth and day-to-day popular experience." Rudé argues that it is necessary, if one wishes to comprehend reality, to bridge "the yawning chasm . . . between the Elect and the non-Elect, which [if unbridged] allows for no historical progression from the one to the other."[3] There is a need to understand ideology as being grounded in complex and diverse life experiences and relationships of the people themselves, shaped by socioeconomic realities and historical developments that generate a variety of ideological currents and counter-currents. These blend (or collide) in different ways for different people depending on time, place, and circumstance. Under certain conditions, the overall ideological balance in a society can tilt leftward, involving an interpenetration (and mutual influence) of "popular ideology of protest" and more developed analyses of revolutionary intellectuals. Thus revolutions involve a dialectic of revolutionary vanguard and insurgent masses, as we shall see.

The Revolutionary Vanguard

Two of the most important historians of the Russian revolution, E. H. Carr and Isaac Deutscher, have offered insights on the nature of Bolshevism. According to Carr, Lenin believed that "the party was to lead and inspire the mass of workers; its own membership was to remain small and select. It would, however, be an error to suppose that Lenin regarded the revolution as the work of a minority. The task of leading the masses was not, properly understood, a task of indoctrination, of creating a consciousness that was not there, but of evoking a latent consciousness; and this latent consciousness of the masses was an essential condition of the revolution. Lenin emphatically did not believe in revolution from above."[4]

Deutscher has commented that "one of the striking features of the Russian labor movement before the revolution of 1917 was the relative insignificance of the trade unions." While similar to the observation offered by Selig Perlman, Deutscher gives it a revolutionary twist: "In suppressing trade unionism, tsardom unwittingly put a premium upon revolutionary political organization. Only the most politically minded workers, those prepared to pay for their conviction with prison and exile, could be willing to join trade unions in these circumstances. But those who were already so politically-minded were, naturally enough, more attracted by political organizations." This contributed to the evolution of a revolutionary vanguard layer within the working class. "The broader and more inert masses," Deutscher concluded, "who were inclined to shun politics but would have readily joined trade unions were not only prevented from forming unions but were gradually accustomed to look for leadership to the clandestine political parties."[5] In fact, the Bolsheviks became the most effective clandestine party in Russia.

The conception of the revolutionaries, the policy of the authorities, and the experience of the masses fit together in a way that generated a mass revolutionary consciousness and upheaval.

The Rise of Bolshevism

Much has been written on the rise of Bolshevism, and elsewhere, particularly in *Lenin and the Revolutionary Party*, I have offered my own detailed interpretation.[6]

One essential reality that merits special emphasis is that the Bolsheviks' "political tradition and organization," as Moshe Lewin has commented, were "rooted in the history of Russian and European Social-Democracy." This has been so often glossed over, minimized, or even denied (by friends and foes and neutrals) that it is worth allowing one of many knowledgeable militants—in this case David Rousset—to provide a most apt elaboration:

> Bolshevism gradually came into being at the heart of this extraordinary and intense period of world activity [in the first decade of the twentieth century]—in the midst of occupation, trade-union, legislative, and political ferment. Its growth took place entirely within the ranks of the Second International, which

on the eve of the war boasted twelve million members from twenty-seven parties in twenty-two countries, in which [Karl] Kautsky and Rosa Luxemburg were closer as partners to the Bolsheviks in Russian affairs than Martov and Plekhanov themselves. We must grasp the vigor and reality of theoretical thought at this time, the power which was contained in the free exercise of critical thought; the efficacy of the free rein of tendencies and factions, and the true significance of the party as a crucible of thought and action. This grasp is necessary to understand the historical breadth of the collapse [of the world socialist movement] which occurred in the First World War. It is also necessary for an understanding of what the first Bolsheviks were and what they were attempting to do in the first congresses of the Third International.[7]

Here we can afford to provide only the barest summary of Bolshevism's history up to 1917. Between 1900 and 1903, Lenin and other Marxists—such as George Plekhanov, the "Father of Russian Marxism," and Julius Martov—struggled to establish the Russian Social Democratic Labor Party (RSDLP) around the revolutionary program and centralized organizational concepts expounded in their influential underground newspaper, *Iskra*. Within the loose networks of RSDLP adherents of this early period, some resisted the shift away from decentralized functioning; some also argued for a concentration on economic and trade union struggles, leaving the leadership of the political struggle against tsarism to the bourgeois liberals; finally, some argued that Marxist intellectuals from nonproletarian backgrounds should not attempt to impose their ideas and leadership on working-class activists. Those holding to variations of these ideas were denounced as "Economists" by the *Iskra*ists. At the 1903 congress of the RSDLP the Economist trend was defeated by a pro-*Iskra* majority, but then the *Iskra*ists themselves split into bitterly counterposed majority-minority (Bolshevik-Menshevik) factions, with Lenin's Bolsheviks advancing the most consistently centralist and uncompromisingly revolutionary orientation (e.g., insisting that the working class, not the bourgeoisie, must take the lead in overthrowing tsarism, and stressing the need for a worker-peasant alliance rather than a worker-capitalist alliance in the revolutionary struggle). In the period leading up to 1905, however, the RSDLP consisted mostly of radicalized intellectuals with a small minority of working-class cadres and a relatively weak base in Russia's proletariat. Far more workers were actually involved in a self-help, social, and cultural movement led by Father Georgi Gapon. Gapon was a rather muddled pro-tsar priest with ties to the secret police yet sympathies for the plight of the workers. In fact, many workers who had been active in earlier RSDLP study circles came to play a central role in the Gapon movement, which grew into a mass phenomenon in St. Petersburg.[8]

The situation changed dramatically in 1905. In the last weeks of 1904, a profound militancy and radicalization was becoming evident in the Gapon movement, with the working class as a whole noticeably in ferment. Related to all of this was a larger ferment in Russian society generated by the Russo-Japanese war, which was going quite badly for the Russian military and therefore bringing discredit to the tsarist regime. Liberal intellectuals with ties to elements among the capitalists and even landowning nobles were beginning to call for major political reforms aimed at modernizing and, to some extent, democratizing Russian society. In January 1905, Gapon and his followers organized a mass demonstration in St. Petersburg. Carrying icons, pictures of the tsar, and a petition respectfully asking their monarch for sweeping social reforms, two hundred thousand men, women, and children marched through the streets singing "God Save the Tsar." When they approached the Winter Palace, however, they were attacked by troops, who inflicted at least hundreds of casualties. A storm of anti-tsarist feeling and furious protest was subsequently unleashed throughout Russia, throwing the country into a turmoil—demonstrations, rallies, strikes, uprisings in the cities, bold and often violent peasant actions against landlords, the nobles' estates, and the authorities in the countryside, with those in the nationally oppressed areas tending to be particularly volatile. The regime vacillated between granting concessions and resorting to massive repression, but major reforms were won—including the legalization of some political and trade union activity, greater freedom of expression, and the establishment of a parliamentary body, the Duma. In this context, both factions of the RS-DLP—swept along by the revolutionary enthusiasm of the workers—made adjustments that won them a mass membership. Lenin's centralism was tempered by the understanding that looser and more democratic norms could help root the party in a dramatically radicalizing working class. The Mensheviks moved closer to the Bolshevik view of the working class leading the anti-tsarist struggle. It appeared that both factions were converging.[9]

There were other political currents that also gained greater coherence during this period. On the left, there were some anarchist currents—anarcho-communists, anarcho-syndicalists, individualists, terrorists and pacifists and adherents of mass action—which played the role of an often influential fringe within the revolutionary movement, though never coming close to enjoying majority support there.[10]

Most substantial was the Party of Socialist Revolutionaries (the SRs), which enjoyed significant support among the radical intelligentsia and some of the peasantry, as well as among workers. Although eventually the SRs assumed minority status within the workers' movement, initially they were keen and sometimes successful competitors with the Social Democrats. Their foremost leaders at the party's founding were Mikhail Gotz, Gregory Gershuni, and Victor Chernov (of whom only Chernov survived to 1917). They fully embraced the heritage of Narodnaya Volya (People's Will), the heroic underground populist-socialists of the late nineteenth century who propagandized for a Russian path to socialism largely based on the village commune that would bypass the oppression of capitalist development and succeed through a mass uprising of the laboring poor of countryside and city. The heroes and heroines of People's Will not only organized an effective underground to spread these ideas among the populace (and to maintain contact with such sympathetic revolutionaries abroad as Marx and Engels), but also to carry out "propaganda of the deed" to show that the most hated and repressive figures in the tsarist regime, even the tsar himself, were not invulnerable. The modern-day SRs retained this terrorist tradition, but they also gave greater attention to mass organizing to prepare for anti-tsarist insurrection. They tended to identify with the Marxist framework in a general way (with many shunning the "Marxist" label) and were—like the RSDLP—affiliated with the Socialist International (also known as the "Second International").[11]

Nonetheless, they lost ground among the workers to the Social Democrats for several reasons: a feeling that the distinctive interests and needs of the proletariat were blurred with those of the peasantry; a sense that individual terrorism undermined the more effective and necessary work of organizing workers for mass struggle; an impression that the specific economic needs and immediate struggles of workers were lost in the SRs' intense focus on tsarist autocracy. There was also a tendency among some SRs, envisioning a far-reaching sociopolitical alliance to bring down tsarism, to conciliate and compromise with bourgeois-liberal forces. This eventually generated a split between the more moderate Right SRs (led by Abram Gotz, Nikolai Avksentiev, Victor Chernov) and the uncompromising Left SRs (represented by such figures as Maria Spiridonova, Mark Natanson, Boris Kamkov). An anarchist-influenced, terrorist-oriented split-off from the SRs, known as the Maximalists, was formed, but their sizeable peasant base after 1905 melted away after particularly severe police repression; this was balanced by a moderate, anti-terrorist split-off called the Popular Socialist Party. A more moderate formation (not a split-off, but associated with the populist tradition) was known as Trudoviks (Labor Group), which came into being as an independent gathering of Duma deputies, with which Alexander Kerensky was associated.[12]

There were two significant parties that essentially represented the bourgeois opposition to tsarism. The most substantial of these was the Constitutional Democratic Party (Konstitutsionno-Demokraticheskaya Partiya), commonly referred to as "Kadets" in reference to the initials of the first two words of the party's name. It came together through the merger of several currents—the radical reformist networks of the Union of Liberation initiated by the ex-Marxist Peter Struve, along with liberal reformers associated with the *zemstvos* (semi-political, semi-social county councils with very little administrative power, concentrating on education and social services in the rural areas); it also included some prominent liberal intellectuals, some of whom had been active in the moderate or legal fringe of the Marxist and populist movements. Given the failure of merchant and industrialist sectors to organize their own party, the Kadets—with a program of parliamentary democracy, social reform, and modernization within the framework of capitalist development—hoped to become a magnet for the Russian bourgeoisie as it came into opposition to tsarism. This goal was not fully realized, although the Kadets did attract many liberals among the professions, gentry, and business community. With its perspective of cross-class alliance against the tsarist autocracy ("for the good of the nation") and its early slogan of "No enemies on the left," it also exerted a strong influence on other oppositional currents. Kadet leaders included the historian Pavel N. Miliukov, Struve, Vasily Maklakov, Nikolai N. Nekrasov. Further to the right was the Octobrist Party, led by Alexander I. Guchkov, functioning as a more moderate—indeed, *loyal*—opposition to tsarism, favoring a constitutional monarchy. It named itself after the tsar's conciliatory October Manifesto of 1905, which had declared freedom of speech, assembly, and organization, and which had upgraded the Duma from a consultative to a legislative body. The Octobrists were the favored party of Russia's industrialists. Between Kadets and Octobrists there were a few less successful and transitory liberal parties.[13]

On the other hand, there were some frankly reactionary pro-tsarist parties that came into being in order to preserve the status quo, particularly in the Duma. And there was the infamous Union of the Russian People and their gangs of thugs known as the Black Hundreds, encouraged and financed by the most right-wing elements in the upper classes and tsarist regime, but drawing in and mobilizing those lower-class elements inclined to hold high the banners of God (as interpreted by the Russian Orthodox Church) and

Tsar (unobstructed by the democratic reforms favored by liberals and revolutionaries) and Motherland (undefiled by Jews and foreigners and radical scum). Shanin describes the Black Hundreds as "the loyalists of the localities, thousands of small owners and traders, petty officials and impoverished nobles, low-grade policemen, pub patriots and some of the peasants," also including some of the more backward elements from the working class, it should be added, who "reacted to the scandal of mass disorders, red flags and what seemed like governmental appeasement of mutineers with fury and dismay." Often guided and organized by the police, the Black Hundreds carried out pogroms "in which thousands of radicals, intellectuals, zemstvo activists, socialist workers and students, as well as 'aliens,' especially Jews, were hunted down and attacked by crowds carrying the Tsar's picture and holy icons, and increasingly armed."[14]

Within the working class, however, the most influential force between 1905 and 1917 turned out to be the RSDLP—and ultimately the Bolsheviks. The Bolshevik triumph, however, was prepared in large measure by a series of splits and factional conflicts, paradoxical as that may seem. Before tracing this development, we should take note of the context.

Despite the defeat of the 1905 uprising, and brutal repression carried out by tsarist forces in city and countryside, some real gains had been won in the 1905–06 period: a parliamentary body, the Duma, was set up; trade unions were legalized; important legislation (involving social insurance, pensions for workers, etc.) was enacted. By 1906 the RSDLP could claim as many as 150,000 members. Then came a sharp reversal initiated by the tsar's newly appointed prime minister. This was Peter Stolypin, who was also minister of the interior (thus directly in charge of the government's repressive forces) and had earned the title "Stolypin the Hangman." He remained in office from 1906 to 1911 and was inclined to deal harshly not only with revolutionaries but also with dumas. The first Duma had been boycotted by the RSDLP and SRs and so was dominated by the bourgeois-liberal Kadets; even this proved too radical a body, and Stolypin ordered it dissolved. New Duma elections resulted in an even more radical body—the RSDLP and SRs won 20 percent of the seats; the Trudoviks, 19 percent; the Kadets, 19 percent; and small-party allies of the Kadets, 18 percent. This anti-tsarist majority, more radical than the last, proved even less tolerable, so Stolypin had the second Duma dissolved in 1907. The third Duma was based on a new electoral law that gave 51 percent of the seats to conservative and reactionary representatives of the landed nobility. In addition, although trade unions were not abolished, they were severely restricted, pushed to be nonpolitical, not permitted to be too militant (or successful), and many union activists were blacklisted. Linked with this, of course, was increased repression against all organizations claiming to be working for a revolution to overthrow the tsar.[15]

At the same time, Stolypin initiated a push for a package of reforms that were designed to advance the modernization process in Russia. He explained that "reforms are necessary in times of revolution because the revolution was born to a considerable degree from the shortcomings of the social system. Only to fight revolution is to remove the results and not the causes." Influenced by the example of Prussia under the "Iron Chancellor" Otto von Bismarck, Stolypin explained: "In places where the government defeated the revolution it did so not by the exclusive use of force but by using its strength to place itself at the head of the reforms." Stolypin's attempt at "revolution from above" included a broad range of reforms: improvements toward a more efficient state apparatus; an agrarian reform that would raise a layer of well-to-do peasants as a bulwark of the regime; tax reform; public education; some modest liberalization for religious minorities; expansion of railways; promotion of the further development of industry; and social welfare reforms. Not all of this was achieved. Powerful reactionaries in the Duma and the state apparatus fiercely resisted many of these reforms. (It is suspected that some of these reactionaries were involved in the prime minister's assassination.) Nonetheless, as Lenin later recounted, under Stolypin "victorious tsarism was compelled to speed up the destruction of the remnants of the pre-bourgeois, patriarchal mode of life in Russia. The country's development along bourgeois lines proceeded apace."[16]

Within this context of repression combined with reform, the RSDLP found it impossible to maintain its previous organizational gains or its unity. Most of those who had returned to Russia in 1905 were forced back into exile, along with many new members. Others were arrested and sent into "internal exile"—Siberia. Many became discouraged and abandoned politics. By 1910, RSDLP membership shrank to ten thousand. Various sources agree that within Russia, for all practical purposes, the organization essentially collapsed. At the same time, there were sharp differences on how to interpret the new situation and on what to do next. The Mensheviks as a whole concluded that they had been too radical in 1905 and should now concentrate on forging a political alliance with the bourgeois-liberals. (Trotsky and a small current disagreed with this shift toward moderation, breaking with the Mensheviks to maintain the perspective of "permanent revolution"—workers must lead the struggle and, allied with the peasants, push it beyond capitalist limits.) The Menshevik-

Bolshevik split reopened larger than before, as Lenin and his comrades found it necessary to counterpose once again a revolutionary alliance of proletariat and peasantry against the Menshevik view of Plekhanov and Martov about the need for bourgeois hegemony in the democratic revolution.[17]

But in addition to this, new fissures appeared. The Mensheviks and Bolsheviks each split three ways (not counting Trotsky's break with the Mensheviks). An important current committed to what was called "liquidation" surfaced among the Mensheviks: the reestablishment of the underground and of illegal work was opposed; instead, the "liquidators" contended, there should be exclusive concentration on building trade unions, cooperatives, social and cultural centers, and so forth, that could advance the workers' conditions and consciousness in practical ways while not provoking tsarist repression. A small current of what came to be known as "Party Mensheviks," led by Plekhanov, favored a fierce struggle against liquidationism and defended the traditional revolutionary perspective of combining legal with illegal work. A larger centrist group led by Julius Martov and Theodore Dan also disagreed with the liquidators but was willing to compromise with them in order to prevent the Bolsheviks from becoming predominant in the RSDLP. Among the Bolsheviks, on the other hand, an ultra-left current led by Alexander Bogdanov insisted that illegal work must be prioritized, trade union work and other "reformist" activity minimized, and electoral work abandoned, in order to prepare for armed insurrection for a new revolutionary wave that would come—Bogdanov felt sure—in the near future. The Bolsheviks who were grouped around Lenin insisted that illegal work remained absolutely necessary and that liquidationism must be repudiated both formally and in practice (therefore putting them at loggerheads with the bulk of the Mensheviks); but the Leninists also insisted that especially in the new period, in the complete absence of a mass revolutionary upsurge, it was essential to devote considerable attention to legal work: trade unionism, elections and parliamentary activity, etc. By 1910 the Leninist Bolsheviks were also irrevocably committed to carrying out a split in the RSDLP in order to establish a cohesive revolutionary organization. This resulted in a new split—the "Party Bolsheviks" or "compromisers," who insisted on maintaining RSDLP unity. This was similar to the conciliationist position of Trotsky's anti-factional faction.[18]

In 1912, the Leninist Bolsheviks engineered a conference in Prague that declared itself a formal congress of the RSDLP, expelled the liquidators, adopted a number of Bolshevik resolutions, and elected a new central committee, essentially launching Bolshevism as an independent party. The other elements of the RSDLP were indignant and rallied to stage a unity conference called by

Trotsky in August of the same year. The deep political differences prevented this "August bloc" from maintaining itself as a united organization, however. This was in stark contrast to the experience of the Bolsheviks. Their Prague conference of 1912 inaugurated a cohesive organization with a coherent political orientation, drawing together activists committed to building an uncompromisingly revolutionary workers' movement that would be rooted in the actual experience and struggles of their country.[19]

This was to have important consequences back in Russia. "The sudden growth of the illegal Bolshevik nuclei was an unpleasant surprise for those Mensheviks who regarded these nuclei as a product of the disintegration of the old prerevolutionary Party organization and doomed to inevitable extinction," the Menshevik leader Theodore Dan recalled many years later. He added that "while the Bolshevik section of the party transformed itself into a battle-phalanx, held together by iron discipline and cohesive guiding resolution, the ranks of the Menshevik section were ever more seriously disorganized by dissension and apathy." This was not simply a product, however, of Lenin's "will power." Russia was, in the period 1911 to 1914, experiencing a general crisis rooted in an economic, social, and cultural upheaval. The upheaval was fueled by the partial "modernization" and great new surge of industrialization that were associated with Stolypin's policies. One manifestation of this was the fact that the industrial labor force grew more than 30 percent between January 1910 and July 1914. Changing realities generate changing consciousness and changed expectations. Working-class militancy increased, reflected in growing strike waves—especially after the massacre of protesting workers in the Lena goldfields in 1912. The Lena incident has been compared by some historians to the 1905 massacre in Petersburg of the demonstrators following Gapon. In the new period of radicalization, Mensheviks lost control of the bulk of trade unions which, especially through the work of the "liquidator" practical organizers, they had led previously. By the summer of 1914, Bolsheviks controlled at least fourteen out of eighteen trade unions in Petersburg, ten out of thirteen in Moscow.[20]

Reginald Zelnik has suggested that the Bolshevik programmatic principle of the worker-peasant alliance helped to win workers, especially since many were newly arrived from the countryside. He writes that workers drawn to Bolshevism had "a uniquely volatile and dynamic mixed consciousness that combined peasant resentment against the vestiges of 'feudalism' (i.e., serfdom) with a proletarian resentment against capitalist exploitation in the factories." Certainly the three key agitational slogans of the Bolsheviks (commonly known as "the three whales of Bolshevism")—the immediate aspirations of workers (the eight-hour workday), the goal of the peasants (confiscation of the big landed estates), and the vision of a democratic republic (via a Constituent Assembly)—would appeal to such dynamically mixed consciousness.[21]

Yet the Russian reality was more complex than this. As a number of historians have pointed out, newly arrived unskilled workers from the countryside were generally inclined to make some quick money and not get into trouble, tending to avoid trade unions—not to mention illegal political activities. The unions, on the other hand, recruited mainly experienced, skilled, and urbanized workers, and many of these workers were in a position—from their own observations and activities over a period of years—to critically evaluate the claims, appeals, and proposals of contending left-wing currents.

There are indications that the Bolsheviks *did* make gains among unskilled and rebellious young workers, but they also had to win over seasoned activists in order to win the unions. In fact, we find a similar pattern developing throughout the Russian workers' movement. An independent investigation by the Second International determined that by 1914 the weekly circulation of the Bolshevik paper *Pravda* was 240,000 compared with 96,000 for the Mensheviks' *Luch*. In the Duma the Mensheviks had seven deputies to the Bolsheviks' six, but the majority of working-class districts tended to vote Bolshevik; thus, out of the nine deputies permitted by law to be selected by the workers' curia (working-class electoral colleges set up under tsarist law), six were Bolsheviks. In elections of the All-Russia Insurance Board, set up by the regime to administer social insurance for workers, 82 percent of those elected by the workers were Bolsheviks.[22]

We need to go beyond raw statistics, however, to get a feel for the dynamics of Bolshevik ascendancy. It's worth considering the reflections of the careful pro-Menshevik scholar Leopold Haimson, who has commented on the Bolsheviks' ability "to strike a note of militance, and yet seemingly a note of realism; to appeal to anger, and also to make [their] expression appear eminently reasonable, if not practical." He continues that "it is because of this multiplicity of the notes they strike, and the varying ways in which they harmonize them, that Bolshevik propaganda and agitation prove so successful by the eve of the war, not only among the explosive strata of the Petersburg working class, but also among the 'less advanced' workers of the more isolated industrial towns and villages."[23]

In 1914, as Dietrich Geyer observes, "not only Soviet researchers but also Americans speak quite properly of a revolutionary situation which did not abate until [the first world] war erupted." Robert Service elaborates on the same point: "In the first half of 1914 alone there were over 3000 strikes, and two-thirds of them were associated with political demands. The slogans were those espoused by the more intransigent Russian Marxists: both V. I. Lenin's Bolsheviks and L. D. Trotsky's faction had cause to cheer. The police's penetration of all revolutionary groupings was as successful as ever; and presumably few workers were even acquainted with the doctrines of Bolshevism."[24]

Here it's worth interrupting to place a question mark over the word *few*, since tens of thousands of workers had been members of the Bolshevik organization and even more read its newspaper, voted for its candidates, and so forth. These formed part of a vital network in the working class throughout Russia, in a variety of ways transmitting Bolshevik ideas and sensibilities to less politicized workmates. But to let Service continue: "Nonetheless the social unrest had reacquired political content. Huge demonstrations against the monarchy shook St. Petersburg in summer 1914. The participants announced clear aims: they wanted a democratic republic, an eight-hour working day in the factories and the expropriation of all gentry-held land. And they wanted no delay in fulfillment."[25]

The eruption of the First World War, however, diverted the rising wave of militancy into patriotic hysteria and slaughter. The Bolsheviks (and those gathered around Trotsky, plus the Menshevik-Internationalists led by Martov) vehemently opposed the Russian war effort and were savagely repressed. In this situation, the reformist (and pro-war) majority of the Mensheviks were able to resume a dominant position in the workers' movement. Yet by 1917 the devastation of the First World War had generated a radicalization among the Russian masses and severely weakened the tsarist regime. There was a resurgence within the working class of the authority enjoyed by the Bolsheviks. Even the Mensheviks holding positions of formal authority in the workers' organizations felt compelled to take increasingly radical positions in order to prevent the total erosion of their following. The programmatic and consequent organizational coherence of the Bolsheviks was made even more dynamic in the mass upsurge of 1917 by a key shift in the thinking of Lenin and the Bolshevik majority: their traditional belief in proletarian hegemony within the revolutionary struggle, during this new period of world crisis and ferment now seemed to place socialist revolution on the agenda—in Russia and throughout the world.[26]

Competing Vanguard Organizations

One of the political terms that has been subject to considerable mystification is *vanguard*—particularly the variant that is often associated with Bolshevism or "Leninism": *revolutionary vanguard party*. In recent years, there has been a well-deserved debunking of this presumably Leninist conceptualization of "a party of a new type" that partisans on both sides of the Cold War—Stalinists no less than militant anti-Communists—insisted was Lenin's hallmark.[27] In fact, such recent debunking restates the point made by more than one knowledgeable activist-scholar—for example, C. L. R. James:

> The theory and practice of the vanguard party, of the one-party state, is not (repeat not) the central doctrine of Leninism. It is not the central doctrine, it is not even a special doctrine. . . . Bolshevism, Leninism, did have central doctrines. One was theoretical, the inevitable collapse of capitalism into barbarism. Another was social, that on account of its place in society, its training and its numbers, only the working class could prevent this degradation and reconstruct society. Political action consisted in organizing a party to carry out these aims. These were the central principles of Bolshevism. The rigidity of its political organization came not from the dictatorial brain of Lenin but from a less distinguished source—the Tsarist police state. Until the revolution actually began in March 1917, the future that Lenin foresaw and worked for was the establishment of parliamentary democracy in Russia on the British and German models. . . . Bolshevism looked forward to a regime of parliamentary democracy because this was the doctrine of classical Marxism: that it was through parliamentary democracy that the working class and the whole population . . . was educated and trained for the transition to socialism.[28]

There is a need to go even beyond this eminently reasonable description of Lenin's Bolsheviks, however, to approximate a conceptualization of *revolutionary vanguard* that is consistent with social science rather than left-wing pretense.

Any systematic examination of social movements and mass struggles in history reveals that it is never the case that a *majority* of the people—of the "masses" of workers or peasants or slaves—are ever involved in an insurgency capable of bringing about a popularly desired power shift. Such mass actions always involve a sizeable minority, generally connected with and supported by a majority, to be sure, and involving sufficient numbers to overwhelm the forces defending the status quo. But even within this minority that is mobilized in such mass actions, there must be—if the struggle is to be effective—a certain number (an even smaller number) of mindful activists, informed by more or less coherent ideological perspectives, having at least a minimum of organizational skills and political experience. This layer of mindful activists must be capable of putting forward a proposed course of action that makes sense to others, and to increasing numbers of others, among the mass of the oppressed group. One can refer to this layer of mindful activists as a *vanguard layer,* and elements of this layer may be drawn to one or another organization or party.

The approach adopted here is to determine what organizations or parties—on the basis of program, organizational cohesion, activity, and influence—demonstrate an ability to attract elements of this vanguard layer (of, for example, the working class), and also demonstrate a capacity for providing effective revolutionary leadership. We can see, in the Russian revolutionary period, a number of competing *vanguard organizations* (as we have defined them here), although not all of these proved capable of functioning as a *revolutionary vanguard organization,* capable of mobilizing a sizeable enough and effective revolutionary insurgency.

As we have noted, there were a number of organizations favoring the overthrow of tsarism. We have seen, however, that a class dynamic played a key role in determining the fate of the various organizations with their competing programs.

The bourgeois-liberal Kadets, despite some success, were denied what could have been powerful support from the major sectors of the capitalist class, because most of the capitalists favored a compromise with tsarism and so supported the Octobrist Party, the most loyal of the opposition parties. One result of this was that the Kadets themselves were pulled to the right. One can argue that none of this is surprising, given the upper-class orientation of these organizations. The only possibility for vanguard organizations to play a consistently revolutionary role, so the argument ran, is if they were rooted in the lower, majority classes and animated by an ideology (for example, some variant of Marxism)—such as the Russian Social Democratic Labor Party (divided most fundamentally into Bolshevik and Menshevik factions with distinct political orientations and organizational structures), the Party of Socialist Revolutionaries (despite seeking to blend Marxism with peasant-oriented populism, they too were divided into more militant Left SRs and more moderate Right SRs), and a number of less organized currents, some drawn to one or another variant of anarchism.

The Mensheviks, seeking an alliance with the liberal bourgeoisie, especially with the Kadets, were similarly affected by that gravitational pull to the right. Despite the proclaimed revolutionary socialist desires of all, they tended to fragment as the "liquidators" began—in practical terms—counterposing modest legal activity in the labor movement (surely palatable to Kadets and, within limits, to Octobrists) to the development of the revolutionary underground; more revolutionary-inclined Mensheviks such as Martov were also drawn along in this undercurrent. The Mensheviks as an *entity* became incapable of functioning as a revolutionary vanguard. One sympathetic historian of Menshevism, John Basil, has bemoaned their "clumsy strategic position" of seeking to make the anti-tsarist revolution through "a socialist-liberal alliance (with the liberals running up front)" while at the same time seeing the liberals as "natural enemies" because "they were the representatives of capitalism," which the Mensheviks hoped to overthrow in the long run: "At the root of the Menshevik dilemma was the incompatibility of their liberal-socialist alliance scheme and their radical mentality encouraged by doctrinaire Marxism." This contradiction generated a disunity of divergent standpoints. "Divisiveness within the party was rife and organizational unity, although sought, was never found. Individuals or small groups firmly convinced of the correctness of their opinions prevented the Mensheviks from enjoying the advantages of unified action."[29] What's more, the notion of the socialist-liberal alliance turned out to be fundamentally flawed. Tsarism was overthrown without the liberals, by what many have described as a more or less spontaneous (but not entirely spontaneous) workers' uprising spearheaded by a diversity of socialist activists. Briefly pushed to center stage in the wake of this revolution, the liberals discredited themselves within months.

"Menshevism as a viable revolutionary program ceased to exist once the Kadets were driven from Russian politics and [Irakli] Tseretelli, Martov and Dan were left without their foil," comments Basil.[30] This is not to say that no Mensheviks were genuine revolutionaries. Many were among the sincerest adherents of Marxism (of non-Leninist coloration, to be sure), the workers' movement, and a socialist future. But at least by 1917 those who remained in the Menshevik organization were trapped in a party incapable of leading a revolution. Many Menshevik activists—including some who had been prominent—finally left to join a Bolshevik Party that had clearly demonstrated a greater capacity for revolutionary leadership.

Aside from the Bolsheviks, we have seen, there was a party on the Russian scene that does seem to have had greater potential for revolutionary leadership than those just examined. This was the Party of Socialist Revolutionaries, the SRs. As Shanin comments, the SRs were less inclined to care about theoretical "orthodoxy" than the RSDLP, a mixed blessing that allowed for greater analytical flexibility but that also "led to a lesser ability to secure inter-generational continuities." Deepening this latter problem was bad luck, which Shanin describes: Mikhail Gotz, "the PSR tough man" roughly equivalent to Lenin (and an adherent of a "permanent revolution" perspective), was severely ill by 1903 and dead by 1906; the most charismatic leader of the SRs, Gregory Gershuni, was imprisoned in the decisive period in 1905 and had died by 1908; the prestigious head of the underground terrorist apparatus, E. Azev, was unmasked as a police spy. Victor Chernov was the only survivor of the Lenin-Martov generation who enjoyed substantial authority among the SRs.[31]

Chernov's self-description (writing about himself in the third-person) is therefore not insignificant: "Rather a theorist, a man of speech, literature, the writing desk and lecture platform than a professional politician. A genuinely Slav breadth of nature, a certain pliancy and adjustability were combined in him with a tendency to withdraw into the world of ideas, of social diagnosis and prognosis, of intellectual initiative and creative imagination, and to leave to others the concrete organization of current work." According to Herbert Ellison, in 1917 "a strong lead from the most prestigious and popular member of the party, Victor Chernov, might well have mobilized the majority of the party behind clear policy initiatives. Regrettably, Chernov repeatedly proved himself incapable of such leadership." But this was part of a general problem—a habit of compromise for the sake of unity that retained in SR ranks some who were not particularly socialist or revolutionary, while also "obscuring issues of doctrine and program that needed clarification." The kinds of issues that divided the SRs were hardly trivial. Ellison notes: "Whereas the moderates could, as early as 1904, conceive of collaboration with liberal political leaders, the Left saw Russian capitalism as a hothouse plant cultivated by the autocracy, and Russian capitalists and their spokesmen in liberal politics as the lackeys of the autocracy. The Leftists' attitude toward liberals was therefore more closely akin to the views of Lenin than to those of the moderates within their own movement." Shanin explains that Chernov "eventually grafted a 'stages theory' onto his own historiography of the future," an orientation which became similar to that of the Mensheviks. In contrast to this, the Left SRs "called for the direct struggle for socialism (the 'permanent revolution' of Mikhail Gotz) and in consequence, for the immediate 'socialization' of the factories—that is, the control of industry by the working class." In any event, the SR central committee had little authority by the end of 1908 (when its ineptness was shown by the humiliating Azev affair), and the party "disintegrated into a number of warring factions and writers." The First World War introduced greater disunity, and the overthrow of the tsar with all the turbulence that followed finally tore the organization in two.[32]

On the other hand, the party had fifty thousand formal members nationwide in 1906 (one-third the number claimed by the RSDLP at that time), and by the summer of 1917 the Left SRs represented forty-five thousand workers in Petrograd alone, according to one of their leaders. The great majority of SRs went over to the Left by the autumn, which is significant given the fact that 58 percent of the (largely) peasant votes in national elections to the Constituent Assembly were for the SRs; even in the more urban Second Congress of Workers' and Soldiers' Soviets in 1917, 250 delegates were Bolsheviks, 159 were SRs, 60 were Mensheviks. Thus the Left SRs, despite obvious organizational weaknesses, had a mass base, mass influence, a proud heritage, rich practical experience, and a revolutionary program. Despite a certain inexperience (understandable under the circumstances), they also had a particularly thoughtful, eloquent, and immensely popular public leader, Maria Spiridonova. Certainly in this period, the Left SRs constituted a revolutionary vanguard. Thus—to run ahead of our story—at the decisive moment they participated fully in the October/November socialist revolution: the Petrograd Soviet's military revolutionary committee that organized the insurrection was essentially a Bolshevik-Left SR body, including Spiridonova. "They by no means saw eye to eye with the Bolsheviks," one of their leaders, Isaac Steinberg, later wrote, "but they believed it possible to settle their differences with them inside the Government [of the new Soviet Republic]. The entry of the L.S.R. into the Government signified a coalition of the two leading parties and the two types of mentality contained within Russian radical Socialism."[33]

The pattern that we see here is a tendency of competing revolutionary vanguard elements to converge as a revolutionary situation develops. This was the case in Russia with the Bolsheviks and elements from the Mensheviks plus Trotsky's faction, and to a lesser extent it also occurred with the Left SRs. It should be noted that even when a tragic split took place between the Bolsheviks and Left SRs, many of the latter—sharply disagreeing with their own leaders—joined the Bolsheviks.

This poses the question of how the Bolsheviks came to be the indisputably hegemonic force. There are two aspects to the answer—one having to do with the quality of the Bolsheviks' Marxism and the other having to do with the quality of their organization.

The difference between the approach to Marxism by the Bolsheviks and Mensheviks was highlighted by Lenin near the end of his life, when he was critically reviewing the massive and insightful memoir of the 1917 revolutions—published by the State Publishing House and widely read within the early Soviet Republic—written by a critical-minded Menshevik, N. N. Sukhanov.

The Mensheviks "all call themselves Marxists, but their conception of Marxism is impossibly pedantic," Lenin complained. "They have completely failed to understand what is decisive in Marxism, namely, revolutionary dialectics." Added to this, "they have even failed to understand Marx's plain statements that in times of revolution the utmost flexibility is demanded, and have even failed to notice, for instance, the statements Marx made in letters—I think it was in 1856—expressing the hope of combining peasant war in Germany, which might create a revolutionary situation, with the working-class movement—they avoid even this plain statement and walk around it like a cat around a bowl of hot porridge."[34]

The approach to Marxism that Lenin is criticizing is explained in this way: "Up to now they have seen capitalism and bourgeois democracy in Western Europe follow a certain path of development, and cannot conceive that this path can be taken as a model only *mutatis mutandis*" (meaning "with the necessary changes having been made"). Quite concretely, "the revolution connected with the first imperialist world war. Such a revolution was bound to reveal new features, or variations, resulting from the war itself, for the world has never seen such a war in such a situation." More abstractly, "while the development of world history as a whole follows general laws it is by no means precluded, but, on the contrary, presumed, that certain periods of development may display peculiarities in either the form or the sequence of this development."[35] Putting it all together, Lenin concluded:

> What if the situation, which drew Russia into the imperialist world war that involved every more or less influential West-European country and made her a witness of the eve of the revolutions maturing or partly already begun in the East, gave rise to circumstances that put Russia and her development in a position which enabled us to achieve precisely that combination of a "peasant war" with the working-class movement suggested in 1856 by no less a Marxist than Marx himself as a possible prospect for Prussia?[36]

Lenin's comments reflect a theoretical and political orientation that not only distinguished the Bolsheviks from the Mensheviks, but was decisive in providing a unique orientation to guide Russia's revolutionary activists in 1917.

There remains the question of the organizational quality of Bolshevism. In assessing the competing vanguards from the vantage point of 1920, the insightful revolutionary activist Victor Serge, one of many anarchists who had recently gone over to the Bolsheviks, commented that "the social revolution in Russia—and everywhere else it has begun—is in large part the work of Bolshevism," and by this he meant the Bolshevism that had been forged by 1912 and sharpened in the early years of the First World War. He conceded that "like all historical judgments, this one is in some ways unfair." He was fully prepared to acknowledge "the enormous and magnificent efforts of all those who, before the time of Bolshevism, *actually practiced* revolution: Social Revolutionary propagandists and terrorists, whose courage was unstinting, anarchists and Mensheviks, whom no persecution could stop." Nonetheless:

> For the first time, during the October revolution, words and actions came together. What had so often been spoken of was put into practice. *The unity of thought and action gave Bolshevism its original power*, without entering into doctrinal questions, we can define Bolshevism as *a movement to the left of socialism—which brought it closer to anarchism—inspired by the will to achieve revolution immediately.*[37]

Central to the movement's ability to do this, Serge argued, was what he termed "the necessity of powerful revolutionary organizations," the meaning of which he elaborated in this way:

> To hope to defeat the capitalist state without strong and flexible combat organizations, without a whole combat apparatus—publications, economic action, illegal action, terrorism, etc.—would be worse than naïve. Revolutionary energy, which by its very nature is multiple and diverse, must be organized, concentrated, coherent and conscious in battle.[38]

It has been demonstrated and documented that in building what ultimately became the Bolshevik Party, Lenin was doing no more than attempting to create in tsarist Russia the kind of mass working-class socialist party that he believed had been built up in Germany—the model being the German Social Democratic Party led by August Bebel, whose primary Marxist theorist was Karl Kautsky. In doing this, he did not conceive of himself as a "Bebel-ite" or a "Kautskyist"—rather, he saw himself as a Marxist (which in the pre-World War I period is also how he conceived of them). The fact remained, as history would show, the kind of party he was actually building—and the kind of party he initially had believed had been created in Germany—was something other than the actuality of the German Social Democracy. Nine years after the Bolshevik revolution, Max Eastman, a thoughtful US radical who was close to John Reed (author of *Ten Days That Shook the World*), after spending time in Russia studying what had happened, sought to make sense of the organization that Lenin had actually helped to forge. It is interesting to consider his description:

It is an organization of a kind which never existed before. It combines certain essential features of a political party, a professional association, a consecrated order, an army, a scientific society—and yet is in no sense a sect. Instead of cherishing in its membership a sectarian psychology, it cherishes a certain relation to the predominant class forces of society as Marx defined them. And this relation was determined by Lenin, and progressively readjusted by him, with a subtlety of which Marx never dreamed.[39]

Aspects of this are certainly overstated. It can be argued, for example, that Lenin's role, centrally important as it was, was one of a number of elements in shaping the Bolsheviks, that there were other comrades plus the larger workers' movement that were decisive in making the party what it was—in certain cases providing balance and correction and revision to some of what Lenin offered. Lenin himself (even when he was frustrated at being outvoted by his Bolshevik comrades, which he sometimes was) was insistent on the democratic and collective nature of the organization. This was not only the reality, but was also essential in making both the party and Lenin's own contributions effective in ways that they otherwise would not have been. Still, Eastman's description contains significant elements of truth.

The Road to Power

It is a common perception that the chaos of war and the impact of military defeat are necessary to weaken the forces (especially the armed forces) of the status quo so as to make revolution possible. Hence, there would have been no 1905 uprising in Russia without the Russo-Japanese War, there would have been no 1917 revolution in Russia without World War I, there would have been no revolution in China or Yugoslavia or Vietnam without World War II, and in general there can be no revolution without a devastating war coming first. Cuba and Nicaragua seem to offer obvious exceptions to this "rule," and additional exceptions can also be cited—including Russia. The Russian experience of 1912–14, touched on earlier, suggests that this common perception of revolution flowing only from war is an illusion. As historian Leopold Haimson has commented, "What the war years would do was not to conceive, but to accelerate substantially" certain "broad forces of polarization that had already been at work in Russian national life during the immediate pre-war period." Suggesting that something akin to the Bolshevik revolution could well have occurred even in the absence of the chaos of the First World War, he has drawn attention to "a set of hypothetical circumstances under which Russia might have undergone—even in the absence of the specific strains induced by the war, though maybe under the stimulus of some other, purely domestic crisis—the kind of radical overturn on which Lenin was already gambling by late 1913–early 1914 and which Russia actually experienced with the October Revolution."[40]

The fact remains that the disaster of the First World War first interrupted and then accelerated, as Haimson notes, a revolutionary process already in motion. The question is posed, war or no, how are the repressive forces, especially the military, to be won over or neutralized or defeated?

One part of the answer can be fraternization: appealing to the rank-and-file soldier, generally from working-class or peasant family, that he not shoot at his class brothers and sisters; finding ways to make friends with him, draw him close, explain the situation to him, encourage him to fight for his own rights and support him in that fight, and so on. There are sometimes at least two serious obstacles to this: 1) certain troops that are so brutalized or "brainwashed" or in some way particularly situated that they would much prefer to kill you than to listen to you; and 2) the vulnerability of even potentially friendly soldiers who—if they disobey orders by listening to you instead of attacking you—can be very severely punished or even killed by their military superiors. Particularly in regard to winning over soldiers in this second category, Trotsky explained the importance of armed struggle during the 1905 upsurge: "Only when the soldiers become convinced that the people have come out into the streets for a life-and-death struggle—not to demonstrate against the government but to overthrow it—does it become psychologically possible for them to 'cross over to the side of the people.'"[41]

One thinks of Carl Sandburg's mocking lines in *The People, Yes*:

> *The czar has eight million men with guns and bayonets.*
> *Nothing can happen to the czar.*
> *The czar is the voice of God and shall live forever.*
> *Turn and look at the forest of steel and cannon*
> *Where the czar is guarded by eight million soldiers.*
> *Nothing can happen to the czar.*[42]

How this actually played out in revolutionary Russia provided a very particular answer to what some revolutionaries (and also some counterrevolutionaries) have advanced as a central aspect of revolution—the role of armed struggle, the relationship between political struggle and military struggle.

In the Russian experience, we see a specific kind of interplay between war and revolution. There is no question that the First World War was one very important factor in bringing on the Russian Revolution. As it turned out, war became a factor in the revolutionary triumph not simply as a cause but also as an effect—and as something that Russia had to go through in order to clinch the revolutionary victory (although, as we shall see, some of the impacts of war also helped to undermine that victory). There was an intervention by hostile foreign powers combined with a foreign-financed and foreign-supported civil war—with all of the killing and horror that war involves. Although military questions at certain points assumed central importance, they were necessarily trumped by political questions.

What masses of people think and feel and do is more decisive than purely military policies and military technology. On the other hand, military realities affect mass consciousness and can affect mass action. A failure to integrate them into a revolutionary perspective means a failure to be serious. The manner in which such integration takes place can affect the confidence and commitment one is able to inspire among activists and the larger population (including sectors of the army). Yet in Russia the armed struggle—recognized beforehand as a necessity by the revolutionaries such as Lenin—organically grew out of the mass struggles of the working class. This brings us to a key question that goes deeper than the issue of armed struggle—the interrelationship of the revolutionary vanguard and the mass struggle, and the mass/vanguard dialectic that has been a legitimate focus for Marxists and post-Marxists alike.

A memoir from a working-class activist who had belonged to the SRs, V. Buzinov, provides a graphic description of how this mass/vanguard dialectic worked in microcosm in the factories: "There were few socialist workers [i.e., party members] and they were supported by the conscious workers. The latter were ten times more numerous as the socialists. . . . Each was, in a way, a 'juridically reasoning individual' capable of understanding all that surrounded him." This is a key—members of the revolutionary organization functioned in a milieu in which respect and authority were not guaranteed but instead had to be earned. At the very least, his or her words would have to make sense to experienced and critical-minded "conscious workers" whose support would be crucial in gaining a general and sympathetic hearing, as well as expanding influence throughout the workplace. As Buzinov explained, such activists essentially understood, from their own life experience, the workers' actual situation and their relationship to the factory owners. Such "conscious workers" could have tremendous impact when agitating among their workmates who—less knowledgeable, less experienced in articulating their own thoughts and feelings—would, when listening to the views of a "conscious worker," exclaim: "That's it! That's just what I wanted to say!"[43]

The dynamic that developed in Russia between vanguard and masses resulted in an interpenetration that changed each. Elements from popular ideology and tradition provided a basis for understanding the new Marxist ideas, in the process altering or adding to those ideas. As the revolutionary movement increasingly took on a mass character, altering the composition of the cadres, a similar alteration took place in the nature of the organization and the struggle. In some cases, this contributed to the generation of insurgencies that were quite unexpected by the vanguard leadership. Such a dynamic, for example, brought the downfall of the tsar of all the Russias.

The Unexpected Rising

Russian entry into the First World War brought an abrupt end to the rising wave of working-class militancy and Bolshevik influence that seemed to have such revolutionary implications in the summer of 1914. Many thousands of the militants were drafted into the armed forces; others whose opposition to the war was too vocal (who came to be known as "internationalists") were arrested or forced to flee abroad. Conscripted "conscious workers" were replaced by new arrivals from the countryside who were not immune from reverence toward the tsar and the patriotic war for which the people were called on to sacrifice. The toughs of the Black Hundreds found it easier to mobilize against "traitors," and even on the left end of the spectrum, significant numbers of Socialist Revolutionaries and Mensheviks rallied to the defense of their homeland (becoming "defensists") against "German imperialism."

It is revealing, however, that from the far right of Russia's ruling elite, an insightful prediction was advanced half a year before the eruption of the First World War. This was offered in a private memorandum to the tsar by Pyotr Durnovo, the former minister of internal affairs who had helped crush the 1905 revolution and now headed the so-called Right Group in the State Council. Durnovo believed a world war would bring revolution in its wake—inevitably originating "in a defeated Germany or a defeated Russia," as Dominic Lieven summarizes. A German revolution would, of course, help to generate revolutionary waves throughout Europe and into Russia. But even before a conclusion of the war, "the needs and casualties of war would destroy the main bulwark of the regime against revolution, namely the peacetime army." Nor could political concessions be made, in such circumstances, to "moderate the fanaticism of the revolutionary parties. More important, the mass of the population—both workers and peasants—were unconscious socialists. This was the product of Russian history and culture. European values—at whose core stood private property—as yet meant nothing to them."[44]

Lieven's gloss on Durnovo traces what would, in fact, be the future course of revolutionary Russia. Amid the disruptions generated by capitalist modernization, "only the authoritarian police state could hold the class war in check. Russia's upper and middle classes could not survive without its support. In any genuinely democratic election, they themselves, their values, and their property would be swept aside." Far from ushering in a liberal, democratic-capitalist political order, in Durnovo's opinion, "tsarism's demise would lead to anarchy and to some version of extreme revolutionary socialism."[45]

And so it was.

The war did not go well for the Tsar's army or for the Russian people, adding new grievances to old. A new wave of working-class radicalization was generated. This was part of a general collapse of the tsarist system and of an even deeper crisis that was overtaking Russian society under the impact of the First World War, which was greatly intensifying the immense problems already created by the processes of industrialization and "modernization." Many millions of people were dramatically affected by the war: fifteen million were mobilized into the army, additional millions were drawn into the factories to keep the economy running, millions more became refugees from the war zones. The absolute destructiveness of the war—six million Russian soldiers were killed, wounded, or captured, and much of the Russian empire's richest lands were lost to German forces—was matched by the breakdown of much of the Russian economy: prices rising far above wages, deteriorating transportation and distribution systems, food and fuel shortages, dramatically worsening living conditions. The faith of the most loyal of Tsar Nicholas's "lowly" subjects began to turn into its opposite as they asked: "If the tsar were a good tsar, why couldn't he save Russia and its people?" Scandalous corruption and ineptness in the highest circles—topped by the amoral intrigues and escapades of the tsar's favorite holy man, Gregory Rasputin—had undermined the confidence of even the most conservative elements of Russia's ruling classes in tsarism's capacity to endure.[46]

Another important factor was the profound weakening of tsarism's repressive forces, particularly the army. Allan Wildman writes that "the soldiers felt they were being used and recklessly expended by the rich and powerful, of whom their officers were the most visible, immediate representatives." Roy

Medvedev adds: "By drafting millions of peasants and workers into the army and training them to handle weapons, the tsarist regime, without intending to, provided military and technical training.... The likely allies of the working class, the peasants, were armed and organized in military garrisons in every major city, with especially large garrisons in Moscow and Petrograd."[47]

William Henry Chamberlin once commented that "the collapse of the Romanov autocracy in March 1917 was one of the most leaderless, spontaneous, anonymous revolutions of all time." This is both true and false—a paradox that sheds much light on the role of the revolutionary party. Historians have noted the growth of war-weariness, despair, and exasperation with the old system throughout Russian society. The only hope for a better life seemed either in a Russian victory in the First World War (which seemed increasingly illusory or even irrelevant) or in some kind of radical social change.[48] These moods and feelings and beliefs, "spontaneously" generated by objective conditions, were certainly the source of the uprising, but the revolutionary parties played an essential role in offering coherent conceptual alternatives to the status quo. Only the organized socialists—defensists as well as internationalists—articulated such alternatives, and their appeals were yielding an increasingly visible response among the Russian workers as 1916 faded into 1917.

It is important to recognize that the Bolsheviks were not the only current playing this crucial role. In Petrograd, for example, the active members of all the revolutionary parties combined constituted no more than 2 percent of the total number of workers, yet they had a profoundly subversive impact. This was true both of moderates and militants, since both favored the overthrow of tsarism. Of course, not all of the different currents were doing their work in the same manner. The Menshevik moderates and their allies were concentrating their efforts in the War Industries Committees and in caucusing with elements of the bourgeois-liberal opposition. The twenty-four thousand Bolsheviks (including two thousand in Petrograd and six hundred in Moscow) were, according to one observer, "buried in a completely different kind of work, keeping the equipment of the movement in repair, forcing the pace for a decisive clash with the tsarist regime, organizing propaganda and the underground press."[49]

According to various observers, the "conscious and tempered workers educated for the most part by the party of Lenin" were not in touch with the central leadership of their organization (repression and war conditions guaranteed that), but they nonetheless played an essential role. Trotsky's description merits attention:

> In every factory, in each guild, in each company, in each tavern, in the military hospital, at the transfer stations, even in the depopulated villages, the molecular work of revolutionary thought was in progress. Everywhere were to be found the interpreters of events, chiefly from among the workers, from whom one inquired, 'What's the news?' and from whom one awaited the needed words. These leaders had often been left to themselves, and nourished themselves upon fragments of revolutionary generalizations arriving in their hands by various routes, had studied out by themselves between the lines of the liberal papers what they needed. Their class instinct was refined by a political criterion, and though they did not think all their ideas through to the end, nevertheless their thought ceaselessly and stubbornly worked its way in a single direction.[50]

Of course, militants from other revolutionary organizations were playing a similar role. Nor were the local Bolsheviks and their sympathizers, or any of the other groups, in control of events—even if their influence was inseparable from what was happening. The overthrow of tsarism involved a far more interesting dynamic.

The stirrings were evident to activists in the know. "You'll have to get to Russia right away or else you won't get in on 'the beginning.' In all seriousness, the letters from Russia are filled with good news." So wrote Nadezhda Krupskaya, a central operative within the Bolshevik organization, to a comrade living in exile more than a month before the initial revolutionary explosion. She quoted a just-received letter from "an old friend, a highly experienced person" on the scene, reporting that "a turn for the better can be seen in the mood of the workers and educated young people" despite the fact that "organization is poor" due to thinning ranks of experienced activists resulting from military conscription. "The influx of women and adolescents into the workforce is lowering organizational capacity but not the mood," and in fact "the organizations are growing."[51]

The Petrograd Bolsheviks were intending to make May 1, the international workers' holiday, the time for massive demonstrations and a general strike that they hoped might culminate in the overthrow of the autocracy. Yet International Women's Day (March 9, or February 23, according to the old Russian calendar) was also a day observed by the workers' movement. It took place amid rising prices, bread lines, and the disappearance of bread from some bakeries, on top of a lockout and militant strike at the massive Putilov works. According to David Mandel, "the mood of the women workers was very militant," and this contributed to unexpected complications. Mandel recounts: "The day began with meetings featuring anti-war speeches, but no other actions were planned. Among the Bolsheviks, who tended to be the most militant, the strategy was to conserve energy for a decisive general strike on May Day. Nevertheless, in the Vyborg District the women workers of several textile mills quit work and, gathering outside the nearby metal-working factories, easily persuaded the men to join them."[52]

Earlier in this study we noted the relative political "backwardness" and passivity of unskilled workers—such as female textile workers—throughout the early history of the workers' movement, as well as the determination of the more "conscious workers" (such as those predominating in the heavily Bolshevik-influenced metal trades) to reach out to them and draw them into the struggle. Now, in a number of instances it was metalworkers who were inspired to take to the streets in response to the appeals of militant textile workers, women who marched through the factory districts on International Women's Day chanting: "Down with the war! Down with high prices! Down with hunger! Bread for the workers!"[53]

Some Bolsheviks were anxious or even indignant that the "undisciplined" workers were not heeding their advice to stay calm and conserve their energy for future battles. But the members of the Bolshevik rank and file threw themselves into the actual struggle that was erupting around them. This is reflected in an up-to-the-minute account written by the Ulyanov sisters, Anna and Mariia (both experienced revolutionary militants) in the Bolshevik paper *Pravda*:

> On Women's Day, February 23, a strike was declared at the majority of factories and plants. The women were in a very militant mood—not only the women workers, but the masses of women queuing for bread and kerosene. They held political meetings, they predominated in the streets, they moved to the city duma with a demand for bread, they stopped trams. "Comrades, come out!" they shouted enthusiastically. They went to the factories and plants and summoned workers to [put] down tools. All in all, Women's Day was a tremendous success and gave rise to the revolutionary spirit.[54]

On the following day demonstrations and strikes spread throughout Petrograd, with a proliferation of anti-war and anti-government banners. The military units of the city for the most part refused to take action against the insurgents, and in some cases even joined them.[55] More and more workers were responding to an appeal issued by an on-the-ground united front:

> We Bolsheviks, Menshevik SDs, and SRs summon the proletariat of Petersburg and all Russia to organization and feverish mobilization of our forces. Comrades! In the factories organize illegal strike committees. Link one district to another. Organize collections for the illegal press and for arms. Prepare yourselves, comrades. The hour of decisive struggle is nearing![56]

There was nonetheless considerable spontaneous action. "Throngs that filled the streets were becoming aggressive," reported Isaac Don Levine. "A well-known bakers' shop was looted and its windows smashed when the crowd of five hundred who waited in line to buy bread were told that only fifty could be served. They broke into the store and found large quantities of bread hidden away for richer customers." Levine noted that "the police had their hands full dispersing the crowds, using their weapons freely."[57] Days of street fighting saw the police take the offensive, fire into the crowds, and then be routed as the workers fought back with growing confidence. As a general strike paralyzed the city, the overwhelming majority of the working class seemed alive with enthusiasm for revolutionary change. By the fourth day of the insurgency, the troops were disobeying the commands of tsarist officers, openly joining the workers in massive numbers, firing on the police stations, helping to free all political prisoners. The tsarist autocracy collapsed. The revolution was triumphant. Historian Michael Melancon has argued that this was not simply the "spontaneous" event that many historians have portrayed, although he acknowledges that "socialists had no specific plans in advance to launch revolutionary disturbances on 23 February and bring them to fruition on 27 February." Rather, there was an interplay between the socialist groups and radicalized working-class layers that were coming into the streets—the initial "orientation to promote strikes and demonstrations" on International Women's Day, followed by a determination "to prolong them and push them toward revolution," as events whirled from protest to insurgency. "Direct and organized socialist involvement and intervention occurred at every single stage."[58]

This was actually reported in 1917 by the knowledgeable *New York Tribune* foreign correspondent Isaac Don Levine. While the "mainstream" politicians in the Duma reared back in fear (with prominent liberal Pavel Miliukov predicting "the revolution will be crushed in fifteen minutes" by tsarist troops), "the leaders of the socialistic, revolutionary, and labor elements organized for a general attack . . . against the old regime." They mobilized "a revolutionary army, composed of soldiers, armed students, and workers," and as they surged forward to victory after victory in the streets, with the tsar's army melting into the revolutionary mass, "red flags were now waving in the air everywhere, and, singing the songs of freedom and revolution, the masses continued their victorious fight. The leaders of the movement commandeered every motor-car they could get, armed it with a machine-gun and a gun crew, and set it free to tour the city and round up agents of the Government."[59]

Many contradictions and most problems remained. As the establishment politicians in the Duma's meeting place, the Tauride Palace, sought to cobble together a "Duma Committee of Safety," at the very same time "the leaders of the revolution, the original labor council, several army representatives and the chiefs of the radical parties met in another hall of Tauride Palace," reported Levine. "Instituting themselves into a temporary committee, the meeting issued an appeal to the entire revolutionary proletariat and soldiery of the city to hold immediate elections for the Council of Workmen's and Soldiers' Deputies"[60]—the Russian word for "council" being *soviet*.

While the local Bolsheviks had played an essential role in the insurrection and in the process leading up to the insurrection, they did not—in their relatively disorganized situation (due to wartime repression)—find themselves in a position to provide a clear direction forward in the wake of the tsar's overthrow. The moderate socialists, whose pro-war position had secured them legality plus valuable contacts with bourgeois liberal political figures, *were* in a position to rally the insurgent masses around a program that seemed to make sense: the workers' soviets and a bourgeois-liberal Provisional Government would be the twin pillars of a unified "revolutionary democracy" that would culminate in a Constituent Assembly from which the framework for a democratic republic would emerge.

"It was the workmen and soldiers that actually fought and shed their blood for the freedom of Russia. The Duma took a hand in the situation only after the revolution had achieved its main success," Levine reported at the time. "The gulf between the Provisional Government and the Council of Deputies is as wide as between the United States Government and Socialism. Only such an upheaval as the revolution could have bridged this chasm between the two extremes." While the Provisional Government "represents . . . business and commerce," Levine noted, "the ultimate aim of the Workmen's Council is social revolution. To achieve this revolution it is necessary to dethrone the political autocrats first, they say. Then the capitalistic system must be attacked by the working classes of all nations as their common enemy."[61]

The bourgeois liberals were, among themselves, far from pleased with this state of affairs. They clearly feared the mass insurgency, despised the "rotters" and "scoundrels in the factories" who were disrupting the war effort, and were agreeable to taking leadership only to prevent a further radicalization. The prominent worker-Bolshevik Alexander Shlyapnikov remarked with surprise "how easily the worker masses were taken in by the trap of national unity and the unity of revolutionary democracy, in which the capitalists were included." There was a logic to this "trap," however: the fear on the part of many thoughtful workers that the working class—a minority class in Russia—would be isolated and crushed, as had happened to the Paris Commune of 1871 and, in a different and less definitive way, in Russia of 1905. It was a complex situation, and the "common sense" solution for even many of the more militant workers seemed to be precisely "the unity of revolutionary democracy, in which the capitalists were included."[62] It should be emphasized, too, that the Bolshevik Party itself—at least up through the better part of April—was not able to articulate a coherent alternative to this "common sense" perspective.

Insurgent Interlude

Thus there was a general spirit of national-democratic unity in which the soviets—while continuing to exist and to develop their own authority—handed much of their power over to a predominantly bourgeois Provisional Government, under the liberal former monarchist Prince Lvov, creating a situation of "dual power." The Provisional Government assumed authority for creating the framework to establish a Constituent Assembly that would draft a new constitution, and it also assumed power for governing the country in the interim. The revolutionary masses hoped that the Provisional Government would initiate far-reaching social reforms, and although they wanted to defend their revolution from any possible assault by German imperialism, they also hoped that the Provisional Government would begin to initiate a Russian withdrawal from the First World War. The soviets, now organized on a national scale (the first All-Russian Congress of Soviets was held in April), with a Menshevik-SR majority, stood for all of these things. "The outstanding figure in the Provisional Government was that of Minister of Justice Kerensky, a Socialist," according to Levine. "As Vice-President of the Council of Workmen's and Soldiers' Deputies, he represented in the Ministry those radical forces which were responsible for the revolution and were in control of the working masses."[63]

As Mark Steinberg notes, the "celebration of freedom and citizenship masked (and only barely, at that) conflicts over power and meaning that lay just beneath the surface." On the one hand, there was the "display of guns and automobiles—symbols of power—in the hands of commoners" as "a leitmotiv of theatricalized power," arms seized and vehicles "requisitioned" by crowds waving red flags, soldiers and workers triumphantly shooting in the air and "even 'girls,' observers noted, . . . 'driving around the city, God knows where, in God knows whose cars.'" Steinberg suggests "the cars and guns and violence were in part symbolic gestures: variously signs of anger and frustration over conditions; of oppression avenged and hierarchies overturned; of liberation from old authority; of a new public power for the poor; and of new ideas of order and justice."[64]

It soon became clear, however, that the Provisional Government was reluctant to go too far or too fast with the hoped-for reforms, and Pavel Miliukov, the Kadet Party leader who was minister of foreign affairs, made it clear that the government remained committed to the war effort. The consequent popular anger and mass demonstrations forced a reshuffling within the regime, with Miliukov and others resigning, as Mensheviks and SRs agreed to assume six ministerial posts in a new coalition government. A polarization began to set in: the bourgeois-liberal Kadets shifted further to the right, while even more reactionary elements became involved in counterrevolutionary plotting; on the other end of the spectrum, growing numbers of workers were enthusiastic about Bolshevik proposals for a Menshevik-SR Provisional Government without any capitalist participation, and for all political power being transferred to the soviets.

Anxious to close down the Eastern Front by pulling their Russian foes out of "the Great War," the German government was happy to funnel anti-war revolutionaries such as Lenin back into their homeland. Taking advantage of this "generosity" of the Kaiser's generals opened Lenin to the charge of being a "German agent." There were other revolutionaries (such as Menshevik leader Julius Martov) who did the same thing while avoiding this stigma, and Lenin has been exonerated of the charge by serious historians. Yet Winston Churchill (from the standpoint of his own class position) certainly hits on something when he writes of the German High Command that "it was with a sense of awe that they turned upon Russia the most grisly of all weapons. They transported Lenin in a sealed train like a plague bacillus from Switzerland into Russia."[65]

A number of Russian revolutionaries, including Bolsheviks, saw the overthrow of the tsar as "a bourgeois-democratic revolution" that would clear the way for the full development of capitalism in Russia, creating the economic abundance and working-class majority required for the eventual transition to socialism. For many Mensheviks and SRs, this suggested the need to support the Provisional Government. Even prominent Bolsheviks, recently returned to the scene, took issue with the growing sentiment among party members to push aggressively against bourgeois liberals and moderate socialists favoring a capitalist consolidation. After all, the Bolshevik line had for more than a decade emphasized the need for a worker-peasant alliance to carry through a bour-geois-democratic revolution—favoring, to be sure, a forceful and uncompromising "democratic dictatorship of the proletariat and the peasantry" to sweep away all vestiges of feudalism, but not to go beyond a capitalist framework.

Upon his return to Russia, Lenin spoke forcefully in favor of his *April Theses*. The Bolshevik sailor Fydor Raskolnikov was present. "This speech produced a complete revolution in the thinking of the Party's leaders, and underlay all the subsequent work of the Bolsheviks," he recalled. "It was not without cause that our Party's tactics did not follow a straight line, but after Lenin's return took a sharp turn to the left." Only then, after a fundamental debate and reorientation, were the Bolsheviks prepared to argue that a dem-ocratic revolution that had been made possible thanks to the revolutionary initiative (and hegemony) of the working class could only be completed by replacing the political power of the bourgeoisie with the political power of the working class itself. This dictatorship of the proletariat (supported by the peasantry) would initiate the socialist transformation of society. "We certainly did not understand the dictatorship of the proletariat as a dictator-ship of the Bolshevik party," explained another Bolshevik militant, Eduard Dune, several years later. "Quite the contrary. We were looking for allies, for other parties willing to go along with us along the path of building soviet power." Dune noted that the left wing of the Menshevik party "was not very far distant from us." Yet another Bolshevik memoirist, Raskolnikov's broth-er A. F. Ilyin-Zhenevsky, later described how pleased he and his comrades were to be working closely with the Inter-District Organization of United Social Democrats (which included Trotsky and his co-thinkers, some of the "party Mensheviks" associated with Plekhanov, and left-Bolsheviks asso-ciated with Alexander Bogdanov and Anatoly Lunacharsky) and how they were initially anticipating, with joy, unity with Martov's Menshevik-Inter-nationalists. While unity with the Inter-District group was achieved, how-ever, Martov pulled away—though some members of his group joined the Bolsheviks individually.[66]

As they advocated the perspective for a new revolution to all who would listen, the Bolsheviks were accused of "spreading anarchy," to which Lenin responded:

> The name of anarchists is reserved for those who decry the necessity of state power; we say that it is unconditionally necessary, and not only for Russia at this moment, but even for a state making a direct transformation to socialism. We

only want that this power should be wholly and exclusively in the hands of the majority of workers,' soldiers' and peasants' deputies.[67]

Reporting in the early summer of 1917, Isaac Don Levine offered this account to US readers:

> The leader of the extremists was Nikolai Lenin. He returned to Russia from Switzerland *via* Germany, and his violent pacifist agitation alienated the large following he has as one of the leaders of the Russian Social Democracy.
>
> To Lenin, a capitalist was worse than a king. An industrial magnate or leading banker was to him more perilous than a Czar or a Kaiser. The working classes, he said, had nothing to lose whether their rulers were German, French, or British. The imperative thing for them to do was to prepare for a social revolution. Meanwhile, preached Lenin, the Russian or any other labor class might as well live under the rule of the Hohenzollerns [the Germans] as be governed by a capitalistic organization.
>
> The Council of Workmen's and Soldiers' Deputies, however, by an overwhelming majority expressed itself against Leninism. Instead it appealed to the German proletariat to rise and overthrow the Kaiser as the only means to the establishment of peace and the union of the European proletariat in the social revolution.[68]

Of course, Lenin also favored the German workers overthrowing the Kaiser and capitalists in Germany, and said so clearly and often. But they would be more apt to do this, he insisted, if the Russian workers moved forward to establish their own political power in Russia, leading the way for the European social revolution that would establish peace and socialism.

Even the clearest articulation of the new Bolshevik perspective could only win majority support among the workers if corroborated by experience. They would have to perceive that the Russian bourgeoisie and its political representatives were—especially through the involvement in the war—far more closely tied to the capitalists and governments of France and Britain than to the needs and aspirations of the Russian working people, that these capitalist politicians were consequently far more committed to curtailing the freedoms won by the workers and soldier-peasants than in allowing serious social reforms to be implemented. But this was exactly the way consciousness shifted in the insurgent working-class districts, as political life in the communities and workplaces dramatically radicalized. A sense of the ferment comes through in Dune's lengthy description of a workers' meeting:

> In May we discussed Lenin's letter [the *April Theses*], which we decided to draw to the attention of a general meeting of the work force. [Timofei] Sapronov first

explained who Lenin was and why he had not been allowed back into Russia before now and went on to talk about the future course of the revolution. He didn't deliver a treatise on revolutionary perspectives or on the bourgeois and socialist revolutions, he spoke in words all those attending could understand. Did we need a government composed of the bourgeoisie and former tsarist officials or should we transfer power into the hands of the representatives of the revolution, the representatives of the working class, the Soviet of Workers' Deputies? The Bolsheviks said the transfer of power to the soviets meant creating what we already had in the factory—a dictatorship of the proletariat. We no longer had guards and police, we worked an eight-hour day at the old rates, yet we earned as much as under the old twelve-hour working day. We lacked the tsar and the police, yet order was better than before the revolution. There was no robbery or stealing, no drunkenness or accompanying hooliganism. If we could organize a revolutionary government in one factory, then why could we not create a similar order across the whole of Russia? Let the bourgeoisie continue to trade and build its mills and factories, but power must rest with the workers, not with the factory owners, traders, and their servants. . . .

Representatives of the workers' aristocracy, the Mensheviks, also spoke. They were against the idea . . . A socialist revolution could occur only when the country was mature economically and culturally, and then the transition from bourgeois-democratic revolution to socialism would be as natural as our revolution had been in February.

The meeting listened carefully to all speakers, but with less attention to arguments about the socialist and bourgeois-democratic revolutions, supported by citations from the works of Bebel and Marx. . . . The Bolsheviks spoke in a way that was more comprehensible. . . .

More people spoke at this meeting than ever before, and those who spoke most were those who had said very little until then. As well as workers from the factory, migrant workers from the countryside and invalid soldiers who had been demobilized also spoke. Some talked of workers' power, others said that the new government must give the landlords' estates to the peasants and bring an end to the futile bloodletting of the war. The meeting continued a long time, but the atmosphere of intense discussion preserved us from exhaustion. . . .[69]

A crescendo of working-class ferment in July culminated in a revolutionary armed demonstration initiated by militants in Petrograd not under any party control. The Bolshevik leaders found it impossible to defuse the volatile situation but also chose not to draw back from their ties with the impatient sectors of the working class that were attempting to push the revolution forward. Their stance was used as a pretext for government repression against the Bolsheviks in the wake of violence that accompanied the armed demonstration. In the face of this, Lenin urged that the Bolsheviks withdraw their call for "all power to the soviets," which under Menshevik-SR leadership seemed, in Lenin's words, to be acting "like sheep brought to the slaughter-house." Instead, he suggested, "we must transfer our main attention to the factory committees," which reflected more dramatically and immediately the working-class radicalization.[70]

Yet the failure of a new Russian military offensive generated a deepening opposition to the war, giving a greater edge to the working-class discontent. The soviets were becoming restive. The pressures of the situation resulted in another governmental reshuffling, with Prince Lvov stepping aside for the moderately radical lawyer Alexander Kerensky, a Trudovik who had become a Right SR. The tensions of the "dual power" situation mounted, however, and Kerensky appointed military strongman General Lavr Kornilov as commander in chief of the Russian army. With this move he hoped to counter the pressure of "unreasonable" workers, who since February had been establishing militant trade unions, setting up aggressive factory committees for workers' control (though not takeovers) of the workplaces, and even organizing their own "red guard" paramilitary groups to help maintain public order and guard against reactionary violence and counterrevolutionary attempts. Although Kerensky was disturbed by such radicalism, right-wingers such as General Kornilov found moderates like Kerensky just as distasteful.

In his memoirs, Kerensky quotes the following message from Kornilov to him, indicating one aspect of the general's intentions:

> I feel sure, when I think of the events of April 20 and July 3 and 4 [involving relative leniency in the face of mass demonstrations], that the spineless weaklings who form the Provisional Government will be swept away. If by some miracle they should remain in power, the leaders of the Bolsheviks and the Soviet will go unpunished through the connivance of such men as [Victor] Chernov. It is time to put an end to all of this. It is time to hang the German spies led by Lenin, to break up the Soviet, and to break it up in such a way that it will never meet again anywhere![71]

Kerensky writes: "Unfortunately, I agreed to this but did not take part in working out the details of the operation." His understanding was that Kornilov intended to leave Kerensky as head of the government. He later discovered, he tells us, that an emissary of Kornilov to conservative and liberal Duma leaders asserted "everything was ready at Headquarters and the front for the removal of Kerensky." Kerensky comments: "The Duma members, being politically mature, refused to discuss with General Kornilov a plot which they considered inept, but they did nothing to stop the conspiracy and did not even bother to inform the person most concerned—myself!" Later historians have debated whether or not Kerensky was correct in asserting that there was a conspiracy to replace him with a military dictatorship under Kornilov. Some argue there was a comedy of errors, miscommunications, misunderstandings. There is little controversy, however, that a decision had been made (initially agreed to by Kerensky himself) to wipe out the Bolsheviks and crush the soviets.[72]

At almost the last minute, in late August, Kerensky concluded that he himself was in danger. As Kornilov moved to march his troops to Petrograd to "save Russia," he vainly sought to dismiss the general and appealed to the workers' organizations (including the Bolsheviks, who were again granted full legality) to rally to the defense of the revolution. The Bolsheviks played an especially aggressive role in mobilizing against the counterrevolutionary attempt, and their authority in the working class soared. In the face of the determined working-class mobilization, and through the efforts of revolutionary agitators who made contact with the soldiers under Kornilov's command, the right-wing military offensive simply disintegrated before reaching Petrograd. Kerensky later described the situation that unfolded in the face of Kornilov's attempted coup:

> The first news of the approach of General Kornilov's troops had much the same effect on the people of Petrograd as a lighted match on a powder keg. Soldiers, sailors, and workers were all seized with a sudden fit of paranoid suspicion. They fancied they saw counterrevolution everywhere. Panic-stricken that they might lose the rights they had only just gained, they vented their rage against all the generals, landed proprietors, bankers and other "bourgeois" groups.
>
> Most of the Socialist leaders who had been in the coalition, fearing the possibility of a counterrevolutionary victory and subsequent reprisals, turned toward the Bolsheviks. During the first few hours of hysteria, on August 27, they welcomed them back with loud acclaim, and side by side with them, set about "saving the revolution."
>
> How could Lenin fail to take advantage of this? . . .[73]

The Bolshevik Revolution

While the Bolsheviks were willing to form a united front against Kornilov, they gave no political support to Kerensky, and once again they raised the demand for "all power to the soviets." Meanwhile, throughout the summer, peasant disorders had been escalating across the Russian countryside, as the rural poor—impatient with government promises of a future land reform that would redistribute agricultural holdings more equitably—on their own began to take over and divide up the great landed estates. Urban discontent was also rising as food shortages hit the cities, with the workers' earlier expectations being frustrated in innumerable ways. The oppressed nationalities throughout the Russian empire, in seething turmoil with hopes excited by tsarism's downfall, were pressing demands for self-determination, toward which the Provisional Government showed obvious reluctance. And Kerensky time and again reaffirmed Russia's participation in the hated World War. Lenin was now convinced that the overthrow of the Provisional Government was a practical possibility, especially as Bolsheviks began to win majorities in the soviets. Bolshevik demands for "peace, land, bread" clearly had majority support throughout the country, but it was clear that the Provisional Government was incapable of satisfying them (which therefore gave them the character of *transitional* demands—enjoying popular support but leading necessarily to revolutionary confrontation). The Socialist Revolutionaries split, with the sizeable grouping of Left SRs supporting Bolshevik proposals. Elements from the Mensheviks also were drawn to the Bolshevik orientation, despite the rigid opposition of their leaders. Lenin was now anxious to see the revolutionary insurrection carried out as soon as possible and therefore urged that it be done by the Bolshevik Party in its own name. Other Bolshevik leaders, closer to the scene, believed that this could be done more effectively through the soviets. They proved to be right.

The Petrograd Soviet, now largely controlled by Bolsheviks and Left SRs, established a Military Revolutionary Committee to coordinate defense of the city against possible German attacks and counterrevolutionary attempts. Under Trotsky's leadership it began covertly to prepare for the overthrow of the Provisional Government. It gained control over government troops in the city when representatives of radicalized military units agreed that only orders that the Soviet confirmed would be obeyed. The Provisional Government made repressive moves against both the Military Revolutionary Committee and the Bolshevik Party, and it also ordered the transfer of loyal troops to Petrograd. In response, the forces of the Military Revolutionary Committee took over the city, storming the Winter Palace where most of the Provisional Government's ministers were then arrested. On the same day, the Second All-Russian Congress of Soviets began. By an overwhelming majority, it approved the Bolshevik-led actions and formed a new government. Similar events in Moscow and other cities consolidated the power of the new workers' state, which began as a coalition of Bolsheviks and Left SRs.

Surveying and summarizing the recent scholarship, Ronald G. Suny writes: "As historians have shifted their attention away from the political elites that formerly dominated explanations of the Russian Revolution and to the people in the streets, the victorious Bolsheviks have appeared less like Machiavellian manipulators or willful conspirators and more like alert politicians with an acute sensitivity to popular moods and desires." Bolshevik membership grew from 24,000 in February, to 80,000 in April, to 240,000 in July, to 350,000 in October. Of the entire Russian working class, it has been estimated that 5.3 percent had enrolled in the Bolshevik Party by October 1917; in Petrograd, 7.04 percent of all industrial workers were Bolsheviks. Workers represented over 60 percent of the Bolshevik membership. Bolshevik influence was, of course, considerably broader than its membership, and the influence of the insurgent working class outside of the organization was also powerfully felt—as we've seen—in Bolshevik ranks. Suny points out that a "heightened feeling of class was forged in the actual experience of 1917 and contained both social hostilities bred over many years and intensified under wartime and revolutionary conditions and a new political understanding that perceived government by soviets as a preferable alternative to sharing power with the discredited upper classes." He summarizes: "With the failure of the coalition [Provisional Government] and its supporters to deliver on the promise of the revolution, the party of Lenin and Trotsky took power with little resistance and with the acquiescence of the majority of the people of Petrograd. The Bolsheviks came to power not because they were superior manipulators or cynical opportunists but because their policies as formulated by Lenin in April and shaped by the events of the following months placed them at the head of a genuinely popular movement."[74]

The Bolshevik insurrection is often described not as a popular uprising but as the destruction of Russian democracy. The Provisional Government under Alexander Kerensky, in the words of influential post-Marxist Sidney Hook, "made Russia one of the freest countries in the world at the time." Hook related how Kerensky himself acknowledged "errors of judgment," the first of which involved "not taking more effective action to repress the insurrectionary potential of the Bolsheviks in July [1917]." Expanding upon his theme in a letter to the *New York Times* printed August 20, 1988, Hook argued, "The elections to the All Russian Constituent Assembly, for which the Bolsheviks agitated under Kerensky's regime, were held in late November 1917 after the Bolsheviks seized power. It was the nearest thing to a free and democratic election ever held in Russia from 1917 to the present day. The Bolsheviks received less than 25 percent of the vote (their count), and forcibly dissolved the Constituent Assembly." He added: "Even Rosa Luxemburg—in a German jail—condemned Lenin's action as a betrayal of democratic socialism."[75]

The common counterposition of Luxemburg to Lenin doesn't hold up to analysis. While voicing criticisms of certain Bolshevik tactics, she argued: "The Bolsheviks, though they were at the beginning of the revolution a persecuted, slandered and hunted minority attacked on all sides, arrived within the shortest time to the head of the revolution and were able to bring under their banner all the genuine masses of the people: the urban proletariat, the army, the peasants, as well as the revolutionary elements of democracy, the left wing of the Socialist Revolutionaries." Leaving aside for a moment the falseness of Hook's claims regarding Luxemburg attitude toward the Bolshevik Revolution, to be examined below, it is worth giving attention to her assessment of the Bolsheviks' growing popularity. This has been corroborated by non-Bolshevik eyewitnesses, such as Raphael Abramovitch (whose history *The Soviet Revolution* contains a laudatory introduction by Sidney Hook). Abramovitch, a prominent Menshevik leader, later noted that "the February bloc" of moderate socialists and bourgeois liberals quickly disintegrated during the spring of 1917, "while Bolshevism received another powerful impetus. The masses were tired of the appeals for patience and self-control which were being made by the leaders of the socialist parties [i.e., the Mensheviks and SRs supporting the Kerensky regime]; they were looking elsewhere for guidance, and the influence of extremist groups was everywhere on the increase." By October "the balance of forces within the all-important Soviets had shifted radically. One Soviet after another was slipping out of the control of the Socialist Revolutionaries and Mensheviks and into the hands of the Bolsheviks and their allies, the Left Social-Revolutionaries." Abramovitch added: "Among the workers in Petrograd, the atmosphere was becoming increasingly tense as the second congress of Soviets approached. Bolshevik slogans were winning support in most of the large factories. . . . The same was true in many plants in Moscow and other industrial centers." Asserting that "the country, as a whole, was not nearly so uniform," Abramovitch admitted that "nevertheless, the trend in October was unmistakable," mentioning growing radicalization among the peasants and soldiers. "The Socialist Revolutionaries and Mensheviks were aware that the rising tide of political and social discontent was carrying the Bolshevik Party toward victory.[76]

The sweeping reforms that the workers and peasants had thought Kerensky represented "remained unimplemented," as Hook acknowledges, largely because Kerensky's foremost commitment was to "the Allied and United States Governments, which urged Kerensky not to slacken the war effort." Sir Robert Bruce Lockhart, a British diplomatic agent in Russia at the time, later recalled that the primary goal of the Allied diplomats at the time was "to cajole or bully Russia into continuing the war."[77]

It is also necessary to qualify the assertion that Kerensky's government was the freest in the world. After the militant July demonstrations against the war and for implementation of the sweeping social reforms promised by the revolution, a fierce repression was unleashed. "Troops of officers, students, Cossacks," recounts Left SR Isaac Steinberg, "came out on the streets, searched passers-by for weapons and evidence of 'Bolshevism,' committed atrocities." The Bolshevik Party became illegal, its headquarters was raided and wrecked, its leaders and most visible militants were arrested or driven underground. What more should have been done to, as Kerensky and Hook put it, "repress the insurrectionary potential of the Bolsheviks"? The US ambassador to Russia at the time, David Francis, may provide a clue in his memoirs, *Russia from the American Embassy,* in which—over and over—he complains bitterly (and asserts that he complained similarly to the Provisional Government at the time) that "Lenin and Trotzky and their fellow conspirators had not been shot as traitors as they should have been," that "had the Provisional Government at this time arraigned Lenin and Trotzky and the other Bolshevik leaders, tried them for treason and executed them, Russia probably would not have been compelled to go through another revolution," that a primary reason why Kerensky failed was that "twice in the brief tenure of his power he blundered fatally; first, when after the attempted Revolution of July, he failed to execute as traitors, Lenin and Trotzky. Second, when during the Korniloff episode, he failed to conciliate General Korniloff and instead turned to the Council of Workmen's and Soldiers' Deputies and distributed arms and ammunition among the workingmen of Petrograd. By this singularly inept stroke he alienated his own army and armed his enemies."[78] Of course, from what we have seen, this seems a bit unfair to Kerensky. But it also suggests that it would have been exceedingly difficult to defeat Bolshevism without suppressing democracy—just as it was exceedingly difficult, if not quite impossible, to realize the desires and goals of the masses of workers and peasants without breaking with the domestic and international bourgeoisie, and fundamentally radicalizing the revolution—which was the Bolshevik program.

There remains Hook's point about the Constituent Assembly. Significantly, the 25 percent of the vote that went to the Bolsheviks included the great majority of the Russian working class. This was, however, a minority class in Russia at the time. The great majority of the peasant votes went to the candidate lists of the Party of Socialist Revolutionaries, approximately

58 percent of the total vote in the country. In his 1918 work *From October to Brest-Litovsk,* Trotsky explained that "numerically, the principal revolutionary party . . . was the party of Social-Revolutionists," of which Kerensky was formally a member, but the larger portion of the SRs had split away to support the Bolshevik insurrection. The SR list of candidates for the Constituent Assembly was destined to win majority support in the countryside, but "since these lists were made up two or three months before the October revolution and were not subject to change, the Left and Right Social Revolutionists still figured in these lists as one and the same party." The result was bizarre: "By the time of the October revolution—that is, the period when the Right Social Revolutionists were arresting the Left and then the Left were combining with the Bolsheviki for the overthrow of Kerensky's ministry, the old lists remained in full force; and in the elections for the Constituent Assembly the peasants were compelled to vote for lists of names at the head of which stood Kerensky, followed by those of Left Social Revolutionists who participated in the plot for his overthrow."[79]

As it turned out, a majority of candidates on the lists drawn up for the SRs had been Right SRs, who had lost majority support of the membership; what's more, the Bolshevik-Left SR coalition was in favor of immediate implementation of the land reform that the Party of Socialist Revolutionaries had traditionally favored (which is why the peasant majority was voting SR), although the Right SRs had opposed such implementation until "later." In short, the Constituent Assembly elections represented something far removed from the repudiation of Bolshevism that Hook's letter suggests.

What of the judgment of Rosa Luxemburg? Her position, in fact, was quite different from that which Hook attributes to her. She quotes at length from Trotsky's work cited here and then writes: "All of this is very fine and quite convincing." And she goes on to agree with the dissolution of the Constituent Assembly but then proposes a different course of action than that taken by the Bolsheviks and their allies. Here is how she put it: "Since the Constituent Assembly . . . composition reflected the picture of the vanished past and not of the new state of affairs, then it follows automatically that the outgrown and stillborn Constituent Assembly should have been annulled, and without delay, new elections to a new Constituent Assembly should have been arranged." This may be a serious criticism, but it is not, as Hook would have it, a condemnation of "Lenin's action as a betrayal of democratic socialism." In fact, she concludes her polemic by asserting that, whatever her criticisms, "the Bolsheviks have shown that they are capable of everything that a genuine revolutionary party can contribute within the limits of the historical possibilities," adding: "In the present period, when we face decisive final struggles in all the world, the most important problem of socialism was and is the burning question of our time. It is not a matter of this or that secondary question of tactics, but of the capacity for action of the proletariat, the strength to act, the will to power of socialism as such. In this, Lenin and Trotsky and their friends were the first, those who went ahead as an example to the proletariat of the world."[80]

Even though not the condemnation of a betrayal, the secondary tactical criticism offered by Luxemburg is not without importance. The fact remains that many revolutionaries in Russia, while remaining committed to socialist democracy, did not see the Constituent Assembly as the best form through which that could be realized. "In the era which we are now entering the old standards no longer suffice," proclaimed the Left SR Maria Spiridonova. "Until recently the phrase Constituent Assembly spelt revolution. It is only recently, when the character of the revolution has made itself more and more clearly felt, that parliamentary illusions began to be dispelled from our minds. It is the people themselves, not parliaments, that can bring about the social release of man. Yes, when the people discovers the secret of its own power, when it recognizes the Soviets as its best social stronghold, let it then proclaim a real national assembly. Let that national assembly be the only one invested with legislative and executive functions."[81] In the opinion of Bolsheviks, Left SRs, even some Mensheviks, not to mention a majority of the Russian working class, the soviets, their own democratic councils, were to be the framework within which genuine democracy would be realized.

We will need to return to the question of the Constituent Assembly later in this study, but here we should give greater attention to the even more fundamental controversy regarding the democratic nature of the Bolshevik revolution. "The refusal to come to terms with the [non-Bolshevik] socialists and the dispersal of the Constituent Assembly," wrote Leonard Schapiro in one of the classic interpretations, "led to the logical result that revolutionary terror would now be directed not only against traditional enemies, such as the bourgeoisie and right-wing opponents, but against anyone, be he socialist, worker or peasant, who opposed Bolshevik rule." But this—according to Schapiro and others sharing his interpretation—was what Lenin had intended all along. As Bertram Wolfe put it: "Thus, what Lenin was aiming at in 1917 was a dictatorship, not only of his self-constituted and self-appointed 'vanguard of the proletariat' over the working class but a dictatorship over the entire population dictating

a positive program to every class of society." Following along the same interpretive pathway in a more recent and influential synopsis, Richard Pipes tells
us the Bolsheviks reached their predetermined goal of "a Bolshevik one-party dictatorship" because Lenin "cleverly camouflaged the seizure of power by
himself and his party as the transfer of 'all power to the soviets,' which slogan
promised grassroots democracy rather than dictatorship."[82]

There is far too much documentation to the contrary—much of it indicated in this study—for such an interpretation to remain credible. An influential work by a widely respected Cold War anti-Communist scholar,
Alfred G. Meyer, provides an account far more consistent with such documentation. In the wake of the overthrow is tsarism, and amid deepening
economic, social, and political crises, Lenin—Meyer notes—"argued that
the masses in Russia were impatient for a radical solution to their problems,
and that they should not be let down by the Bolsheviks as they had by the
bourgeois liberals and by their own petty-bourgeois leaders [Mensheviks
and Socialist Revolutionaries] in 1905 and 1917, respectively." He succeeded
in persuading his comrades that "the seizure of power by the Bolsheviks
would be supported by the vast masses of Russia's workers and peasants."
In fact, "Lenin correctly assessed the revolutionary mood of the common
man," and the Bolshevik-led seizure of power took place, "meeting only sporadic resistance. In a few hours, and with almost no bloodshed, Petrograd
turned Bolshevik and almost the whole country followed suit."[83]

Of particular interest is the vivid account of a prominent Left Socialist
Revolutionary, Sergei Mstislavskii, who comments that "the influence of the
Bolsheviks on the masses grew ever more swiftly and surely, for the Bolsheviks were the only revolutionary group which advocated from the start the
twin slogans of 'realistic peace' and 'expropriation from the expropriators'—
the logical aim of a Social Revolution carried to its conclusion." He adds that
"we, of the then Left wing of the Socialist Revolutionary Party, felt the quick-
ening of the revolutionary pulse of the land no less keenly than Lenin.... We
felt this pulse in our ever growing network of contacts with both the workers
and the peasantry."[84] On the eve of the revolution, he himself wrote in *The
Banner of Labor*, the central organ of the Left SRs, about the concern of many
Left SRs and others regarding what the Bolsheviks' slogans, all too easy yet
compelling, were promising:

> It is difficult for the masses, for the masses in their current state, utterly exhaust-
> ed by their consciousness of a "dead end," to stand firm against the temptations
> of a slogan which so simply, so radically offers to solve all our problems, all our

difficulties, all our vexed questions. You want peace?—Rise up! And tomorrow you'll have peace. You want a world revolution?—Rise up! And tomorrow the world revolution will flare up in an awesome firestorm. You want bread?—Rise up! And tomorrow you'll have bread. You want land?—Rise up! And tomorrow you'll be masters of the land. In brief—one short moment of decisiveness, of enthusiasm, one last tense moment of street fighting—and we shall cross, finally, that last fatal boundary, that boundary that we have been edging towards in indecision for the last eight months.

"We, the Left wing of the Socialist Revolutionary Party, had nothing with which to outbid these slogans," Mstislavskii concluded. "And so, the Bolsheviks became the undisputed masters of the situation."[85]

The fact that Bolshevik leadership was able to become so decisive is summed up by Alexander Rabinowitch:

It cannot be emphasized enough that, during the culminating stage of the struggle for power during the October 1917 revolution in Petrograd, the Bolsheviks drew great strength from their party's representative character, and its close ties and continuing interaction with factory workers, lower ranking military personnel, and a myriad of mass organizations. Another advantage was that party membership in the city totaled roughly fifty thousand, headed by the cream of veteran leaders at all levels of Bolshevik organization. Then, too, tens of thousands of additional workers, including significant numbers of factory women, soldiers of the Petrograd garrison, and Baltic Fleet sailors were enthusiastic supporters of the Bolshevik revolutionary platform.[86]

Alfred Meyer makes an important point that, although the Bolshevik seizure of power was followed by a brutalizing civil war during which severely authoritarian measures were adopted, there was an initial interlude, what he calls "a honeymoon period," that preceded "the years of life-and-death struggle." Another scholar, John L. H. Keep—despite his dominant narrative coinciding with the anti-Leninist spirit of Schapiro and the later Wolfe—provides information and insights consistent with the points we find Meyer making. Thus, in the revolutionary regime's initial functioning, with arbitrary and repressive acts in evidence, "few lives were actually lost as a result of this repression, which seems to have been designed to harass the opposition rather than to eliminate it *tout court.*" Neither was there an effort to make the new order "wholly bureaucratized, for the population was expected to participate actively in 'the construction of socialism,' and this allowed for an awareness of individual and group rights to survive." Keep suggests that "a more authentic soviet order might well have proved more stable, more resilient in times of crisis, more successful in harnessing popular energies for its purposes." The Central Executive Committee (Vee-Tsik) of the Soviets, made up of more than 300 people, functioned as "a revolutionary parliament of sorts," which "debated all the issues of the day that were of interest to the left," and "dissenters were often able to score telling points in debate. They spoke their minds with a forthrightness inconceivable in such a representative body during any later phase of Soviet history." Indeed, "Lenin had no objection to a coalition with non-Bolshevik socialist parties provided that (a) they were committed to the 'soviet' (i.e., Bolshevik) platform and (b) a majority of port-folios, including certain key posts, were reserved to Bolsheviks." Regarding these two provisos, (a) the alluded-to Bolshevik "platform" involved a commitment to *all power to the soviets,* to a worker-peasant alliance, revolutionary internationalism in opposition to imperialist war, and an active commitment to a transition from capitalism to socialism; and (b) the insistence on filling a majority of key positions in a governmental administration is consistent with the orientation of any dominant political party, not necessarily the mark of an authoritarian order.[87]

Indeed, British diplomat Bruce Lockhart—on the scene at the time—later reported that "the Bolsheviks had not yet succeeded in establishing the iron discipline which today [1933] characterizes their regime," adding: "They had, in fact, made little attempt to do so." Lockhart observed what other eye-witnesses reported: that "the only real danger to human life during these early days of the Bolshevik revolution" came from "bands of robbers, ex-army officers, and adventurers, who seized some of the finest houses in the city and who, armed with rifles, hand-grenades, and machine guns, exercised a gangsters' rule over the capital." Terming these "anarchist bands," Lockhart described (again as an eyewitness) how they were finally repressed in March and April 1918. He made a point of contrasting the "comparative tolerance of the Bolsheviks" in the early period "because the cruelties which followed later were the result of the intensification of the civil war," explaining: "For the intensification of that bloody struggle Allied intervention, with the false hopes it raised, was largely responsible."[88]

Meyer notes (in reference to the kind of interpretation represented by Schapiro, Wolfe, and Pipes) that "the distinction drawn here . . . is not general-ly recognized by historians of the Russian revolution," although he goes on to exonerate them: "The honeymoon, after all, was of so short a duration that it is easily forgotten or simply lumped together with the subsequent terror regime of War Communism."[89] Nonetheless, he considers this period important enough to devote more than ten pages to it, beginning with the following paragraph:

The October Revolution brought about the overthrow of all remnants of the old order. It radically destroyed the last shreds of tsarism and the old bureaucracy and relegated the landowner to the realm of dead institutions. The distribution of all gentry land among the peasants, which the Leninist seizure of power guaranteed, was as thorough as it could possibly have been. This was indeed the "bourgeois revolution" of which Lenin had spoken. It carried with it all those changes usually attributed to the complete abolition of the precapitalist order. National self-determination of Russia's many nationalities was, at least for the moment, carried to its logical conclusion. . . . Legal separation of church and state, removal of the old judiciary, reform of the calendar—all these measures were within the European liberal tradition, as part of the "bourgeois revolution." This revolution was also expressed in the social institutions, in science, art, and education—in virtually all functions of public and private life. Everywhere . . . the revolution carried with it maximum freedom of expression and experimentation. Even where political liberties were soon curtailed, a certain degree of personal freedom was not extinguished for several years.[90]

Note on Nationalities

Here we must insert a self-critical admission regarding a serious limitation of the present study. In its focus on Russia, it has given short shrift to the previously noted reality that Russia was, in fact, "a prison-house of nations." All of the dominated areas—Latvia, Estonia, Lithuania, the Ukraine, Georgia, Belarus, Finland, portions of Poland, etc.—constituted important aspects of the story not told here, as we have dealt sweepingly with what is tagged the *Russian* Revolution. Useful sources (hardly exhaustive) on the complexities indicated here are cited in the first chapter of this book.

In this note we can only indicate a few elements of the story. The lengthy quote above from Alfred Meyer fleetingly alludes to one of those elements, which Marc Ferro's social history of the Bolshevik revolution has outlined further. Ferro notes that the Bolsheviks' "nationality policy was . . . only part of a policy aimed at world revolution," with its earliest declarations emphasizing that the Soviet government's foreign policy goals "were meant to achieve, not only the self-determination of peoples that had just been declared valid in Russia, but also the right of the people, the 'proletarian' and individual everywhere to govern himself." In fact, within Russia itself the nationality question "required an immediate solution given that it affected the whole country." Indeed, the struggles of oppressed nationalities had been a significant factor in the fall of the tsarist order. Ferro observes, "The Bolsheviks, who had had to consider the nationality problem for twenty years and regarded it as a purely temporary phenomenon, were caught in an insoluble contradiction: they could recognize the right of self-determination, and the old state would disintegrate; or they cold subordinate this right to the accomplishment of the Revolution, and the revolutionary movement would be split, even in Russia . . ."[91] He summarizes the approach Lenin worked out, which tended to guide early Soviet policy:

> Lenin . . . was at bottom . . . close to Marxist orthodoxy, whether Kautskyist or Luxemburgist, in refusing to see the nation as a homogeneous entity; he analyzed constitution, formation and future in terms of class and culture. However, he had both to use the solvent of nationalism, and to safeguard the future of the great state, which he saw as alone able to solve modern problems of economic development; and he wholly reserved the tactics of his party by laying down the right of self-determination in his theses. The aim was to abolish constraint between nations—though right to divorce was not to mean necessity for divorce. Lenin thought that such an attitude alone would be able to stop the mistrust between Russians and non-Russians and to permit a later reunification under the aegis of the vanguard organizations of both sides.[92]

Avrahm Yarmolinsky summarizes a "Declaration of the Rights of the Peoples of Russia," which was proclaimed by the Soviet government seven days after it came into existence (the Council of People's Commissars, the executive body established by the Congress of Soviets):

> This document, conceived in the flamboyant, slovenly style of the early Soviet proclamations, condemns the Tsar's treatment of subject nationalities as a policy of pitting one people against another, and the attitude of the Provisional Government as one of distrust, hypocrisy and provocation. To effect a union among the workers and peasants belonging to the various peoples of the former empire, the Declaration runs, an open and honest course of action must be pursued. Therefore the Council of People's Commissars pledges itself to the following principles: (1) "The equality and sovereignty of the peoples of Russia. (2) The right of the peoples of Russia to free self-determination, even to the extent of separation and the formation of independent states. (3) The abolition of all national and national-religious privileges and restrictions. (4) The free development of national minorities and ethnic groups inhabiting Russia."[93]

As it turned out, those parts of the old tsarist empire in which "vanguard organizations" were unable to gain hegemony went their own way (Poland, Finland, Latvia, Estonia, Lithuania), while others (the Ukraine, Belarus, Georgia, etc.) formed independent Soviet Republics that quickly affiliated with that of Soviet Russia. E. H. Carr comments that "Soviet nationalities policy . . . was at the outset the crucial factor in Lenin's astonishing achievement of the reassembly of nearly all the former dominions of the Tsars after the disintegration and dispersal of war, revolution, and civil war." More than this, "the absolute rejection of any discrimination between individuals on ground of race or color remained a fixed and rigidly asserted principle in Bolshevik policy and practice, and became a powerful asset in all dealings with former subject peoples."[94]

The Russian Empire (most of which later became the Union of Soviet Socialist Republics) constituted a vast landmass spanning Europe and Asia, with a population in which there was incredible ethnic and linguistic diversity, with almost two hundred distinct peoples and languages. In fact, in 1897, Great Russians made up only 43 percent of the total population, although many of the subject peoples had become "Russified" (two famous examples being the Georgian Josef Djugashvili and the Ukrainian Jew Lev Bronstein—Stalin and Trotsky, respectively). More than this, after the exit of non-Russian Western provinces, Great Russians constituted a slim majority of 52 percent among those remaining 140 million. Of these, 110 million were Slavic; according to Carr, the other 30 million "lacked any kind of cohesion, racial, linguistic or political, among themselves," with as many as 10 million "still in the primitive tribal or nomadic stage."[95]

Despite Bolshevik-Communist support for the elimination of all forms of national, ethnic, and racial oppression, after the 1917 revolution tensions and conflicts were destined to flare up precisely around nationality questions. Lenin himself mused in 1919: "Scratch many a Communist and you will find a Great Russian Chauvinist." The growth of centralizing and bureaucratic tendencies in the government that accelerated during the years of civil war and afterward also had an impact. "Centralization meant standardization," Carr notes, "and the standards adopted were naturally Great Russian standards." More than this, "the bureaucratic mentality against which Lenin inveighed tended almost automatically to become a Great Russian mentality." In fact, such biases could "all too easily disguise itself in Marxist trappings." For example, Commissar of Nationalities Joseph Stalin—while himself intoning against the influence of "Great Russian Chauvinism"—was also inclined to emphasize that "the political foundation of the dictatorship of the proletariat is constituted first and chiefly by the central regions which are industrial and not by the borderlands which represent peasant countries." Of course, differences flared up among Bolsheviks around such matters—one of Lenin's last struggles was, in fact, with Stalin in regard to the nationalities question (and the latter's high-handed attitude and actions) in relation to Soviet Georgia.[96]

"While ... Bolshevik nationalities' policy was not free from those empirical impurities which normally distinguish the application of theory from the theory itself," Carr asserts, "it was still possible to point to substantial advances on bourgeois practice, as well as on bourgeois theory." There is certainly something to be said for this when we recall that the theory and practice on the "national question" of the capitalist powers at this time were manifesting themselves in what has justly been termed "the age of imperialism."[97]

Soviet Democracy

Both of the Russian Revolution's phases—February/March 1917 and October/November 1917—were profoundly democratic developments. The argument that the second was a betrayal of the first is based to a very large extent on the contention that the fruit of the Bolshevik revolution was not a democracy but a one-party dictatorship. In fact, it can be shown that the first fruits of October 1917 involved a soviet democracy accompanied by political pluralism and freedom of expression. A one-party dictatorship certainly did quickly crystallize in the course of events, but we will see that quite different causes explain this development, which was far from Bolshevik intentions.

There are significant counterarguments, based on two undeniable realities: (1) the decision by Lenin and Trotsky and other Bolsheviks (over the protests of yet other Bolsheviks) to reject the formation of an all-socialist coalition government; and (2) the decision, which we have already noted, to dissolve the Constituent Assembly that came into being through nationwide democratic elections in December 1917. These two realities are seen by some analysts as proving the authoritarian intentions of Lenin and his closest comrades. Here we will reaffirm—through an examination of these questions—the initial Bolshevik intention to establish a democratic political order, marked by freedom of expression and political pluralism.

Pluralist Promise

In January 1918, the third All-Russian Congress of Workers' and Soldiers' Deputies opened, merging with the All-Russian Congress of Peasants' Deputies, and proceeded to adopt an initial constitution for the new Soviet Republic as well as a number of other important resolutions. Slightly more than half of the delegates were Bolsheviks, the second-largest group being composed of their Left SR allies. At the conclusion, they elected a new All-Russian Central Executive Committee, the legislative body operating between congresses, with 306 members: 160 Bolsheviks, 125 Left SRs, 2 Menshevik-Internationalists, 3 Anarcho-Communists, 7 SR-Maximalists, 7 Right SRs, and 2 Menshevik-Defensists. As Roy Medvedev comments: "The Bolsheviks obviously recognized the rights of many political minorities at that time and proceeded on a pluralist basis in the representative Soviet bodies."[98]

We have already noted the view of John Keep (a partisan neither of the Bolsheviks nor of the "all power to the soviets" position), namely that the Central Executive Committee (CEC), the Vee-Tsik, of the nationwide federation of soviets might conceivably have lasted as a durable revolutionary parliament—although he comments critically on the fact that the powerful executive body known as the Council of People's Commissars, or the Sovnarkom, was not based on or answerable to this revolutionary parliament. Rather, it had been formed independently under Bolshevik initiative and received independent recognition (as did the Vee-Tsik) from the 1917 Second All-Russian Congress of Soviets. The two bodies coexisted, relatively independent of each other. Although the Sovnarkom initially consulted with and sought approval from the Vee-Tsik, the Central Executive Committee soon began to wither, partly due to overwhelming pressures that we will examine shortly, and partly due to the absence of formal structures governing its relationship with the Soviet government's executive authority. "In theory sovereignty lay with the CEC when the congress of soviets was not in session," Keep notes, "but in practice this sovereignty was nullified by the rights which the people's commissars abrogated to themselves."[99] It may be that this contributed to the erosion of soviet democracy.

There was, in the initial period after the 1917 revolution, no proposal by Lenin and Trotsky to outlaw left-wing oppositional parties or to throw them out of the soviets. (Indeed, there was an appeal for those who had walked out—protesting the insurrection—to return.) In September 1917, after the Bolsheviks had won control of the Petrograd Soviet and as momentum was beginning to build for the seizure of power, Trotsky—as the Soviet's new president—said to his opponents: "We are all party people [i.e., belonging to rival parties], and we shall have to cross swords more than once. But we shall guide the work of the Petersburg Soviet in a spirit of justice and complete independence for all fractions; the hand of the presidium will never oppress the minority." In the same month, Lenin was describing what Soviet democracy would look like, with special reference to freedom of the press: "State power in the shape of the Soviets takes *all* the printing presses and *all* the newsprint and distributes them *equitably*: the state should come first—in the interests of the majority of the people, the majority of the poor, particularly the majority of the peasants, who for centuries have been tormented, crushed and stultified by the landowners and capitalists." His next point makes it clear that, as Bertram Wolfe once acknowledged, "Lenin had no idea of outlawing all other parties and creating a one-party system." For the Bolshevik leader argued: "The big parties should come second—say, those that have polled one or two hundred thousand votes in both capitals [i.e., Petrograd and Moscow]. The smaller parties should come third, and then any group of citizens which has a certain number of members or has collected a certain number of signatures."[100]

Four weeks after the insurrection, Lenin demonstrated his continued commitment to soviet democracy in drafting for the Council of People's Commissars (established by the All-Russian Congress of Soviets) a resolution that stated that "no elective institution or representative assembly can be regarded as being truly democratic and really representative of the people's will unless the electors' right to recall those elected is accepted and exercised. This fundamental principle of true democracy applies to all representative assemblies without exception." Explaining this in the All-Russian Central Executive Committee of Soviets, he provided a significant line of reasoning: "Various parties have played a dominant role among us. The last time, the passage of influence from one party to another was accompanied by an overturn, whereas a simple vote would have sufficed had we the right to recall. . . . The right of recall must be granted the Soviets, which are the most perfect carrier of the state idea, of coercion." (That is, for Lenin, the state idea was inherently coercive; the best form of the state, and the most democratic, was the soviet.) He continued: "Then the passage of power from one party to another will proceed without bloodshed, by means of simple new elections." Early in the following year he was still emphasizing the role of political pluralism in soviet democracy: "If the working people are dissatisfied with their party they can elect other delegates, hand power to another party and change the government without any revolution at all."[101]

Victor Serge has described how in the first months of 1918 the All-Russian Soviet Congress reflected "a whole system of inner democracy. The dictatorship of the proletariat is not the dictatorship of a party, or of a Central Committee, or of certain individuals." He noted that "strict rules" and internal diversity characterized the functioning of the Bolshevik Party as well as of the Vee-Tsik, where Lenin himself was compelled to "brave the fire of the Left SRs, anarchists and International Social Democrats, all doubtful allies, and of the Right SRs and Mensheviks, irreducible enemies." All proposals were subject to vigorous debate, and "here the enemies of the regime enjoy free speech with a more than parliamentary latitude."[102]

Later, the Bolshevik leader Lev Kamenev took issue with those who contended that the Bolsheviks had always sought a one-party dictatorship. He scoffed at the notion that "the Russian Communists came into power with a prepared plan for a standing army, Extraordinary Commissions [the Cheka, secret police], and limitations of political liberty, to which the Russian proletariat was obliged to recur for self-defense after bitter experience." Immediately after power was transferred to the soviets, the opponents of working-class rule were unable to maintain an effective resistance. The revolution had "its period of 'rosy illusions,'" he noted. "All the political parties—up to Miliukov's [Kadet] party—continued to exist openly. All the bourgeois newspapers continued to circulate. Capital punishment was abolished. The army was demobilized." Even fierce opponents of the revolution arrested during the insurrection were generously set free (including pro-tsarist generals and reactionary officers who would soon put their expertise to use in the violent service of their own beliefs). Kamenev described the increasingly severe civil war conditions that finally changed this situation, remarking that "over six months (November 1917 to April–May 1918) passed from the moment of the formation of the Soviet power to the practical application by the proletariat of any harsh dictatorial measures."[103]

Immediately following the October/November seizure of power, the Bolshevik Central Committee had issued a public statement, drafted by Lenin, clarifying how the Bolsheviks viewed what they were doing. Asserting "the basic principle of the new revolution . . . is: *all power to the Soviets*," and that "there must be no other government in Russia but a *Soviet government*," the statement emphasized that "the government can be transferred out of the hands of one Soviet party into the hands of another party . . . simply by a decision of the Soviet, simply by new elections of deputies to the Soviets." Since "the Bolshevik Party was in the majority of the Second All-Russian Congress of Soviets . . . we declare that . . . we have the right and *the obligation* to the people to form a government," but it was also the fact that the Bolsheviks submitted a list of People's Commissars (for the Sovnarkom) and "that the Congress approved this list." The statement emphasized: "*We offered* to share power with the Left SRs and the offer is still open. It is not our fault that *they refused*." The statement also made the point that the Bolshevik Party, in standing "firm on the principle of Soviet power, that is, the rule of the *majority* at the last Congress of the Soviets . . . agreed and *we still agree* to share power with the Soviet minority, on the condition that that minority loyally and honestly undertakes to submit to the majority and carry out the program *approved by the whole* All-Russian Second Congress of Soviets, consisting of gradual but firm and undeviating steps towards socialism."[104]

The Left SRs had won a mass following since the split with their party's right wing. The Left SR leadership was bold, idealistic, full of youthful ardor, yet also "on the whole, ideologically unstable and politically inexperienced" (as the seasoned Menshevik Abramovitch recalled); they "could not match the clear line and full-throated slogans of Bolshevism with their wavering course and their 'yes—but' admonitions," according to the sympathetic historian Oliver Radkey. Still, on December 19, 1917, they finally agreed to the Bolshevik invitation (made from the beginning) to "settle their differences with them inside the Government," as Left SR Isaac Steinberg later put it, adding: "The entry of the L.S.R. into the Government signified a coalition of the two leading parties and the two types of mentality contained within Russian radical Socialism." Seven Left SRs were added to the eleven Bolsheviks in the Sovnarkom. The coalition government held together until March 18, 1918, when the Left SRs decided to walk out, in a disagreement over the Treaty of Brest-Litovsk (to be examined later in this study).

Another element of the revolutionary coalition that had helped make the October 1917 revolution were the anarchists, who were fiercely critical of all government, thus seeking the abolition of, not inclusion in, the Council of People's Commissars; nonetheless, they had also played an important role in the insurrection. Despite their own characteristic disorganization and diversity, they were active in the factory committees, trade unions, soviets, workers' militias, etc., and at first were generally seen as boisterous mavericks who could serve as critical allies (not opponents) of the Bolsheviks.[105]

All-Socialist Government?

Such a coalition had been advocated at the time by what was at first a majority of the central committee of the Bolshevik Party. Everyone was in favor of a coalition with the Left SRs, who had supported the insurrection and soviet power (but who initially refused to join in coalition with the Bolsheviks alone). The disagreement was over whether or not to seek a coalition with the Mensheviks and Right SRs. Lenin was convinced that a coalition would not be viable. After all, the parties which were supposed to join the Bolsheviks in such a coalition had walked out of the second All-Russian Congress of Soviets. They had been and remained hostile to the Bolshevik revolution, with its demand for all power to the soviets.

"Is it permissible to share power with those elements who have hitherto sabotaged the Soviets and who are today fighting from outside against the proletarian state?" asked Trotsky, who added that a so-called socialist coalition government with the Mensheviks and Right SRs was not "capable of carrying out our program.... Nothing whatever can come of merely leaving a few Bolsheviks in a coalition government." This is essentially what the Mensheviks and Right SRs demanded as a condition for their participation in a "socialist coalition" government—adding that Lenin and Trotsky specifically must be excluded from such a government. Lenin held that "to concede to ultimatums and threats from the minority in the Soviets amounts to a complete renunciation not only of Soviet power but of democracy."[106]

Lenin and Trotsky finally won a majority of the Bolshevik leadership to the policy of moving forward without the Mensheviks and Right SRs. In the minds of many, logic and good sense were clearly on their side. Since neither the Mensheviks nor the Right SRs were in agreement with the program approved by the majority delegates in the soviets, they had obviously excluded themselves from the government. One could add that to have a government of elements going in opposite directions would be neither coherent nor viable.

Defending the Bolsheviks' actions, left-wing British suffragist Sylvia Pankhurst advanced an obvious rationale. She commented in 1920 that "bourgeois democrats of capitalist countries" protesting against the Bolsheviks' "dictatorial" decision to form an exclusively Bolshevik government see nothing "unfair in the dictatorship of the Liberal, Conservative, or Coalition Party, whichever happens to form the Government in power in the British Parliament. They do not object to the dictatorship of Republicans or Democrats in America." She added: "When the Party which is successful in the election appoints the Ministers at the head of the great Departments of State, and fills all the seats of Government with its Party friends, no outcry is raised by the partisans of bourgeois democracy."[107]

In the first phase of Bolshevik power, given the democratic elections and political pluralism that were part of the soviet system, Pankhurst's point was well taken.

Dissolving the Constituent Assembly

The decision to dissolve the Constituent Assembly has often been cited as an obvious manifestation of Lenin's authoritarian temper and intentions, giving the lie to all Bolshevik pretense about "workers' democracy." We have already given substantial attention to this matter, but—especially given its importance both in what happened in history and in the polemics and analyses of so many critics of the Bolsheviks—it is certainly worth reflecting on the matter further in arguing that the first fruit of the October Revolution was, in fact, soviet democracy.

Bessie Beatty, in her 1918 eyewitness account *The Red Heart of Russia*, provides a vivid portrait of Lenin speaking at a contentious session of the Central Executive Committee of the All-Russian Soviet. It was composed of delegates from a number of working-class parties, among which Lenin's party had become the dominant force only three months earlier—at which point it had set up a military committee (under Trotsky's leadership) that had quickly moved forward to overthrow Kerensky's Provisional Government under the slogan of "all power to the soviets." At this meeting Lenin had come to defend the decision to dissolve the recently elected Constituent Assembly, which had proved to be a more conservative body than the soviets. One of the members of the body, upon Lenin's arrival, angrily jeered: "Long live the dictator!" This set off a commotion of insults and counter-insults among the delegates. Beatty offers a vibrant description of this historic moment that is worth quoting at length:

> When the chairman had calmed them, Lenin took his place. He stood quietly for a moment, surveying his audience, with his hands in his pockets and an appraising expression in his brown eyes. He knew what was expected of him. He must win the wavering members of his own flock. He must reach out to the larger audience spread over the vast areas of Russia. He must speak so that he would be heard beyond the confines of his country, in that world whose attention was focused for the time on this group of strange new actors in the international drama. Lenin began quietly tracing the historical developments of the Soviet as an institution. He made a critical analysis of the workings of various parliaments, declaring that they had become merely a sparring-place for the verbal contests of socialists.
>
> "In Russia," he said, "the workers have developed organizations, which give them power to execute their aspirations. You are told that we ask you to jump a hundred years. We do not ask you to do anything. We did not organize the Soviets. They were not organized in 1917: they were created in the revolution of 1905. The people organized the Soviets. When I tell you that the government of the Soviets is superior to the Constituent Assembly, that it is more fundamentally representative of the will of the mass, I do not tell you anything new. As long ago as April 4, I told you that the Soviets were more representative of the people than this Constituent Assembly which you wanted to organize."
>
> He explained in detail the political break in the Social Revolutionary Party, and said:

"When the people voted for delegates of the Constituent Assembly, they did not know the difference between the Right S.R.'s and the Left. They did not know that when they voted for the Right Social Revolutionists they voted for the bourgeoisie, and when they voted for the Left they voted for Socialism."

At first he spoke quietly, but before long his hands had come out of his pockets. These, and his brown eyes alternately snapping and smiling, and his eyebrows humorously expressive, all vigorously emphasized his phrases.

It was evident from the faces of the men before him that he was justifying himself and them to their satisfaction.

"The February Revolution was a political bourgeois revolution overthrowing Tsarism. In November a social revolution occurred, and the working masses became the sovereign authority. The Workmen's and Soldiers' delegates are not bound by any rules or traditions to the old bourgeois society. Their government has taken all the power and rights into its own hands. The Constituent Assembly is the highest expression of the political ideals of bourgeois society, which are no longer necessary in a Socialist state. The Constituent Assembly will be dissolved.

"If the Constituent Assembly represented the will of the people, we would shout: 'Long live the Constituent Assembly!' Instead we shout: 'Down with the Constituent Assembly!'" he finished.

In the seat next to me was a little soldier with black beady eyes and a short, bristling mustache. He had a merry face that crinkled when he smiled. Every now and then he gave his head a queer little shake of amazed admiration and whispered: "He's a wise man. He's a wise man."[108]

Not everyone present agreed with the comrade sitting next to Beatty, and there were angry counterarguments—which didn't prevent Lenin from receiving a majority of the votes. Nonetheless, it is worth considering some of the vibrant back-and-forth on this issue.

Actually, the question had been raised in the month preceding the Constituent Assembly's dissolution. "In the duel between the Constituent Assembly and the soviets we see a historical struggle between two revolutions, one bourgeois and the other socialist," insisted Gregory Zinoviev in remarks to the Vee-Tsik on December 22, 1917. The results of the elections "are a reflection of the first, February revolution," while the October revolution was embedded in the living reality of the soviets. "Are there any bourgeois representatives here who would dare to claim, hand over heart, that the overwhelming majority of peasants back the right-wing elements rather than the Bolsheviks and Left SRs? The victory of the left is readily apparent." He added: "Chernov holds it against the soviets that only the most active elements [of the population] take part in elections to them, whereas in the Constituent Assembly elections [everyone down to] the least old woman is involved." But this, Zinoviev insisted, "is a splendid compliment to the soviets," because "the soviets do consist of those who want to fight, who are ready to smash the old [society] and construct a new life. In a transitional revolutionary period it is precisely such organizations that should have the last word."[109]

By this time, the Left SRs were in agreement with the Bolsheviks, as indicated by Prosh Proshyan, one of their outstanding and most respected leaders, who asserted: "If the Constituent Assembly . . . does not recognize soviet power . . . , conflict is inevitable." He added that the Right-SR majority and its allies had "suffered defeat over the war," that its "land policy has proved a fiasco," and that its representatives "have shown themselves bankrupt as statesmen." Proshyan concluded with a militant flourish that if "in their intransigence and stubbornness, they force us to fight them, we are not afraid. The soviets, victorious in every clash with counter-revolution, will pass this test too and will successfully finish off the struggle for fraternity among peoples and for socialism." Representing the left-Mensheviks, N. N. Sukhanov offered the viewpoint of a small minority. "We are now confronting the greatest dangers from without and from within," with "a risk that the country will be carved up between the enemy powers [i.e., Germany] and the Allies," he warned. "In such a situation our only salvation is in a united democratic front such as we had in the days of the Kornilov affair, when the danger dissolved like a puff of smoke." This meant "we need a government which would unite all the forces of democracy," and "such a genuine government can only be the Constituent Assembly . . . capable of rescuing the country from the perils it faces." In response to Lenin's January 1918 defense of the Constituent Assembly's dissolution, left-Menshevik delegate Vasiliy Stroyev repeated Sukhanov's argument, insisting "on the basis of the Constituent Assembly it would have been possible to unite the whole of revolutionary democracy," a position that won almost no support. On the other hand, dissident-Bolshevik David Riazanov argued that the dissolution of the Constituent Assembly had been premature, that it should have been given time to expose itself in the court of popular opinion. "In a single day the people could not assess its [value] or compare their own opinions with its performance. Before dissolving the assembly we should have shown that it had to be dissolved by confronting it with the Third Congress of Soviets and letting the people decide between them."[110]

One of the leading social historians dealing with the Russian Revolution, Rex Wade, has offered a clear criticism of the dissolution of the Constituent Assembly that is accepted by many others. "The dispersal of the Constituent Assembly effectively marked the end of the revolution," he writes. Given Lenin's decision (opposed by more moderate and thoughtful Bolsheviks), "civil war was inevitable and would now determine the future of Russia and its peoples."[111] And as we will see later in this study, the Civil War *did* unleash horrific dynamics of violence and authoritarianism that engulfed and overwhelmed all of the profoundly democratic aspirations and qualities of 1917.

This critique of the Constituent Assembly's dissolution misses three key points: One, it was not simply a Bolshevik decision to disperse the Constituent Assembly—the Left Socialist Revolutionaries and anarchists concurred, because to do otherwise would mean replacing tsarism only with a new capitalist order. Two, the revolutionary process, regardless of complexities and distortions, certainly continued through 1918 and beyond—into the 1920s. Three, more grimly decisive than the dispersal of the Constituent Assembly for the future of Russia and its peoples were international factors—foreign military intervention and funding of antirevolutionary counterinsurgencies, combined with economic blockade, plus the failure of socialist revolution elsewhere, leaving Russia isolated in its backwardness.[112]

For the Socialist Revolutionaries, as W. Bruce Lincoln puts it, the Constituent Assembly had been "a hallowed dream, the culmination of many decades' quest, and the perfect embodiment of popular sovereignty in Russia," and it is quite true that for the Right SRs this would become the central rallying cry in attempting to foment armed struggle against the new Soviet regime. Yet in his careful analysis of the actual Constituent Assembly—or as he puts it "the caricature assembly that convened on January 5, 1918, and died the next day"—the pioneering historian of the SRs, Oliver Radkey, concludes that "it is hard to see how the All-Russian Constituent Assembly could have been a success even if the Bolsheviks had not ended its life after a single session," made up as it was of diverse and divergent forces, a majority of which had questionable authority and no clearly defined program capable of leading the country forward. This dovetails with E. H. Carr's judgment on how the Constituent Assembly's proceedings "served mainly to illustrate the unreality of the assembly and the fundamental differences of doctrine between those who composed it," concluding that by this time it lacked "any solid basis, or any popular support." Hardly a partisan of Bolshevism, Alfred G. Meyer comments that "the unceremonious dissolution of the Constituent Assembly" hardly constituted the inauguration of Bolshevik dictatorship: "For some months afterwards there was no violent terror. The nonsocialist press was not closed until the summer of the same year. The Cheka began its reign of terror only after the beginning of the Civil War and the attempted assassination of Lenin, and this terror is in marked contrast with the lenient treatment that White generals received immediately after the revolution."[113]

4

PROLETARIAN RULE
AND MIXED ECONOMY

Classical Marxism does not define *dictatorship of the proletariat* in the narrow modern-day sense—authoritarian rule by a small minority claiming to represent the interests of working people. Rather, it means political rule by the working class itself. It doesn't imply a one-party state or a generally repressive political culture, but rather the working class winning the battle of democracy. This means establishing a *workers'* democracy facilitated by political pluralism and freedom of expression, and in a form that is more directly available and immediately relevant to the proletarian majority than is the case under capitalist democracy.

Marxism also understands political realities to be grounded in economic realities, historical development as being inseparable from underlying economic development. When we speak of an *economy* we are referring—most elementally—to the activities and relationships people enter into, and the resources they use, to get the things that they need (such as food, clothing, shelter) and the things that they want (such as rings and necklaces and other forms of personal adornment, toys and other playthings, entertaining activities and experiences, forms or sources of music, sources of knowledge—whether from storytellers, books, lecturers, or works of art). Without the essentials—such as food—there will be no life at all, and without at least some of the nonessentials there will be no joy in life.

131

Regarding the activities and resources to create these things, we can see that human labor is primary—making use of tools and technologies to fashion what is needed and wanted from various raw materials and natural resources. In terms of relationships, an economy can involve a small tribal cluster or kin group working cooperatively in hunting and gathering, perhaps ultimately through early agriculture (gardens and flocks, crops and herds), in which all share in the labor and the fruits of their collective labor. It can also involve powerful minorities demanding that laboring majorities provide them with the agricultural surplus, supplemented with surplus labor. It can also involve powerful minorities directly exploiting—one way or another—the labor of diverse majorities. It can involve, over time and with the development of nation-states, the development of increasingly complex relationships and growing interdependence within national economic systems. This growing complexity and interdependence has been deepened and pushed forward, and made increasingly global, by the naturally voracious expansionism inherent in the core dynamics of the capitalist form of economy.

The underlying forces at work in the global economy—captured in the conceptualization of *uneven and combined development*—involve the interplay and coming together of different forms of economy, such as what came into existence in the massive and unstable entity known as tsarist Russia. We have seen that the complexity and instability have resulted in undulating currents, whirlpools, and successive waves of crisis and discontent. This, in turn, contributed mightily to the class conflicts, social struggles, political turmoil, and revolutionary upheaval that have been the focus of this study.

In October/November 1917 this culminated in the triumph of workers' power, supported by the peasantry, led by the Bolsheviks and their allies. The question then became, how would the transition to socialism be accomplished? As Marxists, the Bolshevik leaders knew that it could not be accomplished "just as they pleased"—but only within the context of the actual, material, economic, social, cultural realities within which they had been living their lives and making their revolution. As the saying goes, "it's complicated"—particularly given the complexities, the interdependencies, and the multiple crises, as well as the underlying, overarching, all-encompassing trajectories of historical development previously alluded to. What the Bolshevik leaders did or failed to do would be decisive—but also decisive would be immense realities within Russia and globally, which they might influence but over which they had no control. This must be comprehended as we try to make sense of how the newly dominant institutions of workers' power sought to move in the direction of socialism.

In the present chapter we will examine the earliest economic orientations developed by the Bolshevik regime. It will be argued that what it hoped for was not the direct passage into socialism but instead the creation of a transitional "mixed economy." Such an interpretation is not commonly stressed in regard to the early Soviet Republic. Many analysts view such relative moderation as inconsistent with the extreme radicalism of Bolshevism under Lenin and Trotsky. Everything they did is interpreted as either a heroic or horrific effort to implement "socialism" in economically backward Russia (whose economic backwardness and impoverishment would preclude—as we saw Marx himself insisting in Chapter 1—a genuinely socialist society, since if "want is generalized, and with want the struggle for necessities begins again," then "all the old crap will revive"). In fact, Lenin and Trotsky did not believe socialism was possible in the Russia of 1917–23. They believed that socialism would need to be based on a highly integrated and technologically advanced economy, providing a level of economic abundance that would not be achieved in Russia for many years and could not—given the realities and interdependence of the global economy—be achieved in a single country. Lenin, Trotsky, and their comrades believed that it would be possible and necessary for revolutionary Russia to move in the direction of socialism, but that this could not be completed until working-class revolutions in other countries—especially more advanced capitalist countries—swept more of the planet into a socialist trajectory. The best that revolutionary Russia could do in the period immediately following 1917 would be establishing a state-regulated capitalism, combined with social policies beneficial to the laboring masses, and with the development of some economic sectors operating according to socialist principles— or, what is commonly known as a "mixed economy."

Over the years there has been—from left, right, and center—skepticism over the viability of such a project. It is not possible here to provide a general review of the matter, but aspects of the question were highlighted admirably in a discussion of a different revolution later in the twentieth century. "An economy which is half capitalist and half socialist, which would mean functioning half according to the logic of profit and half according to the logic opposing profit, doesn't exist and cannot exist in any country in the world," wrote the perceptive analyst Adolfo Gilly in 1980, in an article dealing with the Sandinista revolution in Nicaragua. "In all countries adopting the 'mixed economy' label, this only means capitalism with a more or less extensive state sector subordinated to the logic of accumulation for a strong private sector." Gilly pointed out that a strong nationalized sector of the economy in no way "guarantees" a transition to socialism. "It is well known that private enterprise, particularly in industry, in many countries favors and advocates the existence of such a sector as a guarantee to lower costs, to develop the infrastructure and economic resources, freeing them from what would be severe financial commitments."[1] Gilly argued, however, that Nicaragua's "mixed economy" was unlike any in the world, because the mass insurrection led by a consciously revolutionary force had smashed the existing capitalist state and replaced it with new institutions of popular power.

The same can be said of what initially happened in Russia. In each case a special framework was established by the fact that a more or less proletarian government had been brought to power by a working people's revolution. It is that first manifestation of proletarian dictatorship and mixed economy that will be the focus of this chapter.

We will see proliferating contradictions both between each of these two elements (workers' democracy and mixed economy) and within them—contradictions that become increasingly glaring and which, in some cases, would seem to have been predictable. This, in turn, raises obvious questions regarding the clarity of thought on the part of the Bolshevik leadership. If they were as brilliant as some of them seemed to have been, why didn't they understand the profound lack of viability in what they were advocating? Why didn't they perceive the disasters that would obviously result from the revolutionary trajectory they were charting? Such questions take on a sharper edge when we realize that they were being raised at the time by left-wing critics, among the Mensheviks and Right-Socialist Revolutionaries and within the ranks of the Second International (for example, Karl Kautsky). The Bolsheviks denounced such critics for their excessive moderation, but some later historians have been inclined to commend them for their sanity.

Simplistic condemnation of the Bolsheviks and their revolution is easily and commonly employed by those dealing with such questions—but perhaps it is better to take the matter more seriously. It is not necessary to agree with what Lenin, Trotsky, and their comrades chose to do in order to reach for an understanding of why they chose the revolutionary path, and how they proposed to overcome the contradictions that they themselves certainly saw in advance. In the remainder of this study we will give attention to the seemingly shrewd assumptions that were key factors in their revolutionary perspectives, potentialities whose realization they anticipated as providing solutions to the inevitable problems. In doing this, we will also be dealing with miscalculations that would end up deepening the contradictions when the solutions were not forthcoming. We will give attention as well to achievements and positive legacies as we consider, nonetheless, tragic developments that would subvert and overwhelm what was profoundly good in the dreams and efforts of these heroic Communists.

Workers' Democracy and Mixed Economy

The Bolshevik seizure of power was far less violent than many other revolutions. On the other hand, immense devastation had taken place *before* the Bolshevik revolution, largely due to the First World War. In the first three years of the war, 18 million Russians were engaged in the conflict—including many of the most skilled elements from the labor force—and about 2.5 million were killed at the front. We have seen that Russia was not a highly industrialized country, but practically the whole of industry was devoted to war production. Much of the produce of agriculture was also diverted to military needs. The need of tsarist Russia to "keep up" militarily with far more highly industrialized nations put an immense strain on the Russian economy. The country was unable to invest its capital into meeting consumers' needs, into meeting social needs, or even into meeting the needs of the economy (such as repair of infrastructure and machinery). Rather, it was compelled to meet the war crisis by "living on its capital," with disastrous results. Equipment and manpower began to wear out, as debts (including a billowing foreign debt) accumulated and shortages spread throughout the economy. Looking back from 1922, Trotsky commented: "All these circumstances . . . directly predetermined the October Revolution, the triumph of the proletariat and its subsequent difficulties." Indeed, the Bolsheviks faced a bleak situation upon taking power. By October 1917, the number of locomotives needing repair was 5,500, 30 percent of the whole, and this was only "the beginning of the complete breakdown of the railway system," one contemporary scholar noted, "which the Bolsheviks, in spite of extreme efforts, could not check or even retard." It has been estimated that average industrial production in 1916–17 was only 71 percent of prewar levels, and that by the autumn of 1917 it had plummeted further. Given the worsening rate of exchange between town and countryside, peasants found that it made little economic sense to put their grain on the market.[2]

Shortly after the Bolsheviks stormed the Winter Palace, four left-wing journalists from the United States—John Reed, Louise Bryant, Albert Rhys Williams, and Bessie Beatty—gathered together to evaluate the swirl of events. Beatty had been advised by a US official to stock up on sardines and retire to the home of a woman friend for a few weeks, since "the people will be dying of starvation on the streets within a week, and there won't be any *iz-vostchiks* [cab drivers] to carry you around, because the horses will all starve to death." Beatty confided to her friends her concern over the high expectations of the Russian masses supporting the revolution: "I'd hate to be in Lenin's shoes. They expect so much. I just saw [Raymond] Robins [of the American Red Cross]. He says there was only three days' supply of bread when the Winter Palace fell—whenever that was. Yesterday? Anyway . . . Lenin has promised them so much—" Interrupting, Williams snapped: "He has promised them nothing except the chance to run this poor, bankrupt, bewildered, bruised and suffering Russia themselves." As Beatty later recounted, in the early months of Soviet power the Bolsheviks succeeded in their energetic efforts to hold off "the great grey wolf" of famine. "It was not until he [i.e., the wolf] made an alliance with the human enemy of Russia that he finally broke through and brought death to the hungry people." She was referring to the economic embargo, and military invasion and foreign support for the counterrevolutionary Civil War. Even before this catastrophe, however, the economy was clearly in trouble. "It was impossible at any time during the year [from 1917 to 1918] to buy any of the necessities of life without standing in a queue," Beatty reported, and many working women forced to stand in the long lines would grumble to each other: "It is no good for the government to be Socialist if the queue grows longer every day."[3] Indeed, the Bolshevik leaders themselves recognized that this was not the material base on which socialism could come into being.

Before the Bolsheviks took power, Lenin himself stressed this point time and again. In his *April Theses*, he stressed that "it is not our *immediate* task to 'introduce' socialism, but only to bring social production and the distribution of products at once under the control of the Soviets of Workers' Deputies." After the Bolshevik insurrection, such *control* (as opposed to sweeping economic collectivization) defined Bolshevik policy. Nonetheless, "the spontaneous inclination of the workers to organize factory committees and to intervene in the management of the factories was inevitably encouraged by a revolution," notes historian E. H. Carr, "which led the workers to assume that the productive machinery of the country now belonged to them and could be operated by them at their own discretion and to their own advantage." And yet, he insists, "extensive nationalization of industry was . . . no part of the initial Bolshevik program" in the wake of the October/November revolution. In December

1917, prominent University of Wisconsin sociologist E. A. Ross, who was conducting fieldwork in the new Soviet Republic, asked Trotsky if the Bolsheviks intended to nationalize industry. Trotsky replied: "No. We are not ready yet to take over all industry. That will come in time, but no one can say how soon. For the present we expect out of the earnings of a factory to pay the owner five or six percent yearly on his investment. What we aim at now is *control*, rather than *ownership*." Ross asked how new industries would develop. "We can impose on the capitalist to whom we allow a dividend of five or six percent," Trotsky answered, "the obligation to reinvest in some industry a part—say, twenty-five percent—of what he receives." Ross suggested that capitalists would prefer to invest their capital abroad, where they could expect two or three times the return on investments. "They won't be allowed to remove their capital from Russia at will," Trotsky replied. He explained: "We will see to it that the factory is run not from the point of view of private profit, but from the point of view of the social welfare democratically conceived."[4]

Soviet historian Roy Medvedev notes that upon taking power the Soviet government immediately carried out a "list of long overdue and very timely revolutionary reforms," but that "there was nothing socialist *per se* in any of these reforms," although the introduction of workers' control "had a plainly socialist tinge." Medvedev adds that "we can see from Lenin's notes that after the October revolution it was not the intention of the Bolsheviks to nationalize a substantial number of businesses." E. H. Carr explains: "Left to themselves the workers could, in the nature of things, rarely provide the technical skill or industrial discipline or knowledge of accountancy necessary for the running of a factory." The banks were nationalized, and from November 1917 to March 1918 about 850 legislative acts were issued by central authorities, resulting in the nationalization of individual companies, various monopoly groups, and certain mining districts and economic sectors, resulting in an important state sector of the economy. But, as Maurice Dobb pointed out a few years later, there were no moves toward nationalization "in the sudden and sweeping manner the day after the revolution that the popular imagination in Western Europe seems to picture.... The interference of the State in economic affairs was mainly confined to finance, to certain branches of trade and to general regulation and control, such as happened in most belligerent countries during the [first world] war, and as had already under the Tsar acquired the name of 'war socialism.'" Of course, in the context of proletarian revolution and under a workers' state, such measures took on a more "socialist tinge," as Medvedev has put it, and Dobb observed that matters sometimes went further than just described: "When prior to June 28th [1918] specific enterprises were nationalized, this was usually due to some special circumstances applying to that particular business, or to the unauthorized action of local bodies, which tended in the early days to do most things on their own initiative and frequently to be somewhat scornful of centralized authority, particularly in areas where Left S.R. influence was strong."[5]

Despite Trotsky's more conservative comments, an initial Bolshevik drift in this radical direction could be seen in late 1917—which is hardly surprising, given the burst of working-class militancy that brought the Bolsheviks to power in the first place. By early 1918, however, a sharp controversy erupted. Lenin called for an end to the escalating trend of nationalization and expropriation, insisting on a compromise with large capitalists. "The new economic order would rely on limited state ownership," explains Stephen Cohen, "while preserving private (or joint) ownership and management in most enterprises." Lenin utilized the term *state capitalism* to describe what was, as Cohen put it, "a mixed economy combining a limited public sector with a large private one." Lenin saw "no contradiction in the proposition that a proletarian state might preside over a state capitalist economy."[6]

But disagreement over this helped generate a Left Communist faction within Lenin's own party. One of its leaders was Nikolai Bukharin, who protested: "State capitalism under the dictatorship of the proletariat—this is an absurdity, soft-boiled boots." Another leader, Valerian Obolensky (more commonly known by the name N. Osinsky), called for "a decisive liquidation of private property, the introduction of the socialist system, and the direct transition to communism." The Left Communist platform warned against the policy "of agreements with capitalistic businessmen, both the 'patriotic' ones and the international ones who stand behind them," insisting that "the Russian workers' revolution cannot 'save itself' by leaving the international revolutionary path, steadily avoiding a fight, retreating in the face of the pressure of international capital, and making concessions to 'patriotic capital.'" Such a policy of retreat would undermine revolutionary internationalism as well as proletarian democracy. Instead, it was necessary to move forward: "The energetic organization of production on socialist lines will on the one hand strengthen the economic base of the proletariat as a revolutionary force, and on the other will be a new school of class organization and activity for it."[7]

Lenin responded that the workers "have *no experience* of independent work in organizing giant enterprises which serve the needs of scores of millions of people." It was necessary, he insisted, "to learn from the capitalist organizers" and to proceed "cautiously" and "gradually." He stressed: "The difference between socialization and simple confiscation is that confiscation can be carried out by 'determination' alone, without the ability to calculate and distribute properly, *whereas socialization cannot be brought about without this ability.*" Against romantic and impatient conceptions, he insisted that "the bricks of which socialism will be composed have not yet been made." Lenin argued that two preconditions must be realized to allow the development of socialism: (1) "large-scale capitalist engineering based on the latest discoveries of modern science," combined with "planned state organization, which keeps tens of millions of people to the strictest observance of a unified standard in production and distribution," and (2) the proletariat's secure position as "the ruler of the state." He noted that "history . . . has taken such a peculiar course that it *has given birth* in 1918 to two unconnected halves of socialism." In Germany the economic prerequisite of a highly developed and concentrated industrial economy existed, but "the revolution in Germany is still slow in 'coming forth,'" so that the political rule of the working class had yet to be realized. In Russia, on the other hand, the political prerequisite *had* been established, but on the economic plane "petty-bourgeois capitalism prevails," necessitating the building up by the proletarian state of "large-scale state capitalism" which Lenin believed must constitute part of "the period of transition from capitalism to socialism." There are indications that at least some sectors of the Russian bourgeoisie (and even some foreign capitalist firms) were open to participating in such "state capitalist" development.[8]

The Left Communists' opposition to Lenin's perspective seems to have reflected a broader impatience felt by many Russian workers. Dobb pointed out the existence of "syndicalist and centrifugal tendencies among the factory committees," commenting that "in place of nationalization, there was a wholesale and chaotic 'expropriation' of enterprises on local initiative, in some cases in strict violation of Article 9 of the General Instructions on Workers' Control." Alec Nove concurs: "The large majority (over two-thirds) of nationalizations were local, until June 1918, and may have been due to genuinely local decisions. These in turn could have been due to over-enthusiasm, or responses to real or imagined sabotage, or the indignant refusal of employers to accept orders from workers' councils." Nonetheless, a Bolshevik majority lined up behind Lenin's policy of developing a composite system "in which there is large-scale Socialist economy, private capitalist economy, and State enterprises temporarily leased to private capital." Dobb observed that this was "superficially similar in form to what may sometimes be found in capitalist countries, but possessing the fundamental difference that power has been transferred to the organs of the working class."[9]

This is precisely the orientation articulated by Alexei Rykov, who was chosen to head the Supreme Council of National Economy—known as the Vesenkha—established in November 1917. Intended to function as the executive body of a nationwide Economic Soviet (just as Sovnarkom, the executive body of the All-Russian Congress of Soviets, was to function as Soviet Russia's leading political body), the Vesenkha never cohered in that manner amid the economic chaos of the time. But it helped to define the mixed-economy orientation. While emphasizing that he was not questioning the impossibility of a viable economy that would be half-socialist and half-capitalist, Rykov also stressed that "we are in a position to nationalize, and to administer nationalized enterprises, only in a part of industry."[10]

Lenin had insisted in the period leading up to the Bolshevik revolution that "the way to avert a catastrophe is to establish a real workers' control over the production and distribution of goods." He was quite clear on how this was to be implemented:

> To establish such control it is necessary, first, to make certain that in all the basic institutions there is a majority of workers, not less than three-fourths of all the votes, and that all owners who have not deserted their business, as well as the scientifically and technically trained personnel, are compelled to participate; secondly, that all the shop and factory committees, the central and local Soviets of Workers', Soldiers' and Peasants' Deputies, as well as trade unions, be granted the right to participate in such control, that all commercial and bank accounts be open to their inspection, and that the management be compelled to supply them with all data; and, thirdly, that the representatives of all the more important democratic and socialist parties be granted the same right.
>
> Workers' control, already recognized by the capitalists in a number of cases where conflicts arise, should be immediately developed, by way of a series of carefully considered and gradual, but immediately realizable, measures, into complete regulation of the production and distribution of goods by the workers.[11]

It was this orientation that Lenin sought to implement in the wake of the October/November revolution. The eyewitness sociologist E. A. Ross observed that "while there are plenty of syndicalists urging the workmen of each factory to organize, cast out the owner and his agents, and run it as their own, the Bolsheviks are guilty of no such folly." Here he obviously bases his remarks on the policy of Lenin and Trotsky, and of the central government: "They see clearly that such methods would end in anarchy. What they aim for is workers' control of industry. In some matters the capitalist will be free, in others bound by the factory committee, in still others bound by rules laid down by local workers' councils or the central authorities." E. H. Carr reports on instances "in which workers or factory committees, having evicted the managers, later went to them and begged them to return" once they found themselves unable to maintain the factory's operations. Nove comments that "the evidence, though mixed, is still consistent with the intention to maintain a mixed economy for a considerable period." This also corresponds to Joseph Freeman's findings in his early account of *The Soviet Worker.* "On assuming power, the Soviet Government's immediate aim in the economic field was to establish a planned system of production and distribution which would steadily improve the living conditions of the people," wrote Freeman. "It did not, however, plan the immediate nationalization of industry. Lenin looked upon the socialist reorganization of industry as a long and gradual process." Far from trying to create socialism by decree, the Bolshevik leadership thought "the early stages would involve the coordination and control of industry by the workers' state; but the state would at first not take over the actual ownership and management of industry. The workers were to be employed by the old owners and protected by the new state."[12]

It is worth lingering, however, over a complex set of contradictions embedded in the very heart of this mixed-economy approach—the divergent lures, for Russian capitalists, of *cooperation with* and, at the same time, *resistance to* the revolutionary regime. "At a time when the Russian economy, shattered by war and revolution, was plunging downward into a gulf of anarchy and disintegration," according to E. H. Carr, "a certain tacit community of interests could be detected between the government and the more sensible and moderate of the industrialists in bringing about a return to some kind of orderly production." Yet Carr also points out that any such cooperation was necessarily "uneasy, distrustful, and quasi-hostile." How could it be otherwise? Even in this period of presumed Leninist "moderation," as Lars Lih points out, Lenin was declaring: "We will be merciless to our enemies and just as merciless to all wavering elements from our own midst who dare to bring disorganization to our difficult creative work of constructing a new life for the working people." Carr himself offers a similar pronouncement by Lenin from this period, when he described the Vesenkha as "the fighting organ for the struggle with the capitalists and the landlords in the economic sphere, just as the Sovnarkom is in politics."[13]

The Bolsheviks were absolutely committed to the elimination of capitalism altogether as soon as it was deemed possible, and they were doing all that they could to create that possibility. The capitalists, as a class, were absolutely committed to maximizing their profits and to maintaining the economic system that generated such profits—again, by all possible means. Neither side had any illusions about the desires and intentions of the other side. The resulting insecurity ensured a permanently terrible "business climate" that made unlikely the long-term viability of the cooperative relationship.

The resolution to this contradiction would seem to be this: Lenin and his comrades were not assuming that the mixed economy would have a long duration. They assumed the catastrophic world war that had swept Russia decisively on the revolutionary path would sweep other advanced capitalist countries onto the same path. They did not anticipate long-term isolation for the Soviet Republic within a global capitalist economy; they assumed the opposite: the spread of workers' revolutions through eastern Europe, into Germany, Italy, France, Britain, and beyond, creating a United Socialist States of Europe, supplemented in various ways and at various times by revolutionary insurgencies in Asia, Africa, and the Americas. Some of these expectations, and the ways they were frustrated, will be considered in the next chapter. But first we will turn our attention to twists and loops within Bolshevism, the collapse of the mixed-economy orientation, and diverse aspects of the human drama unfolding within such contexts as these.

Twists and Loops

Reality is complex, containing twists and loops, contradictions and complex divergences—and we find abundant examples when we look at revolutionary Russia. We can also find this in the thinking, theorizations, and pronouncements of Lenin and his comrades—divergent trends within Bolshevism, coexisting with those that we have stressed so far, which had an impact on policy and practice in ways that contradicted the basic orientation and undermined the basic goals advanced by Lenin and other leaders of the revolution.

The Bolsheviks' Marxism included more than simply Lenin's thought, but the Marxism of Lenin was a central element within Bolshevism and it contained a dynamic convergence of different elements. Boris Souvarine aptly quotes him during a moment when he reproached some comrades for "repeating a formula divorced from the series of circumstances which had produced it and assured its success, and applying it to conditions essentially different." Sometimes Lenin would seek to "speak French" when Russian realities seemed to approximate those that had brought the French Revolution, and when realities shifted in the opposite direction, he would "speak German," advancing the patient organizational approach reflected in the German Social Democracy's Erfurt Program. But "he never ceased 'speaking Russian,'" Souvarine tells us, "sounding all possibilities, weighing opportunities, calculating the chances of keeping the Party on the right track, avoiding alike belated or premature insurrection inspired by romantic motives, and constitutional and parliamentary illusions." It is worth further following Souvarine's insightful description of Lenin's approach:

> Always to "speak Russian," even when borrowing theory and practice from other revolutionary movements, this was the secret of his superiority over his adversaries. He was a disciple of Marx, but undogmatic, eager in the pursuit of science and knowledge, always alive to the teachings of experience, capable of recognizing, surmounting and making good his errors, and consequently of rising above himself.[14]

Still, the dynamic theoretical methodology, with its consequent incorporation of diverse elements, naturally generated complications in the conceptualizations of Lenin and his comrades. One complication has to do with their conceptualization of the French Revolution of 1789–99, especially the role of the revolutionary Jacobins—and its implications for Bolshevik practice. A second complication relates to Lenin's conceptualization of state capitalism—and, once again, the implications for Bolshevik practice.

The Jacobin Puzzle

In 1920, Albert Mathiez, one of the great historians of the French Revolution, wrote that "Jacobinism and Bolshevism are both dictatorships, born of civil and foreign war; two class dictatorships operating by the same methods: terror, requisition, and taxes, and proposing as a final outcome the same goal, the transformation of society. And not only of Russian or French society, but of universal society."[15]

Indeed, Lenin "remained an impenitent 'Jacobin' of the proletariat, with an unreserved admiration for the 'great French Revolution whose vitality and powerful influence on humanity is demonstrated by the wild hatred which it still provokes,'" according to Souvarine. Of course, being "haunted by the French national tradition of 1793," when the French Revolution radicalized, was not unique to Lenin. At the time of the Bolshevik-Menshevik split in 1903–4, Lenin had been accused of "Jacobinism"—by which was meant (according to one prominent Menshevik, Julius Martov) a "dictatorship by a revolutionary minority" and (according to another prominent Menshevik, Theodore Dan) "a terrorist minority dictatorship."[16] Among Marxists of the time, however, the term generally had a more expansive and complex meaning—and it comes across, for example, if we skim through the writings of Rosa Luxemburg. Although Jacobins were definitely not socialist (and existed before the crystallization of the modern proletariat), she projected them in extremely positive terms:

> [The Jacobins] ardently wished for the complete economic liberation of the people. They sincerely sought to realize the formal equality of all before the law, but also real economic equality. All their speeches and their acts were based on an idea: in the democratic republic, there should be neither wealthy people nor the poor; the democratic republic, that is to say a free country based on popular sovereignty, could not long survive if the people, sovereign politically, found themselves economically dependent on and dominated by the wealthy. . . .
>
> As long as the Mountain [another word for Jacobins] held power, they sought salvation in coercive economic terms, in particular to prevent the people of Paris from dying of hunger.[17]

Twenty-five years later, she would write:

> And what happened in the Great French Revolution? Here, after four years of struggle, the seizure of power by the Jacobins proved to be the only means of saving the conquests of the revolution, of achieving a republic, of organizing a revolutionary defense against inner as well as outer foes, of suppressing the conspiracies of counter-revolution and spreading the revolutionary wave from France to all Europe.[18]

At the same time, she critically characterized the emergency dictatorship established by Robespierre as "a clique affair" and "a dictatorship of a handful of politicians, that is a dictatorship in the bourgeois sense."[19] Nonetheless, she also wrote: "After the fall of the Jacobins, when [Jacobin leader] Robespierre was driven in chains to the place of execution the naked whores of the victory-drunk bourgeoisie danced in the streets, danced a shameless dance of joy around the fallen hero of the revolution."[20]

In the polemics of 1904, Lenin therefore embraced the accusation of "Jacobinism"—he portrayed the Bolsheviks as the "Jacobins of Social-Democracy," while comparing his Menshevik adversaries to the moderate faction of the French Revolution, the Girondins, "inconsistent, wavering, opportunist champions of the cause." He proclaimed: "A Jacobin who wholly identifies himself with the *organization* of the proletariat—a proletariat *conscious* of its class interests—is a *revolutionary Social-Democrat*."[21] As Souvarine later observed, "This definition provided food for controversy for a long time, and that beyond the national field." Rosa Luxemburg, George Plekhanov, Julius Martov, Leon Trotsky, Karl Kautsky, and others "rushed to inform Lenin that the Jacobins were bourgeois revolutionaries whose organization was no model for Social Democracy," as Lars Lih has put it.[22] And yet, as we have seen, some of his critics could themselves be targets of their own objections. Certainly Plekhanov had gone further than Luxemburg in explicit acceptance of the most authoritarian elements of Jacobinism in 1903:

> Every given democratic principle should be examined not on its own merits in the abstract, but in its bearing on what may be called the basic principle of democracy, namely, on the principle that says *Salus populi suprema lex* [the welfare of the people is the highest law]. Translated into the language of the revolutionary, this means that the success of the revolution is the highest law. . . . If it were necessary for the success of the revolution to restrict the effect of one or another democratic principle, it would be criminal to hesitate at such a restriction. . . . If, on an impulse of revolutionary enthusiasm, the people were to elect a very good parliament . . . we should try and make it a long parliament; and if the elections turned out to be unfavorable we should try and dismiss it not in two years' time but if possible in two weeks.[23]

In the early 1900s, Kautsky, too, urged the workers' movement to emulate the Jacobin tradition and reject Girondin moderation.[24]

It is important to recognize the diverse threads of Jacobinism—those associated with the unyielding commitment to revolutionary-democratic goals and ideals, and to inspiring popular mobilizations, as well as those (grounded in the same ideals) associated with emergency dictatorship, authoritarian measures, and the use of violence and terror. Historian Arno J. Mayer has usefully elaborated on this aspect of the Jacobin tradition:

> The establishment and operation of the reign of terror was inseparable from the tangled contingencies of civil war, foreign hostility, economic disorganization, and social dislocation, which called for quick, centralizing and coercive action. The ensuing forced-draft political, military, and economic mobilization and deployment were backed by an enforcement terror, complete with rhetorical intimidation, arbitrary arrests, quasi-legal summary justice, and mass execution. To be effective, the regime of revolutionary terror had to rule by patent fear, which often escaped control.[25]

Lenin—no less than Plekhanov, Trotsky, and Luxemburg—was aware of all aspects of Jacobinism and yet (certainly no less than his critics, when they were not polemicizing against him) continued to identify with the Jacobin tradition. "To make a bogey of Jacobinism in time of revolution is a cheap trick," he insisted, quoting from Marx himself: "The Reign of Terror of 1793 was nothing but a plebeian manner of settling accounts with absolutism and counter-revolution." Lenin added: "We, too, prefer to settle accounts with the Russian autocracy by 'plebeian' methods and leave Girondist methods to [the Menshevik-controlled] *Iskra*." In the same period he hailed the Jacobins as "the most consistent of all bourgeois democrats," and drew attention to 1850 writings of Marx and Engels, pointing to the Jacobin example as a model for the development of strategy and the creation of a revolutionary workers' government.[26]

In June 1917, as Russia was rapidly approaching its second revolution, Lenin gave powerful stress to the Jacobin elements of popular mobilization for revolutionary-democratic goals:

> The Jacobins of 1793 belonged to the most revolutionary class of the eighteenth century, the town and country poor. It was against this class, which had in fact (and not just in words) done away with its monarch, its landowners and its moderate bourgeoisie by the most revolutionary measures, including the guillotine—against this truly revolutionary class of the eighteenth century—that the monarchs of Europe combined to wage war.
>
> The Jacobins proclaimed enemies of the people those "promoting the schemes of the allied tyrants directed against the Republic."
>
> The Jacobins' example is instructive. It has not become obsolete to this day, except that it must be applied to the revolutionary class of the twentieth century, to the workers and semi-proletarians. To this class, the enemies of the people in the twentieth century are not the monarchs, but the landowners and capitalists as a class.
>
> If the "Jacobins" of the twentieth century, the workers and semi-proletarians, assumed power, they would proclaim enemies of the people the capitalists who are making thousands of millions in profits from the imperialist war, *that is,* a war for the division of capitalist spoils and profits.
>
> The "Jacobins" of the twentieth century would not guillotine the capitalists— to follow a good example does not mean copying it. It would be enough to arrest fifty to a hundred financial magnates and bigwigs, the chief knights of embezzlement and of robbery by the banks. It would be enough to arrest them for a few weeks *to expose their frauds* and show all exploited people "who needs the war." Upon exposing the frauds of the banking barons, we could release them, placing the banks, the capitalist syndicates, and all the contractors "working" for the government under workers' control.
>
> The Jacobins of 1793 have gone down in history for their great example of a truly revolutionary struggle against *the class of the exploiters of the working people and the oppressed* who had taken *all* state power into their own hands.[27]

The naïveté of this optimistic scenario matches the observation of Arno Mayer that Lenin and the Bolsheviks—despite the realistic intuition that there would be immense difficulties—were not really prepared for the tidal wave of violence that would be unleashed by the October/November revolution. As we will see, this contributed powerfully to the recessive element in the Jacobin tradition becoming dominant in revolutionary Russia. Yet it was not only these tidal waves of unanticipated difficulties that swept Lenin to the problematical side of Jacobinism. Also drawing the authoritarian element to the fore were complications associated with another theoretical knot associated with Lenin's conceptualizations of state capitalism.

State-Capitalist Conundrums

There is more than one tangle in this theoretical knot, not necessarily having to do with a flaw in the conceptualizations so much as what these conceptualizations implied regarding the question of democracy. Readers should note that we are referring to *plural* conceptualizations of state capitalism—one had been articulated by Lenin's comrade Nikolai Bukharin and two others are associated with Lenin. While Bukharin's actually seems to be in harmony with the revolutionary-democratic orientation of Bolshevism up through 1918, both of Lenin's formulations seem to pose serious challenges to the old orientation.

A merger of politics and economics, according to Bukharin, is what takes place "under the dictatorship of finance capital in its classical, final form," and this is what he terms *state capitalism,* dominated by what he calls "the state capitalist trusts"—composed of "monopolistic employers' associations, combined enterprises, and the penetration of banking into industry." The "cohesion between the economic and the political organizations of the bourgeoisie" that propels forward what would later come to be known as *globalization:* "Having ceased to be 'national' the commodity market, in fact, merely becomes a world market." As "economics fuse organizationally with politics" (in part through the dramatic development of militarization), Bukharin sees the development of "a new model of state power . . . , the classical model of an *imperialist* state."[28]

The fusion of economics with politics had dramatic repercussions for the labor movement, according to Bukharin, which was highlighted by the capitulation of much of the Socialist International to the "all-embracing bourgeois state" with the coming of the First World War: "The treachery of the socialist parties and trade unions was expressed in the fact that they entered the service of the bourgeois state, that they were in fact stratified by this imperialist state and reduced to 'workers' departments' in the military machine." No less significant was the development of global alliances and institutions—what Bukharin refers to as "state 'coalitions' and the 'League of Nations.'"

According to Bukharin, the high degree of economic-political interpenetration and merger, the advance of collectivized and interdependent enterprises, the accelerated globalization are "empirical proof of the 'possibility' of building communism," although this must—as he puts it—be brought about as a process of "state capitalism *in reverse, its own dialectical transformation into its own antithesis.*" The dictatorship of finance capitalism must give way "in the clamor of class struggles" to proletarian rule with "the soviets, the trade unions, the working-class party in power, factory and works' committees and special economic organizations set up after the seizure of power, with a fairly numerous cadre of organizationally and technically skilled workers." He concludes: "Thus the system of state capitalism is dialectically transformed into its own antithesis, the state structure of workers; socialism."[29]

The "state capitalism" theorized by Lenin (to Bukharin's initial exasperation) refers to the nature of the economy that must be overseen *after* the proletarian revolution and the establishment of working-class rule. Far from being something that is "transformed into its own antithesis," Lenin sees state capitalism as something that must be established and built up by the proletarian state. The fusion of economics and politics he envisions, however, seems to have two somewhat different articulations.

One Leninist articulation, according to E. H. Carr, involves the mixed-economy approach to which we have already given attention: "a regime which would leave owners in possession and management of their industrial enterprises while subjecting them to general state supervision," with watchful although relatively moderate workers' control.[30] We have already noted how this tends to collide with the inclinations and aspirations of workers who want to move forward—more rapidly than they are able, if their enterprises are to remain viable—to remove their capitalist exploiters and operate the workplaces under their own management, sharing among themselves the profits produced by their labor.

This impulse of expanding workers' power, which played such an important role in the insurgent mobilizations culminating in the October/November seizure of power, generated new problems, as we have noted, but none was more serious than the decentralizing generation of centrifugal forces to which Carr gives special stress:

Socialism did not seek to subordinate the irresponsible capitalist entrepreneur to an equally irresponsible factory committee claiming the same right of independence of the actual authority; that could only perpetuate the "anarchy of production" which Marx had regarded as the damning stigma of capitalism. The fatal and inevitable tendency of factory committees was to take decisions in the light of the interests of the workers in a particular factory or in a particular region. The essence of socialism was to establish an economy planned and carefully coordinated by a central authority in the common interest of all.[31]

This problem flows into the other Leninist articulation, emphasized by Lars Lih—"state capitalism . . . as a necessary historical stage," in which a proletarian state includes "absolutely everything within the sphere of state regulation." As Lenin suggested on the eve of the October/November revolution, "Socialism is nothing more than the very next step forward from state-monopoly capitalism. In other words: socialism is nothing other than state-monopoly capitalism that is made to serve the whole people and to that extent ceases to be a capitalist monopoly." Shortly after the revolution, Lenin was arguing that the Soviet regime now faced the "organizational task" of compelling "the most strict and universal registration and monitoring" and of creating "an extremely complicated and subtle network of new organizational relations, embracing the systematic production and distribution of products necessary for the existence of tens of millions of people." This variant of state capitalism moved in the right direction (both for immediate survival and for eventual socialism) because it was "something centralized, something allowing for calculation and monitoring, something socialized, and that is exactly what we lack, [for] we are threatened by the atmosphere of petty-bourgeois sloppiness."[32]

Lih gives particular stress to the profound urgency of the accounting and monitoring aspect of this second variant. Consider, first, his apt description of Russian realities on the eve of the Bolshevik seizure of power:

In the fall of 1917 the chain reaction of social disintegration led to a series of explosions—in the countryside on the front lines, and in the capital cities. In the area of food supply the event that lit the fuse was the doubling of fixed prices at the end of August. Generally overlooked amid the high political drama of those days, the decision to double the prices paid to grain producers was not only a signal of the imminent collapse of food supply; it destroyed the morale of the existing political class [clustered around Kerensky's Provisional Government] while confirming the political formula of the Bolshevik political contenders.[33]

After the Bolshevik contenders took power, however, the economic crisis by no means evaporated. The crisis continued to deepen. When preparing to take power, "the Bolsheviks had hoped, or at least had promised, that democratic soviets would provide a basis for a vigorous central authority that could overcome the food-supply crisis", but optimism turned to desperation with "their failure to get grain from the population still under their control" to the war-torn rural areas," with local "separatism" having increasingly devastating impacts on the overall economy, and centrifugal forces by no means being overcome by a flourishing soviet democracy. As one Bolshevik food-supply official sourly commented: "They say that the voice of the people is the voice of God. We harkened to the voice of the people, . . . but what came of it? The most pathetic results possible."[34]

Such realities had a powerful impact on the way Lenin tended to theorize state capitalism in this period. It is instructive to follow his logic in a report delivered April 29, 1918. "Reality tells us that state capitalism would be a step forward," he insisted. "If in a small space of time we could achieve state capitalism in Russia, it would be a victory." Commenting that "the chief enemy is the petty bourgeoisie, its habits and customs, its economic position" (among whom he seemed to include not only small shopkeepers and masses of peasant smallholders but also workers with narrow perspectives), he explained, "To achieve state capitalism at the present time means putting into effect the accounting and control that the capitalist classes carried out." Over and over Lenin stressed that "only the development of state capitalism, only the painstaking establishment of accounting and control, only the strictest organization and labor discipline, will lead us to socialism." He polemicized against Left Communist critics: "When they tell us that the introduction of labor discipline coupled with restoring capitalists as leaders is a threat to the revolution, I say: it is just the socialist character of our revolution that these people have failed to understand, they repeat the very thing that easily unites them with the petty bourgeois, who fear discipline, organization, accounting and control as the devil fears holy water." Arguing that "the tasks of socialist construction demand stubborn, long-continued work and appropriate knowledge, of which we do not have enough," he insisted that "even the more developed generation of the immediate future will hardly achieve the complete transition to socialism." Lenin seems to have sensed divergent moods and inclinations within the working class. On the one hand he argued: "When I express my dissent to those people who claim to be socialists and who promise the workers they shall enjoy as much as they like and whatever they like, I say that communism presupposes a productivity of labor that we do not have at present. Our productivity is too low, that is a fact." On the other hand, he insisted that "the proletariat, which learned discipline from large-scale production, knows that there cannot be socialism until production is organized on a large scale and until there is even stricter discipline."[35]

Both aspects of Lenin's state-capitalism—the *mixed-economy variant* and the *centrally organized variant*—suggest the inadequacy of the genuinely, radically democratic perspectives of 1917 Bolshevism. A majority of the workers as well as a majority of the vast peasantry could not have been expected to have a clear understanding of "the big picture"—whether of the immediate needs of the entire society or of the rational pathway that had to be followed if socialism was to be achieved. Such an understanding of "the big picture" could only have been developed by a central political-economic authority that oversaw the processes involved in monitoring and meeting the urgent needs of the entire population while simultaneously overseeing the process involved in realistically and practically overseeing the transition to socialism. On the other hand, a question can be raised regarding the ability of this central authority to *understand* what was needed and also its ability to *ensure that what needed to be done was actually done.*

Before the end of 1918, the mixed-economy variant of Lenin's state-capitalist conceptualization collapsed, but the monitoring and accounting variant (without the "state-capitalist" label) remained more important than ever. Yet the problematical aspects of implementing this variant hardly disappeared, as we shall see later in this study.

Beyond the Mixed Economy

It is important to recall the point made by Adolfo Gilly—an economy half devoted to the logic of capitalist accumulation and half devoted to the logic running counter to that is an absurdity. This tension is inherent even in the unique variant of the mixed economy that existed in Bolshevik Russia. Yet the implementation of more "radical" economic policies cannot be expected to resolve the problem. The transition from mixed economy to what was called "war communism" dramatically illustrated this fact.

The early orientation of Lenin and Trotsky—a mixed economy under the general control of a workers' state—collapsed within eight months. There were three primary factors that brought this about: the mass radicalization among the workers combined with confusion over the meaning of workers' control; the onset of civil war and foreign invasion; and the growing tendency among Russian capitalists to sabotage, de-capitalize, or simply abandon their enterprises.

Stephen Cohen has noted, in his biography of Bukharin, that there was considerable confusion over the term *workers' control:* "Did it mean management by factory committees, local soviets, trade unions, the Supreme Economic Council, or merely a 'workers' state'?" In fact, it was not clear that workers' control would involve *managing* the factories through any organizational form at all, as we shall see. "There were almost as many Bolshevik opinions as possibilities, and Bukharin himself seemed to hold different ones on different occasions," Cohen recounts. "Knowingly or not, for example, he had adumbrated the eventual statist solution as early as October 1917, when he defined workers' control as meaning that 'state power is in the hands of another class,' the proletariat." Lenin's view of workers' control, as we've seen, did not involve the introduction of socialism or nationalizations. "Such measures as the nationalization of the land," he wrote, "of all the banks and capitalist syndicates, or, at least, the *immediate* establishment of the *control* of the Soviets of Workers' Deputies, etc., over them—measures which do not in any way constitute the 'introduction' of socialism—must be absolutely insisted on, and whenever possible, carried out in a revolutionary way." Control, according to this perspective, precedes nationalizations. Nor did Lenin see workers' control as involving the workers in actually operating or managing the enterprise. His definition is clarified in his comment that "workers' control *can* become a national, all-embracing, omnipresent, extremely precise and extremely scrupulous *accounting* of the production and distribution of goods."[36]

S. A. Smith has criticized Lenin as being, in 1917, "intoxicated by the spectacle of workers, soldiers and peasants taking power into their own hands, and profoundly optimistic about the potential inherent in such self-activity." Smith complains: "It cannot be said that Lenin satisfactorily theorized the relationship between grass-roots workers' control of production and state-wide regulation of the economy." In a sense, however, Lenin *did* theorize a conception of workers' control that fused grassroots control with statewide regulation of the economy. The key was the soviet system, a pyramid of democratic councils—from local to regional to national levels—in which delegates were subject to recall by those who elected them. These were to be the basis of the workers' state that would provide overall coordination of the economy. The factory committees within each workplace were to keep track of how the capitalist owners and managers were running things, preventing irresponsible activity and helping to train workers to assume an increasingly conscious role in the productive process. The trade unions were to defend the rights of workers on the job as well as help shape wage policies and the workers' contribution to industrial productivity. Gradually, private ownership would give way to public ownership, and capitalists would be replaced by managers and answerable to the soviet state, the democratic government of the working class, with the checks and balances of workers' input and safeguards remaining in place through factory committees and trade unions.

It can be argued that there wasn't sufficient theorization here, but it isn't clear that *any* theorization would have been sufficient given the economic calamity that was unfolding. In any event, as Smith observes, "Lenin never developed a conception of workers' self-management. Even after October [i.e., the Bolshevik victory], workers' control remained for him fundamentally a matter of 'inspection' and 'accounting.'" Smith argues that in the period leading up to the revolution, "the Bolshevik formula of 'workers' control of production and distribution' was the one most widely supported by workers in Petrograd." Contrary to some accounts, the mainstream Bolshevik demand was not to nationalize industry with workers managing the factories, but rather to prevent the capitalists from sabotaging the economy and overturning the gains of the workers. "'Sabotage' and 'saboteur' were key words in popular discourse during the revolution and Bolsheviks in the factory committees harped constantly on this theme," Smith points out. "It was the willingness of the Bolsheviks to fight 'sabotage,' in order to protect jobs and the democratic gains of the February Revolution, which was the secret of their rapidly growing popularity in the summer and autumn of 1917." When workers actually took over factories, they often tended to see this as a temporary measure to forestall closure of the factory by greedy or hostile owners.[37]

By the spring of 1918, 40 enterprises in Petrograd had been nationalized, 61 were being temporarily run by factory committees, 207 were under workers' control, and 402 were still being run by their owners. Those in this last category were mainly small workshops, while most of the city's major factories were among the 207 under workers' control. Workers' control meant that within the factory the capitalist management existed alongside the factory committee, but the management's orders could not be effective without ratification by the factory committee or its control commission. The organ of workers' control would oversee the execution of various jobs to be done, also investigating the state of equipment, finances, order books, accounts, fuel, and raw material. In addition, it assumed responsibility for working conditions, productivity, internal order, and laying off workers. The capitalists resented these incursions into the traditional prerogatives of management. Shortly after the Bolsheviks took power, the Society of Factory and Works Owners in

Petrograd denounced "non-state, class control by workers over the country's industrial life (as decreed by the government) since it does not, in practice, pursue national ends and is not recognized by the majority of the Russian people." Unofficially, this organization of Petrograd's major industrial and commercial firms inclined toward closing up business rather than giving in to demands for workers' control, because "the government, by completely handing over management of the factories into the hands of the working class is erecting a barrier to the further participation of capital in industrial life." Yet it was quickly concluded by many that such intransigence was not prudent. "Facing bodies of united workmen," E. A. Ross recounted in 1918, "sometimes with, but often without, the support of their office force, the managers of Russian establishments had to dispense with their familiar means of exploitation and content themselves with what they could get by tact, argument, and personal influence."[38]

Workers' control came to mean different things in different establishments. Ross interviewed two Moscow manufacturers and discovered divergent experiences. "The cotton-mill man threw up his hands. No getting on with the factory committee; they wouldn't let him fire the good-for-nothing fellows. Production was way down," Ross recounted. "The machine-shop man, on the other hand, had no trouble. When he saw the committee about discharging a certain fellow, he stated his case to them in language they could understand, got them to put themselves in his place. He found them always reasonable."[39]

Ross described yet other experiences: "Taking too literally 'the right of labor to the whole produce,' workers have ridden their manager out of the works in a wheel-barrow, only to implore him a few weeks later to come back because they knew not where to buy raw material or what kinds to order. One manager held out till he was let back with complete control of hiring and firing." Ross found in general that Russian capitalists and bourgeois economists agreed that "while the principles upon which state-managed industry may succeed are known, one cannot expect such principles to be followed by a government resting immediately on the Russian proletariat." He predicted that the popular pressures rising from this situation would "therefore result simply in the eventual disappearance of the capital."[40]

We have seen that Lenin and Trotsky sought to avoid such disappearance of capital. Russia was not ready for socialism. But this ran counter to a growing mood of extreme radicalism. A Menshevik observer commented in early 1918 that "the majority of the proletariat, particularly in Petrograd, looks on workers' control as an entry into the kingdom of socialism." Left Communists

pushed for "the complete removal of capitalist and feudal survivals in the relations of production"; they warned that true power to the working class would
not be achieved by some "proletarian elite which will sit with the capitalist elite
on the boards of the [factory] trusts." Such state capitalism, despite Lenin's defense, was attacked with the argument that "a proletarian-peasant dictatorship
which does not entail the expropriation of the expropriators [i.e., of the capital-
ists], which does not eliminate the power of capital in the mines and factories
can only be a temporary phenomenon." This orientation was not restricted to
a party faction. "The process of nationalization went on from below," one Bolshevik later explained, "and the soviet leaders could not keep up with it, could
not take things in hand, in spite of the fact that many orders were issued which
forbade local organizations to enact nationalizations by themselves."[41]

Yet it is not the case that this radical wave simply overwhelmed all in
its path. There was an ongoing struggle among Bolsheviks and also within
the working class. Journalist-historian William Henry Chamberlin aptly describes the stubborn orientation of Lenin and his closest co-thinkers: "When
workers' delegations came to him asking for the nationalization of their factories, Lenin at this time was in the habit of putting embarrassing questions
to them. Did they know accurately what their factories produced, or what
markets could be found for their products? Were they prepared to operate the
factory efficiently if the state placed it in their hands?" Under such questioning, some workers' delegations had second thoughts. "If they could not answer
these questions satisfactorily Lenin would recommend that they make haste
slowly and consent to an arrangement under which the capitalist would have
a share in the management of the factory and would provide technical knowledge and experience for its operation."[42]

Up to a point, such an approach was effective. "If, after all, capital fared
not so badly," reflected Ross, "it was only owing to the amazing reasonableness
of the Russian masses when they were not under the spell of the crowd. . . .
There is no doubt that the Russian, even the illiterate working-man, is one
of the most reasonable beings on earth if someone he trusts approaches him
in the right way and has patience." On the other hand, the economic crisis
in war-torn Russia that we have noted (and which had helped bring about
the revolution) guaranteed deepening discontent. The combination of this
with genuine workers' democracy helped to generate a volatile situation. Ross
commented that "the ease of recalling one factory committee and setting up
another puts reason at a constant disadvantage." Quite aside from the question of whether to allow the capitalist to own and manage enterprises, there

was the question of the extent to which workers would allow themselves to be exploited, and the extent to which the capitalists and their underlings would be permitted to impose discipline. "After an experience of being rolled out of the works in a wheel-barrow, the foremen were pretty limp and said nothing." Productivity fell by 30 to 70 percent. Ross reported: "The labor men I interviewed frankly admitted the great slump in productivity, but insisted labor should not bear all the blame. Part of it was due to the gradual deterioration of the machinery and to the growing difficulty of obtaining a steady supply of raw materials." There were also instances of sabotage by employers desiring a shutdown of operations in order to "bring labor to its senses."[43]

Regardless of the causes of declining productivity (and hence profitability), the indisputable fact of the decline, and the ongoing uncertainty over the future, rapidly ate away at the patience of the business community with this state of affairs. A polarization began to undermine the policies that Lenin sought to advance. Chris Goodey's richly analytical sketch, coinciding with what is described in Ross's account, stresses that "wildcat 'spontaneous' nationalizations" carried out by some workers proved to "undermine the basis of the negotiations going on between Lenin and Trotsky and Western representatives for financial and technical assistance." It also undermined the basis of the compromise that the Bolshevik leaders sought with Russian capitalists. The workers' defiance, according to Goodey, "ensures that the Western representatives will not be enticed into real negotiations, that the capitalist countries will invade, that the civil war will start in earnest, that the proletariat will virtually have disappeared by 1920," thanks to the disintegration of the economy.[44]

Many capitalists—by the spring and summer of 1918 placing their hopes in civil war and foreign invasion—did what they could to facilitate the disintegration of the economy. The incursion of German military forces before the signing of the Brest-Litovsk treaty in March 1918 was followed by the invasion of Allied troops afterward, and French, British, and US support made possible the effective mobilization of indigenous Russian forces by Admiral Kolchak, General Denikin, and others to wage a civil war designed to overturn the Soviet Republic. This encouraged many factory owners who, as Victor Serge observed, "liquidated their stocks, stole or sold their equipment, and vanished with the cash they had realized." While some capitalists might have pragmatically desired to compromise with the Soviet regime, the new dangers escalated the working-class militancy and swept away the moderation of the Bolshevik mainstream. "In June," Ross wrote, "when it had become apparent that the Allies intended to bayonet to death the Soviet regime, general nationalization was prescribed on the ground that in war-time factories had better be in the hands of men loyal if not always competent than in the hands of disgruntled owners, most of whom would practice sabotage on the plant if thereby they might help the cause of the Whites [i.e, counterrevolutionaries]."[45]

The impact of this shift to what came to be called "war communism" was to be profound. All of the reasons for resisting it—unfortunately—were sound. The shift brought about economic chaos and, in a twist of irony, gravely undermined the power of the workers. In April there was one nationalization measure, 7 in May, but an average of 170 a month from July to October. Although in June only 357 enterprises in total had been nationalized, the figure stood at 860 in September, including entire industries—mining, transport, electricity, oil, rubber, sugar, etc. "This expropriation of industry, verging ever closer to total nationalization," wrote Victor Serge, "placed an increasingly numerous population of workers within the responsibility of the Socialist State, and compelled it hastily to establish a body of functionaries, managers and administrators who could not be recruited straight away from among the working class. The bureaucracy was born, and was rapidly becoming a threat." From 1918 to 1919, the government apparatus had grown from 114,539 to 529,841. In roughly the same period the Bolshevik organization, renamed the Communist Party, grew from 115,000 to 251,000. "The functionaries were thus far more numerous than the party membership," Serge noted, "and they infiltrated into the ranks of the party."[46] This was accompanied by the collapse of the economy, the spread of famine, the brutalizing Civil War, which all combined to make war communism a devastating and authoritarian experience, suffused with a desperate heroism and commitment to revolutionary ideals, but no less tragic for all that.

Here we can offer only a few indications of the dimensions of the economic disaster. "Such a decline in the productive forces not of a little community, but of an enormous society of a million people . . . is unprecedented in the history of humanity," according to Bolshevik economist and historian Leonid Kritsman. Alexei Rykov, the Bolshevik president of the Supreme Council of National Economy, reported that from 1918 to 1919 the number of nationalized factories and works rose from 1,125 to about 4,000, which constituted the bulk of the industrial concerns of Soviet Russia, but that by the beginning of 1920 half of these had been forced to close, adding: "The number of operatives is estimated approximately at 1,000,000, which is between one third and one fifth of the numbers of the proletariat in 1914." Victor Serge reports that "the working class was showing numerous symptoms of exhaustion and demoralization," which is not surprising given the fact, for example, that the purchase of food in late 1918 absorbed seven-tenths of the workers' earnings, compared with the previous norm of half. The portion of workers' income separate from their wage earnings had risen from 3.5 percent in 1913 to 38 percent in 1918. "What were the sources of these extras? Simply theft from factories and warehouses." Serge added that the working class's "best sons had left its ranks for the front line or for work in Soviet institutions," and that "famine was forcing it close to the peasants," the class from which many workers had originally come, with many returning to the countryside in search of food. "Production was very low, and the factories lived as best they could, idle more than half the time, and riddled with theft. Raw materials and fuel were lacking and discipline practically non-existent." The stark decline in production is clear in the following figures, given in millions of poods (1 pood = 36.113 pounds): from 1913 to 1918, coal production fell from 1,738 to 731; iron ore, from 57,887 to 1,686; cast iron, from 256 to 31.5; steel, from 259 to 24.5; rails, from 39.4 to 1.1. An index measuring industrial and agricultural production indicates that the former fell by 70 percent, the latter by 40 percent. In Moscow, 1913 saw 23.1 deaths per thousand people, while 1919 saw 45.4 per thousand. The transportation system, vital to any economy, was in shambles—60 percent of the country's railway engines were in need of repair; productivity in transport had fallen by at least 50 percent while running costs had increased by 150 percent. All of this is aside from (but not unrelated to) the millions of people who perished in the famine.[47]

Eyewitness Arthur Ransome, a sympathetic correspondent from the *Manchester Guardian*, gave a vivid sense of how the food crisis affected Moscow—particularly in relation to how *he* was able to eat. He was given a ticket that allowed him to secure his first meal in one of the National Kitchens (replacing private restaurants) that had been set up throughout the city. "The dinner consisted of a plate of soup, and a very small portion of something else," he observed. After he secured a room in a modest hotel, he soon received a card that entitled him to purchase (for a modest amount) one—and only one—dinner daily, between 2:00 and 7:00 p.m., which was "a plate of very good soup, together with a second course of a scrap of meat or fish. . . . Living hungrily through the morning, at two o'clock I used to experience definite relief in the knowledge that now at any moment I could have my meal." Periodically, other delicacies such as a pot of jam or a small quantity of Ukrainian sausage were made available for purchase. Addressing the emergence of an illegal black-market system in which food was selling for exorbitant prices, Ransome commented: "It is obvious that abolition of the card system would mean that the rich would have enough and the poor nothing." A Communist explained to Ransome that the black-market speculation would end when everyone was able to get enough to eat through the card system. "And when will you be able to do that?" The answer: "As soon as the war ends, and we can use our transport for peaceful purposes." Ransome also chatted with the chambermaid who tidied his room: "I asked her how she liked the new regime. She replied that there was not enough to eat, but that she felt freer." In an overheard conversation between two workers on the street one night, one said: "If only it were not for the hunger." The other responded: "But when will that change?"[48]

In this period, the former Bolshevik Party (now Communist Party) and the emerging political system were altered almost beyond recognition. "The party's democratic norms of 1917, as well as its almost libertarian and reformist profile of early 1918," writes Stephen Cohen, "gave way to a ruthless fanaticism, rigid authoritarianism, and pervasive 'militarization' of life on every level.[49] Much more than party norms gave way. The factory committees, trade unions, and soviets were also transformed. The political pluralism of left-wing parties and currents that had flourished up to June 1918 didn't survive inside these proletarian institutions. To a large extent, the widely proclaimed "workers' democracy" slogan became an empty one.

This was not a simple or absolute change, but rather a process that contained contradictions and countervailing tendencies, to which we will give attention in the next chapters. Nor was the rapid elimination of the mixed economy the only causal factor. There was also a civil war, a foreign invasion, and an economic blockade, not to mention a drought plus the loss of rich farmlands and industrial areas to Germany through the Brest-Litovsk treaty. But the premature elimination of the mixed economy was a major factor in creating the disaster that befell the young Soviet Republic.

In much of the discussion of nationalizations and workers' control during the early period of Bolshevik rule, many scholars give considerable attention to the question of "democratic control from below" versus "productivist centralization from above." Under the actual circumstances, the debate seems irrelevant. Maurice Dobb commented that "when a group of workers took over an enterprise . . . they would tend to neglect wider social interests and even to develop a kind of proprietorial feeling of their own," and sometimes this was accompanied by an alluring utopian-libertarian impulse that undermined workshop discipline and industrial productivity. Lenin's wife, Krupskaya, recounted a daytime encounter with a woman worker who, when asked what shift she worked, answered: "None of us are working today. We had a meeting yesterday evening, everyone was behind with her domestic work at home, so we voted to knock off today. We're the bosses now, you know." Even for more disciplined, politically conscious workers, there were serious problems. Under the management of local factory committees, made up of well-meaning but managerially inexperienced workers, the enterprises "were frequently cut off from their former markets and sources of supply," with the result that "the ordinary links between economic units were largely broken down," and the idea of a democratically planned economy was translated into a reality of dreadful chaos. But a top-down approach of central planning provided no solution. "The attempt to nationalize everything from locomotive works to public baths," wrote William Henry Chamberlin, "and to provision the population through state agencies with everything from bread to mushrooms inevitably led to an enormous, unwieldy and incompetent bureaucracy, which stifled all creative initiative and often led to bungling misuse and neglect of the slender resources which the country possessed." Here again, as Lenin had warned, there was the woeful lack of knowledge and expertise, what Chamberlin termed "so much inevitable incompetence and mismanagement, as a result of the sudden influx of uneducated and untrained men into the higher posts of state administration."[50] No matter which way we look at it, no matter what our preference—local initiative or central planning or some hypothetical synthesis—the rapid nationalization of the economy spelled disaster.

One can argue that, under the circumstances, the Bolsheviks had no choice. Unfortunately, sometimes the Bolsheviks themselves did not acknowledge that this was a painful but necessary expedient. "Everything was swept along in a turbulent current, flooded with revolutionary enthusiasm," Bolshevik minister of culture Anatoly Lunacharsky later recalled. "It was necessary above all to give full voice to our ideals and ruthlessly crush whatever did not accord with them. It was difficult to speak about half measures then, about stages, about approaching our ideal step by step. That was taken to be opportunism, even by the most 'cautious.'"[51] Victor Serge wrote:

> The social system in these years was later called "War Communism." At the time it was called simply "Communism," and anyone who, like myself, went so far as to consider it purely temporary was looked upon with disdain. Trotsky had just written that this system would last over several decades if the transition

to a genuine, unfettered Socialism was to be assured. Bukharin was writing his work on *The Economy in the Period of Transition,* whose schematic Marxism aroused Lenin's ire. He considered the present mode of organization to be final. And yet, all the time it was becoming simply impossible to live within it: impossible, not of course for the administrators, but for the mass of the population.[52]

Looking back on this period, Lenin self-critically commented: "In estimating the prospects of development we in most cases—I can scarcely recall an exception—started out with an assumption, perhaps not always openly expressed but always tacitly implied, that we would be able to proceed straight away with socialist construction. . . . We assumed that we could proceed straight to socialism without a preliminary period in which the old economy would be adapted to socialist economy." These comments were made to explain the abandonment of war communism in favor of what came to be called the New Economic Policy (NEP). Dobb described NEP as aiming "to re-establish the proper relationship between the State and its environment which had been rudely broken in June 1918 by the needs of civil war," adding that it "was only new so far as it represented a return to peace after three years of war. It was a return to the path which had been trodden in the spring of 1918."[53] There's an element of truth here, yet Dobb's point is profoundly misleading. There could be no going back. Too much had been destroyed, too many had been killed or horribly injured, too many patterns and policies and precedents had been established. The world, the Russian working class, the Soviet Republic, the Bolsheviks themselves—all had been transformed. Certain possibilities had been eliminated, and qualitatively new problems had been created to confront the revolutionaries—especially problems that they had helped to create, such as the premature socialization of the economy.

The destruction of the mixed economy in 1918 was a disaster. This was matched only by the disaster of Bolshevik Russia's isolation resulting from the failure of socialist revolutions in other countries (especially those that were industrially advanced, such as Germany). Taken together, these two calamities—isolation and premature economic "radicalization"—would be, along with the militarism generated by foreign invasion and brutal civil war, the primary causes of the Soviet Republic becoming a *dictatorship* in the narrow sense of the word.

This dictatorship would persist even with the return to a variant of the mixed economy represented by the implementation of the New Economic Policy.

Workers, Peasants, Cadres

In early 1921, William Z. Foster—a sharp-eyed syndicalist and famed US strike leader seeking a new and more profound meaning for his life—went to Soviet Russia. When he returned to the United States, making his way into the new Communist movement, he sought to employ his perceptions and sensibilities into *The Russian Revolution,* a thick pamphlet issued by the Trade Union Educational League. Included in the pamphlet are related but contradictory narratives reflecting the reality with which he engaged in his journey of discovery.[54]

"The present government of Russia is what the Communists term a dictatorship of the proletariat," he wrote. "This means that the workers have become the ruling class in Russia, and the intention is that they shall remain such, until, through the operations of the new Communist institutions, social class lines are wiped out by all the people physically fit becoming actual producers." Foster went on, deeper in the pamphlet, to define that dramatic term in a quite different way—going beyond the theoretical construct to describe more of what he actually saw:

> The dictatorship of the proletariat, as expressed by the small, strongly organized Communist Party, came into existence because of the general unpreparedness of the masses. Since the various social institutions, made up in the main of these knowing elements, could not function spontaneously in a revolutionary manner, the Communist minorities in them felt compelled to find a way, through organization, discipline, and militancy, to make them do so.[55]

Foster emphasized that the Communist dictatorship was temporary: the elimination of "ignorance and general social backwardness" would make "the dictatorship gradually disappear," and in time the ultimate Communist goal of "a non-government society would be arrived at." While political parties of "the capitalists, aristocrats, and their many hangers-on" were "outlaws," he recorded milder treatment toward what he termed "proletarian parties," among whom he counted the Left-Socialist Revolutionaries, the Mensheviks, and the anarchists. They had been subjected to restrictions and, in some cases, outright repression. "No one deplores more than the Communists this rigid suppression of the opposition, especially honest working class opposition," he wrote. "But it is a supreme necessity of the revolution, something without which the latter could not survive." This was because of the life-and-death struggle against the counterrevolution. "Organized opposition to the Government is forbidden, but individuals talk as freely as in any country in the world," he stressed. "In Russia I heard people criticize the Government more freely than in any country I have ever been in." He made explicit reference to Menshevik, anarchist, and Socialist Revolutionary delegates at the Moscow Soviet denouncing the mistreatment of some of their comrades in the wake of the Kronstadt rebellion, and a Russian anarchist vigorously polemicizing against Communist policy at a session of the Red Trade Union International.[56]

This account has layers of significance. It gives a sense of what an experienced labor activist just embracing Communism (a) wanted to believe, (b) was led to believe by early Russian Communists who were introducing him to their country, and (c) was able to believe based on what he observed in the early Soviet Republic. It also highlights (d) what did *not* come to pass, as well as suggesting (e) what *might have been* if history had taken different turns.

As we sort through the diverse possibilities and "might-have-beens," as well as divergent and contradictory trends and interactions in what actually happened within the historical process that was the Russian Revolution, we need to push against turning such categories as "worker" or "peasant" or "cadre" into simplistic abstractions. Actual human beings, when we place them into such categories (which happens as one develops political, social, and historical analyses), can lose their unique individual qualities as they are blended into some collective entity. They can also all too easily be transformed into some romanticized or vilified construct, preventing us from understanding dynamic realities and potentialities.

Michael Haynes has usefully challenged the recent tendency among conservative historians (e.g., Richard Pipes) as well as some more liberal-minded social historians (e.g., Orlando Figes) to return to a variant of the "grey masses" or "dark masses" conceptualization of Russian peasants and workers. Such historians argue that, given the natural violence and brutality of the lower classes, efforts to generate popular mobilizations to establish "rule by the people" inevitably turn into—to quote an old parody lyric sung to the tune of "Battle Hymn of the Republic"—"arson, rape and bloody murder when the Red Revolution comes." Or as the Russian liberal historian, and leader of the Kadets, Pavel Milyukov, put it: "If the Revolution should come, it will not be so much an uprising as a hateful mutiny. The rabble will be let loose." Yet as Haynes notes, and Christopher Read documents, this vision of popular mayhem unleashed sometimes comes close to being the opposite of the truth.[57]

Of course, it is possible to make all kinds of generalizations about the masses. In the late 1920s, Joshua Kunitz contrasted how nineteenth-century writers such as Ivan Turgenev, Leo Tolstoy, and Nikolai Nekrasov described the peasants with how such writers as Chekov and Gorky described them in the early twentieth century—earlier writers "tended to sentimentalize, idealize, and well-nigh canonize the muzhik [peasant]" as "the store-house of all that was wholesome, religious, and solid in Russia," while later writers "began to harp on the unmitigated backwardness, ignorance, and brutality of the village, on the utter stupidity, servility, and pettiness of the muzhik."[58] And he showed that the working class could be subjected to sweepingly heroic generalizations by early Soviet writers as well, as with the V. Kirillov poem "We," written shortly after the October Revolution:

> *We, the countless, redoubtable legions of Toil,*
> *We've conquered vast spaces of oceans and lands,*
> *Illumined great cities with suns of our making,*
> *Fired our souls with proud flames of revolt.*
>
> *Gone are our tears, our softness forgotten,*
> *We banished the perfume of lilac and grass,*
> *We exalt electricity, steam and explosives,*
> *Motors and sirens and iron and brass. . . .*
>
> *Our souls fused with metal, part of our engines,*
> *We unlearned to wish for and dream of the sky.*
> *It is here on this earth that we want to be happy,*
> *To feed all the hungry, to hush their long cry. . . .*
>
> *O poets and aesthetes, curse, curse the great Demos,*
> *Kiss the fragments of yesterday on the soles of its feet,*
> *Shed tears over ruined and shattered old temples,*
> *While the free and the brave a new beauty shall greet.*
>
> *Our arms, our muscles cry out for vast labors,*
> *The pain of creation glows hot in our breast,*
> *United, we sweeten all life with our honey,*
> *Earth takes a new course at our mighty behest.*
>
> *We love life, and the turbulent joys that intoxicate,*
> *We are hard, and no anguish our spirit can thaw.*
> *We—all, We—in all, We—hot flames that regenerate,*
> *We ourselves, to ourselves, are God, Judge, and Law.*[59]

Social realities such as social classes—collectivities of human beings, people who happen to be part of one or another class—are more complex and diverse than the poem suggests. One aspect of this complexity is generational. Both those who are politically or socially conservative and those of a more revolutionary bent tend to grow older with the passage of time, and they often find that younger innovators (excited by new challenges and possibilities) see their elders' accumulated wisdom and insight as being passé, stodgy, irrelevant, or worse.

One aspect of this generational divide is highlighted within the early Soviet regime's Commissariat of Enlightenment (commonly known by its Russian abbreviation, Narkompros). Heading it was Anatoly Lunacharsky, "a large, untidy man with pince-nez and a benevolent expression," animated by both poetic and tolerant qualities, excited by experiment and modernism, insistent on openness and diversity, and resistant to the repression of *any* cultural trends (traditional as well as radical). Narkompros was an incredibly innovative institution, described by Sheila Fitzpatrick as "incoherent, rambling, malfunctioning, over-staffed with middle-aged intellectuals and under-staffed with proletarian Communists."[60] Within Communist ranks, younger comrades advanced sharp organizational and ideological challenges to the "middle-aged intellectual" approach.

Evgraf Litkens and Platon Kerzhentsev are prominent examples of such younger challengers. The leather-jacketed Civil War veteran Litkens was assigned by the Communist Party to the Commissariat of Enlightenment to help make it more efficient. "Military virtues of discipline, organization and tough-mindedness," as Fitzpatrick puts it, combined in him with the self-presentation "as a hard-headed practical revolutionary, making no concession to sentiment or intellectual self-doubt." Even more harshly, Kerzhentsev—despite multiple political and diplomatic assignments—was vociferous in his assaults on what he saw as the all-too-tolerant ethos represented by Lunacharsky's generation. "It has long been time to bring the fantasy of a few of our Communist poets into the strict but necessary limits of Party discipline," he proclaimed in a direct assault on Lunacharsky in 1920. "Literature for us is a weapon of political education," he insisted, and if independent writers did not give in to "ideological persuasion," then "we do not renounce other methods of struggle, such as taking individual plays off the repertory, forbidding the printing of their works, etc." This approach, which would be triumphant in later years, was taken up by a rising layer of even younger writers, critics, and Party activists dedicated to fighting against "bourgeois attitudes" in the arts and who, as literary historian Marc

Slonim puts it, "behaved like contenders in a civil war, transferring its ruth-lessness and intransigence to the literary field." Not only literature, but all of the arts, academic disciplines, and education in general were to be subor-dinated to this orientation.[61]

This approach was alien to the dominant trend in the Commissariat of Enlightenment, which was basically shared by Lenin himself, who insist-ed: "Proletarian culture must be a legitimate development of all reserves of knowledge mankind has accumulated under the pressure of capitalist society, of landlord society, of bureaucrat society." As Lunacharsky explained, "The laboring masses thirst after education," and the regime's responsibility was to offer "schools, books, theatres, and so on" to facilitate "the people themselves, consciously or unconsciously" so that they evolve "their own culture" under their own democratic control. "But the proletariat must draw on the art of the past in order to produce its own." One of Lunacharsky's closest associates, belonging to the same revolutionary generation as he, was M. N. Pokrovskii, an experienced academic and fierce partisan of Marxist historiography—but also a partisan of scholarly professionalism. Another was Nadezhda Krupska-ya. Immersed in educational efforts from her late teens, she was later cen-tral to the organizational functioning of pre-1917 Bolshevism—"observant, shrewd, immune to flattery, suspicious of pretensions." She was absolutely dedicated to popular education in the spirit of John Dewey and Leo Tolstoy. Krupskaya was six years Lunacharsky's senior, but her sensibilities and her re-lationship with Lenin drew the commissar close to her, and he saw her as "the soul of Narkompros." These three were among the older layer of seasoned, revolutionary Marxist intellectuals. They were resistant to "revolutionary" and "practical" shortcuts to knowledge and culture, which were becoming in-creasingly fashionable among younger cadres in Communist ranks. Krupska-ya "was all for minimizing central authority," according to biographer Robert McNeal. She also complained: "The teachers are being cross-examined about their beliefs in a most detailed way, which is an inadmissible violation of free-dom of conscience."[62]

There was yet another generational divide on cultural questions—with challenges posed to classical and traditional creations by the Russian and So-viet avant-garde, such as the poet Vladimir Mayakovsky, the theater director Vselovod Meyerhold, artists Alexander Rodchenko and Varvara Stepano-va, and others who saw what they offered as the true cultural expression of the revolutionary Russia. While appreciative of the avant-garde innovators, Lunacharsky resisted their pressure to grant them a privileged position as the "official" artistic representatives of the Soviet Republic. "He encouraged Communist artists and scholars," as Fitzpatrick notes, "but not in persecution of their colleagues or bids for monopoly." It is interesting to consider Lenin's views as well. His cultural tastes tended to be relatively conservative. As he explained to the seasoned German Communist leader Klara Zetkin (who tended to agree with him): "It is beyond me to consider the products of expressionism, futurism, cubism and other 'isms' the highest manifestation of artistic genius. I do not understand them. I experience no joy from them." But far from seeking to repress them, he said in the next breath: "Yes dear Klara, it can't be helped. We're both old fogies. For us it is enough that we remain young and are among the foremost at least in matters concerning the revolution. But we won't be able to keep pace with the new art; we'll just have to come trailing behind." Adding that "our opinion on art is not the important thing," he emphasized: "Art belongs to the people. . . . For art to get closer to the people and the people to art we must start by raising general educational and cultural standards."[63]

The generational divide played out differently, and with interesting variations, below the lofty heights of the Commissariat of Enlightenment.

One finds, of course, a similar dynamic of the older leaders resisting what to them are questionable innovations by the less-experienced younger activists. Kunitz explains how many peasants distinguished between Bolsheviks (who had ended the war and allowed them to take the land from the nobles) and the troublesome Communists: "Bolsheviks . . . were those who stood for peace and the confiscation of land; Communists, those who used new-fangled words, attacked the Orthodox Church, the holy saints, the marriage rites, declared woman the equal of man, hailed the poorest peasant [as opposed to those who prospered] as the salt of the earth."[64] Wendy Goldman quotes a *chastushka* (popular short song) that articulates this view:

> *Comrades, your new laws*
> *Are really quite insane,*
> *It's clear they were devised*
> *By someone without a brain.*[65]

But she also notes that increasing numbers of young peasants—joining the Communist Youth and rebelling against the old ways—sang a variety of their own *chastushkas* that expressed quite different views. For example, on religion:

> *God, oh God,*

> *What are you doing?*
> *Instead of working,*
> *The Virgin Mary you're screwing.*[66]

Also on the status of women:

> *I no longer fear my husband,*
> *If we can't cooperate,*
> *I will take myself to court,*
> *And we will separate.*[67]

Sexual freedom:

> *When I was just a little girl*
> *Mama made me bed at home,*
> *But I bed down in the hay*
> *Now that I am grown.*[68]

The right to choose one's own marriage partner:

> *My sweetheart asked me to elope,*
> *But mama scared me so,*
> *Yet even if she hurt me,*
> *I would have to go.*

> *I will elope,*
> *I will make father weep,*
> *I will make father grieve,*
> *I'll take a cow and a sheep.*[69]

There were a number of influences stirring new thinking within the villages. "The twelve million peasants that Russia sent to forty fronts in the great wars [World War I and the Civil War] brought back to the village the ferment of new ideas—the new viewpoint," notes an eyewitness report on the villages by Albert Rhys Williams. Another eyewitness, Samuel N. Harper, who conducted a 1926 study visit, reported the development of three important institutions in the villages—the most important and influential was the Village Assembly (the persistent and spontaneously revitalized old *mir* or *obschina*); less influential but regime-backed was the village soviet (often inclined to defer to the *mir*); and supplementing both was the Peasant Society for Mutual Assistance. Initiated by the Communist Party during the famine of 1921, this third entity was initially designed to provide life-giving assistance from regions not affected by the famine to those that were; it later evolved into a broader self-help movement. "When we have Communism the whole state will be an enormous organization of mutual assistance of all mankind," said the Bolshevik ex-peasant Mikhail Kalinin, serving as the formal president of the Soviet Republic (a more or less figurehead position). "From this point of view the peasant committees of mutual assistance are schools of Communist statecraft for the peasants." This function entailed playing a broad social service role and increasingly important educational and cultural roles for peasants in the villages, but also assisting the increasing number of peasants who had occasion to travel to the cities. "One of the aims of the societies is to further collectivist practices among the peasants," explains Harper. The regime also made sure that the Communist youth organization, the Komsomol, "was given a special role of leadership [in these mutual assistance committees] in order to attract the younger element of the peasantry."[70]

Karl Borders identified the importance not only of the Komsomol branches in the countryside, but also of the Young Pioneers, modeled on the Scout movement in England and the United States but sporting red kerchiefs and interweaving deeper purposes with the hiking, camping, singing, and marching. "From this early age they are inculcated with the ideas of the Communist state and the continued class struggle." wrote Borders. "They are taught habits of neatness and cleanliness. They must not smoke. They are expected to help in every local social undertaking which their ages will permit." An even more active role fell to the somewhat older members of the Komsomol—organizing athletic and cultural activities, to be sure, as well as engaging in social service activities in the community, but also carrying out Communist educational work. They were essentially "protagonists of the soviet regime among the mass of young people."[71] Undoubtedly, such things help explain the proliferation of some of the *chastushkas* reported by Wendy Goldman.

But there were larger forces at play as well in bringing change to the "changeless village." Borders wrote: "There can be no doubt whatever that the Revolution tended to break up still further the old moral and social sanctions which throughout the world were disturbed by the [First World] War. The long drawn out War, civil war, blockade and famine of Russia contributed to an uncertainty and terror to life that brought too early maturity to the children who lived through it all." Some felt the despair expressed by one particular twelve-year-old orphan: "I don't know what I am going to do now. My life is already ruined." Some clung tighter than ever to the old ways. Some rebelled violently, destructively, often self-destructively. "There are plenty of people to tell you, from the village priest to perfectly good Communists, that the youth of the country is going to the devil," said Borders. And yet, as we have seen, some were drawn to the new revolutionary faith.[72] Nothing would ever be the same.

Visiting his old village in the early 1920s, after almost two decades, an amazed Maurice Hindus compared his memories of the way things used to be for peasant children with the new stirrings that were beginning to animate small but growing circles of village youth:

> The world outside scarcely existed for them. Few, very few, ever saw a newspaper, a book, a magazine. Few, very few, went to school, none to college. They lived like their fathers and grandfathers and great-grandfathers before them, in filth, poverty, darkness, with no ambition, no hope, no stimulus to animate them, save their one immemorial dream of someday coming into possession of the landlord's estates. Year after year, generation after generation, the same monotony, the same drudgery, the same dullness. But now? Their imagination had been stirred. They were naïve enough in their outgoing faith in the miraculous power of the Revolution to rid the world forever of want, inequality, sorrow—of all evil and all woe. They knew so little of the perversity of human nature. They gave no thought to forces which some day would bring them no little disillusionment. They were so young and so inexperienced in the ways of man and the world. But their minds teemed with new concepts, new ideas, new beliefs. They *were* aware of a world outside of their village. They *were* awake to the darkness around them and to the need of ushering in enlightenment.[73]

The generational divide is suggested in the shifting attitudes in the village toward the practice of smallpox vaccinations. Williams described his own frustrating discussions with older peasants: "The germ theory sounded far-fetched and fanciful. Better their own theory: To each man his destined lot, and no escaping it; it's fate that metes out good and evil, life, death and smallpox." The idea of preventing disease by scratching people with a needle seemed ridiculous, especially when compared with traditional remedies—"the old charms and conjurations that have stood the test of time," capable of warding off the evil spirits that were obviously the cause of most diseases. "It has happened that the medical corps sent to relieve an epidemic have been taken as the evil spirits themselves," Williams reported. "The peasants sought to get rid of the disease by killing the doctors." In other cases, medical workers were simply locked out, accused of being the Antichrist, with screams: "Go away, you devils! Why do you come here to kill our children?" And yet increasing numbers of older children and young adults, especially those with more experience out in the world, were tipping rural culture in another direction. "The old beliefs . . . are dying. Faith in the old incantations is passing with the passing generation." Williams reported that soon "people on horse and foot" were pushing on to the vaccination center, where "a long line of peasants, sleeves rolled up" were being systematically vaccinated by a white-aproned physician's assistant. Smallpox vaccinations became obligatory in the Soviet Republic, with thirty-one laboratories devoted exclusively to the preparation of vaccines. While there had been 72,236 cases of smallpox reported in 1913, the number had shot up to 152,094 by 1921—yet by 1924, the number was down to 26,744.[74]

Veteran US educator Lucy Wilson—observing "the obvious alertness of peasant children"—suggested that "their life experiences, particularly their first-hand contact with nature, have served admirably as the first school for their mental development." But there were other influences as well. She recounted one journalist's account of riding to pasture with village boys and girls anxious to absent themselves "from the old people who had learned little from the great events of recent years," while "the younger generation was very different, for they had been in the Red Army, they had read books, and they had listened to lectures. None of them, not even the little ones, believed in ghosts or spirits, water nymphs or house goblins."[75] Health worker Anna Haines also commented on the "outside influences" in this cultural revolution:

> More than three-fourths of the Russians are people living in small villages in the country. Their houses, animal sheds and barnyards are still built and maintained after the fashion of their forefathers, but down in the village reading-room, a sort of social center which has appeared almost everywhere within the last ten years, are several disturbing pictures on the wall. On holidays and winter afternoons many of the younger people drift in and read, often with amusement, that one should sleep with windows open, sink one's drinking water well somewhere else than most conveniently to the cattle trough, and that the ever-present malaria comes from a mosquito and not from God as a punishment to this evil generation. And then an ex-soldier, who may be reading in another corner, tells them that these things are so, that he has traveled much and learned the truth; and the next few hours are given over to reminiscences and to forecasting of the future of Russia, with electricity in every house, and water out of hydrants, and tractors.[76]

The generation gap could also been seen among industrial workers. A sixteen-year-old foundry worker, Victor Kravchenko, noted it while listening to lunchtime agitators from the Communist Party in 1921: "The older workers for the most part ignored them, but the younger men and women listened intently. For us it offered hope in a time of general distress and pessimism." He was also attracted to the factory club, "decorated with lithographs of Lenin, Trotsky, Marx and Engels and slogans in crude white letters on strips of red bunting." He adds: "I was caught between the skepticism at home and my own thirst for a faith."[77] He didn't join the group right away, but became increasingly engaged in its activities and meetings.

Kravchenko's father had been a working-class revolutionary, arrested and imprisoned in earlier years, and initially an eloquent supporter of the 1917 revolution. But he quickly became critical, explaining to his son: "I have been fighting to overthrow Tsarism. For freedom, for plenty, not for violence and vengeance. We should have free elections and many parties. If one party dominates, it's the end." His son asked: "What are you, papa? A Menshevik, Bolshevik, a Social Revolutionary?" The father responded: "None of these, Vitya. Always remember this: that no slogan, no matter how attractive, is any indication of the real policy of any political party once it comes to power."[78] Nonetheless, the son eventually decided to join the Komsomol, which (years later) he described in this way:

> Now life had for me an urgency, a purpose, a new and thrilling dimension of dedication to a cause. I was one of the elite, chosen by History to lead my country and the whole world out of darkness into the socialist light. This sounds pretentious, I know, yet that is how we talked and felt. There might be cynicism and self-seeking among some of the grown-up Communists, but not in our circle of ardent novitiates.
>
> My privileges, as one of the elect, were to work harder, to disdain money and foreswear personal ambitions. I must never forget that I am a Komsomol first, a person second. The fact that I had joined up in a mining region, in an area of "industrial upsurge," seemed to me to add a sort of mystic significance to the event. . . .
>
> There was no longer much margin of time for petty amusements. Life was filled with duties—lectures, theatricals for the miners, Party "theses" to be studied and discussed. We were aware always that from our midst must come the Lenins and Bukharins of tomorrow. We were perfecting ourselves for the vocation of leadership; we were the acolytes of a sort of materialist religion.[79]

There were other youth of this period who observed the same qualities in their Communist peers. "The word 'comrade' meant to be closer than family," recalled Mikhail Baitalsky, remembering "boys and girls with sunken eyes in darkened faces [who] studied in literary circles and classes for the rudiments of political knowledge. They nibbled at the granite of science and called for world revolution. We said the words 'world revolution' as often as children say 'mama' and just as easily, without self-righteous pretensions."[80] Baitalsky's description—stressing the qualities of "sincerity and democracy"—matches Kravchenko's:

Our exhilaration with the ideas of the revolution, our feelings toward Lenin, our hatred for the bourgeoisie—all this came from the depths of our soul. One might say to me: You believed in false doctrines. But I am not examining here whether the theories were true or not, only the sincerity of our behavior.

We were sincere above all because we formulated our views in absolute freedom. Those who did not share them did not join the Komsomol.... Komsomol membership brought no privileges... The Komsomol was a voluntary organization and, therefore, was not based on falsehood and hypocrisy. It was based on a Communist faith—pure and unsullied—probably much like the faith of the first pre-Christian societies on the shores of the Dead Sea, with their doctrine of justice and their sacred writings that they read many hours each day. In those days we spent whole evenings in our club without being bored....

Democracy is directly related to sincerity in human relations. I speak not about democracy as a social institution but about democracy as an element of social norms.... It had one important peculiarity: We viewed ourselves as people of the future. This consciousness was not expressed with any solemnity of purpose or arrogance. On the contrary, it seemed natural and ordinary. For us, a commitment to democracy was like being aware of having a kind of mission—a marvelous mission for universal human equality.[81]

The kind of psychology, consciousness, and organizational dynamics that Kravchenko and Baitalsky describe regarding the Komsomol of the years 1919–23 captures a much larger reality within the Russian working-class movement. Mark Steinberg explores such things in an illuminating essay covering the prerevolutionary period in "Vanguard Workers and the Morality of Class." By "vanguard workers" he refers not to those in a specific organization, but to a broader layer within the working class that may be drawn into membership in one or another group—whether it be Menshevik, Bolshevik, Socialist Revolutionary, anarchist (or in the case of Kravchenko's father, none). Steinberg refers to what he calls a "moral judgment," which is central to the way that workers crystallize from a class *in itself* to a class *for itself*, employing a conceptualization articulated by Marx—that is, what is sometimes referred to as "class consciousness."[82]

"Morally literate workers such as these, who were present in most Russian industries during the late nineteenth and early twentieth centuries, were not 'typical' of their class, but played a central role in the collective life of their class, especially in its conscious self-formation as a class," Steinberg notes, commenting that often "vanguard workers did not so much speak *for* other workers as to preach *to* them, challenging them to think and act in unaccustomed ways." Such a dynamic might take the form of relatively insulated, self-important, self-righteous groups marked off from the resistant masses.

"These worker activists were deeply self-conscious, and thus perceived various boundaries between themselves and a majority of workers." But the phenomenon became more interesting "starting in 1905 as the class-conscious
vanguard was given a larger legal arena—trade unions and legal labor press—
and as its message began to attract a mass following (including among them
worker activists who had defected from the camp of class collaboration, as
they now branded it, to the camp of class struggle)." An aspect of the ongoing
"preaching" involved a down-to-earth critique of all that was "ignorant, im-
moral, drunken, and lacking in culture" among their coworkers—particularly
those "ordinary workers" who might prefer "getting drink at the local tavern
to spending . . . time with 'books, theater, and a lively and absorbing discussion
in a close circle of comrades.'" Distinguished from the ordinary worker, these
"conscious workers" helped to articulate the sense that, as a working-class poet
of the late nineteenth century had put it, "we men are not animals, not dumb
beasts."[83] Steinberg elaborates:

> The idea of the human person, . . . of innate human worth and hence natural
> rights, remained at the heart of workers' language of protest in 1905 and after. As
> before, outspoken workers continued to complain of offenses to workers' human
> dignity. They protested that for too long workers had been treated as "animals,"
> "machines," and "slaves," "insulted," verbally abused, physically beaten, and ad-
> dressed as inferiors. The time had come, they said, for employers and supervi-
> sors "to respect the humanity in each human being" . . . , to remember that "those
> who work for them are people, the same if not better than themselves." As was
> common among many other groups of workers, and other subordinate groups,
> injustice was defined first of all as indignity.[84]

Over time, a number of such "conscious workers" became *cadres* in working-
class movements and organizations. The term *cadre* can be understood as one
who has social and political knowledge, who can win people to ideas of what's
what, who can size up a situation, who can speak well about problems and
solutions and how to get from the one to the other, who knows how to make
and distribute leaflets and organize successful meetings, who can work with
others and draw others into the work, and who can transmit all of these skills
to others.

Obviously, not all conscious workers and not all cadres are the same, nor
do they all have the same outlook on vitally important questions. This comes
through in discussions between Kravchenko and his father in the 1920s:

> The passing years had not reconciled my father to the Communists. He was
> willing to acknowledge that many of them were honest and earnest, but the re-

ality of revolution still had too little resemblance to the dream of his youth. He never interfered with my Komsomol activities and at bottom was pleased that I was carving a place for myself in the new environment. But he could not refrain from bitter comment, now and then, on the contrast between the ample life of the officials and top engineers and the misery of the plain workers.

"We talk about unity, son," he would say, "and equality. But look how Comrade N. . . . lives, with his big apartment and motor car and good clothes; then look at the barracks where the new workers from the village are packed like sardines. A clean room and decent food in the administration restaurant, but anything is good enough for the workers' restaurant. . . ."

"Give us time, Papa," I would plead. "So many problems to be solved at once."

"I know about the problems. But I also know that the distance between the upper classes and the lower classes is growing bigger, not smaller. Power is a dangerous thing, Vitya."[85]

The issue of inequality and power abuse was, as we have seen, linked in the father's mind with the question of political freedoms and the need for a multiparty system—what Baitalsky had referred to as a larger "democracy as a social institution" in his reflection on democracy and sincerity within the Komsomol. He himself came to conclude, based on later experience, that the one was eroded and undermined without the other: "One-party rule inevitably led to the need for maximum homogeneity of thought within the ruling party itself." On the issue of material inequality, Baitalsky tells us: "In Lenin's time, there existed a party maximum pay. . . . *Partmaximum* means this: For the same post, a member of the party and a non-party specialist are to receive the same pay; but a Communist has the right to keep only such a sum as shall not exceed a certain figure established by the Central Committee." He notes that "by the end of the 1920s, the *partmaximum* for Moscow was 250 rubles, the average salary of a skilled worker," but that in that period enforcement of the *partmaximum* began to erode, and by 1932 it was totally abolished. "The principle of self-restraint for leading worker-Communists was gradually replaced by the principle of privileges."[86]

It was in this period, however, when young Kravchenko finally decided to take the step of joining the Communist Party. It is worth considering the reasons he gave to his father for taking this step, and also worth taking a look specifically at the leading cadre from the Communist Party most responsible for him taking this step: Comrade Lazarev, an intellectual about thirty years old who gave compelling lectures on problems of socialism. (Actually, Lazarev had recruited him, initially, to the Komsomol.) But first let us consider Kravchenko's explanation to his father for joining the party:

I know that there are plenty of shortcomings, careerism, swinishness and hardship in practical everyday life. I don't like those things any more than you do. But I look on them as phases which will pass. The job of turning a primitive country into a modern industrialized socialist state is gigantic. It can't be done without mistakes and even injustices. But I don't want to stand aside and criticize. I want to work honestly inside the Party, fighting against evil and sustaining what is good.[87]

The eloquent and friendly mentor who recruited him lived, temporarily, in a small apartment away from his actual home, but sought to give a "home-like" quality to his temporary lodgings "in a spotlessly clean room. The divan was covered with a gay rug; books neatly arranged on the desk between bookends; a few flowers in a colored pitcher." On one wall there were family pictures; on another, there were "framed photographs of Lenin and Marx and between them—this was the touch that warmed me and won me over, though I did not know exactly why—the familiar picture of Leo Tolstoy in older age, in the long peasant tunic, his thumbs stuck into the woven belt." Kravchenko describes their discussion in these modest but warm surroundings:

> We talked for hours that night, about books, the Party, the future of Russia. My place was with the Communist minority who must show the way, Lazarev said, and I ought to join the Komsomols and later the Party. Of course, he conceded, the Party wasn't perfect and perhaps its program wasn't perfect, but people are more important than programs.
>
> "If bright, idealistic young people like you stand aloof, what chance will there be?" he said. "Why not come closer to us and work for the common cause? You can help others by serving as an example of devotion to the country. Just look around you in the barracks—gambling, dirt, drunkenness, greed where there ought to be cleanliness, books, spiritual light. You must understand that there's a terrific task ahead of us, Augean stables to be cleaned. We must uproot the stale, filthy, unsocial past that's still everywhere, and for that we need good men. The heart of the question Vitya, is not only formal socialism but decency, education and a brighter life for the masses."
>
> I had been "pressured" by Communists before this. But now, for the first time, I was hearing echoes of the spirit that had suffused my childhood. I argued with Comrade Lazarev; I said I would think it over, but in fact I agreed with him and had already made up my mind.[88]

Kravchenko offers an account from a slightly earlier period during the Civil War that provides, in microcosm, a variety of "types" drawn to the Bolshevik cause. As a young worker, Kravchenko is one of many from his area drawn into the armed self-defense unit organized by his father and older workers. Also drawn in is Grachev, a simple and good-hearted semi-peasant who works as a stableman. In the swirl of confusion and conflict, the two of them meet up with a few others from the Red forces making their way through the area, led by the dedicated and idealistic Lihomanov. Among those in the group were a "gross-looking fellow" in a sailor's uniform who turned out to be a very capable fighter, and a good-looking woman of about thirty, serving as a nurse, who later tells Kravchenko that she had been the daughter of a high tsarist official who—like a significant number of youth from the upper classes—was drawn to the revolutionary cause. As she put it: "When the revolution occurred, I met it with my whole heart. All my life I have loved the plain people and wanted to help them. It was for them that I broke with my family and took courses in the medical school in Kharkov." While not approving of some of the violence on the revolutionary side, she concluded that "my work is healing, not shooting."[89]

The night after the small group of Reds defends itself from a violent attack from White forces, they put up in a small rural house. Kravchenko is awakened by the nurse's nearby screams when the sailor attempts to rape her. The presence of an awake Kravchenko causes the sailor to flee, muttering "dirty bourgeois!" at the weeping nurse. Contrasting the sailor to Lihomanov ("one of the real ones, a true idealist"), the nurse tells young Kravchenko: "We mustn't lose faith or renounce the struggles of thousands of honest men, men like Lihomanov, because of dark and bestial creatures like the man who attacked me tonight." She also commented that her attacker was not even a real sailor, picking up the uniform somewhere and wearing it "because it gave him a certain revolutionary prestige." When Kravchenko later tells Grachev what happened, his friend reflects: "Yes, Vitya, that nurse is right. There's good and bad, in the revolution as in everything. The question is: who will come out on top when the revolution settles down, the honest people or the beasts, the Lihomanovs or the fake sailors."[90]

The Bolshevik ideal conformed to the "honest" ones who won the hearts and minds of such young workers as Baitalsky, Kravchenko, and their friends. Near the end of the period we are examining, in his widely circulated articles on "The New Course," Trotsky explained: "A Bolshevik is not merely a disciplined person; he is a person who in each case and on each question forges a firm opinion of his own and defends it courageously and independently, not only against his enemies, but inside his own party." The Bolshevik leader explained that it was necessary to disagree with something one feels is wrong, even when other comrades, even leaders, disagree with him. "Today, perhaps, he will be in the minority in his organization. He will submit, because it is his party. But this does not always signify that he is in the wrong. Perhaps he saw or understood before the others did a new task or the necessity of a turn." Sometimes it was necessary to dissent: "He will persistently raise the question a second, a third, a tenth time, if need be. Thereby he will render his party a service, helping it to meet the new task fully armed or to carry out the necessary turn without organic upheavals, without factional convulsions."[91]

In the party there were, of course, all kinds. Ante Ciliga, a prominent Yugoslav Communist in Soviet Russia during the late 1920s, later recalled three young women who were active in the Komsomol. Two of them were working-class participants in a study group, one who sat in the front row and "was studying with zeal and success," the other in the back row "who saw everything in black." The latter "at every opportunity spoke of the workers' hard life," with examples of "the most heartbreaking incidents at the factory and at the home," challenging with "subdued indignation" the "contradictions between the workers' realities and the writings in books and papers." For her front-row antagonist, animated by a systematic optimism, "the masses" in the factories and villages were heroic abstractions who followed heroic leaders, and "all the 'shortcomings' and 'accidents' were ironed out by this official optimism." Various classmates were drawn more to one or the other. In contrast to both was the nineteen-year-old daughter of a party official—"beautiful, intelligent, energetic"—who worked in a factory while taking technical courses at night and, on occasion, carrying out "special assignments" with her husband abroad. "Was this not a couple from the vanguard?" Ciliga asked rhetorically. "But looking more closely one discovered the deepest corruption hidden beneath a veil of virtue." He went on to explain: "To that young woman nothing counted but her career and that of her husband. She had the gift of considering everything from the point of view of advancement in the administration."[92]

It was in this period that developments were underway, bringing some of the cadres into very different trajectories. Trotsky, from exile, described the culmination of one of these trajectories in 1932: "On the foundation of the dictatorship of the proletariat—in a backward country, surrounded by capitalists—for the first time a powerful bureaucratic apparatus has been created from among the upper layers of the workers, that is raised above the masses, that lays down the law to them, that has at its disposal colossal resources, that is bound together by an inner mutual responsibility, and that intrudes into the policies of a workers' government its own interests, methods, and regulations." Trotsky was merciless in describing the ex-working-class functionary:

"He eats and guzzles and procreates and grows himself a respectable potbelly. He lays down the law with a sonorous voice, handpicks from below people faithful to him, remains faithful to his superiors, prohibits others from criticizing himself, and sees in all of this the gist of the general line."[93]

5
GLOBAL CONTEXT

*T*he Russian Revolution can only be understood as part of a global upheaval. It was seen by Lenin as an element in a process spanning continents. "The Russian Revolution [of 1905] was followed by revolutions in
Turkey, Persia and China," he wrote in 1913. "It is in this era of storms and
their 'repercussions' in Europe that we are now living." He concluded: "The
frenzied arming and the policy of imperialism are turning modern Europe
into a 'social peace' which is more like a gunpowder barrel."[1]

If anything, Lenin's prophecy was understated. The First World War
broke out in August 1914—flaming through Europe as if it were a terrible
back draft from the long-violated colonies of the major European powers,
with Germany and Austria-Hungary (allied also with the Turkish-based
Ottoman Empire) engaged in a lethal combat with an alliance that included
Britain, France, Russia, and ultimately the United States. Before its conclusion in 1918, among the 65 million men mobilized to fight, there were about 9
million—one soldier out of seven—combat deaths, with an additional 5 million reported missing and 7 million suffering permanent disabilities (out of
approximately 21 million wounded). This was Total War, with the estimated
civilian deaths from the war exceeding the military casualties, with a total
real economic cost estimated at more than $3 trillion (in 2016 US dollars),
and with the horrendous wreckage of cities, farmlands, and countries, not to
mention the brutalization of life, leaving a lasting imprint on all that followed
in the twentieth century.[2]

"Imperialism, nationalism, and the dilemma of modern empire were at the core of World War I's origins," according to the perceptive and decidedly nonrevolutionary historian Dominic Lieven. As he insists, an understanding of modern *imperialism* and *empire* cannot be restricted simply to the quest "for colonial markets and raw materials in Asia, Africa, and the Americas"—it is also relevant to dynamics, conquests, and oppressions within Europe itself. Lieven's misperception that such Marxists as Lenin would have disagreed with such an expansive understanding of terms obscures an important truth, but the historian's key point here helps illuminate the context not only of the First World War but of the Russian Revolution.[3]

"Wars are . . . part of the very nature of capitalism," according to a resolution on "War and Militarism" adopted by the Socialist International (commonly known as the Second International) in 1907. "They will cease only when the capitalist system is abolished or when the enormous sacrifices in men and money required by advances in military technique, and the indignation aroused by the arms race, drive the peoples to abolish this system." The resolution was authored by Rosa Luxemburg and the Russian comrades/opponents (in a period of Bolshevik-Menshevik rapprochement) Lenin and Martov. Emphasizing that all socialists must "exert every effort in order to prevent its outbreak," the resolution concluded that "in case war should break out anyway, it is their duty to intervene for its speedy termination and to strive with all their power to utilize the economic and political crisis created by the war to rouse the masses and thereby hasten the downfall of capitalist class rule."[4] When war finally came, the Second International—beset by its own internal contradictions regarding sharp differences related to the interplay of reform and revolution, a largely uncomprehended process of bureaucratization, and a set of related accommodations to the capitalist status quo—fragmented under the impact of pro-war pressures. "The Socialist parties were by far the largest numerical component of the forces of movement inside each of the major European nations," notes Arno Mayer. He adds that the four major components into which they fragmented consisted of (1) "the right-wing revisionists" who had fully abandoned revolutionary perspectives, (2) the "Social Patriots" who sought to square Marxist perspectives with support for their own country's war effort, (3) the "Independent Socialists" who veered away from outright support for the war but were reluctant to separate from the first two fragments (which were in control of the bulk of the organized socialist movement), and (4) the "Revolutionary Socialists" whose priority was not unity with pro-war socialists—

they wanted no such unity—but adherence to the principles of the Socialist International's 1907 perspective.[5]

"Socialist leaders like Lenin and Rosa Luxemburg, who temperamentally and theoretically were committed to revolution as opposed to evolution, were extremely articulate on the dialectics of wartime destruction," writes Mayer. "Even though they were full of compassion for the innocent victims of bourgeois-capitalist wars, the Socialists considered all battles, whether political or military, national or international, as necessary stages in the unfolding world revolution." Something on the scale of the 1914–18 slaughter signified, as Lenin commented at its beginning, "the beginning of a new epoch."[6] One month after the eruption of the war, the Bolshevik central committee issued a statement that he composed, which sounded themes to which he would return more than once over the next four years:

> In all the advanced countries the war had placed on the order of the day the slogan of socialist revolution, a slogan that is the more urgent, the more heavily the burden of war presses upon the shoulders of the proletariat, and the more active its future role must become in the re-creation of Europe, after the horrors of the present "patriotic" barbarism in the conditions of the tremendous technological progress of large scale capitalism. The bourgeoisie's use of wartime laws to gag the proletariat makes it imperative for the latter to create illegal forms of agitation and organization. Let the opportunists "preserve" the legal organizations at the price of treachery to their convictions—the revolutionary Social Democrats will utilize the organizational experience and links of the working class so as to create illegal forms of struggle for socialism, forms appropriate to a period of crisis, not with the chauvinist bourgeoisie of their respective countries, but with the workers of all countries. The proletarian International has not gone under and will not go under. Notwithstanding all the obstacles, the masses of workers will create a new International.[7]

In his "Letters from Afar," as the February/March revolution was erupting, Lenin emphasized what he repeated over and over again in this period: "The imperialist war was bound, with objective inevitability, immensely to accelerate and intensify to an unprecedented degree the class struggle of the proletariat against the bourgeoisie; it was bound to turn into a civil war between the hostile classes."[8]

The Bolsheviks saw their revolution as only the beginning of a global insurgency. This is captured in "An Appeal to the Toiling, Oppressed, and Exhausted Peoples of Europe," issued by Leon Trotsky in his role as Commissar of Foreign Affairs upon the 1918 signing of the Treaty of Brest-Litovsk, terminating Russia's participation in the war:

After nearly three and a half years of uninterrupted slaughter, with no end in sight, the workers' and peasants' revolution in Russia has opened the way to peace. We have published the secret treaties. We shall continue publishing them in the immediate future. We have declared that these treaties will in no way bind the policy of the Soviet government. We have proposed to all nations the way of open agreement on the principle of the recognition for each nation, great or small, advanced or backward, of the right freely to determine its own destiny. We do not attempt to conceal the fact that we do not consider the existing capitalist governments capable of making a democratic peace. The revolutionary struggle of the toiling masses against the existing governments can alone bring Europe nearer to such a peace. Its full realization can only be guaranteed by the victorious proletarian revolution in all capitalist countries.[9]

For the celebrations taking place on the first anniversary of the Bolshevik revolution, in 1918—with word coming in regarding ferment and insurgency sweeping through Germany, Italy, the now-disintegrated Austro-Hungarian Empire, and elsewhere—Gregory Zinoviev proclaimed:

Republics in Austria and Hungary will be established in the next few days. . . . In Vienna, Budapest, and Prague, state power will be transferred to Soviets of workers and soldiers deputies. Shortly, the revolution will pass from Austria to Italy. . . . The moment when we will see soviets in Milan and Rome is close. . . . The [early] triumph of the German working class is inevitable . . . [and] when a red flag is permanently raised over Berlin, it will signify that the hour when that same red flag is raised over Paris is not far off. . . . It is possible that English capital will survive for a few years alongside socialist regimes in the rest of Europe. But from the moment when socialism in Russia, Austria, Germany, France, and Italy becomes a fact, English capitalism will have reached its end.[10]

Lenin's formulations were far more measured, but their trajectory was similar, as can be seen in his "Letter to American Workers" from August 1918:

We know that help from you will probably not come soon, comrade American workers, for the revolution is developing in different countries in different forms and at different tempos (and it cannot be otherwise). We know that although the European proletarian revolution has been maturing very rapidly lately, it may, after all, not flare up within the next few weeks. We are banking on the inevitability of the world revolution, but this does not mean that we are such fools as to bank on the revolution inevitably coming on a *definite* and early date. We have seen two great revolutions in our country, 1905 and 1917, and we know revolutions are not made to order, or by agreement. We know that circumstances brought *our* Russian detachment of the socialist proletariat to the fore not because of our merits, but because of the exceptional backwardness of Russia, and that *before* the world revolution breaks out a number of separate revolutions may be defeated.

In spite of this, we are firmly convinced that we are invincible, because the spirit of mankind will not be broken by the imperialist slaughter. Mankind will vanquish it. And the first country to *break* the convict chains of the imperialist war was *our* country. We sustained enormously heavy casualties in the struggle to break these chains, but we *broke* them. We are *free from* imperialist dependence, we have raised the banner of struggle for the complete overthrow of imperialism for the whole world to see.

We are now, as it were, in a besieged fortress, waiting for the other detachments of the world socialist revolution to come to our relief. These detachments *exist,* they are *more numerous* than ours, they are maturing, growing, gaining more strength the longer the brutalities of imperialism continue. . . . Slowly but surely the workers are adopting communist, Bolshevik tactics and are marching towards the proletarian revolution, which alone is capable of saving dying culture and dying mankind. In short, we are invincible, because the world proletarian revolution is invincible.[11]

International Frameworks

The response to the Russian Revolution by representatives of one of the dominant world powers, the United States of America, throws some light on the international framework within which the revolution developed. We have seen that the Bolshevik revolution erupted in the midst of the violent denouement of a global power struggle between the United States and the Western European powers on the one hand (especially France and Britain) and Germany combined with Austria-Hungary on the other. The Russian Empire had been committed to the Western Allies. The revolution pulled the massive Eurasian heartland into a new trajectory, which Western geopolitical analysts feared would link German and Russian resources and destinies—resulting in their eventual domination of the world. Consequently, many Western statesmen and policy-makers initially suspected that the Bolsheviks were simply agents of the German Kaiser. After it became clear that the Bolsheviks were very much their own agents, Western statesmen realized, to their horror, that the Bolsheviks did indeed look forward (through the "Bolshevization" of Germany) to a German-Russian Communist alliance designed to overturn "Western civilization." As US secretary of state Robert Lansing commented to President Woodrow Wilson, the Bolsheviks were boldly appealing "to the proletariat of all countries, to the ignorant and mentally deficient, who by their numbers are urged to become masters. Here seems to me to lie a very real danger in view of the present social unrest throughout the world."[12]

US ambassador David R. Francis wrote that the dictatorship of the proletariat "is a worse form of tyranny than absolute monarchy." The ambassador offered two specific points to back up this generalization. First, "no man or woman is allowed to vote who does not perform manual labor." (In fact, those performing other forms of labor were also accepted as voters—but not, it is true, capitalists such as Francis.) The second problem the ambassador cited was that "the decrees of Bolshevism made marriage and divorce so easy that they were to be had for the asking." Warning of "the effect of Bolshevism already seen on the uneducated of every European country," Francis argued (writing in 1921) that "all of the unrest throughout Europe and in this country and in every country on the Western hemisphere can be traced back to the Bolshevik experiment in Russia." Here he seems to refer not to an international conspiracy but rather to a very bad international example. And there remained the danger of the German-Russian connection. Even barring a Communist revolution triumphing in Germany, Francis warned that—despite militarily having lost the First World War—"Germany is using the same means and pursuing the same policy in her economic war, which has not only begun but has made considerable headway with Russia." Writing that "Germany's commercial agents are the only ones admitted into Soviet Russia," he concluded, "The present government of Germany is following in the footsteps of the Imperial government in all matters pertaining to German domination in the commercial world." Arguing against "a temporizing policy with Bolshevism," he advocated "the eradication of Bolshevism in Russia because it is a blot on the civilization of the Twentieth Century, and for the additional reason that it is to our interest to exterminate it in the land of its birth." For this last thought, Francis offered two reasons. "First: If Bolshevism is permitted to thrive in Russia it will promote unrest in all countries. Second: It is our duty to the Russian people to relieve their country of the injury and disgrace inflicted upon it by Soviet Rule."[13]

This sixty-seven-year-old Missouri businessman and politician was not simply an opinionated bigot. He was the chosen representative of the Wilson administration in a sensitive position from 1916 to 1918. The experienced US diplomat George F. Kennan has commented that Francis's "simple, outspoken, American pragmatism provided a revealing contrast to the intensely theoretical controversies that raged around him, and one comes away from the reading of his memoirs with the feeling that America could have been in some ways much worse served, if in other ways better." Assisted by an eager and knowledgeable twenty-six-year-old "Russia expert," Samuel N. Harper, Francis played an active role in mobilizing US support for the Provisional Government and working with such figures as Boris Savinkov and General Lavr Kornilov to "stiffen" the regime's repression of revolutionary elements (Lenin being a special target).[14]

In any event, the concerns and opinions expressed by Francis were not simply his own, but reflected currents of thought dominant in US State Department circles. Indeed, the concerns he expressed were buttressed by additional points of others. A State Department economist in the same period, Alfred W. Kleiforth, cautioned the House Foreign Affairs Committee that "an unwise [i.e., friendly] relation with the present authorities in Russia" could impair US relations with the expected post-Bolshevik regime of the future. These future relations would be important for US commerce. "The upbuilding of the industries of Russia will not only be a great humanitarian work, but will render a patriotic service to the United States," Kleiforth explained. "To foreign investors, Russia will be found a very attractive field." He compared these future possibilities to "the vast opportunities" involved in opening up the American West.[15]

State Department consultant John Spargo agreed: "Even if we put aside every consideration of humanity and confine ourselves to the hard, cold facts of self-interest, we have very profound and important reasons to be concerned in the solution of Russia's great problem." Spargo explained that US interests depended on "the peace and progressive prosperity of the world," that "Europe and Asia are our neighbors" which "touch our life in direct and vital ways," elaborating that "our own economic life is at once affected" by events in these neighboring continents: "We live in an era of international capitalism and our life and progress depend upon international trade exchanges." He noted that this similarly held true for a Germany and for a Russia that might no longer be competitor or antagonist on the world scene: "Even before the war with Germany ended every thoughtful student realized that our own interest, and that of all the Allied nations, required the quickest possible economic rehabilitation of the enemy after the war. Similarly our interest, and the interest of every civilized nation, requires the quickest possible restoration of Russia." It is interesting to note Spargo's insistence that "this is not economic imperialism, but its antithesis." This is true if one is referring to the traditional imperialism associated with acquiring colonies, in the manner of Britain, France, Germany, Belgium, the Netherlands, and so forth. Of the US policy (which would have been identified by the Bolsheviks as a dynamic new variant of imperialism), Spargo preferred to assert: "It is the highest form of international mutualism." From much the same perspective, Secretary of State Lansing pointed out that "Russia is among the largest factors in the complicated system of production by which the world is clothed and fed," going on to stress "the Russian resources should be no longer at the disposal of adventurous revolutionaries, seeking to subvert democratic governments everywhere." President Wilson agreed, expressing alarm that "there is a closer monopoly of power in Petrograd and Moscow than ever there was in Berlin, and the thing that is intolerable is . . . that another group of men more cruel than the Czar himself is controlling the destinies of that great people."[16]

This general orientation was to define the framework of US foreign policy for years to come. "Wilson established the main drift toward an American liberal globalism, hostile both to traditional imperialism and to revolutionary-socialism," historian N. Gordon Levin has explained. "Many who had been associated with Wilson, or who accepted the essentials of his world view, such as Herbert Hoover, Cordell Hull, Franklin Roosevelt, and John Foster Dulles, would continue in later periods to identify America's expansive national interest with the maintenance of a rational and peaceful international liberal order."[17]

It is important to place US policy considerations, however, in the context of broader concerns and considerations of US allies in the 1914–18 global war. At the Versailles Peace Conference, bringing together the Allied victors of the First World War, representatives of "the Big Four" (Britain, France, the United States, and Italy) "individually and collectively . . . spent more time and energy on the Russia question than on any other major issue," notes Arno Mayer. He explains: "During the Conference an outcast regime ruled in Moscow, and this regime was feared not because it just then ruled over a powerful nation but because it was the carrier of highly contagious ideas." Mayer adds that "in order to achieve the overthrow of the Bolshevik regime the Allied and Associated Powers were prepared to compensate their dependent allies in the counterrevolution [such as Finland, Romania, and Poland] with territories which had formerly belonged to Imperial Russia."[18] In fact, he recounts that

> even before the Peace Conference opened, the Allied and Associated Powers singly or in collaboration had taken the necessary steps to complete the naval and military encirclement and the economic blockade of Soviet Russia. Above all, especially with the *Freikorps* [German anti-Bolshevik volunteers] closing the breach in Latvia and Lithuania, the road to East Central Europe was barred. This *cordon sanitaire* [the anti-Bolshevik "sanitary cordon"] was effective in spite of rivalries among the counterrevolutionary powers and the lack of an effective offensive striking force. At best the quarantine—combined with the aid without which the Whites [anti-Bolshevik military forces] could not last—would choke the Soviet regime by denying it basic supplies of food and fuel. At worst the Allies gained a breathing spell during which they could help stabilize Central and East Central Europe while at the same time deciding and preparing their next moves.[19]

War against Revolution

Some among the policy-makers of the old order in Europe and the United States were more aggressive than others. US president Woodrow Wilson's expansively liberal "Fourteen Points" (Mayer suggests it was meant to counter what was represented by Trotsky's "Appeal to the Toiling, Oppressed, and Exhausted Peoples of Europe"), as well as his inclination to consider negotiations with the Bolsheviks, was anathema to France's Prime Minister Georges Clemenceau, who believed that "to make extravagant promises is bad politics" and that it would be imprudent to deal with the Bolshevik regime, which represented (as his minister of foreign affairs put it) the "lowest passions, anarchist oppression, and the negation of every principle of public and private law." (Clemenceau himself saw the high ideals of the Russian Revolution, no less than Wilsonian liberalism, as inconsistent with the natural order of things: "Since remote times peoples have been going at each other for the satisfaction of their appetites and of their selfish interests.") Britain's secretary of war, Winston Churchill, animated by a sense of realpolitik similar to Clemenceau's, wanted to send an army of a million conscripts to help destroy the Bolshevik menace, while Prime Minister Lloyd George leaned more toward Wilson's orientation and agreed with one of his advisors who noted that "the British people were 'thoroughly tired of the war' [and] were determined not 'to embark again on extensive military operations in Russia." Churchill's eager anti-Bolshevism caused the *Daily Express* to term the scaled-down military intervention into Russia as "Churchill's own little war."[20]

The balance struck among the Big Four at Versailles was to support representatives of the old order inside Russia for the purpose of waging war against revolution. Allied troops would be sent to Russia, but their participation in military action against the Bolsheviks was relatively restrained—the primary force to destroy Bolshevism was to be the financially supported White military forces made up of anti-Bolshevik Russians. The "period of open warfare," according to R. Page Arnot, was "at first between the allies and associated powers and the soldiers of the Soviet government, then between the various Czarist generals and Soviet Russia, and lastly between the border States and Soviet Russia."[21] This neat schema hardly captures all the nuance and complexity of foreign intervention, civil war, policies of economic embargo, diplomatic maneuver, and so on, but here we can do little more than briefly survey the sources and extent of the devastation.

Invasion and Civil War

In Russia, by January/February 1918 the revolution had triumphed through-out the country. "Everywhere, from the Baltic Sea to the Pacific Ocean, the masses make the revolution, hail it, defend it, impose it irresistibly," Victor Serge recounted. "Its victory is complete: yet already, in this very period, it comes into collision with the two belligerent coalitions of imperialism, the Central Powers and the Allies. The civil war will continue, or rather be rekindled again by foreign intervention. Victorious at home, the revolution finds itself face to face with the capitalist world." The Bolsheviks were committed to pulling Russia out of the World War. This provoked fierce Allied hostility, breaking as it did a crucial geopolitical link between Russia and the West, as well as weakening the war effort against Germany. The US government, which had already declared an economic embargo with the overthrow of the Kerensky regime, made clear that a separate peace negotiated by Russia would result in the embargo staying in force for as long as the Bolsheviks remained in power. The Soviet regime replied angrily and publicly: "The North American plutocrats are ready to trade locomotives for the heads of Russian soldiers." But the German government—no less hostile despite prospects of peace—wanted to impose a number of humiliating conditions on the Soviet Republic. When Soviet negotiators and leaders balked at this (with the exception of Lenin, who was outvoted), the Germans, with Austrian and Turkish allies, launched an offensive that broke the Bolshevik hold on what had been the bulk of the Russian empire's periphery—Estonia, Latvia, Belorussia, the Ukraine, Finland, and Transcaucasia. This led to the signing of the Treaty of Brest-Litovsk. "The peace we are signing," the Bolshevik Gregory Sokolnikov announced, "has been dictated to us at gun point. Revolutionary Russia is compelled to accept it with clenched teeth."[22]

This concession split Soviet ranks (the Left SRs, many anarchists, and the influential Left Communist faction among the Bolsheviks themselves were vehemently opposed), and it also gave heart to anti-Bolshevik currents in Russia. In addition, it motivated the Allied governments (most importantly, Britain, France, the United States, and Japan, with participation from ten other nations) to launch a military intervention, with a limited commitment of troops, but with a massive amount of military and economic assistance to indigenous anti-Bolshevik combatants.

The military intervention should not be minimized. The overall troop strength has been estimated at three hundred thousand. "We are not at war with Russia," proclaimed President Woodrow Wilson in early 1919, but as historian David Foglesong acidly notes, what *was* involved was "fighting, but not war." In fact, "we were waging war against Bolshevism," according to US Army Captain Hugh S. Martin in the summer of 1919. "Everybody knew that. Yet no Allied government ever stated that it was its policy in intervening."[23] The fact remained, however, that the Allies did not mount a full-scale, well-coordinated military campaign. Their primary purpose was to provide support and assistance to indigenous Russian forces that might be able to overturn the Bolshevik regime.

It is instructive to give attention to the primary left-democratic alternative to Bolshevism and what happened to it. There was in May 1918 the uprising of the Czechoslovak Corps, which had been recruited primarily from Austro-Hungarian prisoners of war by the tsarist regime. (What became the new nation of Czechoslovakia had been part of the Austro-Hungarian Empire.) At first seeking to leave Russia along the Trans-Siberian railway, a plan that the Bolsheviks sought to facilitate, this 40,000-man force, partially in reaction against local Bolshevik efforts to disarm them, soon joined anti-Bolshevik forces led by the Right SRs, some right-wing Mensheviks, Kadets, and others seeking to build a "democratic alternative" with Allied support. The new alternative government, established in Omsk, replete with red flags and socialist slogans, was headed by N. V. Chiakovsky of the Popular Socialist Party, a split-off from the SRs. Chiakovsky was a prestigious symbol for the anti-Bolshevik fighters seeking left and liberal support. He had been a founder and central figure of the first revolutionary-populist group—created in 1869—to overthrow tsarism.[24] Historian David Foglesong describes what happened to the 1919 left-democratic effort in Siberia:

> Although the right SRs guaranteed "personal liberty and private ownership rights," being "socialistic" only in favoring land reform, support for cooperatives, and government control of some major industries, they were nonetheless branded as "extreme socialists." In fact, American diplomats repeatedly portrayed them as being almost indistinguishable from Bolsheviks. On September 24, for example, [US Secretary of State Robert] Lansing forwarded to [President] Wilson a dispatch from [US consul-general in Russia Ernest] Harris which shrilly maintained that the program of the SRs was "so radically socialistic" that it was "practically a Bolshevik plan."[25]

Foglesong notes that "much like Lansing, Harris decided that Russia's generals were the only men who 'really had the power to save Russia' from the despotism of the 'scum of humanity'"—an outlook also held by their British and French counterparts. Harris and the others "therefore favored 'a military dictatorship' which would allow leaders of the Kadet Party and officers like Admiral Kolchak 'to inaugurate a safe and conservative republic.' ... Soon after Kolchak took power, American consuls reported that the situation in Siberia was improving, that order was finally being restored." Despite the satisfaction with the Omsk putsch on the part of the Allied representatives on the scene, according to Foglesong, "it aggravated the declining morale of the Czechs (who sympathized with the democratic socialists) and it led many SRs to side with the Bolsheviks as a lesser evil than reaction." A shrewd independent observer noted that "if it were not for Allied troops, [Kolchak] would be quickly overthrown." More assistance to Kolchak was on the way, with "the United States ... 'shipping Russian rifles and boots' to the Kolchak armies, and ... facilitating the purchase of railroad cars and locomotives with American credits." Kerensky—unhappy with Kolchak's claim to be Russia's "supreme ruler"—commented that British authorities were centrally responsible, citing Winston Churchill's boast to the House of Commons: "We created Kolchak."[26]

Some who were initially inclined to support Kolchak soon pulled away in horror and disgust, describing the "burning of villages, the killing of peaceful Russian citizens by the hundreds, the shooting of representatives of democracy without trial, on the mere suspicion of political unreliability."[27]

Elsewhere, with German acquiescence, the Don Cossacks had launched an anti-Bolshevik offensive. Despite initial losses, the Bolsheviks were able, under Trotsky's leadership, to mobilize a new Red Army of about five hundred thousand (which soon doubled) capable of beating back and finally crushing the challenge. In late 1918, however, under conservative and reactionary nationalist leadership—popularly known as "the Whites"—a more substantial counterrevolutionary offensive was launched. On the Siberian front, Admiral Alexander Kolchak led about one hundred thousand combatants. In the Baltic, General N. N. Yudenich led a force of more than fourteen thousand, which for a time posed a direct threat to Petrograd. In the south, Russia General Anton Denikin—with the assistance of General Lavr Kornilov and General Baron P. N. Wrangel—was able to deploy about one hundred thousand troops against the Reds. The ragged nature of the various conflicts makes it difficult to fix dates with precision, although the Civil War's first stirrings can be traced to January–March 1918, and while the major White armies were vanquished by the end of 1920, what Ronald Suny terms "the final whiff of smoke in the civil war" was in August 1922.[28]

Life in areas controlled by Denikin's forces was hardly better than those under Kolchak's command. Former Kadet leader Pavel Miliukov noted "the high-handed deeds of the demoralized army, the complete neglect of the interests of the liberated population, the predominant influence of the former privileged class of landlords, the elimination of the democratic parties influential among the popular masses"—indeed, a situation in which "looting the population," along with "bribery, drunken orgies, and every kind of violence became customary." On the one hand, for the White forces "the intellectuals, moderate socialists, cooperators [those workers involved in consumers and producers cooperatives]—all were mercilessly confounded ... with the Bolsheviks." On the other hand, increasing numbers of people unsympathetic to the October Revolution were concluding: "This is worse than the Bolsheviks."[29]

Kolchak and Denikin, notes Arno Mayer, "were tsarist, monarchist, and autocratic, and wherever they advanced the land which the peasants had seized was taken back from them, while workers were subjected to White Terror." Some historians see Kolchak, the most successful of the White leaders, as having "high ethical standards and devotion to duty," but lacking in sufficient "strong will" to keep his forces under control, suggesting that "a crowd of intriguers and politicos" controlled him.[30] Mayer, however, gives Kolchak more credit, and makes a broader generalization:

> Admittedly, General Anton Denikin, the commander in chief of the volunteer armies in the south, sought [though often unsuccessfully] to bridle his *enragés* [firebrands]. . . . In Siberia, meanwhile, Admiral Kolchak, the nominal supreme ruler of Russia, remained an undisguised ideological warrior who publicly endorsed the [anti-Semitic forgery] *Protocols of the Elders of Zion*. On the whole, the Whites presented their struggle to restore the old regime and the late empire as a selfless crusade against Jewish, godless, and barbaric communism. Members of the old ruling and governing classes, including high Russian Orthodox clerics, pressed this cause at the headquarters and in the outlying precincts of the counterrevolution.
>
> In the Russian Civil War—as in all civil wars—fanaticism and ruthlessness were characteristic of *both* sides. But the Ukrainian anti-Bolsheviks [such as those led by Simon Petrura] and the Whites easily surpassed the Reds in brutalizing and slaughtering innocent civilians, and these included a disproportionately large number of Jews. . . . Most of this destruction centered on the former Pale of Settlement, which was destined to become the principal locale for the "Final Solution" [perpetrated by Nazi Germany] some twenty years later.[31]

Combined with the devastating work of the White armies under Kolchak, Denikin, and others, and the destructiveness of the Civil War, a general blockade was maintained by the Allies that severed the Russian economy from that of the world. Yet there was not sufficient agreement among the Allied powers to effect a truly unified and massive anti-Bolshevik push—in part because of a radicalization that was sweeping through the working classes, the disillusioned intellectuals, and even rank-and-file soldiers of some of the Allied countries, especially Britain and France. As Winston Churchill, British minister of war, bitterly complained in July 1919:

> The great success achieved by our assistance [to Russian anti-Bolsheviks] shows that we could have effected a complete restoration in Russia by now, if the five victorious Great Powers had given strong and disinterested support from the very beginning. But there are among us a considerable number of people who would be unfeignedly glad to see Kolchak and Denikin, their forces, and all who espouse their cause, beaten and subjected to the Bolshevist Government. They would rejoice to see Lenin, Trotsky and their strange obscure band of Jewish anarchists and adventurers occupy the mighty throne of the Tsars without resistance or rivals, and add the new tyranny of their subversive ideas to the despotic methods of the old regime.[32]

Despite the failure to overthrow Bolshevism, the Civil War, foreign intervention, and trade embargo had a profound impact. In the previous chapter we focused on Bolshevik mistakes that brought devastation to the young Soviet Republic. Here we must give emphasis to other factors. "The collapse of foreign trade was due not only to the prevailing chaos," Alec Nove admits, "but also to the blockade maintained during the civil war by the Western powers." William H. Chamberlin makes the same point,[33] illustrated with table 3.

Table 3: Russian Exports and Imports—1913, 1917–20
(measured in poods)

	EXPORTS	IMPORTS
1913 (pre-blockade)	1,472,100,000	936,600,000
1917	59,600,000	178,000,000
1918	1,800,000	11,500,000
1919	109	500,000
1920	700,000	5,200,000

Source: Chamberlin, *The Russian Revolution*, vol. 2, 112.

George F. Kennan, who like many Western historians is inclined to shrug off the Allied intervention as "confused, half-hearted, and pathetic," nonetheless acknowledges that military aid given to Russian counterrevolutionaries was indeed a "huge expenditure [which] was incurred largely with a view to overthrowing Soviet power." Chamberlin has pointed out that "the material contribution to the White Governments was very considerable, and doubtless prolonged their existence far beyond the time to which they might have been expected to survive if they had been left to their own resources." Chamberlin notes that as an effort to overthrow Soviet power and Bolshevik rule, the Allied intervention was an utter failure, because the Reds definitively defeated the Whites by 1921, and much of the territory lost to Germany was also retrieved by this time. "But intervention had also its defensive, negative aspect," Chamberlin added, "and here it was perhaps more effective than might appear at first sight."[34]

Winston Churchill commented that "the Bolsheviks were absorbed during the whole of 1919 in the conflicts with Kolchak and Denikin," forcing them to concentrate their energies "upon the internal struggle," which provided "a breathing-space of inestimable importance" for creating an anti-Bolshevik buffer zone on Russia's western borders. Without this devastating "interlude" of civil war and foreign intervention, Chamberlin has pointed out, "a triumphant revolutionary Russia would have faced a Europe that was fairly quivering with social unrest and upheaval." The Bolsheviks took their revolutionary internationalism very seriously, so "it was lack of strength, not lack of will, that prevented them from supporting . . . apostles of social revolution in other countries as energetically as Great Britain supported Kolchak and Denikin." As it was, short-lived Soviet Republics were brought into being in Hungary and Bavaria, before being drowned in blood; all of Germany seemed to teeter on the edge of socialist revolution at various points, and the combined impact of the Russian and German revolutions would have sent immense shockwaves throughout the rest of Europe and beyond. In reaction, there was what Mayer has described as an "uneven and uncoordinated drift toward conservatism, reaction, counterrevolution and proto-fascism" that includes British imperial massacres in India (the Amritsar Massacre), the anti-labor Centralia Massacre and "Red Scare" in the United States, the systematic anti-leftist violence of Mussolini's black shirts in Italy, "and in Germany the ready reliance on the *Freikorps* to clean up the Ruhr and Bavaria [of revolutionary workers' insurgencies], with Hitler an interested observer of the bloody liberation of Munich in early May 1919." Germany's socialist revolution was averted, of course, and it would be odd to deny that the Allied anti-Bolshevik offensive played an important role. This was part of the antirevolutionary buffer, or the *cordon sanitaire*, which also saw right-wing dictatorships established in Finland, Hungary,

Poland, and Romania, "welcome allies in the anti-Bolshevik freedom fight."[35]

Of course, the punishment meted out to "the Bolshevik experiment" in the Russian civil war made it something much less pretty to look at than might have been the case otherwise. "Armed and encouraged by foreign capitalism," recounted Angelica Balabanoff (after she had become a critic of Bolshevism), "reactionary generals . . . were leading White armies against the Revolution, assailing a population ruined by war and Tsarist corruption at a moment when the energies of the entire Russian people should have been concentrated upon the reorganization of Russia's internal life and the consolidation of its revolutionary gains." Instead, there was more war, along with the blockade, which generated the desperate fanaticism of war communism (including the economic blunders discussed in the previous chapter). As E. H. Carr puts it, "Soviet Russia's complete economic isolation at this time was a powerful contributory factor to economic experiments which could scarcely have been attempted or persisted in except in a closed system."[36]

The violence and authoritarianism that would become prevalent in the Bolshevik regime's early years—to be discussed later in this study—largely reflected the horrendous conditions imposed on the Soviet Republic by its enemies.

There is controversy over the number of casualties in Russia's civil war. A minimum of 800,000 combatants on both sides died from wounds and from disease—but perhaps there were as many as 2 million. The reality of either can only be seen as calamitous. Then there were the noncombatants, many of whom died from disease and hunger. Deaths from typhus and typhoid climbed from 63,000 in 1917, to 890,000 in 1919 and 1,044,000 in 1920. There were also deaths from dysentery, cholera, influenza. Among those swept away from such causes were prominent Bolsheviks such as Jacob Sverdlov and Inessa Armand, as well as John Reed, author of *Ten Days That Shook the World*. The embargo made medicines, along with much else, quite scarce. There were perhaps three million or more deaths due to an increase in child mortality. The 1921–22 famine killed about five million (though some lives were saved because the blockade—with the end of the Civil War—was called off, and Western countries contributed to the relief effort). Estimates of deaths brought on by Civil War circumstances, from 1918 to 1921, hover around seven or eight million people, about 4 percent of the total population. And of course there was material damage to Soviet Russia (some official estimates run as high as $60 billion), as well as the diversion of much needed resources to military purposes. The wartime and embargo-induced dislocations of the economy—the depletion of fuel, raw materials, spare parts—contributed to disastrous declines, with production falling to about 20 percent of prewar levels. The urban population declined by 30 to 40 percent. There were seven million homeless children. The extreme brutalization of the Civil War experience, and the profoundly heightened impoverishment of the economy caused by the war, seemed to make a mockery of the glowing, idealistic socialist transformation that the revolution was supposed to have ushered in.[37]

Red Army

The relentless war against revolution had other devastating impacts. "Instead of realizing their program of economic betterment for the masses," wrote the on-the-scene witness E. A. Ross (a well-known US sociologist studying the revolution), the Bolsheviks "were obliged to dedicate their best thought, the pick of their followers, and the cream of their productive powers to the creation of a great defensive force." To accomplish this, in Trotsky's words, they were compelled to "plunder all of Russia"—in 1920, for example, consuming 25 percent of all wheat production, 50 percent of other grain products, 60 percent of fish and meat supplies, and 90 percent of all men's boot and shoe wares. Even so, "the clothing supplied to the army was the barest minimum, while the deficiency in equipment was even greater," according to Erich Wollenberg. "The combined effects of the blockade and the separation of the Soviets from important centers of production were seen in the fact that the war commissariat was unable to provide arms for more than 10 percent of the men mobilized."[38]

The problem of military supplies had also been a problem in the much larger tsarist army that had been mobilized for the First World War—a force of 19 million men (about 11 percent of the entire population and almost a quarter of the male population), roughly equivalent to the proportions of soldiers in all the European combatant nations. This force had essentially disintegrated between February and December of 1917, "replaced" by working-class militia groups known as the Red Guard—"a different kind of institution from the old army," writes Carr, "resting on a different class structure and purpose." Designed to defend the workers' movement, the soviets, and the new government against revolutionary intrigues, it was democratic and completely voluntary—a perfect match for the 1917 revolutions. It was not a perfect instrument for opposing and defeating the substantial modern military bodies that were being mobilized to crush the revolution. Consisting of no more than twelve thousand relatively untrained fighters, the Red Guards were numerically no match for the gathering forces of counterrevolution. The decision to create a more substantial Red Army was made in January 1918, and an appeal was made for volunteers—which netted only fifty-five hundred potential fighters. "A country of small peasants, disorganized by war, reduced by it to unheard of misery, is placed in an exceptionally difficult position," Lenin commented grimly. "We have no army and we have to go on living side by side with a bandit armed to the teeth." In April 1918, Trotsky took the assignment of commissar of war, and began the task of developing a real Red Army capable of fighting and winning the battles that were about to erupt, and of staving off the impending counterrevolutionary massacres.[39]

There were, of course, other important Red Army leaders. Among the many officers from the tsarist army that went over to the Reds, some of the most prominent were M. D. Bonch-Bruevich (whose younger brother Vladimir was a prominent Bolshevik), A. A. Brusilov, V. M. Gittis, M. N. Tukachevsky, V. N. Egorov, I. I. Vatsetis, S. Kamenev (no relation to the prominent Bolshevik), and others. While some ex-tsarist commanders and junior officers then switched over to the counterrevolutionary Whites, even more remained loyal to the Red Army. Bolsheviks who played important military roles included V. A. Antonov-Ovseenko, V. K. Blücher, Y. B. Bosch, S. M. Budenny, M. V. Frunze, N. Markin, S. Mrachkovsky, N. I. Muralov, F. F. Raskolnikov, A. P. Rosengoltz, I. N. Smirnov, K. E. Voroshilov, and many others. But as Chamberlin has commented, after a critical-minded appraisal, "when one has made all allowances for the weak sides of Trotsky's military activity, he still remains the outstanding hero of the civil war," a view that Lenin conveyed in a conversation with Maxim Gorky: "Show me another man who could have practically created a model army in a year and won the respect of the military specialists as well. We have got such a man! We have got everything!"[40]

"Trotsky, in these days, was swimming against the stream," wrote Larissa Reissner (a young Bolshevik journalist who became a Red Army volunteer), "against the weariness of four years of war and against the flood-tide of revolution that overflowed the whole land, carrying away with it the wreckage of the old Tsarist discipline and engendering a fierce hatred of everything that recalled memories of officers' orders, barracks and military life." Nonetheless, Trotsky insisted, "in this transition period, the proletariat must assert its class monopoly of government and arms," adding that "until the bourgeoisie give up hope and attempts to organize conspiracies for recapture of governmental power and have been absorbed into the Communist regime, the working class must monopolize the tools of defense." To make this real, there was a need for many more fighters—and a system of military conscription thus was established. "Voluntary recruitment, however agreeable to revolutionary ideology," writes Carr, "proved a failure for bringing adequate man-power into the ranks of the Red Army." Additional forms of compulsion were employed, "setting up an efficient central administration and command," with central organization of the military (and the use of willing "specialists" taken from the old tsarist officer corps, paired with Bolshevik political commissars), disciplined hierarchies, rigorous military drills, and training. Centralized organization increasingly replaced the local initiative, because (as E. A. Ross put it in 1921) "untrained Red Guards and casual bands of partisans are of little avail in coping with forces organized according to military art."[41]

Trotsky "brought discipline to the shattered Bolshevik forces," historian W. Bruce Lincoln tells us, and Geoffrey Swain adds that "the growth of the Red Army was astounding," rising from 372,000 to 475,000 during December 1918, to 1.5 million by the middle of 1919, to 2.5 million by the autumn of 1919, and 5.3 million by the end of 1920. Larissa Reissner emphasized the importance placed on ensuring that the soldiers' everyday needs were attended to— even if there were not enough weapons to enable each soldier to be deployed in battle (nonarmed soldiers being given noncombat duties). Upon Trotsky's arrival at a beleaguered section of the front, "all of [his] organizational genius was promptly manifested." There had been a breakdown in quantity and quality of rations and other supplies, but now "in spite of everything, the rations became obviously better; newspapers, overcoats, and boots arrived. And there, in the place where the boots were being served out, we found a permanent army staff." Yet this staff—Trotsky himself and all officers under his command, as well as "the clerks, telegraphers, ambulance men, and his own body guard," in short, "everyone who could hold a rifle"—was mobilized at the decisive moment to be "hurled at the White Guards, who were then approaching the station." Trotsky insisted that "an officer is a comrade who knows more than an enlisted man," and that (according to the ever-skeptical US journalist George Seldes) "the friendliest relations must prevail between officers and men not on duty, but the strictest discipline while on duty."[42]

What was expected from Red Army soldiers is reflected in the oath that all of them were required to take:

1) I, a son of the toiling people, a citizen of the Soviet Republic, accept the calling of a soldier in the workers-peasants' army.

2) Before the toiling classes of Russia and the whole world, I agree to

follow this calling with honor, to learn faithfully the military duties, and to protect the peoples and the war property from harm and theft as I would my own eye.

3) I agree to observe the revolutionary discipline strictly and infallibly and to obey absolutely all the orders of the commanders, appointed by the authority of the Workers' and Peasants' Government.

4) I agree to abstain and to use my efforts in inducing my comrades to abstain from any actions which cover with shame and lower the dignity of a citizen of the Soviet Republic, and all my actions and thoughts I will direct to the great aim of liberating all the toilers.

5) I agree at the first call of the Workers' and Peasants' Government to come out in defense of the Soviet Republic from all dangers and attempts from all of her enemies, and in the struggle with the Russian Soviet Republic, for the cause of Socialism and brotherhood of peoples, I agree not to spare any of my strength or even life itself.

6) If through evil intention I shall break this my solemn promise, then let my fate be general contempt and let the severe hand of revolutionary law punish me.[43]

For Trotsky, political consciousness was a crucial factor in building a Red Army capable of winning, and he himself was a central force in helping to develop such consciousness. "The front ranks of the masses had to realize the mortal danger of the situation," he later explained. "The first requisite for success was to hide nothing, our weakness least of all; not to trifle with the masses but to call everything by its right name." In his history of the Russian Civil War, W. Bruce Lincoln describes a "revolutionary orator of unmatched brilliance, whose fiery words inspired men and women to face great danger and perform greater feats in the name of the Revolution," adding that Trotsky "sent men and women to Petrograd's defenses with their hearts seared by his revolutionary passion and comforted by his abiding belief in the new world the Bolsheviks were building."[44]

Political consciousness could be developed in more ways than through eloquent speeches. There were contests for prizes that involved giving the correct revolutionary answers to such questions as, "What is the purpose of the dictatorship of the proletariat?" or "What is the difference between the proletarian red army and the capitalistic armies of Europe?" There were, of course, political study groups, leaflets, pamphlets—but many of the soldiers could not read. Literacy classes were widespread but were also highly politicized. Seldes illustrates such an approach by recounting a scene among a group of soldiers:

> In a barracks square, we came upon a girl teaching a group of peasant boy soldiers the rudiments of reading, writing and arithmetic. But instead of the stuff that goes into little children's heads throughout the world, "I am a man," "I see a cat," "This is a dog," the communist girl teacher was calmly writing:
>
> "The Red Army is the instrument of the masses for conquering the world," "Death to the Bourgeois Governments, "Down with the enemies of the Third International."
>
> Everywhere, everywhere, the communist idea pumped into the heads of the communist army.[45]

A more complex form of political education came into play by way of a brutalizing ditty that some of the soldiers were beginning to sing. Troops under White army General Wrangel were singing this: "A steamer is at hand, / Against its side the waves do beat, / When the Red Army men try to land, / We'll give them all to the fish to eat." Red Army soldiers changed the last two lines: "When Wrangel's volunteers try to land, / We'll give them all to the fish to eat." Erich Wollenberg recounts:

> Trotsky issued an army order forbidding this parody, on the ground that Wrangel's volunteers were merely men who had been led astray, and that the Proletarian Revolution would find the way to bring them over to its own side. Such verses, he explained, were merely the products of military brutalization, which soldiers of the Red Army must shun, because they were the human material with which the Socialist State was to be built up.[46]

Yet "military brutalization" there surely was. Geoffrey Swain makes the important point that "the war was, like any war, depressingly brutal." In fact, it has been argued that the "normal" brutality of "any war" was exceeded in this case. "Raw cruelty and fanaticism unlike anything seen in those gigantic battles of the Great War became a part of Russia's Civil War from the beginning," W. Bruce Lincoln points out. The targets of brutality tended to vary, depending on which army was doing the killing: the Reds were inclined to target officers in the opposing army and those from the upper classes, while the Whites targeted enlisted men, Communists, workers, Jews. "Red Army men were instructed to treat the ordinary population well," writes Suny, "but such orders were often not obeyed."[47]

There was the pitiless use of the death penalty in order to force Red Army soldiers to adhere to commanders' orders, as reflected in one of Trotsky's pronouncements as Commander of the Red Army: "I give warning that if any unit retreats without orders, the first to be shot down will be the commissar [Communist political director] of the unit, and next the [military] commander." Sometimes, others would be made examples of as well. As long as there are wars, he later explained, "the command will be obliged to place soldiers between the possible death at the front and the inevitable one in the rear." Yet he insisted, "The strongest cement of the new army was the ideas of the October Revolution." (That this second motivational element was essential is suggested by the fact that of the more than two million desertions from Red Army ranks in the course of the Civil War, more than half were won back into service.) It was a combination of factors that made the Red Army the formidable force that it became—propaganda, organization, revolutionary example, and repression produced the necessary change through which "heterogeneous detachments became regular units buttressed by worker-communists from Petrograd, Moscow, and other places. The regiments stiffened up." And they brought victory.[48]

Various strands to the causes of Red victory are emphasized by different eyewitnesses and historians. Geoffrey Swain retrospectively muses: "The Bolsheviks defeated the White generals because, in the end, they were able to mobilize more of the population to their side."[49] George Seldes, on the scene at the time, added more detail:

> Food, clothing and propaganda have made the army loyal. Trotsky's personality and his knowledge of military strategy were an important factor. . . . Although he has spent most of his life as a red agitator and writer, he has always been a student of military strategy, has written a book on Napoleon's maneuvers and has been given credit for building the keenest morale and using the keenest military strategy in the numerous campaigns in which Russia defeated her enemies in the civil wars.[50]

Regardless of slants, nuances, and details provided by one analysis or another, the victory—and the process through which it was achieved—meant that the Red Army would stand as a central pillar of the Soviet regime. "War encouraged quick, clear, effective decisions on major issues, rather than long deliberations and consultations," Ronald Suny emphasizes. "A habit of command developed among party leaders. Victory in war, some Communists argued convincingly, required coordination and the swift implementation of central state directives," which contrasted with slow-moving deliberations of the more cumbersome soviets, not to mention the niceties of inner-party democracy.[51]

Communist International

Of course, the theoretical pioneers did not envision that socialist transformation would take place in an isolated, industrially underdeveloped, and war-devastated country. Marx and Engels envisioned it as a global process that would be pushed forward and made possible by the industrially developed regions of the Earth—although they had entertained the possibility that a revolution in backward Russia could spark such a process. We have noted Lenin's 1918 insistence that the Soviet Republic was "a besieged fortress, waiting for the other detachments of the world socialist revolution to come to our relief." He noted in the same year that "international imperialism . . . could in no case and under no conditions live side by side with the Soviet Republic," and in the following year repeated that "we live not in a State but in a system of States, and the existence of the Soviet Republic side by side with the imperialist States for an extended period is unthinkable."[52]

Erik van Ree (following a train of thought advanced by Joseph Stalin in the mid-1920s) has argued that Lenin, in fact, believed socialism *could* be fully realized in a single country. He bases what he terms a "hypothetical reconstruction" on an article Lenin wrote in 1915. "The textual evidence on which this hypothetical reconstruction of Lenin's thinking is made is not abundant," he confesses, "but the reconstruction is convincing in light of the known facts."[53] However, much more "textual evidence" can be found, expressed abundantly at various points in time, for the opposite point of view. This has caused many historians to give greater weight to the notion that Lenin actually believed what he himself asserted most often: socialism *cannot* be built in a single country, but must be realized globally.

Necessity of World Revolution

In 1920, Lenin commented that as long as "our Soviet Russia remains a solitary suburb of the whole capitalist world, during that time to think of our complete economic independence and the disappearance of all danger would be an utterly ridiculous fantasy and utopianism." This was not so simply because of the threat of military intervention; there was a more fundamentally economic reason: "We are confronted with a test which is being prepared by the Russian and international market, to which we are subordinate, with which we are bound up, from which we cannot break away. This is a serious test for here they may beat us both economically and politically." On the third anniversary of the October Revolution, he explained: "We knew at that time that our victory would be a lasting one only when our cause had triumphed the world over, and so when we began working for our cause we counted exclusively on the world revolution." He added: "We have always known and shall never forget that ours is an international cause, and until the revolution takes place in all lands, including the richest and most highly civilized ones, our victory will be only a half-victory, perhaps still less." In 1921, after pointing out that "in Russia we have a minority of industrial workers and a vast majority of small agriculturalists," Lenin emphasized that the revolution could be successful if two conditions were met—if there "is an agreement between the proletariat which is exercising its dictatorship, or holds the power of the state in its hands, and the majority of the peasant population," but that "the first condition is that it be supported by a modern social revolution in one of the several advanced countries." He concluded: "We know that only an agreement with the peasantry can save the Socialist revolution in Russia until such time as the revolution takes place in other countries."[54] Addressing the Third Congress of the Communist International in 1921, on the question of the strategic perspectives of the Russian Communist Party, Lenin once again elaborated:

> We thought: either the international revolution comes to our assistance, and in that case our victory will be fully assured, or we shall do our modest revolutionary work in the conviction that even in the event of defeat we shall have served the cause of the revolution and that our experience will benefit other revolutions. It was clear to us that without the support of the international world revolution the victory of the proletarian revolution was impossible. Before the revolution, and even after it, we thought: either revolution breaks out in the other countries, in the capitalistically more developed countries, immediately, or at least very quickly, or we must perish. In spite of this conviction, we did all we possibly could to preserve the Soviet system under all circumstances, come what may, because we knew that we were not only working for ourselves, but also for the international revolution. . . . And, generally speaking, this was correct.[55]

In the same year, Lenin wrote that the Soviet Republic could survive capitalist encirclement—"but not for very long, of course." The following year saw him stating categorically: "We have always proclaimed and repeated this elementary truth of Marxism, that the victory of socialism requires the joint efforts of workers in a number of advanced countries." In the last article he wrote, Lenin again repeated: "We are not civilized enough to pass directly to Socialism though we have the political premises for it," and he posited the goal of "maintaining ourselves . . . until the capitalist countries of Western Europe complete their development to socialism."[56]

This revolutionary internationalist perspective was the common wisdom accepted by all Bolsheviks—until 1924, when Joseph Stalin began emphasizing the possibility of building "socialism in a single country."[57] "The communist revolution can be victorious only as a world revolution," explained Nikolai Bukharin and Eugen Preobrazhensky, in *The ABC of Communism*. "If a state of affairs arose in which one country was ruled by the working class, while in other countries workers . . . remained submissive to capital, in the end the great robber states would crush the workers' State of the first country." Noting that this would be due not simply to military aggression, but also to the fact that "the organization of economic life" would be "a very difficult matter" for an isolated workers' state, they elaborated: "If, however, for the victory of communism, it is essential that there should be a world revolution and that the workers of various lands should render mutual aid to one another, this implies that international solidarity of the working class is an essential preliminary to victory."[58]

Such international solidarity, and the spreading struggle for socialist revolution in all countries, required a global organization to help make it so. The Socialist (or Second) International was supposed to have been such a force, but it fragmented at the beginning of the First World War, as we have noted. "The Second International is dead, overcome by opportunism," Lenin wrote in September 1914. "Down with opportunism and long live the Third International, purged not only of 'turncoats' . . . but of opportunism as well."[59] Over the coming years, Lenin conducted a three-sided struggle, as he organized against the war, for revolution, and for the preparation of a new International. He directed the struggle (1) against thoroughgoing supporters of the war in socialist ranks ("turncoats"), (2) against those whose opportunism (privileging reformist moderation over revolutionary principle) had undermined the militant fiber of the workers' movement, and (3) against the reluctance of many comrades to break from all such elements, some of which had enjoyed considerable prestige and authority before 1914.[60]

First Four Congresses

The Third International was finally launched in 1919 by a small gathering in Moscow. Trotsky was tasked with writing the founding manifesto for the new International. "If the First International [led by Marx] foresaw the road that lay ahead and indicated its direction; if the Second International assembled and organized millions of proletarians; then the Third International is the

International of open mass action, the International of revolutionary realization, the International of the deed," Trotsky wrote. "Workers of the world: in
struggle against imperialist barbarism, against the privileged classes, against
the bourgeois state and bourgeois property, and against all forms and kinds of
social and national oppression—unite!"[61]

A majority of the fifty-some delegates at this founding congress of the Third
International were from Russia and smaller countries within the Russian orbit,
and thirty-five represented organized parties or groups from nineteen different
countries. The German delegate, the only one outside of Russia representing a
substantial force, indicated that he had "no objection in principle" to the creation of a Communist International, but under instruction from his comrades
back home (including Rosa Luxemburg), he urged delay. He observed that "real
communist parties exist in only a few countries; in most, they have been created
only in the last few weeks; in many countries where there are communists today
they have as yet no representation." But he was persuaded to abstain from voting
so as to avoid any "no" votes marring the creation of the new body. "The fact
of the founding of a Third or Communist International, henceforth known as
Comintern, was more important than anything else done at its first congress,"
notes E. H. Carr, adding that it was in a "bleak and hostile world" in which "the
newly founded Communist International took its first steps."[62]

These first steps—sometimes having a heroic quality, other times having
the quality reminiscent of a comic opera—resulted in a dramatic expansion
and consolidation of parties by the time of the Second World Congress in
1920, where the Comintern's second manifesto emphasized: "The Communist International has made the cause of Soviet Russia its own. The international proletariat will not lay down its sword until Soviet Russia is but a link
in the world federation of soviet republics." Comintern president Gregory
Zinoviev optimistically suggested that "probably two or three years will be
needed for the whole of Europe to become a Soviet republic, adding, "We can
express the certainty that, give or take a year or two—we will hold out for a
while yet—we will have the international Soviet republic whose leader will
be our Communist International."[63]

The Comintern was looked upon with horror by some and with utter contempt by others. Combining both of these elements, US journalist
George Seldes—a left-leaning libertarian, at the time fiercely critical of the
Communists—offered readers an eyewitness description of the Comintern
that was part lurid exposé, part comic put-down:

In Moscow, annually, the Third International conspires to grasp the bourgeois scheme of things entire, shatter it to bits, and remold it nearer to Red desire.

It is an open and shut conspiracy; the open part is the congress, the shut part the secret meetings and the distribution of orders and money. But even in the open congress, ways and means of fomenting revolutions in Poland, Germany, China, America, are discussed and the part the Russian army is to play as an international communist army is outlined. . . .

Lenin gave the secret away after listening to reports of progress of the communist plot in all countries, he declared revolution was necessary somewhere adjoining Russia. He preferred Poland or Germany. . . .

The sessions were usually gala affairs full of red banners, mottoes, and sixteen or seventeen renditions of the "Internationale." The Bolshoi Theatre, which houses more than 5,000 people, is usually employed. The heroes sit on the stage and in the boxes; the press in the orchestra pit and the furred proletarian delegates who overwhelm your nostrils with the news that washing water is scarce in all Holy Russia, fill the orchestra and the galleries.[64]

Participants saw it differently. Bertram Wolfe, who perceived the rising movement as something "new, malleable, fresh, spontaneous, and open," later described the impact that Bolshevism had inspired among revolutionaries, old survivors and young converts alike: "From all lands men and women turned in the midst of the darkness of universal war toward the beacon of hope they thought they saw shining from the Kremlin towers."[65] Victor Serge, one of the "impatient rebels" in the center of the Communist International in its earliest years, recalls:

The first days of the International were days of heroic camaraderie. We lived in boundless hope. There were rumblings of revolution in the whole of Europe. . . . The Third International of the early days, for which [people] fought and many died, which filled the prisons with martyrs, was in reality a great moral and political force, not only because following the war the workers' revolution was on the ascendant in Europe and was very nearly victorious in several countries, but because it brought together a multitude of passionate, sincere, devoted minds determined to live and die for communism.[66]

For the Russian Communists themselves, of course, the creation of the Third International was an urgent necessity for making their own efforts in Russia a success. H. G. Wells—British author and Fabian Socialist (wanting socialism through gradual and peaceful social tinkering)—challenged Lenin during a 1920 interview: "But what are you making of the social revolution [in Russia]? Are you making a success of it?" To which Lenin responded: "To make it a success the Western world must join in. Why doesn't it?"[67]

There were significant numbers of revolutionaries coming to Moscow in 1920 who were determined to alter this situation, and their later reminiscences of the Second World Congress of the Comintern do not match the scornful impressions of Seldes or Wells. According to two participant observers (and later harsh critics of the Communist movement), Julian Gumperz and Karl Volk), "hundreds of delegates came from all countries of the world: real labor representatives elected and re-elected a hundred times [to mass workers' organizations], revolutionaries and opportunists, workers from the factories and shrewd attorneys, terrorists and elegant Socialists from the salons of Europe."[68] Alfred Rosmer, a prominent French anarcho-syndicalist throwing in his lot with the Communists, recalled:

> There was something intoxicating about the atmosphere of Moscow in that month of June 1920; the quiver of the armed revolution could still be felt. Among the delegates who had come from every country and every political tendency, some already knew each other, but the majority were meeting for the first time. The discussions were heated, for there was no shortage of points of disagreement, but what overrode everything was an unshakable attachment to the Revolution and to the new-born communist movement.[69]

The Congress was attended by more than two hundred delegates representing relatively substantial organizations in more than thirty-five countries. There were, in addition, an enormous number of supporters and participants from around the world. "For the first time at an international labor congress, the peoples of the Far East were represented—China, Korea, Indo-China, India," wrote Volk and Gumperz, and "with them the Mohammedan tribes of Middle Asia, the Persians and the Turks, all following the lead of the Indian, Manabendranath Roy." It was at this congress that M. N. Roy challenged Lenin himself on strategic perspectives regarding anticolonial and anti-imperialist struggles— and Lenin listened, with both perspectives incorporated into resolutions of the Congress proceedings, to pave the way for further discussions and clarifications. On the other hand, particularly in light of the realization that expected revolutionary victories in Western Europe were being delayed, serious debate on "ultra-left" perspectives took place, with Lenin and the other Russians insisting on a new balance. "Unity of party doctrine under the single and supreme authority of a Communist International seemed to be established beyond challenge," according to Carr. "The minor deviations officially tolerated in 1919 were placed under a ban: no longer was it permissible to differ on the question of participation in parliamentary elections and in trade unions." Communists were expected to overcome all sectarian abstention in regard to mass struggles—reforms were to be fought for as an integral part of revolutionary strategy, as argued in Lenin's new polemic, *Left-Wing Communism, An Infantile Disorder.*[70]

For the most part, however, the debates did not dampen (and in some ways they may have enhanced) the revolutionary mood. "With poetic enthusiasm [the new Comintern president Gregory] Zinoviev welcomed the dawn of victory," Volk and Gumperz recounted. They reproduced his words:

> We have in front of us a picture that is perfect and commands adoration in its simplicity. What could be simpler? The workers of the capitalist countries unite in order to liberate themselves from the weight of oppression. What could at the same time command more adoration? Comrades, listen to the wingbeat of victory! Our earth will be free! Wage slavery will disappear and Communism will triumph all over the world![71]

"A breathless stillness pervaded the hall," wrote Volk and Gumperz, "when Lenin assured the delegates that the Socialist dreams of centuries had become plans, and that action would make the plans into realities. . . . The delegates had heard the wingbeats of victory." Noting that "Lenin's vision encircled the globe," they stressed that "now the Communists of Europe and America knew what the Bolshevists meant when they talked of world revolution. Now they understood that the conquest of power in one separate European country was only a detail in a total plan of more sweeping proportions than ever before conceived." The revolutionary vistas of the Comintern were sweeping: "To the West of the Russian Soviet Republic, a chain of proletarian revolutions carried forward by the industrial workers; to the East, the Soviet movement of the Chinese and the Indians; and the Comintern as the High Command and executor of this plan."[72] A similar point was emphasized by M. N. Roy two years later, as the Communist International continued to grow:

> On the eve of the great Fourth World Congress, Moscow had become the vivid picture of the link that connects the oppressed people of the East with the proletarian masses of the oppressing countries. When we find a representative of the Chinese artisans or of the Turkish peasantry or the Indian coolie eagerly discussing the effects of the split in the Italian Socialist Party or the crisis in the French Communist Party or the tactics that the British Communists should adopt in the present parliamentary crises, the real significance of the Communist International becomes evident. On the other hand, the eagerness with which the representatives of the German, French, English and American proletariat try to find the best ways and means of developing the national struggle in the countries which are dominated by the ruling class of their own countries shows the approach of the Revolution which will liberate the world. To have brought into active life this international solidarity of revolutionary forces in the world is the greatest achievement of the Russian Revolution.[73]

An incredibly severe Twenty-One Conditions for affiliation to the Communist International were adopted at the 1920 Second Congress of the Comintern. The document began with an explanation that there was a powerful attraction to the new International on the part of radicalizing workers from socialist parties of various countries that were not actually in agreement with the revolutionary Marxist program of the new International, some still led by reformist or semi-reformist leaders closely associated with the Second International. This meant that the Comintern "is in danger of being diluted by vacillating and irresolute groups that have not yet broken from the ideology of the Second International." This ideology had led to a general capitulation to the imperialist slaughter of World War I and the suppression of revolutionaries within the various organizations. The conditions were designed to prevent the possibility of such reformist dilution, explicitly excluding any consideration of membership in the Comintern for well-known reformist-socialists and the "centrists" who temporized with them, insisting that Communist principles and organizational perspectives be strictly adhered to, with no organizational ties to the parties and trade unions associated with the Second International being permitted.[74]

Having established the necessity of building uncompromisingly revolutionary Marxist parties, securely interconnected as "national sections" of a "world party," grounded in the Comintern's programmatic framework of revolutionary internationalism, the Communists still had to deal with—and debate—the strategy and tactics required to make it so, particularly given the fact that the triumph of the world revolution was taking longer than initially hoped. One hotly disputed issue had to do with the question of whether a relatively small group of Communists could and should move to take power in their own hands, regardless of what a majority of the workers and the oppressed wanted. Lenin weighed in clearly and forcefully on this question:

> We were victorious in Russia not only because the undisputed majority of the working class was on our side (during the elections in 1917 the overwhelming majority of the workers were with us against the Mensheviks), but also because half the army, immediately after the seizure of power, and nine-tenths of the peasants, in the course of some weeks, came over to our side; we were victorious because we adopted the agrarian program of the Socialist-Revolutionaries instead of our own, and put it into effect. . . .
>
> During our revolutions there were instances when several thousand workers represented the masses. . . . If the movement spreads and intensifies, it gradually develops into a real revolution. We saw this in 1905 and 1917 during three revolutions, and you too will have to go through all this. When the revolution has been sufficiently prepared, the concept 'masses' becomes different: several

thousand workers no longer constitute the masses. . . . The concept of 'masses' undergoes a change so that it implies the majority, and not simply a majority of the workers alone, but the majority of all the exploited. . . . We must win over to our side, therefore, not only the majority of the working class, but also the majority of the working and rural population.[75]

In the period between the Third and Fourth World Congresses of the Comintern, Trotsky made the point that "if the working masses no longer respond today to revolutionary slogans so directly as they did in 1918–19, it is not because they have become less revolutionary but because they are less naïve and more exacting. They want organizational guarantees of victory." A genuinely revolutionary party can gain authority within the working class not merely through "its readiness to fight, i.e., its courage, but also its ability to lead the masses in struggle." This means, he insisted, "its capacity to maneuver in attack or retreat, its skill in leading them out of the line of fire when a situation is unfavorable, its ability to combine and lead all forces for a blow" that can bring a victory for the workers and the oppressed. Attention to such matters, he concluded, was a necessary task for the Communist International.[76]

This line of thought culminated, at the Fourth World Congress, in the call for advancing the *united front* orientation. This was described as "an initiative of the Communists with all workers who belong to other parties and groups, with all unaligned workers, to defend the most basic vital interests of the working class against the bourgeoisie." While the revolution might not be about to break out in one or another particular country, "every struggle for the most limited immediate demand is a source of revolutionary education, for it is the experiences of struggle that will convince working people of the inevitability of revolution and the significance of communism." It was recognized that large numbers of class-conscious workers continued to adhere either to the now thoroughly reformist Second International or to the International Working Union headquartered in Amsterdam. The latter was nicknamed "the Two-and-a-Half International" (because it was positioned politically between the Second and the Third International, consisting of left-wing split-offs from the Second International that did not accept the Twenty-One Conditions for membership in the Comintern).[77]

The united front resolution asserted that "under the impact of the mounting capitalist attack" against workers' rights and standard of living since the end of the World War, "a spontaneous striving for unity has awakened among the workers, which literally cannot be restrained," while "confidence among the broad working masses in the Communists" had only been "gradual." Such workers "have not yet given up their belief in the reformists," the resolution acknowledged, still supporting "the parties of the Second and Amsterdam Internationals," but they increasingly desired to bring their organizations "into struggle together with the Communists against the capitalist attacks." The resolution called for Communist parties to form united fronts with the parties in the reformist internationals, holding up as a model the historic example of the Russian Bolsheviks: "During the fifteen years that elapsed from the appearance of Bolshevism to its victory over the bourgeoisie (1903–17), Bolshevism never ceased in its unremitting struggle against reformism, or Menshevism, which is the same thing. But during these fifteen years, the Bolsheviks frequently arrived at agreements with the Mensheviks." This contributed to the Bolshevik triumph: "A result of this tactic, which varied according to the circumstances, the time, and the location, was that a large proportion of the best Menshevik workers were won over to Communism." Similar results were obtained through unified action with "workers who still follow the anarchists or syndicalists," and who proved that they "can assist in the revolutionary struggle."[78]

Initial Strengths, Deepening Flaw

According to Bertram Wolfe, an early Communist leader in the United States, before 1925 it was *not* the case that "all important decisions for the American Communist Party were being made in Moscow." In fact, in the early 1920s, "the first decisions made in Moscow were salutary and beneficial." He continues: "I rejoiced that the Communist International had pressured us to end our factionalism and set up an open, legal, unified party." He also explains: "However much we were inspired by Lenin's success in Russia and by the revolutionary movements that seemed to be sweeping through Central Europe, we had no thought of becoming a mere adjunct and agency of the Russian Communist party. . . . Even though we were beginning to get peremptory notes from Zinoviev and not too knowledgeable, but forceful and didactic, letters from Lenin, . . . I still believed that they were intended only as helpful suggestions, often exciting ones, and as successful examples to imitate after adapting them to American conditions, but not as categorical commands."[79]

"Lenin, Trotsky, Zinoviev, [Karl] Radek, Bukharin—these were our teachers. We began to be educated . . . in the spirit of revolutionists who take ideas and program very seriously," recalled one of Wolfe's prominent comrades, James P. Cannon, many years later.[80] Yet another leading comrade, Jay Lovestone, reminisced about this period:

In the first stage of the Communist International, Russia really did not control in any mechanical sense, as we speak of it today, but influenced it decisively through its prestige. You see, they had just licked the Tsar and given him a one-way ticket to somewhere. They had gotten rid of the capitalists. They had organized a workers' government. They were living a dream that we had, and naturally we looked up to them. Besides, they tended to treat us as equals, with equal respect—respecting our opinions, and we appreciated that. They were big men, and because they were big men they did not act in little or small ways, but nevertheless the Russian influence was decisive.[81]

Cannon recalled that within the Comintern "the decisive lead was taken by the Russian delegation assigned to permanent work in the Comintern. These were Zinoviev as chairman, Radek and Bukharin." Already a seasoned radical with experience in the Socialist Party of America and the Industrial Workers of the World, and a central organizer and leader of the US Communists, Cannon spent time in Moscow as part of the Comintern's presidium. "I saw these leaders at work and heard them speak on an average of about once a week during the entire period of my stay in Moscow," he later explained to an historian. "There was no question whatever of the leading role played by the Russian representatives. This was taken as a matter of course and was never questioned." Cannon's explanation dovetailed with Lovestone's: "They were the veterans who were schooled in the doctrine and knew the world movement, especially the European section of it, from study and first-hand experience in their years of exile. In addition, they had the commanding moral authority which accrues by right to the leaders of a victorious revolution."[82]

On the other hand, as Alfred Rosmer comments regarding the delegates from around the world attending the Second World Congress, "they all saw the October Revolution and the Third International as something that belonged to them all," and "few of them had come ready to approve every point of the theses submitted to them. . . . All the problems had to be looked at afresh and examined in depth."[83]

Zinoviev played a mixed role in the life of the International of which he was president. Increasingly, he gave "Leninism" an authoritarian twist. "We told our comrades how in the course of the civil war we in Russia had to create a centralized organization of iron, cast from a single pour," he declaimed at the Comintern's Second Congress, "with military discipline that is sometimes extraordinarily hard on every one of us, on the individual member of the party." This was to be the model for all sections of the Communist International: "In the same way, we must now create an International that is cast from a single pour with the same iron discipline and the same centralization, in which we have unconditional confidence in each other and the same self-less readiness to sacrifice ourselves for the common cause of the victory of the proletarian revolution." He emphasized: "It would be very useful for the parties of all countries," he commented, "to be somewhat apprehensive of the Communist International."[84]

In his discussion of Lenin and the party at the time of Lenin's death in 1924, Zinoviev chose to underscore that "the party should be built from above," with "unlimited iron discipline" and "relentless iron discipline." According to Trotsky, Lenin had been a moderating influence on the "centralist predilections" of Zinoviev and others in the Executive Committee, but "when Lenin ceased working, the ultra-centralist manner of handling questions was the one which triumphed." Victor Serge, who worked under Zinoviev, later recalled that "in the International he was a man of shady little schemes; at home the exponent of repression. Into ideological struggles, he introduces intrigue and trickery in increasing doses; by gradual steps he introduces repression in the party." Another who worked under Zinoviev in the International, Alfred Rosmer, wrote in his memoirs of "the 'Zinovievite Bolshevization' undertaken immediately after Lenin's death," through which "communism itself was reduced to the level of maneuver." All too often, practices that had little to do with the successful development of Bolshevism up through 1917—but that were now deemed to be expedient—were elevated to the rank of "principle" and incorporated into what came to be known throughout the world as Leninism.[85]

An additional element also assumed central importance in this period: the increasingly unquestioned dominance of the Russian Communist Party (RCP). It would have fateful and ultimately fatal consequences for the Communist International. It was expressed as early as 1924 in an article entitled "Under the Leadership of Russia," by the Finnish Communist and Comintern functionary O. W. Kuusinen. "Renegades and enemies repeatedly accused the Communist International of aiding the foreign policy of Soviet Russia," wrote Kuusinen. "To us as Communists it would be a matter of joy to be able to render efficient aid to the Socialist power of the Soviets." He also emphasized that "the Communist International possesses in the Russian leadership, in the person of its chairman and of the Russian delegation as well as of the Central Committee of the R.C.P., and accumulated stock of far-reaching revolutionary experience, of Marxian leadership and of proven ability, which are requisite to the historic tasks of the Communist International."[86]

Tied in with RCP predominance was an elemental fact about the Comintern: "It had behind it the facilities and resources which only the control of a governmental apparatus can provide," as one of its initial organizers, the increasingly disaffected Angelica Balabanoff, later noted. "Expensive agencies with numerous personnel were established overnight. The International became a bureaucratic apparatus even before the Communist movement was born." Jay Lovestone later identified the ascendance of the elemental flaw "with Lenin's departure from active life in the Communist International" in 1923. But in his opinion the problematical dynamic was increasing even before that, and he identified it with Zinoviev's leadership. "First there was the beginning of slavishness and mechanical transference, and what I called the Byzantine court at Moscow—kowtowing to the potentates—but it was not yet worked up into a system."[87]

Balabanoff's bitter remarks dovetail with this: "Lenin was guided by what he believed to be the supreme interest of the Revolution. He knew he had in Zinoviev a reliable and docile tool and he never doubted for a moment that he could use that tool to the advantage of the Revolution." Volk and Gumperz add a useful qualifier: "Lenin had little choice other than to make Zinoviev president of the Communist International." Lenin himself was president of the Sovnarkom, Trotsky was organizing and leading the Red Army in the midst of civil war, Bukharin was, in the view of Volk and Gumperz, "too young, too gentle, too emotional, and no organizer." Stalin had never been involved in the international arena and had no knowledge of languages. As someone who was "smart, intelligent, shrewd," Radek might have been able to do it, but he "was not a leader sufficiently integrated into the organism of the Bolshevik Party to be entrusted with such a task." They concluded: "So Zinoviev became the logical candidate, being at home in the international labor movement perhaps even more than in the Russian."[88] Their characterization of Zinoviev is helpful: "He was a peculiar man, full of contradictions—sentimentality that would quickly turn into sharp irony, amiability that would suddenly turn into an insulting harshness, dynamic energy that would abruptly stop in complete passivity. With his fine instinct for mass psychology, he would, nevertheless, make the most fundamental mistakes in his judgments of individual men."[89] Balabanoff's judgment was far more harsh: "Zinoviev was an interpreter and executor of the will of others, and his personal shrewdness, ambiguity, and dishonesty made it possible for him to discharge these duties more effectively than could a more scrupulous man." Indeed, under his watchful eye, "many of our agents and representatives" in the Comintern apparatus "were individu-

als long discredited in the labor movement abroad," in many cases "adventurers, opportunists" prepared to "obey the most contradictory and outrageous
orders quite mechanically and with no sense of responsibility." And yet "as
emissaries of Moscow to the revolutionary workers abroad, they moved in the
reflected glory of the October Revolution." She added: "If the prestige of their
mission impressed thousands of the faithful, the power and money which em-
anated from them attracted new opportunists on every hand."[90]

The contradictory elements in the Communist International reflect the
contradictory elements in the Soviet Republic, in its ruling party, and also
in the entire historical situation. There were the profoundly humanistic and
democratic outlooks and goals that were at the very core of the Third International, yet there were also the militarized models of the desperate Russian
Civil War idealized as appropriate organizational norms for this world party
of revolution. There was the profound sense of international solidarity of the
oppressed and exploited, fighting for liberation, yet there was also, on more
than one level, the centrality of the Russian Communist Party—with all its
strengths and weaknesses—that made its presence felt in every aspect of the
International's functioning. As the forces of world revolution stalled, with one
year giving way to another and yet another, problematical factors began to
proliferate. Such an accumulation of problematical and negative factors, as
the philosopher Hegel would have affirmed, can result in "the transformation
of quantity into quality."

Before the end of the decade, Zinoviev himself was dislodged (as Trotsky
and others had been), both within the Soviet Union as well as in the Communist International, by the political machine headed by Stalin. As the 1920s
shaded into the 1930s, the Stalin regime in the USSR was inclined to impose,
as John Marot has put it, "an ever-increasingly bureaucratic, mechanical subordination of Communist parties abroad to the political dictates of the Kremlin inspired by building 'socialism' at home," adding: "These dictates did not
require paying the closest attention to the working-class movement in Western Europe and America [or elsewhere, for that matter] to help it develop
fruitfully precisely because the fate of the Soviet economy was not directly
intertwined with that of the capitalist economies abroad."[91]

Marot has developed an interesting analysis to explain this degeneration
of the Communist International and its member parties, going beyond both
the simple failure of revolutions outside the Soviet Union or the bureaucratic-
authoritarian degeneration within the Soviet Union. He argues that, contrary
to the understanding of Lenin, Trotsky, Zinoviev, and other leading Bolsheviks,

"the economic interdependence of these countries [that] would have buttressed the political internationalism of the worker's movement" was lacking. Marot's analysis is grounded in the supposition—challenged earlier in this study—that the economic development of tsarist Russia was taking place independently of global capitalism. The presumably "closed, non-capitalist character" of the Russian economy provided, in contradiction to the old Bolshevik assumptions, the "material basis for building socialism autarchically, in one country." Stalin (supported by Bukharin) was in some ways on target in boldly shifting from the pre-1924 stress on revolutionary internationalism to a "socialism-in-one-country" orientation. In defending the old revolutionary internationalism, "Trotsky no doubt interpreted Lenin's writings correctly," Marot argues, but "Bukharin and Stalin could and did make a defensible argument in favor of constructing 'socialism' in Russia... independently of Lenin's thinking, by appeal to Russia's real insubordination to the world-market."[92]

Setting aside any over-emphasis of Russia's economic autonomy (both before and after 1917) from the global capitalist economy, one is struck by Marot's tendency to conflate economic "self-sufficiency" with *socialist* self-sufficiency. In fact, he himself pulls away from that inclination, placing tell-tale quote marks around the word *socialist* as he advances his argument: "The doctrine of building 'socialism' in a closed economy had a weightier material basis than Trotsky allowed because the doctrine reflected the very real insulation of the Soviet economy from the vagaries of world-capitalist accumulation, in the 1920s and beyond."[93] Marot emphasizes that all socialists—including the Bolsheviks of 1917—"took it for granted that the development of socialism was inseparable from the development of democracy," but in his description, the "socialism" created under Stalin's leadership involved "imposing collectivization and industrialization on peasants and workers" by "destroying the lives of millions through shootings, mass-deportations and starvation," transforming "the bureaucracy itself into a ruling class based on state-ownership of property."[94]

The relative isolation of backward Russia within a hostile global economy remains an essential element in explaining both the bureaucratic-authoritarianism that triumphed in Soviet Russia and the consequent degeneration of the Communist International.

There are other essential elements as well, among which one must consider the political disintegration and the extreme brutalization that overtook the revolutionaries, and that helped to create a distinctive political culture within which what came to be called "Stalinism" took form. Yet another essential element is one that Marot has quite appropriately stressed—involving what he considers "the real problems of building socialism in Russia, problems . . . intimately related to the peasant-question."[95]

The next two chapters focus on this tangled cluster of elements, culminating in an exploration of diverse efforts by workers, peasants, cadres, and others to make sense of it all.

6

LOSING BALANCE

As one seeks to understand the Russian Revolution, two of the most insightful guides are the participant-witness Victor Serge and the activist-turned-historian Isaac Deutscher.

Although in his later novels and memoirs Serge would express a highly critical understanding of authoritarianism and terror associated with the aftermath of 1917, in 1920, reflecting his own frame of mind as a Bolshevik activist from within the swirl of events, he was expressing an understanding that is worth looking at, straight in the face.

Revolution "is never the epic festival promised us by historians, who in truth were poets rather than historians," as he tersely put it. "It is a storm in which no one is spared, which uproots the strongest, and where the unforeseen triumphs." He added: "From the point of view of those who are making it, it is a rough and dangerous task, sometimes a dirty task for which you have to wear knee-length boots and roll up your sleeves, not fearing things that will make you sick." He goes deeper: "All the selfishness, the slavishness, the cowardice, the stupidity which lies at the heart of the human beast will be laid bare at certain moments." The good, the bad, and the ugly become inseparable in this relentless process—"no splendid sacrifice, no glorious victory, no stoical idealism in the hearts of the best can eradicate the display of human weakness," deeply rooted in the past and overflowing in the present, as "a profound moral disorder is bound to become rampant."[1]

Within this context Serge explains the necessity of dictatorship and terror.

In explaining the notion of *dictatorship of the proletariat* he goes well beyond the notion of "political rule by the working class." As he puts it:

> Revolution implies violence. All violence is dictatorial. All violence imposes the power of a will by breaking resistance. Since the expropriation of the possessing class is at stake, the revolutionary violence which must accomplish this task can only be that of the non-possessing class, that is, of the most advanced minority of the proletariat. . . . And they cannot rely on the consciousness, the good will or the determination of those they have to deal with; for the masses who will follow them or surround them will be warped by the old regime, relatively uncultivated, often unaware, torn by feelings and instincts inherited from the past.[2]

Inseparable from this is the systematic use of terror, and Serge makes use of the experience of the French Revolution, then applies it to his own time and context:

> From 1917 to 1919, in Red Russia, the same causes . . . could not fail to produce the same effects. Clearly we are observing a general law of the development of revolutions. We have only to recall the circumstances: revolutionary Russia retreated in the face of the need to shed blood as long as it was possible to retreat. But when the ceaseless plotting within found expression in the Yaroslav rising, in the murder of Uritsky in Petrograd, in the attempt on Lenin's life in Moscow; when the Ural region, occupied by Czechoslovaks who were marching on the Volga, became a new Vendée [region of peasant revolts]; when the Russian counter-revolutionary émigrés began to organize armed intervention from Paris and London, while their gangs were devastating the Don country; when white Finland had assassinated eleven thousand defeated Communists—then it became necessary to have recourse to Red terror.
>
> It was necessary on pain of death. For any sign of weakness could have brought about defeat. And defeat means White terror, a hundred times more terrible than Red terror. In 1871 in Paris in a fortnight [after the defeat of the Paris Commune], the Versailles forces killed three times as many people as were victims in the Red terror throughout the whole vast territory of Russia in three years of revolution.[3]

In 1966, not long before his death, Isaac Deutscher—for all of his adult life committed to revolutionary Marxist perspectives and the Bolshevik tradition—engaged in a fascinating discussion with radical pacifists in the United States on questions having to do with Marxism and nonviolence. Speaking of "the great tragedy of the isolation of the Russian Revolution," and of "its succumbing to incredible, unimaginable destruction, poverty, hunger, disease as the result of the wars of intervention, the civil wars, and of course, of the long and exhausting world war," Deutscher elaborated:

Men lost their balance. They lost, even the leaders, the clarity of their thinking and of their minds. They acted under overwhelming and inhuman pressures. I don't undertake to judge them, to blame them or to justify them. I can only see the deep tragedy of this historic process, the result of which was the glorification of violence.

But what was to have been a glassful of violence became buckets and buckets full, and then rivers of violence. That is the tragedy of the Russian Revolution. . . .

To some extent we (and when I say we I mean that generation of Marxists with which I identify morally, I mean Lenin, Trotsky, Bukharin, Zinoviev, the early Communist leaders in Europe) participated in this glorification of violence as a self-defense mechanism. Rosa Luxemburg understood this when she criticized the first faint signs of this attitude.[4]

Initially the Bolsheviks were committed to establishing a genuine workers' democracy in the Soviet Republic corresponding to the criteria outlined in the first chapter of this study. They did not intend to create a one-party dictatorship. Within a fairly short period, however, they were overwhelmed by crises, and the regime consequently moved not simply in the violent direction of which Deutscher spoke, but also in an increasingly authoritarian direction. As Deutscher suggests, the Bolsheviks justified this trajectory in the name of expediency, but also tended to rationalize it by articulating new theoretical principles—some of which were significantly at variance with their earlier democratic perspectives.

For example, far from being premeditated, the formation of the Extraordinary Commission for the Struggle Against Counterrevolution and Sabotage— what would become the notorious Cheka—occurred a month and a half after the Bolsheviks took power, as foreign intervention and civil war were about to become murderously destructive realities. Lenin's reference point was, not surprisingly, the darker side of the Jacobin tradition.[5]

Revolutionary Russia was engulfed by chaos and violence far greater than had been anticipated. The revolutionary-democratic ethos that had been so powerful in 1917 was disintegrating. By 1919, the element in the Jacobin tradition that had been recessive or dormant in Lenin's thought had now come to the fore. As Neil Harding has put it, "the project for universal self-activity transcending the state through a multiplicity of independent communes was replaced by an emphatically centralized dictatorship—the maximization of the state exercised exclusively by the single Party." Instead of the insurgent masses of workers and peasants animated by revolutionary consciousness, which had ceased to be the vibrant reality it had been in 1917, the hope for the future could only be found in a relatively small band of the enlightened and incorruptible, for whom (as George Plekhanov had put it years before) "the success of the revolution is the highest law." Lenin became a Jacobin in this sense "only at the very end, when all other avenues were closed to him."[6]

Disintegrations

The slogan of "all power to the soviets" had been a keystone of the Bolshevik revolution. But this had assumed the continuation within these institutions of the vibrant workers' democracy that had culminated in the soviet revolution. Instead, soviet democracy very quickly disintegrated—partly brought about through Bolshevik repression, as we shall see, but also partly through choices and limitations of the left-wing non-Bolshevik parties themselves.

Bolshevik attitudes toward socialists opposed to the October/November revolution were—as we've noted—extremely negative. The Right SRs tended to support the overturned Kerensky Provisional Government and the soon-to-be-dissolved Constituent Assembly. Many of them became involved in some of the first armed struggles against the Bolshevik revolution, setting up a rival government to the soviets in the early days of the Civil War. They generally agreed with Victor Chernov that before the Bolshevik seizure of power, Lenin had represented an "ultra-revolutionary platform" of the "lumpen-proletariat" of "the urban and village poor," that the Bolshevik revolution "substituted plebianization for democratization," accomplishing "mob rule through the bureaucracy." Chernov saw it not as a true revolution but a coup of which "the overall result will be economic and political regression and not progress." Thus, "objectively Bolshevism is not a revolutionary, but a reactionary or counterrevolutionary force." Such a standpoint naturally justified fighting the Bolsheviks arms in hand, although Chernov himself hesitated to call for this. But as his wife, Olga Chernov, put it in her later memoir, "the Constituent Assembly, that ardent dream of past generations, no longer existed. . . . At the moment there was only one way to stop a Bolshevik dictatorship and set up a People's Government. One must call in more forces and fight them on equal ground."[7]

The Socialist Revolutionaries, explains their conscientious chronicler Oliver Radkey, by the autumn of 1917 had "disintegrated into three warring factions—right, center and left," and "in the heat of factional strife they did not hesitate to malign one another." The Left SRs, as we have noted, finally split away and for a time made common cause with the Bolsheviks. As July sped toward October, many of the others, according to Radkey, "were living in a sort of dream world where fears of counterrevolution mingled with scorn of Bolshevism," with organizational dysfunction in which "deliberations eventuating in formal decisions had given way to fly-by-night conferences between individual members." In the Provisional Government, President Alexander Kerensky and Minister of War Boris Savinkov, both by this point in the SR right fringe, and Minister of Agriculture Victor Chernov, an SR centrist, all were at loggerheads. Chernov vainly sought to adhere to democratic principles, in contrast to his more opportunistic comrades. Kerensky had for some time been an independent operative with only loose ties to the party, while Savinkov—who had been the powerful second-in-command of the SR terrorist apparatus, overseeing assassinations of tsarist officials—was soon to be expelled from the party because he refused to answer for his collusion with General Lavr Kornilov's plotting against Kerensky. According to one writer, Savinkov "would conspire and murder in the name of human freedom against any regime which threatened it," although Radkey has tagged him a "proto-fascist," and Chernov reflected: "Once a brilliant figure among revolutionaries, . . . Savinkov was now inwardly empty. He had lost faith in people and looked down on them. . . . The militant bent in his soul . . . had grown unnoticed into a passion of war for its own sake, a strained, unhealthy, 'apocalyptic' passion." A British agent who had extensive dealings with him commented: "His talents cannot be denied. He wrote several excellent novels. . . . [But] he had mingled so much with spies and agents-provocateurs that, like the hero of his own novel, he hardly knew whether he was deceiving himself or those who he meant to deceive."[8]

After the Bolsheviks came to power, according to a Western intelligence report of May 1918, Savinkov was secretly coordinating a network of up to two thousand operatives (largely made up of army officers), and in July his Union for the Defense of Fatherland and Freedom—banking on a foreign military intervention that failed to materialize—would initiate an abortive uprising in Yaroslav. According to Louis Fischer, from February through June of 1918, "Savinkov mobilized White officers, monarchists, social revolutionaries, and a sprinkling of Mensheviks," in such work, receiving money "from the French mission and the Czecho-Slovaks." It was also the case that "the dominant clique in the [Party of Socialist Revolutionaries, or PSR] Central Committee decided on an armed struggle with Bolshevism in support of Kerensky's effort" to retake power, and even Savinkov's forces "now were welcome to the outraged patriots of the PSR, who were desperate for help." According to a May 26, 1918, report from Bruce Lockhart to his government, "Savinkov's plans for counter-revolution are based on Allied intervention. The French mission has been supporting them and has assured them that intervention is already decided. Savinkov proposes to murder all Bolshevik leaders on night of allies landing and to form a Government which will be in reality a military dictatorship."[9]

The Mensheviks were also divided. Some were inclined to ally themselves with the Right SRs, but the bulk of them followed the nonviolent line developed by Martov, Dan, and Abramovitch. They sought to accept and stay within the legal bounds of the new soviet power, opposing the armed resistance to Bolshevism. At the same time they maintained an implacable political struggle against the Bolsheviks. Martov found the revolution repulsive. "Under the guise of 'proletarian power' . . . the most reprehensible vulgarity is let loose," he wrote, "with all its specifically Russian vices of lack of culture, base careerism, bribery, parasitism, dissoluteness, irresponsibility, and so on." He warned that "we are moving, through anarchy, . . . toward some kind of Caesarism, based on the whole people's loss of faith in the possibility of self-government." (It's interesting to note that both Chernov and Martov initially accused the Bolsheviks not of authoritarianism but of the opposite: helping to unleash impractical popular impulses and expectations. The two critics had predicted that the forces that unleashed would create such social instability that an undemocratic outcome would be the eventual result.) The Mensheviks following Martov sought to establish "the unity of the proletarian movement on the basis of independent class politics and its liberation from anarchistic and utopian adulterations," i.e., from Bolshevik adulterations. They would accomplish this task by "rallying the conscious elements of the proletariat for systematic influence on the backward proletarian masses in all worker organizations and in all arenas of revolutionary struggle." Through such means they hoped that Bolshevik rule would be dissolved democratically by an increasingly sober-minded (or disillusioned) working class. Yet, especially as the Civil War intensified, the Bolsheviks came to feel that all Right SR and Menshevik efforts to dislodge them (whether violent or peaceful) were intolerable, that "if the Russian workers' dictatorship with its Terror collapsed, its place would be taken, not by democracy, but by the White Terror of Kolchak and Denikin," in the words of Karl Radek.[10]

The Right SRs were repressed early; the Mensheviks faced harassment (both official and unofficial) and restrictions almost from the start, culminating in their expulsion from the soviets in the spring of 1918. By 1919, however, Lenin himself was offering assurances that the government would "grant full liberty" to "all those Mensheviks and Socialist-Revolutionaries who are really prepared to help us in our difficult struggle." More than a year later, a delegation of the British Labor Party was able to attend a meeting of the Menshevik central committee, which was held in its public headquarters. Despite serious obstacles, the Mensheviks had forty delegates (out of fifteen hundred) in the Moscow Soviet, including such articulate leaders as Martov, Dan, and Abramovitch (all three of whom Lenin invited to sit on the Vee-Tsik). The fact remains that this period of legal status was precarious and short-lived. Marcel Liebman comments that "it was not until the winter of 1920–21 that the Menshevik Party was suppressed in a systematic way," but suppressed it was.[11]

Regarding his own workplace, one Bolshevik militant, Eduard Dune, later recalled, "the core of Mensheviks consisted of older, thoughtful, and widely read comrades. They were also the most skilled workers in the factory. Their revolutionary ardor had cooled during their lifetimes, but their knowledge and experience were considerable." While initially active in debates and discussions, Dune reports, their support dwindled and they found themselves sidelined by events.[12]

The move to systematic repression was hardly immediate. A very popular Bolshevik leader, V. Volodarsky (Moisei Gol'stein), serving in Petrograd as commissar for press, agitation, and propaganda, had been responsible for suppressing the opposition press in the spring of 1918, but—as Bolshevik militant A. F. Ilyin-Zhenevsky describes it—decided to veer toward a policy of openness as new soviet elections approached in 1918:

> He turned up in a very excited state and said, his eyes shining: "You know, I want to let newspapers of all tendencies appear during the election period. We are so strong now, our achievement is so obvious to everyone, that we have no reason to fear the criticism of the SRs and Mensheviks."
>
> And, sure enough, soon after that, bourgeois, SR and Menshevik papers began to appear, with Volodarsky's permission. But what floods of filth and slander came pouring out from them! Their chronicles of events were specially selected so as to demonstrate all-around ruin, and inability on the part of the Soviet power to cope with the tasks before it. Sometimes they gave deliberately false information aimed at causing panic among the population. There were articles which shamelessly called for open insurrection against the Soviet power. Volodarsky's *beau geste* was not appreciated by his enemies. Worse than that, the treacherous bullet of an SR soon cut short the life of this outstanding tribune and revolutionary. Instead of gratitude he was given death. Such is the cruel law of the class struggle.[13]

Volodarsky's assassination on June 20, 1918, as we will see, contributed powerfully to an incredibly repressive turn of events. Yet the repression of opposition groups was a gradual and uneven development. A young Bolshevik activist assigned to the Belarusian city of Gomel in 1919, Alexander Barmine, later recalled how the initial political pluralism in the soviet evaporated there:

> The overwhelming majority of the delegates were Bolsheviks. But some Menshevik Social Democratic workmen had also been elected, and several members of the Jewish Socialist Bund. There was a good deal to discuss at the sessions. We debated the food scarcity and the military situation. The Bolshevik deputies quite openly criticized the handling of affairs. The Menshevik delegates supported the criticism but held the Soviet power responsible.
>
> After a few days the Bolshevik leaders in the Soviet received from Moscow an order to exclude the elected Mensheviks as enemies of the Revolution. Esther Frumkin, who was then a leader of the Socialist Bund [though later a Communist], protested vehemently against this attack on working-class democracy. In those days I was not very clear in my mind about what was happening. But we were told that such was the decision of the Party. The Menshevik deputies withdrew in a dignified manner, little suspecting that their party had been outlawed for good. I reflect with regret now that one learns only too late the full significance of what is done in the heat of a political moment.[14]

The alliance between the Bolsheviks and Left SRs and anarchists also fragmented fairly quickly. It should be noted, however, that in neither case was this done at the initiative of the Bolsheviks. In both cases, the break was precipitated by the Bolshevik decisions to make concessions to German imperialism in the Treaty of Brest-Litovsk and to resist economic radicalism (such as rapid nationalizations and decentralized forms of workers' control). Not only did this create a breach between the Leninist governmental majority and the Bolshevik allies, with the Left SRs walking out of the government just weeks after entering it, but significant elements among these erstwhile allies resorted to illegal and violent methods. This generated repression that eliminated the Left SRs and anarchists as a force in the mainstream of Russian political life. Paul Avrich, a historian sympathetic to anarchism, observes that by the summer of 1918 "the Bolshevik government had been plunged into a life-and-death struggle with its enemies, both foreign and domestic.... Terrorism reared its head in every corner of the land. Radical SRs launched a grim campaign of assassination against prominent state officials, just as they had done in the days of Nicholas II.... The anarchists, too, resorted to their terrorist ways."[15]

Not all anarchists broke with the Bolsheviks. Some remained absolutely loyal to the Soviet regime, assumed positions of considerable responsibility on its behalf, and in some cases ended up joining the Communist Party, as anarchist historian Martin A. Miller has documented.[16] Of course, the question can be raised about whether such comrades were still anarchists or were now *former* anarchists. Although few question that the oppositional trajectory indicated by Avrich was more common, hardly all engaged in terrorist violence.

The "radical SRs" to whom Avrich refers, however, include the Left SRs initially allied with the Bolsheviks. Despite very definite tensions, the Bolsheviks and Left SRs had appeared for a time to be engaged in a secure and long-term partnership. In the early months of 1918, when Bolshevik strength in Petrograd was significantly depleted due to many militants being drawn into government and military responsibilities, the "partnership with the Left SRs helped ease the difficulties," as Alexander Rabinowitch puts it. "Along with educated, intellectually lively, seasoned, independent-minded revolutionary leaders, the Left SRs were a source of dedicated rank-and-file cadres who were often more capable and reliable than hastily, indiscriminately recruited new Bolsheviks."[17] They were an integral part—nationally and locally—of the new Soviet government, and they were trusted sufficiently by their Bolshevik comrades to be recruited into a number of prominent and sensitive positions within the Cheka—the Extraordinary Commission for the Struggle Against Counterrevolution and Sabotage.

The Treaty of Brest-Litovsk (signed March 3, 1918), concluded between delegates of the Soviet government and of Imperial Germany to allow for the new Soviet Republic to withdraw from the horrific World War, was a shameful document from the standpoint of concessions granted to the arrogant and bullying forces of German imperialism. This was frankly recognized by everyone on the Soviet side. But some refused to accept it, and among the most vociferous of these (despite Maria Spiridonova's appeal for moderation and compromise) were the Left SRs, who promptly walked out of the government with angry public denunciations.

This hardly meant that the Left SRs joined the ranks of the suppressed—they continued their open criticisms of Brest-Litovsk and other Bolshevik policies with which they disagreed. However, while the Left SRs no longer were a government party, their members maintained positions at various levels in the soviets and in the state apparatus, including the Cheka. Kevin Murphy offers a significant account of Left SR activity in a metalworks factory in Moscow that sheds light on key aspects of the situation:

> Worker grievances escalated during the continued economic collapse. Yet as late as 9 May 1918, cooperation between the Left SRs and Bolsheviks evidently continued. A general factory meeting elected four Bolsheviks and two SRs to

the soviets "without debate." However, workers' festering grievances, combined with the intransigence of the national Left SR leadership, contributed to a rapid breakdown of trust between the LSRs and the Bolsheviks. A wild factory meeting (probably in June) included LSR leaders Spiridonova and Steinberg, and Bukharin for the Bolsheviks. "The SRs criticized the Bolsheviks in every possible way" and when Bukharin spoke, "the SRs made noise, whistled, howled like wolves, and did not let him finish his speech," wrote one Bolshevik. The Bolsheviks shut down the meeting and "the next time Lebedev [a popular local LSR metalworker] came to us for permission to organize a meeting, we refused." . . .

Spiridonova . . . may have misread workers' economic grievances as political support for her party. . . . On 5 July . . . the factory committee rejected an LSR proposal to hold another meeting in the factory, but stated that, "if they desire, they may hold a meeting outside the factory." The factory LSRs twice tried to organize meetings before [July 6] . . . but were dispersed by the Red Guards, according to one worker account.[18]

The Left SRs moved decisively out of the ranks of "loyal opposition" on July 6, 1918. According to Left SR leader Isaac Steinberg, his party "was not concerned at that moment with seizing the apparatus of government, it was concerned with bringing about a radical alteration of Soviet policy." Be that as it may, two Cheka officers—under orders from the Left SR leadership— assassinated German ambassador Count Wilhelm Mirbach (in hopes of disrupting the newly negotiated peace). Left SRs "arrested," among others, Cheka director Feliks Dzerzhinsky, took over the central post office and telegraph office, sent out telegrams in the name of "the Left SR party now in power," and opened fire on the Kremlin before being overwhelmed, routed, captured, and disarmed. According to an eyewitness, Lenin himself was stunned when he learned that assassination had been carried out by Left SR Chekists, and "he turned white as he typically did when he was enraged or shocked by a dangerous, unexpected turn of events." Despite Steinberg's comment about simply hoping to pressure the Bolsheviks, "the Left SRs hoped to become leaders of the peasant revolution and form a new government," writes historian Taisia Osipova. She quotes Maria Spiridonova: "Our party must take upon itself the burden of leadership of the insurrection. We shall call upon the masses to rise, we shall incite, ignite, and organize. Only by means of the insurrection shall we be able to overcome that which is moving upon us. . . . We are entering a new stage of political development, a stage when we probably shall be the ruling party." But Communist forces moved quickly, decisively, brutally. Trotsky termed it all a "miserable parody of a revolt." Bolshevik activist A.F. Ilyin-Zhenevsky brooded that "we had ourselves contributed not a little to increasing the influence of the Left SRs through offering them places in the government and drawing them in every way into out Soviet and public work. In our proclamations we spoke of the Left SRs as the party of the rural poor, enhancing thereby the social significance of the group." Such things, he concluded, "went to their leaders' heads. They saw themselves as messiahs destined to save the revolutionary honor of the Russian proletariat by hurling it into armed conflict with European imperialism." They made use "of all the resources that the Soviet power and our Party had given to them," in order to carry out "an act of barefaced treachery," he concluded bitterly. "The Left SR party had committed suicide," reflected Victor Serge.[19]

This foolhardy act by the socialist party closest to the Bolsheviks had particularly tragic consequences. Combined with all of the other calamities—the foreign interventions and civil war, the economic chaos and collapse, and so on—it pulled the Soviet Republic out of the proletarian-democratic trajectory that had defined it from its beginnings. The democratic inclinations hardly ended all at once. Despite the attempted coup, the sixth congress of All-Russia Soviets granted amnesty to arrested Left SRs, and members of the party who did not advocate the overthrow of the regime were able to function, albeit semi-legally, throughout the Civil War. "Seven months after their aborted *coup d'etat* only an estimated two hundred LSRs were in prison," reports Kevin Murphy, "of whom thirty-four were released in June 1920." Some, such as, by this time, Maria Spiridonova, were of the opinion, however, that "the Bolsheviks are the assassins and executioners of freedom, and they must be overthrown as speedily as possible." Her outlook was now similar to that of her Right SR adversary Victor Chernov, who foresaw armed popular rebellion against the Bolsheviks and affirmed: "We will be with the people."[20]

Vladimir Brovkin, hostile as he is among historians dealing with the Bolsheviks, usefully documents fluctuations in the Soviet regime's policies regarding the legality of opposition parties, particularly the Mensheviks and the SRs. He notes a sudden shift in late 1918 away from what had been a growing policy of political repression. Detecting pulls and tugs between moderate and "hard-line" currents among the Bolsheviks, he points out that Lenin "maneuvered between the factions" and that "in his speeches Lenin simply admitted that the policy toward opposition parties was contradictory and inconsistent." Brovkin speculates, "It is quite possible that Lenin was not certain himself how to deal with the opposition parties at this point." However, he also offers a general rationale of Bolshevik policy at that time: "When reforms were contemplated in the direction of the rule of law, economic flexibility, and peasants' private enterprise, the policy toward opposition parties was one of relative toleration; when on the other hand hard-line policy prevailed, repression followed toleration." Not surprisingly, armed uprisings (in which right-Mensheviks and both Left SRs and Right SRs were sometimes involved) and other serious challenges to Bolshevik power were especially likely to generate spikes in repression.[21]

As time went on, political opposition increasingly tended to be equated with counterrevolution, freedom of expression increasingly seemed too dangerous to allow, the death penalty (although abolished but then reinstituted more than once) seemed too necessary to be dispensed with, the use of repression and terror increasingly appeared to be a necessary expedient for preservation of the endangered Soviet Republic. Political pluralism evaporated. One unanticipated consequence was what George Leggett has termed "the stringent overhaul" of the Cheka, with the elimination of the now traitorous or dubious elements; the Left SR rising not only resulted in the identification of the Soviet regime with a single ruling party, but—naturally following from this—the reorganization of the Cheka was "designed to ensure that its commanding cadres stayed unquestioningly loyal to the single-party dictatorship." Victor Serge described another of the consequences: "With the disappearance of political debates between parties representing different social interests through various shades of their opinion, Soviet institutions, beginning with the local Soviets and ending with the Vee-Tsik and the Council of People's Commissars, manned solely by Communists, now function in a vacuum: since all the decisions are taken by the party, all they can do is give them the official rubber-stamp."[22] A similar picture emerges from Lev Kamenev's critical description of the soviets at the end of 1919:

> We know that because of the war the best workers were withdrawn in large numbers from the cities, and that therefore at times it becomes difficult in one or another provincial or district capital to form a soviet and make it function.... [In] the soviet plenary sessions as political organizations often waste away, the people busy themselves with purely mechanical chores.... General soviet sessions are seldom called, and when the deputies meet, it is only to accept a report, listen to a speech, and the like.[23]

Such developments helped to pave the way for the single-party dictatorship that was perfected and glorified with the crystallization of the Stalin regime. This was not, however, the original conception of how things would be—at least not in the mind of a young militant named Alexander Barmine. Though later commenting that as early as 1922 "Stalin was intriguing ... even then to get the threads of power into his grasp," Barmine insisted that this was not the earlier norm:

> During Lenin's time, opposition outside the Party was not yet as rigorously denied expression as it was later "in the paramount interests of the Revolution," and the internal functioning of the Party was democratic. Discussion on all issues was free and open. There was no fear yet of reprisals if one happened to turn out on the wrong side of the fence.
>
> In this connection I want to recall an incident of 1919, the most critical year of the Civil War. I was sent to Simferopol with a Red Army mission to contact the staff of Dybenko, who was in command there. One of our mission, Maxim Stern, was a member of the Central Committee of the Menshevik Party of the Ukraine. Although Simferopol was then under siege, and the White armies of Denikin, holding the eastern Crimea, were only fifty miles away, Stern requested the use of the Simferopol city theater for the purpose of a political meeting. The theater was turned over to him gratis, and he held a mass meeting composed of citizens and Red Army soldiers, to whom he expounded with eloquence the Menshevik point of view and his basic opposition to the principle of one-party dictatorship. In the manner of a town-hall meeting, and with the same good feeling, I myself and two other Bolsheviks replied to him. The discussion was hot, but never passed the bounds of courtesy. Although he had all the time he wanted and said everything he had to say without mincing words, the audience voted by a large majority for our resolution.
>
> I recount this incident because there is a tendency now among critics of Stalin's murderously repressive regime to imagine that something similar dates back to Lenin and the first years of the Revolution.[24]

It is instructive, nonetheless, that the issue discussed and voted on was that of a one-party dictatorship. "The dictatorship of the proletariat is the same as the dictatorship of the Communist Party," Zinoviev explained in 1920 to the delegates at the congress of the Comintern. One can question whether workers' democracy (or any kind of democracy) can be taken seriously if only one party is permitted to function—and indeed, Mikhail Tomsky, a prominent worker-Bolshevik, would later make a joke of it: "There is room for all kinds of parties in Russia, but only one of them is in power and all the rest of them are in prison."[25]

Red Terror

It is important to be clear on the fact that the "Red Terror" of 1918–21 referred to far more than simply the suspension of civil liberties. It involved summary executions of those not only convicted but in many cases simply suspected of

"counterrevolutionary activity," or even of innocent people (members of opposition parties, relatives of real or imagined counterrevolutionaries, vaguely
defined "bourgeois elements," etc.) whom the regime arrested as "hostages" in
order to send an intimidating message to opponents: counterrevolutionary violence against the regime would result in the shooting of those "hostages." The
incorruptible and severe head of the Cheka, Feliks Dzerzhinsky, articulated the
guiding principle as early as June 8, 1918: "We stand for organized terror—this
should be stated frankly—terror being absolutely indispensable in current revolutionary conditions. . . . We terrorize the enemies of the Soviet government
in order to stifle crime at its inception. Terror serves as a ready deterrent."[26]

A scholar hostile to Bolshevism, George Leggett, notes that, despite some
"excesses," before the summer of 1918 the Cheka "had been remarkably restrained," but that especially beginning in July and August it "was increasingly caught up in the crescendo of violence." In August a prominent Bolshevik
(and former Menshevik), M. S. Uritsky—who headed the Petrograd Cheka
but had a reputation for being restrained and humane—was assassinated; on
the same day Lenin was severely wounded by a would-be assassin. Both as-
sailants had Socialist Revolutionary connections. With this the Red Terror
was unleashed without restraint. In Petrograd alone five hundred people were
immediately rounded up and shot. Hundreds more were executed from one
day to the next. From 1918 to 1922, it is estimated that fifty thousand were
killed by the Cheka. Although Lenin placed full confidence in Dzerzhinsky,
and also elaborated a theoretical rationale for Chekist violence, many Bolsheviks still labored to restrain the new institution, whose actions were often
more shocking in the villages than in Moscow and Petrograd. "The Extraordinary Commission tries to free itself of all controls," wrote prominent Bolshevik M. S. Olminsky in December 1918, indignantly detailing Communist
atrocities in the little town of Kakarev to readers of *Pravda*. "The second half
of 1918 was a period when the Red Terror was at its height," wrote N. V.
Krylenko (the Bolshevik who organized the Revolutionary Tribunal system
and began his career as a State Prosecutor in that year), "and it is therefore
completely understandable that, given these exceptional powers, the work of
these commissions [the Cheka] should have brought about a series of excesses
and abnormalities which in turn could not but provoke justifiable reaction."[27]

We have already seen that there had been anti-Bolshevik plotting and
violence at least since early in 1918, but by the summer "events follow one another kaleidoscopically," and a plan "to forge an iron ring around the capital
quickly matures," as Louis Fischer put it. "There are battles, insurrections,

assassinations, invasions—two most exciting months."[28] Fischer provides the following chronology:

July 1. British-French landing in Murmansk.

July 6. Assassination of Count Mirbach, German ambassador in Moscow.

July 6. Left Social Revolutionary insurrection in Moscow.

July 6. Anti-Bolshevik rising in Jaroslav.

July 9. Anti-Bolshevik risings in Murom, Ribinsk and Arzamas.

July 25. Allied diplomats leave Vologda for Archangel.

July 29. Assassination of Eichorn, Commander-in-Chief of German forces in Ukraine.

August 1. Allied landing in Archangel.

August 6. Czecho-Slovaks take Kazan.

August 24. White plot against Soviets revealed in Moscow.

August 30. Uritsky, prominent Bolshevik, assassinated in Petrograd.

August 30. Attempt on life of Lenin in Moscow.

Not all of the items on this list are directly connected to some unified counterrevolutionary plan or conspiracy (though some are), but at the time it was impossible for the Bolshevik regime to know all of the details. "There, you see that's what they do," said Zinoviev to some of his comrades about their opponents. "They are not shy about their methods. But we stand on ceremony with them, we are too soft." Looking back on this moment, A.F. Ilyin-Zhenevsky would conclude that his own earlier "complacent attitude . . . was radically mistaken."[29] His recollection of the mood among people such as himself is vivid and terrible:

> Death! Merciless death to all White Guards must be our answer to these crimes. To the White Terror of the counter-revolution we must reply with Red Terror! They were killing our leaders—we would tear up by the roots their entire wretched class! Such were the slogans that glinted in all the resolutions passed by workers' meetings and on all the banners carried in workers' demonstrations.[30]

In his history of revolutionary Russia, *New York Times* correspondent Harrison Salisbury writes of a salient incident. In the course of a meeting about railroads in the Sovnarkom, Lenin passed a note to Dzerzhinsky: "How many hardened counter-revolutionaries have we in prison?" Dzerzhinsky passed the note back with the answer: "Around 1,500." Lenin read it, put an "X" beside Dzerzhinsky's answer, which he ordinarily did to indicate that he had read the reply, and passed the slip of paper back. Misunderstanding, the Cheka chieftain quietly left the room—and Lenin learned the next day, to his shock, that all fifteen hundred had been shot.[31] Assuming the veracity of the story, even if Lenin hadn't meant for such a thing to happen, he can hardly be absolved from contributing to the culture in which it could take place.

Lenin's role in creating the culture of the Red Terror can be seen by his actions in the wake of the assassination, by a Socialist Revolutionary, of the Bolshevik official V. Volodarsky in June 1918. The ruling body on the scene, the Petrograd Committee of the Communist Party, responded with relative moderation. Alexander Rabinowitch notes that the killing of the popular Bolshevik leader "shocked most workers in neighboring factories and increased the danger of mob violence." Some prominent Party activists "demanded quick vengeance in the form of immediate mass terror for the murder of their leader," and others "formally registered concern about intensified activity by enemies of Soviet power and expressed a desire to settle scores with them"— some expressing a determination that "revolutionary leaders would not be cut down, one at a time." But the majority opinion within the executive committee of the Petrograd Soviet, Rabinowitch tells us, "was that lynch justice should be opposed." The top Bolshevik in Petrograd, Gregory Zinoviev, explained that "we opposed this [vindictive] mood . . . we insisted that there be no excesses."[32] In response, Lenin wrote:

> Comrade Zinoviev! Only today did we hear in the Central Committee that the Petrograd *workers* wanted to reply to Volodarsky's murder by mass terror, and that you (not you personally, but members of the Petrograd Central Committee) restrained them. I emphatically protest! We are compromising ourselves: even in resolutions of the Soviet we threaten mass terror, and when it comes to action, we *obstruct* the *absolutely* correct revolutionary initiative of the masses. This is in-ad-miss-ible! The terrorists will take us for milksops. The time is ultra-martial. It is necessary to encourage the energy and mass-character of the terror against the counter-revolutionaries, and especially so in Petrograd, whose example is *decisive*. Greetings. Lenin.[33]

Although Zinoviev now became an extreme advocate for Red Terror, he continued to be restrained by other leading comrades—including Petrograd Cheka head Moisei Uritsky plus Nikolai Krestinsky and Elena Stasova (both

Bolsheviks since 1903 and prominent in leadership circles), as well as Marxist scholar and trade union leader David Riazanov.[34] But the tide was definitely flowing the other way—particularly after a growing number of violent rebellions combined with additional assassinations and attempted assassinations such as the killing of the moderate Chekist Uritsky, the failed attempt on Zinoviev, and the almost fatal wounding of Lenin—all on August 30, 1918.

Gregory Zinoviev's reputation—including among his comrades—became entwined with some of the worst abuses. "His nerve was badly shaken by the murders of his friends Volodarsky and Uritsky last year," reported on-the-scene journalist Arthur Ransome in 1919, "and he is said to have lost his head after the attack on Lenin, to whom he was extremely devoted. I have heard many Communists attribute to this fact the excesses which followed that event in Petrograd."[35]

The violence against Uritsky and Lenin has commonly been seen as the spark that ignited the explosion, yet Rabinowitch insists that "undeclared Red Terror in all its forms had been underway in Moscow and other Russian cities for months." Earlier in August 1918, for example, Lenin had written to comrades overseeing work in the province of Penza, in which a peasant rebellion was taking place:

> Comrades! The uprising of the five kulak districts should be *mercilessly* suppressed. The interests of the *entire* revolution require this, because now "the last decisive battle" with the kulaks is underway *everywhere*. One must give an example.
>
> 1. Hang (hang without fail, *so the people see*) *no fewer than one hundred* known kulaks, rich men, blood suckers.
>
> 2. Publish their names.
>
> 3. Take from them *all* the grain.
>
> 4. Designate hostages—as per yesterday's telegram.
>
> Do it in such a way that for hundreds of versts [one verst = one kilometer] around, the people will see and tremble, know, shout: they are strangling and will strangle to death the bloodsucker kulaks.
> Telegram receipt and implementation.
>
> Yours, Lenin
>
> P.S. Find some truly hard people.[36]

At the same time, Rabinowitch acknowledges, "it is certainly true that in the former capital the murder of Uritsky, coupled with the failed attempt on

Lenin's life, unleashed a wave of arrests and an orgy of politically motivated seizures of hostages and shootings by the Cheka, district security agencies, and worker and soldier bands that far exceeded anything that had come before, even in Moscow." Samuel Farber comments that while Lenin "did not stand for stupidities [committed by Chekists] or for defense of torture," and although "he often went to considerable lengths to stop Cheka excesses in *individual* cases," he was "equally likely to criticize other Bolsheviks leaders for not being sufficiently zealous in the pursuit of the Red Terror." He adds that "in February 1920, Lenin instructed the Cheka to direct 'revolutionary coercion' against the 'wavering and unstable elements among the masses themselves.'"[37]

Alexander Berkman, the Russian-American anarchist deported to Soviet Russia during the infamous US Palmer Raids and "Red Scare" in 1919–20, was an enthusiastic supporter of the Bolshevik revolution whose ardor quickly cooled. He described the plight of a working-class family headed by his friend Kolya, a tailor, before the man's disappearance: "His wife is ill, the children neglected, dirty, hungry." In his diary covering the year 1920, he explains what happened to Kolya:

> The workers of the clothing factory where my friend is employed have of late been very discontented. Their main complaint concerns the arbitrary methods of the *yatcheika,* the little group of Communists within every Soviet institution. Friction between them and the shop committee resulted in the arrest of the latter. In protest, the workers declared a strike. Three delegates were sent to the Cheka with the request to release the prisoners, but the men disappeared and Kolya was among them. "They call the strikers counter-revolutionists," Kolya's sister said. "They have made a list of the 'opposition' in the shop, and everyday someone is missing."[38]

Intimidation, arrests, and imprisonment were certainly part of the Red Terror. But executions became the essential element. As early as 1918, in the first phase of the Terror, there were 6,300 official executions (including 2,431 charged with participating in open revolts), mostly in the latter part of that year. In 1921, as the official phase of Red Terror was coming to an end, the Soviet authorities documented that the Cheka had executed slightly more than 12,700 people from 1917 to 1920—which is generally seen as a gross underestimate. According to a 1971 study, Arno Mayer tells us, "it was estimated that 200,000 had been executed between 1917 and 1923, while an additional 300,000 to 400,000 were said to either have died in prisons and [prison] camps or been killed in the suppression of peasant revolts, industrial strikes, and military mutinies." Different estimates of total deaths between these two extremes place the numbers at 50,000 and 140,000. "All these estimates," notes Mayer, "are a mixture of incomplete or flawed data and informed conjectures."[39]

Whatever the exact figures, executions on this scale are horrific. Among those who reacted most eloquently was the Left SR Maria Spiridonova, who wrote an open letter to the Bolsheviks from prison. "Your party had great tasks and began them finely," she recalled. "The October Revolution, in which we marched side by side, was bound to conquer, because its foundations and watchwords were rooted in historical reality and were solidly supported by all the working masses." But by November of 1918 this had all changed: "In the name of the proletariat you have wiped out all the moral achievements of our Revolution. Things that cry aloud to Heaven have been done by the provincial Chekas, by the All-Russian Cheka. A blood-thirsty mockery of the souls and bodies of men, torture and treachery, and then— murder, murder without end, done without inquiry, on denunciation only, without waiting for any proof of guilt." Two years later, after surveying the scene with clearer eyes than many sympathizers or critics, Bertrand Russell confirmed: "It is, of course, evident that in these measures the Bolsheviks have been compelled to travel a long way from the ideals which originally inspired the revolution."[40]

Making sense of this detour from the original revolutionary ideals is often done by blaming Lenin's allegedly flawed ideas or personality. Whatever one thinks of that personality and those ideas, however, it is more reasonable to give attention to the larger context. This is the approach of Mayer, who points out that taking account of the White Terror (a matter we will take note of shortly) requires doubling the total casualty figures. He goes on to point out that this period involved a rising crescendo of violence throughout Europe, as the First World War destroyed between ten and thirteen million people, with almost twice that number wounded (not to mention millions more who were traumatized). "By 1917, Russia had suffered about three million casualties, nearly one quarter of its fighting forces," he notes. "There followed the millions of direct and indirect casualties of the civil and foreign war of the Revolution, many of them due to disease furthered by inadequate provisions and medical services. Indeed, the Red and White leaders fought the civil war to the death, *coûte que coûte* [whatever the cost], as Europe seemed once again to be entering a 'valley of the shadow of death.'"[41]

The Furies

Mayer has expressed the tragedy of the Bolshevik revolution more poignantly than most. His apt comment that of all the parties on the scene in 1917, "the Bolshevik party was by far the best organized and disciplined, as well as the most adaptable," is balanced by his observation that "the Bolshevik project was an inconstant amalgam of ideology and circumstance, of intention and improvisation, of necessity and choice, of fate and chance." He emphasizes that "the way the Bolsheviks took power was consistent with their credo of direct and defiant action, and their authoritarian rule following Red October was bound to provoke resistances which they were, of course, determined to counter and repress." We have seen that their initial intention was to help lead the way to socialist revolution, anticipating partnership with other political forces on the working-class and peasant left prepared to follow this course—though some (certainly Lenin) were prepared to go it alone if need be. The fact remains, however, that Lenin's Bolsheviks were not prepared (perhaps no party could have been prepared) for the tidal waves that would hit them. As Mayer puts it, "Just as they were unprepared for the enormity of the crisis, so they were caught unawares by its Furies, which they were not alone to quicken."[42]

George Leggett's important survey of the Cheka's structure and Red Terror atrocities reinforces Mayer's contextualization:

> The summer and autumn of 1918 saw a build-up of economic and military pressures on the Soviet state. Internally it had to contend with hunger in the cities, with scores of peasant rebellions provoked by extortionate grain-requisitioning campaigns, and with a series of armed uprisings such as that of the LSRs in Moscow and Savinkov insurrections. Externally it found itself entangled in the escalating Civil War. The Denikin advance from the Caucasus had been stemmed, but the conflict with the formidable Czechoslovak Corps had exposed the Soviet eastern flank, where a further threat was signaled by the proclamation of Admiral Kolchak as Supreme Ruler on 18 November. Meanwhile the Allied landing in Archangel on 2 August inaugurated the era of foreign intervention, accompanied by Entente blockade of Soviet territory, whilst the collapse of the Central Powers resulted in the emergence of Hetman Skoropadkii's anti-Communist government in the Ukraine, succeeded in December by Petliura's nationalist regime.[43]

While insisting that "terror was implicit in Bolshevism from the start" (whatever that might mean—a matter to be explored later in this study), Leggett acknowledges that Allied intervention, by Britain, the United States, France, and other capitalist powers, "may have been responsible for exacerbating and prolonging the terror, by stoking the Civil War and investing it with the aura of 'capitalist encirclement.'"[44]

If it is not the case that "terror was implicit in Bolshevism from the start," the question still pushes itself forward regarding whether the Bolsheviks had to shoot to kill rather than imprison those seeking to overturn their revolution. The murder of the tsar and his family (mirroring what happened to the royal family during the French Revolution), while eliminating a rallying point for counterrevolutionaries, certainly helped to intensify the conflict. The historical parallel suggests that rage at former oppressors was an essential part of the equation, and that deep and real class hatred helped to drive the conflicts on both sides. Popular rage over the murder of Soviet leaders and the attempt on Lenin's life was also part of the equation.

Christopher Read, whose account of the Bolshevik regime hardly shies away from severe criticism, provides reinforcement for the reciprocal aspect of the unleashed Furies to which Mayer refers: "If the White Terror is anything to go by, the supporters of the old regime could be equally, perhaps even more, murderous. After all, they were the first to embark on mass anti-Semitic pogroms that, according to some accounts, cost the lives of 115,000 Jews in the Ukraine in 1919 alone. Compared with indiscriminate murder on this scale by a much smaller force, the actions on the Red side, although cruel, excessive and unjustifiable, appear, at least, to have been subjected to some serious attempts at control."[45]

This aspect of the Terror (both Red and White) comes through, as well, in the memoir of Hans Kohn. In his later years an academic authority in the United States on nationalism, as a young Austro-Hungarian soldier, Kohn was captured during the First World War by the tsar's military forces and then, as a prisoner of war, he witnessed the carnage of the Russian Civil War. Musing that "even the restraints of international agreements valid in war do not prevail in times of bitter revolutionary and counter-revolutionary conflicts when both sides are locked in a fanatical life-and-death struggle," Kohn wrote: "Compromise is out of the question and any act, no matter how barbaric, is permissible." He continues:

> The "Red" terror during the Russian civil war was frightening, yet the "White" terror, with its disregard for human values, was even more savage and more depressing because it was not motivated by even the dedication to a universal cause that moved the Bolsheviks. Many people shuddered at the execution of the Tsar's family; but few of them cared about the countless other victims on both sides. Looking back on history, I am inclined to believe that this double

standard has been the general rule. The brutalities of the country people in the Peasants' Wars [of the 1500s] could be explained by their long suffering and ignorance; their even more brutal repression by their masters was even more revolting because this cruelty was deliberate and was undertaken in the name of order, civilization, and religion. The same was the case when ruling classes suppressed colonial uprisings, or when the government of [Adolph] Thiers savagely put down the Paris Commune [of 1871]. The ruling classes have never attributed human dignity to peoples in revolt, nor did they ever for a moment believe that the life of one of the subject people could be equal to the life of one of their own class or race.[46]

Kohn "witnessed much of this inhumanity" at close range in Siberia, where he was imprisoned, and where White armies were operating under the command of Admiral Kolchak, "an ostensibly honorable and capable officer." The dominant element among these forces, he observed, were "old-fashioned reactionaries who did not understand the need for change, much less a social revolution, and wished to restore the vast estates seized by the Bolsheviks to their former owners, and to reinstate Russian domination over its subject peoples." Kohn concluded: "The desperate effort to restore a discredited *ancien regime,* the refusal to see its villainies and follies, and to grant the Russian masses' longing for equality and dignity, doomed the 'White' armies in spite of their initial great advantages."[47]

The rationale for the Red Terror was—presumably—to counter and defeat the reactionary terror of the Whites, and also of opponents on the left, such as the Right SRs (and ex-SR adventurers such as Savinkov), who were prepared to use violence against the supporters of the Bolshevik revolution. An official proclamation in September 1918, justifying the Terror in the wake of the Right SR assassination of Uritsky and the attempt on Lenin, proclaimed, "There must be an end to laxity and weakness. All Right Socialist Revolutionaries known to the Soviets must be immediately arrested. A considerable number of hostages must be taken among the bourgeoisie and the officers. Mass shooting must be applied upon the least attempts at resistance or the least movement in the midst of the White Guards."[48] Drawing a military analogy, Trotsky explained in his classic defense of the Red Terror:

> Terror can be very efficient against a reactionary class which does not want to leave the scene of operation. *Intimidation* is a powerful weapon of policy, both internationally and internally. War, like revolution, is founded upon intimidation. A victorious war, generally speaking, destroys only an insignificant part of the conquered army, intimidating the remainder and breaking their will. The revolution works the same way: it kills individuals and intimidates thousands. ...

"But, in that case, in what do your tactics differ from the tactics of Tsarism?" we are asked by the high priests of Liberalism ...

The terror of Tsarism was directed against the proletariat. The gendarmerie of Tsarism throttled the workers who were fighting for a Socialist order. Our Extraordinary Commissions shoot landlords, capitalists, and generals who are striving to restore the capitalist order. Do you grasp this ... distinction? Yes? For us Communists it is quite sufficient.[49]

Yet what actually unfolded was far from being sociologically surgical or ideologically neat. As so often happens in violent contexts such as that of 1917–21, things went whirling far beyond such boundaries, unleashing a terrible inhumanity in the name of defending the revolution. Nowhere is this as clear as with the functioning of the Extraordinary Commissions to which Trotsky refers—in Russian *Chrezvychainaia Komissiia,* whose initials, C. K., would be pronounced "Cheka." (If one adds that it is "All-Russian" or *Vserossiiiskaia,* it becomes "Vecheka.") Formed at Lenin's initiative in 1918, "for Combating Counter-Revolution, Sabotage, and Misconduct in Office," it ballooned under Feliks Dzerzhinsky's capable leadership from several hundred to close to forty thousand. Winston Churchill's cousin, the sculptress Clare Sheridan, who had accepted an offer by Kamenev to sculpt likenesses of various Bolshevik leaders, vividly recalled Dzerzhinsky: "His eyes certainly looked as if they were bathed in tears of eternal sorrow, but his mouth smiled an indulgent kindness." When she commented on his ability to sit so still while posing for her, he commented that "one learns patience and calm in prison," adding—when asked—that he had spent "a quarter of my life, 11 years" in prison. Sheridan commented: "Obviously it is not the abstract desire for power or for a political career that has made revolutionaries of such men, but fanatical conviction of the wrongs to be righted for the cause of humanity and national progress." This finds corroboration from a variety of knowledgeable sources. "Dzerzhinsky's personal integrity has never been in question; his whole adult life was dedicated to the cause of proletarian revolution, and no petty considerations or egoistic ambitions sullied his moral purity," writes the unrelentingly critical chronicler George Leggett. "Any crimes perpetrated on his orders, such as the shooting of hundreds of hostages, were committed 'for the good of the cause.'"[50]

Isaac Deutscher tells us that the Cheka and its incorruptible leader were seen as the "sword of the revolution," although, as we will see, he may overstate things somewhat in writing that "every Bolshevik had been proud to assist it in work directed against the revolution's enemies." Indeed, Dzerzhinsky himself had been heard to comment that "only saints or scoundrels" had the character to do the kind of work the Cheka did. This comes through in two reports by one of his lieutenants, Martyn Ivanovich Latsis. On the one hand: "However honorable the man, and however crystal-pure his heart, work in the Extraordinary Commissions, vested as it is with almost unlimited power and conducted in conditions deeply affecting the nervous system, leaves its mark." On the other hand: "Naturally such a widely ramified apparatus, needing tens of thousands of personnel, could not ensure their universal, unfailing honesty. Often unworthy elements, sometimes even counter-revolutionaries, attached themselves to the Vecheka, some for motives of personal gain."[51]

Even in the case of the most incorruptible of Chekists—as noted in regard to Dzerzhinsky—terrible mistakes and indefensible inhumanity are possible. There is ample documentation to demonstrate that this was even more the case with other Chekists.

The extreme violence of the Red Terror went beyond killing. This comes through in a story told by the left-leaning George Seldes in his articles published for the United Press and the *Chicago Tribune*. While covering Europe during and after the First World War, he was on the scene in Russia in the early 1920s—only to be expelled with several other reporters in 1923 for violating draconian Soviet censorship. His remarkable 1929 classic *You Can't Print That!* contains a dozen chapters (out of twenty-six) on Russia; aside from a fascinating and positive interview with Lenin, his account is unrelenting in its scathing denunciation of bureaucracy and repression under the Bolshevik regime. He concludes this section of the book with a chapter entitled "The Moral Regeneration of Russia," in which he shares the views of Marie Morozova (1890–1933), the daughter of Savva Morozov, the left-leaning capitalist who had contributed so much to cultural, philanthropic, and revolutionary causes before his death in 1905. "She was rich, beautiful, cultured, democratic," Seldes wrote, noting as well that "some called her Santa Maria." Steeped in the cultural reflections of Pushkin, Chekov, and Tolstoy, and deeply stirred by the dynamism and promise of the recent and ongoing insurgencies, she expressed her thoughts to him, in the early 1920s, on the importance of Russia's revolution:

> In the old Russia there was too much wealth for too few persons, too much debauchery, too much disgust with life, too much listlessness, too much seeking after new sensations, too much trying to find something to make life less boring, more worth living. . . .
>
> In the new Russia there is the struggle to get a piece of bread, true, but it keeps all Russia active, active, awake, alive. It is a battle for life . . . and in time of

battle one does not get moody or degenerate, one does not commit suicide out of boredom, out of disgust with life—the result of reading a morbid novel . . . no, one girds himself to the attack. The mind clears . . . the body exerts all its strength . . . moral inspiration comes for victory. . . .

That is the new Russia.

Once there was too much time to kill . . . leisure perverted life. Now there is a tremendous energy, seeking not artistic or noble expression as yet, but the daily bitter black bread. For love and for friendship and for social intercourse, for the amenities of civilized existence, for poetry and art there is today less time and less passion. But that too will come in time. Thank God we have broken with the old Russia. This is the day of moral regeneration.[52]

But countless innocents were swept up in the mad violence of the Red Terror, including supporters of the revolution, Maria Morozov among them. "She was charged with visiting the British mission headquarters and with being too friendly with foreigners," Seldes reported. She had been arrested, jailed, tortured. "When we saw her again, it was in a sanitarium. She had gone mad."[53]

Of course, it was not simply rich people who were targeted—and killing, of course, was definitely central to the Terror. Olga Chernov gives this account from Moscow in the period immediately after the assassination of the Chekist Uritsky and the attempt on Lenin:

The Cheka drew up a list on the following day: fifty people, chosen quite at random, were executed that same night.

Many of our comrades were among the victims: Boris Averkieff—the only son of an old Socialist exiled to Siberia during the Tsar's regime; the two Gousseffs, and Zenaide Mourachkina, a mistress in a communal school. They had been arrested on quite unimportant charges, and were about to be released when this dreadful affair happened.

The other names meant nothing to me, but were quite well known to our host's wife. She was almost weeping as she read down the list of those executed: "That one was a doctor, he used to look after my kids. Such a nice young fellow he was! Let me see, Axeljeff—oh, yes, he was one of the biggest fishmongers here, I knew him quite well. Holy Mother of God, would you believe it? Here's the name of their school master—the kids used to love him, he was always the most popular man in the school. Here's another one, I knew him too. And that man was my chemist [pharmacist], I'm sure he never did anyone any harm. May the Lord have mercy on them, they're all innocent!"

The woman sobbed and went on reading the names. . . . This was a kind of infernal lottery in which the winners were picked out by chance.[54]

An eyewitness later described how the doomed were brought to a ravine in trucks at night and stripped naked—"some were proud and undressed themselves, but the others didn't budge and just stood there, having their clothes torn off them shred by shred"—after which they were blindfolded, roped together in a straight line, and shot. Such scenes, while hardly constant, were not uncommon.[55]

Ripples from such realities could be felt, under the surface in the Soviet Republic, long after the end of the Red Terror. Eugene Lyons, at the time a left-leaning journalist who covered the Soviet Union for the United Press in the late 1920s and early 1930s, describes getting together with two friends—now "humdrum" functionaries in the regime—who were once Chekists. Periodically they felt a compulsion to get together, get very drunk, and relive with each other the horrors of the "good old days." The grotesque account is worth quoting at length:

> "Remember?" Lyova exulted. "I strangled them with these bare hands to save bullets! My fingers are like iron pincers. Here, feel them Gene. . . ."
>
> "Do I remember!" Pyotr snorted. "And the time we lined up five of them and finished them off with one bullet . . . fell neatly, like pushing over a row of tin soldiers, *do, re, mi, fa* . . ."
>
> In his sober incarnation as a factory director, Pytor's hands trembled and he seemed a little scatter-brained. But vodka had a way of steadying his nerves and his brain. . . .
>
> "After the killing of our chief, Lavrov," he said, "we ordered the shooting of every tenth prisoner to put the fear of the Cheka in their rotten hearts. Lyova was with me—weren't you Lyova?—and we lined them up single file and counted—eight, nine, *you* . . . eight, nine, and *you*. . . . That was a girl, a Jewess. 'But Isaak Lasarovich,' she wailed, 'you wouldn't shoot me, would you? We were in school together, you kissed me once.' 'You're a goddam *boorzhooyi* now,' says Isaak. [The word is commonly spelled *burzhui*—a Russified variant of the word "bourgeois."] But he would have spared her if he wasn't afraid of being soft-hearted in our presence. It was very funny."[56]

Noting that Lyova and Pytor "could scarcely have been more than twenty when they served together in the Cheka of their city," Lyons reflected that "it was hard to imagine them as dictators of a whole region," but "when they were far gone with liquor I could no longer doubt their melodramatic past. . . . There were punitive expeditions to peasant villages which had harbored White fugitives, when every man, woman and child was slaughtered and the whole village set on fire." Lyons also notes the similar inhumanity practiced by the White Armies. "There were fearful atrocities against the Reds, and a fearful vengeance wreaked against the next batch of *boorzhooyi* that came to hand," he writes, adding that "once the Petliurists [anti-Bolshevik nationalists of the

Ukraine] came and slit a lot of Jewish throats," and quoting his friend Lyova: "They made our people dig their own graves and climb in and they made their comrades cover them over with earth and trample on the graves." The ex-Chekist concluded: "But we knew as many amusing tricks as they did. And when there were not enough bullets, I strangled them with my own hands. Remember Petya?"[57] Lyons's understanding of these drunken memory-fests is worth considering:

> As they talked I became sharply conscious of the bloody nightmare of remembrance under the humdrum surface of Soviet life. Pytor, Lyova, thousands like them, old Chekists, guerrilla fighters, G.P.U. executioners, carried a staggering burden of memories. They were pinned under the weight, hostages of their past. They dared not question the rightness of what they had done and suffered. Every prompting of conscience was an awesome threat to their peace of mind, their very sanity. To doubt for a moment the revolutionary sanctions of their cruelties—would turn them into fiends in their own eyes. . . . To admit the dignity and sanctity of life would have meant spiritual suicide for these men—it would have turned their heroism into a sordid crime. . . . They were prisoners of their own memories and could not even dream of escape.[58]

The destructive impact of Cheka activities on the psychological-emotional lives of Chekists was noted, as it was happening, by Bukharin: "Do not let us forget how many of them [Chekists] who remain are nervous wrecks and sometimes hopelessly ill. For their work was such torture, demanding such enormous concentration, it was so hellish, that it called for truly iron character."[59]

That many implementing the Red Terror were themselves, in a profound sense, victims of their own inhumanity does not somehow absolve them from the inhumanity to which they subjected so many dozens, hundreds, and thousands of innocents. Nor can an understanding of the larger contexts of violence and inhumanity that generated the Furies of the Red Terror dilute the horrific things that were done to people in its name. At the same time, a keen and honest sense of the horrors does not allow us to turn away from trying to understand how and why these things happened, what they meant, and what they did not mean.

"Truly we cannot hide from ourselves the fact that in some places the word commissar has become a swear word," Zinoviev noted in an early 1919 speech to comrades. "A man in a leather jacket [i.e., a Chekist] has become hateful, as they now say in Perm. To hide this would be laughable. We must face the truth." Candor about such realities permeates early Soviet literature: the devastating *Red Cavalry* stories of Isaac Babel; Victor Serge's inspiring yet horrifying *Conquered City*; the grim account of inhumanity in the service of idealism in Alexander Tarasov-Rodionov's *Chocolate*; Fydor Gladkov's *Cement*—in which (in its earliest version) an up-and-coming Red bureaucrat brutally rapes and thereby destroys an idealistic young female Communist; Mikhail Sholokhov's *And Quiet Flows the Don*, which graphically relates peasant sufferings at the hands of Communists, showing how—as Georg Lukács puts it—"some subjectively outstanding, valuable human beings are destroyed."[60]

Such works, written by people who embraced the Bolshevik revolution, suggest the importance of coming to terms with what happened as best we can. In fact, aspects of these works of art suggest that—contrary to much of what Lenin and Trotsky and others argued—the Red Terror may not have been the only effective way, or the most effective way, of defending the Revolution from the vicious assaults. Regarding the persecution of opposition parties on the left, Samuel Farber comments that "Lenin seems to have been only episodically interested in distinguishing among them . . . on their willingness to be a loyal opposition as opposed to a subversive force aiding the counter-revolution." He imagines "what would have happened if the Bolsheviks had adopted a policy of 'those who are not our active enemies are our friends'" instead of "what seemed to have been Lenin's War Communist policy of 'he who is not with us, is against us.' Such a policy would have been especially welcome at the time of growing isolation and loss of support for the Bolsheviks even before the Civil War broke out in mid-1918. In any case, it may well be that the Red Terror strengthened rather than weakened the determination and even obstinacy of many enemies."[61] In developing this point, Farber quotes from Adam Ulam who—as he says—is "no friend of the Left" but who makes a point worth considering:

> It is arguable that insurgency and bitterness against Communist rule grew in fact in the wake of executions and other inhumanities perpetrated by the Cheka and other authorities, and that many elements, at first friendly or lukewarm in their opposition to the Bolshevik power, became its fanatical enemies because of terror. One does not have to consult White propaganda to reach that conclusion. The most famous novel of the Civil War written by a Communist eyewitness, Mikhail Sholokhov's *And Quiet Flows the Don*, presents an instructive take on how it was mostly through Bolshevik atrocities that the rank-and-file apolitical Don Cossack, like the hero of the novel, Gregory Melenkov, was turned into an anti-Bolshevik fighter. Far from being a regrettable necessity, the extent of the Bolshevik terror was one of the factors that made their victory in the Civil War more difficult.[62]

It was hardly the case that there was agreement among the Bolsheviks that the Red Terror was a necessity. Leggett acknowledges:

> Many idealistic Communists were roused to vehement moral indignation by the cruel and arbitrary character of the Red Terror, and by the spectacle of its wanton application by Chekists, many of whom were criminals and sadists. A ground swell of criticism of the Vecheka manifested itself at Party meetings and in the official Communist press, to the point of demanding that the extra-judicial authority of the Vecheka be quashed and replaced by a proper process of law in open court.[63]

In 1919, resisting growing pressures within the Sovnarkom and party leadership to abolish the Cheka altogether and shift its functions to a reorganized Commissariat for Justice, Lenin won support instead for placing a member of the politburo on the Vecheka Collegium with the right to veto. "Bukharin, who had been campaigning for restriction of the Vecheka's power to execute its prisoners, was nominated for this duty," writes Leggett. "Lenin commented: 'Let him go there himself, and let him try to keep the terror within limits, if it is possible. We shall be very glad if he succeeds.'"[64]

Lenin weighed in decisively about not tolerating grotesque Cheka abuses that had been reported. For example, there is this early 1919 telegram that he wrote in his position as chair of the Sovnarkom, to Zinoviev:

> According to Lunacharsky, Afanasiev, Kromilitsyn, and other members of the Detskoe Selo Cheka have been charged with drunkenness, rape, and other similar crimes. I demand that all the accused be arrested, that no one be released, and the names of all the special investigators be sent to me, because if those guilty are not exposed and shot in a case of this kind, then unheard-of shame will fall on the Petrograd Council of Commissars. Arrest Afansasiev.[65]

According to Leggett's very critical account of the Cheka, "credit must be given . . . to Dzerzhinsky's early and apparently unsolicited initiative for reform. In a significant letter of 13 January 1921, addressed to the Party's Central Committee, Dzerzhinsky set out the Vecheka's views and actions with regard to restriction of the death penalty, contraction of the Vecheka's punitive functions, and the need for systematization of judicial machinery, now that the Civil War was over." This was preceded by a December 24, 1920, order from his office to all Provincial Chekas "forbidding executions without its express sanction, except in cases of open insurrection."[66]

Bolshevik stalwart Lev Kamenev, beginning in 1919, proved one of the most consistent critics of the Cheka's policies during the Red Terror. He was an early advocate for dismantling its power, which took things much further than Dzerzhinsky was inclined to go, but by the end of the Civil War, Lenin was also moving in that direction. "The Vecheka objected to the proposed transfer of its investigative machinery and regarded as premature the separation of political cases from those of major economic damage to the state or of misuse of authority," according to Leggett. "Lenin, however, was determined to reform the Vecheka. In reply to Kamenev he wrote, on 29 November [1921]: 'Comrade Kamenev! My position is closer to yours than to Dzerzhinsky's. I advise you not to give way, and to raise [the issue] in the Politburo. Then we shall make a stand for the very maximum. In addition, we shall make the NKIu [People's Commissariat for Justice] responsible for any failure to report to the Politburo (or Sovnarkom) on the Vecheka's defects and errors."[67]

The fact that by 1921 the Bolsheviks were backing away from the Red Terror, and all of the murderous Furies that this policy had unleashed, does not conjure away the murderous violence and extreme, systematic violations of human rights that resulted from the Terror. Lethal ripples and appalling aftereffects would be felt in Soviet political culture for years to come. The fact remains that they *did* back away. But more than recognizing this, it is necessary, if we wish to understand what happened, to return to the point Arno Mayer made in his study—that the Bolsheviks "*were not alone* to quicken" the Furies. We must consider, as well, Hans Kohn's suggestion that, when all was said and done, the Whites were worse than the Reds. Otherwise, we cannot explain the outcome—Red victory.

Once again, we can gain important insights if we turn to that account of the Right Socialist Revolutionary who was absolutely hostile to the Bolshevik regime, Olga Chernov. She and her family (separated from her husband Victor, who was functioning underground) struggled to avoid arrest as they made their way to the city of Samara—which they saw as a progressive, democratic, and populist haven. In May 1918, Czechoslovak prisoners of war—making their way (with Bolshevik support) along the Trans-Siberian railway toward their homeland—rose in rebellion and linked up with anti-Bolshevik forces, including Kadets, Right SRs, and the prominent old revolutionary N. V. Chiakovsky of the Popular Socialist Party. Chiakovsky was proclaimed the head of a new Russian government with a mildly socialist coloration, and a People's Army was formed—all with support from Allied military forces and funding from Britain, France, the United States, and other foreign powers. Also reinforcing this anti-Bolshevik center in the Siberian north were Russian military forces associated with Admiral Alexander V. Kolchak and others of more conservative orientation.[68]

As Olga Chernov and her family neared their destination, strange and un-expected developments disoriented them as the People's Army appeared to be swept aside by pro-Bolshevik forces. She was soon astonished to reunite with a young peasant woman, Katia, who in earlier days had become part of the SR milieu, but who now was a member of the Communist Party with "all the ardent faith of a new convert." Still harboring feelings of warm friendship, Katia hardly wanted to fight with her old mentor but rather to convert her. "If I had any doubts about the necessity of civil war they are all dispelled after having seen the coun-try delivered from the power of the Whites," Katia said. Chernov replied: "What do you mean? The People's Army has nothing to do with the White Army." To which Katia responded: "That's what you think. But you're badly mistaken. Of course the soldiers aren't Whites, but their leaders, their officers, are all fighting to restore the old regime. Didn't you know that?" She added: "The peasants who used to hate us and who sent their sons to fight against the Red Army have now come back to our side. Their new masters want to give the land back to landed proprietors and have reinstituted corporal punishment for the peasants."[69]

At first Chernov refused to believe her friend, accusing her of spout-ing "political propaganda." But she was unaware of the most recent develop-ments. Sir Alfred Knox, British military attaché to Russia and an advisor to Admiral Kolchak, was of the opinion that Victor Chernov and other Socialist Revolutionaries were undesirables who deserved to be hanged, and he, along with other Allied personnel, felt little regret when Kolchak's force overthrew the socialist-tainted government and proclaimed Kolchak himself Supreme Ruler of Russia. "Anxious to crush all socialists of whatever stamp," as W. Bruce Lincoln notes, Kolchak condoned flogging prisoners with iron rods, and he also executed former members of the Constituent Assembly who had rebelled against his policies before unwisely putting themselves in his care. "We are verging on the death of human civilization and its culture," protest-ed forthright anti-Bolsheviks unable to stomach his policies. "The Kolchak regime's use of terroristic methods to enforce its policies, including flog-gings, pogroms and mass executions," as historian Alan Wood puts it, did little to win popular support.[70]

Finally realizing the truth of Katia's account, Chernov had little with which to counter her young friend's excited remarks:

I've seen a gang of Whites going through a village and beating all the peasants. I've seen it with my own eyes, I tell you! Do you imagine that peasants who have been whipped would not want to join our ranks? If you had seen all that I've seen you'd be with us. . . .

They want to re-establish the whole old regime, even the Tsar. But we are invincible. The peasants will never support them when they find they want to take away their land. . . .

You see what energy and enthusiasm there is in our ranks! We are all brothers and we are going to change the whole of life; we are going to build an earthly paradise for everyone who will march with us. And you and the best of your comrades will belong to our Party. That is my dream![71]

Authoritarian Theorizations

These developments had an impact on Bolshevik theory. Authoritarian elements were introduced that conflicted with the radical-democratic elements that had been characteristic of Bolshevik thought up to 1918. Kamenev, for example, sweepingly generalized the necessity of "the harsh features of a dictatorship: a Red Army, a terrorist suppression of the exploiters and their allies, the limitation of political liberty, becomes inevitable if the proletariat does not wish to give up without a fight the power it has won." Trotsky went further: "Just as a lamp, before going out, shoots up in a brilliant flame, so the State, before disappearing, assumes the form of the dictatorship of the proletariat, i.e., the most ruthless form of State, which embraces the life of the citizens authoritatively in every direction." Lenin's pronouncements in this period assumed a similarly harsh and authoritarian complexion. An example of his extremely sharp formulations (formulations contributing to an atmosphere that would have dire consequences) can be found as early as July 1918, when in open debate with Left SR leader Maria Spiridonova, he snapped: "If there are Left SRs like the previous orator, who say . . . 'we can't work with the Bolsheviks, we are leaving,' we will not regret that for a minute. Socialists who abandon us at such a [critical] time . . . are enemies of the people."[72]

Before critically examining the authoritarian theoretical justifications further, it is worth considering a very influential "defense" of them provided by many academics and others who see such things as representing what scholar George Leggett terms "the very nature of Leninism." Leggett provides a succinct statement of this commonly held view: "It is axiomatic that, once Lenin had seized power for the avowed purpose of single-party rule despite that party's numerical inferiority and in the face of opposition from every quarter, he was committed—whether he wanted it or not (but in fact he did want it, and said so)—to a regime of political terror in which some apparatus was required to implement that terror."[73]

Leggett's (and others') assertions are sharply challenged by much evidence that he himself presents—much of which we have just reviewed: many prominent "Leninists" (including such lieutenants as Olminsky, Bukharin, and Kamenev, not to mention—at times—Cheka head Dzerzhinsky, and certainly Lenin himself) pushed against the alleged "nature of Leninism" that Leggett posits. We have already noted (and, I believe, amply documented the truth of) C. L. R. James's classic assertion: "The theory and practice of the vanguard party, of the one-party state, is not (repeat not) the central doctrine of Leninism. It is not the central doctrine, it is not even a special doctrine." That such things came to be seen as "Leninist" orthodoxy, well after the fact, is another matter. "It was overwhelmingly the force of circumstance which obliged the Bolsheviks to retreat so far from their goals," argues John Rees. "They travelled this route in opposition to their own theory—no matter what rhetorical justifications were given at the time."[74] Central to the actual "Leninist" orientation of Lenin and his comrades over the course of decades, and certainly in the period leading up to the Bolshevik revolution, was the perspective that he articulated, for example, in 1915:

> The proletariat cannot be victorious except through democracy, i.e., by giving full effect to democracy and by linking with each step of its struggle democratic demands formulated in the most resolute terms. . . . We must *combine* the revolutionary struggle against capitalism with a revolutionary programme and tactics on all democratic demands: a republic, a militia, the popular election of officials, equal rights for women, the self-determination of nations, etc. While capitalism exists, these demands—all of them—can only be accomplished as an exception, and even then in an incomplete and distorted form. Basing ourselves on the democracy already achieved, and exposing its incompleteness under capitalism, we demand the overthrow of capitalism, the expropriation of the bourgeoisie, as a necessary basis both for the abolition of the poverty of the masses and for the *complete* and *all-round* institution of *all* democratic reforms. Some of these reforms will be started before the overthrow of the bourgeoisie, others *in the course* of that overthrow, and still others after it. The social revolution is not a single battle, but a period covering a series of battles over all sorts of problems of economic and democratic reform, which are consummated only by the expropriation of the bourgeoisie. It is for the sake of this final aim that we must formulate *every one* of our democratic demands in a consistently revolutionary way. It is quite conceivable that the workers of some particular country will overthrow the bourgeoisie *before* even a single fundamental democratic reform has been fully achieved. It is, however, quite inconceivable that the proletariat, as a historical class, will be able to defeat the bourgeoisie, unless it is prepared for that by being educated in the spirit of the most consistent and resolutely revolutionary democracy.[75]

The fact remains that Lenin's formulations, and those of other comrades, increasingly took on an authoritarian cast in the aftermath of the Bolshevik revolution. In 1917, the essence of the dictatorship of the proletariat for Lenin and his comrades, as we have seen, was to be all power to such Soviets as these. According to Marcel Liebman, "Lenin never depicted what he considered to be a [civil war] necessity as being a virtue or as a really lasting system. On the contrary, some of his remarks—incidental, certainly—allow us to assume that the existence of a plurality of parties accorded better with his political plans." Yet by the summer of 1919, Lenin was matter-of-factly explaining that "the dictatorship of the working class is being implemented by the Bolshevik party," and in the following year Kamenev commented in remarks to the Ninth Congress of the Russian Communist Party that "the Communist Party is the government of Russia. The country is ruled by 600,000 party members." In his 1921 volume of reportage *The Crisis in Russia*, Arthur Ransome—by no means unsympathetic to the Bolshevik revolution—gathered representative quotes from Trotsky and Lenin emphasizing that "a party as such, in the course of the development of a revolution, becomes identical with the revolution" (Trotsky) and that "the words 'Dictatorship of the Proletariat' . . . actually constitutes a party" (Lenin)—in fact, amounting to "the Central Committee of the party" under the circumstances of 1920 (Trotsky).[76]

The logic of this was spelled out in a central work of 1919, written by Party theorists Nikolai Bukharin and Eugen Preobrazhensky in their elaborate explanation of the Communist Party's just-adopted program, *The ABC of Communism*. In their discussion of the nature of the Communist Party, they assert that all political parties represent social classes, but that "nowhere and at no time has any party been able to enroll all the members of the class which it represents; never has any class attained the requisite degree of consciousness." Rather, "those who organize themselves into a party are the most advanced members of a class; those who best understand their class interests; those who are most daring, most energetic, and most stubborn in the fight," which naturally means that "the number of adherents of the party is always considerably less than the number of those composing the class whose interests the party represents." This essentially amounted to identifying the dictatorship of the proletariat with the dictatorship by the Communist Party: "In no other way than through the victory and the strengthening of the proletariat is there any possibility of rebuilding life on new foundations. But, since the victory of the proletariat can only be secured through the organization of the workers and through the existence of a strong, solid, and resolute party, we must draw into our ranks all those who labor, all those to whom the new life is dear, all those who have learned to think and to fight like proletarians."[77]

By the end of 1920, Lenin was again matter-of-factly explaining what most Russian Communists had by then concluded:

> The dictatorship of the proletariat cannot be exercised through an organization embracing the whole of the class, because in all capitalist countries (and not only over here, in one of the most backward) the proletariat is still so divided, so degraded, and so corrupted in parts (by imperialism in some countries) that an organization taking in the whole proletariat cannot directly exercise proletarian dictatorship. It can be exercised only by a vanguard that has absorbed the revolutionary energy of that class.[78]

The vanguard of the working class could be represented only by a single party, the Communists—the other contenders had discredited themselves as wavering, petit bourgeois, potentially or actually traitorous entities. As Lenin put it in 1919, "in regard to the Mensheviks and the Right and Left Socialist-Revolutionaries, we must draw a lesson from our most recent experience." Lenin acknowledged that much of the supporting periphery of these parties was shifting "towards Soviet power," in opposition to the reactionary forces led by Admiral Kolchak and General Anton Denikin, and that the Bolsheviks must move to connect with such forces. But he also noted other elements in this milieu—"some deliberate and malicious, others unwitting and because of their persistence in their old mistakes"—that involved "the type of Menshevism and Socialist-Revolutionarism which leans towards Kolchak and Denikin." Lenin concluded:

> Our task is to put the question bluntly. What is better? To ferret out, to imprison, sometimes even to shoot hundreds of traitors from among the Cadets, non-party people, Mensheviks and Socialist-Revolutionaries, who "come out" (some with arms in hand, others with conspiracies, others still with agitation against mobilization, like the Menshevik printers and railwaymen, etc.) *against* Soviet power, *in other words, in favor of Denikin?* Or to allow matters to reach such a pass that Kolchak and Denikin are able to slaughter, shoot and flog to death tens of thousands of workers and peasants? The choice is not difficult to make.[79]

Some revolutionary Marxists warned against what they saw as a dangerous turn of events. Rosa Luxemburg argued as early as 1918: "Without general elections, without unrestricted freedom of press and assembly, without a free struggle of opinion, life dies out in every public institution, becomes a mere semblance of life, in which only the bureaucracy remains as an active element." The Bolsheviks felt the criticism was unfair. "If our November revolution had taken place a few months, or even a few weeks, after the establishment of the rule of the proletariat in Germany, France, and England," Trotsky argued, as if in response to Luxemburg, "there could be no doubt that our revolution would have been the most 'peaceful,' the most 'bloodless' of all possible revolutions on this sinful earth." Instead, the Russian Revolution was the first socialist revolution, thus putting Russia alone among nations, the most powerful of which were responding with murderous hostility, and "in the moment of greatest peril, foreign attacks and internal plots and insurrections," the Bolshevik regime resorted "to severe measures of State terror." He insisted: "Without the Red Terror, the Russian bourgeoisie, together with the world bourgeoisie, would throttle us long before the coming of the revolution in Europe."[80]

Here Luxemburg was prepared to agree. "All of us are subject to the laws of history, and it is only internationally that the socialist order of society can be realized," she acknowledged. "The Bolsheviks have shown that they are capable of everything that a genuine revolutionary party can contribute within the limits of historical possibilities." This is a remarkable admission. "They are not supposed to perform miracles," she added. "For a model and faultless proletarian revolution in an isolated land, exhausted by world war, strangled by imperialism, betrayed by the international proletariat, would be a miracle."[81] The "betrayal" by the workers of other countries—that is, their failure to make socialist revolutions in their own lands, which would bring relief to the Russian Soviet Republic—was a circumstance that Luxemburg herself sought to alleviate in Germany, before she was murdered by *Freikorps* death squads under the Social Democrat Gustav Noske in 1919.

If Luxemburg was willing to concede so much, what then was the point of her initial critique? She herself explained it in this way: "The danger begins only when they make a virtue of necessity and want to freeze into a complete theoretical system all the tactics forced upon them by these fatal circumstances and want to recommend them to the international proletariat as a model of socialist tactics." By trying to place into socialism's theoretical arsenal "as new discoveries all the distortions prescribed in Russia by necessity and compulsion," Luxemburg warned, the Bolsheviks would introduce disastrously "false steps" for those seeking to follow their example.[82]

7
MAJORITY OF THE PEOPLE

*H*istorically, there had been a decades-long controversy among Russian revolutionaries over how the overthrow of tsarism and how the movement toward socialism might be accomplished. From the late 1880s down to 1917 and beyond, the two basic positions to emerge were that of the "populists" and that of the Marxists—the first positing a revolution based on the vast peasantry (in some cases assuming that capitalism could be bypassed altogether), the second positing a revolution based on the rising working class (in all cases insisting that capitalism was already and inevitably triumphing in Russia).[1]

In what follows, I will try to do justice to different lines of argument (each of which grasps aspects of the complex reality), but for the sake of clarity, I will state here that my own view tilts in the direction of Marxists who embrace Socialist Revolutionary insights.

Among Russia's revolutionary Marxists, Lenin arguably developed the most insightful and the shrewdest approach to "the peasant question." Russian Marxists—guided by the central thrust of Marx's own analysis—focused on the modern proletariat that arose within the dynamic development of industrial capitalism. Lenin was no exception, and until 1917 he shared the general conviction that industrially backward, overwhelmingly agricultural Russia would first have to experience a thoroughgoing *bourgeois-democratic revolution* that would sweep away the authoritarian tsarist system of semi-feudalism/semi-capitalism—allowing for the full development of industrial capitalism and a bourgeois-democratic polity within which a dramatically expanding proletariat could both become the majority of the people and wage the ultimately triumphant struggle to "win the battle of democracy" (as the *Communist Manifesto* had put it).

Yet Lenin seems to have had a keener sense than many of the limitations and unreliability of the Russian bourgeoisie. More important, he had a keener appreciation of the combined oppression and revolutionary potential of the Russian peasantry. In contrast to his mentor George Plekhanov and other comrades who became Mensheviks, Lenin and (largely thanks to him) his Bolshevik comrades were able to develop a more radical, consistent, and uncompromising approach to the bourgeois-democratic revolution that was based on the central strategic conception of a worker-peasant alliance.

It can be argued that as a consistent Marxist, Lenin also had a decisive edge over the revolutionary populists of the Socialist Revolutionary Party, who were influenced by Marxism, to be sure, but maintained a critical distance from the Marxist mainstream that traditionally gave short shrift to the peasants. The nature of the working class was in important ways qualitatively different from that of the peasantry. The working class was concentrated more compactly than the peasants in a collective labor process, often within an industrial capitalist workplace, and these new proletarian layers were stimulated to think critically of their often new and dynamically changing surroundings. Increasing numbers of workers were becoming literate and in many cases were experiencing a growing scientific awareness, at the same time enduring what was increasingly and obviously the oppressive exploitation of their labor-power from which actual labor was squeezed in order to enrich their employers. All of this generated study circles, discussion groups, trade unions, reform struggles, and political organizations—and the consequent labor movement and class struggles gave the edge to the revolutionary struggle that could not be found so easily within the vast peasantry. A discussion of the difference between the worker and the peasant by one of Lenin's protégés, Nikolai Bukharin, is suggestive of how Bolsheviks saw the matter:

> Every worker becomes accustomed to *working back to back with other workers in the same position.* Concentrated in enormous masses, the workers live and work in gigantic factories and plants, in the mines and pits. Not only do they learn to hate and mistrust the bourgeoisie, to unmask every betrayal, but they also learn to strike back *in unison.* They grow steadily more accustomed to the belief that they can defeat the enemy only through *joint action,* and that once the enemy has been defeated, *only jointly* can they reconstruct the entire economy and administer the

country they have taken from the bourgeoisie. Urban culture places at their disposal the means with which the workers can build their ranks into a structured army, do battle against the domination of the landlords and the capitalists, and unravel all the guile of the enemy. With the peasant, matters are quite different. The peasant works by himself, on his *own farm*, with his family and his household. With few exceptions (for instance, mowing, etc.) he is unaccustomed to working in common along with his fellow villagers. He has his own separate, *private* farm; and he is concerned, first and foremost, with the interests of *his own* petty undertaking. The conditions of rural life are such that he is seldom beyond the outskirts of the village. Even today there are still peasants who have never been so far as the district capital, and others have never traveled on a railroad.[2]

The contrast perhaps contains overstatement and distortion, but few would argue that it has no correspondence to social realities in early twentieth-century Russia. Either because of this proletarian edge, or coinciding with it, Lenin's vision and political instincts certainly proved to be sharper than those of the Socialist Revolutionaries. And the practical-political results of Lenin's approach—grounded as it was in the labor movement—ultimately proved to be far more effective than what the SRs were able to accomplish. At the same time, it can also be argued, Lenin's Marxist insights tended to tilt in the direction of applying a schematic approach to rural Russia's complex actualities to which the Socialist Revolutionaries were actually more sensitive. On some level, Lenin perceived this, adapting at decisive moments (but not, as we shall see, at all moments) to their perspectives.

The day after their 1917 seizure of power, the Bolsheviks submitted two decrees for consideration to the All-Russia Congress of Soviets, and both were unanimously approved. One was a decree for peace, declaring Russia's withdrawal from the First World War. The other was a decree for land—essentially giving Russia's agricultural lands to the peasants. Specifically, it declared the abolition of private property, with all lands held by landlords, the state, and the Russian Orthodox Church to be placed "at the disposal of rural district land committees and of county Soviets of Peasants' Deputies pending the Constituent Assembly." Wording on the detailed execution of this measure (which also exempted from confiscation the smallholdings of working peasants) was taken directly from the program of the Socialist Revolutionary Party, which Lenin now termed "the expression of the unconditional will of the vast majority of the conscious peasants of the whole of Russia."[3] To the assertion that the Bolsheviks were simply advancing the position of the SRs, thereby abandoning their own long-held position favoring nationalization of the land and the development of collective farming, Lenin responded:

> Does it matter whose work it is? We, as a democratic government, cannot evade the decision of the rank and file of the people, even if we do not agree with it. In the fire of life, by applying it in practice, by carrying it out on the spot, the peasants themselves will come to understand what is right. . . . Life is the best teacher and will prove who is right; let the peasants starting from one end, and us starting from the other, settle this question.[4]

Of course, the new regime was simply legalizing an established fact. "Decree or no decree the land was destined to pass into the hands of the peasant," Maurice Hindus points out. "The peasant was seizing it by force of arms." The Bolshevik triumph had been rooted, in part, in the powerful reality (noted by Lenin in September 1917) that "peasant revolt is flowing everywhere in a broad stream," and—initially—Lenin and his comrades derived their orientation from this dynamic, which was also grounded in their historic commitment to a worker-peasant alliance. "In order to prove to the peasants that the proletarians want not to order them about, not to dictate to them, but to help them and be their friends, the victorious Bolsheviks did not put *a single word of their own* into the decree on the land, but copied it word for word from the peasant ordinances (the most revolutionary, it is true) which had been published by the SRs in the SR newspaper."[5]

There were sound reasons for this initial adaptation to the SR approach. We have already noted that the peasantry, roughly 80 percent of the entire population, constituted by far the largest chunk of "the people." Failure to involve them in the decisive decisions affecting their lives would prove to be highly problematical for any government claiming to represent and advance the interests of the toiling masses—not to mention a government claiming to be more democratic than the constitutional republics of the bourgeois world. In addition, it can be argued, the SR Party—through many years of experience, analytical study, and struggle in close contact with the Russian peasants—had a far better understanding of "the peasant question" than did the Russian Social Democratic Labor Party, not only Mensheviks but Bolsheviks as well.

An alternative analysis to pro-SR interpretations indicates that, on the contrary, it was the Bolsheviks who had the superior understanding, realizing that the term *peasantry* itself masked decisive class divisions. "The poor and landless peasants were more likely to engage in the violent and revolutionary break-up of the landlords' estates than the more prosperous peasants whose own small possessions might suffer," writes historian E. H. Carr. "In this sense the SRs—especially the Right SRs—were a less revolutionary party than the Bolsheviks, and had an analogy with the Mensheviks who represented the skilled groups of workers in the towns."[6] As will be suggested, however, this Bolshevik view of things may itself have failed to comprehend important complexities.

The fact that the initial radical-democratic approach of the Bolsheviks was not sustained highlights what became a problematical aspect of that regime—that its perspectives and policies quickly diverged from the outlooks and desires of the majority of the people. We have so far explored a number of reasons why this was so, and in this chapter we will add to our understanding of how that came to be. One problem was that *the Bolshevik understanding of "the peasant question" oversimplified realities better grasped by the SRs and Left SRs, their sometime allies.* We will also consider perspectives of others who struggled to develop a different Marxist analysis and socialist policy than that projected by Lenin and his co-thinkers.

Divergent Understandings of the Peasantry

"The Communist Party, being Marxist, was consequently hostile to the peasants," was the bitter judgment of Socialist Revolutionary Olga Chernov. "It had proclaimed the nationalization of the land, but had disfigured the meaning of this law." She then got to the heart of the matter: "It had always classed the peasants as petit-bourgeois and treated them as enemies of the proletariat. The Communists were town-dwellers, with no understanding of country life or the needs and struggles of the farmers." She concluded: "They only excited the hatred of the country districts."[7]

Lenin's perceptions were far more complex and interesting than Chernov seems to allow.[8] Alert, as were all Marxists, to the voraciously expansive globalization dynamics inherent in the capitalist mode of production, Lenin was able to document the permeation of the Russian economy by these dynamics and the persistent absorption of agriculture, including peasant life, into the vortex of a commodity economy. "Even in the central agricultural belt (which is the most backward in this respect compared with the south-eastern border regions or the industrial gubernias), the peasant is completely subordinated to the market on which he is dependent in regards both his personal consumption and his farming, not to mention the payment of taxes." Throughout Russia, he argued, agricultural and village communities were being dramatically affected by capitalist dynamics—"competition, the struggle for economic independence, the grabbing of land (purchasable and rentable), the concentration of production in the hands of a minority, the forcing of the majority into the ranks of the proletariat."[9]

Like many observers of the Russian scene at this point in time, but unlike many populists, Lenin believed that the traditional village commune (the *mir* or *obschina*) could no longer be seen as a barrier or alternative to such capitalist development. "The system of economic relations in the 'community' village," he insisted, "does not at all constitute a special economic form ('people's production,' etc.), but is an ordinary petty-bourgeois one," he wrote, adding that "the Russian community peasantry are not antagonists of capitalism, but, on the contrary, are its deepest and most durable foundation." Capitalist penetration and transformation of the countryside was generating "differentiation of the peasantry," creating "two new types of rural inhabitants." One, according to Lenin, was "the rural bourgeoisie or the well-to-do peasantry . . . [who] include the independent farmers who carry on commercial agriculture in all its forms," plus "the owners of commercial and industrial establishments, the proprietors of commercial enterprises, etc." On the other end of the rural social spectrum was "the rural proletariat, the class of allotment-holding wage-workers. This covers the poor peasants, including those that are completely landless." While each of these new types reflect the increasingly "commodity, money character" of the rural economy, the intermediate layer, what Lenin terms the *middle peasantry*, "is distinguished by the *least* development of commodity production," but in the new circumstances its position "is an extremely precarious one"—a process "specifically characteristic of capitalist economy takes place, the middle members are swept away and the extremes are reinforced—the process of 'de-peasantizing.'"[10] One could argue with Olga Chernov and her comrades that this analysis reflected aspects of reality in rural Russia, as Lenin contended, and that such an analysis is hardly one that makes peasants "enemies of the proletariat." On the other hand, defenders of traditional peasant life would certainly take umbrage with such a conclusion as this one by Lenin:

> One has only to picture to oneself the amazing fragmentation of the small producers, an inevitable consequence of patriarchal agriculture, to become convinced of this progressiveness of capitalism, which is shattering to the very foundations the ancient forms of economy and life, with their age-old immobility and routine, destroying the settled life of the peasants who vegetated behind their medieval partitions, creating new social classes striving of necessity towards contact, unification, and active participation in the whole of the economic (and not only economic) life of the country, and of the whole world.[11]

At the same time, however, Lenin seems to have grasped that it was just this devastating impact of capitalism on traditional peasant life that was radicalizing masses of peasants, causing them under certain circumstances to rail against the established order. This was the basis for the worker-peasant alliance that he began projecting at least as early as 1903. In *To the Rural Poor,* he extols the peasant struggles of previous centuries: "In the period of serfdom the entire mass of the peasants fought against their oppressors, the landlord class, which was protected, defended, and supported by the tsarist government." After the 1861 abolition of serfdom, "the peasants remained without rights, remained an inferior, tax-paying, 'black' social-estate, remained in the clutches of serf bondage." Lenin went on to extol the peasant uprisings of 1902, explaining "they rose against the landlords, broke open their barns, shared the contents among themselves, distributed among the starving the grain that had been sown and reaped by the peasants but expropriated by the landlord, and demanded a new division of the land. . . . The peasants decided—and quite rightly—that it was better to die fighting the oppressors than to die of starvation without struggle." He continued that "the Russian working class will always honor the memory of the martyrs who were shot down and flogged to death by the tsar's servants."[12] And he concluded:

> The day will soon come when the urban workers will rise not merely to march shouting through the streets, but for the great and final struggle; when the workers will declare as one person: 'We shall win freedom or die in the fight!'; when the places of the hundred who have been killed, fallen in the fight, will be taken by thousands of fresh and still more resolute fighters. And the peasants, too, will then rise all over Russia, will go to the aid of the urban workers, will fight to the end for the freedom of the workers and the peasants.[13]

But Lenin never seems to have discarded the basic schema that projected onto the complex peasant reality edifyingly clear conceptualizations of "well-to-do" peasants (later given the problematically expansive tag of *kulaks*), seen as up-and-coming peasant-capitalists, atop the very large but presumably shrinking segment of "middle peasants" (many of whom wished to become peasant-capitalists), and the presumably swelling number of poor and proletarianizing peasants. Insightful as Lenin's analyses were, they missed important countervailing tendencies that helped make a different reality than what he perceived. More than this, the limitations of his own approach were replicated, made even simpler (more limited), and at times applied—with destructive insensitivity and brutality—by many who had rallied to the Bolshevik cause. This finds reflection in Olga Chernov's harsh criticism.

Latter-day historians (including those who are not unsympathetic to the goals of the Bolshevik revolution) have been able to identify the problematical limitations of the Bolshevik approach to "the peasant question." Teodor Shanin has offered a particularly effective critique, noting that aspects of Lenin's analysis are well taken, but that he presents a "sharply over-polarized picture" of class divisions within the peasantry inconsistent with the findings of "contemporary rural specialists, Marxist and non-Marxist alike." Particularly problematical was that "his bourgeois-capitalist stratum was a conjecture, and a strongly over-stated conjecture at that, as Lenin was to learn and to admit in the period of the revolution and the civil war in 1917–21." Shanin notes recent scholarship regarding "the limited use of wage labor within agriculture and the consequent limited advance of capitalism within it," which is consistent with Lenin's own 1906 conclusion that his earlier estimate of capitalist development in agriculture had been "overstated." Shanin also emphasizes that the accumulation of land in the hands of a few and the spread of large-scale units of production . . . confidently expected by the early liberal and Marxist analysis . . . did not happen." In addition, "the 'kulaks' as understood by the Russian peasants and indeed by everybody with a sufficient knowledge of the Russian countryside . . . cannot be equated with capitalist entrepreneurship. Arguably, the opposite holds true, that is, the 'kulaks' hampered rather than advanced the development of capitalist farming."[14]

In different ways, either directly or tangentially, sometimes implicitly and sometimes quite explicitly, a number of scholars in the late twentieth and early twenty-first century—such as Viktor Danilov, Moshe Lewin, Lars Lih, Wendy Goldman, and perhaps most pointedly John Marot—have put forward ways of understanding the Russian peasantry more or less consistent with Shanin's approach. Some scholars, such as S. A. Smith, have challenged Shanin and others for envisioning some sort of "moral economy" of the peasantry—a controversy that need not divert us from endorsing Shanin's criticism of the all-too-common Marxist inclination to overstate "class divisions" and "capitalist" consciousness within the peasantry.[15]

But even in Lenin's time, there were people—adhering to, or influenced by, Marxist perspectives—who articulated a more balanced understanding that took up aspects of the reality missing from Lenin's analysis. Most famous was Rosa Luxemburg, who in a substantial note in *The Accumulation of Capital* (1913) attached to a rich discussion of the debates on capitalist development in Russia, wrote:

Obviously, it is an empty abstraction to divide the peasantry among all the categories of capitalist production, and to conceive of the peasant as entrepreneur, wage laborer, and landlord all in one person. The economic particularity of the peasantry—if it is to be treated as an undifferentiated category ... consists precisely in the fact that it belongs neither to the class of capitalist entrepreneurs nor to that of the waged proletariat; it does not represent capitalist production at all, but rather simple commodity production.[16]

Of course, Luxemburg's comments were made in passing, embedded in a complex work taking up many issues in Marxist theory and global capitalist development. And a scant five years later, in her posthumously published critique *The Russian Revolution*, she seems to have reversed herself—sharply criticizing Lenin for opportunistically taking slogans from "the much condemned Socialist-Revolutionaries, or rather, from the spontaneous peasant movement," rather than sticking to the original Bolshevik program of a nationalized and centralized program of agricultural production. Now, she warned, "it was the rich peasants and usurers who made up the village bourgeoisie possessing the actual power in their hands in every Russian village, that surely became the chief beneficiaries of the agrarian revolution." Beginning her next sentence with the revealing words "without being there to see," she nonetheless confidently asserted that "anyone can figure out for himself that in the course of the distribution of the land, social and economic inequality among the peasants was not eliminated but rather increased, and that class antagonisms were further sharpened." Her 1918 conclusion: "The Leninist agrarian program has created a new and powerful layer of popular enemies of socialism on the countryside, enemies whose resistance will be much more dangerous and stubborn than that of the noble large landowners."[17] This flies in the face of her 1913 characterization of the peasantry—and corresponds instead to problematical underlying notions common among Marxists (certainly among the Bolsheviks as well as the Mensheviks) at the time.

There were others, however, who did provide more detailed and sustained interpretations. Of course, some Bolsheviks sought to develop nuanced and complex analyses of peasant life—for example, Nikolai Bukharin, who emphasized that "the peasantry is *far from homogeneous*," explaining:

The well-to-do tavern-keeper, the village moneylender, and the *kulak* are all referred to as peasants. The large-scale proprietor, who keeps several agricultural workers in harness in order to profit from their labor, is also called a peasant. The toiling proprietor, who works for himself along with his family and does not live at the expense of other people's labor, is similarly a peasant. There are also poor peasants, who do not even own a horse and are scarcely able to make ends meet by taking odd jobs on the side. And finally, there are peasants who are farm laborers for part of the time, urban workers for the balance, and whose farms are but a secondary source of income. In the capitalist system the vast majority of the peasants are condemned to a type of existence in which they barely make ends meet.[18]

But Bukharin is, in fact, offering a sophisticated restatement of Lenin's early schema. Others went well beyond it.

The independent-minded left-wing Menshevik Nikolai N. Gimmer—commonly known by his revolutionary *nom de plume* N. N. Sukhanov—in the early 1900s had been an articulate SR theorist, and in the 1920s sought to integrate earlier insights into a nuanced Marxist approach to Soviet Russia's agricultural development. Even more substantial were the research and analyses provided by Alexander Chayanov, primarily a scholar who devoted his life to the integration of sociology, economics, and agricultural policy, with special reference to rural realities in tsarist and early Soviet Russia. Neither man was an uncritical supporter of the Bolshevik revolution, but both stayed in Soviet Russia and sought to assist the regime in considering and developing policies that might be beneficial to the workers and peasants, and to the socialist cause generally.[19]

Sukhanov approached matters in an independent and critical-minded manner that took issue with various elements on the left. In his 1909 study *On the Problem of the Evolution of Agriculture,* revised in 1924, he challenged, on the one hand, revisionist-Marxist and reformist trends in the international socialist movement favoring small peasant farms (he held that large mechanized farms were superior if organized along cooperative lines), and, on the other hand, the more "orthodox" Marxists—both Bolsheviks and Mensheviks—seeing the triumph of capitalism in Russian agriculture as inevitable. In his massively documented study, he contrasted the "vitality and stability" of non-capitalist Russian peasant farms (which should be supported, in his opinion) with problematical capitalist agriculture. On the other hand, he increasingly differentiated himself from the mainstream populism of the SRs (eventually going over to the Russian Social Democratic Labor Party), arguing that in contrast to the workers, peasants had greater potential for *opposing* socialism (although they continued to manifest "communal psychology, customs, and practices," and—he insisted—correct policies could pull them in a socialist direction). Consequently, he urged the SRs to stop self-identifying as a "peasant party" and to merge with the Marxists. He also began to question whether the traditional *obschina* was durable in the face of aggressive tsarist policies to undermine them in order to advance capitalist development—for which SR leader Victor Chernov severely criticized him, insisting that once tsarist anti-*obschina* policies were ended, "you will be surprised how quickly many of the wounds inflicted will be healed."[20]

In the early 1920s, Sukhanov moved away from his pessimistic doubts as the *obschina* did indeed experience a remarkable revitalization in post-tsarist Russia—a matter to be taken up later in this chapter. From an explicitly and aggressively Marxist perspective, he polemicized against Leonid Kritsman and other influential Communist theorists who were "shell shocked by one sentence in the second chapter of Lenin's *Development of Capitalism in Russia* which read, 'The peasantry ceases to exist, it is transformed on the one hand into a proletariat and on the other hand into a bourgeoisie.'" Sukhanov went on to scoff that "ever since, Kritsman has been knocking himself out in the search for capitalism in the peasant economy, determined to find it wherever it does and does not exist." Instead, this peasant economy operated according to quite different principles. A revolutionary workers' party in Russia moving forward to build a socialist society, would not find "proletarian cadres" among the lower strata of the peasantry with whom to ally in a struggle to vanquish the "kulaks"—instead it would find, if it moved forward in that manner, "vast masses of dispersed and reactionary petty [peasant] proprietors who are hostile to socialism." In contrast to this barren approach, "the agrarian program of a workers' party must always be a peasant program." This would include providing for the economic and cultural needs of all, supporting peasant smallholders with a supply of land—though collectively owned, rather than private property—and encouraging voluntary, large-scale production with strategic offerings of agricultural technology.[21]

From a more scholarly, less activist vantage point, Alexander Chayanov influentially worked amid an important, somewhat diverse current of other scholars and policy-advocates focused on agrarian realities. He developed a theorization of the peasant economy shortly before the 1917 revolution, and further developed it in the succeeding years. In contrast to Sukhanov, he does not appear to have been critical of the Bolsheviks taking power, and although his analyses were controversially (though nonpolemically) in opposition to the perspective of Lenin's *Development of Capitalism in Russia*, Lenin intervened to enable Chayanov to work and publish without interference, "because we need wise heads, we are left with too few of them." Chayanov insisted that into the first quarter of the twentieth century, 90 percent or more of the farms in Russia still had no hired labor (which is the key qualifier, in his opinion, that would make them "capitalist"). Instead, they were distinctive "family farms," a key element in his own conceptualization of *peasant economy.*[22]

Not all families were the same, and the specifics of each were important: the number of children and other household members, their ages, the amount of work each could do, the amount of food each would need. These essentials had to do with labor and consumption—"the family labor force and consumption units," as Chayanov put it—which meant that *"every family,* depending on its age, is in its different phases of development a completely distinct labor machine as regards labor force, intensity of demand, consumer-worker ration and the possibility of applying the principles of complex cooperation." Such governing dynamics (that is, "the peculiar features of their economic behavior") counterposed "the family to the capitalist farm" (a counterposition that he also tagged "the labor farm" in opposition to "the farm based on hired labor"). Even if both existed within the context of a capitalist economy—which Chayanov was prepared to acknowledge was increasingly the case in tsarist Russia—he saw "a difference between the phase of capitalist development in which the number of family undertakings comprise a substantial part of production and the phase in which they have lost any significance."[23]

Chayanov—in contrast to many populists—was not inclined to argue against the Marxist insistence that capitalist development was becoming the dominant factor in the Russian as well as the global economy. In fact, he acknowledged, "the peasant farm almost everywhere has been drawn into the system of the capitalist commodity market; in many countries it is influenced by finance capital, which has made loans to it and coexists with capitalistically organized industry and, in some places, agriculture also." Capitalist relations had become hegemonic in the Russian economy, and "the world's agriculture, ours included, is being more and more drawn into the general circulation of the world economy, and the centers of capitalism are more and more subordinating it to their leadership." Yet the fact remained that in Russian agriculture the head of production most generally "does not sit in the entrepreneur's chair, but is the organizer of family production." To construct a theory of Russian agricultural economics as essentially capitalist "is clearly one-sided and is inadequate for learning about economic reality in all its actual complexity."[24]

Chayanov's moderately but firmly stated conclusions were based on careful research (which seems to have coincided, more or less, with that of Sukhanov):

> Simple, everyday observation in the countryside shows us elements of "capitalist exploitation." We suppose that, on the one hand, proletarianization of the countryside and, on the other, a certain development of capitalist production forms

undoubtedly take place there. However, in our opinion, these social processes should be sought out, not by means of classifying sown areas, and so on [that is, on the basis of what are the more prosperous farms], but on direct analysis of capitalist factors in the organization of production, i.e., hired labor on farm, not brought in to help their own, but as the basis on which to obtain unearned income, and oppressive rents and usurers' credit. . . .

On the basis of agricultural statistics, we might establish the proportion of labor and capitalist agriculture in different countries, and almost everywhere we would observe, together with purely labor farms, capitalist forms. In Russia, this type of farm has not become very widespread among the peasants. . . .

Within the Russian peasantry, social differentiation is still in its initial stages, and we will not undertake to judge how far the semi-labor, semi-capitalist "farmer" type unit will be able to improve its position with the present tendency of the Russian peasantry for enclosed farms. We must hope that the labor farm, strengthened by cooperative bodies, will be able to defend its positions against large-scale, capitalist type farms as it did in former times.[25]

Chayanov added an interesting and important observation to his account of what had been happening in rural Russia: "While the elements of capitalist organization of production did not develop much among Russian peasants, the proletarianization of part of the peasantry in densely populated areas proceeded very rapidly before the Revolution." What he is referring to is the reality that we noted earlier in this study regarding the dramatic growth of the Russian proletariat: "It was of a clearly industrial character and took the form of a completely regular stream of rural population porting into industrial and urban centers."[26]

Along with insisting that agriculture of tsarist Russia and the early Soviet period could not be understood by theoretically mutilating peasant realities to make them fit the Procrustean bed of "bourgeois/proletarian relations" in the countryside, Chayanov offered an insightful and prescient description of how the global capitalist economy was powerfully bringing about its own mutilation of peasant life throughout the world. "In a *production sense* concentration in agriculture is scarcely reflected in the formation of a new large-scale undertakings, *in an economic sense* capitalism as a general economic system makes great headway in agriculture," he commented in 1924, elaborating: "The dynamic processes of agricultural proletarianization and concentration of production, leading to large-scale agricultural production units based on hired labor, are developing throughout the world, and in the USSR in particular, at a much slower rate than was expected at the end of the nineteenth century." In fact, "the area swept by agrarian revolutions has even, as it were, strengthened the position of the small farm." He then noted an aspect of capitalist penetration:

Repeating the stages in the development of industrial capitalism, agriculture comes out of a semi-natural existence and becomes subject to trading capitalism that sometimes in the form of very large-scale trading undertakings draws masses of scattered peasant farms into its sphere of influence and, having bound these small-scale commodity producers to the market, economically subordinates them to its influence. By developing oppressive credit conditions, it converts the organization of agricultural production almost into a special form of distributive office based on a "sweatshop system." In this connection, it is enough to recall the examples of capitalist exploitation which Knop, the Moscow cotton firm, applied to the Sart cotton growers, buying up their harvest in the spring, giving out advances for food, and giving them credits for seed and means of production.

These trading links that convert the natural, isolated family farm into one of a small commodity producer are always the first means of organizing scattered peasant farms and of opening the first path for the penetration of capitalist relations into the countryside.[27]

The fact that Chayanov's analyses, far from being widely considered, were marginalized in preference to Lenin's early conceptualizations would have profound implications for practical policy, and for people's lives, in the early Soviet Republic.

Agrarian Tragedy

It is impossible to make sense of the early agricultural policies of the Soviet regime simply by referring to Lenin's and the Bolsheviks' theoretical perspectives on the peasantry. According to Lars Lih, "one of the central features of this whole period of war, revolution, and civil war was a food-supply crisis that was both symptom and intensifier of the overall dislocation and then breakdown of national economic and social life."[28] Even before the Bolsheviks took power, Lenin was pointing to the crisis that was overtaking the country—a crisis facing the Provisional Government, and one that had been developing under tsarism as well. It was a crisis of hunger, and the solution was (in his opinion) the rapid application of the Bolshevik program:

> Dire necessity is knocking at the door of the entire Russian people. This dire necessity consists in the fact that it is impossible to continue farming in the old way. If we continue as of old on our small farms, even as free citizens on free land, we shall still be faced with inevitable ruin.... Individual husbandry on individual plots, even though it be "free labor on free land," offers no way out of the terrible crisis.... It is essential to go over to joint cultivation on large model farms.[29]

"In fall 1917 the chain reaction of social disintegration led to a series of explosions—in the countryside, on the front lines, and in the capital cities," Lih has emphasized, pointing to unmistakable signs "of the immanent collapse of food supply," which "destroyed the morale of the existing political class while confirming the political formula of the Bolshevik contenders."[30] E. H. Carr has placed this crisis in larger context:

> What came to be called "war communism" was, as its chief contemporary historian wrote, "an experiment in the first steps of the transition to socialism." The period from 1918 to 1920 was in every way a testing time for the new regime; and while it defeated with impressive ease enemies whose only program was to restore the old order, the exigencies of the civil war threw into relief the fundamental dilemma confronting it. The economic backwardness of Russia had smoothed the path for the political triumph of the revolutionaries, since they had been opposed only by the survivals of an obsolete feudalism and by an undeveloped and still inefficient capitalism. But the same fact made the subsequent socialist construction infinitely difficult, since they were called on to build a socialist order without the solid democratic and capitalist foundation which Marxist theory had treated as indispensable.[31]

We have seen that the Bolsheviks' vision was ultimately to consolidate the peasant smallholdings into larger enterprises that would be worked collectively with all the most modern techniques. Thus, in 1917 the land was not simply declared the property of the individual peasants. Rather, it was nationalized but then distributed more equitably to peasant households (by the peasants themselves) for their use. Or this is how it was officially, legally rationalized largely after the fact—"the fact" being that the peasants, with Bolshevik blessing and encouragement, simply took the land and carried on their own redistribution. For all practical purposes, the peasants reasoned, the land was theirs—with the support of the new government. Lenin's notion was that the peasants were vital allies that must be won over gradually to collectivized agriculture. As with much else, however, harsh realities generated far more brutal policies than had been anticipated in theory.

The Bolsheviks' lack of close ties with the countryside had an impact on government policy in the Civil War period. Especially serious in this regard was the tragic break between the Bolsheviks and the Left Socialist Revolutionaries, whose base was especially strong among the working peasantry (i.e., those who worked their own land without significant help from hired labor). In April 1918, Spiridonova had argued for a reversal of her party's decision to break with the Bolsheviks. "Our chief duty is to bring about the socialization of the land," she said. "The mentality and principles of the Bolsheviks are alien to this task. It is we who must carry it out. How can we do it unless we take part in the business of government?"[32] Unfortunately, she was not able to win a majority of her party to this perspective. Despite their pragmatic adoption of the Socialist Revolutionary Party's call for redistribution of the landed estates to the peasantry, the Bolsheviks were theoretically opposed to the "petit bourgeois" smallholdings as anything more than a temporary expedient. This in itself created potential for a collision between the Bolshevik regime and much of the Russian peasantry, a collision that the Left SRs might have helped to avert. On the other hand, it would be wrong to see "Bolshevik dogmatism" as the only cause for the clash with the peasants. The new regime faced a complex reality that lent some credence to the Bolsheviks' long-standing preference for centrally coordinated collectivization of land and rural labor, which was anathema to the Left SRs and to their peasant constituents.

With famine threatening the country, the Bolshevik leaders took desperate measures. Historian Roy Medvedev, sympathetic to the Bolsheviks, has put it bluntly: "They chose to take grain from the peasants by force in order to feed the starving industrial and office workers in Russia's urban regions." A "Food Army," largely composed of enthusiastic young worker-Bolsheviks, was sent to obtain food by any means necessary. A national network of poor peasants' committees was also organized to pit those with little or no land against the "rich peasants" (many of whom were poor by Western standards) but also against middle peasants, or working peasants, who were perceived as "hoarding surpluses." Although this was a positive development in that it created a ramshackle rural support base for the Bolshevik crusade and was hailed by Lenin and others as bringing "socialist revolution" to the countryside, it actually created a new layer of smallholders (with holdings too small to produce a surplus) and had a devastating impact on village life. One Bolshevik proclamation declared: "Workers and starving peasants, comrades, you know where the grain is. Almost all the surplus grain is in the hands of the village kulaks. . . . The detachments you form, together with the disciplined units of the Red Army, led by experienced and tested revolutionaries and specialists in food procurement, will march out to win the grain from the village bourgeoisie." As Gregory Zinoviev expressed it: "We are very well aware that we cannot carry through the proletarian revolution without crushing the village kulaks and without annihilating them psychically and, if necessary, physically." He added, with "revolutionary" swagger, that "the revolution in the village should take the kulak by the throat and strangle him by all the rules of soviet art; it is precisely for this that we need a genuine, operative worker-peasant machine for strangling kulaks."[33]

Yet this so-called "village bourgeoisie" turned out to comprise majority sectors of the rural population that had largely supported the Bolshevik revolution but that did not want to simply turn over the fruits of their labor to these outsiders in exchange for well-meaning promises and practically worthless paper money. According to historian Taisia Osipova:

> In fact, this definition of kulak was nothing but a rhetorical abstraction. Despite their social differentiation, the wealthier peasants in central Russia had not broken with the traditional peasant commune. They still followed the same patriarchal laws as the rest of the peasants. . . . Although there were too few of the better-off peasants to pose a danger to the government, their affinity with peasants at large and their leadership role in the countryside gave them strength. What united them with the middle-income peasants and some of the poor peasants was their resistance to the Bolsheviks' policy of coercion. For three years rebellions shook Russia, on the periphery and in the central provinces, as peasants fought against this state coercion.[34]

Moshe Lewin also argues that "the kulak was a hard-working peasant, who sometimes (though not always) employed one or, more rarely, two paid workers, and owned a few agricultural machines which he would hire out to his neighbors. He cannot therefore be defined as either a 'capitalist' or a 'semi-capitalist.'"[35]

Journalist Maurice Hindus, visiting his old village after living nineteen years in America, offered a memorable description of one such "kulak" (at least, he had that distinction in the eyes of Soviet officials): "His manner of living varied but little from that of the average muzhik. Hens strutted about the house. In the corner under the sleeping platform lay a little brown pig, stretched out at full length and snoring hoarsely. The rough board floor was crusted with mud and littered with potato skins and bits of manure tracked in from outdoors. The little windows were dim with dust and fly-specks, and cobwebs hung in the corner directly over the icon."[36]

All too often, the "surplus grain" targeted by Soviet requisition detachments was a normal cushion for hard times. Sometimes it was grain for future planting, the confiscation of which would mean hunger for all in the future. After such policies were abandoned, Lenin described what had happened in precisely these terms, while offering what Carr has called "the only possible excuse for such measures," namely that such policies were wartime measures necessary "to cover the costs of the army and to maintain the workers" in the life-and-death struggle against the armies of the landlords and capitalists.[37]

Mikhail Baitalsky, an enthusiastic Komsomol activist at the time, still recalled years later one of the outcomes, remembering "the burial of several boys and girls—seventeen-and-eighteen-year-old Young Communists killed by peasants for demanding that they turn over grain requisitioned by the state. In response, the peasants killed these boys and girls, slit open their stomachs, and filled them with grain." Baitalsky wrote:

> The cruelty of the peasants—who did not want to turn over their grain to the state—made a deep impression on me. I have not been able to forget it—these tormented boys and girls, these Communist youth. In the years that followed, I witnessed a great deal; but this impression has stayed with me forever because it was my first such experience.
>
> The cruelty of the peasants, whose grain was being forcibly confiscated, was the cruelty of despair, the impotent vengeance of the embittered. It cannot be justified, but it must be distinguished from the cruelty exhibited by the machinery of the state.[38]

"One-fifth of the workers in the food-supply detachments were killed between May and December" of 1918, writes Lars Lih, who adds that "in the months of July through September the conflict with the peasants led to more than ten thousand state and party casualties."[39] But it was the Bolsheviks who had initiated this destructive struggle in the countryside, which generated fierce rebellions and considerable violence. Fortunately for the Bolsheviks, the bulk of the peasants feared the White armies (which symbolized a return of the big landlords) more than they feared the obviously anti-landlord Reds, who at least promised a better future for the peasants once the Civil War was won. Otherwise the conflict in the countryside might have overturned the revolution.

The Left SRs had attempted to persuade the Bolsheviks that the key "class" distinction among the peasantry must be based not on whether one had an ill-defined "surplus" or an extra cow or an "advanced" piece of farm equipment, but on whether or not one used hired labor. (It has been estimated that only 1 percent of all peasant households employed more than one laborer.) After an initial vacillation, the Bolsheviks rejected this argument, deciding to procure the "hoarded surpluses" by force while at the same time striking at the rural base of the Left SRs. "In late 1918," notes Lih, "Zinoviev compared the middle peasant to the middle strata in the towns." The petty bourgeois elements in the towns were soon made to realize that "we weren't fooling around and that there was no other master [but us] nor could there be."

Lih follows Zinoviev's analogy: "In the village this realization would soon occur when the kulaks were crushed and the middle peasant saw that the poor peasant was now 'the true master of the Russian land.'" The Bolshevik struggle of "intensifying the class struggle in the countryside" to obtain food for the cities and to undermine the Left SRs combined with the Bolshevik vision of large-scale, centralized agricultural industry replacing "petty-bourgeois" peasant smallholdings. "The government is already running big estates with workers instead of peasants where conditions are favorable," Lenin explained to H. G. Wells in 1920. "That can spread. It can be extended first to one province, then another." His next comment speaks volumes: "The peasants of the other provinces, selfish and illiterate, will not know what is happening until their turn comes!" In fact, these experiments in collectivized agriculture remained relatively ineffective and miniscule in the period we are discussing.[40]

The Bolsheviks had been popular among the peasants in late 1917 because they supported the peasants taking the land. But the mood changed. "We are Bolsheviks, but not Communists," peasants were reported as saying. "We are for the Bolsheviks because they drove out the landowners, but we are not for the Communists because they are against individual holdings."[41]

Bolshevik-turned-Communist policy as it unfolded in 1918 generated hundreds of desperate uprisings among the peasantry, at various moments, throughout Russia. It has been estimated that between 1918 and 1921, peasant rebels killed at least 100,000 people, "mostly civilian Soviet functionaries, Communists, and other representatives of authority," according to Taisia Osipova. Such rebellions were suppressed by the Red Army and the Cheka, which inflicted much higher casualties upon the recalcitrant peasantry. Among armed peasant detachments were fighters who were neither Red nor White but called themselves "Green" (such as followers of anarchist Nestor Makhno), disaffected deserters from the Red Army, and others. It is estimated that as many as a million rebels perished on the battlefield, through executions and through deaths in prisons and concentration camps, and undoubtedly there were additional casualties on the Communist side in the fighting. The famine of 1920–21—flowing from traumas of the First World War and the Red-White conflict, but also from the effects of Communist conflicts with the peasantry—swept away millions more.[42]

A lengthy Cheka report by high-level Bolshevik stalwart, V. A. Antonov-Ovseenko, clearly explained the causes of the uprisings. A few sentences give a sense of the report's perspective:

The peasant uprisings develop because of widespread dissatisfaction, on the part of small property-owners in the countryside with the dictatorship of the proletariat, which directs at them its cutting edge of implacable compulsion, which cares little for the economic peculiarities of the peasantry and does the countryside no service that is at all perceptible.... The peasantry, in their majority, have become accustomed to regarding the Soviet regime as something extraneous in relation to themselves, something that issues only commands, that gives orders most zealously but quite improvidently.... [The Soviet regime] is a force which issues instructions from the outside and not the acknowledged guide of the peasant farmer; in the eyes of the peasants it is tyrannical and not a system that, before all else, organizes and ministers to the countryside itself.[43]

Antonov-Ovseenko was not the only one drawing such conclusions. The Bolsheviks-turned-Communists on the ground were learning—some more quickly than others—from the bitter lessons they were being taught by the actual peasants who refused to conform to schematic "Marxist" conceptualizations.

The result was a series of policy shifts. "One common view of the later years of the time of troubles is as a period when the Bolsheviks and the peasants grew dangerously apart after their alliance in 1917," writes Lars Lih. "Only after a series of peasant revolts in late 1920 and 1921 did the Bolsheviks come to their senses by making the long-overdue changes necessary to placate the peasants," in the form of the New Economic Policy inaugurated in March 1921. But in a detailed examination of the period, Lih finds "a different story." He concludes:

The Bolshevik-peasant alliance of 1917 was compatible with mutual incomprehension, and it was only in 1918 that the Bolsheviks and the peasant realized how little they understood each other. In the years that followed, this lack of knowledge began to be overcome, thus laying the groundwork for the introduction of the food-supply tax. The policy changes of 1921 [the New Economic Policy] were not a repudiation of the achievements of the civil war period but their continuation.[44]

Shifting Policies

In August 1917, almost three months before the Bolshevik revolution, Pavel Ryabushinsky arose at the second All-Russian Commercial and Industrial Congress to deliver a speech that was widely reported afterwards. A powerful, very wealthy Russian industrialist and banker, also a patron of the arts and a moderately liberal opponent of the tsarist autocracy, Ryabushinsky had played an influential role on the political scene leading up to and following the overthrow of the tsar. Feeling strongly that the insurgent workers' movement was going too far in its radical demands, he said:

> Our commercial and industrial class will do its job to the end [to assist crisis-ridden Russia] without expecting anything for itself. But at the same time it feels at present it is unable to convince anybody or influence people in leading positions.
>
> Therefore our task is very difficult. We must wait—we know that the natural course of life will go on its way and unfortunately it will severely punish those who destroy economic laws....
>
> We feel that what I have said is inevitable. But unfortunately it is necessary for the bony hand of hunger and the people's poverty to grab by the throat the false friends of the people, the members of the various committees and soviets, before they come to their senses. The Russian land groans in their comradely embrace. The people at present do not understand this, but soon they will, and they will say: "Away, deceivers of the people." (*Stormy applause*)[45]

Some historians have seen these remarks as reasonable, others as vitriolic—but at the time, and for some time afterward, the threat of "the bony hand of hunger" was seen by revolutionaries as a threat from the upper classes to sabotage the economy and to blackmail the suffering masses of people in order to defeat the revolution. To a significant degree, this is the context within which many Bolsheviks were inclined to view the food crisis threatening the country in 1918. Ryabushinsky's remarks "demonstrated better than any other argument that the struggle with hunger was a class struggle," according to a later Soviet source. "There is no doubt that this is a definite plan, worked out in the quiet of bourgeois offices a long time ago," proclaimed the prominent and popular Bolshevik orator Gregory Zinoviev, who projected the capitalists to be saying "we have a way of controlling you: the bony hand of hunger, and it will smother your revolution." He called for "holy violence against those kulaks who fulfilled Ryabushinsky's program." This was by no means simply his own orientation—it reflected the official statement of the Sovnarkom (Council of People's Commissars), which declaimed in May 1918: "All that is steadfast, disciplined, and conscious in a single organized food-supply order! Unhesitating fulfillment of all directives of the central authority! No separate actions! War on the kulaks!"[46]

Such a mind-set contributed powerfully to generating the agrarian tragedy we have examined. In fact, the Bolsheviks were attempting to deal with a food crisis brought on by disruptions in food production and distribution resulting from civil war and foreign intervention. There were other, longer-term causes for the crisis that merit attention. The 1917 revolution had swept away the large landed estates as well as the modernization fostered by the Stolypin reforms under the tsar. The purpose of those reforms, it will be remembered, had been to facilitate the formation of a peasant stratum that would be more prosperous than the rest, more inclined to maintain (tsarist) law and order, more open to the modernization efforts being fostered by Prime Minister Stolypin.

With the Bolshevik revolution, the village communal institution, the *obschina* or *mir*, naturally came to the fore again. Land was distributed more equitably by the *mir*, through less efficient traditional strips located in widely separated fields. Modern crop rotations, although more productive than the old three-field system of rotation, didn't fit in with *mir* arrangements and therefore weren't used. There was a greater reliance than ever on the tried-and-true technology of the past, such as the wooden plow. This also made practical sense in the face of the decline of manufactured goods in this period, and also given the likelihood that if one produced more than the others the result might be dangerous accusations that one was a "rich peasant" or "kulak."

The dynamic of the revolution thus strengthened the impulses toward the more tradition-bound and self-sufficient communities of subsistence farmers and weakened those of the ambitious and individualistic commercial farmers; the ranks of the latter were hard hit by assaults on "the greedy kulak," while the ranks of the former were expanded by the demotion of the more well-to-do as well as the acquisition of small parcels of land by many of the landless or near-landless rural poor. Agricultural productivity was set back by the mighty waves of egalitarianism and social justice that swept the countryside. "Thus the effect of the revolution was, in a technical sense, reactionary," notes Alec Nove.[47]

Before coming to power, the Bolsheviks had called for dealing with the collapse of both political authority and food supply with the most thoroughgoing revolutionary democracy. "Democratic soviets could overcome the food-supply crisis by crushing the sabotage that was its main cause," is Lih's summation of the initial strategy. "But events quickly revealed that the soviets and other local organizations would not make real sacrifices to support the new authority unless direct local benefit was obvious." As a frustrated Bolshevik functionary complained: "They say that the voice of the people is the voice of God. We hearkened to the voice of the people, . . . but what came of it? The most pathetic results possible." For many, "all power to the soviets" had meant *all power to the localities*—which was disastrous for the effort to ensure that people throughout the new Soviet Republic would have enough to eat.[48] Lih recounts: "The response unveiled by the Bolsheviks in the spring of

1918 was called the food-supply dictatorship. The legislative underpinnings of the food-supply dictatorship were set forth in a series of dramatic decrees passed in late May and early June. . . . Its aim was to reconstitute authority in the face of the spiraling growth in intensity of centrifugal forces that had continued since the fall of 1917."[49]

According to Lih, despite levying "well-aimed" criticisms at various aspects of Bolshevik policy, neither the Mensheviks nor the Left SRs proved able to articulate any "positive alternatives" that might prove more effective than the Bolsheviks' "food-supply dictatorship" in supplying food throughout Russia in this moment of crisis.[50] Yet this emergency measure dovetailed with other authoritarian developments. "Bolshevik rhetoric on the food-supply crisis took place in a growing atmosphere of invective and threats against the other socialist parties," Lih points out. We can see this in an angry speech by Lenin following a critique offered by Left SR leader Maria Spiridonova. "A thousand times wrong is he who says (as do sometimes careless or thoughtless Left SRs) that this is a struggle with the peasantry," Lenin argued. "No, this is a struggle with an insignificant minority of village kulaks—this is a struggle to save socialism and distribute bread in Russia." He added ominously: "It is untrue that this is a struggle with peasants. Anyone who says this is the greatest of criminals, and the greatest of misfortunes will happen to the person who lets himself be hysterically carried away to the point of saying such things." Trotsky spoke in a similar vein: "Don't poison the worker masses with lies and slander, for this whole game might end in a way that is to the highest degree tragic," warning that "the soviet political authority will act more decisively and radically" against such things. He commented on the evaporating lines of demarcation separating counterrevolutionaries, monarchists, exploiters, and kulaks from Mensheviks and Socialist Revolutionaries: "No, there is no such line: they are united in one black camp of counter-revolutionaries against the exhausted worker and peasant masses."[51]

In regard to moving beyond emergency measures to longer-term solutions, there was agreement among revolutionaries of different persuasions that larger production units and greater coordination among the peasants was needed to increase agricultural productivity and increase food production and distribution. Yet the most successful form of collectivism in the countryside had involved voluntary communes and cooperatives, of which the Left SRs were enthusiastic partisans. They argued for a reliance on these organizations, combined with incentives to grow more, incentives that had been obliterated by wholesale requisitioning. The most commonsense incentive would have been to allow the peasants to keep part of their surpluses, which could then be used to exchange for goods they needed through consumer cooperatives and through the market, which had been abolished (actually, driven underground) by the Bolsheviks.

Left SR leader Spiridonova complained: "While we were organizing peasant families in agrarian communes in a number of provinces, the Bolshevik commissars came out and upset the work of these communes." Against her Bolshevik adversaries in the All-Russian Congress of Soviets in the summer of 1918, she thundered: "You may have a majority in this Congress, but you have not a majority in the country. You want to transform the property of the landlords into state-controlled economic units controlled by your commissars, but unfortunately the working peasants of Russia see in that nothing but a return to slavery." Her comrade Isaac Steinberg later recalled: "The policy on which Lenin was now recklessly embarked showed Bolshevism in an entirely new light. The freedom of the peasants, their cooperation with the workers, the freedom of the Soviets, were all imperiled." Speaking on behalf of the Left SRs at the Soviet Congress, Spiridonova insisted: "We declare that the peasantry also has an independent way of life and a right to a historical future."[52]

Unfortunately, the Left SRs were in the process of removing themselves from all positions through which they might have positively influenced the situation—first by their withdrawal from the government after the Treaty of Brest-Litovsk, then by their suicidal campaign of terror and insurrection designed to renew war with Germany and challenge Bolshevik power. The role they might have played, one based on the insights and experience gained through their rural base, could have helped shape policies by which the Soviet regime would have avoided the devastating confrontation with the peasantry. As it was, the kind of approach championed by the Left SRs was finally embraced by Lenin and his comrades in the New Economic Policy of 1921.

As Lih points out, Lenin and his comrades, through successive approximations, gradually shifted in this direction in the course of a series of painful experiences from 1918 to 1920.

Early on, they recognized the absolute necessity of reigning in and replacing (as much as possible) abusive, incompetent, and corrupt "enforcers" of Bolshevik policy. One early Bolshevik chronicler, N. Orlov, commented on the abusive manner of initial worker-detachments sent to the countryside to secure grain—such as "some drunken vagabond, accidentally occupying the post of a requisition detachment." Another Bolshevik organizer, Alexander

Schlichter, referred to another detachment as "worthless trash" that failed to understand that "without the assistance of the peasantry it would be impossible to accomplish anything, and the practice of simple raids on the village and of armed requisition was a bad one." A state monitoring report, responding to peasant complaints, found that "too many products and commodities spill over into the pockets of the soviet bureaucracy, their families, lovers, acquaintances, and relations," and there was, as Lih indicates, a "drive to impose the discipline of the center on the food-supply apparatus as a whole."[53]

It also did not take long to overcome illusions regarding the "poor peasants," with Communist officials concluding, according to Lih, that "the poor peasants and semi-proletarians were more a nuisance than a staunch ally." Orlov commented that the much-touted Committees of the Poor had proved "pitifully small, self-seeking and benighted groups of poor peasants, making clams to *all* the grain of their area and conquering the resistance of the entire peasant mass only by help of detachments from the cities and from the north." Other objections accused them of "timidity and sloth," and yet others complained "everywhere the unenlightened poor peasant covers up for the rich peasant simply for fear of losing someone who will give loans." There was also a decided shift away from the "anti-kulak" ferocity, coupled with a new stress on the *middle peasants'* central importance. By the end of 1918, Lenin was emphasizing that the kulaks were not a target for expropriation as the big landowners had been, and by 1920 he commented that "we got carried away with the fight against the kulaks"; the term *kulak* tended to disappear from official decrees, and smashing kulaks ceased to be projected as the solution to the food-supply crisis. Bolshevik food-supply official P. K. Kaganovich referred to kulaks "not so much as an economic force as a psychological phenomenon," and references were made to a "kulak mood" flowing from "mutual misunderstanding." It was the middle peasant who was increasingly seen, Lih tells us, as "the key not only to grain collection but also to political stability." A Communist food-supply official in the Ukraine, Miron Vladimirov, explained in 1920 the need to help "the poor villagers and the loyal strata of the middle peasantry [to] rise up the social ladder" as a means for "asking them to help solve and carry out tasks" that would help the Soviet Republic while "strengthening their own position." The three-tier schema superimposed on the peasantry (kulak/middle peasant/poor and proletarianized peasant) was never fully abandoned—but it was softened, blurred, minimized in practice and even in propaganda. Alexander Smirnov, a seasoned Bolshevik who headed the People's Commissariat of Agriculture from 1923 to 1928, distinguished himself in challenging (as historian James Heinzen notes) "the accepted over-simplified categories into which peasants fell—poor, middle, and rich—and refusing to accept the vague and simplistic categories of rural class analysis commonly used in the party." Smirnov sought to "minimize the number of peasants who could be labeled as kulaks."[54]

Yet these "accepted categories" had already been eroding under the impact of stubborn realities. Increasingly, compromise and flexibility found their way into Bolshevik policy. As early as the summer of 1918, Lenin had shifted from uncompromising appeals for a crusade against kulaks in the villages to a call "to neutralize the greatest possible number of peasants in the civil war," in part through paying peasants higher fixed prices for grain, encouraging greater use of cooperatives, and relying more heavily on commodity exchange, as well as applying greater discipline over food-supply detachments. All these steps represented on-the-ground efforts to precisely enact the regime's new policy shifts. A new *razverstka* (quota assessment) system was established. "Instead of a strategy based on class struggle and overcoming sabotage," Lih writes, "the *razverstka* system aimed at neutralization of the peasantry and possibly even a partnership with it." In Soviet appeals issued in 1919 to the peasants regarding their "moral duty to the socialist fatherland and the Red Army," the regime insisted that "the state demands from the peasant and for the worker only that amount that the worker can give [in return] to the peasant." Worker-detachments to the villages now became "travelling squads of agitators," which, in addition to securing grain, sought to assist peasants with the harvest and with repairs. A shift away from the "village-splitting tactics of class struggle," *razverstka* "assigned a definite amount to the village" to be given in grain, with a promise "to leave the village alone once the amount was paid"—seeking to present a strong but reasonable image of a state "taking only the surplus and not anything that was really needed for consumption and farm needs."[55]

In the 1920s, Maurice Hindus quoted the judgment of Communist theorist V. Karpinsky: "How soon the socialization of land will become universal all over Russia, depends first upon the sentiment of the people of the country with respect to socialization, and secondly on the possibility of the [Soviet-run] agricultural communes, which are in a minority, to convince the majority of private owners of the land, of the practicability and greater profitableness of communistic agricultural labor."[56] Such seemingly reasonable shifts were undermined by multiple factors, not least of which were, in the words of Lih, "all the hardships of the complete economic breakdown of 1920, when the economy was rapidly spiraling toward utter destruction," making it impossible to keep all of the well-intentioned promises. For example, there was the tendency to con-fiscate from the middle peasant whatever the food detachment could find, "on the assumption that the peasant could subsist on what was hidden." There was also the powerful temptation to collect the *razverstka* not just once, as promised, but two or three times. Despite the intention to exchange useful commodities for whatever grain was taken, the devastated condition of Soviet industry made this problematical. The regime attempted to offset this with "peasant weeks"—designated periods in which workers volunteered to help with farm work—which Eugen Preobrazhensky described as "the beginning of the payment for grain and for labor obligations," although it is not clear that this was deemed a satisfactory trade by most the peasants. "We must show the village that soviet authority takes the peasant surplus, while giving almost nothing in return," he continued, "only because of its poverty." This too could be expected to bring scant comfort to rural areas. Also problematical was the fact that the moderate policies associated with *razverstka* were viewed as a temporary compromise, "forced by the urgency of military survival" but destined to be abandoned once the Civil War was over.[57]

On August 8, 1920, Alexander Schlichter—newly appointed chair of the provincial executive committee for food supply in Tambov Province—addressed a conference of comrades. A veteran revolutionary and longtime Bolshevik, Schlichter enjoyed a reputation for increasing grain procurements with an intelligence and sensitivity that had prevented peasant uprisings. In his remarks, he emphasized that those under his direction must "work like law-abiding revolutionaries" in order to overcome the "bitter memories of food supply workers, especially of what they were doing two or three months ago." Only by interacting with the peasantry in a qualitatively better man-ner would it become possible for them in the future to "safely walk in the countryside." But it was too late. Three weeks later, a food procurement team was massacred, which was only the initial moment of a massive peasant rebel-lion—precisely in Tambov Province. This was one of several uprisings taking place in this period.[58]

The peasants' "loyalty to the Bolshevik regime and reluctant submission to the requisitions had been inspired mainly by fear of a 'white' restoration and the loss of their lands," E. H. Carr tells us. "Once this fear was finally removed, the way was open for a revival of normal resentments at oppressive exactions." As many peasant soldiers from the Red Army demobilized and returned to their villages, there was a proliferation of rural rebellion, with increasingly violent outbreaks from September 1920 to March 1921. Some of the more effective of the uprisings were led by Right SRs, carrying out the decision of their underground Central Committee, in some cases effectively utilizing well-thought-out tactics of guerrilla warfare. Their slogans were "Down With State Monopoly on Grain Trade" and "Soviets Without Communists." Tens of thousands participated in the rebellions. The casualty rates were devastating, with noncombatants caught in the cross fire and horrific atrocities committed by both sides. Red Army forces led by Civil War heroes M. N. Tukhachevsky and I. P. Uborevich, utilizing sweepingly brutal tactics, finally won decisive victories. Delano DuGarm, a historian of the Tambov rebellion, writes that the impact of this popular rising on the regime was that "it forced a reassessment of the sources of peasant discontent, especially the forced grain procurement system." His colleague Taisia Osipova offers the more sweeping judgment that "the peasants overturned [the policies of war communism] through armed struggle," and that "in this sense the peasants won on the internal front of the civil war."[59]

Under the New Economic Policy, the confiscation of agricultural "surpluses" was replaced by a "tax in kind," a food tax that was far more modest than the previous requisitioning targets. Food that remained after payment of the tax was free to be used as the peasant saw fit—including being sold on the market, which was revived with the legalization of private trade, although consumer cooperatives were officially encouraged and enjoyed some success. "Everyone, once the first shock of surprise was over, accepted NEP as a necessity," notes Carr, but "it was accepted by some willingly, by others with an uneasy conscience; and the justification of NEP was a theme reaching back to the beginnings of the regime and pointing forward to the economic controversies of the future." To the extent that "war communism was building on a foundation of what had gone before" in the state-capitalism model, employing "centralized control and management," its policies were retained, despite revisions in scope and detail. On the other hand, war communism's "substitution of a 'natural' economy for a 'market' economy," involving "an unprepared plunge into the unknown," had proved problematical and was "decisively rejected by NEP." David Rousset states the case with admirable clarity: "NEP was based on the necessity to resort to capitalism in order to save the economy from suffocation, to uproot agriculture from village autarchy, to put a broken down industry on its feet, to fill the holes made by the civil war, and to put basic goods back into circulation: in other words, to recreate a dynamic of production."[60]

This shift in Bolshevik policy also contained problems (which will be touched on later), but it meant a new lease on life for the peasantry, as well as for the entire population, not to mention the Bolshevik regime. The destructive impact of the earlier war communism policies didn't simply evaporate into thin air, however. In addition to being a nightmarish memory for the peasants who survived, it was to be a precursor of a far more devastating collectivization campaign launched by the Stalin regime in the early 1930s. And while the earlier aggressive policies under Lenin were largely a tragic product of civil war and economic crisis, they were also related to an analysis of—and attitude toward—the peasantry that, despite the historic Bolshevik tradition of the "worker-and-peasant alliance," made the peasant a second-class citizen under the Bolshevik conception of "the dictatorship of the proletariat."

It is conceivable that a different course could have been followed. Had the Bolshevik–Left SR coalition held together, perhaps policies would have been developed to give the rural population greater political rights and equality in this early period, sparing them victimization from government violence that was all too common in 1918–21. This could have helped lay the sociopolitical basis for greater nationwide democracy than the Bolsheviks by themselves provided.

The initial "pro-peasant" policy (and the return to it, as we shall see), while viewed by leading Bolsheviks as necessary and much preferable to policies antagonistic to peasant aspirations, appears to have been linked with the development of capitalist market mechanisms that necessarily generate socio-economic inequality. This raises obvious questions about the socialist project in Russia and also about the possibilities of realizing the ideal of proletarian democracy. Such realities were inseparable from the unanticipated fact that the Soviet revolution remained isolated in a global capitalist economy.

Even before NEP, Maurice Hindus was asking, "In a country which is so overwhelmingly agricultural, can communism in industry exist side by side with individualism in agriculture?"[61]

Limitation or Expansion of Democracy?

The Bolsheviks saw the peasants as the most important allies of the workers, but they believed that it was the working class as such that must be the politically dominant class in Soviet Russia—a bold notion, considering the fact that 80 percent of the country's population was peasant and less than 20 percent proletarian. "The industrial urban proletariat," according to the 1919 program of the Russian Communist Party, "comprising that portion of the toiling masses which is highly concentrated, most united, most enlightened, and most perfectly tempered for the struggle, must be the leader in all rev-olutions." Explaining this, Bukharin and Preobrazhensky argued that "the peasants (the middle peasants and even some of the poor peasants) were far from steadfast," adding: "They were only successful when they joined forces with the proletariat. Conversely, whenever the peasants took a different line from the proletarians, they were inevitably enslaved by Denikin, Kolchak, or some other representative of the landlords, the capitalists, or the military caste." Consequently, peasant electoral representation was given less weight than that of the urban working class. In the All-Russian Congress of Soviets, one rural delegate would represent every 125,000 inhabitants, while one ur-ban delegate would represent every 25,000 electors. The party program spoke of "the temporary character of these privileges," but they were to stay in place until the "historical conditions" that brought them into being had given way to "the socialist organization of the villages." It is worth adding that the Men-sheviks shared this non-peasant bias, and even when they were in opposition after the Bolsheviks took power, as Vladimir Brovkin notes, "the Mensheviks welcomed concessions to peasants but feared the one-man, one-vote princi-ple," being inclined to agree with the Bolsheviks that "a workers' revolution in Russia could succeed by the resolute leadership of a revolutionary minority."[62]

The Bolsheviks had traditionally seen themselves as a working-class par-ty, not as some sort of workers-and-peasants party. While many of its working-class members may have had peasant roots, at the end of 1917 there were only 4,122 members in its rural cells, out of a Bolshevik Party membership of 115,000 (and out of a rural population of 100 million).[63]

It is also crucial to recall that in pre-Bolshevik Russia there was no pre-tense of democracy. The tsar was absolute ruler. When some quasi-democratic reforms were forced through by the 1905 upsurge, the tsarist policy-makers made use of the Prussian model: different classes elected representatives to an electoral college, and these various electoral colleges were allowed to select a particular percentage of legislators; representation in the legislature was always skewed toward those chosen from the electoral colleges of the socioeconomic elite. In Russia, when the worker ascended to the throne of the tsar, it did not seem as odd for him to give his peasant ally a smaller voice in policy-making than numbers would seem to call for. Sociologist E. A. Ross, who made several visits to Russia in the wake of the October Revolution, elaborated:

> It is obvious that in this system the industrial workers are a privileged class. . . .
> The Constitution speaks of "inhabitants" when referring to the rural population
> and of "voters" when referring to the urban population. If about two fifths of

"inhabitants" are "voters," then the townspeople would have double the political weight of an equal number of country people. Their advantage is further enhanced by their being represented on higher and lower bodies at the same time, i.e., on county soviets and provincial congresses, and on the national Congress. Probably the political weight of a town worker is about *four times* that of a peasant. The Communists justify this inequality of representation on the ground that the peasants are centuries behind the factory workers in civic consciousness and political ripeness.[64]

There are ways in which this circle can be squared, through reference to the argument of social scientists—cited in the "Defining Democracy" section of this study's appendix—that an "economic threshold" and a "sociocultural" or "literacy threshold" must be reached before democracy becomes a practical possibility, at least in relation to large and complex enterprises and societies. If democracy is not always, everywhere, and under all circumstances possible because it requires certain cultural and social preconditions, the goal of a revolutionary government could be to help advance processes that facilitate the development of such necessary preconditions. One might add that such processes should be advanced not simply "from the top down," but with increasing degrees of popular inputs and participation on the part of more and more people in society. If such processes, inputs, and participation increase quantitatively, the whole system could change qualitatively into a genuinely democratic polity.

Yet the contradiction, in regard to the peasantry, between democratic rhetoric and undemocratic practice stubbornly refused to evaporate—deeply grounded, as it was, in what N. N. Sukhanov had tagged "simplistic clichés and schemes invoked in the name of a falsely understood Marxism."[65] Bertram Wolfe—as he wrestled in the late 1940s with his own residual revolutionary socialist commitments—insightfully identified the problem (in retrospect, to be sure, and imparting to it a whiff of inevitability):

The Marxists in Russia, Bolsheviks as well as Mensheviks, tended to look upon the Russian peasantry with distrust and suspicion. Having set him down as a petty bourgeois, unconsciously the Marxist workingmen looked upon him as a potential enemy. Hence it became easy in Soviet Russia for the Bolshevik workingmen to sanction the use of force against the peasant majority and the use of police overseers over them: first to requisition grain and stop "profiteering" or private trading, then to police the planting and harvesting and the marketing of the crops, then to marshal them in droves into the collective farms. But this same peasantry was really the overwhelming majority of the Russian people, so that to sanction a police overseership over them would inevitably exclude the possibility of democracy—in the simple sense of government of, for and by the majority of the people. And a police apparatus huge enough to police the planting and harvesting all over vast, rural Russia, would it not tend to spill over into the very organizations of the advanced city workers who had sanctioned it: into their state, their unions and their party?[66]

The problem that Wolfe emphasizes here definitely posed itself with special violence during the Civil War between 1918 and 1920—and even more so with the "revolution from above" initiated by the Stalin regime beginning in the late 1920s, which carried out forced collectivization of the land, brandishing such slogans as "eliminate the kulaks as a class," and which resulted in millions of deaths through pitiless repression and devastating famine. "Preserving a democratic workers' state now meant, at the very least, preserving peasant support," John Marot has aptly noted. "For the question of democracy in the very broadest, 'popular' sense of the term—support of the majority for the gains of the October Revolution—came down, in the final analysis, to retaining the support of the peasant-majority."[67]

The period between 1920 and 1928 saw the consequent implementation of the New Economic Policy, advanced by Lenin in part for the purpose of "adapting" to actualities that did not conform to Bolshevik preconceptions regarding class dynamics and economic-developmental realities in Russian agriculture. New pathways toward increasing freedom and democracy, which are at the heart of the socialist promise, seemed to open up. Maurice Hindus has described it expansively but accurately:

> The New Economic Policy, with its legalization of private enterprise, the removal of the ban on hired labor on the farm, the extension of greater political sovereignty to the village, the periodic slashings of prices of necessaries at a colossal loss of the government, the recent broadening of the New Economic policy with its further concessions to private enterprise, have been put into force primarily to placate this Russia, to meet the needs of the peasant. Certain it is that the fortunes of the Revolution are interwoven with the fortunes of the muzhik.[68]

"This, it will be said, is a concession to the muzhik. That is just what it is," Trotsky approvingly commented in 1922. "If we had not made this concession, the Soviet Republic would have been overthrown. How many years will this phase of the economy last? We don't know know—two years, three, five, or ten: until the Revolution comes in Europe." Bolshevik economist Eugen Preobrazhensky made a similar point in the same year: "NEP is, assuredly, a slow flanking tactic on the part of the proletarian government of a country that has not been supported by proletarian revolution in other countries and that has been obliged to build socialism in isolation within a hostile capitalist encirclement." But he added that "it is at the same time the economic policy of the proletariat of a *peasant* country that finds itself in this situation. In analyzing what NEP is today and what it promises for tomorrow, we must therefore take both of these aspects into account." Noting that the Bolsheviks won the Civil War due to "the strong military alliance between the workers and the peasants of our country," Bukharin emphasized in 1925 that "we will triumph fully and completely, we will really build a new society of labor only if we are able once more, in these new, peaceful, postwar conditions, to strengthen anew that alliance between the working class and the peasantry that was the guarantee of our victory throughout the entire revolution."[69]

At the Fourth World Congress of the Communist International in 1922, Trotsky was tasked with explaining all of this to the assembled delegates. It is worth lingering over some of what he told them. Addressing the idea that the NEP constituted "a retreat from socialism," he insisted: "We never had socialism, nor could we have had it." He went on to describe the actualities of what had been tagged "war communism" in this way: "We nationalized the disorganized bourgeois economy, and during the most critical period of life-and-death struggle we established a régime of 'Communism' in the distribution of articles of consumption." But this was hardly the goal for which the 1917 revolution had been made. He continued:

> By vanquishing the bourgeoisie in the field of politics and war, we gained the possibility of coming to grips with economic life and we found ourselves constrained to reintroduce the market forms of relations between the city and the village, between the different branches of industry, and between the individual enterprises themselves.
>
> Failing a free market, the peasant would be unable to find his place in economic life, losing the incentive to improve and expand his crops. Only a mighty upsurge of state industry, enabling it to provide the peasant and agriculture with all its requirements, will prepare the soil for integrating the peasant into the general system of socialist economy. Technically this task will be solved with the aid of electrification, which will deal a mortal blow to the backwardness of rural life, the muzhik's barbaric isolation, and the idiocy of village life. But the road to all this is through improving the economic life of our peasant-proprietor as he is today. The workers' state can achieve this only through the market, which stimulates the personal and selfish interests of the petty proprietor. The initial gains are already at hand.
>
> This year the village will supply the workers' state with more bread-grains as taxes in kind than were received by the state in the period of War Commu-

nism through confiscation of the grain surpluses. At the same time, agriculture is undoubtedly on its way up. The peasant is satisfied—and in the absence of normal relations between the proletariat and the peasantry, socialist development is impossible in our country.[70]

Of course, as Trotsky emphasized at the same World Congress, "it is perfectly self-evident that the tempo of our future [socialist] construction will in the highest measure depend upon the development of the revolution in Europe and in America."[71]

It could be argued, however, that the seeming pause in the advance toward socialism, represented by the NEP, opened up more time and greater space within which there was an opportunity to further develop Communist theoretical and policy perspectives regarding rural policies. Such a deepening of Marxism might have helped transcend the contradictions afflicting Bolshevik policy. While there are indications that Lenin—had he lived long enough—may have been able to carry out such creative work (as he had done in the past), this was not to be.[72] The leading theorists in the Russian Communist Party likewise failed to come up with a coherent breakthrough. Trotsky, for all his insight and innovative brilliance, never got past the traditionally restrictive categories that hampered so much of Marxist analyses on the peasantry. Bukharin's boldly creative efforts became fatally entangled in his alliance with Stalin—who finally and brutally dispensed with the bright but imprudent factional partner, coming up with his own horrific "resolution" of the peasant question.

Yet this outcome need not have been the foregone conclusion that Bertram Wolfe seems to suggest. There were significant realities, along with the development of interesting theorizations within Soviet Russia beyond Bolshevik ranks, that indicated pathways for a new understanding of how "the peasant question" might fit into the forward movement of socialism. In the period leading up to 1917, populist "illusions about peasant socialism" had given way to liberal and Marxist analyses, and also to relentless capitalist economic development in Russia, and many agreed that what was supposed to have been (according to populist dogma) the bridge from tsarism to Russian socialism, the *obschina* or *mir,* seemed to be in irreversible decline, according to Moshe Lewin. "Oddly enough, however, there was a revival of the *mir* during and after the revolution. It was the *mir* which undertook the confiscation and redistribution of the estates of the landed gentry." Compared with the *mir,* he adds, the rural soviets were "something of a Cinderella." Soviet statistics indicated that in the mid-to-late 1920s, 90 to 95 percent of the peasantry belonged to these 380,000 village communes existing throughout Russia.[73]

This opened the possibility of a line of thought that Sukhanov developed with enthusiasm. (The former Menshevik found employment as a minor researcher for the Soviet regime and was active in the agrarian section of the Communist Academy.) He was able to cite manuscripts from Marx's 1881 writings—newly published by Bolshevik scholar David Riazanov of the Marx-Engels Institute—to document that Marx himself had seen the *obschina* (in Marx's own words) as "a natural basis for collective appropriation" that could (with infusions of technology) help to generate "a combined and mechanized form of farming." Sukhanov argued that—contrary to his own earlier pessimism (and the accepted "wisdom" of most pre-1917 Marxists)—Marx's 1881 notions still made sense and should be implemented, through a merger of the village soviets with the *obschinas* and the necessary infusions of technology. "In the context of Russia's industrial development and of the Soviet revolution, the *obschina* could have played an important part in modernizing and socializing soviet agriculture," argues Sukhanov's biographer Israel Getzler. Yet the critical-minded Sukhanov, seeking to assist the Soviet regime while sporting two albatrosses around his neck—his ex-populist and ex-Menshevik credentials—had neither a following nor allies. As Sukhanov himself commented, "It is sufficient for me to put forward an idea to have it rejected out of hand."[74] Moshe Lewin has observed the irony of this: "And so we are left with a paradoxical situation, in which the village organization which stood for all the collectivist aspects of village life, and which had been rooted in the village for centuries, was given no part whatsoever to play in the collectivization of the peasantry. And this was done in the face of constant criticism and complaints from those in power about the individualism of the peasant who would not give up his strip of land."[75] Interestingly, not only was Sukhanov's pro-*obschina* partisanship dismissed by Communist hard-liners, but it was ignored by Alexander Chayanov as well.

It may be that Chayanov was tactfully avoiding this specific conflict with the hard-liners, but there may have been other considerations, such as those put forward in a 1920 study by Maurice Hindus. Land improvement was impossible, according to Hindus, as long as the peasant producer was "a slave of the commune, its customs, traditions, institutions." Regularly redistributing strips of land—with the unproductive, the mediocre, and the good being circulated among various peasants, with all being restricted at the same time to less productive agricultural practices—the *obschina* or *mir* "tended to promote inefficiency, extravagance and waste" on the part of the peasant, and "contributed substantially toward his economic ruin." Hindus also argued that the form of "communism" represented by the village commune—"that is the equitable periodic redistribution of the land"—involved a system in which "the peasant could do what he pleased with his stock, implements and crops. The land belonged to the commune, but the muzhik worked it as his private property and gathered and disposed of his crops as he chose." This generated individualistic impulses and practices cutting across general agricultural productivity and the well-being of the larger society.[76]

Chayanov's skepticism about the viability or need of the *obschina* was offset by his insistence that the noncapitalist peasant family farm was the firmly rooted reality on which Russia agriculture was based, and on which it must continue to be based. Chayanov offered an additional duo of concepts—*vertical concentration* and *horizontal concentration*—to explain alternate lines of agricultural development. The first (as Viktor Danilov puts it) involves a "path of growing diversity and interaction between different forms and scales of the organization of production processes and economic ties, both of the co-operative and the non-co-operative varieties." The second involves "a form of concentration under which a multitude of very small and geographically scattered enterprises were merged, not only in the economic but in the technical sense, into one gigantic whole." Chayanov saw vertical concentration as preferable if it "assumes not capitalist, but cooperative or mixed forms." In fact, "in its cooperative form this process goes much deeper than in its capitalist ones, since the peasant himself hands over to cooperative forms of concentration sectors of his farm that capitalism never succeeds in detaching from it in the course of their struggle."[77]

In his 1924 studies, Chayanov utilized Lenin's category of state capitalism to describe Russia's current economic reality as a transitional phase between "normal" capitalism and socialism, asserting that "we ought to introduce elements into the future organization of agriculture, the further development of which *would itself outgrow state capitalism and might be the basis for a future socialist economic system*." Horizontal concentration—forcing peasant smallholdings into nationalized enterprises that are "large and technically quite well-organized farms," or a system of "grain and meat factories," with a "further proletarianization of the peasantry"—was "completely inapplicable," he insisted. Instead, "the course of cooperative collectivization" through vertical concentration (not obliteration) of peasant smallholdings "is the sole course possible in our conditions to introduce into peasant farming the elements of large-scale farm industrialization and the state plan." Cooperatives had already been utilized by smaller farms "in their struggle for existence in capitalist society," and with state support and the introduction of agricultural technologies, "the scheme is converted into one of the main components of the socialist production system."

Chayanov envisioned "that this process will last for a long while," involving "a system of cooperative combines and unions to establish a direct link between each peasant farm and central bodies of state capitalism, thus bringing it into the general stream of the planned economy."[78]

Technological inputs and supportive modernizing policies would be essential: "With a parallel development of electrification, technical installations of all kinds, systems of warehouses and public buildings, networks of improved roads, and cooperative credit, the elements of social capital and the social economy increase quantitatively so much that the whole system changes qualitatively." Such a process would hardly need the kind of "police apparatus huge enough to police the planting and harvesting all over vast, rural Russia," as Bertram Wolfe had put it. Instead, such a system—freely, democratically—could be, in Chayanov's words, "converted from one of peasant farms that have formed cooperatives for some sectors of their economy to one of a social cooperative economy, founded on socialized capital, that leaves in the private farms of its members the technical fulfillment of certain processes almost on the basis of a technical commission."[79]

This path, while consistent with the ideals and goals of the October Revolution, was the one not taken. The actual path that was ultimately blazed by the Stalin regime beginning in 1929, indicated in Wolfe's comments, would contribute powerfully to the betrayal of the revolution's ideals and goals.

In the years 1918–21, however, the realities were more fluid, soviet power was more fragile, and the ideals and dedication were fresh. Yet the revolutionaries were imperfect, they were human, and the difficulties they faced were overwhelming. "The inhuman energy of a handful of dreamers—the progressive proletarians and party workers—is sustaining the chain of state and class that as yet holds us together," mused Bolshevik N. Orlov. "It seems that if this handful vanished tomorrow, we would be scattered and torn apart from each other like the atoms of a substance subjected to strong heat."[80] This is one facet of Communism's tragedy in the period we are considering.

"If we could tomorrow give 100,000 first-class tractors, supply them with benzene, supply them with mechanics," Lenin commented in 1919, "the middle peasant would say: 'I am for the commune (i.e., for communism).'" He added: "But in order to do this, it is first necessary to conquer the international bourgeoisie, to compel it to give us these tractors." He made the same point differently in 1922, in comments to the Communist International, when he described Russia as having still "a minority of workers in industry and a vast majority of small cultivators," and then elaborated:

A socialist revolution in such a country can be finally successful only in two conditions. First, on the condition of its support at the right moment by a socialist revolution in one or several leading countries. As you know, we have done very much compared with what was done before to bring about this condition, but far from enough to make it a reality.

The other condition is a compromise between the proletariat which puts its dictatorship into practice or holds the state power in its hands and the majority of the peasant population.[81]

To place the tangled realities in perspective, we might conclude as follows. Despite limitations in his 1890s analyses, Lenin's pioneering insights on the peasantry (reflected, for example, in his 1903 pamphlet *To the Rural Poor*) became central to Bolshevism's very definition after 1905. The Bolshevik political strategy of "hegemony" was based on the idea of the socialist proletariat providing leadership to the peasants. The peasants were seen as an ally principally because of the complete clash of interests between them and the gentry landowners (and Lenin's problematical theories of class structure in the village played very little role in this political calculation).

An essential part of Lenin's peasant program from the beginning was that local peasant committees should decide what to do with the land (although this was certainly distorted by the mistaken 1918 effort by the Bolsheviks to mobilize "poor peasants" against more fortunate neighbors). During the Civil War, terrible pressures were placed on the peasants in order to support the Red Army, keep industry going, and so forth. We have seen that such pressures generated a violent peasant backlash. On the other hand, the triumph of the Red Army over the Whites, and the ability to keep industry going and to expand it, were ultimately *in the direct interest* of the peasants themselves, preserving their possession of the land and ensuring their well-being by getting the overall economy up and running again. That a significant number of peasants recognized such realities ultimately ensured the salvation of Lenin's worker-peasant alliance despite tragic lapses during the Civil War.

Yet the persistence of vulgar Marxist blind spots among Bolsheviks-turned-Communists would, when the 1920s flowed into the 1930s, help generate murderously brutal policies toward the peasant majority as the Stalin regime launched its "revolution from above."[82]

8

LIBERTY UNDER
THE SOVIETS

A problematical tendency among many looking at the trajectory of
the Russia Revolution, with the culmination of Bolshevik triumph
into Communist tragedy, is to draw a straight line between the desperate repressions of the Civil War period (1918–21) and the even greater crescendo
of repressive violence represented by Stalinism from the early 1930s on to
the end of that decade. But there was an incredibly important interlude of
creativity, relative freedom, and genuine accomplishment in the 1920s, which
seemed to be consistent with the promise of 1917. It stands in stark contrast to
much of what came after. This omission of a vital decade constitutes one of
the most serious distortions within the historiography and political discourse
regarding the meaning and legacy of the Russian Revolution.

It is impossible to do justice to these realities of the 1920s in this short
space. But some indication of the creative and life-affirming qualities of the
decade can be suggested here. It is important, as well, to indicate serious
ambiguities and problems that were also making themselves felt at the same
time, involving contradictions of the NEP, severe limitations on democracy,
and intensifying dynamics of bureaucratic power and privilege.

"The Russian system of government at the present time is like that to
which the population has been accustomed for centuries," commented John
Dewey after a visit in the late 1920s, and "like the old system it has many

293

repressive traits." But there was more to be said than this obvious truth, in his opinion. The Soviet regime "is one that has opened to [the masses] doors that were formerly shut and bolted; it is as interested in giving them access to sources of happiness as the only other government with which they have any acquaintance was to keep them in misery. This fact, and not that of espionage and police restriction, however excessive the latter may be, explains the stability of the present government, in spite of the comparatively small number of communists in the country."[1]

On the basis of further developments and experiences, Dewey would later dramatically revise this judgment. He himself was insightful and even prophetic in emphasizing that the Soviet Republic was "in a state of flux, of rapid alterations, even oscillations," elaborating: "If I have learned nothing else, I learned to be immensely suspicious of all generalized views about Russia; even if they accord with the state of affairs in 1922 or 1925, they may have little relevancy to 1928, and perhaps be of only antiquarian meaning by 1933."[2] Yet his judgment in the late 1920s was based on the developments and experiences of that decade. These were the subject of an impressive number of studies carried on by researchers coming from outside of Soviet Russia. It is worth surveying some of what they reported—which included a number of critical concerns but also an impressive accumulation of achievements.

"Personal reactions color most of what is written about Soviet Russia. Where one puts emphasis is a matter of feeling and opinion." So wrote Roger Baldwin, a radical libertarian profoundly influenced by anarchist and socialist traditions, conscientious objector imprisoned during World War I, onetime member of the Industrial Workers of the World, and longtime leader of the American Civil Liberties Union. "Life under the Soviets is so packed with contrasts and contradictions, that anyone can prove almost any case his bias dictates—and prove a case against them, if he likes, out of the mouths of the Bolsheviks themselves." He added: "On no subject is it more difficult to convey a fair view than on issues of liberty and repression, because viewpoints and facts are both so contradictory."[3]

Fluctuations of Repression and Freedom

Baldwin also served as chairperson of the International Committee for Political Prisoners, a body including such people as Jane Addams, Clarence Darrow, Eugene V. Debs, W. E. B. Du Bois, Elizabeth Gurley Flynn, Felix Frankfurter, Norman Thomas, Oswald Garrison Villard, and others. For this committee, and with the assistance of Isaac Don Levine, he had seen through to publication a 1925 book entitled *Letters from Russian Prisons*, a volume, according to its own scrupulously accurate self-description, that consisted of "reprints of documents by political prisoners in Soviet prisons, prison camps and exile, and reprints of affidavits concerning political persecution in Soviet Russia, official statements by Soviet authorities, excerpts from Soviet laws pertaining to civil liberties, and other documents." Baldwin's introduction to this volume clearly indicates the nature of its contents (and of his own views):

> Russia presents the unique spectacle of a revolutionary government based on working-class and peasant power imprisoning and exiling its political opponents in other revolutionary parties. Old comrades in the struggle to overthrow the Tsar, who served terms together in exile and prison, are now split into hostile camps. The Bolsheviks in power send again to a new exile and prison their former comrades in suffering under the Tsar....
>
> [This study] does not touch the many Tsarists and others outside the radical parties who have also been imprisoned or exiled for their views.... We have tried to exclude all references to prisoners who joined active counter-revolutionary movements of violence, as did a considerable number of those in the revolutionary parties opposed to the Soviet Government.... The essential fact stands out clear and unchallenged—that the Soviet Government exiles and imprisons political opponents for their political activities and expressions in speech and print. Socialists, Syndicalists, Anarchists are the principle targets for attack, but Zionists and Tolstoyans have also suffered....
>
> [H]igher standards are expected of a new State devoted to the revolutionary conceptions of "the cooperative commonwealth," producers' control and the abolition of classes. Friends of social progress see no need for the perpetuation of the evil practices of Tsardom. They realize that the period of transition as defined by the Bolsheviks may last fifty years, and that it may continue indefinitely to be used as the excuse for political tyranny, though the Soviet Government appears to be the most secure in Europe. No claim of comparative virtue in the light of more vigorous persecution by reactionary governments is warranted....
>
> The material presented here ... was obtained chiefly from officials of the persecuted revolutionary parties in Berlin and Paris for the most part—the Social Democrats (Mensheviks), the Socialist-Revolutionaries of the Right and Left, and the Anarchists. Their letters and testimony may be expected to represent the worst conditions of imprisonment and exile, and in that sense may be considered an exaggerated picture of the situation. Furthermore, prison letters frequently reflect a prison psychology prone to exaggerate and distort the picture of conditions as a whole. But even making allowances for the sources of information, it constitutes a clear case for a complete change of policy.[4]

In his study that was published three years after the release of *Letters from Russian Prisons*—following an extensive fact-finding visit to Soviet Russia, free from "official chaperonage" and with relatively free access not only to Soviet officials and institutions but also to critics and opponents of the regime— Baldwin by no means repudiated any of what he wrote in the first volume. In fact, in the course of his 1928 volume, he repeated all of the critical points. Yet as he noted, "my prejudices are amply conveyed in the title of this book," explaining: "Though over half of it is devoted to a description of the controls by the Soviet state, I have chosen to call it *Liberty under the Soviets* because I see as far more significant the basic economic freedom of workers and peasants and the abolition of privileged classes based on wealth; and only less important, the release of non-Russian minorities to develop their national cultures, the new freedom of women, the revolution in education—and, if one counts it as significant, liberty for religion—and anti-religion." In fact, as Kevin Murphy documents, "during the entire NEP period the Soviet Union incarcerated very few of its citizens. The entire Soviet prison population was no higher than 150,000, with a tiny minority imprisoned for political offenses."[5]

Baldwin goes on to make the interesting point that "the regime is dominated by the economic needs of workers and peasants," and that "their economic power, even where unorganized, is the force behind it." His next point: "Their liberties won by the Revolution are the ultimate dictators of Soviet policy. In this lies the chief justification for the hope that, with the increasing share by the masses in all activities of life, the rigors of centralized dictatorship will be lessened and all creative forces be given free rein." He elaborates: "Peasants and workers are keenly aware of their new liberties won by the Revolution. Anywhere you can hear voiced their belief, whatever their criticism and discontent, that they are 'free.' And they constitute over ninety percent of the Russian people." He adds that "if one is not speculatively minded about revolutionary progress, the next fairest test by which to judge liberty in Russia is to compare it with what liberty the Russian people enjoyed under tsarism. And on that basis it is clear that the Russian people enjoy more of essential liberties than at any time in their history, and more of some sorts than any people in the world."[6]

Twenty-five years later, Baldwin edited another book, entitled *A New Slavery, Forced Labor: The Communist Betrayal of Human Rights*. This contained documentation of forced labor camps in Russia and other Communist countries, where guards brutally and often murderously oppressed many hundreds of thousands, ultimately millions, of people. The story became sensationalized in the 1970s with Alexander Solzhenitsyn's *The Gulag Archipelago*, but in 1947 had been fully highlighted in David Dallin and Boris Nicolaevsky, *Forced Labor in Soviet Russia*, and more recently has been reliably corroborated and more fully described in Oleg V. Khlevniuk, *The History of the Gulag: From Collectivization to the Great Terror.*[7]

It is especially interesting to read Baldwin's foreword to the 1953 volume. In it there is no repudiation of what was reported in his book of 1928. Instead, he simply takes issue "with what now seems a naïve optimism, that despite the single-party dictatorship, buttressed by its powerful secret police and universal censorship, the evidence was stronger of tendencies toward the ultimate human rights and freedoms which Marxist principles prophesied."[8] What changed his mind, he notes, were developments taking place *after* he completed the previous book, which created a qualitatively new reality. The situation was quite different in the 1920s:

> [T]hen there was no forced collectivization of the peasants' land with its terrible toll in starvation and exile; the trade unions had not been brought under rigid party control; education had not been Stalinized; the dictatorship had not rigidly cracked down on all opposition and dissent; the Communist Party had not been purged of all divergences. Forced labor was unheard of. The only evidence resembling it concerned the then comparatively small numbers of political prisoners either exiled to remote Siberian camps, as under the Tsars, or segregated in what the secret police with some pride called it "model labor camps." Evidently, it was from these origins that the vast system of forced labor grew. . . . Reports of the wholesale liquidation of peasant opposition to land collectivization in the early 1930s shook the faith of many; the purges and trials of many "old Bolsheviks" in 1936 and after shocked many more of us into incredulity and revulsion.[9]

What can be determined here is that at the time of Lenin's death in 1924, paraphrasing Hannah Arendt, the roads seemed to be open to different possibilities of development. A period during the 1920s involving a significant phase of relative freedom—connected to the ideals and goals of the October Revolution—stood as a vital and suggestive interregnum between the repressions of war communism and the murderous onslaughts of Stalinism.

On the other hand, there is no controversy over the fact that socialism was not established in Soviet Russia; nor can it be seriously argued that the quality of democracy idealized in classical Marxism was realized under the Bolshevik regime. Nonetheless, some theorists operating within the Marxist tradition have demonstrated an inclination to argue in favor of the inevitability of those things they desire, and to look very favorably, with the generous benefit of multiple doubts (in the manner of apologists), on such a regime as the one we have been examining. Others identifying with the same tradition have seemed content simply to denounce the harsh realities that fail to measure up to their ideal.[10] A more interesting question is whether such a proletarian revolution as described in this study created the *possibility* for greater freedom, real democracy, and eventual socialism.

Anomalies

At the same time it is important, in surveying the broad sweep of history, to catch the inevitable anomalies that also contribute to our understanding of different facets of the reality. There are, in fact, innumerable "anomalies"—some clustering together to constitute what are, in fact, trends and counter-tendencies that are an essential part of the story. Here, we will focus on only one, discovered by a young Maurice Hindus, who as a child was carried by immigrant parents from rural Russia to the United States, and later in the early 1920s—as a journalist and researcher—revisited his old peasant village.[11]

He couldn't help but notice, at various social events and meetings, a young woman "whose manner and garb set her apart from the other girls," someone not only more "well bred" but also "who seemed a favorite with the 'intellectual' boys" clustered in the local branch of the Komsomol. Her name was Manka, and Hindus learned that she was the daughter of a peasant. But many years before, her father had gone into the military and risen to the rank of officer, settled in Kiev and done well, marrying a city-born woman with whom he raised a family. Manka was born in Kiev, grew up in very comfortable circumstances, and graduated from school—the gymnasium—with "a passion for books and music and an abundant life."

The Revolution turned the lives and circumstances of all in her family upside down. They lost all their property, privileges, and urban comforts. The father then brought the family back to his old peasant village, where his family support network made it possible for his own immediate family to survive. Manka's father had made the adjustment without seeming difficulty: "The shift from a life of ease and luxury in the city to one of toil and penury in the village seemed to affect neither his body nor his disposition. He was always jovial, always full of talk and warmth, always eager to listen to a good jest and still more eager to tell one, and when he laughed he threw his head back and his body shook." His two sons—younger than Manka (who was now twenty-two)—appeared to have adjusted well. The older one dreamed of becoming an explorer in the far North, the younger talked like a pint-sized Communist revolutionary. His wife and then-teenage daughter, on the other hand, were at first utterly devastated, and Manka at one point even tried to run away to return somehow to her beloved city life—after which she adjusted and matured.

Manka's maturing did not involve deadening herself in any way, but rather engaging in self-discovery. "Labor was a disgrace in my silly old world," she recounted to Hindus. "I was the daughter of a muzhik; yet I never thought of that. I always thought of myself as a daughter of an officer in the army, a person of privilege.... You see I lived in a world that was hollow and silly." Her daily circumstances had changed dramatically. "Now she had to trudge in the mud, carry big pails of water to the house, bring in heavy armfuls of wood, drive the pigs to pasture, clean stalls, and do other heavy chores around the house and farm." Yet she had a quality about her, perhaps a reflection of her father, of cheerful resignation. One saving grace was a particular quality that Hindus noticed in her—she was "an affectionate soul," and "the sight of any act of cruelty always filled her with revulsion." He recounted: "More than once I saw her go over to little boys and girls who were amusing themselves by throwing sticks and stones at stray dogs and cats and reprimand them for their lack of feeling for dumb beasts." This element in her character also helped her become aware of the humanity of those around her—people who in earlier years would have struck her as part of the "dark masses," who "seemed not human beings but beasts, monsters, coarse, smelly, horrid." These old attitudes evaporated.

Particularly important were boys in the Soviet who reached out to her:

They talked to me. They gave me books to read. They invited me to lectures, to mass-meetings, to parties. They offered me a position as a teacher in a Soviet school. A new world was beginning to open to me. New ideas were filtering into my mind. I saw in life something beyond myself, my immediate wishes and pleasures. I read and read, talked and talked, argued and argued, and nights I lay awake thinking and wondering. It was all so new to me, these new ideas, new friends, new interests. I was stirred. The village, the muzhiks, even the mud in the street, assumed a new color and a new meaning for me. I began to perceive the why and wherefore of it all. I began to forget myself, to grow less and less self-conscious.

Her new friends clearly meant a lot to her, yet her own sensibilities prevented her from accepting them uncritically:

I liked the boys at the Soviet and the other youths who used to come to the meetings and the lectures. They were crude and unschooled, but they were so sincere, so strong-willed, so cheerful. They lived not for themselves but for a social purpose.... I never expect to be a Communist, and there is something else about these boys that grieves me; they hate the bourzhuis [bourgeoisie—more generally, those from the old privileged social strata] too much. They think nothing of hurting their feelings. They look at them as useless creatures. I have talked myself hoarse arguing on this point. I have told them that if they are real earnest Marxists then they must consider man the product of his circumstances, his materialist environment, and the bourzhuis is no more to blame for his state of mind, for his past deeds or misdeeds, than the proletarian for his....

Still, they are so courageous. They have ideas. They are all the time talking about building new schools and new playgrounds and organizing social centers and educating the muzhiks. So many of them are so strong and determined and so jolly and good-hearted. And they read books and arrange lectures and study all the time, and mingling with them has changed me, changed me so complete-ly that I sometimes wonder if I am the same Manka that used to live in Kiev.

Manka's relationships with others in the village also changed qualitatively:

I began to draw close to our neighbors. I went to their homes. I didn't seem to mind their squalor. I hardly noticed the pigs rooting around the floor grunting. I was no longer repulsed by the sight of a whole family eating with their hands from the same big earthen dish. I became interested in their problems, in their worries and needs. I perceived how unenlightened and dark-minded they were, and yet how simple and kindly and hospitable and sincere, and I was seized with a sudden yearning to do something, to scrub the dirt and squalor out of their homes, to teach them to read and write, and to explain to them the need for fresh air and sunshine in the home.

She became particularly interested in the everyday realities of peasant women. In her description of a typical young girl, she noted:

She marries young. She has never been outside of the village unless to vis-it another village in the neighborhood. She knows nothing of the world. She never reads anything. She knows nothing of love. She talks of it with a kind of light-hearted earnestness, but has no conception of its meaning, its purpose, its power of exalting the individual. Unlettered, unread, inexperienced, she mis-takes a fleeting physical passion for love, and how fleeting it is she finds out soon enough. After marriage her life becomes a deadly routine, an endless round of toil and worry and dullness....

Heavens! Look at our women when they are thirty—beauty gone, gaiety gone—misshapen, shriveled, flat-chested creatures, irritable, morbid, given to swearing and cursing their husbands, their neighbors, their children, and beat-ing them, too, without mercy, with fists and feet and clubs, and often crippling them for life ... women, mothers!... No rest, no pleasure, no diversion, no inspi-ration, no love, no sympathy—nothing but toil and quarrels and beatings ... of course our men beat their wives with fists and whips . . . beastly creatures! And the wives don't hesitate to strike back and strike hard.

Sometimes when our men scold their women they call them hags, and I have often thought that the word fits them well, that many of our peasant women are mere hags, drained of the beauty, sweetness, glory, with which they glowed when they were girls, and turned into coarse, callous, sharp-tongued creatures . . . yes, such is the lot of our peasant women. It is the lot of a slave, and it must be changed. The muzhik girl must be taught to understand herself and the world. Her *I* must be awakened, so that she can come to regard herself as somebody, not a mere drudge but a human being, a woman, with a life all her own and entitled to her share of joy and inspiration.

Such perceptions were shaping Manka's own life choices:

I have found my life-work, and I have found myself too, and I am really quite happy. In winter during the day I teach school, and evenings I hold meetings with girls and women and sometimes with men, and we discuss everything we can think of. I read stories, poems, plays, newspapers, and make comments and invite remarks on the various happenings of the day. I have started a chorus and once a week we have rehearsals and sing new and old songs. I am especially eager to draw older women into these diversions. They are the loneliest of the lonely! Day and night they toil, and they never see anything but this village and the muzhiks—nothing to freshen their minds and buoy their hearts. And next winter, with the help of one of the other teachers in this district, I hope to produce a play here with the muzhiks themselves taking the various parts—a real play, too, one of the very best of our literature.

It is impossible to quantify how many such anomalies were percolating within the early Soviet Republic.

Fluid Realities, Divergent Trajectories

In his valuable exploration of the way that British intellectuals and writers on the political left dealt with Soviet Union in the years 1929–41, Paul Flewers has usefully distinguished between the more critical-minded studies such people produced before 1929 and what was generally more apologetic material produced in the 1930s. "What distinguishes the sympathetic visitors of the Soviet republic in the early years from those who went later, particularly in the 1930s, is that the former were far less inclined to overlook the more negative aspects of Soviet society" he writes. "There were visitors who didn't ask themselves whether the nicely turned-out factories, farms and sanatoria they saw were typical examples. Yet many sympathetic observers openly expressed their concern about certain features of the regime, especially the Cheka, described the dreadful hardships they saw, asked awkward questions of Soviet leaders, and sought out oppositional figures for their opinions."[12]

In far more bitter terms, the disillusioned Eugene Lyons made exactly the same point about similar observers from the United States. Left-wing sympathizers such as John Reed, Louise Bryant, Albert Rhys Williams, Bessie Beatty, and others "showed a romantic, almost lyrical acceptance of the revolution," but "the facts, no matter how harsh, were usually admitted and assimilated as part of the agony of birth." In contrast, in the 1930s "the attitude in most pro-Soviet writings is . . . for the most part a literature of apologetics, ranging from panicky rationalization and self-deception to complete concealment." The difference, he suggested, was between "inspired prophets of an embattled revolution" versus "press agents of a going, if rather unpleasant, business." He added: "The emphasis of the new recruits is no longer on the coming freedom and equality. It is upon factories, percentages, machinery, tractors. Few of them reveal any awareness that socialism ever meant more than the government ownership of all life and its rigid organization under a police regime."[13] This is harsh but—comparing what was written at the time with what is now commonly known—not entirely untrue.

What this suggests is that a critical utilization of sympathetic sources from the 1920s might provide useful information on revolutionary achievements of the Soviet Republic in that time. A series of such studies was commissioned by Vanguard Press, an independent radical publisher, and a dozen volumes, collectively known as the Vanguard Studies of Soviet Russia, were published in 1927–28 under the general editorship of Dr. Jerome Davis of Yale University. The authors produced sympathetic yet critical-minded works providing information on their impressions of accomplishments in the Soviet Republic and perceptions of current problems and future possibilities. In a similar key is journalist William Henry Chamberlin's *Soviet Russia: A Living Record and a History,* capturing the particular historical moment of the 1920s. Another is Samuel Harper's 1929 volume *Civic Training in Soviet Russia*, a transitional and informative work by a scholar who had been an anti-Soviet Russia expert serving the US State Department in 1917–22 before evolving into a Soviet sympathizer in the 1930s.[14]

There were many independent observers who registered the existence of a considerable degree of liberty in this phase of Bolshevik power. After a monthlong tour of the Soviet Union in late 1924, a sympathetic but not uncritical British delegation, officially representing Britain's Trade Union Congress, commented that "as to the persistent assertions in the Press that the present regime in Russia is a 'reign of terror,' the Delegation would wish to put on record its conviction that this could not be honestly believed by any unprejudiced person travelling within the [Soviet] Union and talking to its citizens."[15]

Even during the earlier years of war communism, all was not quite unmitigated terror and repression. Certain freedoms and democratic opportunities existed that a dozen years later (and even sixty years later) would have been unthinkable. There were mass demonstrations organized at the funerals of Plekhanov and Kropotkin in 1918 and 1921, respectively, by Menshevik and anarchist opponents. Their newspapers and other publications were fully legal at first, though they quickly ran into Bolshevik censorship and suppression as soon as the Civil War began in earnest. Their oppositional literature and activities (and also those of the SRs, particularly the fragment of the Left SRs that renounced violence against the regime) often exercised visible influence throughout most of the period under review, although—in the case of the Mensheviks and SRs—this became increasingly difficult as the country's crises deepened.[16]

The aftermath of the 1921 Kronstadt revolt included the permanent outlawing of all opposition parties. And yet both contemporaries and later scholars have documented the persistence of considerable intellectual and cultural freedom in the early Soviet Republic up to the late 1920s. Independently published material, some of it critical of official ideology, and the circulation of foreign publications were possible. There was considerable free expression and controversy among artists and writers, philosophers, social and natural scientists, and others both inside and outside of the Communist Party; some of this involved far-reaching social and political criticism of a kind that would not be allowed in later years. Despite continuing political restrictions, many who had formerly identified with non-Bolshevik political groupings (as well as dissident Bolsheviks) were able to find some outlets for their "unorthodox" views.[17]

What of those who were not among the narrow layers of intelligentsia? Many contemporary observers, especially after the violence of the Civil War period, agreed with Roger Baldwin that for working people there was *more* freedom. "In general the common man in Russia today," Chamberlin wrote of the late 1920s, "has the sense of release, of social liberty, that comes with the disappearance of classes which are visibly above him in wealth and opportunity, culture and social status." For example, "the worker does not have to cringe before the 'red dictator' of the Soviet factory as, in pre-war times, he cringed before the private owner of the factory. He can write letters to the press complaining of conditions in the factory and suggesting changes, something which a worker would scarcely do with impunity even in democratic capitalist countries, where factories are private and not public concerns." Chamberlin added other considerations, such as "greater freedom for women, more humane treatment of the soldier in the Red Army, recognition of the right of racial minorities to use freely their own languages, greater liberty for children in the schools," concluding: "I should think it probable that the number of people in Russia who consciously feel liberated as a result of the Revolution probably exceeds the number who feel more oppressed than they were under Tsarism."[18]

Kevin Murphy has documented the existence and vitality of open and quite vocal dissident currents inside the massive Hammer and Sickle Metal Works (before the revolution, the Moscow Metal Works Company) through the early 1920s, particularly from Left SRs, and then from the 1923 Opposition grouped around Leon Trotsky. This particular factory—before, during, and after 1917—had a reputation as "a hotbed of dissident activity," but such a phenomenon was not unique to that particular workplace.[19] Anna Louise Strong reported that in the early 1920s, "the factories that had an opposition bragged about it." She quotes a worker from one:

> We had the best election in town. Three different parties and lots of attacks. A Social Revolutionary got up, and denounced the government for failing to keep its promises. "Two years ago they promised you a new world," he said. "Now they offer you a better water-supply and a few more electric lights." There is some interest in that kind of election.[20]

Journey down the Volga

In 1922, Max Eastman traveled down the Volga River, and wrote in his autobiography years later (well after abandoning his socialist beliefs and becoming an anti-Communist) that his long-ago experiences stood as a "refutation of the notion that things were 'just as bad' under Lenin and Trotsky as they became after Stalin seized his despotic power." At this time he "wandered freely, talking with all kinds of people," and "no man or woman ever hesitated to enter into friendly relations with me, or withheld, so far as I could judge, his frank opinion both of the Communist idea in general and of the government." He spoke, of course, with strong supporters of the regime—both "idealistic Communists and the hardboiled place-hunters [those who hunt after government positions]"—and he especially liked the former, "those young, gentle and intelligent Communists" who frankly admitted that they were taking him on a propaganda tour. However, "the joyous hope in their eyes was not propaganda," and "they fervently believed . . . that a new and better world was coming to being along the lines indicated by Marx and by Lenin and Trotsky."

Quite different were the opinions of a fish merchant, who frankly complained, "There can't be much improvement so long as labor dictates the conditions. You've got to set a limit on what labor can do." This man's friend did not hesitate to chime in: "What you've got to do is restore private property. At least the government has got to encourage private enterprise. They've got to quite stifling us with arbitrary taxation." When asked what he thought about Bolshevism, a ragged old man sitting in a shanty responded: "It's all damn nonsense, if you want my opinion. Liberty! The Russian people haven't got enough spunk to be free. Communism—*Phh!* What they need is just what they had before, an oak club over the back. All this nonsense is ruining the country. The only thing that would put things to rights is a Tsar!" An attractive young woman whose opinion Eastman asked regarding the Bolsheviks "had evidently done some thinking about the question, for she answered instantly and with an earnestly regretful shake of her beautiful head: 'They haven't done enough killing.'" A woman from the nobility, now living an extremely modest lifestyle, described her husband, who had been a tsarist officer, and although he had opposed the anti-Bolshevik hostilities, had been executed by the Bolsheviks. "I resent that accident, that unnecessary misfortune, but I have no personal resentment against the Communists because he was shot. That is the way the war was conducted," she mused. "That is what a revolution is, I suppose, and the revolution was bound to come, I can see that. I don't know whether any good will come of it or not. I am afraid there are too many beasts in the world."[21]

Of particular interest is a discussion Eastman had, over the course of more than an hour, with a group of twenty workers, "day laborers and mechanics, [who] were grouped around an outdoor table over the riverbank." When asked about conditions in the Soviet Republic, one responded: "We're sick—that's our condition. We *were* sick, but we're beginning to get well." Pointing to the factory he proudly added: "You can hear those wheels going round." A younger worker said: "It may be possible to develop a society under the Communist dictatorship, but it will take a long time. . . . We Russian people are accustomed to a life where everybody has his own private ambition. Everybody wants a little to get a little piece of property." The question was posed, did this mean the Bolsheviks didn't represent them? "Self-appointed representatives!" was the response of another worker leaning against a tree. The young man explained, "All the important offices in our trade union are occupied by Communists, and they are decided from above." Indicating that he himself was more representative of the workers in his shop, he concluded: "They can't elect me to an important post because I'm not a Communist. I have no power, I can't decide anything." No one disagreed, but a deep, warm voice intoned: "God give us peace! That's what we want—peace!" There was general agreement. What did they think about Lenin and Trotsky? "I'll tell you what we think of Lenin," said one, seeming to speak for all. "If there were ten of him there wouldn't be any problem." A young mechanic chimed in: "Trotsky is also a big man—he has respect of all the workers." The man against the tree expressed a different view. "Lenin we can acknowledge. He's a Russia citizen and speaks for the Russians," he said. "Trotsky's a Jew, and Jews are always for the Jews." The worker with the large, warm voice disagreed: "All men ought to meet each other as men. And I say if a man is defending the working class, he's a good leader." The tree-leaner was willing to concede the point: "All right. That's all right, if he works for the working class." A milder voice insisted: "If he works for the population!" There was no concession: "The working class!"[22]

Workers and Peasants in the Soviet Republic

Murphy's *Revolution and Counterrevolution: Class Struggle in a Moscow Metal Factory* extensively and persuasively documents the existence of a considerable degree of ferment, critical-mindedness, and organized working-class power in the early half of the 1920s. The crescendo of class-conscious activism and labor militancy in the factories of 1917 extends into 1918, he finds, but is then largely dissipated thanks to the crescendo of civil war and economic collapse. With NEP, however, a new dynamic gets going—one that "was inherently contradictory," facilitating market forces and demanding labor discipline, but also reviving the economy and highlighting workers' rights. The 1922 Labor Code did many things not provided for in other countries: it guaranteed an eight-hour workday (six hours for youth); ensured that overtime work would be compensated at 150 percent; provided for trade unions, with worker bargaining rights and the right to ratify contracts (that would determine wages and working conditions); established Rates Conflict Commissions with equal representation from workplace management and workers to handle noncontract disputes; and guaranteed that women would receive sixteen weeks' paid maternity leave. Communist Party membership in the Hammer and Sickle Metal Works (which had a workforce of about 3,000) climbed from 60 in 1921 to 240 in 1924 and 690 by 1926. In part, this was because in the early years of the NEP the Communist Party generally supported the demands put forward by the workers—often in well-attended and "stormy" meetings. The trade union, occupying a contradictory position (loyally supporting the Soviet regime and its policies but seeking to reflect the moods and needs of the workers), helped to fight for and win gains in the early 1920s. On the other hand, as the regime began shifting in a more intolerant and "productivist" direction in the late 1920s, trade union leaders tended to follow Mikhail Tomsky, head of the All-Russian Central Council of Trade Unions in 1922–29 (successor to dissident-Communist Alexander Shlyapnikov), who "was content to conduct an orderly retreat, saving what he could on the way."[23]

Murphy's corrective is crucial for those wanting to transcend the flat and distorted accounts that were prevalent among Cold War anti-Communists. Yet the realities were even more complicated, and the demons of repression were themselves at liberty even in the "good old days" of the early 1920s, as Steven Smith indicates:

> Instances of heavy-handed tactics in the capital [Moscow] are not hard to find. One group of workers who were a constant thorn in the side of the regime were those at the Aleksandrovskie railway shops. Following a protest at non-payment of wages, the authorities sacked the entire workforce on 31 March 1918 and sent twelve Menshevik and SR workers for trial to a revolutionary tribunal. In August 1920 . . . tram workers in Moscow went on strike and were all fired, the authorities subjecting them to "re-registration" to decide who should be taken back. No opposition party members were involved in the dispute. Again, on 25 March 1921, Bromley workers, once stalwarts of the Bolshevik Party, passed a Left SR resolution supporting the Kronstadt rebels (the only instance of support for the rebels in the capital). The Cheka accused them of "demagogically blackening with filth the Communist Party and soviet power," arrested the Left SR leaders, shut down the plant, and announced that an entirely new workforce would be taken on.[24]

The fact remains that throughout the 1920s, in addition to a number of strikes (some of which were successful), there were multiple cases of audacious free expression, critical-minded protest against abuses, and outspoken pushes from below for positive change in the Soviet Republic. For example, "wall newspapers" were proliferating and commonly utilized, with the general encouragement of the regime and the Communist Party—"an institution of practically all Soviet institutions, at least in the more politically active urban centers," according to Samuel Harper—with large sheets of paper filled with frank discussions of social and workplace problems, naming names (managerial bullies, for example, or inept party and soviet officials, or malingering coworkers) and citing specific grievances. The wall newspapers were prominently displayed in the hallways of workers' clubs, workplaces, and so on, but also in community centers in some rural areas. Committees of laborers would create them and compose their content, or solicit contributions from coworkers and fellow activists. Some of the wall papers were quite elaborate in their makeup, with bright colors and illustrations; others were plain but neat, some handwritten and others typed. Members of the Communist Party or Communist youth in the particular institution were expected to participate in initiating and producing the wall newspaper, but it was supposed to be the product of the whole group, not just the Communist element. Special "how-to" manuals circulated to help those carrying out such work. Sometimes, the criticisms expressed would result in efforts to censor or retaliate against critics—although such actions were officially forbidden and were not always successful. "The estimated 40,000 wall newspapers, generally appearing every two weeks, represent a simple form of civic activity for a very considerable army of writers," Harper reported.[25]

Another significant phenomenon of the early 1920s—in this case developing without Communist input—was the phenomenon of what journalist Arthur Ransome tagged *non-partyism*, "much more than a cloak for invisibility for enemies or conditional supporters of the Communists." Particularly in country districts, despite "every kind of agitation" on behalf of the Communist Party, delegates sent to the soviets were overwhelmingly nonparty. He elaborated: "The local Soviets in these districts are also non-party, and they elect usually a local Bolshevik to some responsible post to act as it were as a buffer between themselves and the central authority. They manage local affairs in their own way, and, through the use of tact on both sides, avoid falling foul of the more rigid doctrinaires in Moscow."[26] According to Ransome, non-partyism was "the peasants' way of expressing their aloofness from the revolution and, at the same time, their readiness to defend that revolution against anybody who attacks it." The underlying dissident sensibility reflected in all of this corresponded, in his opinion, to currents reflected "in the Kremlin itself at an All-Russian Conference of the Communist Party. A workman, Sapronov, turned suddenly aside in a speech on quite another matter, and said with great violence that the present system was in danger of running to seed and turning into an oligarchy, if not autocracy." Ransome reported that "until the moment when he put his listeners against him by a personal attack on Lenin, there was no doubt that he had with him the sympathies of quite a considerable section of an exclusively Communist audience." Ransome went on to speculate: "Non-partyism may well be the protoplasmic stage of the future political opposition of the peasants."[27]

Divergent Trajectory

William Henry Chamberlin's political evolution, like that of Max Eastman and a number of other left-wing intellectuals of the 1920s and early 1930s, was pushed sharply to the right largely under the impact of Soviet experience.[28] It could be argued that their commitment to reporting the truth as they saw it was responsible for this critical shift as realities became increasingly ugly. However, for no other reason than that elemental commitment to the truth, they never retracted their relatively positive (though hardly uncritical) reports of Soviet Russia in the 1920s. It's worth giving somewhat more sustained attention to this particular journalist because Chamberlin was among the most knowledgeable, and also because he had opportunity and possible motivation (given his changing political convictions) to retract earlier observations, but in later years, he chose to stand by them, with a shifting interpretation, to be sure.

Chamberlin's grandfather had shifted from a farming background to journalism, which was also the profession of his urban-oriented father, and which became his profession as well. Influenced by the liberal and mildly socialist outlook of his father, he himself became increasingly drawn to radical and socialist views and activities, moving to New York City to find himself within the city's bohemian intellectual and cultural scene. Finding employment as a journalist, he also wrote articles, under a pen name, for the Socialist Party's daily newspaper, *The Call*. He was a firm opponent of the First World War and enthusiastically greeted the Bolshevik revolution. In this period he had met and married a Russian immigrant who shared his left-wing orientation. Assigned as the *Christian Science Monitor*'s Russia correspondent in 1922, he benefitted from his wife Sonya's Russian language skills.[29]

Sharp observation and elemental thoughtfulness made it impossible for Chamberlin and his wife to maintain their youthful, unadulterated enthusiasm. In the early 1920s, they witnessed a meeting of students where those "who could not prove their red-blooded proletarian origin or their devotion to the principles of Marx were being turned out of a workers' high school," and in reaction to the meanness of the procedure, Chamberlin recalled, Sonya angrily "wrote down in firm letters: 'I am *not* a Communist' and passed the declaration of unfaith to me with a challenging gesture." (Prominent Communists—such as Anatoly Lunacharsky and Nadezhda Krupskaya—were also disturbed by such developments and "protested in vain the punishment of children for the social status of their parents," as a later scholar has noted.) This was one of a number of sobering experiences. "Sometime in 1924 the last traces of partisanship slipped away, and I no longer experienced even an unconscious desire to report developments from the standpoint of an apologist," he later reflected. "But it would be inaccurate to suppose that I saw only the dark sides of Soviet life," he added. "The psychological stage which succeeded partisanship was neutrality and detachment." It was in this spirit that he would write *Soviet Russia: A Living Record and a History* (produced in the late 1920s and published in 1930). "We had Communist friends whose sincerity and devotion we respected, and who helped us to see the more constructive aspects of Soviet life: the educational work among women, the rabfacs, or special schools for workers, the crèches and clinics and sanatoria which were a part of the new program of social legislation."[30]

Chamberlin's *Soviet Russia* is an important reflection of a particular historical moment, captured at a particular moment in his own political trajectory from enthusiastic support for the revolutionary regime to shock and reorientation under the impact of harsh realities.

He and Sonya soon witnessed the persecution of "nonparty" experts and specialists in the 1929–30 public trials. It seemed clear to them that the authorities had arraigned, reviled, and forced false confessions from such people as Nikolai Sukhanov and Alexander Chayanov (whose analyses of the peasantry were discussed in a previous chapter), and the well-known economist Nikolai Kondratiev.[31] Not long after came bitter disillusionment as the Stalin regime crystallized through the propagation of extreme authoritarian and murderous policies (recorded in his 1934 analysis *Russia's Iron Age*)—which caused Chamberlin to abandon his socialist beliefs altogether, as reflected in his 1937 volume *Collectivism: A False Utopia* and his eventual evolution into a strident Cold War anti-Communist and explicit identification as a political conservative.

Looking back, in his 1940 memoir *Confessions of an Individualist*, he commented that "when my views of the Soviet regime had become sharply more negative because of changed conditions . . . I sometimes regretted the publication of this work," *Soviet Russia*. Nonetheless, in his opinion, "it was a pretty faithful reflection of my views of the Soviet Union during the period of the NEP, with perhaps a 10 percent allowance for the restraining influence of censorship." (Chamberlin's reference to this restraint refers to the need to get his material past Soviet censors, and also to ensure his continued ability to enter, travel in, and report from the Soviet Union). It was written as he "tried to cast up a balance sheet of the Soviet regime," and at the time "I held the balance pretty even."

In his 1940 reflections he commented that "there was a depressingly low quality about Soviet life, a lack of savor about its censored books and magazines, as about its badly prepared food," as well as "the harrying of the intelligentsia" and political repression, which by his account entailed the "killing and exiling [of] far more people" than occurred under the tsar. (Such negative comments were related to that "10 percent" he had set aside or diluted in earlier reporting.) Another element in the compromised 10 percent was what turned out to be the fleeting but absurd claim (toward the end of his 1930 book) that there was "some solid basis for Communist optimism regarding the possibility of ultimately making socialist forms prevail in agriculture." Ironically, this turned out to be the disastrous and murderous forced collectivization of agriculture, Stalin's so-called revolution from above, which was initiated as Chamberlin was completing his book, and which caused his final disillusionment.[32]

On the other hand, far from repudiating the content of the other 90 percent of *Soviet Russia,* Chamberlin reaffirmed it in his critical-minded summary of 1940:

> More people certainly knew how to read and write than before the Revolution, although what was offered to them in contemporary literature and journalism was a good deal less worth reading. Social insurance measures were not altogether lacking in Tsarist Russia; but they had been greatly extended. Hours of labor had been shortened. There was more opportunity for members of the poorer classes to obtain education, to rise to state service. Discriminations against non-Russian nationalities had been abolished. Women were given full legal equality with men.[33]

Chamberlin's *Soviet Russia* generously elaborates on all of this, in rich detail that still rewards those seeking information on Soviet Russia in the 1920s. Further discussions of these and related matters can be found in the previously cited Vanguard Studies of Soviet Russia series: Roger Baldwin's *Liberty under the Soviets,* H. N. Brailsford's *How the Soviets Work,* Lucy L. W. Wilson's *The New Schools of New Russia,* Anna J. Haines's *Health Work in Soviet Russia,* Scott

Nearing's and Jack Hardy's *The Economic Organization of the Soviet Union*, Robert W. Dunn's *Soviet Trade Unions*, Karl Borders's *Village Life under the Soviets*, Avrahm Yarmolinsky's *The Jews and Other Minor Nationalities under the Soviets*, Jessica Smith's *Woman in Soviet Russia*, Julius F. Hecker's *Religion under the Soviets*, R. Page Arnot's *Soviet Russia and Her Neighbors*, and (originally scheduled as part of the series, but appearing independently in 1930) *Voices of October: Art and Literature in Soviet Russia* by Joseph Freeman, Joshua Kunitz, and Louis Lozowick. Some of these were works as critical-minded as Chamberlin's work, others less so, but all were informative.

Contradictions of NEP

Also of particular importance, however, are Chamberlin's comments on the New Economic Policy. Within the NEP itself, and its impacts on Soviet Russia, there were also contradictory trajectories. While there may be a temptation to identify the relative prosperity and liberality of the NEP period with the virtues of mixed economy as such, there are reasons to be skeptical of such an easy analytical pathway. Chamberlin also mentions two key problems that underlay what would produce the disastrous crisis generating the classical Stalinist "solution": "The Socialist reconstruction of Russia is . . . handicapped by the comparative isolation of the country from the markets of world capital and by the failure, as yet, to make a smooth working adjustment with the peasants."[34]

Although emphasizing that "the New Economic Policy marked a turning in the history of the Russian Revolution," Chamberlin identified accumulating problems that were leading to its breakdown. "One of the weak links in the economic life of the country, and especially in the relations between city and countryside, is the sharp and chronic shortage of manufactured goods," he wrote, citing "the frequent waiting lines outside the stores which sell textile and woolen goods, the bare or scantily supplied shelves of the rural cooperatives, which sometimes offer the peasants little in exchange for their grain," as well as the Soviet government's refusal "to import goods for immediate consumption, concentrating its purchases abroad on machinery and essential raw material," which deepened "the chasm between internal supply and demand." There was also the matter of "the inferior quality of present-day goods," making it necessary to renew them more frequently," which contributed to making "the goods shortage . . . one of the most visible Soviet economic problems for the last few years." He went on to cite a top Soviet economic official's identification of three major problems: "the disproportion between industrial and agricultural prices (the former being much higher); the disproportion between the demand for agricultural raw material (cotton, leather, wool, etc.) and its supply; and the disproportion between the number of working hands in the villages and the possibility of using them economically (the agrarian over-population)." The shoddiness of consumer goods and their exorbitant prices—and in insufficient quantities to keep pace with growing worker and peasant purchasing power—dovetailed with the inability of the industrial sector to make it worthwhile for peasants to exchange agricultural produce for manufactured items that weren't actually there.[35]

Chamberlin perceived two related afflictions of the Soviet economic system. One he stressed prominently in *Soviet Russia*, the other he confessed in his 1940 memoir. "If one were asked to sum up in one word the greatest evil of this system, the chosen word, I am sure, would be 'bureaucracy,' using that term in its worst Russian sense," he emphasized. "Anyone who has had extended experience in dealing with Russia offices knows what an extraordinary expenditure of time and energy is often necessary to obtain some very trifling thing—a stamp on an official paper, for instance." He contextualized the problem, noting that "from time immemorial Russian officialdom" had been the epitome of bureaucratic inefficiency—but he added that "the introduction of socialism inevitably involved a spread of the bureaucratic tradition over a wide field of industry and trade." On the other hand, at the opposing end of the economic spectrum in the mixed economy of the 1920s, there was "the horrible vulgarity of the NEP, the extremely unprepossessing types, more like pigs than human beings, which burgeoned forth as the new parvenu class after the restrictions on private trade were withdrawn."[36]

Of course, what Chamberlin tags "the introduction of socialism" was no such thing—unless one is inclined to equate economic democracy with economic bureaucracy. Nor was the "capitalist" aspect of this mixed economy capable of providing a coherent solution. Increasingly, the NEP was proving to be an unstable intersection of divergent economic trajectories. A discussion of the debates over the NEP crisis and their ultimate resolution goes well beyond the scope of the present study.[37] But it was clearly a crisis that was not offset by the genuine achievements that had been won within the framework that the NEP had provided. This is a matter to which we will return in the next chapter.

It is worth giving some attention to certain negatives embedded within the positives that can be associated with the NEP.

Commenting on the NEP's implementation during the 1920s, Donald Filtzer writes, "Despite the imposition of one-man management and a hierarchical command structure within the industrial enterprise and a considerable erosion of their collective power compared to the period when the factory committees had exercised authority, the individual worker enjoyed far greater rights and liberties then her or his capitalist counterpart." He continues: "A very liberal Labor Code studiously protected workers against dismissal except in flagrant cases of absenteeism or violations of discipline." Through the trade unions and other mechanisms, there existed a number of protections "not only against dismissals and the levying of disciplinary penalties, but also over grievances concerning wage rates, output quotas, and conditions of work," with avenues for exercising "a good deal of control over the pace and organization of work." The Bolshevik expectation that worker satisfaction would result in dramatic increases in industrial productivity was disappointed, "although productivity rose steadily, albeit modestly, through most of the decade."[38]

The peasants were also benefitting significantly. "Well into the twenties, the peasants enjoyed the fruits of their labor on their house-hold plots, making the NEP, all proportions maintained, a golden era for them," according to John Marot. The NEP's elimination of the compulsions and forced extractions imposed by the tsarist system, and then by war communism, gave the peasants control both of the *necessary product* required for peasant survival and of the *surplus product* that had routinely been expropriated by the authorities. The surplus—the Bolsheviks anticipated, given the peasants' presumed "petty-bourgeois" instincts—would flow into the enhanced market provided by NEP, but things didn't work out that way. Instead, "they decided to keep in their hands much of the surplus formerly exported, converting it into extra meat, a few more eggs, more milk, larger reserves of gain in case of drought or flood, better footwear, sturdier housing, more free time, etc." He adds: "Peasants ate better, and, to round out the picture, so did workers."[39]

The granting of greater economic freedom to the peasants did not cause them to become more capitalistic (which would have been the case if they were motivated by the desire to maximize profits). Had they gone in that direction, they would have found ways to improve efficiency and productivity, and create more of the surplus much needed by a Soviet economy lacking the capital to industrialize (not to mention more of the agricultural surplus needed to feed a growing urban labor force). Instead, peasants were inclined simply to carry on in the traditional ways, which contributed to the growing "goods shortage."

This shortage (which could have been overcome through improvements and expansion in industrial production), in turn encouraged peasants to hold back even more of the much-needed surplus. As Marot argues, "The structure of the peasant mode of production ruled out systematic gains in the productivity of agricultural labor, thus systematically ruling out regularly transferring labor from agriculture to industry—adding workers—undermining the growth of the urban economy." What's more, the worker-friendly situation in the factories described by Filtzer, Marot points out, "ruled out systematically increasing the intensity of work and/or the length of the working day with the existing labor force." This had an impact in the agrarian sector of the economy. As Rousset has nicely put it, "The peasantry was driven into crisis not by political hostility but by the failures of state industry, which was incapable of supplying them with urgently needed goods in sufficient quantities or at advantageous prices." In some cases, he adds, "the peasantry dealt with the town speculator, because he paid more for cord and supplied them with products of higher quality." These speculators were petty businessmen ambitiously striving to make profits and were commonly labeled "Nepmen." Both Nepmen and peasants, according to Rousset, turned "against the state because it was behaving like an insolvent debtor." In other cases, as Marot emphasizes, because most peasants were not capitalistically inclined, they simply kept the surplus for themselves.[40]

According to E. H. Carr, "the essence of NEP" meant that "agriculture had remained a quasi-independent enclave in the economy, functioning on its own lines, and resisting any attempt from without to alter them." Yet by the late 1920s, "the belief on which NEP was founded, that the cities could be fed through a combined system of voluntary deliveries to the state and free sales on the market had broken down." Carr notes that peasant-state relations "turned sour," leading by decade's end to "a declaration of war between the authorities and the well-to-do peasant who held large available stocks in the countryside." Marketable grain was, in 1927, only 37 percent of what it had been in 1913, according to Maurice Hindus: "Cleverly and audaciously the muzhik was on strike against the city, which couldn't supply him with the consumer goods he demanded in exchange for his grain and other foods."[41]

An additional complication arose concerning Soviet Russia's relations with global capitalism. The economic survival and revitalization generated by the NEP also involved the restoration and development of foreign trade, especially with Weimar Germany after the 1922 Rapallo Treaty (between Germany and Soviet Russia, pledging economic cooperation and renouncing all territorial and financial claims against each other related to the Treaty of Brest-Litovsk and the First World War). "We are living not merely in a state, but in a system of states," Lenin had commented in 1919, "and it is inconceivable for the Soviet Republic to exist alongside of the imperialist states for any length of time. One or the other must triumph in the end." No early Communist leader was inclined to disagree—both Trotsky and Stalin would cite Lenin's comment more than once over the years—but the fact remained that the improvement of the international position of the Soviet contributed powerfully to life-giving internal economic improvements. Although this rapprochement with the capitalist West was not perceived as a permanent position but rather a temporary stance adopted to meet Soviet Russia's current political realities, by 1925 Stalin was nonetheless moved to comment that "what we at one time regarded as a brief respite after the war has become a whole period of respite. Hence a certain equilibrium of forces and a certain period of 'peaceful co-existence' between the bourgeois world and the proletarian world." Peaceful coexistence or world revolution? To the extent that Lenin's 1919 comment was true (and was perceived to be true by Soviet leaders), the global implications of the NEP represented yet another growing and irresolvable tension.[42]

The contradictory and divergent trajectories inherent in the economic realities of the 1920s meant the consolidation that the Soviet Republic achieved in that period was neither stable nor permanent. It would soon give way to a momentous political shift, what is generally seen as the Stalinist era. The contradictory socioeconomic dynamics—with all of their positive and negative elements—found reflection in the realm of culture.

Culture and Consciousness

An entity known as "living newspapers" were, according to Samuel Northup Harper, another important outlet for political expression and social criticism, although they were also a form of cultural activity percolating in workers' clubs, village reading-rooms, and elsewhere. "Led by an organization of professionals under the name of the Blue Blouses, local groups in these institutions stage skits on current topics of the day, combining music, dancing, acting, and a kind of gymnastics in the technique of presentation," Harper wrote. Often the little skits "are very caustic in their portrayals of actual conditions" and "mock at the fundamental principles of the Revolution" (or, one might suspect, the hypocrisy of some individuals who identified themselves with such principles). "The ideal is for a local amateur group to give two or three different performances a week, so that the living newspaper will in fact become a powerful weapon of agitation and propaganda." The political education of both performers and audiences were to be advanced through such activities. And, Harper added, "through the living newspapers a sense of humor which was noticeably absent in the first years of the Revolution is able to express itself."[43]

Professionals such as the Blue Blouses were sometimes "criticized for tending toward 'bourgeois cabaret' methods," Harper noted—but while some undoubtedly were associated with the cabaret scene that was flourishing in 1920s urban centers, one can question the "bourgeois" labeling that some leftists rigidly insisted upon. In his remarkable history of Russian art and culture, W. Bruce Lincoln discusses precisely that scene:

> In those days, Moscow teemed with back-alley theaters, cellar cabarets, and literary cafés, in which Russia's artists and poets tested their new freedom. Bearing such names as Tenth Muse, Domino, Pittoresque, Red Cockerel, Music Box, Three-Leaved Clover, Pegasus's Trough, The Forge, The Imagists' Café, these provided forums for Futurists, Cubists, Suprematists, Imagists, Expressionists, Acmeists, Constructivists, Accidentists, Anarchists, and a virtually untranslatable group called the *Nichevoki* (the Nothing-ists). All of them cursed the past and hailed the future, shouting and roaring, and urgently whispering in a cacophony of sounds and visions that left no literary avenue unexplored.[44]

This flows directly into the much broader and deeper literary, artistic, and cultural ferment that constituted one of the most important arenas of "liberty under the Soviets"—as well as of the growing complications and limitations that such liberty was running into. We can do no better, here, than to link up with an old man's vivid memories of the time when, as a perceptive and enthusiastic US Communist, fluent in Russian, he personally engaged with the remarkable cultural scene of Soviet Russia in the 1920s. "In the days of civil war, famine, chaos and peril—they had monuments in Moscow to Dostoyevsky, Bakunin, Marx, Danton and Robespierre. There was also a monument to Human Thought and they planned monuments to Tolstoy, Cezanne and Rimsky-Korsakov," recalls Joseph Freeman. Theaters for plays, operas, ballet, and symphonies were now completely open to the entire population, and "in 1920, Moscow audiences saw and heard plays and operas by Wedekind, Wilde, Marinetti, Debussy, Offenbach, Richard Strauss, Wagner, Mozart, Shakespeare, Merejkowski, Alexander Blok and Puccini. There was Mayakovsky's *Mysteria-Bouffe* and Romain Rolland's *Storming of the Bastille*."[45]

In prerevolutionary Russia, artistically daring avant-garde currents had flourished among Russia's young artists, with shapes and forms and colors utilized in dynamically abstract ways. These—and much else—were among the diverse range of cultural expressions that were embraced and promoted by the Commissariat of Education, headed by Anatoly Lunacharsky. An International Art Bureau for Promoting Relations between Russian and European Artists was established, consisting of Lunacharsky, Kazimir Malevitch, Wassily Kandinsky, and Vladimir Tatlin.[46]

Of these, Wassily Kandinsky—with his "rejection of materialism in favor of the spiritual," and his view of art "as a vehicle of transcendence . . . aspiring from the concrete to the abstract"—had the least affinity to Soviet realities. Experiences in Russia during the 1914–21 cataclysm of war and revolution, he later related, "shattered me to the depths of my soul [and] raised me to ecstasy," but despite his desire to work in the new revolutionary context, he experienced such frustrations that he finally left the country. This was so despite the lavish praise that some Bolsheviks provided for Kadinsky. For example, in 1920, Konstantin Umansky (a cultured young Bolshevik militant serving in a high position within the Foreign Office) "published a book about Soviet art in the first three years of the revolution. It was a hymn of praise to modern art, above all to Kandinsky and Malevitch," which included the judgment that "Kandinsky's creation more than characterizes the new Russian art. It is a brilliant document of the tempo of Russian art as a whole and it stands out for the well-nigh prophetic role it plays in the world of art."[47]

Kazimir Malevitch was an incredibly innovative painter. From 1900 through 1920 (a period during which he was influenced by Pablo Picasso and Georges Braque), he shifted from impressionism to primitivism to a style featuring peasant figures "with cylindrical, robotlike arms, legs, and bodies," with "lavish use of metallic greens, blues, and bronzes"—transitioning, then, to reflecting "Galileo's famous dictum that 'nature speaks the language of mathematics and the letters of this language are circles, triangles, and other mathematical figures.'" He inspired a new school of Suprematists (one of the best known being El Lissitzky), who "soon transferred their lessons to the functional arts—architecture, ceramics, book design, even clothing," notes art historian John Bowlt. "Their geometric vocabulary left an indelible print on early Soviet design." Vladimir Tatlin was Malevitch's close associate and fierce rival, and founder of Constructivism (which attracted such major artists as Liuba Popova, Varvara Stepanova, and Alexander Rodchenko). He "started his career as a sailor before turning to painting," then "blazed a new trail" that "rejected the idea of transcendental inspiration and the personal genius, arguing for an alliance with engineering," reflected in his remarkable drawings and models for a Monument to the Third International. The structure, which ended up never being built, was conceived as a massive and functional headquarters for the Comintern. This artistic current, Bowlt tells us, sought to prepare "a new generation for direct involvement in the industrial and democratic demands of the revolutionary ethos."[48]

Theater in 1926, Freeman reports, was especially vibrant. Particularly impressive were the innovations of the world-famous producer-director Vsevolod Meyerhold:

> Among other things, I saw Meyerhold's production of *The Inspector General*, starring his wife, Zinaida Reich. He based it on Gogol's entire output in order to show the implications of the play for our own time and to create a monumental spectacle consistent with the scope of the enterprise.
>
> Gogol wanted to ridicule the high and mighty among the Czarist bureaucracy. Fear for the censor obliged him to choose a small, nameless town and a picayune hero for *The Inspector General*. Meyerhold restored Gogol to his true proportions. He made use of all the versions of the play, as well as of incidents and scenes in *Dead Souls*. He invested the main characters with greater importance and placed them in courtly splendor. The fifteen episodes into which the play was divided were mounted on trapezoid platforms, and moved on and off stage by motor power during intermissions. Within these episodes Meyerhold succeeded in laying bare the lust, gluttony and hypocrisy of Gogol's grotesque world. In this many saw a reflection of the world around them.
>
> The revolution in art, represented by Kandinsky and Malevitch, was still alive. In the Sholem Aleichem play I saw at the Yiddish Kamerny Theatre the sets were by Chagall. This was a manifestation of the contemporary breakthrough via expressionism which Paul Tillich has described as "a more radical disruption of the surface of things, a more intensive piercing into their elements, a more sensitive vision of their demonic depth than has happened in centuries."[49]

A powerfully influential cultural current arose in the wake of the October Revolution that projected the triumph of a new Communist art and literature based on the political triumph of the proletariat. It crystallized in 1920 in "the famous organization of the *Prolecult*... the purpose of which was to direct the fight for proletarian culture on an international scale," according to Marc Slonim, who notes that this generated a variety of conflicting subgroups within the broader movement. Some called for repression of "nonparty" elements and for a "literary dictatorship" that vanquish "bourgeois ideology and counter-revolutionary tendencies," revolutionizing art and literature "as the Bolsheviks had revolutionized the social-political order."

Naturally, the question was posed regarding which was the true representative of this revolution. In reaction to this, such prominent figures as Trotsky, Lunacharsky, and Alexander Voronsky (an influential Communist literary critic whose cultural views were close to those of Lenin and left-dissident Maxim Gorky) emphasized, as Slonim paraphrased it, "that many elements had to be taken from bourgeois art and literature and that it was impossible to create a proletarian literature by purely exterior governmental means." Lunacharsky insisted: "To demand the immediate birth of a genuine proletarian culture is to demand a miracle." Trotsky agreed that artistic quality trumped theoretical manifestos: "The issue between bourgeois and proletarian art depends of quality." Voronsky launched a substantial journal, *Red Virgin Soil,* with the participation of Gorky and Lenin, in part to provide a literary outlet for nonproletarian writers who, while in sympathy with socialist and revolutionary ideals, were not attempting to enunciate a Communist Party line. In fact, a formal Party resolution insisted: "The Party must fight against all thoughtless or contemptuous treatment of the old cultural heritage as well as of the literary specialists. . . . It must also fight against a purely hot-house proletarian literature" and foster "the free rivalry of various tendencies and groups in the literary sphere."[50]

The development of cinema opened the pathway to another incredibly important cultural medium, although as W. Bruce Lincoln has pointed out, this could not be fully realized until the NEP: "Only when the fighting stopped could Sergei Eisenstein and Vsevolod Pudovkin begin work on the first great Soviet films that would earn them undisputed places among the world's best film directors in barely more than five years." Joseph Freeman commented that in 1926, when Eisenstein's *Potemkin* hit New York City, "the critics were unanimously enthusiastic. They felt that by American standards the picture lacked 'entertainment value'; some of them were a little uncomfortable under its propaganda; but all recognized the arrival of a new force in the art of film." This was, of course, a cultural form capable of embracing millions of people throughout Soviet Russia—"intelligible to millions of workers and peasants unaffected by poems, novels or theatres," Freeman noted. "In a country like Russia, with vast distances to be covered, with many levels of culture, some of them quite primitive, an art which could reach everybody was bound to take first place."[51] Inherently inclusive, it provided a means to "raise consciousness" and "the cultural level of the masses," in a sense getting everyone on "the same page," as determined by the filmmakers and government authorities, to be sure. But once thinking and sensibilities are stirred

among many millions, it is hardly a foregone conclusion that a central authority can *keep* everyone on that particular "page."

When he went to Moscow in the spring of 1926, Freeman later recalled,
it was shortly after an editorial in the *New York Times* announced that the Soviet government was "growing susceptible to the susceptibilities of the masses." This was, it speculated, thanks to the victory of "the Stalin moderates at
the recent Communist Congress" (also led, then, by NEP enthusiast Nikolai
Bukharin), which was a victory "for a policy of reconciliation." The *Times*
added that the "conversion of the muzhik to Marxism" had been "indefinite-
ly postponed." Freeman adds that "the Party had prohibited the Komsomol
from putting on anti-religious plays," and that Trotsky himself "had emphasized the need for finding a place within the sphere of the Communist regime
for those elements 'who cannot go all the way with us.' Those elements, the
Times noted, 'comprise the vast majority of the Russian people.' It was obvious
that 'the crusading temper was showing signs of being spent.'"[52] While not
agreeing that the Russian Revolution was now "spent," Freeman certainly saw
1926 as a moment in which all paths still seemed open, yet the future seemed
fraught with—if anything—revolutionary promise:

> Like everybody in Russia at that time, the writers lived in a world beleaguered
> and inspired. Fresh was the memory of the Great War, the fall of the Winter Pal-
> ace, the October Revolution, the civil war, the Good News that world socialism
> was on the way or eventually bound to come and to fulfill its historic mission of
> transforming man and the world for an ever better life. Lenin was dead only two
> and a half years; his spirit was omnipresent, his successor undetermined.
>
> Civil war songs were still sung throughout Russia and in the Hotel Lux, too
> [where foreign Communists were often quartered]. We sang Kirpichiki, Molo-
> daya Gvardia, Krasnaya Armya: The White Army, the black baron, are once
> more preparing for us a Czarist throne, but from the taiga to the British sea, the
> Red Army conquers them all. Before the decade was over I translated from the
> Yiddish a civil war song by Yitzik Feffer: "Over towns and villages, black clouds
> sweeping, blond Komsomol girls through battle are creeping. . . . Bullets are
> whistling, trains are hooting, somewhere the foe's machine guns are shooting;
> a comrade falls whom the smoke has blinded; turn your white apron round the
> wound and bind it. What if Mom weeps, what if Pop is stern? Lenin! Trotsky!
> Youth Comintern!"
>
> The future was immense with promise. In spite of everything, and because of
> everything, it was still that dawn when it was bliss "to be alive, but to be young was
> very Heaven." The present was immense with peril. On the peaks of history the
> gods were engaged in mortal combat for dominion; round the republic there was
> the mounting menace of fascism [Mussolini had triumphed in Italy and Hitler's

Nazi movement was becoming an increasingly ominous force in Germany] and war [the threat of new imperialist military interventions, and the slowly gathering clouds of a Second World War].[53]

What we see in the cultural, literary, artistic developments of the 1920s are reflective of larger political and social realities. Despite imbalances and limitations, there is considerable evidence of improvements in the conditions of the masses, the flourishing of diversity and critical-mindedness within growing sectors of the population, the existence of some important liberties and outlets for popular expression, and the countrywide popularization of egalitarian and socialist ideals. There seemed to be grounds, in the opinion of many, for the Soviet Republic to crystallize into a workers' democracy in the foreseeable future, with guarantees of freedom and well-being for all.

"What there is in Russia is an experiment having two purposes," reflected John Dewey in the late 1920s. "The first and more immediate aim is to see whether human beings can have such guarantees *against* want, illness, old-age, and *for* health, recreation, reasonable degree of material ease and comfort that they will not have to struggle for purely personal acquisition and accumulation, without, in short, being forced to undergo the strain of competitive struggle for personal profit." Regarding the second purpose, related to Dewey's own profoundly democratic concerns as a philosopher and educator,

> it is an experiment to discover whether the familiar democratic ideals—familiar in words, at least—of liberty, equality and brotherhood will not be most completely realized in a social regime based on voluntary cooperation, on conjoint workers' control and management of industry, and an accompanying abolition of private property as a fixed institution—a somewhat different matter, of course, than the abolition of private property as such. . . . When economic security for all is secured, and when workers control industry and politics, there will be the opportunity for all to participate freely and fully in a cultivated life. That a nation that strives for a private culture from which many are excluded by economic stress cannot be a cultivated nation was an idea frequently heard [by Dewey while visiting Soviet Russia] from the mouths of both educators and working people.[54]

Dewey was naturally drawn especially to what J. P. Nettl notes, which is that in the 1920s "perhaps the most exciting experiments were introduced in the educational field." Nadezhda Krupskaya, herself a teacher by training, played a central role in educational reforms contrasting the authoritarian norms in the tsarist system—characterized by "a spirit of bigotry" and "servile loyalty to the authorities," in which "discussion of the realities of life was taboo"—to seeing schools as "an embryo and a symbol of the future society without classes." The innovations were most pronounced in city schools. There was an emphasis on racial, ethnic, gender, and social equality (and new coeducational classes). "Above all, the traditional and disciplinarian relationship between teachers and pupils tended to give way to new forms of collaboration," Nettl comments, citing official policy to the effect that "the teacher must be an organizer, an assistant, an instructor and above all an older comrade, but not a superior officer." Among the innovations, "an attempt was made to integrate children's work around one large theme, known as the complex method, instead of dividing it into separate and distinct subjects. Group work among students was encouraged." In addition, "visiting factories, museums, theatres and other places of public entertainment became an essential part of the school curriculum," and was tagged the "excursion method." Not all went smoothly—innovation could generate disorganization, and all too often there were "great shortages of buildings, teachers, and books"—although Lucy Wilson, a US educational researcher who closely studied the Soviet school system throughout the 1920s, was able to report positive changes for the years 1925–27 that seemed "almost incredible to me, an eyewitness."[55]

In this context, it is worth considering a remarkable personal letter from the same period. It was reproduced in an account by Olga Chernov, like her husband, Victor (exiled leader of the Socialist Revolutionary Party), a bitter critic of Bolshevik rule. She received the letter from a friend whom we met earlier in this volume, a young peasant-turned-worker and former SR named Katia. "Life is always hard," she writes, describing difficult living conditions. She has taken her young son and left her Communist husband because she felt he was "profiting from injustice and privileges." Katia asserts: "But we are going to do away with these new privileges as well as the old! We workers are strong. I am staying with those who work and suffer and believe in the future." She writes that "we are destroying the past to construct the future, but sometimes the destruction gets a bit too energetic." Specifically, she complains: "We sometimes destroy those feelings considered like the rest of the past *bourgeois*—sensibility, kindness, tenderness, and also the courage to tell the truth when it runs contrary to the dominating ideas." Yet she remains committed to the ideals of the Bolshevik revolution: "I cannot describe my state of mind to you in a letter, sometimes my strength is lacking for the double—the multiple—fight. For I have to fight for my life and my son's, and I also have to fight for our class and our Party, side by side with those who—in my opinion—are turning it from the right path." Working in a factory by day, Katia attends evening classes at the Workers' University, studying science but also the literature of ancient Greece. Referring to the legend of the Golden Fleece and the myth of the Garden of Golden Apples, she writes:

> I am not so simple as I used to be. I know that our generation will never reach the Fleece nor the Apple. We thought we held it in our hands, but it rolled away into the dirt and blood. Then, still splashed and stained, we saw how it shone as it rolled along. It is the light that leads us.
>
> Apple-red apple,
> Where are you rolling? . . .
>
> Do you still remember that tune which everyone used to sing? That apple is rolling towards the happiness of the whole world, dear Olga Elissevna, I am certain of that. Will my son live to see that day?[56]

There were others who also had hopes for the future. The former Menshevik Simon Liberman, who worked as a "nonparty specialist" for the Soviet government from 1918 to 1926 (and then fled abroad to the freer atmosphere of France and the United States) later critically characterized "Russia's socialists of the non-Bolshevik variety" as people who had "failed to place themselves at the head of the popular forces, which, at this juncture of history, longed above all for a firm leadership to take them onward to well-defined ends." This only the Bolsheviks had been prepared to do, and many intellectuals such as Liberman decided to work with them because "they realized that the new government, no matter how bad, was nevertheless a government of the people and for the people." Also looking back after his own disillusionment, US journalist Louis Fischer still termed this period of Bolshevik rule as "a churning process which ground the former ruling castes into dust and brought vital new forces to the surface," constituting "an experiment in the interest of the downtrodden majority," which "glorified the common man and offered him land, bread, peace, a job, a house, security, education, health, art, and happiness." Indeed, the British delegation representing the Trade Union Congress asserted in 1925 that "the Soviet system of representation and its scheme of constitutional and civil rights, so far from being undemocratic in the widest sense of the word, gives in many respects a more real and reasonable opportunity of participation in public than does parliamentary and [pluralist] party government." The delegation noted that in important respects "such participation is still severely restricted," particularly because "the system has been kept under close control by its originators," although this Communist control was exercised "with the tacit consent of an immense majority of their fellow electors." The Communist Party's "permanence in power" did not seem a necessary feature of the soviet system to the delegation (it predicted the eventual emergence of "a two-party system and a constitutional opposition"), and it believed that in the foreseeable future "there are certainly as great—and possibly greater—possibilities than elsewhere in respect of popular government, political peace, and social progress."[57]

There were even deeper and more extensive aspirations associated with the Soviet "experiment," to use the term preferred by the democratic educator-philosopher John Dewey. He himself conveyed these as he paraphrased how, during an extensive discussion with him and others, Nadezhda Krupskaya—Lenin's widow and herself an educator and veteran Bolshevik organizer—sought to sum up the task of the Soviet regime:

> Its purpose is . . . to enable every human being to obtain personal cultivation. The economic and political revolution that had taken place was not the end; it was the means and basis of a cultural development still to be realized. It was a necessary means, because without economic freedom and equality, the full development of the possibilities of all individuals could not be achieved. But the economic change was for the sake of enabling every human being to share to the full in all the things that give value to human life.[58]

Was this all a beguiling illusion, or did such potential for democracy and freedom exist? Even if it did, it certainly could not be realized in Soviet Russia under the continuing and combined pressures of impoverishment and technological backwardness on the one hand and isolation in a hostile capitalist world on the other. As it was, the failure of socialist revolution in the industrially advanced West guaranteed new crises, including the rise of fascism and Nazism, the 1930s Depression, and the coming of a Second World War.[59]

Under such circumstances, the negative potential of corruption and authoritarianism (what Marx had warned of as "the same old crap") triumphed over the positive potential of liberty. The countervailing tendencies pushing toward liberty, the persisting revolutionary commitments, the residual elements of 1917 workers' democracy—vibrant as they all may have been—were overtaken by the darker forces also inherent in the complex realities of revolutionary Russia.

More rigid, restrictive, authoritarian tendencies were in evidence. In the realm of art and literature, some pioneers of what would become the restrictive new cultural orthodoxy of "socialist realism" referred to their production in the 1920s as "heroic realism"—although one critic ridiculed it as "heroic servilism." Joseph Freeman later commented, "The dragon of false realism in art, boon companion of false abstraction in politics, was raising its head. . . . After 1930 the Party and the government dominated Soviet literature with catastrophic results." It is instructive to consider two opposing approaches to culture, noted by J. P. Nettl: one, Lenin's conviction that "culture was not something which intellectuals tossed at each other but a process in which everyone in society was involved"; the other, Stalin's conceptualization in which "culture ceased to be social self-expression and became an enormous process of brutally simplified learning."[60]

9

CONSOLIDATION OF
THE SOVIET REPUBLIC

*I*n 1924, the year that Lenin died, it could be said that the Soviet Republic had finally consolidated. Some have been inclined to see this as the moment when Stalin triumphed, the moment when the bureaucratic authoritarianism of "Stalinism" displaced the original revolutionary-democratic Bolshevism.

That strikes me as mistaken. Too much of the complex and contradictory "liberty under the Soviets" we have been examining continued to flourish into the later years of the 1920s. It could be argued that there was no thoroughgoing "Stalinism" until the destruction of the New Economic Policy—that Stalinism finally crystallized in the *process* advanced through the successive defeats of the Left Opposition of Trotsky (1923–24), the United Opposition of Zinoviev-Kamenev-Trotsky (1926–27), and then the Right Opposition of Bukharin-Rykov-Tomsky (1928–30), culminating in the "revolution from above" that carried out the forced collectivization of land and the rapid development of industry characterizing the Soviet Union from 1929 through 1934—obliterating the 1924 "consolidation" in the process. There were significant countervailing tendencies to this—reflected in the oppositions just mentioned, and in others arising earlier. Grounded in some of the dynamics explored in the previous chapters, these emancipatory tendencies would also, by necessity, push beyond the 1924 consolidation.

Thus, the "consolidation of the Soviet Republic" was neither a finished nor stable reality—it faced difficulties, not least of which were the contradictions of the NEP, the partial basis for the 1924 consolidation. It contained germs that would bring about further transformation. Some of these germs were qualitatively different from what came to be known as Stalinism. Possibilities existed for overcoming the contradictions along pathways that were quite different from those that Soviet Russia actually followed in the 1930s.

But it is certainly also the case that the germs of what became Stalinism, already latent in Bolshevism in 1917 (largely related to "blind spots" identified later in this chapter), were growing dramatically and spreading rapidly through the body politic of Soviet Russia during the period we have been examining. That authoritarian crystallization came to be identified, by a variety of political analysts and in the popular mind, with the *dictatorship of the proletariat* that had presumably been established by the October Revolution of 1917. We have already noted that the original meaning of that term is the opposite of what it came to mean.

The conceptualization labeled *dictatorship of the proletariat*—meaning "proletarian rule"—has been central to (1) Marxist theory in general, (2) Trotsky's theory of permanent revolution, which has played a role in the present study, and (3) the ideology and claims of the Bolsheviks. If utilized in a critical-minded way (taking it seriously but not employing it as a magical incantation), the concept can have value in helping us understand not simply the mind-set of the revolutionaries under examination but also the realities of Russian political life. To approach this seriously, we must determine the particular realities that allow us to say whether or not "proletarian rule" existed in Bolshevik Russia of 1917–24.

Defining Proletarian Dictatorship

For some, the regime issuing from the October Revolution was certainly a "proletarian dictatorship," representing the evaporation of bourgeois participation in the political life of the country. In the wake of the Bolshevik seizure of power, parties of the conservative and liberal bourgeoisie received only 13 percent of the vote in the 1917 elections for the Constituent Assembly, with 87 percent of the vote going to the various socialist parties. All socialists committed to conciliation with capitalists were quickly marginalized within the dynamic framework of the soviets, and in Russia generally, by those committed to working-class rule. With the dissolution of the Constituent Assembly, and in some cases even before, bourgeois political forces worked exclusively to overthrow the Bolshevik regime by force and violence. Actual members of the capitalist class generally had only the most circumscribed means for expression of their ideas, no right to organize politically, and in most cases no right even to vote. In the Civil War period many were victimized by the policies of the "Red Terror." The destruction of the Russian bourgeoisie as a political force coincided with the nationalization of the economy—taking place, again, under the banner of working-class rule.[1]

In what sense was there actually "proletarian rule"? For Marx, political rule by the working class was seen as "winning the battle of democracy," involving full freedom of expression, a flourishing pluralism of parties, institutionalized forms of direct democracy in society from top to bottom, and so forth.[2]

We have seen that this was projected by the Bolsheviks in 1917 but fairly quickly went out of existence. The Bolshevik regime, nonetheless, was clearly (1) committed to carrying out policies and establishing programs beneficial to the proletarianized (and semi-proletarianized) layers constituting the majority of working people, (2) prepared to realize that priority at the expense of the capitalist class, (3) dependent for its existence on support of these proletarianized working people who saw it as a force representing their interests, and (4) committed to ensuring that a very high percentage of those involved in government decision-making and administration were from the working class.[3]

The combination of these factors—it could be argued—adds up to something consistent with the classical Marxist dictatorship of the proletariat, even if the radical-democratic ideal of classical Marxism is not sustained. That tended to be the position of the Russian Communists, although the extent to which the reality diverged from the radical-democratic ideal of *workers' democracy* (elaborated in the section of this volume's appendix titled "Defining Democracy") raises important questions, to be explored in this chapter. If we accept the notion that some variant of dictatorship of the proletariat existed, based simply on the restricted adherence to the four-point definition just provided in the paragraph above, additional questions can be raised. In particular, it would seem that if the combination of factors adds up to proletarian rule, then the elimination of any of the factors would raise a question about whether a proletarian dictatorship continued to exist.

This suggests that a failure of the regime to improve (or prevent the decline of) the situation of the proletariat might erode, and ultimately eliminate, proletarian support for the regime. In fact, the mixed-economy project of the Bolsheviks sometimes resulted in the regime favoring certain policies at the expense of the workers' immediate needs and desires—although this was defended as being in the long-range interests of the proletariat. In the latter period of war communism in 1920–21, the so-called proletarian dictatorship more than once came into conflict with the actual proletariat and proved fully prepared to repress the workers. It can be argued that such a narrative oversimplifies a far more complex process, but to state it so baldly helps to pose the question more sharply.

We have already reviewed the crises that overwhelmed the democratic-libertarian dreams of the Bolsheviks, resulting in an authoritarian trajectory. Within the Communist Party itself there were angry protests as the scope and momentum of authoritarianism increased—something that had initially been accepted under the circumstances but which many now pushed against as the circumstances changed. "When the enemy had you by the throat, it was no time for philosophy," commented the militant Red Guard Eduard Dune. He elaborated:

> From our position in the Red Army we looked in front of us, at the enemy; we had little opportunity to glance behind us and to see the bitter soviet reality. We were unwilling to see that at home, in the party, political appointees were replacing elected committees, and that the dictatorship of the proletariat was falling into the hands of a dictator; that the soviet constitution and self-government were being replaced by administrative debauchery. It seemed that these transformations were not actions of an enemy but "small defects in the larger mechanism." We more readily explained the huge peasant rebellions that originated after the war as intrigues by enemies of the revolution than by their truer causes.[4]

But at the end of the Civil War, young worker-Bolsheviks and militants such as Dune found that the "bitter soviet reality" raised multiple questions in their minds about what was really what, and "amidst these bewildering questions we confronted the end of the civil war, debating, even after the [party] congress, the questions of inner-party democracy and the next stage of the revolution, the New Economic Policy."[5]

Even before the NEP, debates raged and the push toward revolutionary democracy proved to be powerful in the wake of the Red Civil War victory. "As the war disappeared, there arose a new wave of opposition to the authoritarian regime in the Communist Party," notes Robert V. Daniels. A salient aspect of this was advanced by one of the authors of the party handbook *The ABC of Communism*, Eugen Preobrazhensky, "who remained sensitive to infringements of democracy, even though he was now one of the top party secretaries," and who drafted a set of critical theses on the problem of bureaucracy in the party in preparation for the Ninth Congress of the Russian Communist Party in 1920—where oppositionists pushed the question even further. Discussions and debates at the congress revealed, according to Daniels, that "the actual differences between the leadership and the Opposition . . . were more a matter of emphasis than principle." The agreed-upon resolution that came out of the congress was "a rousing manifesto of democratic intent," which insisted on "broader criticism of the central as well as the local party institutions," an end to the appointment of local party secretaries by the party's national center, and a prohibition on "any kind of repression against comrades because they have different ideas." And there was a sweeping affirmation of the principles that would make the "dictatorship of the proletariat" a genuinely democratic expression of political rule by the working class and by the toiling masses in general. The resolution stressed "the need again to direct the attention of the whole party to the struggle for the realization for greater equality: in the first place, within the party; secondly, within the proletariat, and in addition within the whole toiling mass; finally, in the third place, between the various offices and various groups of workers, especially the 'spetsy' [bourgeois specialists] and responsible workers, in relation to the masses."[6]

Despite such stated intentions, the hoped-for realities—according to Simon Pirani—were "confounded by circumstances and pushed back by the state," certainly not in a "uniform or unidimensional" manner, and most definitely against pressures from "workers, communists, and others [who] kept trying to push the revolution forward." Such revolutionary pushing was not always grounded in an understanding of the difficult realities—Pirani notes that "in the mood of the civil war communists . . . there was a streak of super-optimism, i.e., and exaggerated confidence, based on the victories achieved in 1917–19, in their own ability to change the world." At the same time, according to one of these militants, "in the heart of every conscious comrade from the front, who at the front has become used to almost complete equality, who has broken from every kind of servility, debauchery and luxury—with which our very best party comrades now surround themselves—their boils hatred and disbelief." Under the pressure from the ranks at the 1920 party congress, Gregory Zinoviev—not known for being a consistently democratic figure in this period—advanced perspectives (summarized by Pirani) that targeted "accumulation of power in the *glavki* [bureaucracy]; the negative consequences of militarism, which had imbued some communists with arrogant, authoritarian methods; the integration of some communists into circles of *spetsy* with whom they worked and consequent corrupt relations; and the party's failure to counter these tendencies." But for many, this was not enough. One radical worker called for "a third revolution in production" to match the two revolutions of 1917, and Pirani concludes: "The central role that the state played in reproducing and reinforcing hierarchical social relations, and the exploitative nature of those relations in the economy, were only rarely alluded to by any participants in the discussions of 1920–21. Soon, the tenth congress would silence what discussion there had been, and strengthen the authoritarian tendencies that the dissidents of 1920, albeit partially and incoherently, tried to resist."[7]

One of the most articulate critiques was advanced by the Workers' Opposition, a faction inside the Russian Communist Party and led by Alexander Shlyapnikov and Alexandra Kollontai. Shlyapnikov was a veteran working-class activist and longtime Bolshevik organizer, leader of the Metalworkers' Union, and the first commissar of labor in the Soviet government, and the feminist intellectual Kollantai, also an experienced revolutionary activist, was the first commissar of social welfare. Both had been closely associated with Lenin, especially as he had pushed forward to the revolution of October 1917—and now they crossed swords with him around the meaning of proletarian rule. "Some of the Bolsheviks' most ardent supporters among the proletariat had begun to declare openly that the time had come for a real workers' democracy, with decent food, decent housing, and full representation in decision making," notes Barbara Evans Clements. The Workers' Opposition was castigated for being anti-leadership—to which Kollontai responded: "Workers know there is something wrong. But instead of running to Ilyich's [Lenin's] office for a chat, as many of our more timid comrades do, we have proposed a series of practical measures to cleanse our ranks and revive our relations with them [i.e., the workers]." The Opposition was also accused of representing an "anarcho-syndicalist deviation," because of its call for a decisive trade union role in running the economy. Shlyapnikov responded that this was false, that the Workers' Opposition did "not repudiate political struggle, the dictatorship of the proletariat, the party's leading role, nor the significance of the soviets as bodies of power."[8]

In a widely distributed document entitled *The Workers' Opposition*, this dissident faction protested against the rise of a "bureaucratic state system" that had replaced the "self-activity of the working masses" with "a hierarchy of 'permissions' and 'decrees,'" adding: "We give no freedom to class activity, we are afraid of criticism, we have ceased to rely on the masses: hence we have bureaucracy with us." The dissidents attributed the problem to the fact that many nonrevolutionary elements had been drawn into the state apparatus and also that any party standing at the head of the Soviet state is compelled to consider the needs of nonproletarian layers in society (the vast peasantry, urban petty bourgeoisie, and so on) and the pressures of world capitalism, creating a gap between leaders of the party and state on the one hand and the working class on the other. The Workers' Opposition observed that "during these three years of the revolution, the economic situation of the working class, of those who work in factories and mills, has not only not been improved, but has become more unbearable." The faction perceived the outlook of "the working masses" in this way: "The leaders are one thing, and we are something altogether different. Maybe it is true that the leaders know better how to rule over the country, but they fail to understand our needs, our life in the shops, its requirements and immediate needs; they do not understand and do not know." In fact, the leaders, "having severed all ties with the masses, carry out their own policy and build up industry without any regard to our opinions and creative abilities," and "distrust of the workers by the leaders is steadily growing." The solution seemed simple enough: "The Workers' Opposition has said what has long ago been printed in *The Communist Manifesto* by Marx and Engels: the building of communism can and must be the work of the toiling masses themselves. The building of communism belongs to the workers."[9]

To speak of building communism under conditions existing in Russia at that time was an illusion. The criticisms voiced by *The Workers' Opposition* document reflected terrible realities, but the solution offered was based on this false assumption: "Since the October revolution, unprecedented opportunities for economic creation have now opened new, unheard-of forms of production, with an immense increase in the productivity of labor." As we have seen, the opposite was the case. And yet the polemic of the Workers' Opposition gave voice to discontent felt throughout the country among those who had been inspired by the Bolshevik revolution. "During the winter months popular anger developed on a wide front," Paul Avrich recounts, "embracing sailors and soldiers as well as peasants and workers, who yearned for the anarchic freedom of 1917 while craving at the same time a restoration of social stability and an end to bloodshed and economic privation."[10]

In addition to uprisings in the countryside, a rash of strikes and demonstrations broke out in Petrograd. The influence of Mensheviks, anarchists, and both Left and Right SRs could be felt in these heterogeneous protests. Workers turned out in the streets with banners focusing not only on economic demands but also on the restoration of civil liberties, pluralism, soviet democracy. Some (particularly those influenced by the Right SRs) appealed for a return of the bourgeois-democratic Constituent Assembly. There were others less liberal: "Down with the Communists and Jews." According to Avrich, "an open breach occurred between the Bolshevik regime and its principal mainstay of support, the working class." Yet this is far too categorical—Avrich himself acknowledges that "for many intellectuals and workers" in Russia at this time "the Bolsheviks, with all their faults, were still the most effective barrier to a White resurgence and the downfall of the revolution."[11]

If we are to understand the class realities of this period, there is another key point that must be grasped. The multifaceted and diverse reality of the Russian working class discussed earlier in this study did not simply evaporate after 1917. As Mary McAuley has put it, "There will always be a number of different demands and disagreements within the working class. At times they may cluster together to create a relatively unified set. In October [1917], with its program of a Soviet government, an end to war, an attack on privilege and wealth, the Bolshevik party did express just such a set." The working class in its great majority cohered into a powerful force to make the Bolshevik revolution. But with the profound change in the political, social, and economic realities, "the [working-class] demands no longer formed the same set as they had in October." In fact, there tended to be different "sets" for different fractions and layers. "Throughout 1917–1920, worker activists in the factories differed significantly from ordinary workers," observes William Husband. "Even among the most advanced workers of Petrograd, those who served on the factory committees and held trade union offices were more sophisticated politically than the worker on the factory floor." He adds that "outside Petrograd and in industries in which unskilled workers predominated, this gap became critical" under changing conditions. (Husband goes on to make the interesting point that while many of the more skilled and politically confident "conscious workers" of Petrograd may have desired less centralized forms of workers' control, which would give them greater authority, other layers of the working class—lacking such expertise and confidence—preferred greater centralization, for which the state and party provided direction.)[12]

An element in Husband's argument adds a crucial dimension to the problematic we are considering. The cadres who assumed responsibility in the Bolshevik regime were in many cases the kind of worker activists he describes. At what point can we decide that they were no longer part of the working class? Perhaps such people, after a period of enjoying privilege and power in a stabilized and consolidated new social order, could be said to have become transformed from dedicated worker activists into a social layer of ex-workers who have risen above their class. But we are dealing, in 1920–21, with an intense and incredibly fluid situation, in which what is ostensibly a proletarian state is fighting for its life, in which the mobilization of working-class support is crucial for its survival, and in which the "worker activists" in question—still fired by socialist ideals and revolutionary enthusiasm, and not more than three years away from the workbench—are themselves making great sacrifices and often taking incredible risks. This doesn't mean that all of them are necessarily free from narrowness, arrogance, pettiness, selfishness, and various other faults that crop up in human groups (whether workers, capitalists, bureaucrats, or whatever). But it is still too soon in 1921 to decide that they have passed, as a group, from the ranks of the proletariat to the ranks of a self-interested bureaucracy. In fact, it was from this layer of worker activists that many prominent members of the Workers' Opposition arose. Other such worker activists disagreed with that opposition—and among these, some would evolve into bureaucrats while others would evolve into opponents of bureaucratic privilege.

This brings us to the Kronstadt uprising of 1921, when a majority of the sailors and workers at a key naval base outside of Petrograd—impatient with economic shortages and dictatorial restrictions—rose up, arms in hand, calling on the workers and peasants of Russia to carry out a new revolution that would reestablish soviet democracy, which some interpreted as "soviets without Communists." In an appeal to "the laboring masses of the East and of the West," the Kronstadt rebels declared there was "no middle ground in the struggle against the Communists and the new serfdom that they have erected," elaborating: "Here is raised the banner of rebellion against the three-year-old violence and oppression of Communist rule, which has put in the shade the three-hundred-year yoke of monarchism. Here in Kronstadt has been laid the first stone of the third revolution, striking the last fetters from the laboring masses and opening a broad new road for socialist creativity." They were able to count on Menshevik, Socialist Revolutionary, and anarchist support—and anticommunist forces and governments watched expectantly from abroad. The uprising was brutally suppressed by the Bolshevik regime, but it is important to recognize that this would not have been possible without a substantial residue of loyalty to that regime among the workers, peasants, and others—soldiers, sailors, civilians—who went into battle against the Kronstadt rebels: about fifty thousand participated in the assault on Kronstadt, of whom an estimated ten thousand were killed or wounded. Even the Workers' Opposition participated in quelling the rebellion.[13] One eyewitness who was sympathetic to the rebels, Victor Serge, explained why he and others like him finally supported the Bolshevik side in this tragic dispute:

> If the Bolshevik dictatorship fell, it was only a short step to chaos, and through chaos to a peasant rising, the massacre of the Communists, the return of the émigrés, and in the end, through the sheer force of events, another dictatorship, this time anti-proletarian. Dispatches from Stockholm and Tallinn testified that the émigrés had these very perspectives in mind; dispatches which, incidentally, strengthened the Bolshevik leaders' intention of subduing Kronstadt speedily and at whatever cost. We were not reasoning in the abstract. We knew that in European Russia alone there were at least fifty centers of peasant insurrection. To the south of Moscow, in the region of Tambov, Antonov, the Right Social-Revolutionary school-teacher, who proclaimed the abolition of the Soviet system and the re-establishment of the Constituent Assembly, had under his command a superbly organized peasant army, numbering several tens of thousands. He had conducted negotiations with the Whites. (Tukhachevsky [famed Red Army general] suppressed this Vendée around the middle of 1921.)[14]

It is simply not the case, then, that Kronstadt represented the working class and the Party turning against each other. Closer to the truth is an analysis that comprehends that members of a decimated, fragmented, demoralized working class were swept into a violent conflict with each other over the question of whether the existence of the Bolshevik regime continued to be in their interests. The proletarian unity of 1917, and the "historic partnership" of the working class as a whole with the Bolshevik Party, no longer existed. In what remained of the Russian working class in 1921, however, enough men and women were prepared to accept the Bolshevik regime (and enough were prepared even to fight and die for it) that its survival was ensured. And over the next few years, as the country recovered from the triple curse of civil war, foreign hostilities, and economic collapse, the regime was able to bring important benefits to the reviving working class, and "the historic alliance began to re-form on a tentative basis," in the phrasing of William Chase.[15] In significant ways, despite continuing difficulties and contradictions, it can be argued that Soviet Russia remained a proletarian state.[16]

Yet Isaac Deutscher has put forth apt imagery in his description of oppositional Bolsheviks of the 1920s as they increasingly "clashed with the party 'apparatus' as the apparatus grew independent of the party and subjected party and state to itself." He emphasizes a growing cleavage between "the power and the dream"—and the deepening contradiction felt by the Bolsheviks who had created a machine of power to make the dream a reality. "They could not dispense with power if they were to strive for the fulfillment of their ideals; but now their power came to oppress and overshadow their ideals."[17]

Intertwined with this contradiction was the problem of holding the country together, of holding off the forces of counterrevolution, as well as the forces of disintegration and chaos and starvation—which seemed to make "iron dictatorship" an absolute necessity. "Despite its mistakes and abuses," Victor Serge wrote at the time, "the Bolshevik Party is at present the supremely organized, intelligent, and stable force that, despite everything, deserves our confidence. The Revolution has no other mainstay, and is no longer capable of any thorough-going regeneration."[18] For some of the central Communist leaders, the most serious issue was how to overcome the inefficiencies and disorganization generated by the inept bureaucratic tangles of war communism—embattled with a debilitating and further disorganizing "localism"—that threatened to wash away both the "machine and the dream."

Trotsky became an exponent of increased centralization, which is not surprising in light of his role as head of the Red Army. "Under the form of the 'struggle against despotic centralism' and against 'stifling' discipline, a fight takes place for the self-preservation of various groups and subgroupings of the working class, with their petty ward leaders and their local oracles," he wrote in this period. "The entire working class, while preserving its cultural originality and its political nuances, can act methodically and firmly without remaining in the tow of events and directing each time its mortal blows against the weak sectors of its enemies, on the condition that at its head, above the wards, the districts, the groups, there is an apparatus which is centralized and bound together by an iron discipline."[19]

This came to a head in a debate on the trade unions. The Workers' Opposition insisted that an increasingly empowered trade union movement—independent of control by the party leadership and restrictions from the Soviet state—should enable the working class to direct the country's economic development. Trotsky argued for "the militarization of labor," insisting that the working class was already in power, having its own workers' state (the dictatorship of the proletariat), so it made no sense to counterpose the trade unions to this. Instead, the workers' state, led by the workers' party, should be in undisputed control—including of the trade unions.

Taking a centrist position, and (with essential assistance from Zinoviev and Stalin) mobilizing a majority within the party for it, Lenin himself emphasized: "A workers' state is an abstraction. What we actually have is a workers' state with this peculiarity, firstly, that it is not the working class but the peasant population that predominates in the country, and, secondly, that it is a workers' state with bureaucratic distortions." Because of this, while insisting on state control of economic development, he favored independent trade unions that would "protect the workers from their state."[20]

In later years, Serge reflected on the dilemma and thinking of this time:

> The great ideas of 1917, which had enabled the Bolshevik Party to win over the peasant masses, the army, the working class, and the Marxist intelligentsia, were quite clearly dead. Did not Lenin, in 1917, suggest a Soviet form of free press, whereby any group with the support of ten thousand votes could publish its own organ at the public expense? He had written that within the Soviets power could be passed from one party to another without any necessity for bitter conflicts. His theory of the Soviet State promised a state structure totally different from that of the old bourgeois states, "without officials or a police force distinct from the people," in which the workers would exercise power directly through their elected Councils and keep order themselves through a militia system.
>
> What with the political monopoly, the Cheka and the Red Army, all that now existed of the "Commune-State" of our dreams was a theoretical myth. The war, the internal measures against counter-revolution, and the famine (which created a bureaucratic rationing apparatus) had killed off Soviet democracy. How could it revive, and when? The Party lived in the certain knowledge that the slightest relaxation of its authority would give the day to reaction.[21]

Working-Class Rule?

If the Soviet government of 1917 was a genuine expression of workers' democracy and was consequently what Marx meant by *dictatorship of the proletariat* (some also use the term *workers' state*), what sense can one make of what existed by the early 1920s? Some scholars have drawn on Lenin's own partial explanation: "An industrial proletariat . . . in our country, owing to the war and the desperate poverty and ruin, has become declassed, i.e., dislodged from its class groove, and has ceased to be a proletariat. . . . Since large-scale capitalist industry has been destroyed, since the factories and works are still at a standstill, the proletariat has disappeared." Lenin's view was that only the Communist Party, largely composed of those who had been workers and who were committed to a revolutionary working-class program, could hold the new Soviet Republic together. Isaac Deutscher made this a central component of his own influential account of Russia's post-revolutionary realities.

More recent historians such as Diane Koenker have effectively challenged this interpretation as exaggerated, though Koenker's own data indicates elements of truth in Lenin's formulation: dramatic socioeconomic disruptions, combined with the enlistment of revolutionary workers into the Red Army and state apparatus, obviously affected the vitality and political cohesion of the Russian workers' movement. "A desperate, individualistic, and apolitical atmosphere permeated factory life," notes Kevin Murphy. "The shortage of party workers was very keenly felt" in 1919, as "the most ardent believers in the revolution volunteered for the war effort, and the few Communists who remained had neither the resources nor the influence to combat the multitude of problems."[22]

The fact remains—as Simon Pirani has observed in his important study *The Russian Revolution in Retreat*—that "the working class was far from non-existent, and when in 1921, it began to resuscitate soviet democracy," responses from powerful elements in the Communist Party worked not for its revival but its limitation and even elimination.[23]

Eduard Dune, who became involved in the oppositional Democratic-Centralist group, later cited Lenin's explanation in his own wry criticism, asking, "Is not the existing party of a nonexistent class no longer a vanguard but something separate and apart?" He elaborated: "If Lenin's argument was true, that the victory over the counter-revolution was marked by the disappearance of the class in whose name we triumphed, then had not the slogan of the dictatorship of proletariat become only a myth? A non-existing class could not have a vanguard—its own party."[24]

In any event, there now existed a "workers' state" that was independent of any actual control by the working class. A disillusioned party member explained in a letter of resignation: "I cannot be that sort of idealist communist who believes in the new God That They Call the State, bows down before the bureaucracy that is so far from the working people, and waits for communism from the hands of pen-pushers and officials as though it was the kingdom of heaven." In 1920, a leader of the Democratic-Centralist faction in the Communist Party snapped: "Why talk about the proletarian dictatorship or workers' self-activity? There's no self-activity here!"[25]

A 1923 manifesto from the dissident Workers' Group (not to be confused with the Workers' Opposition) asserted: "What are we being told? 'You sit quietly, go out and demonstrate when you're invited, sing the Internationale—when required—and the rest will be done without you, by first-class people who are almost the same sort of workers as you, only cleverer.' ... But what we need is a practice based on the self-activity of the working class, not on the party's fear of it."[26]

Among the early working-class oppositional groups in and around the Russian Communist Party, the best known is the Workers' Opposition, but other formations merit attention—the Democratic Centralists, led by Timofei Sapronov and Valerian Osinskii; Workers Truth, whose activists included such female militants as Polina Lass-Kozlova and Fania Shutskyever; and the Workers' Group, whose leading personality was the tough, thoughtful worker-Bolshevik militant Gavriil Miasnikov. It is one of the great tragedies of Bolshevism that such oppositional currents were crushed by 1923, and that aspects of their perspectives, rooted deeply in the Bolshevism that culminated in the 1917 triumph, and initially enjoying significant working-class support, were not allowed the space to challenge the ominous, ultimately murderous, bureaucratization.[27]

Nonetheless, elements in the central core of the Bolshevik leadership who had promoted "iron dictatorship" to defend the revolutionary dream would eventually go into opposition as "the machine of that dictatorship when it began to devour the dream." Beginning with Lenin himself, and then Trotsky, Zinoviev, Kamenev, Bukharin, Rykov, and others (all of whom had "pragmatically" yet myopically worked to eliminate previous oppositional currents), the bureaucratic-authoritarian onslaught dealt them defeat after defeat after defeat. Ironically, it was Leon Trotsky, the very symbol of the militaristic-authoritarian element within the Bolshevism of 1918–1921, who became the most prominent and one of the most consistent leaders in opposing the bureaucratic dictatorship, incorporating and developing many of the oppositional insights which he had once haughtily dismissed.[28]

As one sifts through the perspectives and policies being developed in 1918–1923 by these revolutionaries—Lenin and all of the central leaders of the new Communist regime—amid the overwhelming challenges and pressures that they faced, one gets a sense of a dedicated political collective animated by an immense swirl of brilliant insights, horrified desperation, terrible blind spots, beset by an ongoing clash of egos, each buoyed up by an absolute confidence in the positive qualities of their own commitments. And one sees an accumulation of decisive moments, involving decisions that carry them further and further from the goals to which they were committed. Reality is often like that; history is like that—one often has no clear awareness of a transformative error that one is in the process of making.

Marxist-feminist scholar Soma Marik believes one such decisive moment occurred at the Tenth Party Congress of the Communist Party in March 1921, when a ban on organized opposition was codified both inside and outside of the Communist Party. "Yet, in 1921, it seemed to be only another temporary measure," she writes. "Lenin pleaded for time, thereby creating the impression that eventually, in one or two years, matters would change. But the effect of the changes of 1921 was devastating. The danger of bureaucratization had been ever present from the early days of the revolution. Once workers' democracy was throttled, this bureaucratization could proceed unhindered."[29]

It is worth reflecting, however, on Trotsky's classic essay of 1937, "Stalinism and Bolshevism," in which he identifies the primacy of larger forces that shaped the destiny of the revolution:

> As far as the prohibition of the other Soviet parties is concerned, it did not flow from any "theory" of Bolshevism but was a measure of defense of the dictatorship [of the proletariat, i.e., the workers' state] in a backward and devastated country, surrounded by enemies. For the Bolsheviks it was clear from the beginning that this measure, later completed by the prohibition of factions inside the governing party itself, signaled a tremendous danger. However, the root of the danger lay not in the doctrine or in the tactics but in the material weakness of the dictatorship, in the difficulties of its internal and international situation. If the revolution had triumphed, even if only in Germany, the need to prohibit the other Soviet parties would immediately have fallen away.[30]

Marik also suggests a key problem embedded in Leninist theory. "The lack of discussion about the role of political parties in *The State and Revolution* remains a significant flaw," she writes. "Lenin's account of representative democracy can be criticized for being silent on the question of plurality, rival programs within the workers' state, and on the distinction between counter-revolution and opposition." In fact, Lenin, Trotsky, and other leading Bolsheviks idealized the Communist Party under their leadership as the only legitimate political expression of Russia's revolutionary working class. This was, of course, related to the fact that most non-Bolshevik parties, initially elected by the workers, peasants, and soldiers to represent them in the soviets of 1917, "decided to turn their backs on the Soviets," as Marik puts it, and in some cases "even to join hands with a bourgeois-aristocratic counter-revolution." But she also insists that multiparty socialism was the key to avoiding the disaster that befell Soviet Russia.[31]

There were others, as we have seen, who were insisting on the same point at the very moment when Lenin and Trotsky were inadvertently helping to engineer the revolution's defeat. A 1922 declaration of the Workers' Group, calling for "the resurrection of workers' democracy in the form of workplace-based soviets," seems to hit the nail on the head, in Simon Pirani's analysis. He writes:

> It argued that, whereas during the civil war the emphasis had been on suppressing the exploiters, NEP required rebuilding such soviets as the "basic cells" of soviet power. There could be no free speech for those who oppose revolution, "from monarchists to SRs," and curtailing democracy during the civil war had been an unavoidable necessity. But under NEP 'a new approach' was needed, including free speech for all workers: "there is no such thing in Russia as a communist working class, there is just the working class, with Bolsheviks, anarchists, SRs and Mensheviks in its ranks," among whom "not compulsion, but persuasion" had to be used. . . . The manifesto lambasted the use of "bureaucratic appointments that brush aside the direct participation of the working class" to run industry.[32]

The fact remains, of course, that while some of the oppositional groups won significant working-class support, none won the support of the working class as a whole. Even many working-class Bolsheviks and pro-Bolshevik workers were not inclined to engage in oppositional activity. Some undoubtedly chose—out of naïve idealism or hard-headed opportunism—simply to accept for good coin the proposition that *they* were the rulers of the country because their benevolent leaders were ruling in their interests and in their name. (In history, such dynamics are hardly unique to the Soviet Republic of the early 1920s.) For others there developed, instead, a profound sense of alienation. One worker swept up in the 1930s purges, befriended by Communist Joseph Berger in the prison camps, explained why he and many workmates had avoided participation in any of the oppositions of the 1920s:

> We would have joined anyone—Shlyapnikov [of the Workers' Opposition] or Sapronov [of the Democratic Centralists] or Trotsky himself—if we had thought it would do any good. What we thought was needed was a shift in power or at least a change of attitude towards the workers. But whichever group won, it would only mean a change at the top. And there was something else. It seemed to us that already then, and especially after Lenin's death, it was too late. They were doomed to fail because a new order was already established. The Party was no longer the Party we had known. We no longer had its confidence. But the last thing we could do was to stop trusting it. It was our whole life. It was still the Party . . . It was what we believed in. . . . We *were* the Party and the State, and yet the State and the Party were somehow outside us. They were our religion, but they were no longer ourselves.[33]

Kevin Murphy's intensive research regarding a single metal factory in Moscow before, during, and after October 1917 highlights the dynamic. "In the first year of the revolution, workers in the Moscow Metalworks approximated the Marxist ideal of a united, irrepressible social force. . . . In the politically charged atmosphere of the late summer and early fall [of 1917], the Bolsheviks in the Moscow Metalworks won the political argument for a Soviet government, as they succeeded in doing throughout the Russian empire." But afterward, "War Communism had fractured the relationship between the Soviet government and an exhausted, demoralized working class."[34]

Inequality and Apparatus

Socialism—the profound economic democracy, the society of the free and the equal for which the October Revolution had been made—was beyond reach. Eduard Dune, and not he alone, asked "was it that without a world revolution we had given birth to a classless, starving collection of people, with silent factories and mills? When could we expect help from the world revolution? Was it only when the 'crayfish whistles'?" He concluded, in the words of Alexander Shlyapnikov: "Another 'better' working class we will not have, and we need to satisfy the one we do have."[35] And to accomplish this, it obviously became essential to move beyond starvation and silent factories.

This brings us back to a consideration of the New Economic Policy. We have already given this considerable attention, but its importance in the development toward and crystallization of Stalinism calls out for additional examination.

The inability of the Soviet Republic to move forward to socialism in a capitalist world economy made inevitable far-reaching compromises with such capitalist hallmarks as market relationships and socioeconomic inequality. While Russia was vast and resource-rich, with immense economic potentialities, it was hardly economically self-sufficient. The extent to which the Soviet Republic was cut off from the world capitalist economy took a devastating toll. The failure of socialist revolutions in the advanced industrial countries contributed to the Bolshevik economic retreat of 1921 from war communism.

On the other hand, as Anna Louise Strong noted in 1923, "it was not the kind of communism that anyone wants again." Trotsky, her mentor in this period, told her: "Our acts in those years were dictated not by economic good sense but by the need of destroying the enemy." He explained: "Economic good sense would have taken over only the industries we could manage; but if we had followed this plan, we would not have survived to celebrate now the fifth anniversary of our Revolution." Trotsky saw in the tragedy a dialectical necessity that paved the way for its own negation. "The whole policy of war communism was forced by the blockade, by the regime of a military fortress, with disorganized industry and exhausted resources," he explained. "The military victory which was impossible without this severe policy, at last allows us to exchange it for measures of economic good sense. Here is the origin of the New Economic Policy."[36]

It is beyond the scope of this study to engage in detailed exploration of the many facets of rich experience associated with the NEP and the era of Soviet history it shaped. Our primary focus here will be restricted to the question of how democracy and workers' power were affected in the early years of NEP, as the Soviet Republic was becoming consolidated.[37]

Alec Nove has explained that the NEP "was a form of mixed economy, with an overwhelmingly private agriculture, plus legalized private trade and small-scale manufacturing," though the Bolshevik regime maintained state ownership and control of "the commanding heights" of the economy (banking, foreign trade, most industrial enterprises, mechanized transport, natural resources). Even these now tended to operate under the influence of capitalist norms, according to the mechanism of "profit and loss," with Lenin insisting that this shift in the direction of capitalism was "seriously meant and for a long time." As Lenin himself had put it, "Only an agreement with the peasantry can save the socialist revolution in Russia until the revolution has occurred in other countries." According to Simon Liberman (in charge of the Soviet timber industry in this period), Lenin "envisaged for Russia and its Communist regime a kind of advanced capitalist economy to be brought about by giving concessions to foreigners," and in the opinion of some leading Bolsheviks (such as Abel Yenukidze), Lenin would have "brought NEP to its logical conclusion" by giving "light industry back to its owners" if he had lived a few years longer. Things didn't go this far, however, nor did foreign capitalist enterprise become as significant a factor in Russia's economic development as some had hoped. Even with its more limited application, Liberman noted, "while releasing private initiative, it led to a new variety in life." There were continuities with some of what came before. "Under the revived (but also revised) notion of 'state capitalism,' Lenin stressed the paramount importance of reestablishing the link (*smychka*) between town and country on the basis of market relations," writes Lewis Sieglebaum. "The state would regulate the exchange of commodities, educate the masses of small producers, the peasants, in the advantages of soviet power, and invigilate against those who might seek to take advantage of the state's retreat." According to the critical-minded Anatole Mazour, "a balanced budget was attained within a few years and a degree of prosperity was achieved within a relatively short period. The recuperative power of the nation was a marvel to many people at home and abroad."[38]

William Henry Chamberlin saw the NEP, when it was still in effect, as marking "a turning point in the history of the Russian Revolution," noting that its adoption "coincided with the stoppage of attacks from without and the gradual restoration of peace and order within the country," in his view marking "the dividing line between the destruction of the old and the building up of the new Russian social order."[39]

In multiple ways, the peasantry benefitted immensely. "Not only had the peasant for the first time since the revolution a surplus to sell and legal authority and encouragement to sell it, but the terms of trade were exceptionally favorable to him," writes E. H. Carr, who adds: "If the countryside was profiting at the expense of the town, the town was deriving visible benefits, however unequal the distribution and however high the eventual cost, from the greater abundance of supplies." While "in agriculture NEP quickly provided the indispensable stimulus to production which launched Soviet Russia on the path of economic rehabilitation," achievements in industry "were slower, less direct and dangerously one-sided." Specifically:

> The peasant had been placed by NEP in a position, for the first time for many years, to sell his surplus production, after meeting the requirements of his family and of the tax-collector, at his own price. Those peasants who, in the winter of 1921–1922, had surpluses to sell were conscious of their strength and not unwilling to recoup themselves for what they had suffered at the hands of the cities under war communism.
>
> The situation of industry was more complex. The freedom of trade and loosening of state controls under NEP, which stimulated and encouraged the peasant, meant something quite different for large-scale industry which suddenly found itself thrown on its own resources and on the tender mercies of *khozraschet* [profitability]: from the autumn of 1921 onwards, more and more enterprises were cut off from state credits and state supplies of raw materials and food, and told to shift for themselves.[40]

What this meant for workers, E. H. Carr tells us, was the replacement of guaranteed rations with "payment in a currency of uncertain and constantly declining purchasing-power," as well as "a period of serious and widespread unemployment, due to drastic dismissals of workers both by public services and by industrial enterprises reorganizing themselves in response to the dictates" of profitability— so that, for workers, in less than a year NEP had reproduced the characteristic essentials of a capitalist economy." Despite the improvements brought by NEP, the hardships for workers were intense in regard to food, clothing, and shelter, and "people were swallowed up by poverty," as Jay Sorenson put it.[41]

The beneficial situation of the peasants should not be overstated. Chamberlin, in his journalistic investigations during the NEP, caught a key element of its complex meaning in the vast countryside in two different interviews—one with a Communist official "of the most devoted, fanatical, and uncompromising type," uneasy with aspects of NEP, and the other a Cossack peasant woman who represented the direction in which that policy seemed to be tipping. "We didn't fight through the civil war, we didn't beat the White generals and landlords and capitalists, and the Allied troops who came to help them . . . to let capitalism creep back in veiled forms," the official said. "Our policy is to unite the poor and the middle-class peasants in cooperatives and collective farms and raise the living standard of all the peasants gradually, instead of letting a few grow rich while the rest remain poor." The peasant woman argued: "We can't all be equal, because some of us will always work harder than others." She implored: "Let me work as much land as I can with my own arms and I'll gladly pay rent and taxes to the state for it, and sell my grain too, if I can get a fair price and some goods to buy with the money." She rejected the old war communism norms: "Nothing will ever come out of this idea of making us all *byedniaks* [poor peasants] and calling everyone who is a capable hard worker a bloodsucker and a kulak. That sort of thing keeps us poor, and keeps the state poor too."[42]

In fact, this reflects tensions and conflicts in the policies of the Soviet regime. By the late 1920s Alexei Rykov, Soviet premier in the NEP period, was angrily asserting:

> We can't fight for culture in the village if we reckon as kulaks peasants who are using metal spoons instead of wooden ones, and there are such cases. If we consider the peasant who has a radio receiver a kulak, then for a sewing machine we should call him a *pomyeschik* [feudal landlord]. If the peasant works the soil well, without exploitation of others, they burden him with the individual tax. Then who will undertake to work the land well? I don't think there will be any such idiots who will do this when they know that for this they will be subject to the individual tax, their children will be driven out of school, and they themselves will be deprived of electoral rights.[43]

Privilege and Power

But, of course, even for peasants who had the right to vote, the bottom line was still the same as what had become true in the period of war communism—political power remained concentrated in the hands of the Communist Party dictatorship.

There was a dramatic transformation of urban social realities. *New York Times* correspondent Walter Duranty recorded that for the surviving members of Russia's old ruling classes,

> NEP was a respite from pressure, to restore perhaps a semblance of the respect and position that they had lost, and if the fates were kind, a chance to escape abroad. To the Communists and to the small group of proletarian leaders who had benefited by the Military Communist period NEP was doubtless repugnant, but to the mass of workers it brought jobs that would henceforth be paid in money instead of valueless paper or moldy rations, and the certainty that with money they could buy the food and necessities of life that had previously been lacking. To the traders NEP meant opportunity and the dawn of better days.

It is worth noting how Duranty's account differs from that of Carr—the former calls the guaranteed rations for workers "moldy" and suggests that they were benefitting from the shift to money payment; the latter suggests the shift represented hardship and uncertainty. Duranty went on to stress the NEP's "rapid acceleration, its confusion, its opportunities for quick and easy profit, and the immense stimulus it gave to employment of all kinds. Not to mention its growing contempt for the rules and restrictions which had previously been enforced by the Bolsheviks." By 1925–26, the NEP had restored the economy to pre–World War I levels. On the other hand, the utilization of capitalist mechanisms to revive industry and increase productivity generated speedups and overtime in the factories and also relatively high rates of unemployment. Nor was this period free from shortages of goods, as well as rampant inflation. While benefitting from the NEP in many ways, the working class more than any other group in society found itself making the greatest sacrifices for the policy's achievements.[44]

This was in contrast to the rise of the "Nepmen"—who to a significant degree introduced a jarring element into the young Soviet society. The description by Eugene Lyons is worth considering:

> A new middle class of Nepmen—private merchants, artisans, small-scale manufacturers, professional men, bureaucrats in comfortable berths, more prosperous peasants, the criminal elements which are the excrescence of private initiative—had come into being. Some of them were resuscitated middle-class [bourgeois] people of the pre-revolutionary era, others were tasting affluence and the sweets of privilege for the first time.
>
> No more extraordinary class has ever been called into being and blown into oblivion in the memory of humankind. Because it was young, born in chaos and in some measure outside the law, because it was at bottom uncertain of its tenure and therefore desperately eager to make the most of its advantages immediately, it was exceptionally vulgar, profiteering, crude, and noisy. Under capitalism

the bourgeoisie has the poise and self-assurance that come with power. It has a culture of its own and an ideology of self-justification. In NEP Russia, for the first time, there was the anomaly of a large bourgeoisie without political power, without culture, without respect for its own class.[45]

"Already in the first year of the New Economic Policy abuses of freedom had made their appearance," recalled Associated Press correspondent William Reswick. "Parvenues, grown rich in less than a year, were wary of government banks. They persisted in spending their big profits as fast as they made them. . . . Debauchery, wild orgies, drunken all-night parties with nudity as a feature became the vogue among the *nouveau riche*. This went on side by side with widespread unemployment and a rapidly dwindling currency that soon restricted the peasants' produce to the Nepmen." Duranty's account is similar, detailing as well the dramatic rise of gambling, prostitution, the proliferation of opium, cocaine, and heroin, and gangsterism, as well as widespread corruption in official circles. And yet, he emphasized, "in a single year the supply of food and goods jumped from starvation point to something nearly adequate, and prices fell accordingly. This was the rich silt in NEP's flood, whereas the gambling and debauchery were only froth and scum."[46] There is certainly truth to this, and yet something of the "froth and scum" must have penetrated more deeply than Duranty seems to allow. Consider the reminiscences of the year 1926 by Serge:

> The sordid taint of money is visible on everything again. The grocers have sumptuous displays, packed with Crimean fruits and Georgian wines, but a postman earns about fifty roubles a month. There are 150,000 without jobs in Leningrad alone: their dole varies between twenty and twenty-seven roubles a month. Agricultural day-workers and female servants get fifteen, with their board added, it is true. Party officials receive from 180 to 225 roubles a month, the same as skilled workers. Hordes of beggars and abandoned children; hordes of prostitutes. . . . Our aim is still to be a party of poor men, and little by little money becomes master, money corrupts everything—even as it makes life blossom everywhere. In less than five years, freedom of trade has worked miracles. There is no more famine, and an intoxicating zest for life arises about us, sweeping us away, giving us the unfortunate sensation of slipping downhill very fast.[47]

The contradictions were sometimes intense. In the early 1920s, food rations were so short that the daily norm of nutrition for a worker laboring for eight hours was one pound of bread and one-and-a-half pounds of vegetables—with one-and-a-quarter pounds of bread for each additional two hours of overtime. These figures were reported by Premier Rykov, who added that

1.2 million workers could not be provided for at all. Angry gangs of young workers, often sporting leather jackets and organized into Communist Youth groups, took it upon themselves to deal brutally with the pervasive corruption they perceived, sometimes coordinating their efforts with the Cheka.[48]

Even Anna Louise Strong, who resisted pessimistic perceptions with an almost religious passion, acknowledged the existence in the NEP of "a many-sided conflict" in which forces destructive of her own communist ideals exerted a powerful influence: "I have seen graft honey-combing whole [government] departments. On the Murmansk [railroad] line most of the sleeping compartments were pre-empted by train officials, who exacted little bribes in addition to the regular fare, before they surrendered them.... Private merchants were handing money to workers in the Housing Department, to secure favored locations quickly.... During these two years I have seen certain small officials install themselves comfortably, and entrench themselves in bureaucratic methods."[49]

Strong also cited what she believed to be essential countervailing tendencies, represented particularly by idealistic party activists who stressed to her: "We must see that the Communist Party remains a party of workers, and clean out bureaucrats and white collar men.... The workers of Russia will never sell out; as long as we keep our Party disciplined and clean, we are safe." They argued that despite the corruption and the threatening rise of capitalist influences, "the power of the State is in our hands, and the lands, and the natural resources, and the basic industries, and also the press and the schools." The influence and seductive materialism of the Nepmen could not compete, ultimately, with the powerful analyses of Marxism and transcendent ideals of socialism, which "are discussed in the newspapers" and whose adherents envision "the development of a vast Republic of free workers" and "even have in mind the dream of World Revolution, in which all countries will some day follow what they have begun, and all history will look back on them as founders of a new epoch."[50]

Strong and her friends believed, then, that the Russian working class, led by the most far-sighted, incorruptible, and highly principled elements in the Communist Party, would transcend the backwardness, inequality, and brutality of their situation and achieve a full-bodied proletarian democracy and eventually a socialist society. Of course, reality unfolded differently.

Amid the complexities of Soviet Russia in this period, William Henry Chamberlin struggled to hold on to his earlier socialist convictions. Long after his final disillusionment, he recalled that initially he had "imagined a dictatorship of idealists . . . whose ruthlessness would be redeemed and offset by absolute devotion to their cause." In fact, "there were such men and women, many of them, in Russia at that time, mostly among the veteran revolutionaries of prewar times. Whenever I met one I would feel strengthened in my original faith." But, according to Chamberlin, there were three different layers in the Russian Communist Party of this time, and not all were dedicated to the cause. "The old revolutionaries at the top, the manual workers at the bottom of the Communist hierarchy contained a large proportion of honest and devoted men," he wrote, but especially in the middle layers, "there was a host of careerists and adventurers who had flocked into the Communist ranks because they sniffed the loaves and fishes of power." Such middle layers found assignments, and employment, in the bureaucracy (all too often "puffed up with the arrogance of the small official") that "had spread and multiplied since the revolution had given the state so many economic functions to fulfill." The NEP did not eliminate this problem. That the "social differentiation came into being everywhere, as much in the town as in the village," has been pointed out by many, including David Rousset, who writes: "The state was not spared. The bureaucracy acquired its functional independence gradually, but quickly. This took on a more and more accentuated social character; the authorities gave themselves privileges in a most matter-of-fact fashion."[51]

"Cadres Decide Everything"

The inequalities associated with the relative prosperity flowing from the NEP became part of a chemistry not anticipated by Strong and her Bolshevik comrades. For it was not the workers who had power. Nor was it the peasants or the Nepmen or the majority of the members of the Russian Communist Party. Power was in the hands of the hierarchical apparatus of the party, which had become an interpenetrating entity—as we have seen—with the hierarchical apparatus of the Soviet state, what has been commonly referred to as the bureaucracy. For some, the fact that the social class of those making up this bureaucracy was predominantly proletarian meant that political power was in the hands of the working class, but "the functional separation between the worker who had become an industrial and administrative cadre and the worker at his machine at the work-place," as Rousset has put it, "took on the dimensions of an open divorce and was transformed into social differentiation."[52]

The newly appointed general secretary of the Russian Communist Party's Central Committee, tasked with overseeing the organization's functioning and assignments of various members to government positions was a long-time Bolshevik organizer with considerable underground experience, Joseph Stalin. Keenly aware of the necessity of efficient "technique" to maintain "factories, mills, collective farms, state farms, a transport system, an army," he viewed as an absolute necessity the development and placement of cadres imbued with such technique. Also crucial was the cadres' absolute loyalty to the leadership of the Russian Communist Party. In 1935 he would comment that "the old slogan, 'technique decides everything,' which is a reflection of a period already passed, a period in which we suffered from a dearth of technique, must now be replaced by a new slogan, the slogan 'Cadres decide everything.'" This was literally true in 1935 (when the multifaceted administrative apparatus in the USSR constituted at least 12 percent of the population), and it was becoming a reality in the 1920s.[53]

In the Marxism of the Bolsheviks, there is no clear conceptualization of or attention to the question of *bureaucracy*. One can find references to governmental inefficiency such as with the tsarist regime, or to the undemocratic and opportunistic qualities explaining the failure of the German Social Democratic Party in 1914, but there are no general theorizations along the lines one finds in writings by Max Weber, Robert Michels, Jan Waclaw Makhajsky—and certainly no anticipation of bureaucracy as a problem that would flow from making a revolution in Russia. "The 'dictatorship of the proletariat' was supposed to end up in the withering away of the state," notes Moshe Lewin. "Bureaucracy, a service layer of the state and of the ruling class, wasn't supposed to represent much of a problem." That it was a growing and intractable and increasingly problematical reality beginning in 1917 resulted in expressions of "bewilderment and helplessness, from the early pronouncements of Lenin through those of [Sergo] Ordzonikidze [prominent Communist, associated with Stalin], of Bukharin in 1934," and others.[54]

"The basis of bureaucratic rule is the poverty of society in objects of consumption, with the resulting struggle of each against all," Trotsky wrote. "When there is enough goods in a store, the purchasers can come whenever they want to. When there is little goods, the purchasers are compelled to stand in line. When the lines are very long, it is necessary to appoint a policeman to keep order. Such is the starting point of the power of the Soviet bureaucracy. It 'knows' who is to get something and who has to wait."[55] And yet, this alone does not define the problem. Looking back on the development of the bureaucracy, Trotsky suggested that the NEP affected this development in two essential ways. The first factor relates to the NEP's necessity. "The young bureaucracy, which had arisen at first as an agent of the proletariat, began now to feel itself a court of arbitration between two classes," he pointed out. "Its independence increased from month to month." The second factor relates to the NEP's successes:

> In its first period, the Soviet regime was undoubtedly far more equalitarian and less bureaucratic than now. But that was an equality of general poverty. The resources of the country were so scant that there was no opportunity to separate out from the masses of the population any broad privileged strata. At the same time the "equalizing" character of wages, destroying personal interestedness, became a brake upon the development of the productive forces. Soviet economy had to lift itself from its poverty to a somewhat higher level before fat deposits of privilege became possible. The present state of production is still far from guaranteeing all necessities to everybody. But it is already adequate to give significant privileges to a minority, and convert inequality into a whip for the spurring on of the majority.[56]

There are different ways to understand this, however. For example, while an excellent study by Michal Reiman describes the bureaucracy under Stalin in the late 1920s as "separated from the people and hostilely disposed toward it," Trotsky insists that "even when the bureaucratic rust was already visible on the party, every Bolshevik, not excluding Stalin, would have denounced as a malicious slanderer anyone who should have shown him on a screen the image of the party ten or fifteen years later." Stalin brought to his task "the prestige of an old Bolshevik, a strong character, narrow vision, and close bonds with the political machine," but "the success which fell on him was a surprise." This involved "the friendly welcome of the new ruling group, trying to free itself from the old principles and from control of the masses, and having need for a reliable arbiter in its inner affairs." He shared with others in the apparatus the inclination "to approach the inner life of the party exclusively from the viewpoint of convenience in administration," and became the "indubitable leader." Yet for many of the leading elements in the apparatus, their *consciousness* was by no means simply that of greedy or power-hungry opportunists. Stalin's very conception of himself, Robert C. Tucker persuasively argues, involved a profound identification with Lenin: "Stalin always needed to think of himself as acting like Lenin when he embarked upon a major project."[57]

Stalin's self-conception was consistent with that of many in the Russian Communist Party as well as in the apparatus—including those who were oppositionists and those who were not, certainly through the 1920s and into the 1930s. They *did not see themselves* as "separated from the people and hostilely disposed toward it," but instead believed themselves to be genuinely *revolutionary* cadres, doing their very best to be true to the ideals of the Bolshevik revolution.

Yet there was, at the same time, a quite different reality unfolding—what Marc Ferro calls "a rapid evaporation of the early Bolsheviks, who were submerged by new members." In 1917, there were twenty-four thousand party members, and of these, twelve thousand remained in 1922 and eight thousand in 1927—but by 1920 there were already six hundred thousand party members, and one million in 1927. At the same time, the apparatus of full-time functionaries in the party soared from 700 in 1919, to 15,300 in 1922, to more than 100,000 by the end of the decade. The immense growth of the apparatus was, of course, even greater beyond the Communist Party—those servicing the state and economy ballooned to 5.8 million by 1920.[58]

The cadres who had lived through underground work, revolution, and civil war—absolutely committed to the revolutionary program for which they sometimes took great risks—would naturally be different from cadres without such experience who were holding a majority of apparatus positions in the era of the NEP. And if "being determines consciousness" as Marx insisted, then for some of the dedicated older comrades remaining, consciousness—the way of understanding things—would be subtly altered by their changed life circumstances.

Germs of Stalinism

"It is often said that 'the germ of Stalinism was in Bolshevism at its beginning.' Well, I have no objection," Victor Serge once commented. "Only, Bolshevism also contained many other germs—and those who lived through the enthusiasm of the first years of the victorious revolution ought not to forget it. To judge the living man by the death germs which the autopsy reveals in a corpse—and in him since birth—is this very sensible?"[59]

It is essential in medical science not to lose a sense of the interplay between endogenous and exogenous factors, and in our case between subjective and objective factors—the interaction between what was internal in the makeup of Bolshevism and what were the decisive socioeconomic dynamics of the larger reality. "It is rare for history to provide such an example, such a powerful demonstration of the impossibility of revolutionary action prevailing in a lasting way over the real technological level," as David Rousset has aptly put it. The profoundly democratic, libertarian-socialist, and humanistic aspirations of the October Revolution, the triumph of soviet democracy, the amazing innovations and achievements in cultural life could not endure in the absence of the necessary material basis required for sustaining such things. The Bolsheviks understood that tsarist Russia could not provide such a material basis, but their hope and expectation was that their bold and life-affirming revolutionary initiative would help—in the specific and momentous context of their time—to generate similar initiatives throughout the world. This in turn would provide a material basis, global in reach, capable of sustaining the creative and democratic developments that they were initiating in Russia, and which they anticipated would be enriched by similar developments around the world. The failure of revolutions in other countries and the extended isolation of Soviet Russia provided, as Rousset notes, "a rigorous demonstration of the scientific validity of the principles on which the Marxist theory of society is based." The consequence: "the irrevocable downfall of the Marxist leadership, tragic because of its victims and because of the intellectual regression which accompanied it," as well as the loss of so much of the political and social and cultural achievement that flowed from the triumph of October.[60]

In order to explore this further, it might be helpful to define what is meant here by *Stalinism*. A succinct definition of Stalinism might be "authoritarian modernization in the name of socialism." (Kevin Murphy has suggested a similarly succinct definition with more of an edge: "The primary function of Stalinism was to make possible the accumulation of capital for expanding production at the expense of the cultural and material needs of the populace.") The democratic core of socialism—rule by the people over the economy—evaporates. "Our Soviet society is a socialist society, because the private ownership of the factories, works, the land, the banks and the transport system has been abolished and public ownership put in its place," Stalin explained to journalist Roy Howard in 1936. "The foundation of this society is public property: state, i.e., national, and also co-operative, collective farm property." The primary purpose of such a society would be industrial and agricultural development to advance living standards and cultural levels of the population, and to strengthen the nation. At the same time, he explained (for example, in his report to the 1930 Party Congress), "correct leadership by the Party" is essential for such efforts: "The Party should have a correct line; . . . the masses should understand that the Party's line is correct and should actively support it; . . . the Party should . . . day by day guide the carrying out of this line; . . . the Party should wage a determined struggle against deviations from the general line and against conciliation towards such deviations;

. . . in the struggle against deviations the Party should force the unity of its ranks and iron discipline." Erik van Ree has suggested that this approach was consistent with Stalin's view of democracy, which he saw not as rule by the people but as "policies alleged to be in the interest of the people" and as "a system that allowed the population to participate at least in state organs, even without having a determining say in it."[61]

What has come to be termed *Stalinism* may be summarized as involving five interrelated components:

1) A definition of socialism that excludes democracy as an essential element, positing a one-party dictatorship over the political, economic, and cultural life of a country.

2) An insistence that it is possible to create "socialism" in one country— by which is actually meant some variation of socioeconomic modernization.

3) A powerful and privileged bureaucratic apparatus dominating both party and state, generally with a glorified authoritarian leader functioning as the keystone of this political structure. (For some analysts, the existence of extensive material privileges and outright corruption among the powerful bureaucratic layers are key aspects of the crystallization of Stalinism.)

4) The promotion of some variant of a so-called "revolution from above"—often involving populist rhetoric and mass mobilizations— driven by the state and party bureaucracy, on behalf of modernizing policies but often at the expense of the workers and peasants that the party dictatorship claims to represent.

5) Related to the authoritarian modernization: extreme and often murderous repression, as well as propagandistic regimentation of education and culture and information, and systematic persecution of dissident thought.[62]

A Stalin admirer, *New York Times* correspondent Walter Duranty, captured something of this in his comment that "Stalinism was progressing from Leninism (as Lenin had progressed from Marxism) towards a form and development all its own," adding: "Stalin deserved his victory because he was the strongest, and because his policies were most fitted to the Russian character and folkways in that they established Asiatic absolutism and put the interests of Russian Socialism before those of international Socialism."[63] Of course, to grasp the actual meaning of the "Russian Socialism" to which Duranty refers, one must understand what *Stalin* meant by it—which would not have been accepted by the Bolsheviks of 1917.

A number of serious historians have emphasized that Lenin and Trotsky themselves bear significant responsibility for what happened, yet this truth must be contextualized if it is not to be transformed into a falsehood. "They never pursued power for power's sake," as Rousset has pointed out. "In their very actions they were indomitable adversaries of parasitic bureaucracy. Their entire lives were not merely *devoted* to the proletarian revolution, but were *integrated* into it." For Rousset the military suppression of the 1921 Kronstadt uprising, overseen by Lenin and Trotsky and the other central Bolshevik leaders, "definitively sapped workers' power." But this was only one element in a more extensive and profound process, explored earlier in this chapter. Nonetheless, their role in the early stages of this process—understandable and even well-intentioned as it may have been—"accelerated the ruin of the workers' state," as Rousset puts it. "With their own hands they prepared their own defeat."[64] When they sought to push back some of the increasingly negative effects of what they had done, it was too late.

What came to be known as Stalinism was not what Lenin and his comrades intended. Nor did it happen all at once—this was a complex process involving an interplay of "objective factors" influencing Russia's revolution and post-revolution efforts, and "subjective factors" inherent in the revolutionary movement.

A primary and decisive factor was the isolation of revolutionary Russia in a hostile capitalist world—the *failure* of the anticipated world revolution that had been central to the strategic orientation, and that had been part of the very justification for the Bolshevik revolution. It is not possible to create the kind of socialism that Marx and his Russian followers envisioned in any country that is trying to exist and survive within a global capitalist economy.

Combined with this was Russia's economic and cultural "backwardness." On the one hand, that oft-used word referred to the industrial and agricultural conditions that provided far too low a level of productivity to sustain the hoped-for socialism; on the other hand, it meant the widespread and deep illiteracy, poverty, and brutalization flowing from centuries of the tsarist order, which also created barriers to the realization of a socialist polity. Along with not having the resources, internally, to sustain socialism in the Marxist sense, it could be the case that the economic and cultural thresholds allowing for a genuine and thoroughgoing democracy—rule by the people—to shape the economic and political life of society were far from being reached. Added to this were the multiple layers of raw and horrific devastation brought on by the First World War, the Allied war against the revolution, and the persistence of a civil war whose counterrevolutionary forces were sustained through outside financing.

This would most likely have been enough to ensure the failure of the revolutionary project. But there were theoretical blind spots within the Bolshevik movement to which we have given much attention, and which must be listed as part of any discussion regarding "germs of Stalinism" within the original, heroic Bolshevism of 1917. It should be repeated: even without these blind spots, the objective realities related to war, invasion, blockade, and economic collapse generated massive pressures toward authoritarianism. But the blind spots we are identifying made it harder to resist and triumph over negative consequences of such authoritarian pressures.

One blind spot involved an insufficient theorization and comprehension of the dynamics and requirements of democracy, which too easily allowed for naïve assumptions regarding (1) the possibility of sustaining genuinely mass-democratic involvement in the decision-making and problem-solving required in the early Soviet Republic; (2) the fatal dangers to the revolutionary process, as Rosa Luxemburg famously and aptly emphasized, in closing off organized diversity—particularly eliminating the existence of different parties—within the soviets and Russian political life, and in utilizing brutally repressive "emergency measures" to limit freedom of expression.[65]

This requires additional clarification. On the one hand, there is no question that the Bolsheviks, as Marxists, were profoundly committed to political and economic democracy as their end goal, and certainly into the early days of the Russian Revolution, rule by the people was also the *means* for attaining that end—such notions can be found in their theorizations, programmatic statements, internal discussions, and agitational appeals. On the other hand, we cannot find so clear an articulation of the *complexities* of democracy. Most people have the capacity to function in a purely democratic manner in order to sustain a relatively small group, the internal dynamics of a workplace or community (the size of a neighborhood or village), but this is not so easily transposed to larger contexts. To govern effectively—democratically or otherwise—a complex nation-state and national economy require the attainment by the decision-makers of certain educational and cultural thresholds involving literacy, knowledge, sensibilities (related to what Dewey and Krupskaya referred to as "personal cultivation"). At the same time—since no single person or current of people can be all-wise and all-knowing—effective decision-making, as well as the very possibility of democracy, requires the freedom to articulate diverse perceptions and points of view. There must be the possibility for those who will shape decisions to freely develop and express such perceptions and understandings. Those in agreement with such understandings must be free to join together in order to develop and argue for them—implying the need for different parties (and sometimes for organized tendencies within parties). While many Bolsheviks understood this, we cannot find a clear articulation of such understanding within the Bolshevik Party as a whole, and it is certainly missing from certain desperate pronouncements of its central leaders at moments of extreme crisis.

A second blind spot involved the peasantry, which was a far more complex entity than the standard Bolshevik theorizations allowed for. As the majority of the people, the peasants could be subjected to policies, based on faulty or arrogant assumptions, only at the peril of the revolutionary-democratic goals to which the Bolsheviks had dedicated themselves. Yet this blind spot in Bolshevik theorizations lent legitimacy to Stalin's forced collectivization of the land—a policy "shattering to the structure of peasant society," as Maurice Hindus described it at the time, adding with transparent wonder, "It was an audacious decision, a stupendous gamble!" Beyond simply solving "the question of food for export and for home consumption," this "revolution from above" was seen by its partisans as bringing "death to private property in the village," clearing "the road to the Communist millennium." While Hindus at that time was inclined to give the Communist regime the benefit of the doubt, in later years he would lament that "the overwhelming mass of poor and so-called middle peasants, especially wives and mothers, opposed it as violently as did kulaks," and that "millions of them died during the resulting famine in the autumn and winter of 1932–33, when the kulaks were already liquidated." Hindus saw forced collectivization as bringing a momentous modernization—as he put it, "Stalin was a monster killer but he was also a monumental builder"—yet adds: "The victory would have been easier and far less costly had not he been the tyrant that he was."[66] Yet it would have been problematical even if it were less murderously implemented.

A third blind spot involved a lack of awareness of the nature of bureaucracy, and the danger—even the very possibility—that this phenomenon could, in more than one way, undermine and overwhelm the best of revolutionary intentions. Although Marx and Engels wrote extensively on the question of bureaucracy, they did not offer any systematic analysis of this phenomenon, and their attention on it was not focused on the working-class movement. The tendency among Marxists was to associate the term with the existence of a governmental or organizational apparatus of functionaries that may facilitate efficiency or, if it were malfunctioning, result in inefficiency, and—within the trade union movement—perhaps reflect alien class influences through overly close contact with employers. But as J. P. Nettl notes, for theorists in the Second (Socialist) International "the notion of a bureaucracy developing a will of its own *and for its own benefit* was unthinkable." As Karl Kautsky had put it, there was no serious danger of bureaucratic degeneration "in the period preceding" the working class taking power or "in the period in which the predictable consequences of this victory are developed." Among Bolshevik theorists, the possibility was not perceived until it was too late. In 1916, Gregory Zinoviev discussed the development of an undemocratic and opportunistic reformism dominating the apparatus of the workers' movement, but he saw it as inconsistent with anything associated with the revolutionary component of the movement. In 1917, Lenin's discussion of *The State and Revolution* envisioned proletarian revolution inexorably moving in the direction of a vibrant and thoroughgoing workers' democracy. In 1921, Nikolai Bukharin argued in *Historical Materialism* that tendencies toward bureaucratic degeneration would be overcome by the growth of productive forces and the spread of education. It was not until 1928 that Trotsky acknowledged that a "bureaucratic hierarchy . . . with all its ministries and departments" had "raised itself over and above society."[67]

Obviously, these blind spots interconnected, they reinforced each other, and under the immense "objective" pressures that we have noted, they provided the basis for the crystallization of a "cadres decide everything" approach that was an essential element in the Stalinist ethos. A second essential element affording a deeper *material basis* for that ethos was provided by the relative prosperity generated by the NEP. This created the basis for inequalities and privileges that added new and vital dimensions to the self-interest of these "cadres."

We noted earlier that the NEP created elements affecting the chemistry of the situation, which brought a qualitative change in the nature of the bureaucracy—a powerful element of material privilege. We have already met the Yugoslav Communist Ante Ciliga, a thoughtful and dedicated activist doing international work in the early Soviet Republic (1926–29). He was able to observe how those well placed in the bureaucracy lived, and noted that while "their salaries were relatively modest," they often benefitted from certain advantages:

First they received payment in kind from the State. They paid a ridiculously low rent, and furniture, cars, holidays, theatres, books, and children's education cost them nothing at all. Next they had introduced into the administration the tacit understanding that the shops should reserve for them the entire stock at their disposal of the first-rate goods from the factory or from the contraband confiscated in the harbor of Leningrad. When the food shortage began, this illegal but efficacious system spread gradually to foodstuffs. Later on the system was perfected and legalized by the creation of a distributive network reserved to the bureaucracy.[68]

In fact, Ciliga's own initial trajectory in the late 1920s carried him into the highest levels of the privileged elite, what he calls "the upper ten thousand." In addition to having unlimited access to books and "periodicals of all tendencies, a fruit forbidden to the ordinary run of mortals and to plain Communists," he was able to make himself at home "in the magnificent and well-kept halls," as well as his private study, in Moscow's Communist University. "I lived in truly splendid, well-furnished apartments at the Party House, which was one of the largest palaces of the most aristocratic quarter of the town." He enjoyed a fair amount of leisure time to devote himself to literature, languages, and other studies, and "Russia's finest watering places, travel, and entertainments were within my reach."[69] Life could have been very comfortable—except that he was becoming critical of the regime and still believed deeply in the kinds of things that had caused him to join the revolutionary movement. But many in or near this stratum were not so afflicted.

"Limousines for the 'activists,' fine perfumes for 'our women,' margarine for the workers, stores 'de luxe' for the gentry, a look at delicacies through the store windows for the plebs—such socialism cannot but seem to the masses a new refacing of capitalism, and they are not far wrong," Trotsky wrote in *The Revolution Betrayed*, published in 1937. He went on to refer to Marx's earlier-quoted comment that communism needed to be built on the basis of abundance rather than scarcity: "On the basis of 'generalized want,' the struggle for the means of subsistence threatens to resurrect 'all the old crap,' and is partially resurrecting it at every step."[70]

More than a dozen years earlier, in Moshe Lewin's judgment, the Russian Communist Party had "reinvented itself for new tasks and realities, while retaining the original labels," and he marks the year 1924 as the end of Bolshevism. "For a few more years, one group of old Bolsheviks after another was to engage in rearguard actions in an attempt to rectify the course of events in one fashion or another," he writes, as the organization's political traditions "were rapidly swept aside by the mass of new members and new organizational structures which pressed that formation into an entirely different mode." Lewin adds: "The process of the party's conversion into an apparatus—careers, discipline, ranks, abolition of all political rights—was an absolute scandal for the oppositions of 1924–8. But their old party was dead." He concludes that "people should not be misled by old names and ideologies: in a fluid political context, names last longer than substances."[71]

And yet, well beyond 1924 there were still Communists who were genuinely engaged with Marxism, who believed in the old ideals, who truly adhered to the revolutionary commitments written into the program of the Communist Party. Some of them were uncritically inclined to follow the Stalin leadership—or *any* leadership of the Russian Communist Party—and others were inclined to be more critical-minded.[72] Among those critical-minded ones in the Soviet Republic, some had helped to make the 1917 revolution and to win the Civil War, and others—often younger—had been inspired by such things and were won to them. Some were not yet facing the contradictions between "the dream and the machine" of which Isaac Deutscher spoke. Others had begun to see what was happening and (like Ciliga) were moving into opposition. If there had been a revolutionary victory in Germany or China (in both cases there were genuine possibilities), the chemistry of world politics, of the Communist movement, and of the Soviet Republic would have been altered, in which case the positive qualities of these genuine Communists might have decisively come into their own. And there remained, after 1924, positive aspects of the new order with which to identify. Despite terrible contradictions and limitations, there were, as we have seen, immense gains within early Soviet society that were being fought for and in some cases won in the late 1920s. Although there is much truth in what Lewin has written, in some ways it seems premature to mark 1924—the year of Lenin's death—as the end of the October Revolution. One is left almost stammering, *If, if, if . . .*

The fact remains, however, that what happened did actually happen. For more than one reason, many have been inclined to see this actual outcome as what was fated to be.

Songs of Life and Death

Throughout the 1920s, as we have seen, fierce controversies raged among artists, writers, critics, and others, with a multiplicity of trends. Perhaps the clearest and most portentous conflict of views—as stark as the contrast between life and death—can be found in positions articulated by Anatoly Lunacharsky, who headed the early Soviet regime's Commissariat of Enlightenment, and an extremely combative group of writers and critics, a rising young layer of militants within the Communist Party, gathered around the journal *At the Post*.

Lunacharsky's views were nicely summarized by US Communist cultural writer Joseph Freeman in 1930:

> Many years of preoccupation with pre-revolutionary art had created in Lunacharsky a profound respect for the past; he considered bourgeois culture a great treasure-house of esthetic pleasure and wisdom; he looked upon it as a means of understanding life and believed that it brought order out of chaos. At the same time he was anxious that art should develop new forms, and was therefore friendly to all kinds of experiments. Science, he argues, deals with abstract forms, but art is experience; the artist's task is to concentrate life and intensify it, thus helping men to experience as much as possible.... Convinced that art in all its aspects is one of humanity's greatest achievements, he established a network of institutions for the preservation of the art of the past, to serve not only as a source of pleasure, but as a stimulus for new creations.... Furthermore, he said, the workers cannot possibly create their own class esthetics without a knowledge of the art of the past. By accepting both the bourgeois past and the proletarian future in art, Lunacharsky became the intermediary between extreme views.... In direct opposition to the views of *Na Postu* [*At the Post*], Lunacharsky maintained that all art is useful if it shows talent."[73]

The militants of *At the Post* insisted in their manifesto that "the basic criterion for the estimation of a literary tendency is its social significance," elaborating: "Only that literature can be useful from a social point of view in our time which organizes the mind and consciousness of the reader, especially the proletarian reader, in the direction of the final aims of the proletariat as the creator of communist society—namely, proletarian literature. All other kinds of literature which act otherwise on the proletariat aids the rebirth of bourgeois and petit-bourgeois ideology."[74] This orientation—ferreting out and denouncing such "incorrect" ideologies in Soviet cultural life and insisting on an art and literature that it deemed "useful from a social point of view"—inspired fierce controversies within the incredibly creative "cultural chaos" of the 1920s, but it increasingly came into its own in the Soviet Union's cultural life as time went on. To gain a sense of the vibrancy and complexity of the early Soviet period, however, one must focus on the rich variety of trends that flourished before the triumph of what became known as Socialist Realism.

Three poets—representing, successively, the very different trends known as Symbolism, Futurism, and Imagism—highlight some of the ambiguities inherent in Russia's revolutionary process. A poem is characteristically dialectical—an interplay of words in movement, with different and sometimes opposite meanings inherent in the same vibrant image. Marc Slonim's sympathetic appreciations (from the vantage point of the early 1930s) of poets Alexander Blok, Vladimir Mayakovsky, and Sergei Essenin are worth lingering over. Taken together, they are profoundly suggestive of the ambiguities of the early Soviet experience.

The oldest of the trio, and a poetic idol of prerevolutionary Russia, Blok (1880–1921) was from a privileged and highly cultured background. Victor Serge remembered his blue eyes and "long, serous face that hardly ever smiled . . . restrained in his gestures, with a fine dignity about him." His sympathies were with the lower classes, not with the tsarist order, and in the wake of the Bolshevik triumph, he refused to join family and friends leaving Russia. A friend of his, ready to leave with his bags packed, noticed Blok's bags were not. Over the telephone, the friend asked: "Are you by any chance going with the Bolsheviks?" To which Blok responded, "Yes, if you like to put it that way, I prefer to stay with the Bolsheviks" (although Serge comments that he also felt a strong affinity to the Left Socialist Revolutionaries).[75] Slonim wrote:

> A wonderful lyric poet, Blok had sung the dream and passions of a generation: he foresaw the Revolution and welcomed it. . . . His poem *The Twelve*, published in 1918 . . . pictured the riotous sweep of the revolutionary elements. The heroes of the poem are Red soldiers, who march light-heartedly to plunder and murder. They march through a Petersburg blizzard as bandits and dreamers inspired by hatred of the bourgeois world and by a confused belief in a better life. Christ Himself may be their invisible leader and inspirer. Thus the twelve bandits become identified with the twelve apostles and out of the blood and filth of the Terror and anarchy emerges a new Evangel, justifying all the cruelty and destruction of Bolshevism.[76]

Mayakovsky (1893–1930), drawn into the revolutionary socialist movement (and active as a Bolshevik while a teenager), became immersed in poetry that boldly, impertinently challenged social and cultural traditions. "Mayakovsky was a mighty and big-striding animal—physically more like a trained-down prize-fighter than a poet—and with a bold shout and dominating wit and nerves of leather," writes Max Eastman, who tells us he "knew Mayakovsky and enjoyed him." Living longer than Blok and Essenin, he more than they felt the constriction of a growing ideological-artistic orthodoxy—and seeking to be a disciplined soldier of the Revolution, he sought to adapt. Victor Serge's severe judgment was that Mayakovsky "wasted his best talent in a weary quest for God knows what ideological line, demanded of him by petty pedants who made a living out of it."[77] Slonim wrote:

> Mayakovsky is an outstanding example of reaction against Symbolism, against its airiness, musicality, and isolation. His language was course, pungent, and colloquial, his rhythm was militant and emphatic, and his effects crudely expressive, based upon street jokes and poster vividness. Mayakovsky's poetry is essentially declamatory, and belongs to the street and the platform; his words are emphatic and weighty, his similes material, rough and ready, and he intersperses circus jokes with political quips and newspaper sensations.
>
> Mayakovsky made his mark in Russian poetry in those years of battle when the poet's role was to rouse men to battle and celebrate victories. Subsequently, he devoted his raucous voice and great inventive talent to the service of the Revolution, and to his very death he continued apostrophizing all the wrongs of the day: he wrote verses about bread prices, the New Economic Policy, the food supply, international events, the Chinese Revolution, and a party comb-out. . . . Mayakovsky, by stressing the communal function of poetry, exercised an enormous influence on Soviet literature. He personified the new generation, its revolutionary materialism and contempt of sentiment, its striving towards a collective construction and love of big numbers. His motto of participation was enthusiastically adopted by dozens of young poets.[78]

The youngest of the three, Essenin (1895–1925)—whose poems were like "tender moonlight over rural Russia with bells ringing in the steeples," as Max Eastman put it—was a blond, blue-eyed boy-wonder, a blend of innocence and arrogance, alternately gentle and wild. To a friendly Communist critic, he said: "I am also on the side of Soviet power, but I love Rus'. I do things my own way. I won't allow anyone to put a muzzle on me, and I won't dance to anyone's fiddle." On the one hand, he proclaimed: "The moon is the tongue / In the bell of the sky, / My country's my mother / A Bolshevik I." On the other hand, it is said that he also had sympathies with the "Green" revolutionaries associated with the Tambov peasant rebellion and with anarchist Nestor Makhno's peasant forces. In one poem he taunts, "Not even Lenin is god to me," and he mocks a Communist speaker: "*Das Kapital,* her Bible, by her side, / She talks of Marx, / Of Engels . . . / By the way, / I've never read them—I've not even tried." The young peasant-poet baited the Bolsheviks: "It's not so simple, comrade communists. You're going to have to huff and puff a bit when it comes to our dear little peasants. You're not necessarily doing so well with them." Yet various Communists—Voronsky, Serge, Trotsky, Freeman—would write of him with respect and affection. His short life was a chaos, blending drunkenness and scandals with brilliant verses and masterful performances.[79] Slonim wrote:

Essenin came to the front in 1920–21 as the spokesman of the Imagist movement, which reproached the Futurists for forgetting that the "image" was the quintessence of poetry. The Imagists hoped to reform poetry by the creation of fresh images, unexpected similes, and daring metaphors, all profoundly hostile to the Symbolist stylistic tradition. For just as Mayakovsky may be said to typify the dynamism of Bolshevik assertion and to prove the poet of the city and the worker, so Essenin, a peasant by birth, stands out as the poet of peasant Russia and of that spiritual schism, which was, in those years, common to both intellectuals and peasant representatives.

It was his heavy lot, in those years of tragedy and brazen war, to be a purely lyric poet, with a bent for elegy and a thirst for idyll and calm. His poems of, very often, coarse pathos are always haunted by the image, and at the same time mirage, of a reminiscent and yet ideal "village," whose dawns, fields, cows, and horses replenished his stock of images.... His greatest enemy was the machine, that "iron guest" which menaced the village of his dreams with destruction and his own life with annihilation. He foretold his death in many poems, and at last took his own "superfluous life" in December 1925.

Essenin's influence is attributable not only to his considerable talents but also to the fact that his poems, as contrasted with Symbolist sophistries, Futurist war-whoops, and the theoretical argumentativeness of other revolutionary movements [among artists, poets, critics, etc.], spoke of simple human sufferings and told of the tragedy of a personality which was unable to adapt itself to the necessities of a historic schism.[80]

Anticommunists have often been tempted to portray the early death of each poet as proof of the heartlessness at the core of the communism to which each had hopefully looked. In some cases the accusation almost boils down to the revolutionary regime, like a cruel parent, not embracing the beautiful, sensitive child-poet. But, of course, reality is more complex than that.

Blok, Essenin, and Mayakovsky each consumed too much alcohol (Essenin was certainly an alcoholic), and all three had very complex and unhappy personal relationships (again, Essenin went through eight marriages in his short life). Unlike the other two, Blok did not kill himself but died from an illness not clearly identified, though variously chalked up to a heart condition, to venereal disease acquired through an obsession with prostitutes, and to severe depression (he suffered from all of these). At the same time, shortly before his own unhappy death, Blok spoke of an earlier poet from the tsarist era, Pushkin (who also died young, in a foolish duel), saying of this artistic hero that in the repressive society of his own time, he had found it impossible to survive. The necessities of peace and freedom can be taken away, Blok noted: "Not the outward peace but the creative. Not the childish freedom, the freedom of being liberal, but the freedom of creation, the secret freedom. And the poet dies because he can no longer breathe: life has lost its meaning."[81] It is generally agreed that this reflects Blok's frame of mind as he himself stopped living in the difficult year of 1921.

The year 1925 was not as difficult—either for the Soviet Republic as a whole or for the peasantry with which Essenin so strongly identified. The sympathetic critic Alexander Voronsky, after one of the poet's drunken ruckuses, found him alone in a room weeping: "I have nothing left. I feel terrible. I don't have any friends, or people close to me. I don't love anyone or anything. All I have left are my poems. I gave them everything, do you understand, everything. Once there was the church, the village, the countryside, the fields, the forest. Now they have left me all by myself."[82] He wrote his farewell with the blood from a cut wrist, before hanging himself: "There is nothing new about dying in this life / But there is surely nothing new about living either."[83]

Yet the suicide was not simply the outcome of personal problems. It is interesting to see how different defenders of the Soviet regime—fellow poet Mayakovsky and the recent commander of the Red Army, Leon Trotsky—addressed this matter. Essenin was "a fine, fresh and genuine poet," commented Trotsky, and "under the crust of his affected brazenness there throbbed the peculiar tenderness of an unshielded, undefended soul." He went on to suggest that while Essenin was "a lyric poet, . . . ours is not a lyrical era," that his poetry "is intimate, tender, lyrical; the Revolution is public, epic and catastrophic." Trotsky concluded: "His lyrical spring could have expanded to the end only in a society alive with song, harmonious and happy, in which not only struggle, but friendship, love and tenderness rule. Such a day will come." Mayakovsky, on the other hand, sternly lectured the departed poet: "We must wrest / delight / from the future's grasp. / Let me tell you, friends, / dying is no trick, / Making life worth living / is a harder task."[84]

It was in the difficult year of 1930 that Mayakovsky himself felt sufficient despair to give up the struggle and fire a bullet into his heart. He was contending with a tangle of personal complexities, to be sure, but it is also clear that he was wrestling with a convergence of political pressures and disappointments. In a poetic 1929 "Talk with Comrade Lenin," he had focused on the proliferation of powerful and self-important bureaucrats: "Some people / without you / got out of hand. / Many a rogue, / many a scoundrel / rove to and fro / and around our land. / Who can tell / their names / and their numbers! . . . Chest thrown out. They stalk along / proudly, / all decked with badges / and fountain pens." Nor was he happy over what was happening with his own poetry. "I've suppressed myself, / setting my foot / on the throat /

of my own song," he wrote in an unfinished poem before his death. He had spent the night before his death drinking, in bitter argument with friends who challenged him for accommodating to Communist Party hacks.[85]

Poetry reflects a vibrant life force that, when turned in on itself, can self-destruct. With each of these three poets, we can perceive multiple causes for his death—external barriers and blockages related to the conditions of the time and the dynamics of the new regime, as well as internal occlusions and conflicts. Each of these remarkable people—despite soaring hopes, and despite a capacity to deeply move so many other people with their passion and creativity—was finally pulled under by terrible and relentless demons. Yet the poetry, with all of its multiple meanings, endured and triumphed even with the tragic passing of the poet, continuing to affect the perceptions, thoughts, feelings, lives of many, many others over time. The poetry, with all its effervescent ambiguity, its blend of triumph and tragedy, continues to echo down to our own time.

10
INEVITABILITIES
AND OTHERWISE

As we reach for conclusions about the legacy of the Bolshevik revolution, we should recall the strands that interweave throughout this entire study. The utility of what has been broadly categorized as historical materialism, along with its connection to the possibility of democracy, merits additional comment. Related to this are the larger matters of historical inevitability and human freedom, and where the Bolshevik triumph and the Communist tragedy fit in to the questions of life's meaning and of what to do next.

On this final point, we should recall Engels's assertion, in a February 24, 1893, letter to Russian economist Nikolai Danielson, that "history is about the most cruel of all goddesses, and she leads her triumphal car over heaps of corpses, not only in war, but also in 'peaceful' economic development."[1] Yet Marxists insist history and economic development are the work of humanity, the product of human action and human labor. And it is a dubious proposition to claim that we individuals bear no responsibility for our actions—that the Goddess of History (or Economic Forces) *makes* us do what we do. And, in fact, We may not make history exactly as we please, but we do make our own history—whether or not the outcomes are good, as they sometimes are, or evil, as they sometimes are. We must bear responsibility for our actions—even those we "didn't mean to do."

What are we to do with this implication that inhumanity is inherent in humanity? How does this relate to the matters explored in this volume, and what does it mean for the future? Such questions could certainly tilt in a conservative direction—toward the conviction that efforts to create a better world are doomed because people are inherently incapable of being better than they actually are. As William Henry Chamberlin emphasized in the 1950s—after he became a political conservative—"Human nature is fallible, even downright wicked," and he approvingly quotes John Adams (the brilliant revolutionary-conservative Founding Father) to back up his contention that "every moral theorist will admit the selfish passions in the generality of men to be the strongest."[2] Conservatism as a political philosophy assumes the wisdom of conserving traditional power structures and customs, which naturally means opposing such revolutions as that led by the Bolsheviks. Even many liberals incline toward some form of conservatism in this sense.

There are crude and sophisticated varieties of conservatism. The crude variety portrays the Bolsheviks as monsters, cynically mouthing idealistic slogans in order to empower themselves through the suffering of all others. This understanding of historical reality is inconsistent with much of what is presented in these pages—and, I would argue, is inconsistent with what actually happened. The sophisticated variant of conservatism, on the other hand, can draw strength from what is presented here. If one's opponents are worthy (as humane, intelligent, and truly well-meaning as a person can be), and if—despite all that—they are overwhelmed by the circumstances they seek to improve, and despite all of their best efforts they fail disastrously, then one has a powerful argument for the conservative proposition that "there is no alternative" (or at least none that is desirable) to traditional power structures and customs.

Opponents of revolution consider it inevitable that revolutions must turn out badly—that mass action to challenge and overturn existing power structures, for the purpose of creating a better society, will instead unleash the Furies of murder and mayhem, violence, and terror leaving in their wake something no better, or even far worse, than what existed before. Some tell us this is because "the masses" are too narrow or stupid or loutish or wicked—"the crooked timber of humanity." A society of the free and the equal in which the free development of each is the condition for the free development of all remains an impossibility, human nature being what it is. Efforts to improve life qualitatively will always come to a bad end.

Dark Masses and Original Sin

Speaking personally, I have trouble with the underlying assumption in this conservative challenge. I know that my own people come from and are part of "the masses." I have, in the course of my life, known many others like me. And I know that there has been narrowness, stupidity, loutishness, and wickedness among us—but I am inclined to see as an absolute truth that there is also much more, and much better, than that.

The psychological-emotional dimension of this truth deserves attention. As we live out our lives, it is very clear to me (I have been watching closely), some of us seem sometimes to be possessed by demons—crystallizing through *complex combinations* not only of innate passions and lusts and yearnings related to our genetic codes (including quirks that one or another of us may inherit), but also through the impacts and imprints of mistakes and sometimes horrific abuses from family members in our early life, as well as terrible pressures and oppressions from the larger society. But I have also seen what seem to be innate drives for self-determination (freedom), for creative activity, for genuine community with others. I have seen people caring about each other, nurturing, loving. I have seen families that are dysfunctional and families that—despite inevitable problems and conflicts—are vibrant and life-affirming. I have seen people who are troubled and do terrible things, and others who have been able to find and share happiness and reveal wondrous qualities. I have seen people struggle with and sometimes overcome their demons—in some cases only for a time, in other cases for the rest of their lives.

I have seen much of this played out in that quintessential human quality—humor. I have seen humor that is incredibly cruel, on many levels and in many ways. But I have also seen humor that is liberating and loving and fine—a manifestation of the healthiest, the most spontaneously creative and delightfully quirky, the best that is in humanity.

It is, of course, the broader historical canvass that is the focus of the present study—but here too the sweeping assertions of our collective wickedness and of the impossibility of a better world are not convincing. I confess that, as much as I know about history, there is still much that I do not know or comprehend. But from what I do know, I *am* aware of qualitative improvements in the human condition, by multiple measurements (greater life expectancy, greater health, greater knowledge, an expansion of rights for more and more people), despite the persistent—and sometimes increased—oppressions and dangers of our time. Revolutionary insurgencies have sometimes unleashed horrors, but sometimes they have unleashed admirable qualities in people, and have made it possible for things getting better for more and more people. What happened in ancient Athens that culminated in democracy, and certain things that happened in America that were animated by aspirations in the 1776 Declaration of Independence, and reflected in the 1863 Gettysburg Address and in the 1963 "I Have a Dream" speech, can be best understood not as bringing perfection or "changing human nature" (whatever that is supposed to mean) but as improving the human condition.

If, however, we do not accept the sweeping strictures against revolution we must still take seriously the specific critiques of the Bolshevik revolution. In fact, the present volume also offers a particular critique. But the quite common critique positing the *inevitability* of what has come to be known as "Stalinism" (a repressive and sometimes murderous bureaucratic tyranny)—arguing that this was the logical and necessary outcome of the "Leninism" animating the Bolshevik revolution—is highly problematical. This is demonstrated by the fact that the party led by Lenin, which made the revolution, was animated by a vibrant internal democracy, while the party led by Stalin from the late 1920s onward was profoundly undemocratic. In fact, it was deemed necessary to repress and/or kill a majority of Lenin's closest comrades—in the name of "Leninism," to be sure.

If we are seeking an "original sin" to explain the post-1917 Communist tragedy, I would argue that it is not embedded in the ideas of Lenin and the structure of his party, nor can it be found simply in the personality of Stalin. We would be better served by turning our attention to larger and deeper historical realities. One aspect of what happened can be found in the context of foreign intervention, civil war, and economic embargo and collapse, which—as we have seen—generated authoritarian and brutalizing qualities that acquired immense potency among the Communists, within the ranks no less than within the leadership. Those who were Communists were people (neither demons nor angels)—and people are shaped by many elements, some genetic and others "environmental." We have seen the traumas of violence in the Civil War that could not fail to generate never-ending ripples in conscious and unconscious thought and emotional life, partly repressed in the relative peace and mellowness of the NEP period, but quite capable of surfacing again, as they did, in the 1930s.

For that matter, there were traumas of horrific violence, impacting millions of people, generated *before* the Bolshevik revolution. One must consider the realities of the First World War and the ruthless imperialism and dehumanizing militarism inseparable from it. One must also consider—stretching down through the centuries—the multiple impacts of the tsarist autocracy and oppression from powerful landowners; the centuries of serfdom, with systematic violence combined with the persistent impacts of economic backwardness, famine, disease, and stunting cultural realities. The brutalizing effects of such things on peasant families involved destructive experiences of one generation rippling down in various ways into the emotional and psychological dynamics within families of the next, making themselves felt in the hearts and minds of multiple individuals in succeeding generations. Such experiential and successive intergenerational "rippling" would, obviously, have affected not only the vast peasant majority but also the working class, as well as all other strata of the population.

Regarding that *rippling effect*, psychologist Irvin Yalom notes that "each of us creates—often without our conscious intent or knowledge—concentric circles of influence that may affect others for years, even generations," that "the effect we have on other people is in turn passed on to others, much as the ripples in a pond go on and on until they're not longer visible but continuing at a nano level." Through such rippling, you are "leaving behind something of your life experience; some trait; some piece of wisdom, guidance, virtue, comfort that passes on to others, known or unknown."[3] Long after some profound experience has taken place, long after one or another individual passes away, the impacts continue to be felt. Naturally, wisdom and virtue are not the only qualities that can ripple down from parent to child, from one person to another, down through generations.

The great writer Maxim Gorky, reflecting on the post-1917 violence and the Civil War asked: "Who was crueler, the Whites or the Reds?" He concluded: "Probably they both were alike. You see, both one side and the other were Russians." He complained that "the folk wants as far as possible to eat more and work less, have all rights and no duties," although the continual violation of people's rights throughout society and down through the generations caused the writer to add darkly that "the atmosphere of rightlessness in which ... the folk is accustomed to live convinces it of the lawfulness of lawlessness." The result can be terrible cruelty among those who are oppressed. Gorky—whose own youth was spent in the countryside—added that "cruelty . . . is what has tormented me all of my life." Recounting Gorky's bitter remarks of 1917–22, Bertram Wolfe notes that Gorky feared "Lenin's seizure of power and his demagogic appeals for terror from below would give free rein to peasant cruelty until it wiped out the cities which to him were the center of culture and humaneness." Wolfe continues that Gorky "saw the workingman as yesterday's peasant, with the same limited horizon, anarchic cruelty and laziness." Such comments correspond to Victor Serge's troubling recollection that in the course of the Russian Revolution "a sort of natural selection of authoritarian temperaments" could be observed, adding that "the victory of the revolution deals with the inferiority complex of the perpetually vanquished and bullied masses by arousing in them a spirit of social revenge, which in turn tends to generate new despotic institutions. I was witness to the great intoxication with which yesterday's sailors and workers exercised command and enjoyed the satisfaction of demonstrating that they were now in power!"[4]

Character Structures

A problem with such somber reflections on Russia's "dark masses" is that their truth is undermined through overstatement. We have noted, in the course of this study, diverse personalities, different kinds of people—certainly the bad and the ugly, but also the insightful and caring and good. This is true of people in all strata of society. Relevant to this is an extensive sociopsychological study of German workers in 1929, conducted by researchers from the Institute for Social Research, commonly known as the Frankfurt School. The study, according to Erich Fromm (one of those directing the study), held that "the character structure" of the mass of human beings "forms the basis for . . . a political and social structure," and it sought to determine character structures among a broad survey of German workers, largely to determine the likelihood of Adolf Hitler coming to power.[5]

One of the questions was, "Which men in history do you admire most?" Would the answer reflect an admiration for the powerful or those benefitting humanity? A respondent was deemed to have given an *authoritarian* answer if his or her list included the following choices: Alexander the Great, Julius Caesar, Napoleon, Marx, Lenin (admiration of the revolutionary leaders as authority figures and as conquerors). On the other hand, a *democratic* answer might correspond with choices such as these: Socrates, Kant, Pasteur, Marx, Lenin (admiration of the revolutionary leaders as men of principle and as innovators). An accumulation of such answers would give a sense of a person's deep-held convictions, grounded in the structure of his or her character, which was shaped by various experiences, family life dynamics, social structures, economic conditions, and more over a period of years. According to Fromm, the study concluded that 10 percent of the respondents were classified as having authoritarian character structures, 15 percent were deemed to have democratic character structures, and 75 percent "were people whose character structure was a mixture of both extremes."[6]

Fromm went on to distinguish various "character types" that might emerge within the revolutionary struggle. "Anyone can acquire an opinion," he noted, "just as one can learn a foreign language or a foreign custom, but only those opinions which are rooted in the character structure of a person, behind which there is the energy contained in his character—only these opinions become convictions. The *effect* of ideas, while these are easy to accept if the majority proclaims them, depends to a large extent on the character structure of a person in a critical situation." Specifically, "anyone can, for a number of reasons, participate in a revolution, regardless of what he feels."[7] Among those swept up in a revolutionary upheaval, and taking hold of revolutionary ideas (having to do with such things as "liberty, equality, fraternity" and "power to the people"), one can find what Fromm identifies as *authoritarians*, *rebels*, and *fanatics*, as well as those with genuinely *revolutionary character*.

In his discussion of a person with an *authoritarian* character structure, Fromm reflects that such a person "feels himself strong when he can submit and be part of an authority which (to some extent backed by reality) is inflated, is deified, and when at the same time he can inflate himself by incorporating those subject to his authority." Fromm goes on to give a distinctive definition to the term *rebel* as "the person who is deeply resentful of authority for not being appreciated, for not being loved, for not being accepted." This kind of rebel "wants to overthrow authority because of his resentment and, as a result, to make himself the authority in the place of the one he has overthrown." A *fanatic*, as Fromm uses the term, "has chosen a cause, whatever it may be—political, religious, or any other—and he has deified this cause. He has made this cause an idol." Fromm concludes, "By complete submission to this idol, he receives a passionate sense of life, a meaning of life; for in his submission he identifies himself with the idol, which he has inflated and made into an absolute."[8]

Those manifesting a *revolutionary* character structure, Fromm writes, are free from "symbiotic attachment to the powerful ones above"—whether these be tsars or commissars or revolutionary idols. According to Fromm, "Full freedom and independence exist only when the individual thinks, feels, and decides for himself." A person can be conditioned by conscious efforts and struggles to attain "a productive relatedness to the world outside himself, which permits him to respond authentically." More than this, because he is "not caught up in the parochial worship" of existing custom and authority, and able to see alternative potentialities (for freedom, creative labor, genuine community) in himself and others, "the revolutionary character is the one who is identified with humanity and therefore transcends the narrow limits of his own society, and is able, because of this, to criticize his or any other society from the standpoint of reason and humanity." Fromm adds that because of this, "the revolutionary character thinks and feels in what might be called a 'critical mood'—in a critical key, to use a symbol from music," which is "by no means anything like cynicism," but rather "an insight into reality, in contrast to the fictions that are made a substitute for reality." In addition, "power never becomes sanctified, it never takes on the role of truth, or of the moral or good. . . . He who is morally impressed by power is never in a critical mood, is never a revolutionary character." Fromm concludes that this is "not necessarily a character type which has its place only in politics . . . but also in religion, in art, and in philosophy."[9]

There are two other points Fromm makes, in passing, that deserve further development. One is that he is referring "not to a behavioral concept, but to a dynamic concept" (suggesting, therefore, the possibility of growth and change). The other is that "the majority of people of course have never been revolutionary characters," but "there have always been enough revolutionary characters to get us out of the caves and their equivalents."[10] One could argue that the rippling effects that have helped to shape the character structures of the innumerable individuals who make up humanity have left us all with elements of the creative and destructive, of wisdom and fanaticism, of authority-worship and violence as well as profoundly humane and caring qualities. These—in different proportions—are latent in all of us. Elements of creativity and community have made their way into each of us, just as we all suffer damage, in more than one way, from the demons of the past. Among those with authoritarian character structures and those with revolutionary character structures, the combinations have decisively tilted one way or another, but each has been able to find a response among "the majority of people" precisely because such elements are latent in all of us. There exist dramatically different possibilities.

Such reflections bring to mind a line of thought developed almost four decades ago by Marshall Berman in his remarkable essay "All That Is Solid Melts into Air." If all of us are an integral part of an inherently and dynamically "demonic" (self-absorbed/dehumanizing) system, then how can any of us free ourselves from the demonic forces? Berman says that this notion "cuts deeply against the twentieth-century Leninist 'vanguards' who . . . claim to transcend the vulgar world of need, interest, egoistical calculation and brutal exploitation." He adds that "it raises questions about Marx's own romantic image of the working class"—in fact, "how can we expect *anybody* to transcend all this?" He answers his own question by acknowledging the tension between Marxism's critical insights and radical hopes, and then insisting on the necessity of demanding and struggling for genuine transcendence over the destructiveness—concluding that "to give up the quest for transcendence is to . . . betray . . . ourselves."[11]

The Revolutionary Wager

Relevant here is Lucien Goldmann's atheistic utilization of the "Pascalian wager"—a reference to the argument by philosopher Blaise Pascal (1623–1662) that all people bet with their lives either that God exists or does not. It makes more sense—according to Pascal—to live as though God exists (and to seek to believe in God). For the person who chooses God, if it turns out that God doesn't exist, there is no great loss (only passing up the enjoyment of sinful but transient "pleasures"), while if God does exist such a person will receive the infinite pleasures of Heaven. "In his book *The Hidden God*," comments Michael Löwy, Goldmann compares "religious faith and Marxist faith: both . . . believe in trans-individual values—God for religion, the human community for socialism. A similar analogy exists between the Pascalian gamble on the existence of God and the Marxist gamble on the liberated future: both presuppose risk, the danger of failure, and the hope of success. Both come down to a question of faith and are not demonstrable on the exclusive level of factual judgments."[12] One might add that for the Marxist, the only hope for "winning" such a wager is to recognize (as Abraham Lincoln once said) that "we cannot escape history," that we must engage actively with it. One must commit one's life to the revolutionary wager by (1) working with others to develop an understanding of the political, economic, and social dynamics of our age; (2) employing the most effective insights regarding the ongoing development of the analyses, strategies, tactics, and organizational forms needed for such change; and (3) on the basis of such understanding and insights, winning others to helping bring the changes that are needed.

Lenin and his comrades made such a wager with the whole of their lives. They gambled and ultimately they lost—but, we have suggested, the gamble made sense. There were inspiring triumphs that came from their efforts, and the ultimate loss was not inevitable. The greater failure would have been never to have tried. To hold back, it can be argued, ensures the triumph of the demons of violence, oppression, and degradation. In struggling to free oneself from the grasp of the powerful demons that have taken shape out of rippling experiences of past devastations, there are no certainties and perhaps no "happily-ever-afters."

The brutal fact remains that despite all of the deep-felt idealism and immensely heroic efforts, despite all of the powerful insights and inspiring achievements associated with the 1917 revolution, the demons of inhumanity were ever present. In addition to the revolutionary triumph, there was the triumphant crescendo of bureaucratic and murderous tyrannies we associate with Stalinism. Yet there were people—part of the 1917 triumph—who stood fast for what they believed in, and who resisted as best they could, and with the whole of their lives, the horrific degeneration. One can argue that the existence and struggles of this saving remnant have helped honor and preserve all that was good in the 1917 struggle for liberation.

The tragedy should not blind us to the moments of imperishable triumph. Nothing in the past ever vanishes—so the triumph is permanent, not transient. Even if all who experienced it, and all memories of it, were to vanish—what happened in the past will *always* be what happened in the past, and what we thought and felt and did (and all that we *tried* to do, even if we failed) will continue to have been so, forever. More than this, those living today and tomorrow can learn from the triumphs and tragedies of the past—and comprehending such things may help those who have made the wager for a better world avoid or overcome further tragedies, and to create human triumphs of creative labor, of life-enhancing freedom, and of genuine community.

Historical Materialism

Historical materialism, the analytical tradition associated with Karl Marx, focuses on the development of economic systems—activities and relationships that people enter into, and resources (including technologies) they use, to get the things that they need and the things that they want—as a decisive force in the shaping of culture, politics, and history. Related to this are three other fundamental suppositions: (a) the sense that socioeconomic classes (essentially, powerful minorities enriching themselves through the exploitation of laboring majorities)—with tensions and conflicts between them—play a decisive role in such development and shaping of culture, politics, and history; (b) the sense that there has been a succession of different economic systems interrelated with specific forms of class societies; and (c) the sense that the system assuming global dominance in the time of Marx—capitalism—was not only the most dynamic form of economy in human history but also one providing possibilities for a dramatic expansion of human freedom. Specifically, according to Marx, the working-class majority has the capacity to organize for the purpose of replacing capitalism with a liberating socialism. By successfully struggling to take power into its own hands, it can bring into being a new system, the economic democracy of socialism. We have obviously made use of such perceptions in the present study.

We have also made use of Leon Trotsky's articulation (under the rubric of *permanent revolution*) of what Isaac Deutscher has termed a "quintessential element in classical Marxism."[13] This linked the revolutionary struggle for democracy—freedom of expression, end of feudal privilege, equal rights for all, rule by the people—with the struggle for socialism, a society in which the great majority of people would own and control the economic resources of society to allow for the full and free development of all. This orientation also linked the struggle for revolution in Russia with the cause of socialist revolution throughout the world. Applied to Russia, this involved three key points:

1) The revolutionary struggle for democracy in Russia could only be won under the leadership of the working class with the support of the peasant majority.

2) This democratic revolution would begin in Russia a transitional period in which all political, social, cultural, and economic relations would continue to be in flux, leading in the direction of socialism.

3) This transition would be part of, and would help to advance, and must also be furthered by, an international revolutionary process.[14]

In another, related application of Trotsky's articulation of the theory of *uneven and combined development*, our study of the Russian Revolution has placed Russia—both in its tsarist and early Soviet phases—somewhere on the continuum of "underdeveloped" or "developing" societies, with the interpenetration of capitalist political-economic "modernization" and precapitalist (or "premodern") political culture. That continuum sits within the larger framework of a capitalist world economy involving an "international division of labor" or "economic interdependence and mutualism" or "imperialist relations" (all three of these may aptly describe the reality), shaping the internal development of that country. We have seen that this sets up a dynamic in regard to the incapacity of indigenous bourgeoisies to give consistent leadership to "bourgeois-democratic" revolutionary change (or democratic "modernization"). Rather, the contradictions and crises of the situation tended to generate a radicalization of struggles for democratic reforms, pushing them beyond the bounds of capitalist hegemony. An examination of the revolutionary process has given support to the utilization of Marxist class categories, particularly to the concept of "proletariat" and "proletarianization," although we have been compelled to examine the concepts critically and utilize them flexibly (in the manner of Marx himself, we would argue). At the same time, it could be suggested that a more flexible utilization of the categories may have helped revolutionaries avoid some of the rigidities afflicting Bolshevik policies in regard to the peasantry.

We have also seen the importance in the revolutionary process of the interpenetration of popular ideologies and aspirations on the one hand and revolutionary theories and programs on the other, the dynamic (not manipulative) interplay between the projects of revolutionary vanguards and the inclination of masses of people to resist oppressive situations. We have noted that consciously organized groups competed to play such a vanguard role, and through a process somewhat akin to natural selection, a specific grouping cohered and evolved (with a programmatic orientation fundamentally independent from capitalist political currents) into a force capable of rallying mass support for a radical-democratic revolution. We have noted the great impact the revolution had internationally; in fact, the revolutionary leadership counted on revolutionary triumphs elsewhere to assist their own situation. On the other hand, the same fact inevitably generated the hostile international reaction among "the great powers" of the capitalist world, and we have taken note of the extremely negative effects that this reaction has upon the revolutionary process.

We have observed that the revolutionary leadership proposed a gradual transition from capitalism to socialism, via a left-wing variant of "mixed economy." Our findings suggest a possible link between the mixed-economy policy and the ability to realize some measure of the "proletarian democracy" ideal. This notion is further supported by the fact that by 1923, thanks to the New Economic Policy (a modified mixed-economy variant), Russia's Soviet Republic had attained a new stability accompanied by an abatement of political terror and by an expansion of channels allowing some free expression and a genuine measure of popular participation in shaping social policy.

The fact remains that what existed in the Soviet Republic was by no means an actual democracy, and the situation soon took a drastically authoritarian turn—although things might have been different had socialist revolutions triumphed in other countries. There were hopes that the mixed economy of the NEP might bring the tenuous development toward pluralist democracy, although we have also noted that the policy contained its own contradictions and was entering a crisis that raised questions about its long-term viability. In fact, we know that after the interlude of the NEP, the USSR experienced an intensification of authoritarianism and terror in the 1930s (to the degree that many peasants as well as workers and veteran Bolsheviks were destroyed).

One could argue that the revolutionaries were faced with a choice: either make such far-reaching compromises through the NEP that the revolutionary project (the "proletarian state" as well as socialist hopes) would pass out of existence, or shift to more radical, centralized anticapitalist policies. In either case, an increase in authoritarianism could have resulted. For those adhering to the original socialist project, the resolution, ultimately, involved not simply the internal resources of the revolutionaries and their country, but more decisively what happened outside of their country. In particular, there were two counterposed dynamics: on the one hand, the efforts of hostile powers to isolate, damage, and destabilize the revolution; on the other hand, the efforts of the revolutionaries of other lands (including those of the "hostile powers") to draw their own countries onto the trajectory of "proletarian revolution" and postcapitalist development. To the extent that this latter effort failed, there was a diminished possibility of the revolution we have studied to achieve its stated goals.

The line of analysis developed in this study suggests that Russia's revolution may have been necessary for the positive future development of that country. It can also be demonstrated that such revolutionary regimes as the early Soviet Republic—especially to the extent that hostile governments are not engaged in attempting to strangle or overturn them—can bring genuine material benefits to the working people and the oppressed (particularly in regard to health, education, social welfare, and so forth). What remains in question is the issue of democracy as defined by revolutionary Marxists, which also involves the *possibility* of socialism (by definition, an inherently democratic economic system)—as opposed to some form of authoritarian and bureaucratic rule over a collectivized economy.

A very common belief is that, as such post-Marxists as Max Nomad and James Burnham have most lucidly and powerfully argued, political and economic *democracy* (defined as majority rule or self-government by the people)— which is central to the definition of socialism—is humanly impossible.

In examining the historical record, not to mention contemporary realities in the second decade of the twenty-first century, it is impossible to point to a socialist democracy that came into being anywhere. The most we can see in the historical experience is people making strides toward that goal. Sometimes they faced agonizing choices, as well as sometimes making painful and tragic mistakes in the process of trying to realize their socialist vision. In some cases, the "mistakes" were so terrible as to constitute crimes, and those struggling *against* such self-described "revolutionaries" have been the ones making a contribution toward realizing the socialist goal. As one socialist theorist, Hal Draper, once tried to explain regarding genuine *rule by the people*: "It is a direction, not a dogma. *It is a line of struggle,* not a finished utopia."[15]

In a similar manner, Charles Tilly has projected the struggle for democracy as a kind of never-ending story, insisting that in modern times "democratization and de-democratization occur continuously, with no guarantee of an end point in either direction." The processes that advance possibilities of rule by the people, according to Tilly, are determined by three processes. One process involves the development and integration into public politics of what he terms "trust networks"—which can include kinship groups, religious sects, revolutionary organizations, neighborhood and workplace councils, and locally rooted social movements. Another process essential for the advance of actual democracy is the limiting and pushing back of "categorical inequality"—social and economic no less than political. A third process involves limiting and overcoming the existence of autonomous and coercive power centers that operate outside the control of public politics.[16]

If we consider the material presented in this study, we can see that victories *have* been won by revolutionaries seeking to build revolutionary mass movements to overthrow oppressive tyrants and initiate basic social change. Victories have also been won over local and outside forces utilizing powerful resources to roll back or at least contain the revolution—although this victory exacted an incredibly high sacrifice of human lives, material needs, and hoped-for social programs, and to some extent the sacrifice of democratic and humanistic impulses and ideals.

Revolutionary movements, mass upheavals, and popular struggles against adverse conditions embrace and unleash a variety of tendencies. Under conditions of economic disaster and war, tendencies toward elitism and intolerance often win out over tendencies toward genuine egalitarianism and tolerance; this is exacerbated if there are scarce resources, because a minority will naturally tend to ensure its acquisition of material privileges, which requires intensified doses of ideological elitism and repressive intolerance to hold back the others. And this gives credence to the argument of Nomad and Burnham.

On the other hand, we have seen that sometimes—with the change of conditions—countertendencies can come to the fore allowing greater pluralism, tolerance, opportunities for egalitarianism and popular participation, and so on. Of course, "conditions" are complex and subject to being affected by such diverse factors (which often have contradictory effects—for example, the mixed blessings of the New Economic Policy). It is therefore risky to think in terms of the *inevitability* of oligarchy, socialism, or anything else. The fact that human beings are involved in all of this means, for example, that lessons learned from past experience can be applied to new realities in order to deflect repetitions of negative experience. It also becomes a factor in making the future difficult to predict. This suggests, too, that what *did* happen did not *have* to happen, that different outcomes were possible in history and that different outcomes are therefore possible in the future.

This does not mean that everything is "up for grabs" or that *anything and everything* can be possible. Specific dynamics and tendencies inherent in socioeconomic and political realities—as well as in the physical, material universe—happen to exist and will be part of (and part of determining) any future that unfolds. It would seem that the extent to which people are aware of these dynamics, tendencies, and realities correlates with how they make choices and decisions that can shape the future in such a way that generates a cooperative commonwealth—characterized by freedom, creativity, community, a decent life, and the flowering of human potential for each person. What we do—and what we fail to do—makes a difference.

The struggle for human liberation, for a society of the free and the equal, has been going on for centuries. There are many men and women whose efforts and sacrifices we can learn from, from whom we can gain strength and inspiration. In her 1918 critique of the Russian Revolution, for example, Rosa Luxemburg makes reference to a figure from German history, Ulrich von Hutten (1488–1523), a humanistic poet-activist who challenged the immense power of princes and churches, and her praise for the Russian revolutionaries links them with past heroes and heroines like Hutten as well as the future ones destined to endure:

> What is in order is to distinguish the essential from the non-essential, the kernel from the accidental excrescencies in the politics of the Bolsheviks. In the present period, when we face decisive final struggles in all the world, the most import-

ant problem of socialism was and is the burning question of our time. It is not a matter of this or that secondary question of tactics, but of the capacity for action of the proletariat, the strength to act, the will to power of socialism as such. In this, Lenin and Trotsky and their friends were the *first,* those who went ahead as an example to the proletariat of the world; they are still the *only ones* up to now who can cry with Hutten: "I have dared!"

This is the essential and *enduring* in Bolshevik policy. In *this* sense theirs is the immortal historical service of having marched at the head of the international proletariat with the conquest of political power and the practical placing of the problem of the realization of socialism, and of having advanced mightily the settlement of the score between capital and labor in the entire world. In Russia, the problem could only be posed. It could not be solved in Russia. And in *this* sense, the future everywhere belongs to "Bolshevism."[17]

The tragedies overwhelming such people as Luxemburg, Lenin, Trotsky, and the millions inspired by them cannot erase the triumph of who they were. Because of what they did and attempted, nothing can ever be the same.

METHODOLOGICAL APPENDIX:

ANALYTICAL TOOLS

*R*egarding the French Revolution, Albert Soboul noted: "Through the recollection of struggles for freedom and for independence, as well as by its dream of fraternal equality, the Revolution, child of enthusiasm, still excites men and women, or else arouses their hatred." The same is true of the revolution examined here. Yet it would be a mistake to think the hatred that is aroused belongs simply to those whose privileges are threatened, though there is, of course, such hatred from that source. Yet there are also some who were once touched by the enthusiasm, but who came to be bitterly disappointed, and they have advanced the belief that revolutionary illusions—from before the French Revolution down to our own time—are generally a mask for terror and tyranny. As the premier theorist of disillusionment, Max Nomad, once summarized: "The process of revolution is always the same: seizure of power; organization of a revolutionary government; its defense against the reactionaries at first; and then its consolidation against the masses as well as in the interest of a better paid aristocracy of office-holders, technicians, and other members of the educated layers of society."[1] Some speak of "Stalinism," but in fact this notion goes far beyond the tragic despotism arising in Soviet Russia of the 1930s. It is a generalization about all of history, all of humanity, and it is an essential element in what has for many years been the dominant ideology in the United States, reflected in cynical "street smarts" as well as in the accepted wisdom of academe.

In this study, we have made use of this accepted wisdom as a prod to explore more deeply the historical process of revolution. Our focus has been on realities and events in Russia from 1917 to 1924. At the same time that we have made use of the accepted wisdom, however, we reached beyond it—in part because we are not inclined to abandon the enthusiasm inspired by the revolutionary vision. The study of such things as revolution is profoundly shaped by the assumptions and analytical constructs that one brings to that study. The sets of assumptions and constructs one uses must be made explicit in order to make clear the meaning of such a study's results. Those who tell us that they are simply dealing with "reality" while leaving ideology to others are trying to fool us, and perhaps themselves as well. (The prevailing ideological assumptions are most effective when unconsciously absorbed by those who believe they have gone beyond ideology.) This means that critical attention must be given to the approach that we bring to this study.

The eminent historian of the French Revolution whom we've already cited, Albert Soboul, commented that "the history of the Revolution, like any historical subject, is structured and thus thinkable, scientifically knowable, like any other reality." That this was not a platitude became clear with his next sentence: "The goal of the historian is to achieve, if not certitudes, at least probabilities or networks of probabilities, or even better, as Georges Lefebvre said, tendential laws." Soboul warned against two pitfalls: "on one hand, an all-purpose schematization that impoverishes and dessicates the rich historical subject; on the other hand, a cursory empiricism that, in the name of the complexity of the real, considers and treats only one particular case." Soboul concluded that "if the historian intends to understand and arrive at some explanation of causes and effects, it is essential to have recourse to some theory connecting ideas to the needs and pressures of society." The Marxist influence in Soboul's work—as in that of Georges Lefebvre and Albert Mathiez, not to mention Jean Jaurès, before him—involved an interpretive framework that brought to the fore economic relationships and development, social transformations and crises, class tensions and struggles, and revolutionary transitions from one socioeconomic system to another.[2]

This "historical materialist" approach is found in the present study. Of course, there are many variants of Marxism. The tradition we draw upon here is that identified with not only Karl Marx and Frederick Engels but also Rosa Luxemburg, V. I. Lenin, Leon Trotsky, and Antonio Gramsci.[3]

Gramsci's views on ideology, "organic" intellectuals, and class hegemony are particularly useful. The same is true regarding Luxemburg's conception of "mass strike" and the interplay of mass insurgencies and socialist vanguards. Similarly, we make use in our study of Lenin's approach to the masses-vanguard dialectic, his insight regarding the nature of revolutionary crises, and his grasp of strategic and tactical dynamics within nationally specific as well as international contexts. Of central importance to this study are Trotsky's theory of uneven and combined development and his theory of permanent revolution. Hopefully none of these theoretical tools deteriorate into the "all-purpose schematization" that flattens and blurs the rich and complex historical realities, against which Soboul warned.

Although considerable attention is given to "social history" in these pages, readers can regard this largely as a work of intellectual history. It involves the study of ideas and theories, but it can also be seen as part of a long tradition of *developing* ideas and theories under the impact of studying revolutions.

We have noted that the manner in which revolutions are interpreted and understood often becomes intertwined with the question of whether to condemn or defend them. By the two hundredth anniversary of the French Revolution, historiographical fashion tilted toward the conclusion that the Revolution began with splendid aspirations but quickly became a disaster that left France a sorrier place than it had been beforehand. Of course, this was also the argument of Edmund Burke at the time—countered by the partisan defense of Thomas Paine, who saw in it a vital affirmation of "the rights of man."[4]

For that matter, the first American Revolution continues to be the subject of controversy. The "second American Revolution," the Civil War of 1861–65, combined with the era of Reconstruction of 1865–77, has also been the focus of fierce disputes. As in the study of the French Revolution, Marxist-oriented scholars have made remarkable advances, but their interpretations cannot be said to have won universal acceptance.[5]

Of course, these are "bourgeois-democratic" revolutions. The "proletarian" revolutions—beginning with the Paris Commune of 1871, including the Bolshevik seizure of power in 1917, and often somewhat problematically involving a variety of overturns during the twentieth century—have generated even greater passions. The first great defender and interpreter of the Paris Commune was Karl Marx himself, whose pamphlet *The Civil War in France* was followed by the massive *History of the Commune of 1871* by the Communard Prosper O. Lissagary. The first coherent account of the Bolshevik revolution was left-wing journalist John Reed's *Ten Days That Shook the World* (1919), followed in 1932 by a participant's unrivaled panorama—Trotsky's *History of the Russian Revolution*. Sympathetic historians have followed the lead of Reed and

Trotsky, just as unsympathetic historians have followed the leads of hostile contemporaries (e.g., well-known historians Woodrow Wilson and Winston Churchill). A perusal of this study's bibliography will reveal the consumption of many gallons of printers' ink in such enterprises.[6]

The present study approaches revolution under the inspiration of Paine, Marx, and Trotsky. This is so not simply in regard to partisanship for the cause of human liberation, but also in regard to the quest to see reality in a new way and to further develop our analytical tools. On this last point, Paine sought the further clarification of democratic political theory; Marx sought the deeper understanding of class struggles and also of the state and its transformation; Trotsky sought a better grasp of revolutionary dynamics. The present study also seeks to advance our understanding of these and related questions.

The Post-Marxist Challenge

The perspective that Marx and Engels sketched in the *Communist Manifesto* of 1848 called for workers of all countries to unite in order to lose their chains and win the world, referring to the workers' movement as a movement of the great majority in the interests of the great majority—all of which was more a forecast of future realities than a description of what actually existed in the middle of the nineteenth century. In many ways it seemed profoundly relevant in the century *following* its publication, as the capitalist system secured global predominance, drawing ever-increasing numbers of people into the labor market. As Belgian economist Ernest Mandel commented in the late twentieth century: "There are today a billion wage workers in the world, incomparably more numerous and better educated than their predecessors 80, 50 or even 30 years ago."[7] This trend has not diminished as "globalization" has continued its work in the twenty-first century.

As one decade succeeded another, the organized labor movement became a force in the political life of more and more countries. What's more, revolutions influenced by Marxism triumphed in a succession of countries—from Russia in 1917 to similar overturns through much of the twentieth century. It seemed possible, even in the late 1980s given the way things were going, that a revolutionary resurgence and triumph might be experienced in the advanced capitalist countries of the twenty-first.

Critics of Marxism, on the other hand, were able to point to an accumulation of striking contradictions and problems appearing to throw the whole perspective into question. The triumphant "Marxist" revolutions had occurred not in the most industrialized and proletarianized areas but in largely agricultural societies where the working class seemed to be a small minority. In the advanced industrial countries that the *Communist Manifesto* implied would see the first revolutionary triumphs, the labor movement appeared to have accommodated itself to the capitalist status quo. In the "backward" countries where revolutions occurred, serious questions could be raised regarding whether the proletariat had won "the battle for democracy" and established its own political rule, as the Manifesto had predicted, or whether power was exercised only in the name of the proletariat and the rural poor by authoritarian and increasingly bureaucratic elites.

By the 1990s and into the 2000s, it all seemed to fall apart for the Marxists. Capitalism played a colossal trick—what Marx and Engels had proclaimed in the *Communist Manifesto* became true for the once-confident Marxists: "All that is solid melts into air." The revolutionary wave had run its course and now receded into nothingness. Actual or pretended Communist regimes collapsed (or, in the case of the People's Republic of China, embraced capitalism), and the great Soviet experiment turned out to be the road to nowhere. ("What is Communism?" began one joke in the former Soviet Union. The answer: "The longest road from capitalism to capitalism.") The working class increasingly seemed to lose its dynamism. The organized labor movement—its crimson banners fading in the sunshine of capitalist prosperity, its militants foiled and befuddled by the amazing new dynamics of "globalization" and in some cases frantically accommodating to triumphant capitalism—eroded. In some cases it collapsed and in others it morphed ever further into a bureaucratic apparatus, integrated into the capitalist status quo, on close terms with business and government elites, removed from the daily lives of ordinary workers.

There have been recent waves of disillusioned leftists and post-Marxists in the late twentieth and early twenty-first centuries, but their contributions seem to me not to go qualitatively beyond earlier waves: a few in the 1920s, more in the 1930s and 1940s, culminating as the "established wisdom" of the 1950s, providing an analytical alternative to Marxism, developed largely by people once "infected" with some variant of Marx's vision. Utilizing their Marxian-influenced intellectual tools, they dug their way out of earlier attachments, going on to settle accounts—sometimes bitterly, sometimes with generous nostalgia, but often perceptively—with the failed vision. In this study, it is the perspectives of these post-Marxists to which we have given attention: Selig Perlman, Max Nomad, Sidney Hook, James Burnham, Bertram Wolfe, W. W. Rostow, Daniel Bell, but there have been many others who could also be cited. There are substantial disagreements among such people (as there are among Marxists), yet there are important perspectives they shared in their maturity.[8]

Their general outlook has remained hegemonic in the intellectual life of the United States since the 1940s—from the extreme conservative to the extreme liberal spaces on the political spectrum—aside from a leftward vacillation in the late 1960s (and perhaps another shaping up in the early twenty-first century). One of their most effective representatives, Daniel Bell, explained that "we have all become post-Marxists," arguing that the validity of Marx's approach—rooting "social change in social structure or institutions" and "seeking to lay bare the sources of that determinism in social relations between men"—is combined for post-Marxists with the understanding that "the working class will not inherit the world," making it necessary for serious thinkers to go beyond Marx.[9]

As a pioneering post-Marxist and labor historian, Selig Perlman was one of the first to articulate the view that Marx was wrong to see the working class as a force for socialist revolution. While agreeing with Marx that the two primary social classes of modern times consist of capitalists and workers, Perlman believed that the Marxist conception of working-class consciousness is simply the invention of intellectuals like Marx who see working people as "an abstract mass in the grip of an abstract force." The notion of "proletarian revolution" is simply unnatural. The "homegrown" outlook of real workers, "the organic psychology of the manualist," involves an inherent "urge towards collective control of job opportunities, but hardly toward similar control of industry." In fact, only the capitalists have "the demonstrated capacity . . . to survive as a ruling group," because they "know how to operate the complex economic apparatus of modern society upon which the material welfare of all depends," and they have a psychology of "limitless opportunities" (unlike the narrow "scarcity consciousness" of the workers) and a "will to power" necessary to run industrial society. Rather than seeking to overthrow capitalism, workers naturally seek to create organizations that will struggle with capitalists only "for an enlarged opportunity measured in income, security and liberty in the shop and industry." A modest "wage and job conscious" trade unionism—not class-conscious radicalism leading to a revolution, a workers' state, and socialism—is the best vehicle reflecting that actual psychology and advancing the real interests of workers.[10]

Another post-Marxist, W. W. Rostow, noted that "Marx belongs among the whole range of men of the West, who, in different ways, reacted against the social and human costs of the drive to [economic] maturity and sought a better and more humane balance in society." Rostow stressed both the grandeur and the immense failure in the contributions of this passionate logician of revolution: "Driven on—in his father's phrase—by a 'demonic egoism,' by an identification with the underdog and a hatred of those who were top-dog, but also disciplined to a degree by a passion to be 'scientific' rather than sentimental, Marx created his remarkable system: a system full of flaws but also full of legitimate partial insights, a great formal contribution to social science, a monstrous guide to public policy."[11]

Obviously, if the proletariat was incapable of creating a cooperative commonwealth, then the keystone of Marx's proposals for "public policy" would fall away. What made it all truly monstrous, however, was the fact that Marx's ultrademocratic vision became a cover for the most brutal despotism. James Burnham saw the Marxist movement of the twentieth century as a new variant of Bonapartism: "Mature Bonapartism is a popular, a democratic despotism, founded on democratic doctrine, and, at least in its initiation, committed to democratic forms." According to Burnham, "The primary object, in practice, of all rulers is to serve their own interest, to maintain their own power and privilege. There are no exceptions. . . . The demagogues of the opposition say their victory will be the triumph of the people; but they lie, as demagogues always do." He added: "The Marxists and the democratic totalitarians claim that freedom can now be secured only by concentrating all social forces and especially economic forces in the state which, when they or their friends are running it, they identify with the people. . . . Their arguments and programs are . . . simply myths that express, not movements for political liberty, but a contest for control over the despotic and Bonapartist political order which they . . . anticipate. The concentration of all social forces in the state would in fact destroy all possibility of freedom."[12]

As the twentieth century progressed to the twenty-first, however, the shiny wonders of capitalist globalization became increasingly tarnished. Many people around the world (especially the sector identified by Marx and Engels as *working class*, those who make a living through selling their labor-power) have been experiencing declining living conditions, increased exploitation, growing cultural and environmental degradation, deteriorating communities, and growing social instability, not to mention the seemingly never-ending story of violence, terrorism, war. Such "Marxist" realities naturally resurrect the post-Marxist narrative.

Defining Democracy

The literal definition is simple: government by the people, or rule by the people. This is the content of what is elaborated by Thomas Jefferson in the beginning of the Declaration of Independence and Abraham Lincoln in the Gettysburg Address. John Dewey, in his discussion of Jefferson, offered interesting reflections on democracy's underpinnings:

> The will of the people as the moral basis of government and the happiness of the people as its controlling aim were so firmly established with Jefferson that it was axiomatic that the only alternative to the republican position was fear, in lieu of trust, of the people. Given fear of them, it followed, as by mathematical necessity, not only that they must *not* be given a large share in the conduct of government, but that they must themselves be controlled by force, moral or physical or both, and by appeal to some special interest served by government—an appeal which, according to Jefferson, inevitably meant the use of means to corrupt the people. Jefferson's trust in the people was a faith in what he sometimes called their common sense and sometimes their reason. They might be fooled and misled for a time, but give them light and in the long run their oscillations this way and that will describe what in effect is a straight course ahead.[13]

In contrast to this, Joseph A. Schumpeter, in his critique of democracy, has taken issue with the underlying assumption of *rule by the people*—that people know what they want when actually most people's "will" consists of "an indeterminate bundle of vague impulses loosely playing about given slogans and mistaken impressions." Schumpeter was quite willing to acknowledge that "there is truth in Jefferson's dictum that in the end the people are wiser than any single individual can be, or in Lincoln's about the impossibility of 'fooling all the people all the time.'" But, he insisted, history "consists of a succession of short-run situations that may alter the course of events for good," and that "all the people can in the short run be 'fooled' step by step into something they do not really want," and such "short-run" realities recur over and over and over.[14]

Related to this is James Burnham's uncompromising perspective: "'Democracy' is usually defined in some such terms as 'self-government' or 'government by the people.' Historical experience forces us to conclude that democracy, in this sense, is impossible." While the quest for such democracy would lead to despotism, he insisted, liberty could be secured through the acceptance of government in the hands of a ruling class—but a ruling class divided into at least two strong factions. "Political freedom," according to Burnham, "is the resultant of unresolved conflicts among various sections of the elite." Hope for the future involved "a purge of the ranks of the ruling class . . . and the recruitment of new leaders" with the managerial expertise necessary "to promote those variants of the evolving social order that permit at least the minimum of liberty and justice without which human society is degraded to merely animal existence."[15]

This raises a question that is a central focus of the present study: What is the relationship of democracy to the revolution under examination? I would argue that for the nonrevolutionary post-Marxists, there is a fundamental (though, in many cases, covered-over) agreement with Burnham's views on democracy. A key to their rejection of Marxism is the conviction that—unlike the capitalists (and their managers)—the working class is incapable of ruling society. While some liberals and conservatives raise the word *democracy* as a banner, it is important to understand that this word has often been redefined in a way that is consistent with Burnham's perspective. Attention to the work of different democratic theorists will help to clarify this point.

In an influential study by Henry B. Mayo, *An Introduction to Democratic Theory*, we find respectful reference to Burnham's perspective: "The charge of inevitable oligarchy . . . is supported by much empirical evidence" and by "impressive arguments." In response, Mayo asserted that democratic theory can accept the necessity of "leadership" and that "democracy need not presuppose any large proportion of the politically active, or even a high proportion of voters." According to Mayo: "Democracy obviously stands or falls by its method of selecting its leaders, and rests on the explicit assumption that elections are the best, or least bad, method of choosing the wisest and best [leaders]." Fleetingly acknowledging the possibility that "a traditional ruling class is necessary" and the fact of "the power of money to pervert administration or legislation," he insisted that democracy involves not an attempt to achieve "the highest ideals" but rather to secure a situation which is "tolerable and . . . acceptable for the time being . . . and which the public may be persuaded to accept.[16]

Robert A. Dahl, in his similarly influential *A Preface to Democratic Theory*, offered a similarly "precise" (or narrowed) definition of democracy and of the function of elections. "We expect elections to reveal the 'will' or the preferences of a majority on a set of issues," he reflected. "This is one thing elections rarely do, except in an almost trivial fashion." Commenting that "majority rule is mostly a myth," Dahl asserted: "Elections and political competition do not make for government by majorities in a very significant way, but they vastly increase the size, number and variety of minorities whose preferences must be taken into account by leaders making policy choices."[17]

A careful reading of their works suggests that this is generally the kind of "democracy" defended by many political theorists who remain attached to the word.[18]

In any event, we should remember this approach to defining democracy as we critically survey Russian realities: *democracy exists when the political leaders of a society conduct elections designed to persuade the populace of policies preferred by the leadership, while at the same time facilitating efforts of various minorities (or interest groups) to have leaders take their own particular concerns into consideration.* Such a definition would certainly allow us to take a rather generous view of the early Bolshevik regime. Whether this in any way amounts to "rule by the people" seems highly questionable.

Approaching the question from a more historical standpoint, John Dewey, observed that "the development of political democracy came about through substitution of the method of mutual consultation and voluntary agreement for the method of subordination of the many to the few enforced from above." C. B. Macpherson has elaborated: "It cannot be too often recalled that liberal democracy is strictly a capitalist phenomenon. Liberal-democratic institutions have appeared only in capitalist countries, and only after the free market and the liberal state have produced a working class conscious of its strength and insistent on a voice."[19]

This raises the obvious question: since modern democracy has appeared only under capitalism, or is "a strictly capitalist phenomenon," as Macpherson puts it, can democracy exist independently of capitalism? A hint is contained in what is stressed in Macpherson's second sentence—regarding "a working class conscious of its strength and insistent on a voice," a matter to which we must return.

On the other hand, what are we to make of the diluted "democracy" that mainstream theorists have felt compelled to articulate under modern capitalism? "Owing to the dramatic growth of elite power," Peter Bachrach has noted, traditional democratic theory (e.g., of Paine, Jefferson, and Lincoln) has come to be seen as "an anachronism," generating "cynicism toward democracy as it becomes evident that the gap between the reality and the ideal cannot be closed." This has required—in the view of influential theorists such as Dahl and Mayo (and among such post-Marxists as Rostow and Bell)—an effort to "recast democracy" in a manner reflecting "a receptiveness toward the existing structure of power and elite opinion-making in large industrial societies," a way of defining the term that reflects "a profound distrust of the majority of ordinary men and women, and a reliance upon the established elites to maintain the values of civility and the 'rules of the game' of democracy."[20]

John Dewey noted the problem as well. "After democratic political institutions were nominally established," he mused, "beliefs and ways of looking at life and of acting that originated when men and women were externally controlled and subjected to arbitrary power, persisted in the family, the church, business and the school," contributing to "a subtle form" of exclusion from meaningful participation in decision-making that is "perhaps economic, certainly psychological and moral.... Others who are supposed to be wiser and who in any case have more power decide the question for them and also decide the methods and means by which subjects may arrive at the enjoyment of what is good for them." Such a mode of operation often "is habitual and embodied in social institutions," seeming "the normal and natural state of affairs," with the mass of people "unaware that they have a claim to a development of their own powers." The persistence of such realities, he concludes with typical understatement, means the "political democracy is not secure."[21]

Harold Laski highlighted some of the relevant issues with admirable clarity. Commenting that the way "in which economic power is distributed at any given time and place will shape the character of the legal imperatives which are imposed in that same time and place," he challenged the notion that simply basing the state on the democratic principle of universal suffrage would result in "rule by the people." Democracy means that power is exercised by the people, or at least their majority. But "power depends for its habits upon a consciousness of possession, a habit of organization, an ability to produce an immediate effect," and even with the equal and universal distribution of the right to vote for the government's elected representatives, "in a democratic state, where there are great inequalities of economic power," such habits and abilities that Laski refers to are precisely what the majority of people do not have. He elaborates: "They do not know the power that they possess. They hardly realize what can be effected by organizing their interests. They lack direct access to those who govern them. Any action by the working classes, even in a democratic state, involves risk to their economic security out of all proportion to the certainty of gain." Laski's bluntness stands in contrast to the formulations preferred by many post-Marxist theorists:

> The division of society into rich and poor makes the legal imperatives of the state work to the advantage of the rich.... Their power compels the agents of the state to make their wishes the first object of consideration. Their conception of good insensibly pervades the mental climate of the administration. They dominate the machinery of the state. By justice they mean the satisfaction of their demands. By the lessons of history they mean the deposit of their experience.... [T]he quality of public opinion depends upon the truth of the information upon

which it is based, and its power to make an impression is a function of the degree to which it is organized. . . . News becomes propaganda as soon as its substance can affect policy; and, in an unequal society, the incidence of news is tilted to the advantage of the holders of economic power.[22]

If the first question about democracy pondered its relationship with revolution, Laski's conclusions raise (and suggest a negative answer to) a second question: *Can genuine democracy actually exist under capitalism?* This second question assumes a more broadly conceived notion of democracy.

A democratic ethos is at the heart of the Marxist tradition. Revolutionary socialists in the tradition of Marx and Lenin have insisted that genuine, living democracy can only be realized by going beyond the capitalist framework, a notion also embedded in Trotsky's theory of permanent revolution.[23]

The classical tradition of revolutionary Marxism, indeed, holds to a vision of democracy far more expansive and demanding than is the case of many liberal-democratic theorists of the mid-to-late twentieth century. "The system of workers' councils, the separation of state and party, multiparty representation, inner-party democracy, workers' self-management and union rights," in the words of Marxist theorist George Novack, identifying with the Leninist-Trotskyist tradition, "can be the keystones of a healthy postcapitalist state and the best curatives for the diseases of bureaucratism." Novack goes further, explicitly stressing the need for such a socialist democracy to generate "the uprooting of women's oppression" and to advance the emancipation, empowerment, and self-determination of "weak, poor, oppressed and under-developed nationalities" existing within society.[24]

Novack also stresses the necessity of freedom of expression and political pluralism, arguing that this is in harmony with the Leninist conceptualization of the revolutionary vanguard party. "A plurality of parties is not only most favorable to the political vitality of the state in the transitional period [from capitalism to socialism] but also useful to the ruling party as well," he asserts. "The existence of competition and criticism, the presentation of alternative policies and courses, the direct confrontation of differing orientations act as a prod to keep the party from deviating too far from the correct course." He adds, significantly: "They can prepare a peaceful and legal replacement if the vanguard should degenerate to the point of failing to fulfill its role as the best representative of the forward march to socialism."[25]

From all of this we can construct a seven-point "democratic state" checklist for evaluating (for example) the extent to which revolutionary Russia achieved democracy:

1) a system of governmental bodies under the control of popularly elected representatives;

2) a distinction between the governing party and the state apparatus (making possible a change in governing parties);

3) a plurality of political parties participating in the electoral process and able to offer opposing orientations on major questions;

4) freedom of expression (speech, press, etc.);

5) the existence of popular civic organizations controlled by their members (including trade unions), capable of formulating and winning support for alternate political policies;

6) some forms of genuine control over workplaces by those who work there; and

7) equal rights for all citizens in society, with special attention given to the elimination of the special oppression historically experienced by women, oppressed nationalities and racial groups, and so forth.

As we can see, this is a more demanding definition of democracy than that culled from such theorists as Mayo and Dahl, one which obviously would be far more difficult to live up to in the real world. A somewhat similar but more modest articulation of the "concept of democracy" is offered by three other theorists, Dietrich Rueschemeyer, Evelyne Huber Stephens, and John D. Stephens: "It entails, first, regular, free and fair elections of representatives with universal and equal suffrage, second, responsibility of the state apparatus to the elected parliament (possibly complemented by the direct election of the head of the executive), and third, the freedoms of expression and association as well as the protection of individual rights against arbitrary state action." They link this with a conceptualization in their comparative analysis of the emergence of democracy in various capitalist countries, that (1) the working class (not the capitalist class) has played a central role in the process of democratization, (2) "it is the struggle between the dominant and subordinated classes over the right to rule that—more than any other factor—puts democracy on the historical agenda and decides its prospects," and (3) democracy has historically been "a product of the contradictions of capitalism, and the process of democratization [has been] primarily a product of the action of the subordinate classes." In his panoramic history of democracy, Brian Roper finds that this has been more generally true throughout history: "The social forces that have most consistently fought for, and defended, democracy are the 'poor and middling folks' in various societies: peasant citizens in the Athenian city-state; the middle classes, urban petite-bourgeoisie (sans-culottes), poorer members of the clergy, wage-laborers and sections of the peasantry in France during the 1790s; workers and peasants in Russia during the first two decades of the twentieth century; workers, students, farmers and members of the middle classes in the advanced capitalist societies during the twentieth century." In her outstanding study *The History of Human Rights,* Michelene Ishay similarly demonstrates that "the struggles for universal suffrage, social justice, and workers' rights . . . were socialist in origin."[26]

In other words, while capitalism generates socioeconomic blockages to the actual realization of "rule by the people," the development of capitalism has nonetheless generated powerful struggles for democracy, pushed forward by the laboring "lower classes." If it turns out, however, that they prove unable to achieve and sustain the kind of rule elaborated in the seven points derived from Novack's discussion, we are brought back to Burnham's challenge regarding the extent to which genuine democracy can be realized at all.

Less sweeping than Burnham's universal rejection of democracy's possibility is the rejection of democracy's *universal applicability.* There is the question, raised by conservative scholars such as Howard J. Wiarda, of whether such things as democracy can be "exported" or expected to flourish in all cultures. Others have responded that this "cultural relativist" approach in fact serves US foreign policy inclinations to side with traditionalist elites and "modernizing" authoritarians who are willing to accommodate the interests of elites within the US political economy. Some social scientists argue that, given the achievement of an "economic threshold" and a "sociocultural," or "literacy threshold," democracy—while not inevitable—is possible.[27] Harold Laski emphasized a sort of "general education threshold" in his primer on politics: "Knowledge is essential, and the right to education is therefore fundamental to citizenship. For without education, at least as a general rule, a man is lost in a big world he is unable to understand. He cannot make the most of himself; he cannot be critical about the meaning of experience. The uneducated man amid the complexities of modern civilization is like a blind man who cannot relate cause and effect."[28] Regardless of what geographical location or which people we have in mind, then, this suggests that if such "thresholds" are realized, rule by the people could be a practical possibility. It also suggests that without their realization, Novack's Marxist vision of what genuine democracy looks like cannot be achieved. On the other hand, Novack himself acknowledges that such democratic principles cannot be realized under all conditions.

"Scrupulous as a workers' regime may be in observing the rights of the people," he tells us, "its democratic functioning will be vitiated in the long run unless and until two fundamental tasks are solved." One task, we will see, was not solved in Russia during the period covered in our study: "The productivity of labor must be developed to the point where enough goods are available for everyone's needs, there are no sharp divisions between the haves and the have-nots, and penury, misery and gross inequality are overcome." The other task, according to Novack, is even more decisive in "fortifying the processes of democratization," though it also remained unrealized—"a series of victories for the working class over capitalism in the industrialized metropolises, where the greatest powers of production are concentrated and the greatest enemies of socialism are located." Some might understandably respond: if these are seen as preconditions for securing democracy in early Bolshevik Russia (or anywhere else), then democracy is inevitably doomed.[29]

Nonetheless, a focal point of this study involves an exploration of the extent to which actual democracy can be said to have been realized, or not realized, in Bolshevik Russia. This is rooted in an acceptance of the vision to which such revolutionaries as Marx and Engels, Luxemburg, Lenin, Trotsky, and Gramsci committed their lives. And it connects with the belief that if popular revolutions—such as the Russian Revolution of 1917—have resulted in bureaucratic dictatorships instead of socialist democracies, this can best be explained not by the abstract "impossibility" of socialism or democracy but by specific historical circumstances, which can be understood and ultimately overcome.

Politics of Uneven and Combined Development

Marxism fuses together a view of history, an engagement with current realities, and a strategic orientation for replacing capitalism with socialism. The dominant interpretation of history shared by Marxists of the early twentieth century went something like this: since the rise of class societies (with small, powerful upper classes of exploiters enriched by vast laboring majority classes), there have been a succession of historical stages characterized by different forms of economy—ancient slave civilizations giving way to feudalism, which has given way to present-day capitalism.[30]

The growth of capitalism was facilitated by democratic revolutions that swept away rule by kings and the power of landed nobles, making way for increasingly democratic republics and market economies. The victory of the capitalists (bourgeoisie) paves the way for the triumph of industrialization and modernization. This creates economic productivity and abundance making possible a socialist future (a thoroughly democratic society of freedom and plenty, in which there will be no upper class and lower class). Capitalism also creates a working-class (proletarian) majority that potentially has an *interest* in, and the *power* required for bringing into being, a socialist future.

Many Marxists consequently believed that there must first be a bourgeois-democratic revolution, followed by industrialization and modernization, before the necessary preconditions for a proletarian-socialist revolution can be created. There was a crying need for such a bourgeois-democratic revolution in an economically "backward" country such as Russia in the early 1900s, oppressed by the tsarist autocracy and landed nobility (to which capitalists were subordinated as junior partners), with a small working class and a large impoverished peasantry. Many Marxists concluded they should fight for the triumph of such a revolution, so that capitalist development could eventually create the economic and political preconditions for a working-class revolution that would eventually bring about socialism.

In his distinctive conceptualization of *uneven and combined development*, Trotsky rejected this "pedantic schematism" as a distortion of the realities experienced by "the backward countries" of the world. "Under the whip of external necessity their backward culture is compelled to make leaps," he argued. "From the universal law of unevenness thus derives another law which, for the lack of a better name, we may call the law of *combined* development—by which we mean a drawing together of the different stages of the journey, a combining of separate steps, an amalgam of archaic with more contemporary forms."[31]

Particularly in the 1960s and '70s, this perspective became an issue in debates over dependency theory in Latin America. Marxist theorists, in many cases associated with Communist Parties in Latin America, argued that most of Latin America was economically equivalent to a semifeudal stage of development, and that there was a need for a profound bourgeois-democratic makeover (led through a coalition of workers, peasants, and progressive capitalists)—which would someday pave the way for a transition to socialism. There were also nonsocialist "modernization theorists" such as W. W. Rostow who advanced a different variant, through which foreign aid from more advanced countries such as the United States could help the underdeveloped countries "mature" through social and economic modernization, paving the way for democracy and abundance (and no need for socialism).

Other theorists, supportive of revolutionary strategies, advanced what was termed "dependency theory," in some cases utilizing a variant of the theory of uneven and combined development. Its application to twentieth-century realities was summed up, during the debate, in this way by Timothy Harding: "Capitalism as it spread everywhere across the world swallowed up earlier systems without totally destroying them and employed them in modified ways for the capitalist purpose of commodity production for profit." The economically less advanced areas would be blocked from developing in the way that the more advanced (and now dominant) areas had developed. This approach differed profoundly from the "orthodox Marxist" (and later Rostow's) "orderly pattern of historical development," as Trotsky put it, "according to which every bourgeois society sooner or later secures a democratic regime, after which the proletariat, under conditions of democracy, is gradually organized and educated for socialism" (or in Rostow's case, for "post-maturity" and "high mass consumption"). The "orthodox" perspective "considered democracy and socialism, for all peoples and countries, as two stages in the development of society which are not only distinct but also separated by great distances of time from each other."[32] Given the dynamics that Trotsky perceived, however, the old schema was profoundly unrealistic.

Many Russian Marxists (especially the Mensheviks, influenced by "the father of Russian Marxism," George Plekhanov) disagreed, insisting on the long-held understanding that Russia must first have a bourgeois-democratic revolution, which would clear the way for extensive economic, social, and political developments eventually culminating in the possibility for a proletarian-socialist revolution. For the Mensheviks, this meant building a worker-capitalist alliance to overthrow tsarism. Lenin and his Bolsheviks—revolutionary Marxists, profoundly skeptical of the revolutionary potential of Russia's capitalists—called instead for a radical worker-peasant alliance that would carry the anti-tsarist struggle to victory. But even they did not question the "orthodox" schema: first a distinct bourgeois-democratic revolution paving the way for capitalist development; later—once conditions were ripe—a working-class revolution to bring about socialism.

Yet from a Marxist point of view, this schema provides a theoretical and political puzzle. If the working class is as essential to the democratic revolution as the Mensheviks claimed, and their direct exploiters are the capitalists with whom they are engaged in class struggle that is "constant, now hidden, now open" (as the *Communist Manifesto* tells us), then how can these mortal enemies be expected to link arms as comrades in a common struggle? And if—as

Lenin insisted—the workers must, in fact, turn their backs on the capitalists (in alliance with the peasantry) to overthrow tsarism, what sense would it make for them in the moment of victory to turn power over to their exploiters?

It was Trotsky, Michael Löwy has noted, who was best able to dramatically "grasp the revolutionary possibilities that lay beyond the dogmatic construction of the democratic Russian Revolution which was the unquestioned problematic of *all* other Marxist formulations." One can find anticipations of this in other Marxists, and Trotsky himself insisted that his "permanent revolution" conception overlapped with perspectives of others. It flows naturally from the revolutionary conceptualizations inherent in the analyses and methodology of Marx himself. "Trotsky is deeply committed to one element in classical Marxism," as Isaac Deutscher has observed, "its quintessential element: permanent revolution." Revolutionary-minded theorists and activists—seeking to apply such Marxism to the world around them—will naturally come up with formulations going in a "permanentist" direction.[33]

In Trotsky's sparkling prose we see several interrelated elements formulated more clearly and boldly than can be found in other theorists. Trotsky's formulation linked the struggle for democracy—freedom of expression, end of feudal privilege (especially land reform), equal rights for all, rule by the people—with the struggle for socialism, a society in which the great majority of people would own and control the economic resources of society to allow for the full and free development of all. It also linked the struggle for revolution in Russia with the cause of socialist revolution throughout the world.

Trotsky's version of the theory contained three basic points: (1) The revolutionary struggle for democracy in Russia could only be won under the leadership of the working class with the support of the peasant majority. (2) This democratic revolution would begin in Russia a transitional period in which all political, social, cultural, and economic relations would continue to be in flux, leading in the direction of socialism. (3) This transition would be part of, and would help to advance, and must also be furthered by, an international revolutionary process.

The first point in the theory is quite suggestive when one examines the actualities of Russia's 1917 revolution. While the bourgeoisie tended to be too weak and compromised to lead the militant struggle necessary for a triumphant democratic revolution, the same was not true for all other social layers. Majority sectors of the population—the newly proletarianized labor force, the impoverished peasant masses, aspiring and democratic-minded elements among the petty bourgeoisie (artisanal, petty commercial, and professional layers)—*did* have a vital interest in the achievement of the democratic tasks. Among these forces, the *urban working class* had sufficient cohesion, leverage, and (through educational and organizing efforts of the revolutionary socialist movement) the necessary consciousness and will to provide consistent leadership in the democratic struggles. An alliance with the massive Russian peasantry would, of course, be a precondition for victory—but so would proletarian leadership. This would consequently give the revolution a dual character. "So far as its direct and indirect tasks are concerned," Trotsky wrote, "the Russian revolution is a 'bourgeois' revolution because it sets out to liberate bourgeois society from the chains and fetters of absolutism and feudal ownership. But the principal driving force of the Russian revolution is the proletariat, and that is why, so far as its method is concerned, it is a proletarian revolution." This working-class hegemony in the struggle had a logic, Trotsky insisted, that "leads directly . . . to the dictatorship of the proletariat and puts socialist tasks on the order of the day."[34]

By *dictatorship of the proletariat*, of course, Marxists have not meant authoritarian rule by an elitist dictatorship, but rather political rule by the working class (often conceived as involving greater actual democracy, as we have seen, than does political rule by the capitalist class). Nor did it exclude other (nonproletarian) layers of society. "The dictatorship of the proletariat in no way signifies the dictatorship of the revolutionary organization over the proletariat," Trotsky insisted. He quoted Marx's description of the Paris Commune as "the true representative of all the healthy elements of French society, and therefore the truly national government." He argued that in Russia "the dictatorship of the proletariat will undoubtedly represent all the progressive, valid interests of the peasantry—and not only the peasantry, but also the petty bourgeoisie and the intelligentsia." The broad social alliance that brought the revolution to victory would, he felt, probably be reflected in the composition of the new revolutionary government. Instead of *dictatorship of the proletariat* he was quite willing to utilize other labels: "workers' democracy," or "dictatorship of the proletariat supported by the peasantry," or "coalition government of the working class and the petty bourgeoisie." But he insisted that the reality must involve the "dominating and leading participation" of the working class, "the rule of the proletariat."[35]

The second point in Trotsky's theory of permanent revolution—involving a transition period going in the direction of socialism—requires more careful examination. Some partisans of Trotsky's perspective have assumed that the establishment of proletarian rule must coincide with the rapid replacement of a capitalist economy with the nationalization of the means of production and centralized planning (as opposed to maintenance of market mechanisms) in order to ensure the meeting of society's needs. Seeming confirmation of this assumption exists in the form of historical experience: within months of the Bolsheviks coming to power in Russia, sweeping nationalizations destroyed capitalism in that country. This is not consistent, however, with the actual thrust of Trotsky's theory.

Under the impact of the 1905 revolutionary upsurge in Russia, and partially through restudying the experience of history's first "proletarian dictatorship," the Paris Commune of 1871, Trotsky made the obvious point that the dictatorship of the proletariat is not premised on the establishment of a collectivized, planned economy. He believed the reverse to be true: "The Paris Commune of 1871 was not, of course, a socialist commune: its regime was not even a developed regime of socialist revolution. The commune was only a prologue. It established the necessary premise of the socialist revolution."[36] Trotsky believed that national-democratic struggles in "backward" capitalist countries would result—if carried out in a consistent, uncompromising manner under proletarian hegemony—in the establishment of working-class rule and would move in a socialist direction. But he did not believe that this would necessarily mean rapid nationalizations of the various sectors of the economy.

On the contrary, Trotsky insisted that "it would be absurd to think that all the proletariat has to do is acquire power and it can replace capitalism by socialism by means of a few decrees. . . . A government of the proletariat does not mean a government of miracles." He envisioned substantial reforms, such as the eight-hour work day and a heavily progressive (comparatively speaking) income tax, and also some nationalizations "with those branches which present the least difficulties." But for all practical purposes, he envisioned a form of mixed economy, a significant public sector but also a large private sector, with proletarian controls but a substantial degree of capitalist enterprise: "In the first period the socialized sector of production will have the appearance of oases connected with private economic enterprises by the laws of commodity exchange."[37] While Trotsky believed that the revolution would not be stabilized at this "mixed economy" stage, he insisted that—particularly in a country with such "underdeveloped" technology and productivity as Russia—it would not be possible to move forward to the realization of socialism in a single country.

This brings us to the third essential point in Trotsky's theory. "The Russian proletariat . . . will be able to carry its great cause to its conclusion," he stressed, "only under one condition—that it knows how to break out of the national framework of our great revolution and make it the prologue to the world victory of labor." Many critics and some would-be defenders of Trotsky's theory fail to give sufficient attention to this key international factor: "A national revolution is not a self-contained whole; it is only a link in the international chain. The international revolution constitutes a permanent process, despite temporary declines and ebbs." In fact, the theory loses coherence without this dimension. As he put it in 1929, the Marxist approach to socialist construction is grounded in the class struggle "on a national and international scale." In a world dominated by the capitalist economy, a socialist revolution in one country "must inevitably lead to explosions, that is, internally to civil wars and externally to revolutionary wars." Far from being an afterthought, this was at the heart of Trotsky's perspective. "Therein lies the permanent character of the socialist revolution as such," he explained, "regardless of whether it is a backward country that is involved, which only yesterday accomplished its democratic revolution, or an old capitalist country which already has behind it a long epoch of democracy and parliamentarism."[38]

There is a significant corollary to this third point. A failure to break out of the national framework, Trotsky ultimately concluded, would result either in the overturn of the revolution in a country such as Russia or in its bureaucratic degeneration.

BIBLIOGRAPHY

Abraham, Richard. *Alexander Kerensky: The First Love of the Revolution*. New York: Columbia University Press, 1987.

Abramovitch, Raphael. *The Soviet Revolution, 1917–1939*. New York: International Universities Press, 1962.

Acton, Edward, Vladimir Iu. Cherniaev, and William G. Rosenberg, eds. *Critical Companion to the Russian Revolution, 1914–1921*. Bloomington: Indiana University Press, 1997.

Alexinsky, Gregor. *Modern Russia*. London: T. Fisher Unwin, 1915.

Ali, Tariq, ed. *The Stalinist Legacy: Its Impact on World Politics*. Harmondsworth, UK: Penguin Books, 1984.

Allen, Barbara C. *Alexander Shlyapnikov, 1885–1937: Life of an Old Bolshevik*. Chicago: Haymarket Books, 2016.

Anweiler, Oskar. *The Soviets: The Russian Workers, Peasants, and Soldiers Councils, 1905–1921*. New York: Pantheon Books, 1974.

Aptheker, Herbert. *American Negro Slave Revolts*. New York: International Publishers, 1969.

———. *The American Revolution*. New York: International Publishers, 1960.

Arendt, Hannah. *The Origins of Totalitarianism*. 2nd ed. New York: Meridian Books, 1958.

Arnot, R. Page. *Soviet Russia and Her Neighbors*. New York: Vanguard Press, 1927.

Arshinov, Peter. *History of the Makhnovist Movement, 1918–1921*. London: Freedom Press, 2005.

Avrich, Paul. *Kronstadt, 1921*. New York: W. W. Norton, 1974.

———. *The Russian Anarchists*. New York: W. W. Norton, 1978.

Bachrach, Peter. *The Theory of Democratic Elitism: A Critique*. Boston: Little, Brown, 1967.

Baitalsky, Mikhail. *Notebooks for the Grandchildren*. Atlantic Highlands, NJ: Humanities Press, 1995.

Balabanoff, Angelica. *My Life as a Rebel*. Bloomington: Indiana University Press, 1973.

Baldwin, Roger N. *Liberty under the Soviets*. New York: Vanguard Press, 1928.

———. *A New Slavery, Forced Labor: The Communist Betrayal of Human Rights*. Dobbs Ferry, NY: Oceana Publications, 1953.

Baran, Paul. *The Political Economy of Growth*. New York: Monthly Review Press, 1962.

Barber, John. *Soviet Historians in Crisis, 1928–1932*. New York: Holmes & Meier, 1981.

Barmine, Alexander. *One Who Survived: The Story of a Russian under the Soviets*. New York: G. P. Putnam's Sons, 1945.

Baron, Samuel H. *Plekhanov: The Father of Russian Marxism*. Stanford, CA: Stanford University Press, 1963.

———. "The Transition from Feudalism to Capitalism in Russia: A Major Soviet Historical

Controversy." *American Historical Review*, 77, no. 3 (1972): 715–29.

Basil, John D. *The Mensheviks in the Revolution of 1917*. Columbus, OH: Slavica Publishers, 1984.

Bater, James H. "St. Petersburg and Moscow on the Eve of the Revolution." In *The Workers' Revolution in Russia, 1917: The View from Below*, edited by Daniel H. Kaiser, 20–57. Cambridge: Cambridge University Press, 1987.

Beatty, Bessie. *The Red Heart of Russia*. New York: The Century, 1918.

Bebel, August. *My Life*. Chicago: University of Chicago Press, 1913.

Bell, Daniel. *The Coming of Post-Industrial Society: A Venture in Social Forecasting*. New York: Basic Books, 1973.

———. *The End of Ideology: On the Exhaustion of Political Ideas in the Fifties*. Rev. ed. New York: The Free Press, 1965.

Berger, Joseph. *Shipwreck of a Generation: The Memoirs of Joseph Berger*. London: Harvill, 1971.

Berkman, Alexander. *The Bolshevik Myth*. New York: Boni and Liveright, 1925.

Berman, Marshall. *Adventures in Marxism*. London: Verso, 1999.

———. *All That Is Solid Melts into Air: The Experience of Modernity*. New York: Simon and Schuster, 1982.

Blanc, Eric. "Anti-Imperial Marxism: Borderland Socialists and the Evolution of Bolshevism on National Liberation." *International Socialist Review*, no. 100 (Spring 2016): 111–40.

Bobroff, Anne. "The Bolsheviks and Working Women, 1905–1920." *Radical America* (May–June 1976).

Bone, Ann, ed. *The Bolsheviks and the October Revolution: Central Committee Minutes of the Russian Social-Democratic Labour Party (Bolsheviks), August 1917–February 1918*. London: Pluto Press, 1974.

Bonnell, Victoria E. *Roots of Rebellion: Workers' Politics and Organizations in St. Petersburg and Moscow, 1900–1914*. Berkeley: University of California Press, 1983.

———, ed. *The Russian Worker: Life and Labor under the Tsarist Regime*. Berkeley: University of California Press, 1983.

Borders, Karl. *Village Life under the Soviets*. New York: Vanguard Press, 1927.

Bottomore, Tom, ed. *A Dictionary of Marxist Thought*. Cambridge: Harvard University Press, 1983.

Boudin, Louis B. *The Theoretical System of Karl Marx*. Chicago: Charles H. Kerr, 1907.

Bowlt, John E. "Art." In *The Cambridge Companion to Modern Russian Culture*, edited by Nicholas Rzhevsky, 213–49. Cambridge: Cambridge University Press, 1998.

Brailsford, H. N. *How the Soviets Work*. New York: Vanguard Press, 1927.

Braune, Joan. *Erich Fromm's Revolutionary Hope: Prophetic Messianism as a Critical Theory of the Future*. Rotterdam: Sense Publishers, 2014.

Braverman, Harry. *Labor and Monopoly Capital: The Degradation of Work in the Twentieth Century*. New York: Monthly Review Press, 1974.

Brody, David. "Selig Perlman." In *Dictionary of American Biography*, Supplement Six, 1956–60, edited by John A. Garraty. New York: Charles Scribner's Sons, 1980.

Broido, Vera. *Lenin and the Mensheviks: The Persecution of Socialists under Bolshevism*. Boulder: Westview Press, 1987.

Brook-Shepherd, Gordon. *Ironmaze: The Western Secret Services and the Bolsheviks*. London: Pan Books, 1998.

Brovkin, Vladimir N. *Behind the Front Lines of the Civil War: Political Parties and Social Movements in Russia, 1918–1922.* Princeton, NJ: Princeton University Press, 1994.

———, ed. *The Bolsheviks in Russian Society: Revolution and the Civil Wars.* New Haven, CT: Yale University Press, 1997.

———. *The Mensheviks after October: Socialist Opposition and the Rise of the Bolshevik Dictatorship.* Ithaca, NY: Cornell University Press, 1987.

———. *Russia after Lenin: Politics, Culture and Society, 1921–1929.* New York: Routledge, 1998.

Brower, Daniel R. *Estate, Class, and Community: Urbanization and Revolution in Late Tsarist Russia.* Carl Beck Papers in Russian and Eastern European Studies, no. 302. Pittsburgh: Russian and Eastern European Studies Program, University of Pittsburgh, 1983.

Bryant, Louise. *Six Red Months in Russia.* London: Journeyman Press, 1982.

Bryusov, A., A. Sakharov, A. Fadeyev, Y. Chermensky, and G. Golikov. *Outline History of the USSR.* Moscow: Foreign Languages Publishing House, 1960.

Bukharin, Nikolai. *Historical Materialism: A System of Sociology.* Ann Arbor, MI: University of Michigan Press, 1969.

———. *The Politics and Economics of the Transition Period.* London: Routledge and Kegan Paul, 1979.

———. *Selected Writings on the State and the Transition to Socialism.* Edited by Richard B. Day. Armonk, NY: M. E. Sharpe, 1982.

———, and Eugen Preobrazhensky. *The ABC of Communism.* Ann Arbor, MI: University of Michigan Press, 1966.

Burbank, Jane. *Intelligentsia and Revolution: Russian Views of Bolshevism, 1917–1922.* New York: Oxford University Press, 1986.

Burnham, James. *The Machiavellians: Defenders of Freedom.* New York: John Day, 1943.

———. *The Managerial Revolution.* Bloomington: Indiana University Press, 1962. See esp. the preface to the book.

Burston, Daniel. *The Legacy of Erich Fromm.* Cambridge, MA: Harvard University Press, 1991.

Bushnell, John. "Peasant Economy and Peasant Rebellion at the Turn of the Century: Neither Immiseration nor Autonomy." *Russian Review,* 47, no. 1 (1988): 75–88.

Byres, T. J. "Peasantry." In *A Dictionary of Marxist Thought,* edited by Tom Bottomore, 412–14. Cambridge, MA: Harvard University Press, 1983.

Cannon, James P. *The First Ten Years of American Communism.* New York: Lyle Stuart, 1961.

———. *The History of American Trotskyism.* New York: Pathfinder Press, 1972.

Carr, E. H. *The Bolshevik Revolution.* 3 vols. London: Macmillan, 1950–53.

———. *History of Soviet Russia.* 14 vols. London: Macmillan, 1950–78.

———. "Marx, Lenin and Stalin." In *Revolutionary Russia: A Symposium,* edited by Richard Pipes, 361–76. Garden City, NY: Anchor Books, 1969.

———. *The Russian Revolution from Lenin to Stalin, 1917–1929.* New York: Palgrave Macmillan, 2004.

———. *Twilight of the Comintern, 1930–1935.* New York: Pantheon Press, 1982.

Caute, David. *The Fellow Travellers: A Postscript to the Enlightenment.* New York: Macmillan, 1973.

———. *Isaac and Isaiah: The Covert Punishment of a Cold War Heretic.* New Haven, CT: Yale University Press, 2013.

Chamberlin, William Henry. *The Confessions of an Individualist.* New York: Macmillan, 1940.

———. *The Evolution of a Conservative.* Chicago: Henry Regnery, 1959.

———. *The Russian Revolution, 1917–1921.* 2 vols. New York: Grosset & Dunlap, 1965.

———. *Russia's Iron Age.* Boston: Little, Brown, 1934.

———. *Soviet Russia: A Living Record and a History.* Boston: Little, Brown, 1930.

Chase, Stuart, Robert Dunn, and Rexford Tugwell, eds. *Soviet Russia in the Second Decade: A Joint Survey by the Technical Staff of the First American Trade Union Delegation.* New York: John Day, 1928.

Chase, William J. *Workers, Society, and the Soviet State: Labor and Life in Moscow, 1918–1929.* Urbana: University of Illinois Press, 1987.

Chayanov, A. V. *The Theory of Peasant Cooperatives.* Columbus, OH: Ohio State University Press, 1991.

———. *The Theory of Peasant Economy.* Edited by Daniel Thorner, Basile Kerblay, and R. E. F. Smith. Madison: University of Wisconsin Press, 1986.

Chernov, Olga. *See* Tchernoff.

Chernov, Victor. *The Great Russian Revolution.* New Haven, CT: Yale University Press, 1936.

Chilcote, Ronald H., and Joel Edelstein. *Latin America: Capitalist and Socialist Perspectives of Development and Underdevelopment.* Boulder, CO: Westview Press, 1986.

Chilcote, Ronald H., and Dale L. Johnson, eds. *Theories of Development: Mode of Production or Dependency?* Beverly Hills, CA: Sage Publications, 1983.

Christian, Shirley. "Shultz on a Latin Tour, Carries Capitalist Word." *New York Times,* August 8, 1988.

Churchill, Winston S. *The Aftermath (the World Crisis, 1918–1928).* New York: Charles Scribner's Sons, 1929.

Ciliga, Ante. *The Russian Enigma.* London: Ink Links, 1979.

Clark, Ronald W. *Lenin: A Biography.* New York: Harper & Row, 1988.

Clements, Barbara Evans. *Bolshevik Feminist: The Life of Aleksandra Kollontai.* Bloomington: Indiana University Press, 1979.

———. *Bolshevik Women.* Cambridge: Cambridge University Press, 1997.

Cliff, Tony. *Lenin.* 4 vols. London: Pluto Press, 1975–79.

Cohen, Stephen. *Bukharin and the Bolshevik Revolution.* New York: Vintage Books, 1975.

Commission of the Central Committee of the CPSU(B), *History of the Communist Party of the Soviet Union (Bolsheviks): Short Course.* New York: International Publishers, 1939.

Countryman, Edward. *The American Revolution.* New York: Hill & Wang, 1985.

Courtois, Stéphane, Nicolas Werth, Jean-Louis Panne, Andrej Paczkowski, Karel Bartošek, and Jean-Louis Margolin. *The Black Book of Communism: Terror, Crimes, Repression.* Cambridge, MA: Harvard University Press, 1999.

Cox, Michael, ed. *E. H. Carr: A Critical Appraisal.* New York: Palgrave Macmillan, 2000.

Cox, Terry. *Peasants, Class, and Capitalism: The Rural Research of L. N. Kritsman and His School.* Oxford, UK: Clarendon Press, 1986.

Crossman, Richard, ed. *The God That Failed.* New York: Bantam Books, 1965.

Curtiss, John Shelton. *The Russian Revolutions of 1917.* New York: Van Nostrand, 1957.

Dahl, Robert A. *A Preface to Democratic Theory.* Chicago: University of Chicago Press, 1973.

Dallin, David, and Boris I. Nicolaevsky. *Forced Labor in Soviet Russia.* New Haven, CT: Yale

University Press, 1947.

Dan, Fedor [Theodore] Il'ich. *Two Years of Wandering: A Menshevik Leader in Lenin's Russia.* London: Lawrence and Wishart, 2016.

Dan, Theodore. *The Origins of Bolshevism.* New York: Schocken Books, 1970.

Daniels, Robert V. *The Conscience of the Revolution: Communist Opposition in Soviet Russia.* New York: Simon & Schuster, 1969.

———, ed. *A Documentary History of Communism.* 2 vols. New York: Vintage Books, 1962.

Danilov, Viktor P. *Rural Russia under the New Regime.* Bloomington: University of Indiana Press, 1988.

Davies, R. W. *The Soviet Economy in Turmoil, 1929–1930.* Cambridge, MA: Harvard University Press, 1989.

Davis, Horace B. *Socialism and Nationalism: Marxist and Labor Theories of Nationalism to 1917.* New York: Monthly Review Press, 1967.

Dawley, Alan. *Class and Community: The Industrial Revolution in Lynn.* Cambridge, MA: Harvard University Press, 1980.

Day, Richard B., and Daniel F. Gaido, eds. *Witnesses to Permanent Revolution: The Documentary Record.* Chicago: Haymarket Books, 2011.

Delany, William. "The Role of Ideology: A Summation." In *The End of Ideology Debate,* edited by Chaim I. Waxman, 291–314. New York: Funk and Wagnalls, 1968.

Deutscher, Isaac. *Marxism in Our Time.* Edited by Tamara Deutscher. Berkeley, CA: Ramparts Press, 1971. See esp. "Trotsky in Our Time," 31–61, and "Marxism and Nonviolence," 79–91.

———. *The Non-Jewish Jew and Other Essays.* New York: Oxford University Press, 1968.

———. *The Prophet Armed: Trotsky, 1879–1921.* New York: Oxford University Press, 1954.

———. *The Prophet: The Life of Leon Trotsky.* London: Verso, 2015.

———. *The Prophet Outcast: Trotsky 1929–1940.* New York: Vintage Books, 1965.

———. *The Prophet Unarmed: Trotsky 1921–1929.* New York: Vintage Books, 1965.

———. *Soviet Trade Unions.* London: Royal Institute of International Affairs, 1950.

———. *Stalin: A Political Biography.* New York: Oxford University Press, 1967.

———. *The Unfinished Revolution: Russia 1917–1967.* London: Oxford University Press, 1970.

Dewey, John. *Impressions of Soviet Russia and the Revolutionary World.* New York: New Republic, 1929.

———. *Intelligence in the Modern World: John Dewey's Philosophy.* Edited by Joseph Ratner. New York: The Modern Library, 1939. See esp. chap. 5, "The Modes of Societal Life," and subsection 5, "The Democratic Form," originally published as "Democracy and Educational Administration" in the journal *School and Society,* April 3, 1937.

———. *The Living Thoughts of Thomas Jefferson.* New York: Fawcett Books, 1957.

Diggins, John P. *Up from Communism: Conservative Odysseys in American Intellectual History.* New York: Harper & Row, 1975.

Dimitrov, Georgi. *The United Front.* New York: International Publishers, 1938.

Dobb, Maurice. *Russian Economic Development since the Revolution.* New York: E. P. Dutton, 1928.

Draper, Hal. *The "Dictatorship of the Proletariat" from Marx to Lenin.* New York: Monthly Review Press, 1986.

———, ed. *Karl Marx and Frederick Engels: Writings on the Paris Commune.* New York:

Monthly Review Press, 1972.

————. *Karl Marx's Theory of Revolution*, vol. 2, *The Politics of Social Classes*. New York: Monthly Review, 1978.

————. *Karl Marx's Theory of Revolution*, vol. 3, *The "Dictatorship of the Proletariat."* New York: Monthly Review Press, 1986.

————. "Reply to Max Nomad: Is Oligarchy Inevitable?" *New Politics* 5, no. 3 (1966), 65–71, and no. 4 (1966), 70–75.

————. *The Two Souls of Socialism*. Berkeley: Independent Socialist Clubs, 1966.

Du Bois, W. E. B. *Black Reconstruction in America, 1860–1880*. New York: Atheneum, 1985.

DuGarm, Delano. "Peasant Wars in Tambov Province." In *The Bolsheviks in Russian Society: The Revolution and the Civil Wars*, edited by Vladimir N. Brovkin, 177–98. New Haven CT: Yale University Press, 1997.

Dune, Eduard M. *Notes of a Red Guard*. Urbana: University of Illinois Press, 1993.

Dunn, Robert W. *Soviet Trade Unions*. New York: Vanguard, 1928.

Duranty, Walter. *I Write as I Please*. New York: Halcyon House, 1935.

Dutt, R. Palme. *The Life and Teachings of V. I. Lenin*. New York: International Publishers, 1934.

Eastman, Max. *Artists in Uniform: A Study of Literature and Bureaucratism*. New York: Octagon Books, 1972. First published 1934 by Knopf.

————. *Love and Revolution: My Journey through an Epoch*. New York: Random House, 1964.

————. *Marx, Lenin and the Science of Revolution*. London: George Allen and Unwin, 1926.

Easton, Loyd D., and Kurt H. Guddat, eds. *Writings of the Young Marx on Philosophy and Society*. Garden City, NY: Anchor Books/Doubleday, 1967.

Edwards, Stewart. ed. *The Communards of Paris, 1871*. Ithaca, NY: Cornell University Press, 1973.

————. *The Paris Commune, 1871*. New York: Quadrangle Books, 1973.

Ellison, Herbert J. "The Socialist Revolutionaries." *Problems of Communism* 16, no. 6 (1967): 76–85.

Elwood, Ralph Carter. *Inessa Armand: Revolutionary and Feminist*. Cambridge: Cambridge University Press, 1992.

————, ed. *Reconsiderations on the Russian Revolution*. Cambridge, MA: Slavica Publishers, 1976.

————. *Russian Social Democracy in the Underground*. Assen, the Netherlands: Van Grocum, 1974.

Engels, Frederick. *The Condition of the Working-Class in England*. Moscow: Progress Publishers, 1973.

————. Letter to Nikolai Danielson, 24 February 1893, www.marxists.org/archive /marx/works/1893/letters/93_02_24.htm.

Engelstein, Laura. *Moscow, 1905: Working-Class Organization and Political Conflict*. Stanford, CA: Stanford University Press, 1982.

Engerman, David C. "John Dewey and the Soviet Union: Pragmatism Meets Revolution." *Modern Intellectual History* 3, no. 1 (2006): 33–63.

————. *Know Your Enemy: The Rise and Fall of America's Soviet Experts*. New York: Oxford University Press, 2009.

————. *Modernization from the Other Shore: American Intellectuals and the Romance of Russian Development*. Cambridge, MA: Harvard University Press, 2004.

———. "Modernization from the Other Shore: American Observers and the Cost of Soviet Economic Development." *American Historical Review* 105, no. 2 (2000): 383–416.

Enteen, George M. *The Soviet Scholar-Bureaucrat: M. N. Pokrovskii and the Society of Marxist Historians*. University Park, PA: Pennsylvania State University Press, 1978.

Erlich, Alexander. *The Soviet Industrialization Debate, 1924–1928*. Cambridge, MA: Harvard University Press, 1960.

Etzioni-Halevy, Eva, ed. *Classes and Elites in Democracy and Democratization: A Collection of Readings*. New York: Garland Publishing, 1997.

Farber, Samuel. *Before Stalinism: The Rise and Fall of Soviet Democracy*. London: Verso, 1990.

Ferro, Marc. *The Bolshevik Revolution: A Social History of the Russian Revolution*. London: Routledge and Kegan Paul, 1985.

———. *Nicholas II*. New York: Oxford University Press, 1993.

Figes, Orlando. *A People's Tragedy: A History of the Russian Revolution*. New York: Viking Press, 1996.

Filtzer, Donald. *Soviet Workers and Stalinist Industrialization*. London: Pluto Press, 1986.

Fischer, Louis. *Men and Politics: An Autobiography*. New York: Duell, Sloan and Pearce, 1941.

———. *The Soviets in World Affairs: A History of the Relations between the Soviet Union and the Rest of the World*. 2 vols. Princeton, NJ: Princeton University Press, 1951.

Fitzpatrick, Sheila. *The Commissariat of Enlightenment: Soviet Organization of Education and the Arts under Lunacharsky, October 1917–1921*. Cambridge: Cambridge University Press, 1970.

———. *The Cultural Front: Power and Culture in Revolutionary Russia*. Ithaca, NY: Cornell University Press, 1992.

———, ed. *Cultural Revolution in Russia, 1928–1931*. Bloomington: Indiana University Press, 1978.

———. *Everyday Stalinism: Ordinary Life in Extraordinary Times in the 1930s*. New York: Oxford University Press, 2000.

———. *The Russian Revolution*. 2nd ed. New York: Oxford University Press, 1994.

Fitzpatrick, Sheila, Alexander Rabinowitch, and Richard Stites, eds. *Russia in the Era of NEP: Explorations in Soviet Society and Culture*. Bloomington: Indiana University Press, 1991.

Flewers, Paul. *The New Civilization? Understanding Stalin's Soviet Union 1929–1941*. London: Francis Boutle Publishers, 2009.

Foglesong, David S. *America's Secret War against Bolshevism: U.S. Intervention in the Russian Civil War, 1917–1920*. Chapel Hill: University of North Carolina Press, 1995.

Foner, Eric. *Politics and Ideology in the Age of the Civil War*. New York: Oxford University Press, 1980.

———. *Reconstruction: America's Unfinished Revolution, 1863–1877*. New York: Harper & Row, 1988.

———. *Tom Paine and Revolutionary America*. New York: Oxford University Press, 1976.

Foner, Philip S., ed. *The Bolshevik Revolution: Its Impact on American Radicals, Liberals, and Labor; A Documentary Study*. New York: International Publishers, 1967.

———. *Labor and the American Revolution*. Westport, CT: Greenwood Press, 1976.

———, ed. *Mother Jones Speaks: Speeches and Writings of a Working-Class Fighter*. New York: Pathfinder Press, 1983.

Foster, William Z. *The Russian Revolution*. Chicago: Trade Union Educational League, 1921.

Francis, David R. *Russia from the American Embassy, April, 1916–November, 1918*. New York: Charles Scribner's Sons, 1921.

Frank, André Gunder. *Capitalism and Underdevelopment in Latin America*. New York: Monthly Review Press, 1967.

Frankel, Edith Rogovin, Jonathan Frankel, and Baruch Knei-Paz, eds. *Revolution in Russia: Reassessments of 1917*. Cambridge: Cambridge University Press, 1992.

Freeman, Joseph. *An American Testament: A Narrative of Rebels and Romantics*. New York: Farrar and Rinehart, 1936.

———. "The Soviet Cinema." In *Voices of October: Art and Literature in Soviet Russia*, by Joseph Freeman, Joshua Kunitz, and Louis Lozowick, 217–64. New York: Vanguard Press, 1930.

———. *The Soviet Worker: An Account of the Economic, Social and Cultural Status of Labor in the USSR*. New York: Liveright, 1932.

———. "A Year of Grace." *New Politics*, Winter 1965. http://www.unz.org/Pub/NewPolitics-1965q1–00108.

Freeman, Joseph, Joshua Kunitz, and Louis Lozowick. *Voices of October: Art and Literature in Soviet Russia*. New York: Vanguard Press, 1930.

Fromm, Erich. *The Crisis of Psychoanalysis: Essays on Freud, Marx, and Social Psychology*. Greenwich, CT: Fawcett, 1971.

———. *The Dogma of Christ and Other Essays on Religion, Psychology, and Culture*. Garden City, NY: Anchor Books, 1966. See esp. chap. 6, "The Revolutionary Character."

———. *The Working Class in Weimar Germany: A Psychological and Sociological Study*. Cambridge, MA: Harvard University Press, 1984.

Furet, François. *Interpreting the French Revolution*. Cambridge: Cambridge University Press, 1981.

Furr, Grover. *The Murder of Sergei Kirov: History, Scholarship and the Anti-Stalin Paradigm*. Kettering, OH: Erythros Press and Media, 2013.

Gabriel, Mary. *Love and Capital: Karl and Jenny Marx and the Birth of Revolution*. New York: Little, Brown, 2012.

Galili, Zeva. *The Menshevik Leaders in the Russian Revolution: Social Realities and Political Strategies*. Princeton, NJ: Princeton University Press, 1989.

Gardner, Lloyd. *Architects of Illusion: Men and Ideas in American Foreign Policy, 1941–1949*. Chicago: Quadrangle Books, 1972.

———. *Imperial America: American Foreign Policy since 1898*. New York: Harcourt Brace Jovanovich, 1976.

———, Walter F. LaFeber, and Thomas J. McCormick, eds. *Creation of the American Empire*. 2 vols. Chicago: Rand McNally, 1976.

Gardner, Virginia. *Friend and Lover: The Life of Louise Bryant*. New York: Horizon Press, 1982.

Gasper, Phil, ed. *The Communist Manifesto: A Road Map to History's Most Important Political Document by Karl Marx and Frederick Engels*. Chicago: Haymarket Books, 2005.

Gatrell, Peter. *The Tsarist Economy, 1850–1917*. London: B. T. Batsford, 1966.

Geertz, Clifford. *The Interpretation of Cultures*. New York: Basic Books, 1973.

Geier, Joel. "Zinovievism and the Degeneration of World Communism." *International Socialist Review*, no. 93, Summer 2014, 41–73.

Genovese, Eugene. *The Political Economy of Slavery.* New York: Vintage Books, 1967.

Georgakas, Dan. "October Song." In *Abandon Automobile: Detroit City Poetry 2001,* edited by Melba Joyce Boyd and M. L. Lieber, 132. Detroit: Wayne State University Press, 2001.

Getty, J. Arch. *Origins of the Great Purges: The Soviet Communist Party Reconsidered, 1933–1938.* Cambridge: Cambridge University Press, 1985.

Getty, J. Arch, and Oleg V. Naumov. *The Road to Terror: Stalin and the Self-Destruction of the Bolsheviks, 1932–1939.* New Haven, CT: Yale University Press, 1999.

Getzler, Israel. "The Mensheviks." *Problems of Communism,* November–December 1967.

———. *Nikolai Sukhanov: Chronicler of the Russian Revolution.* New York: Palgrave, 2002.

Geyer, Dietrich. *The Russian Revolution.* New York: St. Martin's Press, 1987.

Gilly, Adolfo. *La Nueva Nicaragua: Antiimperialismo y lucha de clases.* Mexico City: Editorial Nueva Imagen, 1980.

Gladkov, Fydor Vasilievich. *Cement.* Evanston, IL: Northwestern University Press, 1994.

Glickman, Rose L. *Russian Factory Women: Workplace and Society, 1880–1914.* Berkeley: University of California Press, 1984.

Goldman, Wendy Z. *Women, the State and Revolution: Soviet Family Policy and Social Life, 1917–1936.* Cambridge: Cambridge University Press, 1993.

Gollwitzer, Heinz. *Europe in the Age of Imperialism, 1880–1914.* New York: W. W. Norton, 1979.

Goodey, Chris. "Factory Committees and the Dictatorship of the Proletariat (1918)." *Critique* 3, no. 1 (1974): 27–47.

Gordon, Manya. *Workers before and after Lenin: Fifty Years of Russian Labor.* New York: E. P. Dutton, 1941.

Gorky, Maxim. *Untimely Thoughts: Essays on Revolution, Culture and the Bolsheviks 1917–1918.* New Haven, CT: Yale University Press, 1995.

Graham, Loren R. *Science and Philosophy in the Soviet Union.* New York: Vintage Books, 1974.

Gramsci, Antonio. *Selections from the Prison Notebooks.* New York: International Publishers, 1973.

Gray, Camilla. *The Russian Experiment in Art, 1863–1922.* London: Thames and Hudson, 1986.

Green, Philip, ed. *Democracy.* Atlantic Highlands, NJ: Humanities Press, 1993.

Greene, Jack P., ed. *The Reinterpretation of the American Revolution.* New York: Harper & Row, 1968.

Greenlaw, Ralph W., ed. *The Social Origins of the French Revolution: The Debate on the Role of the Middle Classes.* Lexington, MA: D. C. Heath, 1975.

Gregor, Richard, ed. *Resolutions and Decisions of the Communist Party of the Soviet Union,* vol. 2, *The Early Soviet Period, 1917–1929.* Toronto: University of Toronto Press, 1974.

Guerin, Daniel. *Class Struggle in the First French Republic.* London: Pluto Press, 1977.

Haimson, Leopold H., ed. *The Mensheviks from the Revolution of 1917 to the Second World War.* Chicago: Chicago University Press, 1974.

———. "The Problem of Social Identities in Early Twentieth Century Russia." *Slavic Review* 47, no. 1 (1988): 1–20.

———. "The Problem of Social Stability in Urban Russia, 1905–1917." *Slavic Review* 23, no. 4 (1964): 619–42, and 24, no. 1 (1965): 1–22.

———. "The Russian Workers Movement on the Eve of the First World War." Unpublished paper, delivered at the annual meeting of the American Historical Association, December 1971.

———, in collaboration with Ziva Galili y Garcia and Richard Wortman. *The Making of Three Russian Revolutionaries*. Cambridge: Cambridge University Press, 1987

Haines, Anna J. *Health Work in Soviet Russia*. New York: Vanguard Press, 1928.

Harding, Neil. *Lenin's Political Thought*. 2 vols. New York: St. Martin's Press, 1975 and 1981.

Harding, Timothy. "Dependency, Nationalism and the State in Latin America." *Latin American Perspectives* 3, no. 4 (1976): 3–11.

Harper, Samuel Northrup. *Civic Training in Soviet Russia*. Chicago: University of Chicago Press, 1929.

———. *The Russia I Believe In: The Memoirs of Samuel N. Harper, 1902–41*. Edited by Paul V. Harper, with the assistance of Ronald Thompson. Chicago: Chicago University Press, 1945.

Hasegawa, Tsuyoshi. *The February Revolution: Petrograd, 1917*. Seattle: University of Washington Press, 1981.

Haslam, Jonathan. *The Vices of Integrity: E. H. Carr, 1892–1982*. London: Verso, 2000.

Haupt, Georges, and Jean-Jacques Marie, eds. *Makers of the Russian Revolution: Biographies of Bolshevik Leaders*. Ithaca, NY: Cornell University Press, 1974.

Haynes, Mike. "The Debate on Popular Violence and the Popular Movement in the Russian Revolution." *Historical Materialism* 2, no. 1 (1998): 185–214.

———, and Jim Wolfreys, eds. *History and Revolution: Refuting Revisionism*. London: Verso, 2007.

Haywood, Harry. *Black Bolshevik: The Autobiography of an Afro-American Communist*. Chicago: Liberator Press, 1978.

Hecker, Julius F. *Religion under the Soviets*. New York: Vanguard Press, 1928.

Heinzen, James W. *Inventing a Soviet Countryside: State Power and the Transformation of Rural Russia, 1917–1929*. Pittsburgh: Pittsburgh University Press, 2004.

Heller, Henry. *The Bourgeois Revolution in France, 1789–1815*. New York: Berghahn Books, 2006.

Hicks, John, and Robert Tucker, eds. *Revolution and Reaction: The Paris Commune, 1871*. Amherst: University of Massachusetts, 1971.

Hillquit, Morris. *From Marx to Lenin*. New York: The Hanford Press, 1921.

Hindus, Maurice. *Broken Earth*. New York: International Publishers, 1926.

———. *House without a Roof: Russia after Forty-Three Years of Revolution*. Garden City, NY: Doubleday, 1961.

———. *Humanity Uprooted*. London: Jonathan Cape, 1931.

———. *The Kremlin's Human Dilemma: Russia after Half a Century of Revolution*. Garden City, NY: Doubleday, 1967.

———. *The Russian Peasant and the Revolution*. New York: Henry Holt, 1920.

Hobsbawm, Eric. *The Age of Extremes: A History of the World, 1914–1991*. New York: Vintage Books, 1996.

Hook, Sidney. "Bolshevik Coup Lacked Popular Support" (letter to the editor). *New York Times*, August 20, 1988.

———. *Out of Step: An Unquiet Life in the 20th Century*. New York: Harper & Row, 1987.

———. *Towards the Understanding of Karl Marx: A Revolutionary Interpretation*. New York: John Day, 1933.

Hornblower, Margot. "Liberté, Egalité, Fraternité? 200 Years Later, the French Are Still Quarreling about the Revolution." *TIME*, May 1, 1989.

Horne, Alistair. *The Terrible Year: The Paris Commune, 1871*. New York: Viking Press, 1971.

Horowitz, David, ed. *Isaac Deutscher: The Man and His Work*. London: Macdonald, 1971.

Hudis, Peter. *Marx's Concept of the Alternative to Capitalism*. Chicago: Haymarket Books, 2013.

Hunt, Richard N. *The Political Ideas of Marx and Engels*. 2 vols. Pittsburgh: University of Pittsburgh Press, 1974 and 1984.

Husband, William. *Workers' Control and Centralization in the Russian Revolution: The Textile Industry of the Central Industrial Region, 1917–1920*. Pittsburgh: The Carl Beck Papers in Russian and Eastern European Studies, University of Pittsburgh, 1985.

Iarov, Serge V. "Workers." In *Critical Companion to the Russian Revolution*, edited by Edward Acton, Vladimir Iu. Cherniaev, and William G. Rosenberg, 604–18. Bloomington: Indiana University Press, 1997.

Ilyin-Genevsky, A. F. *The Bolsheviks in Power: Reminiscences of the Year 1918*. London: New Park, 1984.

———. *From the February Revolution to the October Revolution, 1917*. New York: Workers Library Publishers, 1931.

International Committee for Political Prisoners. *Letters from Russian Prisons*. New York: Albert and Charles Boni, 1925.

Isaacson, Walter. "The World According to Mr. X." Review of *George Kennan and the Dilemmas of U.S. Foreign Policy*, by David Mayers. *New York Times Book Review*, December 18, 1988.

———, and Evan Thomas. *The Wise Men: Six Friends and the World They Made*. New York: Simon & Schuster, 1988.

Ishay, Micheline. *The History of Human Rights: From Ancient Times to the Globalization Era*. Berkeley: University of California Press, 2008.

James, C. L. R. "Lenin and the Vanguard Party." In *The C. L. R. James Reader*, edited by Anna Grimshaw, 327–30. Oxford: Blackwell, 1992.

———. *World Revolution 1917–1936: The Rise and Fall of the Communist International*. New York: Pioneer Publishers, 1937.

Jaurès, Jean. *A Socialist History of the French Revolution*. London: Pluto Press, 2015.

Jellinek, Frank. *The Paris Commune of 1871*. New York: Grosset & Dunlap, 1965.

Johnstone, Monty. "Socialism, Democracy and the One-Party System." *Marxism Today*, August, September, and November 1970.

Joravsky, David. *Soviet Marxism and Natural Science, 1917–1932*. New York: Columbia University Press, 1961.

Kahn, Albert E. *High Treason: The Plot against the People*. New York: Lear Publishers, 1950.

Kaiser, David H., ed. *The Workers' Revolution in Russia, 1917: The View from Below*. Cambridge: Cambridge University Press, 1987.

Kameneff [Kamenev], L. *The Dictatorship of the Proletariat*. Detroit: The Marxian Educational Society [1920?].

Kanatchikov, Semën. *A Radical Worker in Tsarist Russia: The Autobiography of Semën Ivanovich Kanatchikov*. Stanford, CA: Stanford University Press, 1986.

Kaplow, Jeffry, ed. *New Perspectives on the French Revolution: Readings in Historical Sociology.* New York: John Wiley & Sons, 1965.

Karlinsky, Simon. "Died and Survived." Review of *Selected Poems*, by Alexander Blok. *New York Times*, May 9, 1982. www.nytimes.com/1982/05/09/books/died-and-survived .html?pagewanted=all.

Katznelson, Ira, and Aristide R. Zolberg, eds. *Working-Class Formation: Nineteenth-Century Patterns in Western Europe and the United States.* Princeton, NJ: Princeton University Press, 1986.

Kazin, Alfred. *New York Jew.* New York: Vintage Books, 1979.

———. *Starting Out in the Thirties.* Boston: Little, Brown, 1965.

Keep, John L. H., ed. *The Debate on Soviet Power: Minutes of the All-Russian Central Executive Committee of Soviets, October 1917–January 1918.* Oxford: Clarendon Press, 1979.

Kenez, Peter. *The Birth of the Propaganda State: Soviet Methods of Mass Mobilization, 1917–1929.* Cambridge: Cambridge University Press, 1985.

Kennan, George F. *Russia and the West under Lenin and Stalin.* Boston: Little, Brown, 1961.

Kerblay, Basile. "A. V. Chayanov: Life, Career, Works." In *The Theory of Peasant Economy*, by A. V. Chayanov, xxv–lxxv. Madison: University of Wisconsin Press, 1986.

Kerensky, Alexander. *Russia and History's Turning Point.* New York: Duell, Sloan and Pearce, 1965.

Khlevniuk, Oleg V. *The History of the Gulag: From Collectivization to the Great Terror.* New Haven, CT: Yale University Press, 2004.

Kingston-Mann, Esther. *Lenin and the Problem of Marxist Peasant Revolution.* New York: Oxford University Press, 1983.

Kingston-Mann, Esther, and Timothy Mixter, eds. *Peasant Economy, Culture and Politics of European Russia, 1800–1921.* Princeton, NJ: Princeton University Press, 1991.

Kir'ianov, Iu. I. "On the Nature of the Russian Working Class." *Soviet Studies in History* 22, no. 3 (1983): 8–60.

Kochan, Lionel. *The Making of Modern Russia.* Harmondsworth, UK: Penguin Books, 1971.

Koenker, Diane. *Moscow Workers and the 1917 Revolution.* Princeton, NJ: Princeton University Press, 1981.

Koenker, Diane, William Rosenberg, and Ronald Grigor Suny, eds. *Party, State, and Society in the Russian Civil War: Explorations in Social History.* Bloomington: Indiana University Press, 1989.

Kohn, Hans. *Living in a World Revolution: My Encounters with History.* New York: Pocket Books, 1965.

Kollontai, Alexandra. *Selected Writings.* New York: W. W. Norton, 1980.

Krausz, Tamás. *Reconstructing Lenin: An Intellectual Biography.* New York: Monthly Review Press, 2015.

Kravchenko, Victor. *I Chose Freedom: The Personal and Political Life of a Soviet Official.* New York: Charles Scribner's Sons, 1946.

Krupskaya, N. K. *Reminiscences of Lenin.* New York: International Publishers, 1970.

Kunitz, Joshua. "Men and Women in Soviet Literature." In *Voices of October: Art and Literature in Soviet Russia*, by Joseph Freeman, Joshua Kunitz, and Louis Lozowick, 66–173. New York: Vanguard Press, 1930.

————. *Russia: The Giant That Came Last.* New York: Dodd, Mead, 1947.

Kuusinen, O. W. "Under the Leadership of Russia." *Communist International*, no. 1 (1924): 132–46.

La Feber, Walter. *America, Russia, and the Cold War, 1945–1980.* New York: John Wiley & Sons, 1980.

Lapidus, Gail Warshofsky. "Educational Strategies and Cultural Revolution: The Politics of Soviet Development." In *Cultural Revolution in Russia, 1928–1931,* edited by Sheila Fitzpatrick, 78–104. Bloomington: Indiana University Press, 1978.

————. *Women in Soviet Society: Equality, Development, and Social Change.* Berkeley: University of California Press, 1978.

Lasch, Christopher. *The Agony of the American Left.* New York: Vintage Books, 1969.

Laski, Harold J. *Introduction to Politics.* London: George Allen and Unwin, 1962.

Le Blanc, Paul. "Bolshevism and Revolutionary Democracy." *New Politics,* Winter 2009.

————. *From Marx to Gramsci: A Reader in Revolutionary Marxist Politics.* Chicago: Haymarket Books, 2016.

————. "Ideology and Revolution." *Monthly Review,* December 1971.

————. *Lenin and the Revolutionary Party.* Atlantic Highlands, NJ: Humanities Press, 1989. New ed. Chicago: Haymarket Books, 2015. Page references are to the Haymarket edition.

————. "Lenin Studies: Method and Organization," *Historical Materialism* (forthcoming 2017).

————. *Leon Trotsky.* London: Reaktion Books, 2015.

————. *Marx, Lenin, and the Revolutionary Experience: Explorations in Communism and Radicalism in the Age of Globalization.* New York: Routledge, 2006.

————. "Reflections on the Meaning of Stalinism." *Crisis and Critique,* 3, no. 1 (2016). http://crisiscritique.org/ccmarch/blanc.pdf.

————. *Revolutionary Studies.* Chicago: Haymarket Books (forthcoming 2017).

————. "Uneven and Combined Development and the Sweep of History." *International Viewpoint,* September 21, 2006. http://www.internationalviewpoint.org/spip.php?article1125.

————. *Unfinished Leninism: The Rise and Return of a Revolutionary Doctrine.* Chicago: Haymarket Books, 2014.

————. "Workers and Revolution: A Comparative Study of Bolshevik Russia and Sandinist Nicaragua." PhD. diss. University of Pittsburgh, 1989. Ann Arbor, MI: University Microfilms International, 1990.

————, Dianne Feeley, and Thomas Twiss. *Leon Trotsky and the Organizational Principles of the Revolutionary Party.* Chicago: Haymarket Books, 2014.

Lefebvre, Georges. *The French Revolution.* 2 vols. New York: Columbia University Press, 1962.

Lefebvre, Henri. *Dialectical Materialism.* London: Jonathan Cape, 1968.

Leggett, George. *The Cheka: Lenin's Political Police.* Oxford: Clarendon Press, 1986.

Lenin, V. I. *Collected Works.* 45 vols. Moscow: Progress Publishers, 1960–70.

————. *The Development of Capitalism in Russia.* Moscow: Progress Publishers, 1967.

————. *On Culture and Cultural Revolution.* Honolulu, HI: University Press of the Pacific, 2001.

————. *On Trade Unions.* Moscow: Progress Publishers, 1970.

————. *On Workers' Control and the Nationalization of Industry.* Moscow: Progress Publishers, 1970.

————. *Revolution, Democracy, Socialism: Selected Writings.* Edited by Paul Le Blanc. London: Pluto Press, 2008.

————. *Selected Works.* 3 vols. New York: International Publishers, 1967.

Lenoe, Matthew E. *The Kirov Murder and Soviet History.* New Haven, CT: Yale University Press, 2010.

Levin, Dan. *Stormy Petrel: The Life and Work of Maxim Gorky.* New York: Appleton-Century, 1965.

Levin, Jr., N. Gordon. *Woodrow Wilson and World Politics: America's Response to War and Revolution.* New York: Oxford University Press, 1973.

Levine, Bruce. *The Fall of the House of Dixie: The Civil War and the Revolution That Transformed the South.* New York: Random House, 2013

————. *Half Slave and Half Free: The Roots of the Civil War.* New York: Hill and Wang, 2005.

Levine, Isaac Don. *Eyewitness to History: Memoirs and Reflections of a Foreign Correspondent for Half a Century.* New York: Hawthorn Books, 1973.

————. *The Man Lenin.* New York: Thomas Seltzer, 1924.

————. *The Russian Revolution.* New York: Harper and Brothers, 1917.

Leviné-Meyer, Rosa. *Inside German Communism: Memoirs of Party Life in the Weimar Republic.* London: Pluto Press, 1977.

Lewin, Moshe. *Lenin's Last Struggle.* New York: Vintage Books, 1970.

————. *The Making of the Soviet System: Essays in the Social History of Interwar Russia.* New York: The New Press, 1994.

————. *Russian Peasants and Soviet Power: A Study of Collectivization.* New York: W. W. Norton, 1975.

————. *Russia/USSR/Russia: The Drive and Drift of a Superstate.* New York: The New Press, 1995

————. *The Soviet Century.* London: Verso, 2005.

Liberman, Simon. *Building Lenin's Russia.* Chicago: University of Chicago Press, 1945.

Lichtheim, George. *Collected Essays.* New York: Viking Press, 1974.

————. *Marxism: An Historical and Critical Study.* New York: Frederick A. Praeger, 1961.

Liebich, André. *From the Other Shore: Russian Social Democracy after 1921.* Cambridge, MA: Harvard University Press, 1997.

Liebman, Marcel. *Leninism under Lenin.* London: Merlin Press, 1980.

Lieven, Dominic. *The End of Tsarist Russia: The March to World War I and Revolution.* New York: Penguin Books, 2016.

Lih, Lars T. *Bread and Authority in Russia, 1914–1921.* Berkeley: University of California Press, 1990.

————. "The Fortunes of a Formula: From DEMOCRATIC Centralism to Democratic CENTRALISM." *Links: Journal of Socialist Renewal*, April 14, 2013. http://links.org.au/node/3300.

————. "The Ironic Triumph of Old Bolshevism: The Debates of 1917 in Context." *Russian History* 38, no. 2 (2011): 199–242.

————. "Kautsky When He Was a Marxist" (2011), www.historicalmaterialism.org

/journal/online-articles/kautsky-as-marxist-data-base.

———. *Lenin.* London: Reaktion Books, 2011.

———. *Lenin Rediscovered: What Is to Be Done? in Context.* Chicago: Haymarket Books, 2008.

———. "Zinoviev: Populist Leninist." In *Martov and Zinoviev: Head to Head in Halle,* edited by Ben Lewis and Lars Lih, 39–60. London: November Publications, 2011.

Lincoln, W. Bruce. *Between Heaven and Hell: The Story of a Thousand Years of Artistic Life in Russia.* New York: Viking, 1998.

———. *In War's Dark Shadow.* New York: Simon and Schuster, 1983.

———. *Passage through Armageddon.* New York: Simon and Schuster, 1986.

———. *Red Victory.* New York: Simon and Schuster, 1989.

Lissagary, Prosper O. *The History of the Commune of 1871.* New York: Monthly Review Press, 1967.

Lockhart, R. H. Bruce. *British Agent.* New York: G. P. Putnam's Sons, 1933.

Longley, D. A. "The Division in the Bolshevik Party in March 1917." *Soviet Studies* 24, no. 1 (1972): 61–76.

Losurdo, Domenico. *War and Revolution: Rethinking the Twentieth Century.* London: Verso, 2015.

Lovell, Stephen. *The Soviet Union: A Very Short Introduction.* Oxford: Oxford University Press, 2009.

Lovestone, Jay. "Testimony of Jay Lovestone before House Un-American Activities Committee." In *The "American Exceptionalism" of Jay Lovestone and His Comrades, 1929–1940,* edited by Paul Le Blanc and Tim Davenport, 605–65. Leiden, Netherlands: Brill, 2015.

Löwy, Michael. *On Changing the World: Essays in Political Philosophy, from Karl Marx to Walter Benjamin.* Chicago: Haymarket Books, 2013. See esp. chap. 3, "Marxism and Religion."

———. *The Politics of Combined and Uneven Development: The Theory of Permanent Revolution.* London: Verso, 1981.

Lunacharsky, Anatoly. *Revolutionary Silhouettes.* New York: Hill and Wang, 1968.

Luxemburg, Rosa. *The Accumulation of Capital.* In *The Complete Works of Rosa Luxemburg,* vol. 2, *Economic Writings 2,* edited by Peter Hudis and Paul Le Blanc, 1–342. London: Verso, 2015.

———. *Rosa Luxemburg Speaks.* Edited by Mary-Alice Waters. New York: Pathfinder Press, 1970.

———. *Socialism or Barbarism: The Selected Writings of Rosa Luxemburg.* Edited by Paul Le Blanc and Helen C. Scott. London: Pluto Press, 2010. See esp. chap. 2, "The French Revolution," and chap. 16, "The Russian Revolution."

Lyashchenko, Peter I. *History of the National Economy of Russia to the 1917 Revolution.* New York: Macmillan, 1949.

Lyons, Eugene. *Assignment in Utopia.* New York: Harcourt, Brace, 1937.

———. *The Red Decade: The Stalinist Penetration of America.* Indianapolis: Bobbs-Merrill, 1941.

Macpherson, C. B. *Democratic Theory: Essays in Retrieval.* Oxford: Clarendon Press, 1973.

Magdoff, Harry. *Imperialism: From the Colonial Age to the Present.* New York: Monthly Review Press, 1978.

Makhno, Nestor. *The Struggle against the State and Other Essays.* San Francisco: AK Press, 1996.

Malia, Martin. *The Soviet Tragedy: A History of Socialism in Russia 1917–1991*. New York: Free Press, 1995.

Malle, Silvana. *The Economic Organization of War Communism, 1918–1921*. Cambridge: Cambridge University Press, 1985.

Malloy, James M., and Mitchell A. Seligson, eds. *Authoritarians and Democrats: Regime Transition in Latin America*. Pittsburgh: University of Pittsburgh Press, 1987. See esp. chaps. 1 and 8, "Democratization in Latin America: The Current Cycle," and "Development, Democratization, and Decay: Central America at the Crossroads."

Mandel, David. *The Petrograd Workers and the Fall of the Old Regime*. New York: St. Martin's Press, 1983.

———. *The Petrograd Workers and the Soviet Seizure of Power*. New York: St. Martin's Press, 1984.

Mandel, Ernest. "The Gulag Archipelago: Solzhenitsyn's Attack on Stalinism and the October Revolution." *Inprecor*, May 9, 1974. www.marxists.org/archive /mandel/1974/05/solzhenitsyn-gulag.html.

———. "History Advances over Skepticism." *International Viewpoint*, June 2, 1986.

———. *The Place of Marxism in History*. Montreuil, France: International Institute for Research and Education, 1986.

———. *Power and Money: A Marxist Theory of Bureaucracy*. London: Verso, 1992.

Mandel, Ernest, David Mandel, Leon Trotsky, Rosa Luxemburg, V. I. Lenin, and Paul Le Blanc. *October 1917: Workers in Power*. Edited by Fred Leplat and Alex de Jong. London: Merlin Books, 2016.

Mandel, Ernest, and George Novack. *The Revolutionary Potential of the Working Class*. New York: Pathfinder Press, 1974.

Manning, Roberta Thompson. *The Crisis of the Old Order in Russia, Gentry and Government*. Princeton, NJ: Princeton University Press, 1982.

Marcuse, Herbert. *Reason and Revolution: Hegel and the Rise of Social Theory*. Boston: Beacon Press, 1960.

Marik, Soma. *Reinterrogating the Classical Marxist Discourses of Revolutionary Democracy*. Delhi: Aakar Books, 2008.

Marot, John Eric. *The October Revolution in Prospect and Retrospect: Interventions in Russian and Soviet History*. Chicago: Haymarket Books, 2013.

Marx, Karl. *Capital*, vol. 1. New York: Vintage Books, 1977.

———. *Political Writings*, vol. 1, *The Revolutions of 1848*. Edited by David Fernbach. London: Penguin Books, 1973.

Marx, Karl, and Frederick Engels. *On Colonialism*. New York: International Publishers, 1972.

———. *Selected Works*. 3 vols. Moscow: Progress Publishers, 1973.

Marzani, Carl. *The Education of a Reluctant Radical*, book 2, *Growing Up American*. New York: Topical Books, 1993.

Mason, Edward S. *The Paris Commune*. New York: Macmillan, 1930.

Mason, Paul. *Live Working or Die Fighting: How the Working Class Went Global*. Chicago: Haymarket Books, 2010.

Matgamna, Sean, ed. *The Fate of the Russian Revolution: Lost Texts of Critical Marxism*. London: Phoenix Press, 1998.

Mathiez, Albert. "Bolshevism and Jacobinism." *Dissent* 2, no. 1 (1955).

———. *The French Revolution.* London: Williams and Norgate, 1927.

Mawdsley, Evan. *The Russian Civil War.* Boston: Unwin & Allen, 1987.

Mayer, Arno J. *The Furies: Violence and Terror in the French and Russian Revolutions.* Princeton, NJ: Princeton University Press, 2000.

———. *Politics and Diplomacy of Peacemaking: Containment and Counterrevolution at Versailles, 1918–1919.* New York: Alfred A. Knopf, 1967.

———. *Why Did the Heavens Not Darken? The "Final Solution" in History.* New York: Pantheon Books, 1988.

———. *Wilson vs. Lenin: Political Origins of the New Diplomacy, 1917–1918.* New York: Median Books, 1964.

Maynard, Sir John. *Russia in Flux: Before the October Revolution.* New York: Collier Books, 1962.

Mayo, Henry B. *An Introduction to Democratic Theory.* New York: Oxford University Press, 1960.

Mazour, Anatole G. *Soviet Economic Development: Operation Outstrip, 1921–1965.* New York: D. Van Nostrand, 1967.

———. *The Writing of History in the Soviet Union.* Stanford, CA: Hoover Institution Press, 1971.

McAuley, Mary. "Party and Society in Petrograd during the Civil War." *SBONIK: Study Group on the Russian Revolution,* no. 10 (1984): 43–51.

McCall, Leslie. "The Complexity of Intersectionality." *Signs* 30, no. 3 (2005): 1771–1800.

McDaniel, Tim. *Autocracy, Capitalism and Revolution in Russia.* Berkeley: University of California Press, 1988.

McDermid, Jane, and Anna Hillyar. *Midwives of the Revolution: Female Bolsheviks and Women Workers in 1917.* Athens: University of Ohio Press, 1999.

McNeal, Robert H. *Bride of the Revolution: Krupskaya and Lenin.* London: Victor Gollancz, 1973.

McPherson, James M. *Abraham Lincoln and the Second American Revolution.* New York: Oxford University Press, 1992

———. *Battle Cry of Freedom: The Civil War Era.* New York: Oxford University Press, 2003.

Medvedev, Roy. *Let History Judge: The Origins and Consequences of Stalinism.* New York: Columbia University Press, 1989.

———. *The October Revolution.* New York: Columbia University Press, 1979.

Meiksins, Peter. "Beyond the Boundary Question: The Sociology of Class Politics." *New Left Review,* no. 157 (1986): 101–20.

———. "New Middle Class or Working Class?," *Against the Current,* Winter 1984.

Melancon, Michael. *Rethinking Russia's February Revolution: Anonymous Spontaneity or Socialist Agency?* The Carl Beck Papers in Russian and East European Students, no. 1408. Pittsburgh: University Center for International Studies, University of Pittsburgh, 2000.

———. *The Socialist Revolutionaries and the Russian Anti-War Movement, 1914–1917.* Columbus: Ohio State University Press, 1990.

Merli, Frank J., and Theodore A. Wilson, eds. *Makers of American Diplomacy: From Theodore Roosevelt to Henry Kissinger.* New York: Charles Scribner's Sons, 1974.

Meszaros, Istvan. *Philosophy, Ideology and Social Science.* New York: St. Martin's Press, 1986.

Meyer, Alfred G. *Leninism.* New York: Frederick A. Praeger, 1962.

Michel, Louise. *The Red Virgin: Memoirs of Louise Michel.* Tuscaloosa, AL: University of Alabama Press, 1981.

Middlebrook, Kevin J., and Carlos Rico, eds. *The United States and Latin America in the 1980s: Contending Perspectives on a Decade of Crisis.* Pittsburgh: University of Pittsburgh Press, 1986. See esp. essays by Howard J. Wiarda, Guillermo O'Donnell, Rafael Braun, Margaret E. Crahan, Giuseppe Di Palma, and Edelberto Torres-Rivas.

Miliband, Ralph. *Marxism and Politics.* Oxford: Oxford University Press, 1977.

Miliukov, Paul N. *Russia Today and Tomorrow.* London: Macmillan, 1922.

Miller, Martin A. "Anarchists in the State: New Perspectives on Russian Anarchist Participation in the Bolshevik Government, 1917–1919." *Anarchist Studies* 20, no. 2 (2012): 48–54.

Mills, C. Wright. *The Marxists.* New York: Dell Publishing, 1962.

Montgomery, David. *Beyond Equality: Labor and the Radical Republicans, 1862–1872.* New York: Alfred A. Knopf, 1967.

Morgan, Kenneth O. *Keir Hardie: Radical and Socialist.* London: Weidenfeld & Nicholson, 1997.

Morrison, Walter, ed. *The Collected Stories of Isaac Babel.* New York: World Publishing, 1960.

Mstislavskii, Sergei. *Five Days Which Transformed Russia.* Bloomington: University of Indiana Press, 1988.

Munck, Jørgen Larsen. *The Kornilov Revolt: A Critical Examination of Sources and Research.* Aarhus, Denmark: Aarhus University, 1987.

Murphy, Kevin. *Revolution and Counterrevolution: Class Struggle in a Moscow Metal Factory.* Chicago: Haymarket Books, 2007.

Nash, Gary B. *The Urban Crucible: Social Change, Political Consciousness, and the Origins of the American Revolution.* Cambridge, MA: Harvard University Press, 1979.

Nash, Gary B., Billy G. Smith, and Dirk Hoerder. "Laboring Americans and the American Revolution." *Labor History* 24, no. 3 (1983): 418–35.

Nash, George H. *The Conservative Intellectual Movement in America since 1945.* New York: Basic Books, 1976.

Nation, R. Craig. *Lenin, the Zimmerwald Left, and the Origins of the Communist International.* Chicago: Haymarket Books, 2009.

Nearing, Scott, and Jack Hardy. *The Economic Organization of the Soviet Union.* New York: Vanguard Press, 1928.

Nettl, J. P. *Rosa Luxemburg.* 2 vols. London: Oxford University Press, 1966.

———. *The Soviet Achievement.* New York: Harcourt, Brace and World, 1967.

Nimtz, August H. *Lenin's Electoral Strategy from Marx and Engels through the Revolution of 1905: The Ballot, the Streets—or Both.* New York: Palgrave Macmillan, 2014.

———. *Lenin's Electoral Strategy from 1907 to the October Revolution of 1917: The Ballot, the Streets—or Both.* New York: Palgrave Macmillan, 2014.

Nomad, Max. *Dreamers, Dynamiters and Demagogues.* New York: Waldon Press, 1964.

———. "Is There a Socialism from Below?" *New Politics* 5, no. 2 (Spring 1966): 94–100.

Novack, George. *Democracy and Revolution.* New York: Pathfinder Press, 1971.

Nove, Alec. *An Economic History of the USSR.* Harmondsworth, UK: Penguin Books, 1982.

Occleshaw, Michael. *Dances in Deep Shadows: The Clandestine War in Russia, 1917–20.* New York: Carroll and Graf, 2006.

Olgin, Moissaye J. *The Soul of the Russian Revolution*. New York: Henry Holt, 1917.

Orlovsky, Daniel. "The Lower Middle Strata in 1917." In *Critical Companion to the Russian Revolution*, edited by Edward Acton, Vladimir Iu. Cherniaev, and William G. Rosenberg, 529–33. Bloomington: Indiana University Press, 1997.

Osipova, Taisia. "Peasant Rebellions: Origin, Scope, Dynamics, and Consequences." In *The Bolsheviks in Russian Society: The Revolution and the Civil Wars*, edited by Vladimir N. Brovkin, 154–76. New Haven CT: Yale University Press, 1997.

Owen, A. L. Riesch, ed. *Selig Perlman's Lectures on Capitalism and Socialism*. Madison: University of Wisconsin Press, 1976.

Owen, Thomas C. *Capitalism and Politics in Russia: A Social History of the Moscow Merchants, 1855–1905*. Cambridge: Cambridge University Press, 1981.

Pankhurst, Sylvia. *Soviet Russia as I Saw It*. London: The "Workers' Dreadnought" Publishers, 1921.

Pells, Richard H. *The Liberal Mind in a Conservative Age: American Intellectuals in the 1940s and 1950s*. New York: Harper & Row, 1985.

Pelz, William A. *A People's History of Modern Europe*. London: Pluto Press, 2016.

Perlman, Selig. Review of *Marxism: Is It Science?*, by Max Eastman." *The American Political Science Review*, October 1941.

———. *A Theory of the Labor Movement*. New York: Macmillan, 1928.

Perrie, Maureen. "The Social Composition and Structure of the Socialist-Revolutionary Party before 1917." *Soviet Studies* 24, no. 2 (1972): 223–50.

Piatnitsky, O. *Memoirs of a Bolshevik*. New York: International Publishers, 1930.

Pipes, Richard. *Alexander Yakovlev: The Man Whose Ideas Delivered Russia from Communism*. DeKalb: Northern Illinois University Press, 2015.

———. *Communism: A History*. New York: Random House, 2003.

———, ed. *Revolutionary Russia: A Symposium*. Garden City, NY: Anchor Books, 1969.

———. *The Russian Revolution*. New York: Alfred A. Knopf, 1990.

———. *Struve: Liberal on the Right, 1905–1944*. Cambridge, MA: Harvard University Press, 1980.

———, ed. *The Unknown Lenin*. New Haven, CT: Yale University Press, 1996.

Pirani, Simon. *The Russian Revolution in Retreat, 1920–1924: Soviet Workers and the New Communist Elite*. London: Routledge, 2008.

Pisarev, I. *Population of the USSR*. Moscow: Progress Publishers, 1962.

Pokrovskii, M. N. *Russia in World History: Selected Essays*. Ann Arbor, MI: University of Michigan Press, 1970.

Polonsky, Vyacheslav. "Lenin's Views on Art and Culture." Reproduced in *Artists in Uniform: A Study of Literature and Bureaucratism*, by Max Eastman, 217–52. New York: Octagon Books, 1972.

Polunov, Alexander. *Russia in the Nineteenth Century: Autocracy, Reform, and Social Change, 1814–1914*. Armonk, NY: M. E. Sharpe, 2005.

Popov, N. *Outline History of the Communist Party of the Soviet Union*. Moscow-Leningrad: Cooperative Publishing Society of Foreign Workers in the USSR, 1934.

Poretsky, Elisabeth. *Our Own People: A Memoir of 'Ignace Reiss' and His Friends*. Ann Arbor, MI: University of Michigan Press, 1970.

Porter, Cathy. *Alexandra Kollontai: A Biography*. Updated edition. Chicago: Haymarket Books, 2014.

Preobrazhensky, E. A. *The Crisis of Soviet Industrialization: Selected Essays*. Edited by Donald A. Filtzer. Armonk, NY: M. E. Sharpe, 1979.

Priestland, David. *The Red Flag: A History of Communism*. New York: Grove Press, 2009.

Purcell, A. A., et al. (Trades Union Congress General Council Delegates). *Russia Today: The Official Report of the British Trade Union Delegation*. New York: International Publishers, 1925.

Rabinowitch, Alexander. *The Bolsheviks Come to Power: The Revolution of 1917 in Petrograd*. New York: W. W. Norton, 1976.

———. *The Bolsheviks in Power: The First Year of Soviet Rule in Petrograd*. Bloomington: University of Indiana Press, 2007.

Rabinowitch, Alexander, and Janet Rabinowitch, with Ladis K. D. Kristof, eds. *Revolution and Politics in Russia: Essays in Memory of B. I. Nicolaevsky*. Bloomington: Indiana University Press, 1972.

Radek, Karl. *Proletarian Dictatorship and Terrorism*. Detroit: The Marxian Educational Society, 1921.

Radkey, Oliver H. *The Agrarian Foes of Bolshevism*. New York: Columbia University Press, 1958.

———. *The Sickle under the Hammer: The Russian Socialist Revolutionaries in the Early Month of Soviet Rule*. New York: Columbia University Press, 1963.

Radosh, Ronald. *American Labor and United States Foreign Policy*. New York: Random House, 1969.

Rakovsky, Christian. *Selected Writings on Opposition in the USSR, 1923–1930*. London: Allison and Busby, 1980.

Ransome, Arthur. *The Crisis in Russia*. New York: B. W. Huebsch, 1921.

———. *Russia in 1919*. New York: B. W. Huebsch, 1919.

Raskolnikov, F. F. *Kronstadt and Petrograd in 1917*. London: New Park, 1982.

Read, Christopher. *From Tsar to Soviets: The Russian People and Their Revolution, 1917–21*. New York: Oxford University Press, 1996.

Reavey, George, and Marc Slonim, eds. *Soviet Literature: An Anthology*. New York: Covici-Friede, 1934.

Reed, John. *Ten Days That Shook the World*. New York: International Publishers, 1926.

Rees, John. *The Algebra of Revolution: The Dialectic and the Classical Marxist Tradition*. London: Routledge, 1998.

Rees, John, with Robert Service, Sam Farber, and Robin Blackburn. *In Defence of October: A Debate on the Russian Revolution*. London: Bookmarks, 1997.

Regler, Gustav. *The Owl of Minerva*. New York: Farrar, Straus, and Cudahy, 1960.

Reiman, Michal. *The Birth of Stalinism: The USSR on the Eve of the "Second Revolution."* Bloomington: Indiana University Press, 1987.

Reswick, William. *I Dreamt Revolution*. Chicago: Henry Regnery, 1952.

Riazanov, David. *Karl Marx and Friedrich Engels: An Introduction to Their Lives and Work*. New York: Monthly Review Press, 1973.

Riddell, John, ed. *Founding the Communist International: Proceedings and Documents of the First Congress, March 1919*. New York: Pathfinder Press, 1987.

————, ed. *Lenin's Struggle for a Revolutionary International, Documents: 1907–1916, the Preparatory Years.* New York: Monad/Pathfinder, 1984.

————, ed. *To the Masses: Proceedings of the Third Congress of the Communist International, 1921.* Chicago: Haymarket Books, 2016.

————, ed. *Toward the United Front: Proceedings of the Fourth Congress of the Communist International, 1922.* Chicago: Haymarket Books, 2013.

————, ed. *Workers of the World and Oppressed Peoples, Unite! Proceedings and Documents of the Second Congress, 1920.* 2 vols. New York: Pathfinder Press, 1991.

Riga, Liliana. *The Bolsheviks and the Russian Empire.* New York: Cambridge University Press, 2012.

Rigby, T. H. *Lenin's Government: Sovnarkom, 1917–1922.* Cambridge: Cambridge University, Press, 1979.

Robertson, Ann. *Marxism's Lessons for Today.* San Francisco: Socialist Action, 1987.

Rochester, Anna. *Lenin on the Agrarian Question.* New York: International Publishers, 1942.

Rogovin, Vadim Z. *1937: Stalin's Year of Terror.* Oak Park, MI: Mehring Books, 1998.

————. *Stalin's Terror of 1937–1938: Political Genocide in the USSR.* Oak Park, MI: Mehring Books, 2009.

Roper, Brian S. *The History of Democracy: A Marxist Interpretation.* London: Pluto Press, 2013.

Rosenberg, William G., ed. *Bolshevik Visions: First Phase of the Cultural Revolution in Soviet Russia.* Ann Arbor, MI: Ardis, 1984.

Rosenstone, Robert A. *Romantic Revolutionary: A Biography of John Reed.* Cambridge, MA: Harvard University Press, 1990.

Rosmer, Alfred. *Moscow under Lenin.* New York: Monthly Review Press, 1972.

Ross, Edward Alsworth. *The Bolshevik Russian Revolution.* New York: The Century, 1921.

————. *Russia in Upheaval.* New York: The Century, 1918.

————. *The Russian Soviet Republic.* New York: The Century, 1923.

Rostow, W. W. *The Dynamics of Soviet Society.* New York: New American Library, 1958.

————. *The Stages of Economic Growth: A Non-Communist Manifesto.* 2nd ed. Cambridge: Cambridge University Press, 1971.

————. *The United States in the World Arena: An Essay in Recent History.* New York: Harper & Row, 1960.

————. *The World Economy: History and Prospect.* Austin: University of Texas Press, 1980.

Rousset, David. *The Legacy of the Bolshevik Revolution.* New York: St. Martin's Press, 1982.

Roy, M. N. *Selected Works of M. N. Roy,* vol. 1, *1917–1922.* Edited by Sibnarayan Ray. Delhi: Oxford University Press, 1987.

Ruckman, Jo Ann. *The Moscow Business Elite: A Social and Cultural Portrait of Two Generations, 1840–1905.* DeKalb: Northern Illinois University Press, 1984.

Rudé, George. *The French Revolution.* New York: Weidenfeld & Nicolson, 1988.

————. *Ideology and Popular Protest.* New York: Pantheon Books, 1980.

Rueschemeyer, Dietrich, Evelyne Huber Stephens, and John D. Stephens. *Capitalist Development and Democracy.* Chicago: University of Chicago Press, 1992.

Rühle, Jürgen. *Literature and Revolution: A Critical Study of the Writer and Communism in the Twentieth Century.* New York: Frederick A. Praeger, 1969.

Russell, Bertrand. *The Practice and Theory of Bolshevism.* London: George Allen and Unwin,

1954.

Rzhevsky, Nicholas, ed. *The Cambridge Companion to Modern Russian Culture.* Cambridge: Cambridge University Press, 1998.

Salisbury, Harrison E. *Black Night, White Snow: Russia's Revolutions 1905–1917.* New York: De Capo Press, 1977.

Sandburg, Carl. *The People, Yes.* New York: Harcourt, Brace & World, 1936.

Schama, Simon. *Citizens: A Chronicle of the French Revolution.* New York: Alfred A. Knopf, 1989.

Schapiro, Leonard. *The Communist Party of the Soviet Union.* New York: Vintage Books, 1960.

Schumpeter, Joseph A. *Capitalism, Socialism and Democracy.* 3rd ed. New York: Harper & Row, 1962.

Schwarz, Solomon. *The Russian Revolution of 1905: The Workers' Movement and the Formation of Bolshevism and Menshevism.* Chicago: University of Chicago Press, 1967.

Seldes, George. *You Can't Print That! The Truth behind the News, 1918–1929.* New York: Payson and Clarke, 1929.

Senn, Alfred. *The Russian Revolution in Switzerland: 1914–1917.* Madison: University of Wisconsin Press, 1971.

Serge, Victor. *Conquered City.* New York: New York Review of Books, 2011.

———. *From Lenin to Stalin.* New York: Monad/Pathfinder Press, 1980

———. *Memoirs of a Revolutionary.* New York: New York Review of Books, 2012.

———. *Revolution in Danger: Writings from Russia, 1919–1921.* London: Red Words, 1997.

———. *Russia Twenty Years After.* Atlantic Highlands, NJ: Humanities Press, 1996.

———. *Year One of the Russian Revolution.* Chicago: Holt, Rinehart and Winston, 1972.

———, and Natalia Sedova Trotsky. *The Life and Death of Leon Trotsky.* Chicago: Haymarket Books, 2015.

Service, Robert. *Lenin: A Biography.* Cambridge, MA: Harvard University Press, 2000.

———. *The Russian Revolution, 1900–1927.* London: Macmillan, 1986.

Seward, William H. "The Irrepressible Conflict" (speech). October 25, 1858. Transcript. https://archive.org/details/irrepressiblecon00insewa.

Shachtman, Max. "Revolution and Counter-revolution in Russia." *New International,* January 1938.

Shandro, Alan. *Lenin and the Logic of Hegemony: Political Practice and Theory in the Class Struggle.* Chicago: Haymarket Books, 2015.

Shanin, Teodor, ed. *Late Marx and the Russian Road: Marx and "the Peripheries of Capitalism."* New York: Monthly Review Press, 1983.

———, ed. *Peasants and Peasant Societies: Selected Readings.* Harmondsworth, UK: Penguin Books, 1971.

———. *The Roots of Otherness: Russia's Turn of the Century.* 2 vols. New Haven, CT: Yale University Press, 1985.

———. *Russia, 1905–07: Revolution as a Moment of Truth.* New Haven, CT: Yale University Press, 1986.

———. *Russia as a "Developing Society."* New Haven, CT: Yale University Press, 1986.

Sheridan, Clare. *Mayfair to Moscow—Clare Sheridan's Diary.* New York: Boni and Liveright, 1921.

Shlyapnikov, Alexander. *On the Eve of 1917.* London: Allison & Busby, 1982.

Sholokhov, Mikhail. *And Quiet Flows the Don.* New York: Vintage Books, 1989.

Shukman, Harold, ed. *The Blackwell Encyclopedia of the Russian Revolution.* Oxford: Basil Blackwell, 1988.

Siegelbaum, Lewis H. *Soviet and State Society between Revolutions, 1918–1929.* Cambridge: Cambridge University Press, 1992.

Siegelbaum, Lewis H., and Ronald Grigor Suny, eds. *Making Workers Soviet: Power, Class and Identity.* Ithaca, NY: Cornell University Press, 1994.

Simmons, Ernest J. "The Origins of Literary Control." *Survey,* April–June 1961.

Slonim, Marc. *Soviet Russian Literature: Writers and Problems, 1917–1977.* Oxford: Oxford University Press, 1977.

Smith, Jessica. *Women in Soviet Russia.* New York: Vanguard Press, 1928.

Smith, S. A. "'Moral Economy' and Peasant Revolution in Russia: 1861–1918." *Revolutionary Russia* 24, no. 2 (2011): 143–71.

———. *Red Petrograd: Revolution in the Factories, 1917–1918.* Cambridge: Cambridge University Press, 1986.

———. Review of *Revolution and Counterrevolution,* by Kevin Murphy. *Historical Materialism* 15, no. 4 (2007): 167–85.

———. *The Russian Revolution: A Very Short Introduction.* Oxford: Oxford University Press, 2002.

Snyder, Louis L. *The World in the Twentieth Century.* Princeton, NJ: Van Nostrand, 1964.

Soboul, Albert. *The French Revolution 1787–1799.* New York: Vintage Books, 1975.

———. *Understanding the French Revolution.* New York: International Publishers, 1988.

Solzhenitsyn, Alexander. *The Gulag Archipelago: An Experiment in Literary Investigation.* Abridged. New York: Harper Perennial, 2007.

Sorenson, Jay B. *The Life and Death of Soviet Trade Unionism.* New York: Atherton Press, 1969.

Souvarine, Boris. *Stalin: A Critical Survey of Bolshevism.* New York: Alliance Book Corporation, 1939.

Soviet Union. *50 Years, Statistical References.* Moscow: Progress Publishers, 1969.

Spargo, John. *Bolshevism: The Enemy of Political and Industrial Democracy.* New York: Harper and Brothers, 1919.

———. *Russia as an American Problem.* New York: Harper and Brothers, 1920.

Stalin, Joseph V. "Address to the Graduates of the Red Army Academies." In *Soviet Union 1935,* edited by A. Fineberg, 3–14. Moscow: Co-operative Publishing Society of Foreign Workers in the USSR, 1935.

———. *Collected Works.* 14 vols. Moscow: Foreign Languages Publishing House, 1954.

———. "Interview between J. V. Stalin and Roy Howard" (March 1, 1936). Marxist Internet Archive. www.marxists.org/reference/archive/stalin/works/1936/03/01.htm.

———. "Political Report to the 14th Congress of the CPSU(B)" (December 18, 1925). Marxist Internet Archive. www.marxists.org/reference/archive/stalin/works/1925/12/18.htm.

———. "Political Report to the 16th Congress of the CPSU(B)" (August 27, 1930). Marxist Internet Archive. www.marxists.org/reference/archive/stalin/works/1930/aug/27.htm.

———. *Problems of Leninism.* Peking: Foreign Languages Press, 1976.

Stampp, Kenneth M., and Leon F. Litwack, eds. *Reconstruction: An Anthology of Revisionist Writings*. Baton Rouge: Louisiana University Press, 1969.

Starr, S. Frederick. "Tsarist Government: The Imperial Dimension." In *Soviet Nationality Policies and Practices*, edited by Jeremy R. Azrael, 3–38. New York: Praeger Publishers, 1978.

Steinberg, Isaac. *Spiridonova: Revolutionary Terrorist*. Freeport, NY: Books for Libraries Press, 1971.

Steinberg, Julius, ed. *Verdict of Three Decades: From the Literature of Individual Revolt against Soviet Communism, 1917–1950*. New York: Duell, Sloan and Pearce, 1950.

Steinberg, Mark D. "Vanguard Workers and the Morality of Class." In *Making Workers Soviet: Power, Class and Identity*, edited by Lewis H. Siegelbaum and Ronald Grigor Suny, 66–84. Ithaca, NY: Cornell University Press, 1994.

———. *Voices of Revolution, 1917*. New Haven, CT: Yale University Press, 2001.

Steinfels, Peter. *The Neoconservatives: The Men Who Are Changing America's Politics*. New York: Simon & Schuster, 1979.

Stepniak [Sergey Mikhaylovich Stepnyak-Kravchinsky]. *Russia under the Tzars*. New York: Charles Scribner's Sons, 1885.

Stites, Richard. *The Women's Liberation Movement in Russia: Feminism, Nihilism, and Bolshevism, 1860–1930*. Princeton, NJ: Princeton University Press, 1978.

Stone, W. T. "Peaceful Coexistence." *Editorial Research Reports 1954*, vol. 2. Washington, DC: CQ Press. http://library.cqpress.com/cqresearcher/cqresrre1954112600.

Strong, Anna Louise. *I Change Worlds*. New York: Holt, Rinehart and Winston, 1935.

———. *The First Time in History: Two Years of Russia's New Life (August, 1921 to December, 1923)*. New York: Boni and Liveright, 1924.

Suhr, Gerald D. "Petersburg's First Mass Labor Organization: The Assembly of Russian Workers and Father Gapon." *Russian Review*, July 1981 and October 1981.

Sukhanov, N. N. *The Russian Revolution 1917: A Personal Record*. Princeton, NJ: Princeton University Press, 1984.

Suny, Ronald Grigor. "Nationalism and Class in the Russian Revolution: A Comparative Discussion." In *Revolution in Russia: Reassessments of 1917*, edited by Edith Rogovin Frankel, Jonathan Frankel, and Baruch Knei-Paz, 219–46. Cambridge: Cambridge University Press, 1992.

———. *The Soviet Experiment: Russia, the USSR, and the Successor States*. New York: Oxford University Press, 2010.

———. "Toward a Social History of the October Revolution." *American Historical Review* 88, no.1 (1983): 31–52.

Suny, Ronald Grigor, and Arthur Adams. *The Russian Revolution and Bolshevik Victory*. 3rd ed. Lexington, MA: D. C. Heath, 1990.

Swain, Geoffrey. *Russian Social Democracy and the Legal Labor Movement, 1906–1914*. London: Macmillan Press, 1983.

———. *Russia's Civil War*. Stroud, UK: History Press, 2008.

Sweezy, Paul M. *The Theory of Capitalist Development*. New York: Monthly Review Press, 1968.

Tarasov-Rodionov, Alexander. *Chocolate*. Garden City, NY: Doubleday Doran, 1932.

Tchernoff [Chernov], Olga. *New Horizons: Reminiscences of the Russian Revolution*. London:

Hutcheson, 1936.

Thatcher, Ian D. *Trotsky.* London: Routledge, 2003.

Thompson, E. P. *The Making of the English Working Class.* New York: Vintage Books, 1963.

Thompson, John M. *Revolutionary Russia, 1917.* New York: Charles Scribner's Sons, 1981.

Tillich, Paul. *Perspectives on 19th and 20th Century Protestant Theology.* New York: Harper & Row, 1967.

———. *The Socialist Decision.* New York: Harper & Row, 1977.

Tilly, Charles. *Democracy.* Cambridge: Cambridge University Press, 2007.

Timasheff, N. S. *The Great Retreat: The Growth and Decline of Communism in Russia.* New York: E. P. Dutton, 1946.

Timberlake, Charles E., ed. *Essays on Russian Liberalism.* Columbia: University of Missouri Press, 1972.

Trepper, Leopold. *The Great Game: The Memoirs of the Spy Hitler Couldn't Silence.* New York: McGraw-Hill, 1977.

Trotsky, Leon. *The Challenge of the Left Opposition, 1923–25.* New York: Pathfinder Press, 1975.

———. *The Challenge of the Left Opposition, 1928–29.* New York: Pathfinder Press, 1981.

———. *The First Five Years of the Communist International.* 2 vols. New York: Pathfinder Press, 1972.

——— [Trotzky]. *From October to Brest-Litovsk.* Brooklyn: Socialist Publication Society, 1919.

———. *The History of the Russian Revolution* (Three Volumes in One). New York: Simon & Schuster, 1936.

———. *How the Revolution Armed: The Military Writings and Speeches of Leon Trotsky.* 5 vols. London: New Park Publications, 1979–81.

———. *Leon Trotsky on the Paris Commune.* New York: Pathfinder Press, 1970.

———. *Leon Trotsky Speaks.* Edited by Sarah Lovell. New York: Pathfinder Press, 1972.

———. *My Life.* New York: Pathfinder Press, 1970.

———. *1905.* New York: Vintage Books, 1972.

———. *Permanent Revolution and Results and Prospects.* New York: Pathfinder Press, 1978.

———. *Portraits, Political and Personal.* New York: Pathfinder Press, 1977.

———. *The Revolution Betrayed.* Garden City, NY: Doubleday, Doran, and Co., 1937.

———. *Stalin.* New York: Stein & Day, 1967.

———. *The Stalin School of Falsification.* New York: Pathfinder Press, 1972.

———. *The Struggle against Fascism in Germany.* New York: Pathfinder Press, 1971.

———. *Terrorism and Communism.* Ann Arbor, MI: University of Michigan Press, 1961.

———. *The Third International after Lenin.* New York: Pathfinder Press, 1970.

———. *The Transitional Program for Socialist Revolution.* New York: Pathfinder Press, 1974.

———. *War and the International.* Ceylon: Young Socialist Publications, 1971.

———. *Writings of Leon Trotsky, 1929–1940.* 14 vols. Edited by George Breitman et al. New York: Pathfinder Press, 1973–79.

———. *The Young Lenin.* Garden City, NY: Doubleday, 1972.

Tucker, Robert C. *The Marxian Revolutionary Idea.* New York: W. W. Norton, 1969.

———. *Stalin as Revolutionary: 1879–1929.* New York: W. W. Norton & Company, 1988.

———. *Stalin in Power: The Revolution from Above, 1928–1941.* New York: W. W. Norton & Company, 1990.

Twiss, Thomas M. *Trotsky and the Problem of Soviet Bureaucracy.* Chicago: Haymarket Books, 2015.

Ulam, Adam B. *The Bolsheviks: The Intellectual, Personal, and Political History of the Origins of Russian Communism.* New York: Macmillan, 1965.

Van der Linden, Marcel. *Western Marxism and the Soviet Union: A Survey of Critical Theories and Debates since 1917.* Chicago: Haymarket Books, 2009.

Van Ree, Erik. "Lenin's Conception of Socialism in One Country, 1915–17." *Revolutionary Russia* 23, no. 2, (2010): 159–81.

———. *The Political Thought of Joseph Stalin: A Study in Twentieth-Century Revolutionary Patriotism.* London: Routledge Curzon, 2002.

Vidali, Vittorio. *Diary of the Twentieth Congress of the Communist Party of the Soviet Union.* Westport, CT: Lawrence Hill, 1984.

Volkogonov, Dmitri. *Lenin: A New Biography.* New York: Free Press, 1994.

Volobuev, P. V. "The Proletariat—Leader of the Socialist Revolution." *Soviet Studies in History* 22, no. 3 (1983): 61–82.

Voronsky, Aleksandr Konstantinovich. *Art as the Cognition of Life: Selected Writings, 1911–1936.* Detroit: Mehring Books, 1998.

Wade, Rex A. *Red Guards and Workers' Militias in the Russian Revolution.* Stanford, CA: Stanford University Press, 1984.

———. *The Russian Revolution, 1917.* Cambridge: Cambridge University Press, 2000.

Wald, Alan. *The New York Intellectuals: The Rise and Decline of the Anti-Stalinist Left from the 1930s to the 1980s.* Chapel Hill: University of North Carolina, 1987.

Wallace, Sir Donald MacKenzie. *Russia on the Eve of War and Revolution.* New York: Vintage Books, 1961.

Walling, William English. *Russia's Message: The People against the Czar.* New York: Adolf A. Knopf, 1917.

Waxman, Chaim I., ed. *The End of Ideology Debate.* New York: Funk and Wagnalls, 1968.

Wellenreuther, Hermann. "Labor in the Era of the American Revolution: A Discussion of Recent Concepts and Theories." *Labor History* 22, no. 4 (1981): 573–600.

Wells, H. G. *Russia in the Shadows.* New York: George H. Doran, 1921.

Westbrook, Robert B. *John Dewey and American Democracy.* Ithaca, NY: Cornell University Press, 1991.

Westwood, J. N. *Endurance and Endeavour: Russian History, 1812–1992.* Oxford: Oxford University Press, 1992.

Wheatcroft, Stephen. "Crises and the Condition of the Peasantry in Late Imperial Russia." In *Peasant Economy, Culture and Politics of European Russia, 1800–1921*, edited by Esther Kingston-Mann and Timothy Mixter, 128–72. Princeton, NJ: Princeton University Press, 1991.

Wiarda, Howard J. *Can Democracy Be Exported? The Quest for Democracy in U.S.-Latin American Policy.* Woodrow Wilson International Center for Scholars, Latin American Program, no. 157. Washington, DC: The Wilson Center, 1984.

Wildman, Allan K. *The Making of a Workers' Revolution: Russian Social Democracy, 1891–1903.* Chicago: University of Chicago Press, 1967.

Wilentz, Sean. *Chants Democratic: New York City and the Rise of the American Working Class,*

1788–1850. New York: Oxford University Press, 1986.

Williams, Albert Rhys. *Journey into Revolution: Petrograd, 1917–1918.* Chicago: Quadrangle Books, 1969.

———. *Lenin: The Man and His Work.* New York: Scott and Seltzer, 1919.

———. *The Russian Land.* New York: The New Republic, 1928.

———. *Through the Russian Revolution.* New York: Boni and Liveright, 1921.

Williams, Robert C. *The Other Bolsheviks: Lenin and His Critics, 1904–1914.* Bloomington: Indiana University Press, 1986.

Williams, William Appleman, *The Tragedy of American Diplomacy.* 2nd ed. New York: Dell Publishing, 1982.

Wilson, Edmund. *To the Finland Station: A Study in the Writing and Acting of History.* New York: Farrar, Straus and Giroux, 1972.

Wilson, Lucy L. W. *The New Schools of New Russia.* New York: Vanguard Press, 1928.

Wolf, Eric R. *Peasant Wars of the Twentieth Century.* New York: Harper & Row, 1973.

Wolfe, Bertram D. *The Bridge and the Abyss: The Troubled Friendship of Maxim Gorky and V. I. Lenin.* New York: Frederick A. Praeger, 1967.

———. *An Ideology in Power: Reflections on the Russian Revolution.* New York: Stein and Day, 1970.

———. *Lenin and the Twentieth Century: A Bertram D. Wolfe Retrospective.* Edited by Lennard D. Gerson. Stanford, CA: Hoover Institution, 1984.

———. *A Life in Two Centuries: An Autobiography.* New York: Stein and Day, 1981.

———. *Marxism: One Hundred Years in the Life of a Doctrine.* New York: Dell Publishing, 1967.

———. *Three Who Made a Revolution.* New York: The Dial Press, 1948.

Wollenberg, Erich. *The Red Army.* London: New Park Publications, 1978.

Wood, Alan. "The Revolution and Civil War in Siberia." In *Critical Companion to the Russian Revolution,* edited by Edward Acton, Vladimir Iu. Cherniaev, and William G. Rosenberg, 706–18. Bloomington: Indiana University Press, 1997.

Wood, Ellen Meiksins. *The Retreat from Class: A New "True" Socialism.* London: Verso, 1986.

Yakovlev, Alexander N. *A Century of Violence in Soviet Russia.* New Haven, CT: Yale University Press, 2002.

Yalom, Irvin D. *Staring at the Sun: Overcoming the Terror of Death.* San Francisco: Jossey-Bass, 2008.

Yarmolinsky, Avrahm. *The Jews and Other Minor Nationalities under the Soviets.* New York: Vanguard Press, 1928.

———. *Road to Revolution: A Century of Russian Radicalism.* New York: Collier Books, 1962.

Ypsilon [Karl Volk and Julian Gumperz]. *Pattern for World Revolution.* Chicago: Zeff-Davis Publishing, 1947.

Zavalishin, Vyacheslav. *Early Soviet Writers.* New York: Frederick A. Praeger, 1958.

Zelnik, Reginald E. "Russian Bebels: An Introduction to the Memoirs of the Russian Workers Semen Kanatchikov and Matvei Fischer." Parts 1–2. *Russian Review* 35, no. 3 (1976): 249–89; 35, no. 4 (1976): 417–47.

———. "Russian Workers and the Revolutionary Movement." *Journal of Social History* 6, no 2 (1972): 214–36.

———, ed. *Workers and Intelligentsia in Late Imperial Russia: Realities, Representations, Reflec-*

tions. Berkeley: International and Area Studies, University of California, 1999.

Zinoviev, Gregory. *History of the Bolshevik Party: A Popular Outline.* London: New Park Publications, 1973.

———. "Nikolai Lenin." *Communist International,* no. 1 (1924).

———. "The Social Roots of Opportunism" (1916), *New International* 8, nos. 2–5, March–June 1942, www.marxists.org/archive/zinoviev/works/1916/war/opp-index.htm.

NOTES

Preface

1. On labor, community, and freedom, see Easton and Guddat, *Writings of the Young Marx*, 275, 293, 394–395, 457. On the radical expansion of democracy and the free development of each and all, see Gasper, *The Communist Manifesto*, 69, 71. On Marx, his comrades, and their ideas, see Gabriel, *Love and Capital*; Riazanov, *Karl Marx and Friedrich Engels*; Le Blanc, *From Marx to Gramsci*.
2. Le Blanc, "Workers and Revolution."
3. Le Blanc, *Revolutionary Studies*.
4. E. Mandel, D. Mandel, Trotsky, Luxemburg, Lenin, and Le Blanc, *October 1917: Workers in Power*.
5. Berman, *Adventures in Marxism*, 58.
6. E. Wilson, *To the Finland Station*, 547; Berman, *Adventures in Marxism*, 62. A limitation built into Wilson's classic is an explicit misunderstanding and rejection (210–33) of the dialectical approach to reality—the notion that all elements of our ever-changing reality are alive with the interplay of contradictory dynamics, whose accumulation generates qualitative transformations. Marshall Berman's writings are infused with this dialectical sensibility, and attentive readers will see it in the present volume as well. See Marcuse, *Reason and Revolution*; H. Lefebvre, *Dialectical Materialism*; Rees, *The Algebra of Revolution*.
7. Berman, *Adventures in Marxism*, 63.

Chapter 1: Nothing Can Ever Be the Same

1. Reed, "First Proletarian Republic Greets American Workers," *New York Call*, November 22, 1917, reprinted in P. Foner, *The Bolshevik Revolution*, 54.
2. Bryant, *Six Months in Red Russia*, x, xi. Also see V. Gardner, *Friend and Lover*.
3. Beatty, *The Red Heart of Russia*, 479–80.
4. A. Williams, *Through the Russian Revolution*, 275. Also see the later and partly autobiographical Williams, *Journey into Revolution*.
5. Reed, *Ten Days That Shook the World*, xii. Also see Rosenstone, *Romantic Revolutionary*.
6. Trotsky, *History of the Russian Revolution*; Chamberlin, *The Russian Revolution*. The en-

dorsements of Trotsky's work can be found in Marzani, *The Education of a Reluctant Radical*, 198; and Thatcher, *Trotsky*, 187. On Chamberlin, see Engerman, "Modernization from the Other Shore," 383–416; as well as Chamberlin's two outstanding books of reportage—*Soviet Russia* and *Russia's Iron Age*—and his memoir, *The Confessions of an Individualist*, 63–159; Fitzpatrick's endorsement can be found on the back cover of the 1987 Princeton University Press reprint of his two-volume *The Russian Revolution*.

7. Commission of the Central Committee, *History of the Communist Party of the Soviet Union*, 196, 206, 224; Dimitrov, *The United Front*, 78, 280.

8. Wolfe, *An Ideology in Power*, 187, 188; Meyer, *Leninism*, 282–83; Daniels, ed. *A Documentary History of Communism*, vol. 1, xl; Daniels, *The Conscience of the Revolution*, 410; Rostow, *The Stages of Economic Growth*, 160. For an informative general discussion, see Engerman, *Know Your Enemy*.

9. Carr's *History of Soviet Russia* is summarized in Carr, *The Russian Revolution from Lenin to Stalin*. Deutscher's foremost works are *Stalin*, and his three-volume biography of Trotsky, now gathered into one, *The Prophet*. Also see Haslam, *The Vices of Integrity*; M. Cox, *E. H. Carr*; Horowitz, *Isaac Deutscher*; Deutscher, *The Non-Jewish Jew and Other Essays*; and Caute, *Isaac and Isaiah*.

10. Tucker, *Stalin as Revolutionary*; Tucker, *Stalin in Power*.

11. Cohen, *Bukharin and the Bolshevik Revolution*; Lewin, *Lenin's Last Struggle*, *The Making of the Soviet System*, and *The Soviet Century*.

12. Among the relevant texts here are: Liebich, *From the Other Shore*, esp. 271–326; Haimson, *The Mensheviks from the Revolution*, and *The Making of Three Russian Revolutionaries*; Rabinowitch, Rabinowitch, and Kristof, eds., *Revolution and Politics in Russia*. Influential Menshevik contributions to the historiography (in some ways consistent with what Reed, Chamberlin, and Trotsky present) include Sukhanov, *The Russian Revolution 1917*; Dan, *The Origins of Bolshevism*; and Abramovitch, *The Soviet Revolution*.

13. Avrich, *The Russian Anarchists*, and *Kronstadt, 1921*; Shanin, *The Roots of Otherness*.

14. Suny, "Toward a Social History of the October Revolution"; Kaiser, ed., *The Workers Revolution in Russia 1917*; Lincoln, *In War's Dark Shadow*, *Passage through Armageddon*, and *Red Victory*; Acton, Cherniaev, and Rosenberg, eds., *Critical Companion to the Russian Revolution*. Rabinowitch's *The Bolsheviks Come to Power*, published in 1976, was the earliest and one of the most influential of the new contributions.

15. Malia, *The Soviet Tragedy*; Pipes, *The Russian Revolution*; Volkogonov, *Lenin*; Yakovlev, *A Century of Violence in Soviet Russia*; Pipes, *Alexander Yakovlev*; Courtois, Werth, Panne, Paczkowski, Bartošek, and Margolin, *The Black Book of Communism*. Relevant to all of this is the critique offered by Domenico Losurdo in *War and Revolution*—and particularly effective is his considered demolition of the moral authority of *The Black Book of Communism*, with its indefensible silences on the terror, crimes, and repression associated with both liberal and illiberal capitalism, not to mention colonialism and imperialism (280–326). Also see Le Blanc, *Marx, Lenin, and the Revolutionary Experience*, 11–12.

16. Getty, *Origins of the Great Purges*, 203. Even broader social and cultural scope is provided in Fitzpatrick, *Everyday Stalinism*.

17. Getty and Naumov, *The Road to Terror*, 14; Fitzpatrick, *The Russian Revolution*, 8–9.

18. Figes, *A People's Tragedy*, 736, 823–24.

19. See Bebel, *My Life*; Michel, *The Red Virgin*; Morgan, *Keir Hardie*; P. Foner, ed., *Mother Jones Speaks*; and Allen, *Alexander Shlyapnikov*. Also relevant—among many other works—is P. Mason, *Live Working or Die Fighting*.

20. Wade, *The Russian Revolution*, 283.

21. McCall, "The Complexity of Intersectionality."

22. Freeman, *The Soviet Worker*, 9–10; Wade, *The Russian Revolution*, 89.

23. See Siegelbaum and Suny, *Making Workers Soviet*.

24. Wade, *The Russian Revolution*, 91–97.

25. Haimson, "The Problem of Social Identities," 5, 6. Also see Orlovsky, "The Lower Middle Strata in 1917"; and Iarov, "Workers," in Acton, Cherniaev, and Rosenberg, eds., *Critical Companion to the Russian Revolution*, 529–33, 604–18.

26. Marxist theoretical perspectives are examined in Davis, *Socialism and Nationalism*, including an exposition of Lenin's important defense of the right of oppressed nations to self-determination—but the realities are messier. Important discussions of evolving perspectives of revolutionaries (Lenin first of all) and practices before 1917 are explored in Suny, "Nationalism and Class in the Russian Revolution"; Riga, *The Bolsheviks and the Russian Empire*; and Blanc, "Anti-Imperial Marxism."

27. Clements, *Critical Companion to the Russian Revolution*, 592–603.

28. Lapidus, *Women in Soviet Society*, 48, 51; Clements, *Bolshevik Women*, 18, 20, 105–8; Wade, *The Russian Revolution*, 118.

29. Lapidus, *Women in Soviet Society*, 44, 51–52; Stites, *The Women's Liberation Movement in Russia*, 301; Clements, *Bolshevik Women*, 12; McDermid and Anna Hillyar, *Midwives of the Revolution*, 1; Wade, *The Russian Revolution*, 117.

30. Lapidus, *Women in Soviet Society*, 37, 40, 48, 49; Stites, *The Women's Liberation Movement in Russia*, 289, 317; Clements, *Bolshevik Women*, 11, 12–13; Wade, *The Russian Revolution*, 118, 121, 124.

31. A. Williams, *Lenin*, 86, 87–88; I. Levine, *The Man Lenin*, 192, 193.

32. Service, *Lenin*; Lih, *Lenin Rediscovered*, and *Lenin*.

33. Le Blanc, *Lenin and the Revolutionary Party*; Dune, *Notes of a Red Guard*; Serge, *Year One of the Russian Revolution*; Lih, "Kautsky When He Was a Marxist"; Krausz, *Reconstructing Lenin*; Shandro, *Lenin and the Logic of Hegemony*.

34. Lih, "Zinoviev, Populist Leninist," *Martov and Zinoviev*, and "The Ironic Triumph of Old Bolshevism"; Krupskaya, *Reminiscences of Lenin*; Lunacharsky, *Revolutionary Silhouettes*; Haupt and Marie, *Makers of the Russian Revolution*.

35. Elwood, *Russian Social Democracy*; Nimtz, *Lenin's Electoral Strategy from Marx and Engels through the Revolution of 1905*, and *Lenin's Electoral Strategy from 1907 to the October Revolution*; Zinoviev, *History of the Bolshevik Party*; Lih, "The Fortunes of a Formula." The yet-to-be-translated Russian work cited by Lih is V. Nevskii, *Istoriia RKP(b)*. St. Petersburg: Novyi Prometei, 2009.

36. Lewin, *The Making of the Soviet System*, 199.

37. Reed, *Ten Days That Shook the World*, 129.

38. A. Williams, *Through the Russian Revolution*, 276–77, 278. Outstanding contemporary critiques, holding up disturbingly well down to the present, are Bertrand Russell's crisp *The Practice and Theory of Bolshevism* and Alexander Berkman's passionate *The*

Bolshevik Myth. Leggett's devastating account, *The Cheka*, adds important detail, as does Rabinowitch, *The Bolsheviks in Power.* A broader elaboration can be found in Farber, *Before Stalinism*, usefully engaged with in Rees et al., *In Defence of October.* Koenker, Rosenberg, and Suny, *Party, State, and Society* is invaluable, and aspects of the debate are deepened in Pirani, *The Russian Revolution in Retreat*; and Murphy, *Revolution and Counterrevolution.* Also relevant is Mayer, *The Furies.*

39. Luxemburg, "The Russian Revolution," in *Rosa Luxemburg Speaks*, 375, 391, 393.

40. Arendt, *The Origins of Totalitarianism*, 318–19. Corroboration regarding the relatively positive aspects of the 1920s, consistent with what Arendt says, can be found in Chamberlin, *Soviet Russia*; Fitzpatrick, Rabinowitch, and Stites, eds.,*Russia in the Era of NEP*, and Brovkin; *Russia after Lenin.*

41. Duranty, *I Write as I Please*, 179, 181.

42. In addition to materials already presented—from scholars as diverse as Deutscher, Tucker, and Getty—see Ali, ed., *The Stalinist Legacy*; Medvedev, *Let History Judge*; Rogovin, *1937*, and *Stalin's Terror of 1937–1938*; Lenoe, *The Kirov Murder*; and Khlevniuk, *The History of the Gulag.* For a sample of Furr's prodigious output, see *The Murder of Sergei Kirov.*

43. An outstanding textbook is Suny, *The Soviet Experiment*; but also useful is S. A. Smith, *The Russian Revolution*; combined with Lovell, *The Soviet Union.*

44. Van der Linden, *Western Marxism*; Trotsky, *The Revolution Betrayed.* Trotsky's perspective is brilliantly contextualized and analyzed in Twiss, *Trotsky and the Problem of Soviet Bureaucracy.*

45. Trotsky, *The Revolution Betrayed*, 56. This passage from Marx's *The German Ideology*, quoted by Trotsky, can also be found in a slightly different translation in Marx and Engels, *Selected Works*, Vol. 1, 37.

46. Trotsky, *The Revolution Betrayed*, 59. A useful account of the Communist International, related to issues discussed by Trotsky, can be found in James, *World Revolution.* John Riddell and his collaborators have produced multiple volumes documenting the Communist International in Lenin's time; the vitally important first four congresses are covered in *Founding the Communist International*; *Workers of the World and Oppressed Peoples, Unite!*; *To the Masses*; and *Toward the United Front.* On consequences of Stalin's reorientation for the Comintern, see Carr, *Twilight of the Comintern.*

47. Gasper, ed., *The Communist Manifesto*, 69, 71; Hudis, *Marx's Concept of the Alternative to Capitalism.*

Chapter 2: Prerevolutionary Russia

1. Rostow, *The Dynamics of Soviet Society*, 250; Timasheff, *The Great Retreat, the Growth and Decline of Communism in Russia*, 34, 394–95; Shanin, *Russia as a "Developing Society,"* 174; Rostow, *The World Economy*, 428.

2. Lichtheim, *Collected Essays*, 310, 325, 326–27. Lichtheim's own interesting interpretation of Marxism is available in *Marxism: An Historical and Critical Study*, positing that "modern society has moved beyond the stage with whose analysis Marx was primarily

concerned," making it possible at last "to understand Marx because we have reached a point where neither his own modes of thought, nor those of his nineteenth-century opponents, are altogether adequate to the realities" (xx).

3.   Shanin, *Russia as a "Developing Society,"* 186, 183. Among Soviet historians in the 1960s there was also a tendency to revive—without acknowledgement to Trotsky—the conception of uneven and combined development, according to Baron, "The Transition from Feudalism to Capitalism in Russia," 724. The classic works that in the 1960s helped advance the debate on "dependency" were Baran, *The Political Economy of Growth*, and Frank, *Capitalism and Underdevelopment in Latin America*.

4.   Gatrell, *The Tsarist Economy*, 82–83; Bushnell, "Peasant Economy and Peasant Revolution at the Turn of the Century," 78–79, 80, 82; S. A. Smith, "'Moral Economy' and Peasant Revolution in Russia,"145–46.

5.   Bushnell, "Peasant Economy and Peasant Revolution," 81; S. A. Smith, *The Russian Revolution*, 6, 8.

6.   Polunov, *Russia in the Nineteenth Century*, 174, 176, 189, 190, 193, 201; Westwood, *Endurance and Endeavour*, 186–87.

7.   Wheatcroft, "Crises and the Condition of the Peasantry in Late Imperial Russia," 128–29, 136–46, 158, 165–66, 171–72.

8.   Alec Nove, *An Economic History of the USSR*, 25–28.

9.   Marot, *The October Revolution in Prospect and Retrospect*, 21–26.

10. Pokrovskii, *Russia in World History*, 48, 71, 72, 73–74, 75, 78, 80–81.

11. For an early critique, see Trotsky, *1905*, 327–45. On later controversies see Szporluk, introduction to Pokrovskii, *Russia in World History*, especially 10–12, 35–46, and Barber, *Soviet Historians in Crisis, 1928–1932*, 47–79. More recent interpretations and controversies are described in Baran, "The Transition from Feudalism to Capitalism in Russia," cited in note 3 above.

12. Shanin, *Russia as a "Developing Society,"* 93, 97, 101, 141.

13. Ibid., 25. Klyuckevskii also quoted on 25.

14. Kochan, *The Making of Modern Russia*, 18–19; Bryusov, Sakharov. Fadeyev, Chermensky, and Golikov, *Outline History of the USSR*, 23–135; Maynard, *Russia in Flux*, 19; Shanin, *Russia as a "Developing Society,"* 147; Wolf, *Peasant Wars of the Twentieth Century*,

15. Stepniak, *Russia under the Tzars*, 1.

16. Ibid., 2, 6.

17. Kerensky, *Russia and History's Turning Point*, 96; Lenin, *The Development of Capitalism in Russia*, excerpted in Lenin, *Revolution, Democracy, Socialism*, 95, 99–100.

18. Wallace, *Russia on the Eve of War and Revolution*, 287; Maynard, *Russia in Flux*, 34–38; Wolf, *Peasant Wars of the Twentieth Century*, 58–64; Shanin, *Russia as a "Developing Society,"* 93.

19. Borders, *Village Life under the Soviets*, 107–8.

20. Shanin, *Russia as a "Developing Society,"* 67, 72–81, 82, 165..

21. Hindus, *The Russian Peasant and the Revolution*, xi–xii, 80, 81, 92.

22. Hindus, *The Kremlin's Human Dilemma*, 185.

23. Shanin, *Russia as a "Developing Society,"* 66–72, 165–173, 82, 152, 147, 146, 141; Maynard, *Russia in Flux*, 50. A *dessiatin* is an archaic land measurement in tsarist Russia, equal to 2.702 English acres or 10,925 square meters.

24. Gatrell, *The Tsarist Economy*, 34; L. Wilson, *The New Schools of New Russia*, 11.

25. See Kingston-Mann, *Lenin and the Problem of Marxist Peasant Revolution*, and Shanin, *Russia, 1905–07*, 279–305.

26. Trotsky, *The History of the Russian Revolution*, 317.

27. Byres, "Peasantry," *A Dictionary of Marxist Thought*, 413 (which provides the Kritsman quote). For a substantial study of the analytical orientation developed by Kritsman and his co-thinkers, see Cox, *Peasants, Class, and Capitalism*.

28. Shanin, *Russia as a "Developing Society,"* 82, 83.

29. Ibid. Also see Chayanov, *The Theory of Peasant Economy*, and Danilov, *Rural Russia under the New Regime*.

30. Lewin, *Russian Peasants and Soviet Power*, 21-2.

31. Gorky quoted in Shanin, ed., *Peasants and Peasant Societies*, 370–71.

32. Lewin, *Russian Peasants and Soviet Power*, 21–22.

33. Gorky, *Untimely Thoughts*, 44, 45.

34. Ibid., 39–40; Lewin, *Russian Peasants and Soviet Power*, 25.

35. Olgin, *The Soul of the Russian Revolution*, 26–27.

36. Hindus, *The Russian Peasant and the Revolution*, 10.

37. Walling, *Russia's Message*, 108, 109, 113, 145.

38. Ibid., 110, 111, 115.

39. *The Accumulation of Capital* in *The Complete Works of Rosa Luxemburg*, vol. 2, *Economic Writings 2*, Hudis and Le Blanc, eds., 192.

40. Danilov, *Rural Russia under the New Regime*, 47, 49–51.

41. Alexinsky, *Modern Russia*, 114–15, 117, 146, 147. (Economist M.I. Tugan-Baranovsky, whose major study *The Russian Factory in Past and Present* appeared in 1898, is quoted by Alexinsky on 117.)

42. Ferro, *Nicholas II*, 1–4, 7, 87. Pavlova quoted in I. Levine, *The Russian Revolution*, 132.

43. Lieven, *The End of Tsarist Russia*, 83.

44. I. Levine, *The Russian Revolution*, 133.

45. Kochan, *The Making of Modern Russia*, 24; Volkov cited by Baron, "The Transition from Feudalism to Capitalism," 727.

46. Wallace, *Russia on the Eve of War and Revolution*, 100, 101, 104–5, 106.

47. Trotsky, *1905*, 45–46; Manning, *The Crisis of the Old Order in Russia, Gentry and Government*, 3.

48. Wallace, *Russia on the Eve of War and Revolution*, 158–59.

49. Shanin, *Russia as a "Developing Society,"* 33–49; Trotsky, *Permanent Revolution*, 41, 50; Kochan, *The Making of Modern Russia*, 175–77; Bryusov et al., *Outline History of the USSR*, 155; Dobb, *Russian Economic Development since the Revolution*, 70; Nove, *An Economic History of the USSR*, 18; Lyashchenko, *History of the National Economy of Russia to the 1917 Revolution*, 716, 717; but also see Gatrell, *The Tsarist Economy*, 227–28, who suggests that the extent of foreign domination may be overstated. Also see Wallace, *Russia on the Eve of War and Revolution*, 500–506.

50. Wallace, *Russia on the Eve of War and Revolution*, 193; Shanin, *Russia as a "Developing Society,"* 120 (also 118–21); Trotsky, *Permanent Revolution*, 53; Trotsky, *1905*, 39–40; T. Owen, *Capitalism and Politics in Russia: A Social History of the Moscow Merchants, 1855–*

1905, ix, 211; Ruckman, *The Moscow Business Elite*, 208, 209. Also see Brower, *Estate, Class, and Community*, 5–6.

51. Kunitz, *Russia: The Giant That Came Last*, 255, 258; Westwood, *Endurance and Endeavour*, 178; Lincoln, *In War's Dark Shadow*, 74–82; Gatrell, *The Tsarist Economy*, 91, 208; McDaniel, *Autocracy, Capitalism and Revolution in Russia*, 178, 239, 264.

52. D. Levin, *Stormy Petrel: The Life and Work of Maxim Gorky*, 76, 106–10; Lincoln, *In War's Dark Shadow*, 83–85; R. Williams, *The Other Bolsheviks*, 58–61.

53. Elwood, *Inessa Armand*, 40–41; "Interview with George Denike," in Haimson, with Galili y Garcia and Wortman, *The Making of Three Russian Revolutionaries*, 384, 385; Wolfe, *The Bridge and the Abyss*, 24.

54. Liberman, *Building Lenin's Russia*, 55–56.

55. McDaniel, *Autocracy, Capitalism and Revolution*, 405. On the earlier "irrepressible conflict," see Seward, "The Irrepressible Conflict," and B. Levine, *Half Slave and Half Free*.

56. McDaniel, *Autocracy, Capitalism and Revolution*, 29.

57. Dobb, *Russian Economic Development*, 71; Nove, *An Economic History of the USSR*, 18–19; Shanin, *Russia as a "Developing Society,"* 187.

58. Nove, *An Economic History of the USSR*, 28.

59. Lieven, *The End of Tsarist Russia*, 166.

60. Pokrovskii, *Russia in World History*, 109, 115–16; Shanin, *Russia as a "Developing Society,"* 58–59; Maynard, *Russia in Flux*, 140–41; Suny, "Nationality Policies," in Acton, Cherniaev, and Rosenberg, eds., *Critical Companion to the Russian Revolution*, 659, 660; Polunov, *Russia in the Nineteenth Century*, 8, 52–53; Yarmolinsky, *The Jews and Other Minor Nationalities under the Soviets*, 6. (Herzen quoted in Polunov, 8).

61. Maynard, *Russia in Flux*, 152–53; Riga, *The Bolsheviks and the Russian Empire*, 4.

62. Shanin, *Russia, 1905–07*, 66, 72; Suny, "Nationality Policies," 665; Riga, *The Bolsheviks and the Russian Empire*, 4.

63. The simplest definition is offered by Engels in an 1888 footnote to the *Communist Manifesto*, Marx and Engels, *Selected Works*, vol. 1, 108. Also see Boudin, *The Theoretical System of Karl Marx*, 191–214; E. Mandel and Novack, *The Revolutionary Potential of the Working Class*; Braverman, *Labor and Monopoly Capital*, 24–30; 377–423; Meiksins, "New Middle Class or Working Class?"; Meiksins, "Beyond the Boundary Question"; E. Wood, *The Retreat from Class*.

64. Bonnell, *Roots of Rebellion*, 24, 25. The quotation in Bonnell's remarks is from E. P. Thompson.

65. Lenin, *The Development of Capitalism in Russia*, 563–67, 587–88, 602, 603, 604–5, 606.

66. Ibid., 588–89.

67. Shanin, *Russia as a "Developing Society,"* 118, 117; Glickman, *Russian Factory Women*, 83; Nove, *An Economic History of the USSR*, 17; Bonnell, *Roots of Rebellion*, 23, 35; Bater, "St. Petersburg and Moscow on the Eve of the Revolution," , 25, 27, 28; Bryusov et al., *Outline History of the USSR*, 156, 162, 163; Trotsky, *1905*, 20, 21, 339; Freeman, *The Soviet Worker*, 9–10, 26.

68. Bater, "St. Petersburg and Moscow," 31; Shanin, *Russia as a "Developing Society,"* 63–64, 120, 121, 123. Regarding living conditions, community life, and consciousness, see Freeman, *The Soviet Worker*, 12–13; Brower, *Estate, Class, and Community*, 18–19, 28–33;

Glickman, *Russian Factory Women*, 2–3; Haimson, "The Problem of Social Identities," 4–5. Also see Bonnell, introduction to Bonnell, ed., *The Russian Worker*, 14–19.

69. Glickman, *Russian Factory Women*, 3.

70. Glickman, *Russian Factory Women*, 6, 7, 8; Freeman, *The Soviet Worker*, 10, 20, 25; Gordon, *Workers before and after Lenin*, 23–24.

71. Freeman, *The Soviet Worker*, 11, 18–19.

72. P. I. Denisov quoted in Kanatchikov, *A Radical Worker in Tsarist Russia*, 318–19.

73. Glickman, *Russian Factory Women*, 14–15, 85–87, 90; Freeman, *The Soviet Worker*, 10–11, 25; Bonnell, ed., *The Russian Worker*, 118.

74. Glickman, *Russian Factory Women*, 11–14; Freeman, *The Soviet Worker*, 12–13; Bater, "St. Petersburg and Moscow," 49–50; Bonnell, ed., *The Russian Worker*, 21, 22, 23.

75. Bonnell, ed., *The Russian Worker*, 23–24; Bater, "St. Petersburg and Moscow," 22; Freeman, *The Soviet Worker*, 26.

76. Bonnell, ed., *The Russian Worker*, 24–28; Glickman, *Russian Factory Women*, 16, 17, 18; Denisov quoted in Kanatchikov, *A Radical Worker in Tsarist Russia*, 320.

77. Zelnik, "Russian Bebels," part 1, 277, 278; Kir'ianov, "On the Nature of the Russian Working Class," 42.

78. Bonnell, ed., *The Russian Worker*, 39, 50.

79. Lyashchenko, *History of the National Economy of Russia*, 542–45; Trotsky, *The Young Lenin*, 148–50; Wildman, *The Making of a Workers' Revolution*, 35.

80. Zelnik, "Russian Bebels," part 1, 264.

81. Ibid., 265–66. On the Socialist Revolutionaries, see Radkey, *The Agrarian Foes of Bolshevism*; Ellison, "The Socialist Revolutionaries"; Perrie, "The Social Composition and Structure of the Socialist-Revolutionary Party before 1917." On workers' Marxism, see Zelnik, "Russian Bebels," part II, 423.

82. Zelnik, "Russian Bebels," part 1, 271, 274, 281.

83. Kollontai, *Selected Writings*, 41–42.

84. Zelnik, "Russian Bebels," part 1, 277, 284; D. Mandel, *The Petrograd Workers*, 13, 23–24, 26.

85. Bonnell, ed. *The Russian Worker*, 11; D. Mandel, *The Petrograd Workers*, 17.

86. Haimson, "The Problem of Social Identities in Early Twentieth Century Russia," 5, 6.

87. Zelnik, "Russian Bebels," part 2, 434, 435, 436, 439; Engelstein, *Moscow, 1905*, 58.

88. Zelnik, "Russian Bebels," part 2, 443.

89. Wildman focuses on the worker/intellectual conflict in *The Making of a Workers' Revolution*. On the Zubatov unions, see Schwarz, *The Russian Revolution of 1905*.

Chapter 3: Revolutionary Triumph

1. Bell, *The End of Ideology*, 334, 336, 352, 353, 355; Perlman, review of *Marxism: Is It Science?*, 972.

2. Koenker, *Moscow Workers and the 1917 Revolution*, 6; Le Blanc, "Ideology and Revolution," 3. Also see Waxman, ed., *The End of Ideology Debate*.

3. Geertz, *The Interpretation of Cultures*, 216; Delany, "The Role of Ideology," in Wax-

man, *The End of Ideology Debate*, 296; Rudé, *Ideology and Popular Protest*, 23, 24. Especially important to this analysis is Gramsci's theorization of the struggle for intellectual-cultural hegemony between classes and the key role of "organic intellectuals" organized in the revolutionary party. See Gramsci, *Selections from the Prison Notebooks*, for example, 5–23, 144–47, 150–55, 185, 188–90, 195–200, 204–5, 323–25, 340.

4. Carr, "Marx, Lenin and Stalin," 372.

5. Deutscher, *Soviet Trade Unions*, 1.

6. In particular, see Le Blanc, *Lenin and the Revolutionary Party*, new ed., with additional material in Le Blanc, *Unfinished Leninism*; Lenin, *Revolution, Democracy, Socialism*.

7. Lewin, *The Soviet Century*, 308; Rousset, *The Legacy of the Bolshevik Revolution*, 86.

8. See discussion in Schwarz, *The Russian Revolution of 1905*, 267–84, and in Suhr, "Petersburg's First Mass Labor Organization."

9. In addition to works by Schwarz and Suhr just cited, see Trotsky, *1905*, and Engelstein, *Moscow, 1905*.

10. Avrich, *The Russian Anarchists*.

11. In addition to works by Radkey, Perrie, and Ellison cited above in chapter 2, note 81, see Chernov, *The Great Russian Revolution*; I. Steinberg, *Spiridonova*, and Shanin, *Russia, 1905–07*.

12. Radkey, *The Agrarian Foes of Bolshevism*, 65–67; Melancon, *The Socialist Revolutionaries and the Russian Anti-War Movement, 1914–1917*, 11–12, 20–40.

13. Pipes, *Struve*, 174–84; Hasegawa, *The February Revolution*, 14–18; Timberlake, ed., *Essays on Russian Liberalism*.

14. Shanin, *Russia, 1905–07*, 23, 43.

15. See ibid., 236–51, for a useful discussion of Stolypin.

16. Ibid., 238; Lenin, *Selected Works*, vol. 3, 343.

17. Useful works on this period include Elwood, *Russian Social Democracy in the Underground*, and Piatnitsky, *Memoirs of a Bolshevik*.

18. For an interesting account of this period from a "conciliator" standpoint, see Swain, *Russian Social Democracy and the Legal Labor Movement*. Covering the same period, pages 85–161 of Trotsky's *Stalin* offer a more insightful and knowledgeable account by a former "conciliator."

19. In addition to sources cited in footnotes above, see Zinoviev, *History of the Bolshevik Party*, and Krupskaya, *Reminiscences of Lenin*.

20. Dan quoted in Popov, *Outline History of the Communist Party of the Soviet Union*, vol. 1, 283, and in Dutt, *The Life and Teachings of V. I. Lenin*, 34. Information on the state of the revolutionary movement can be found in: Haimson, "The Problem of Social Stability in Urban Russia," part 1, 631–32; Bonnell, *Roots of Rebellion*, 393–408.

21. Zelnik, "Russian Workers and the Revolutionary Movement," 217–18.

22. Haimson, "The Problem of Social Stability," part 1, 630–31; Krupskaya, *Reminiscences of Lenin*, 242; Lenin, *Collected Works*, vol. 20, 466. Also see Bonnell, *Roots of Rebellion*, 410–17.

23. Haimson, "The Russian Workers Movement on the Eve of the First World War," 83–84, 85.

24. Geyer, *The Russian Revolution*, 27; Service, *The Russian Revolution*, 23.

25. Service, *The Russian Revolution*, 23.

26. Useful sources on this period are Shlyapnikov, *On the Eve of 1917*; Trotsky, *History of the Russian Revolution*, vol. 1; Hasegawa, *The February Revolution*.

27. Lih, *Lenin Rediscovered*. Also see Le Blanc, "Lenin Studies: Method and Organization."

28. James, "Lenin and the Vanguard Party," 327.

29. Basil, *The Mensheviks in the Revolution of 1917*, 15, 16, 18, 19, 179, 182.

30. Ibid.

31. Shanin, *Russia, 1905–07*, 224.

32. Chernov, *The Great Russian Revolution*, 398–99; Ellison, "The Socialist Revolutionaries," 4, 5; Shanin, *Russia, 1905–07*, 224, 227, 228.

33. Ellison, "The Socialist Revolutionaries," 3, 4, 10; I. Steinberg, *Spiridonova*, 179, 181, 182, 187.

34. Lenin, "Our Revolution (Apropos of N. Sukhanov's Notes)," *Collected Works*, vol. 33, 476.

35. Ibid., 477.

36. Ibid., 478.

37. Serge, *Revolution in Danger*, 88, 90.

38. Ibid., 94, 95.

39. Eastman, *Marx, Lenin and the Science of Revolution*, 159–60.

40. Haimson, "The Problem of Social Stability in Urban Russia," part 1, 627–29; Haimson, "The Problem of Social Stability in Urban Russia" part 2, 17.

41. Trotsky, *1905*, 269.

42. Sandburg, *The People, Yes*, 221.

43. D. Mandel, *The Petrograd Workers*, 16.

44. Lieven, *The End of Tsarist Russia*, 303, 306–7

45. Ibid., 307.

46. J. Thompson, *Revolutionary Russia, 1917*, 9–16.

47. Ibid., 11; Medvedev, *The October Revolution*, 39.

48. J. Thompson, *Revolutionary Russia, 1917*, 21, 11.

49. Hasegawa, *The February Revolution*, 140; Medvedev, *The October Revolution*, 40.

50. Zinoviev, *History of the Bolshevik Party*, 192–93; Trotsky, *History of the Russian Revolution*, vol. 1, 154, 153.

51. McDermid and Hillyer, *Midwives of the Revolution*, 3.

52. D. Mandel, *The Petrograd Workers*, 63–64.

53. Ibid., 64.

54. McDermid and Hillyer, *Midwives of the Revolution*, viii.

55. D. Mandel, *The Petrograd Workers*, 65.

56. Melancon, *Rethinking Russia's February Revolution*, 22.

57. I. Levine, *The Russian Revolution*, 216.

58. Melancon, *Rethinking Russia's*, 35.

59. I. Levine, *The Russian Revolution*, 219–20, 223, 225. Levine, who had emigrated from Russia to the United States in 1911 (at the age of 19), would later spend time in the early Soviet Republic as a US journalist in the early 1920s, but in April 1917 the newspaper for which he was a foreign correspondent, the *New York Tribune*, acquired a remarkable set of leaflets and news bulletins from revolutionary Russia that enabled him to write, as he later noted, "the first authoritative inside account of the

revolution." I. Levine, *Eyewitness to History*, 37.

60. I. Levine, *The Russian Revolution*, 226.

61. Ibid., 227, 271, 276, 278.

62. D. Mandel, *The Petrograd Workers*, 80, 85, 227; Liebman, *Leninism under Lenin*, 119–20.

63. I. Levine, *The Russian Revolution*, 257–58.

64. M. Steinberg, *Voices of Revolution, 1917*, 63, 64.

65. Clark, *Lenin*, 196–99, 202–11, 216–17, 219. (Churchill quoted on 197.)

66. Longley, "The Division in the Bolshevik Party in March 1917," 75; Raskolnikov, *Kronstadt and Petrograd in 1917*, 77; Dune, *Notes of a Red Guard*, 56; Ilyin-Zhenevsky, *From the February Revolution to the October Revolution 1917*, 80, 85–86. The outstanding study of the complexities among the Mensheviks in this period is Galili, *The Menshevik Leaders in the Russian Revolution*. Although the common interpretation of Lenin "correcting" some of his "old Bolshevik" comrades in 1917 has recently been challenged—particularly by Lih, "The Ironic Triumph of Old Bolshevism," a number of eyewitnesses and participants remember what happened in ways consistent with the older interpretation—for example, Raskolnikov, cited above, as well as Krupskaya, *Reminiscences of Lenin*, 348–51, and the alert Menshevik critic Sukhanov, *The Russian Revolution 1917*, 282–92.

67. Lenin quoted in Carr, *The Bolshevik Revolution*, vol. 2, 31.

68. I. Levine, *The Russian Revolution*, 275–76.

69. Dune, *Notes of a Red Guard*, 48–49.

70. Rabinowitch, *The Bolsheviks Come to Power*, 62.

71. Kerensky, *Russia and History's Turning Point*, 368.

72. Ibid., 370–71. The historical controversies are capably reviewed in Munck, *The Kornilov Revolt*, and a well-researched narrative is offered in Abraham, *Alexander Kerensky*, 247–87.

73. Kerensky, *Russia and History's Turning Point*, 400.

74. Suny, "Toward a Social History of the October Revolution," 51, 54; also see Rabinowitch, *The Bolsheviks Come to Power*, xvii, 311–12; Volobuev, "The Proletariat—Leader of the Socialist Revolution," 67, 68.

75. Hook, "Bolshevik Coup Lacked Popular Support."

76. Luxemburg, *Rosa Luxemburg Speaks*, 372; Abramovitch, *The Soviet Revolution, 1917–1939*, 57, 75, 76, 77; also see Sidney Hook's introduction on pages vii–xii, as well as an earlier, less hostile discussion of Bolshevism in *Towards the Understanding of Karl Marx*, which offers a more positive—and I believe more useful, less distorted—understanding of Marxism in general than can be found in his disillusioned works after 1939.

77. Quoted in Abramovitch, *The Soviet Revolution*, 70.

78. Hook, "Bolshevik Coup Lacked Popular Support"; Francis, *Russia from the American Embassy*, 141, 143, 193–94.

79. Trotzky [Trotsky], *From October to Brest-Litovsk*, 78. This analysis was not held by the Bolsheviks alone. The Left SRs also saw the realities in precisely this way, which is presented in Isaac Steinberg's *Spiridonova*. Steinberg was a Left SR leader who soon became an uncompromising opponent of Bolshevism but still viewed the attempt to establish soviet power as profoundly democratic. Hook recounts that even while living in the United States during the early Cold War period, Steinberg—although now a firm anti-Communist—continued to defend this analysis, which validated the

October Revolution and the dismissal of the Constituent Assembly in favor of rule by the soviets. See Hook, *Out of Step*, 316–17. E. H. Carr's analysis of the Constituent Assembly also corresponds to that of the Bolsheviks and Left SRs—see Carr, *The Bolshevik Revolution*, vol. 1, 109–21.

80. Luxemburg, *Rosa Luxemburg Speaks*, 385, 395.

81. Quoted in I. Steinberg, *Spiridonova*, 191.

82. Schapiro, *The Communist Party of the Soviet Union*, 183; Wolfe, *An Ideology in Power*, 172; Pipes, *Communism: A History*, 38–39.

83. Meyer, *Leninism*, 175, 176.

84. Mstislavskii, *Five Days Which Transformed Russia*, 112, 114.

85. Ibid., 116–17.

86. Rabinowitch, *The Bolsheviks in Power*, 392.

87. Meyer, *Leninism*, 196; Keep, ed., *The Debate on Soviet Power*, 24, 31, 32, 35, 339.

88. Lockhart, *British Agent*, 239–40, 255–56.

89. Meyer, *Leninism*, 196.

90. Ibid., 185–86. What Meyer says here can be further buttressed by two summary accounts written in the 1950s and 1990s by respected US academics; both feature ample collections of documents and articles—see Curtiss, *The Russian Revolutions of 1917*, and Suny and Adams, *The Russian Revolution and Bolshevik Victory*.

91. Ferro, *The Bolshevik Revolution*, 100–103.

92. Ibid., 103.

93. Yarmolinsky, *The Jews and Other Minor Nationalities under the Soviets*, p 8.

94. Ferro, *The Bolshevik Revolution*, 103–11; Carr, *The Bolshevik Revolution*, vol. 1, 365, 379.

95. Carr, *The Bolshevik Revolution*, vol. 1, 254.

96. Carr, *The Bolshevik Revolution*, vol. 1, 367, 370, 373; Lewin, *Lenin's Last Struggle*, 43–64.

97. Carr, *The Bolshevik Revolution*, vol. 1, 272. See Gollwitzer, *Europe in the Age of Imperialism*; Sweezy, *The Theory of Capitalist Development*, 287–328; and Magdoff, *Imperialism*.

98. Medvedev, *The October Revolution*, 115.

99. Keep, ed., *The Debate on Soviet Power*, 31, 32, 33, 34.

100. Deutscher, *The Prophet Armed*, 287; Cliff, *Lenin*, vol. 3, 162; Wolfe, *Lenin and the Twentieth Century*, 179; Lenin, *Collected Works*, vol. 25, 378.

101. Cliff, *Lenin*, vol. 3, 10; Shachtman, "Revolution and Counter-revolution in Russia," 10; Lenin, *Collected Works*, vol. 26, 498.

102. Serge, *Year One of the Russian Revolution*, 243.

103. Kameneff [Kamenev], *The Dictatorship of the Proletariat*, 9, 10.

104. Bone, ed., *The Bolsheviks and the October Revolution*, 144–45, 146, 147. Valuable works on the governmental structures and the functioning of the Soviets and the Sovnarkom are Brailsford, *How the Soviets Work*, Anweiler, *The Soviets*, and Rigby, *Lenin's Government*.

105. Abramovitch, *The Soviet Revolution*, 120; Radkey, *The Sickle under the Hammer*, 155; I. Steinberg, *Spiridonova*, 187; Avrich, *The Russian Anarchists*.

106. Trotsky, *The Stalin School of Falsification*, 119, 120; Bone, ed., *The Bolsheviks and the October Revolution*, 137; Brovkin, *The Mensheviks after October*, 21–35.

107. Pankhurst, *Soviet Russia as I Saw It*, 68.

108. Beatty, *The Red Heart of Russia*, 431–34. This lengthy passage is reproduced from Le

Blanc, *Marx, Lenin, and the Revolutionary Experience*, 85–86. The text of Lenin's speech can be found in Lenin, *Revolution, Democracy, Socialism*, 280–84, in Lenin's *Collected Works*, vol. 26, 437–41, and in Keep, ed., *The Debate on Soviet Power*, 260–64.

109. Keep, ed., *The Debate on Soviet Power*, 243–44.

110. Ibid., 247–48, 249, 264–65, 265–66.

111. Wade, *The Russian Revolution, 1917*, 282. The well-documented account in Rabinowitch, *The Bolsheviks in Power*, 104–27, lends credence to Wade's reasoned critique, as does the less restrained account in Lincoln, *Passage through Armageddon*, 475–79.

112. This passage is reproduced from Le Blanc, *Marx, Lenin, and the Revolutionary Experience*, 270n20.

113. Lincoln, *Passage through Armageddon*, 476; Radkey, *The Sickle under the Hammer*, 456–58; Carr, *The Bolshevik Revolution*, vol. 1, 118, 121; Meyer, *Leninism*, 193.

Chapter 4: Proletarian Rule and Mixed Economy

1. Gilly, *La nueva Nicaragua*, 45–46.

2. Freeman, *The Soviet Worker*, 31–32; Dobb, *Russian Economic Development*, 71–77, 82–83; Trotsky, *1905*, 344.

3. A. Williams, *Journey into Revolution*, 137; Beatty, *The Red Heart of Russia*, 313, 314, 316.

4. Lenin, *Selected Works*, vol. 2, 15; Carr, *The Bolshevik Revolution*, vol. 2, 69, 81; Ross, *Russia in Upheaval*, 208, 212.

5. Medvedev, *The October Revolution*, 94, 118–19; Carr, *The Bolshevik Revolution*, vol. 2, 70; Dobb, *Russian Economic Development*, 31, 33, 50.

6. Cohen, *Bukharin and the Bolshevik Revolution*, 70, 71.

7. Ibid., 76; Medvedev, *The October Revolution*, 131; Daniels, *A Documentary History of Communism*, vol. 1, 152, 154, 155.

8. Lenin, *Selected Works*, vol. 2, 692, 697–98, 699, 707; Medvedev, *The October Revolution*, 132; Carr, *The Bolshevik Revolution*, vol. 2, 87; Dobb, *Russian Economic Development*, 47–57.

9. Dobb, *Russian Economic Development*, 44–45; Nove, *An Economic History of the USSR*, 53.

10. Carr, *The Bolshevik Revolution*, vol., 73–78, 97.

11. Ibid., 60–61.

12. Dobb, *Russian Economic Development*, 50; Ross, *Russia in Upheaval*, 284; Carr, *The Bolshevik Revolution*, vol. 2, 70; Nove, *An Economic History of the USSR*, 54; Freeman, *The Soviet Worker*, 33.

13. Carr, *The Bolshevik Revolution*, vol. 2, 75, 78, 81; Lih, *Bread and Authority in Russia, 1914–1921*, 152.

14. Souvarine, *Stalin*, 121–22.

15. Mathiez, "Bolshevism and Jacobinism," 76.

16. Ibid., 121. Dan and Martov quoted in Draper, *The "Dictatorship of the Proletariat" from Marx to Lenin*, 74.

17. Luxemburg, "On the Occasion of the Hundredth Anniversary of 1793," *Socialism or Barbarism*, 41–42.

18. Ibid., 226.

19. Ibid., 234.

20. Ibid., 170.

21. Lenin, *Collected Works*, vol. 7, 380, 381; Lenin, *Collected Works*, vol. 8, 222.

22. Souvarine, *Stalin*, 63; Lih, *Lenin Rediscovered*, 524.

23. Quoted in Draper, *The "Dictatorship of the Proletariat,"* 70–71.

24. Kautsky cited in Lenin, *Collected Works*, vol. 21, 98.

25. Mayer, *The Furies*, 119–20.

26. Lenin, *Collected Works*, vol. 8, 393, 432; Lenin, vol. 10, 136–37.

27. Lenin, *Collected Works*, vol. 25, 57–58.

28. Bukharin, *The Politics and Economics of the Transition Period*, 48, 60, 63, 76.

29. Ibid., 79, 96, 101, 104, 105, 106.

30. Carr, *The Bolshevik Revolution*, vol. 2, 88.

31. Ibid., 72.

32. Lih, *Bread and Authority*, 149, 150, 151.

33. Ibid., 105.

34. Ibid., 134, 136, 137.

35. Lenin, *Collected Works*, vol. 27, 293, 294, 297, 300, 301, 303–4, 305.

36. Cohen, *Bukharin and the Bolshevik Revolution*, 71; Lenin, *On Workers' Control and the Nationalization of Industry*, 31; Lenin, *Selected Works*, vol. 6, 265 (italics in original); S. A. Smith, *Red Petrograd*, 155.

37. S. A. Smith, *Red Petrograd*, 156, 167, 226, 228, 237–38.

38. Ibid., 231, 240; Ross, *Russia in Upheaval*, 271.

39. Ross, *Russia in Upheaval*, 275.

40. Ibid., 283, 284–85.

41. S. A. Smith, *Red Petrograd*, 224, 229, 230, 239.

42. Chamberlin, *The Russian Revolution*, vol. 1, 415.

43. Ross, *Russia in Upheaval*, 271, 272, 273, 275.

44. Goodey, "Factory Committees and the Dictatorship of the Proletariat (1918)," 42–44.

45. Serge, *Year One of the Russian Revolution*, 235; Ross, *The Russian Soviet Republic*, 341–42.

46. Serge, *Year One of the Russian Revolution*, 353, 356.

47. Chamberlin, *The Russian Revolution*, vol. 2, 110; Ross, *The Russian Soviet Republic*, 342; Serge, *Year One of the Russian Revolution*, 241, 350, 351; Nove, *An Economic History of the USSR*, 68; Chase, *Workers, Society, and the Soviet State*, 21, 308; Serge and Sedova [Trotsky], *The Life and Death of Leon Trotsky*, 104. (The quotes from Kritsman and Rykov can be found in Chamberlin and Ross, respectively.)

48. Ransome, *Russia in 1919*, 30, 38, 40, 41, 42, 62–63.

49. Cohen, *Bukharin and the Bolshevik Revolution*, 79.

50. Dobb, *Russian Economic Development*, 44, 45; Chamberlin, *The Russian Revolution*, vol. 2, 113, 114. Krupskaya's anecdote is cited in Robertson, *Marxism's Lessons for Today*, 23.

51. Medvedev, *The October Revolution*, 130.

52. Serge, *Memoirs of a Revolutionary*, 135. Also see Nove, *An Economic History of the USSR*, 46–82; and Dobb, *Russian Economic Development*, 98–165.

53. Medvedev, *The October Revolution*, 134–35; Dobb, 163, 165.

54. This draws from Le Blanc, *Marx, Lenin, and the Revolutionary Experience*, 124.

55. Foster, *The Russian Revolution*, 40–42.

56. Ibid., 43.

57. Haynes, "The Debate on Popular Violence and the Popular Movement in the Russian Revolution," 193; also see Haynes and Wolfreys, eds., *History and Revolution*; Read, *From Tsar to Soviets*, 86–88, 114–17.

58. Kunitz, "Men and Women in Soviet Literature," in Freeman, Kunitz, and Lozowick, *Voices of October*, 96–97.

59. Ibid., 80–81. For more on Kirillov and his sad fate, see Zavalishin, *Early Soviet Writers*, 149–53.

60. Fitzpatrick, *The Commissariat of Enlightenment*, xii, xiv.

61. Ibid., xiii, 79–80, 154; Chamberlin, *Soviet Russia*, 300; Slonim, *Soviet Russian Literature*, 34, 38.

62. Slonim, *Soviet Russian Literature*, 36; Fitzpatrick, *The Commissariat of Enlightenment*, xii–xiii, xiv, xv–xvi, 26, 29–30, 54, 97; Enteen, *The Soviet Scholar-Bureaucrat*, 3, 26, 27; McNeal, *Bride of the Revolution*, 192–94, 198–99.

63. Fitzpatrick, *The Commissariat of Enlightenment*, xv–xvi; Lenin, *On Culture and Cultural Revolution*, 233, 234, 247.

64. Kunitz, "Men and Women in Soviet Literature," 98.

65. Goldman, *Women, the State and Revolution*, 162.

66. Ibid., 163

67. Ibid., 171.

68. Ibid., 168.

69. Ibid., 170.

70. A. Williams, *The Russian Land*, 15; Harper, *Civic Training in Soviet Russia*, 197–200.

71. Borders, *Village Life under the Soviets*, 151.

72. Ibid., 152.

73. Hindus, *Broken Earth*, 185–86.

74. A. Williams, *The Russian Land*, 9, 11, 13–16; Haines, *Health Work in Soviet Russia*, 98–99.

75. L. Wilson, *The New Schools of New Russia*, 45–46, 164.

76. Haines, 163–64.

77. Kravchenko, *I Chose Freedom*, 30–31.

78. Ibid., 21.

79. Ibid., 38.

80. Baitalsky, *Notebooks for the Grandchildren*, 56, 58.

81. Ibid., 9–10.

82. M. Steinberg, "Vanguard Workers and the Morality of Class," 66. This is also discussed in Le Blanc, *Lenin and the Revolutionary Party*, 28–42, 106–14, 178–85, 247–57, 260–63.

83. Steinberg, "Vanguard Workers," 67, 68, 69, 74; Kunitz, "Men and Women in Soviet Literature," 73.

84. Steinberg, "Vanguard Workers," 78–79.

85. Kravchenko, *I Chose Freedom*, 43.

86. Baitalsky, *Notebooks for the Grandchildren*, 11, 59, 60.

87. Kravchenko, *I Chose Freedom*, 54.

88. Ibid., 36, 37. On Lazarev's own later dissidence and purging, see 86–87, 251–52.

89. Ibid., 27–28.

90. Ibid., 27–29.

91. Trotsky, *The Challenge of the Left Opposition, 1923–25*, 127.

92. Ciliga, *The Russian Enigma*, 79–80.

93. Trotsky, *The Struggle against Fascism in Germany*, 213.

Chapter 5: Global Context

1. Lenin, *Revolution, Democracy, Socialism*, 221, 222.

2. This passage draws from an editor's note in Lenin, *Revolution, Democracy, Socialism*, 216. The statistics are taken from Snyder, *The World in the Twentieth Century*, 35 (including the figure of the war's total cost, which Snyder calculated to be $400 billion).

3. Lieven, *The End of Tsarist Russia*, 4–5. There is a vast literature on varied Marxist analyses of imperialism, but for a partial summary see Le Blanc, *From Marx to Gramsci*, 38–43.

4. Riddell, ed., *Lenin's Struggle for a Revolutionary International*, 34, 35.

5. Mayer, *Wilson vs. Lenin*, 37, 41.

6. Ibid., 24.

7. Riddell, *Lenin's Struggle for a Revolutionary International*, 161.

8. Lenin, *Collected Works*, vol. 23, 299.

9. Trotsky, *Leon Trotsky Speaks*, 90.

10. Quoted in Rabinowitch, *The Bolsheviks in Power*, 376–77.

11. Lenin, *Revolution, Democracy, Socialism*, 299–300.

12. L. Gardner, LaFeber, and McCormick, eds., *Creation of the American Empire*, vol. 2, 336. The interpretation offered here obviously owes much to W. Williams, *The Tragedy of American Diplomacy*. Also of value are LaFeber, *America, Russia, and the Cold War, 1945–1980*, and L. Gardner, *Imperial America*.

13. Francis, *Russia from the American Embassy*, 332, 333, 334, 335.

14. Kennan, *Russia and the West under Lenin and Stalin*, 50–51; Harper, *The Russia I Believe In*, 91–106. Regarding Kennan, who later helped shape US foreign policy in the early Cold War years following World War II, biographer-historian Walter Isaacson remarks that he was himself a man "of decidedly anti-populist, even anti-democratic attitudes" (Isaacson, "The World According to Mr. X," 16); see also Isaacson and Thomas, *The Wise Men*. This assertion seems consistent with the sensibilities of Francis, Lansing, President Woodrow Wilson, and their colleagues, at least in regard to Russian realities.

15. L. Gardner, *Architects of Illusion*, 9.

16. Spargo, *Russia as an American Problem*, 10, 11. Spargo had for many years been a prominent intellectual in the Socialist Party of America, but the First World War propelled him into being a supporter and foreign policy advisor of the US government—a trajectory followed by others who came to be called "State Department socialists." See Radosh, *American Labor and United States Foreign Policy*, 185–267.

17. N. Levin, Jr., *Woodrow Wilson and World Politics*, 234, 235, 260.

18. Mayer, *Politics and Diplomacy of Peacemaking*, 284, 285.

19. Ibid., 343.

20. Ibid., 184–88, 320–23, 340, 457–58; Occleshaw, *Dances in Deep Shadows*, 284, 289, 290.

21. Mayer, *Politics and Diplomacy of Peacemaking*, 656–57, 813–14; Fischer, *The Soviets in World Affairs*, 188–237; Arnot, *Soviet Russia and Her Neighbors*, 24.

22. Serge, *Year One of the Russian Revolution*, 139, 143–44, 168; Carr, *The Bolshevik Revolution*, vol. 2, 131. Also see Shukman, ed., *The Blackwell Encyclopedia of the Russian Revolution*, 141–46.

23. Wollenberg, *The Red Army*, 92; Foglesong, *America's Secret War against Bolshevism*, 188.

24. On the old "Chiakovsky Circle" and Chiakvoksy's later evolution, see Yarmolinsky, *Road to Revolution*, 175–85, 187.

25. Foglesong, *America's Secret War against Bolshevism*, 178.

26. Ibid., 178–79, 180; Kerensky, *Russia and History's Turning Point*, 507.

27. Miliukov, *Russia Today and Tomorrow*, 162.

28. Mawdsley in Shukman, ed., *The Blackwell Encyclopedia of the Russian Revolution*, 141–46; Suny, *The Soviet Experiment*, 73–74, 82.

29. Miliukov, *Russia Today and Tomorrow*, 168, 170, 171, 172.

30. Mayer, *Politics and Diplomacy of Peacemaking*, 486; Brovkin, ed., *The Bolsheviks In Russian Society*, 127.

31. Mayer, *Why Did the Heavens Not Darken?*, 57.

32. Quoted in Wollenberg, *The Red Army*, 101–2.

33. Nove, *An Economic History of the USSR*, 68; Chamberlin, *The Russian Revolution*, vol. 2, 112.

34. Kennan, *Russia and the West*, 118–19; Chamberlin, *The Russian Revolution*, vol. 2, 170.

35. Chamberlin, *The Russian Revolution*, vol. 2, 171; Mayer, *Politics and Diplomacy of Peacemaking*, 563.

36. Chamberlin, *The Russian Revolution*, vol. 2, 171; Balabanoff, *My Life as a Rebel*, 184; Carr, *The Bolshevik Revolution*, vol. 2, 245.

37. Mawdsley, *The Russian Civil War*, 285–88; Kahn, *High Treason*, 5–6; Chamberlin, *The Russian Revolution*, vol. 2, 112; Freeman, *The Soviet Worker*, 39.

38. Ross, *The Russian Soviet Republic*, 83; Wollenberg, *The Red Army*, 110–11.

39. Wollenberg, *The Red Army*, 5; Carr, *The Bolshevik Revolution*, vol. 3, 60–64.

40. Mawdsley, *The Russian Civil War*, 59–62, 169; Lincoln, *Red Victory*, 17, 18, 21, 82–84, 190–92; Chamberlin, *The Russian Revolution*, vol. 2, 37–40; Wollenberg, *The Red Army*, 162; Serge and Sedova [Trotsky], *The Life and Death of Leon Trotsky*, 85.

41. Reissner quoted in Wollenberg, *The Red Army*, 153; Ross, *The Russian Soviet Republic*, 84; Carr, *The Bolshevik Revolution*, vol. 3, 66, 67.

42. Lincoln, *Red Victory*, 189; Mawdsley, *The Russian Civil War*, 242; Reissner quoted in Wollenberg, *The Red Army*, 152–54; Seldes, *You Can't Print That!*, 193.

43. Ross, *The Russian Soviet Republic*, 87.

44. Trotsky, *My Life*, 397; Lincoln, *Red Victory*, 295–96.

45. Seldes, *You Can't Print That!*, 189–90.

46. Wollenberg, *The Red Army*, 156–57.

47. Suny, *The Soviet Experiment*, 71; Lincoln, *Red Victory*, 48; Swain, *Russia's Civil War*, 148.

48. Swain, *Russia's Civil War*, 145, 150; Trotsky, *My Life*, 401, 407, 411; Chamberlin, *The Russian Revolution*, vol. 2, 30.

49. Swain, *Russia's Civil War*, 150.

50. Seldes, *You Can't Print That!*, 192.

51. Suny, *The Soviet Experiment*, 128. Also see Lincoln, *Red Victory*, 478–79.

52. Lenin quoted in C. L. R. James, *World Revolution*, 131.

53. Van Ree, "Lenin's Conception of Socialism in One Country, 1915–17," 160.

54. Lenin quoted in James, *World Revolution*, 131, 132; Lenin, *Collected Works*, vol. 31, 397, 399.

55. Lenin, *Collected Works*, vol. 32, 479–80.

56. Lenin quoted in Lewin, *Lenin's Last Struggle*, 3–4; James, *World Revolution*, 132.

57. See, for example, "Fundamentals of Leninism" and "Concerning Questions of Leninism," in Stalin, *Problems of Leninism*, 36, 208–11. At the time, US journalist Walter Duranty commented: "Stalin deserved his victory [i.e., winning leadership of the Communist Party of the Soviet Union in the mid-1920s] because he was the strongest, and because his policies were most fitted to the Russian character and folkways in that they established Asiatic absolutism and put the interests of Russian Socialism before those of international socialism" (Duranty, *I Write as I Please*, 274). Also see Tucker, *Stalin as Revolutionary*, 368–94.

58. Bukharin and Preobrazhensky, *The ABC of Communism*, 138–39.

59. Riddell, ed., *Lenin's Struggle for a Revolutionary International*, 164.

60. See Senn, *The Russian Revolution in Switzerland*, and Nation, *Lenin, the Zimmerwald Left, and the Origins of the Communist International*.

61. Riddell, ed. *Founding the Communist International*, 231–32.

62. Carr, *The Bolshevik Revolution*, vol. 3, 119–23, 131.

63. Riddell, ed., *Workers of the World and Oppressed Peoples, Unite!*, 105, 825.

64. Seldes, *You Can't Print That!*, 163, 164.

65. Wolfe, *A Life in Two Centuries*, 564.

66. Serge, *From Lenin to Stalin*, 36, 38.

67. Wells, *Russia in the Shadows*, 155.

68. Ypsilon [Volk and Gumperz], *Pattern for World Revolution*, 19.

69. Rosmer, *Moscow under Lenin*, 46.

70. Ypsilon [Volk and Gumperz], *Pattern for World Revolution*, 22; Carr, *The Bolshevik Revolution*, vol. 3, 188, 191.

71. Ypsilon [Volk and Gumperz], *Pattern for World Revolution*, 19.

72. Ibid., 21–22.

73. Roy, *Selected Works of M. N. Roy*, vol. 1, 468.

74. Carr, *The Bolshevik Revolution*, vol. 3, 191–96; Riddell, ed., *Workers of the World and Oppressed Peoples, Unite!*, 763–71.

75. Lenin, *Revolution, Democracy, Socialism*, 316, 317, 318.

76. Trotsky, *The First Five Years of the Communist International*, vol. 1, 295.

77. Riddell, ed., *Toward the United Front*, 1158.

78. Riddell, ed., *Toward the United Front*, 1164, 1165, 1171, 1173.

79. Wolfe, *A Life in Two Centuries*, 229, 373–75.

80. Cannon, *The History of American Trotskyism*, 14–15.

81. Lovestone, "Testimony of Jay Lovestone," in Le Blanc and Davenport, eds., *The "American Exceptionalism" of Jay Lovestone and His Comrades*, 640.

82. Cannon, *The First Ten Years of American Communism*, 65, 78, 85.

83. Rosmer, *Moscow under Lenin*, 63.

84. Riddell, ed., *Workers of the World and Oppressed Peoples, Unite!*, 410, 804.

85. Zinoviev, "Nikolai Lenin," 14; Trotsky, *The Third International after Lenin*, 155–56, 238; Serge, *From Lenin to Stalin*, 43; Rosmer, *Moscow under Lenin*, 57. Also see Geier, "Zinovievism and the Degeneration of World Communism."

86. Kuusinen, "Under the Leadership of Russia," 134.

87. Lovestone, "Testimony of Jay Lovestone," 640.

88. Balabanoff, *My Life as a Rebel*, 221; Ypsilon [Volk and Gumperz], *Pattern for World Revolution*, 15–16.

89. Ypsilon [Volk and Gumperz], *Pattern for World Revolution*, 16.

90. Balabanoff, *My Life as a Rebel*, 223.

91. Marot, *The October Revolution in Prospect and Retrospect*, 27.

92. Ibid., 26–28.

93. Ibid., 28.

94. Ibid., 16, 18.

95. Ibid., 28.

Chapter 6: Losing Balance

1. Serge, *Revolution in Danger*, 90, 91.

2. Ibid., 92.

3. Ibid., 93–94.

4. Deutscher, *Marxism in Our Time*, 86–87.

5. Mayer, *The Furies*, 256–57; Leggett, *The Cheka*, 16, 22.

6. N. Harding, *Lenin's Political Thought*, 326; on Plekhanov, see his 1903 comment, quoted in Draper, *The "Dictatorship of the Proletariat,"* 70–71.

7. Burbank, *Intelligentsia and Revolution*, 83, 84; Chernov, *The Great Russian Revolution*, 417, 419; Tchernoff, *New Horizons*, 106.

8. Radkey, *The Sickle under the Hammer*, ix, 4, 17, 18, 21; Chernov, *The Great Russian Revolution*, 326–27; Lockhart, *British Agent*, 178–79; Shukman, ed., *The Blackwell Encyclopedia of the Russian Revolution*, 374–75.

9. Brook-Shepherd, *Ironmaze*, 34–35; Fischer, *The Soviets in World Affairs*, vol. 1, 118; Radkey, *The Sickle under the Hammer*, 453; Occleshaw, *Dances in Deep Shadows*, 137.

10. Burbank, *Intelligentsia and Revolution*, 19–20, 21; Radek, *Proletarian Dictatorship and Terrorism*, 51. On Menshevik policy and aspects of Bolshevik response, see Dan, *Two Years of Wandering*, and especially the informative essay by the book's translator and editor, Francis King, on pages 1–45.

11. Lenin, *Collected Works*, vol. 29, 273; Johnstone, "Socialism, Democracy and the One-Party System," part 2, *Marxism Today*, 181; Russell, *The Practice and Theory of Bolshevism*, 41; Broido, *Lenin and the Mensheviks*, 68–70; Serge, *Year One of the Russian*

Revolution, 243–44; Liebman, *Leninism under Lenin*, 251.

12. Dune, *Notes of a Red Guard*, 48.

13. Ilyin-Zhenevsky, *The Bolsheviks in Power*, 102–3; Rabinowitch, *The Bolsheviks in Power*, 314.

14. Barmine, *One Who Survived*, 66.

15. Avrich, *The Russian Anarchists*, 183–84, 185–86, 188.

16. Miller, "Anarchists in the State."

17. Rabinowtich, *The Bolsheviks in Power*, 393.

18. Murphy, *Revolution and Counterrevolution*, 159.

19. I. Steinberg, *Spiridonova*, 216, 194–217; Serge, *Year One of the Russian Revolution*, 261–62; Chamberlin, *The Russian Revolution*, vol. 2, 42–83; Rabinowitch, *The Bolsheviks in Power*, 292, 294–95; Osipova, "Peasant Rebellions," 157; Trotsky, *How the Revolution Armed*, vol. 1, 370–402; Trotsky, *Leon Trotsky Speaks*, 109–12; Ilyin-Zhenevsky, *The Bolsheviks in Power*, 110–11.

20. Murphy, *Revolution and Counterrevolution*, 160; Read, *From Tsar to Soviets*, 207; Carr, *The Bolshevik Revolution*, vol. 1, 170–79; Brovkin, *Behind the Front Lines of the Civil War*, 249, 251.

21. Brovkin, *Behind the Front Lines of the Civil War*, 26, 27, 50, 51, 56, 239–69.

22. Leggett, *The Cheka*, 85; Serge, *Year One of the Russian Revolution*, 264.

23. Quoted in Anweiler, *The Soviets*, 235.

24. Barmine, *One Who Survived*, 92–93.

25. Zinoviev in Riddell, ed., *Workers of the World and Oppressed Peoples, Unite!*, 152; Tomsky quoted in Matgamna, ed., *The Fate of the Russian Revolution*, 173.

26. Quoted in Shukman, ed., *The Blackwell Encyclopedia of the Russian Revolution*, 182.

27. Leggett, *The Cheka*, 104–5, 119–20; Chamberlin, *The Russian Revolution*, vol. 2, 66–83.

28. Fischer, *The Soviets in World Affairs*, vol. 1, 117.

29. Ilyin-Zhenevsky, *The Bolsheviks in Power*, 18, 104.

30. Ibid., 109.

31. Salisbury, *Black Night, White Snow*, 566.

32. Rabinowitch, *The Bolsheviks in Power*, 314–16.

33. Leggett, *The Cheka*, 67.

34. Rabinowitch, *The Bolsheviks in Power*, 324, 331, 332, 342–43.

35. Ransome, *Russia in 1919*, 17.

36. Rabinowitch, *The Bolsheviks in Power*, 314, 330; Pipes, ed., *The Unknown Lenin*, 50.

37. Rabinowitch, *The Bolsheviks in Power*, 330; Farber, *Before Stalinism*, 134.

38. Berkman, *The Bolshevik Myth*, 240.

39. Read, *From Tsar to Soviets*, 207; Mayer, *The Furies*, 310.

40. I. Steinberg, *Spiridonova*, 235, 236; Russell, *The Practice and Theory of Bolshevism*, 54.

41. Mayer, *The Furies*, 310–11.

42. Ibid., 230–31.

43. Leggett, *The Cheka*, 84.

44. Ibid., 102.

45. Read, *From Tsar to Soviets*, 207.

46. Kohn, *Living in a World Revolution*, 107–8.

47. Ibid. Kohn's point that the White Terror was worse than the Red Terror in important ways is corroborated by the fact that the high estimate some scholars give for total

Cheka executions during the entire Civil War period (140,000) is lower than the number of Jews killed by White forces in just one area, the Ukraine, in the single year of 1919—Rees et al., *In Defence of October,* 89n124.

48. Chamberlin, *The Russian Revolution,* vol. 2, 66.
49. Trotsky, *Terrorism and Communism,* 58, 59.
50. Sheridan, *Mayfair to Moscow,* 95; Leggett, *The Cheka,* 252.
51. Deutscher, *The Prophet Unarmed,* 109; Leggett, *The Cheka,* 162, 188.
52. Seldes, *You Can't Print That!,* 243–44.
53. Ibid., 245.
54. Tchernoff, *New Horizons,* 125.
55. Ibid., 128. Other reports describe the same mode of operation, periodically through-out the Red Terror, in Odessa, for example. See Berkman, *The Bolshevik Myth,* 254–55.
56. Lyons, *Assignment in Utopia,* 470–71.
57. Ibid., 471, 472–73.
58. Ibid., 473.
59. Quoted in Leggett, *The Cheka,* 162.
60. Zinoviev quoted in Brovkin, *Behind the Front Lines of the Civil War,* 60; Zavalishin, *Early Soviet Writers,* 189–94, 215–17, 288–98; Rühle, *Literature and Revolution,* 43–77; Lukács quoted in Rühle, *Literature,* 74. The works mentioned can be found in Morrison, ed., *The Collected Stories of Isaac Babel;* Serge, *Conquered City;* Tarasov-Rodionov, *Chocolate;* Gladkov, *Cement;* and Sholokhov, *And Quiet Flows the Don.*
61. Farber, *Before Stalinism,* 128, 129.
62. Ulam, *The Bolsheviks,* 426.
63. Leggett, *The Cheka,* 117.
64. Ibid., 162.
65. Pipes, ed., *The Unknown Lenin,* 61.
66. Leggett, *The Cheka,* 340.
67. Ibid., 136, 137, 163–64, 342.
68. A. Wood, "The Revolution and Civil War in Siberia," in Acton, Cherniaev, and Rosenberg, eds., *Critical Companion to the Russian Revolution,* 712–13; Serge, *Year One of the Russian Revolution,* 252–54, 343–46.
69. Tchernoff, *New Horizons,* 147.
70. Lincoln, *Red Victory,* 241–42, 254, 255; A. Wood, "The Revolution and Civil War in Siberia," 715.
71. Tchernoff, *New Horizons,* 147–48.
72. Kameneff, *Dictatorship of the Proletariat,* 11; Trotsky, *Terrorism and Communism,* 109, 169–70; Trotsky, *On the Paris Commune,* 53; Clark, *Lenin,* 353–429; Le Blanc, *Lenin and the Revolutionary Party,* 270–279; Rabinowitch, *The Bolsheviks in Power,* 289.
73. Leggett, *The Cheka,* 340.
74. James, "Lenin and the Vanguard Party," 327; Rees, *The Algebra of Revolution,* 83.
75. Lenin, *Revolution, Democracy, Socialism,* 233–34.
76. Liebman, *Leninism under Lenin,* 267; Lenin, *Collected Works,* vol. 29, 559; Kamenev quoted in Cliff, *Lenin,* vol. 3, 175; Ransome, *The Crisis in Russia,* 52–53.
77. Bukharin and Preobrazhensky, *The ABC of Communism,* 84, 91.

78. Lenin, *Collected Works*, vol. 32, 21.

79. Lenin, *Collected Works*, vol. 2, 451, 452–53.

80. Luxemburg, *Rosa Luxemburg Speaks*, 391; Trotsky, *Terrorism and Communism*, 57, 59, 64.

81. Luxemburg, *Rosa Luxemburg Speaks*, 395.

82. Ibid., 394–95.

Chapter 7: Majority of the People

1. This is usefully surveyed in Kingston-Mann, *Lenin and the Problem of Marxist Peasant Revolution*, 19–37.

2. Bukharin, *Selected Writings on the State and the Transition to Socialism*, 218.

3. Carr, *The Bolshevik Revolution*, vol. 2, 34–35.

4. Quoted in ibid., 35–36.

5. Hindus, *The Russian Peasant and the Revolution*, 281; Carr, *The Bolshevik Revolution*, vol. 2, 36.

6. Carr, *The Bolshevik Revolution*, vol. 2, 39.

7. Tchernoff, *New Horizons*, 137.

8. This draws from Lenin's late nineteenth-century tome *The Development of Capitalism in Russia* and his remarkable 1903 pamphlet *To the Rural Poor*, both excerpted in Lenin, *Revolution, Democracy, Socialism*. Book-length studies of Lenin's thought on "the peasant question" can be found in Kingston-Mann, *Lenin and the Problem of Marxist Peasant Revolution*, and Rochester, *Lenin on the Agrarian Question*, but also see Shanin, *Russia, 1905–07*, 279–305.

9. Lenin, *Revolution, Democracy, Socialism*, 94.

10. Ibid., 95, 96, 97.

11. Ibid., 99–100.

12. Ibid., 145, 146.

13. Ibid., 151.

14. Shanin, *Russia as a "Developing Society,"* 99, 154, 155, 156, 158.

15. See, for example: Danilov, *Rural Russia under the New Regime* in its entirety; Lewin, *Russian Peasants and Soviet Power*, 21–28; Lih, *Bread and Authority*, 139–52; Goldman, *Women, the State and Revolution*, 144–52; and Marot, *The October Revolution in Prospect and Retrospect*, 11–86. On the critique of the "moral economy" argument, see S. A. Smith, "'Moral Economy' and Peasant Revolution in Russia."

16. Luxemburg, *The Complete Works of Rosa Luxemburg*, vol. 2, 497–98.

17. Luxemburg, *Rosa Luxemburg Speaks*, 377, 378.

18. Bukharin, *Selected Writings*, 218–19.

19. Both were victimized in the late 1920s—arrested, put on trial, successfully pressured to confess to phony charges, and imprisoned—as the crystallizing Stalin dictatorship was beginning to prepare for its "revolution from above," in a precursor to later "purge trials" that would savage the ranks of old Bolsheviks in 1936–38 (in the wake of which the already incarcerated Sukhanov and Chayanov were exterminated, with so many others). For biographical information, see Getzler, *Nikolai Sukhanov*,

and Kerblay, "A. V. Chayanov," in *The Theory of Peasant Economy.*

20. Quoted in Getzler, *Nikolai Sukhanov*, 11–15, 16, 17.
21. Ibid., 128, 133.
22. Shanin, "Chayanov's Message," and Thorner, "Chayanov's Conception of the Peasant Economy," both in Chayanov, *The Theory of Peasant Economy*, 17, xiii.
23. Chayanov, *The Theory of Peasant Economy*, 55, 60, 225.
24. Ibid., 49, 224, 225–26, 257.
25. Ibid., 255, 256.
26. Ibid., 257.
27. Ibid., 257–58.
28. Lih, *Bread and Authority*, 1.
29. Quoted in Carr, *The Bolshevik Revolution*, vol. 2, 32.
30. Lih, *Bread and Authority*, 105.
31. Carr, *The Bolshevik Revolution*, vol. 2, 270.
32. I. Steinberg, *Spiridonova*, 203.
33. Medvedev, *The October Revolution*, 153, 155, 156, 157; Lih, *Bread and Authority*, 175.
34. Osipova, "Peasant Rebellions," 155
35. Lewin, *Russian Peasants and Soviet Power*, 78.
36. Hindus, *Broken Earth*, 137.
37. Carr, *The Bolshevik Revolution*, vol. 2, 149–50.
38. Baitalsky, 4–5.
39. Lih, *Bread and Authority*, 187–88.
40. Malle, *The Economic Organization of War Communism*, 365; Lih, *Bread and Authority*, 197; Nove, *An Economic History of the USSR*, 62–63, 108; Wells, *Russia in the Shadows*, 160.
41. Carr, *The Bolshevik Revolution*, vol. 2, 165.
42. Osipova, "Peasant Rebellions," 173. Also see Arshinov, *History of the Makhnovist Movement*, and Makhno, *The Struggle against the State and Other Essays.*
43. Quoted in Tony Cliff, *Lenin*, vol. 3, 141, 142.
44. Lih, *Bread and Authority*, 199.
45. Lincoln, *Passage through Armageddon*, 191, 376–77; A. Williams, *Journey into Revolution*, 82; D. Mandel, *The Petrograd Workers*, 211–12; Lih, *Bread and Authority*, 100–102.
46. Lih, *Bread and Authority*, 102, 154, 167.
47. Nove, *An Economic History of the USSR*, 106.
48. Lih, *Bread and Authority*, 136, 137.
49. Ibid., 126.
50. Ibid., 165.
51. Ibid., 146–47, 154–55.
52. I. Steinberg, *Spiridonova*, 212–13, 237; Carr, *The Bolshevik Revolution*, vol. 2, 174; Lih, *Bread and Authority*, 161.
53. Lih, *Bread and Authority*, 169, 194, 211–12.
54. Ibid., 175, 176–77, 195, 201, 202; Heinzen, *Inventing a Soviet Countryside*, 156.
55. Lih, *Bread and Authority*, 168, 170, 171, 173, 190, 191, 196–97.
56. Hindus, *The Russian Peasant and the Revolution*, 279.
57. Lih, *Bread and Authority*, 196, 198, 212, 214, 217, 218.

58. DuGarm, "Peasant Wars in Tambov Province," 177.

59. Carr, *The Bolshevik Revolution*, vol. 2, 271; Osipova, "Peasant Rebellions," 171–72, 173; DuGarm, "Peasant Wars in Tambov Province," 177–78, 194.

60. Nove, *An Economic History of the USSR*, 84; Carr, *The Bolshevik Revolution*, vol. 2, 272–73; Rousset, *The Legacy of the Bolshevik Revolution*, 18–19.

61. Hindus, *The Russian Peasant and the Revolution*, 277.

62. Bukharin and Preobrazhensky, *The ABC of Communism*, 186–87, 382. Similar reasoning, predominating in the late 1920s, was offered to British observer H. N. Brailsford, who passed it on in *How the Soviets Work*, 65–66. On the Menshevik perspective, see Brovkin, *Behind the Front Lines of the Civil War*, 241.

63. Medvedev, *The October Revolution*, 161; Gregor, ed., *Resolutions and Decisions of the Communist Party of the Soviet Union*, vol. 2, 16; Farber, *Before Stalinism*, 50.

64. Ross, *The Russian Soviet Republic*, 317.

65. Getzler, *Nikolai Sukhanov*, 128.

66. Wolfe, *Three Who Made a Revolution*, 117.

67. Marot, *The October Revolution in Prospect and Retrospect*, 37.

68. Hindus, *Broken Earth*, 15.

69. Trotsky, *How the Revolution Armed*, vol. 5, 365; Preobrazhensky, *The Crisis of Soviet Industrialization*, 20; Bukharin, *Selected Writings*, 215, 216–17.

70. Trotsky, *The First Five Years of the Communist International*, vol. 2, 232–33.

71. Ibid., 192.

72. Shanin, *Russia, 1905–07*, 294–95, 302, 305; Lewin, *Russian Peasants and Soviet Power*, 23–24, 93–94, 318–19.

73. Lewin, *Russian Peasants and Soviet Power*, 26; Getzler, *Nikolai Sukhanov*, 130.

74. Getzler, *Nikolai Sukhanov*, 129, 130, 132, 134. On the newly discovered works of Marx to which Sukhanov referred, see Shanin, ed. *Late Marx and the Russian Road*.

75. Lewin, *Russian Peasants and Soviet Power*, 93.

76. Hindus, *The Russian Peasant and the Revolution*, 82–84, 272–73. By the late 1960s, Hindus seems to have reversed himself: "The folk democracy of the muzhik was a solid foundation on which the Soviets, had they chosen to do so, could have built a modern-style democracy" (*The Kremlin's Human Dilemma*, 186).

77. Chayanov, *The Theory of Peasant Cooperatives*, xxxi, 3; Chayanov, *The Theory of Peasant Economy*, 263–64.

78. Chayanov, *The Theory of Peasant Economy*, 265–68.

79. Ibid., 269. It is interesting to note that this approach is consistent with the 1920 suggestions of the US researcher who himself had been born and reared in a Russian peasant village, Maurice Hindus—see Hindus, *The Russian Peasant and the Revolution*, 285–90.

80. Lih, *Bread and Authority*, 195–96.

81. Carr, *The Bolshevik Revolution*, vol. 2, 165, 277.

82. These closing reflections respond to an insightful critique of an earlier draft of this book from Lars Lih.

Chapter 8: Liberty under the Soviets

1. Dewey, *Impressions of Soviet Russia and the Revolutionary World*, 67–68.
2. Ibid., 22. For valuable discussion and contextualization of Dewey's experience and reflections, see Engerman, "John Dewey and the Soviet Union."
3. Baldwin, *Liberty under the Soviets*, 1–2.
4. International Committee for Political Prisoners, *Letters from Russian Prisons*, iii, xiii, xiv–xv.
5. Baldwin, *Liberty under the Soviets*, 2–3, 7–9; Murphy, *Revolution and Counterrevolution*, 105. The matter of religion in the early Soviet Republic is usefully explored at length in Hecker, *Religion under the Soviets*—although the relative freedom of religion Hecker describes would soon be destroyed in the midst of Stalin's "revolution from above," and Hecker himself would be executed.
6. Baldwin, *Liberty under the Soviets*, 3–4, 7.
7. Solzhenitsyn, *The Gulag Archipelago*; Dallin and Nicolaevsky, *Forced Labor in Soviet Russia*; Khlevniuk, *The History of the Gulag*. Solzhenitsyn famously argued that the infamous gulag was designed and inaugurated under Lenin, and many have followed him in such assertions, but the data in Dallin and Nicolaevsky, Khlevniuk, and others tell a different story. Also see E. Mandel, "The Gulag Archipelago."
8. Baldwin, foreword to Baldwin, ed., *A New Slavery, Forced Labor*, 18–19.
9. Ibid., 19, 20.
10. A shrewd analytical account of the former is provided in Flewers, *The New Civilization?*, and samples of the latter can be found in J. Steinberg, ed., *Verdict of Three Decades*.
11. This account is based on chapter 11 of Hindus's *Broken Earth* (cited above), particularly 229, 230, 232, 233, 234, 238, 239, 241, 242, 243, 244, 245, 246–47.
12. Flewers, *The New Civilization?*, 40–41.
13. Lyons, *The Red Decade*, 111–12. An outstanding and informative study dealing with Lyons, William Henry Chamberlin, Walter Duranty, Maurice Hindus, and Louis Fischer, among others, is Engerman, *Modernization from the Other Shore*.
14. Caute, *The Fellow Travellers*, 186–87; also see Harper, *The Russia I Believe In*.
15. Purcell et al., *Russia Today*, 48–49.
16. On demonstrations, see Burbank, *Intelligentsia and Revolution*, 38; Baron, *Plekhanov*, 354; Avrich, *The Russian Anarchists*, 227; Serge, *Memoirs of a Revolutionary*, 144–45; Rosmer, *Moscow under Lenin*, 99–102. On the press, see Avrich, *The Russian Anarchists*, 179–85, 191–95, 199–202, 237, 244; Brovkin, *The Mensheviks after October*, 103–10; Broido, *Lenin and the Mensheviks*, 113–15, 138.
17. Baldwin, *Liberty under the Soviets*, 136; Mazour, *The Writing of History in the Soviet Union*, 4; Kenez, *The Birth of the Propaganda State*, 240, 245–47; Eastman, *Artists in Uniform*, 33–38; Slonim, *Soviet Russian Literature*, 43, 48; Graham, *Science and Philosophy in the Soviet Union*, 10. Also see: Freeman, Kunitz, and Lozowick, *Voices of October*; Joravsky, *Soviet Marxism and Natural Science*; Rosenberg, ed., *Bolshevik Visions*; Barber, *Soviet Historians in Crisis*.
18. Chamberlin, *Soviet Russia*, 397–98, 399, 401.
19. Murphy, *Revolution and Counterrevolution*, 155, 161–64.

20. Strong, *The First Time in History*, 51.

21. Eastman, *Love and Revolution*, 357–58, 359–60, 361, 370–71, 372, 380–81.

22. Ibid., 366–68.

23. Murphy, *Revolution and Counterrevolution*, 73–74, 82, 83, 86, 87, 91, 96, 98, 114.

24. S. A. Smith, review of *Revolution and Counterrevolution*.

25. Harper, *Civic Training in Soviet Russia*, 96–98.

26. Ransome, *The Crisis in Russia*, 178–79.

27. Ibid., 180, 181, 183.

28. See, for example, Diggins, *Up from Communism*.

29. Chamberlin, *Confessions of an Individualist*, 1–2, 15–16, 28–32, 40–43, 45–50, 64, 65, 66, 97.

30. Ibid., 65, 88, 100. On Lunacharsky's and Krupskaya's dissent, see Lapidus, "Educational Strategies and Cultural Revolution," 92.

31. Chamberlin, *Confessions of an Individualist*, 145–48. These fake show trials—which were an integral element in pushing forward the Stalinist "revolution from above" of forced collectivization of the land and breakneck industrialization—are discussed in more detail in Lyons, *Assignment in Utopia*, 357–61, 369, 370–80. On these early persecutions, see also Serge, *Russia Twenty Years After*, 83–85, 173–74; R. W. Davies, *The Soviet Economy in Turmoil*, 110–25, 406–11; André Liebich, *From the Other Shore*, 199–214. Further exploration and contextualization can be found in the essays in Fitzpatrick, ed., *Cultural Revolution in Russia, 1928–1931*, and in Fitzpatrick, *The Cultural Front*, 91–148.

32. Chamberlin, *Confessions of an Individualist*, 102–3; Chamberlin, *Soviet Russia*, 417.

33. Chamberlin, *Confessions of an Individualist*, 102.

34. Chamberlin, *Soviet Russia*, 148–49.

35. Ibid., 36, 149, 150–51, 152, 155–56.

36. Ibid., 157–58; Chamberlin, *Confessions of an Individualist*, 68.

37. Siegelbaum, *Soviet State and Society between Revolutions*, 188–223; Davies, *The Soviet Economy in Turmoil*, 60–75; Filtzer, *Soviet Workers and Stalinist Industrialization*, 13–33; Erlich, *The Soviet Industrialization Debate*.

38. Filtzer, *Soviet Workers and Stalinist Industrialization*, 20–21, 156.

39. Marot, *The October Revolution in Prospect and Retrospect*, 62–63, 64.

40. Ibid., 45; Rousset, *The Legacy of the Bolshevik Revolution*, 31.

41. Carr, *The Russian Revolution from Lenin to Stalin*, 124, 128, 161; Hindus, *House without a Roof*, 217.

42. Lenin, *Collected Works*, vol. 29, 153; Stalin, *Collected Works*, vol. 7, 268. Also see Stone, "Peaceful Coexistence."

43. Harper, *Civic Training in Soviet Russia*, 102–3.

44. Ibid., 103; Lincoln, *Between Heaven and Hell*, 321–22.

45. Nettl, *The Soviet Achievement*, 110, 111, 114; Freeman, "A Year of Grace," 108.

46. A valuable discussion of the prerevolutionary cultural avant-garde and aspects of its interconnection with the early Soviet Republic can be found in Lincoln, *Between Heaven and Hell*, 267–331. On the remarkable cultural work of Lunacharsky and his colleagues, see Fitzpatrick's excellent study, *The Commissariat of Enlightenment*.

47. Bowlt, "Art," 210; Lincoln, *Between Heaven and Hell*, 365; Gray, *The Russian Experiment*

in Art, 235; Freeman, "A Year of Grace," 108–9.

48. Lincoln, *Between Heaven and Hell*, 291–92, 352; Gray, *The Russian Experiment in Art*, 143–83; Bowlt, "Art," 217, 218.

49. Freeman, "A Year of Grace," 110.

50. Slonim and Reavey, eds., *Soviet Literature*, 23–26; Voronsky, *Art as the Cognition of Life*, 260–65, 401–33; see also Polonsky, "Lenin's Views on Art and Culture," 217–52.

51. Lincoln, *Between Heaven and Hell*, 327; Joseph Freeman, "The Soviet Cinema," 217, 221.

52. Freeman, "A Year of Grace," 108;

53. Freeman, "A Year of Grace," 111.

54. Dewey, *Impressions of Soviet Russia*, 115–16.

55. Nettl, *The Soviet Achievement*, 111–12; L. Wilson, *The New Schools of New Russia*, 11–12, 61, 159. Further details are provided in Chamberlin, *Soviet Russia*, 275–88.

56. Tchernoff, *New Horizons*, 284, 285, 286.

57. Simon Liberman, *Building Lenin's Russia*, 200; Fischer in Crossman, ed., *The God That Failed*, 180, 182, 183; Purcell et al., *Russia Today*, 46, 49.

58. Dewey, *Impressions of Soviet Russia*, 112.

59. See, for example, Pelz, *A People's History of Modern Europe*, 127–56; and Hobsbawm, *The Age of Extremes*, 85–177.

60. Freeman, "A Year of Grace," 110, 112; Nettl, *The Soviet Achievement*, 111.

Chapter 9: Consolidation of the Soviet Republic

1. Interesting information on anti-bourgeois policies of the Bolsheviks can be found in Hillquit, *From Marx to Lenin*, 133–36, and also Brailsford, *How the Soviets Work*, 61–64. Does the "dictatorship of the proletariat" mean that capitalists are necessarily denied rights as citizens to vote, express themselves, and organize politically? Hillquit's argument that (according to Marx) it doesn't—assuming that there is no effort by these capitalists to overturn proletarian rule by force and violence—has been corroborated in Draper's *The "Dictatorship of the Proletariat" from Marx to Lenin*.

2. See Hunt, *The Political Ideas of Marx and Engels*; Draper, ed., *Karl Marx and Frederick Engels*.

3. For sources consistent with this perspective, see Chamberlin, *Soviet Russia*; S. Chase, Dunn, and Tugwell, eds., *Soviet Russia in the Second Decade*; Purcell et al., *Russia Today*.

4. Dune, *Notes of a Red Guard*, 228.

5. Ibid., 228, 230.

6. Daniels, *The Conscience of the Revolution*, 115–16, 117–18.

7. Pirani, *The Russian Revolution in Retreat*, 1–2, 45, 53, 66, 69, 71.

8. Clements, *Bolshevik Feminist*, 179; Allen, *Alexander Shlyapnikov*, 160; Porter, *Alexandra Kollontai*, 351–52.

9. Kollontai, *Selected Writings*, 163–64, 168–69, 171–72, 189, 192, 199–200.

10. Ibid., 175; Avrich, *Kronstadt, 1921*, 33.

11. Avrich, *Kronstadt, 1921*, 35, 36, 51.

12. McAuley, "Party and State in Petrograd during the Civil War," 53; Husband, *Workers' Control and Centralization in the Russian Revolution*, 8.

13. Avrich, *Kronstadt, 1921*, 202, 211, 242, 243.

14. Serge, *Memoirs of a Revolutionary*, 150–51. Avrich's scholarship lends credence to this analysis, as does that of Farber, *Before Stalinism*, 184, 189–95.

15. I'm offering here a slightly modified version of the analysis in W. Chase, *Workers, Society, and the Soviet State*, 294–97.

16. Such terminological matters are, of course, secondary to the fluid actualities of the time—an issue admirably wrestled with in Twiss, *Trotsky and the Problem of Soviet Bureaucracy*, and van der Linden, *Western Marxism and the Soviet Union*.

17. Deutscher, *The Prophet Unarmed*, 54, 73.

18. Serge, *Memoirs of a Revolutionary*, 151.

19. Trotsky, *Leon Trotsky on the Paris Commune*, 56.

20. See excerpts from Lenin, "The Party Crisis" and "On the Trade Union," in *Revolution, Democracy, Socialism*, 336.

21. Serge, *Memoirs of a Revolutionary*, 155.

22. Lenin cited and his comments discussed, along with Koenker's critique, in Le Blanc, *Lenin and the Revolutionary Party*, 274, 347n31. Also see Koenker, *Party, State, and Society in the Russian Civil War*, 81–104; Murphy, *Revolution and Counterrevolution*, 73–74.

23. Pirani, *The Russian Revolution in Retreat*, 22–23.

24. Dune, *Notes of a Red Guard*, 229–30.

25. Pirani, *The Russian Revolution in Retreat*, 55, 91–92.

26. Ibid., 142.

27. All of these groups are discussed in Pirani's challenging work; see also Daniels, *Conscience of the Revolution*.

28. See Paul Le Blanc, *Leon Trotsky*, from which portions of this section are reproduced. This section also draws substantially from my review essay "Bolshevism and Revolutionary Democracy," *New Politics*, Winter 2009, which expresses differences I have with some of the analysis presented by Simon Pirani's *The Russian Revolution in Retreat*.

29. Marik, *Reinterrogating the Classical Marxist Discourses of Revolutionary Democracy*, 477.

30. *Writings of Leon Trotsky, 1936–37*, 426.

31. Marik, *Reinterrogating the Classical Marxist Discourses*, 379–80.

32. Pirani, *The Russian Revolution in Retreat*, 195–96.

33. Berger, *Shipwreck of a Generation*, 70–71.

34. Murphy, *Revolution and Counterrevolution*, 73, 74.

35. Dune, *Notes of a Red Guard*, 230.

36. Strong, *The First Time in History*, 36–38.

37. For a rich survey of the issues, most of which cannot be dealt with here, see Fitzpatrick, Rabinowitch, and Stites, eds., *Russia in the Era of NEP: Explorations in Soviet Society and Culture*.

38. Nove, *An Economic History of the USSR*, 86; W. Chase, *Workers, Society, and the Soviet State*, 53–56, 295; Liberman, *Building Lenin's Russia*, 95, 144; Murphy, *Revolution and Counterrevolution*, 83; Reswick, *I Dreamt Revolution*, 119, 164–65; Mazour, *Soviet Economic Development*, 30.

39. Chamberlin, *Soviet Russia*, 36.

40. Carr, *The Bolshevik Revolution*, vol. 2, 294, 295, 309–10, 312.

41. Ibid., 321–22, 323; Sorenson, *The Life and Death of Soviet Trade Unionism*, 179.

42. Chamberlin, *Soviet Russia*, 415–16.

43. Quoted in ibid., 201.

44. Duranty, *I Write as I Please*, 139, 140.

45. Lyons, *Assignment in Utopia*, 84–85.

46. Reswick, *I Dreamt Revolution*, 53, 54; Duranty, *I Write as I Please*, 138–50.

47. Serge, *Memoirs of a Revolutionary*, 233, 234.

48. Sorenson, *The Life and Death of Soviet Trade Unionism*, 179, 183–84.

49. Strong, *The First Time in History*, 244, 245.

50. Ibid., 236, 237, 241, 239.

51. Chamberlin, *Confessions of an Individualist*, 68–69; Rousset, *The Legacy of the Bolshevik Revolution*, 28.

52. Rousset, *The Legacy of the Bolshevik Revolution*, 25.

53. Stalin, "Address to the Graduates of the Red Army Academies," 7; Trotsky, *The Revolution Betrayed*, 137.

54. Lewin, *Russia/USSR/Russia*, 171, 175, 198.

55. Trotsky, *The Revolution Betrayed*, 112.

56. Ibid., 90, 112–13.

57. Reiman, *The Birth of Stalinism*, 119; Trotsky, *The Revolution Betrayed*, 93, 95, 96–97; Tucker, *Stalin in Power*, 266.

58. Ferro, *The Bolshevik Revolution*, 275; Lewin, *The Making of the Soviet System*, 200; E. Mandel, *Power and Money*, 72–73; S. A. Smith, *The Russian Revolution*, 69.

59. Serge, *Memoirs of a Revolutionary*, xxx.

60. Rousset, *The Legacy of the Bolshevik Revolution*, 21. In his account, Rousset tends to see 1921—with the brutal Kronstadt suppression and the "retreat" into the NEP—as representing the decisive defeat for the October Revolution. My own view, argued in this account, is that the process was more complex and extended, but this does not erase the validity of Rousset's more general point.

61. Murphy, *Revolution and Counterrevolution*, 187; Stalin, "Interview Between J. V. Stalin and Roy Howard," and "Political Report to the 16th Congress of the CPSU(B)"; Van Ree, *The Political Thought of Joseph Stalin*, 3–4.

62. This and other portions of this section are taken from Le Blanc, "Reflections on the Meaning of Stalinism," 87, 97–98.

63. Duranty, *I Write as I Please*, 262, 274.

64. Rousset, *The Legacy of the Bolshevik Revolution*, 87.

65. Trotsky's subsequent sensitivity and insights regarding this matter are presented in Le Blanc, Feeley, and Twiss, *Leon Trotsky and the Organizational Principles of the Revolutionary Party*. An interesting and thoughtful discussion can also be found in Rousset, *The Legacy of the Bolshevik Revolution*, 81–83.

66. Hindus, *Humanity Uprooted*, 162–65, 167, 169–70; Hindus, *The Kremlin's Human Dilemma*, 188, 193, 194.

67. Nettl, *Rosa Luxemburg*, vol. 1, 406; Zinoviev, "The Social Roots of Opportunism"; Bukharin, *Historical Materialism*, 311; Twiss, *Trotsky and the Problem of Soviet Bureaucracy*, 32, 239. Trotsky's analysis dovetails with the important contributions of Rakovsky,

Selected Writings on Opposition in the USSR, 1923–30, 124–36, 158–65.

68. Ciliga, *The Russian Enigma*, 121.

69. Ibid., 82.

70. Trotsky, *The Revolution Betrayed*, 120.

71. Lewin, *The Soviet Century*, 308.

72. The persistence of vibrant revolutionary ideals and commitments among many people in the international Communist movement, including in the USSR, during the post-1924 period comes through clearly in a number of memoirs, including Fischer, *Men and Politics*; Freeman, *An American Testament*; Haywood, *Black Bolshevik*; Leviné-Meyer, *Inside German Communism*; Poretsky, *Our Own People*; Regler, *The Owl of Minerva*; Strong, *I Change Worlds*; Trepper, *The Great Game*; and Vidali, *Diary of the Twentieth Congress of the Communist Party of the Soviet Union*, as well as already-cited accounts by Barmine, Berger, and Kravchenko.

73. Freeman et al., *Voices of October*, 50, 51.

74. Ibid., 45.

75. Rühle, *Literature and Revolution*, 5–6; Serge, *Memoirs of a Revolutionary*, 177, 178.

76. Reavey and Slonim, eds., *Soviet Literature*, 18.

77. Eastman, *Artists in Uniform*, 63; Serge, *Memoirs of a Revolutionary*, 310.

78. Reavey and Slonim, eds., *Soviet Literature*, 20–21.

79. Eastman, *Artists in Uniform*, 50; Voronsky, *Art as the Cognition of Life*, 236, 241; Zavalishin, *Early Soviet Writers*, 121, 123.

80. Reavey and Slonim, eds., *Soviet Literature*, 21–22.

81. Karlinsky, "Died and Survived"; Lincoln, *Between Heaven and Hell*, 274–80, 315–17; Zavalishin, *Early Soviet Writers*, 20, 21, 22; Serge, *Memoirs of a Revolutionary*, 177, 178; Rühle, *Literature and Revolution*, 9.

82. Voronsky, *Art as the Cognition of Life*, 240.

83. Quoted in Serge, *Memoirs of a Revolutionary*, 229.

84. Trotsky quoted in Freeman, "Year of Grace," 112; Mayakovsky quoted in Zavalishin, 81.

85. Rühle, *Literature and Revolution*, 17; Zavalishin, *Early Soviet Writers*, 77; Serge, *Memoirs of a Revolutionary*, 310.

Chapter 10: Inevitabilities and Otherwise

1. Engels, letter to Nikolai Danielson, 24 February 1893.

2. Chamberlin, *The Evolution of a Conservative*, 63.

3. Yalom, *Staring at the Sun*, 83, 84.

4. Wolfe, *The Bridge and the Abyss*, 33, 34, 36; Serge, *Memoirs of a Revolutionary*, 156

5. Fromm, "The Revolutionary Character," in *The Dogma of Christ and Other Essays*, 151. The full study can be found in Fromm, *The Working Class in Weimar Germany: A Psychological and Sociological Study*. Theoretical perspectives related to the study can be found in Fromm, *The Crisis of Psychoanalysis*. Also see Braune, *Erich Fromm's Revolutionary Hope*, 3–46, and Burston, *The Legacy of Erich Fromm*, 98–132—both of which provide scholarly examinations of the 1929 study, its context and implications, and Fromm's explication of "social character."

6. Fromm, "The Revolutionary Character," 152–53.
7. Ibid., 151–52, 154.
8. Ibid., 153, 154, 155–56.
9. Ibid., 157–58, 159–60, 162, 163–64, 165–66, 168.
10. Ibid., 170, 171.
11. Marshall Berman, *All That Is Solid Melts into Air*, 118–20. For a characterization of capitalist civilization as having this "demonic" quality, see Tillich, *Perspectives on 19th and 20th Century Protestant Theology*, 59–60, 85–88, 151, 155–56, 170, 184–85; and *The Socialist Decision*, 131–34, 172–73.
12. Löwy, "Marxism and Religion," *On Changing the World*, 27–28.
13. Deutscher, "Trotsky in Our Time," in *Marxism in Our Time*, 36.
14. Summary drawn from Le Blanc, "Uneven and Combined Development and the Sweep of History."
15. This is based on a fascinating polemic during the 1960s between Hal Draper and Max Nomad. Draper's original contribution, a minor classic entitled *The Two Souls of Socialism*, has been published in a number of places as an article and pamphlet. In my opinion, his harmonization in that essay of democracy with the revolutionary Marxist tradition is fundamentally correct yet, as this entire study suggests, is tidier and more schematic than the realities. Nomad criticized it in "Is There a Socialism From Below?," and Draper responded with a two-part rejoinder: "A Reply to Max Nomad: Is Oligarchy Inevitable?" (the important qualification cited here appearing on page 70 of the first part of the rejoinder).
16. Tilly, *Democracy*, 24, 74, 76, 110–20, 204, 205.
17. Luxemburg, "The Russian Revolution," in *Socialism or Barbarism*, 237.

Methodological Appendix: Analytical Tools

1. Soboul, *The French Revolution 1787–1799*, 612; Nomad, *Dreamers, Dynamiters and Demagogues*, 236.
2. Soboul, *Understanding the French Revolution*, 271. See also Jaurès, *A Socialist History of the French Revolution*; Mathiez, *The French Revolution*; and Lefebvre, *The French Revolution*, 2 vols.
3. For discussion of this variant of Marxism, see Le Blanc, *From Marx to Gramsci*, and E. Mandel, *The Place of Marxism in History*. Impacts on the twentieth century are the focus of many volumes, including Mills, *The Marxists*, and Priestland, *The Red Flag*.
4. Burke's *Reflections on the Revolution in France* and Paine's *The Rights of Man* can be found in numerous editions. On 1989 controversies, see Hornblower, "Liberté, Egalité, Fraternité?" Earlier scholarly debates are reflected in Kaplow, ed., *New Perspectives on the French Revolution*, Greenlaw, ed., *The Social Origins of the French Revolution*. Assaulting the Marxist position are Furet, *Interpreting the French Revolution*; and Schama, *Citizens: A Chronicle of the French Revolution*. Marxist perspectives are elaborated in the works of Soboul, cited above, and—from a somewhat different slant—Guerin, *Class Struggle in the First French Republic*; also see Rudé, *The French Revolution*, and Heller, *The*

Bourgeois Revolution in France.

5.   On the first American Revolution, there are many recent Marxist-influenced contributions, including G. B. Nash, *The Urban Crucible*; Countryman, *The American Revolution*; E. Foner, *Tom Paine and Revolutionary America*. Controversial interpretations by earlier Marxist historians include Aptheker, *The American Revolution*, and P. Foner, *Labor and the American Revolution*. Literature on contending interpretations includes Greene, ed., *The Reinterpretation of the American Revolution*; Wellenreuther, "Labor in the Era of the American Revolution"; G. B. Nash, Smith, and Hoerder, "Laboring Americans and the American Revolution." On the "second American Revolution," i.e., the Civil War and Reconstruction, see: Du Bois, *Black Reconstruction in America*; Aptheker, *American Negro Slave Revolts*; Genovese, *The Political Economy of Slavery*; Montgomery, *Beyond Equality*; Stampp and Litwack, eds., *Reconstruction: An Anthology of Revisionist Writings*; E. Foner, *Politics and Ideology in the Age of the Civil War*; E. Foner, *Reconstruction: America's Unfinished Revolution*; McPherson, *Battle Cry of Freedom* and *Abraham Lincoln and the Second American Revolution*; B. Levine, *Half Slave and Half Free* and *The Fall of the House of Dixie*.

6.   The literature on the Paris Commune contains sharply conflicting interpretations. For Marx's interpretation, see Draper, ed., *Writings on the Paris Commune*, by Marx and Engels. The classic history is Lissagary, *The History of the Commune of 1871*. Scholarly conservative interpretations can be found in E. Mason, *The Paris Commune*, and Horne, *The Terrible Year: The Paris Commune 1871*, while scholarly left-wing accounts can be found in Jellinek, *The Paris Commune of 1871*; Edwards, *The Paris Commune, 1871*. Also see Hicks and Tucker, eds., *Revolution and Reaction*. An excellent account of how Wilson defined the challenge of the Russian Revolution can be found in N. Levin, Jr., *Woodrow Wilson and World Politics*; Churchill eloquently speaks for himself in Churchill, *The Aftermath*.

7.   E. Mandel, "History Advances over Skepticism," 4.

8.   Valuable memoirs that give a vivid sense of the development of this intellectual current are Kazin, *Starting Out in the Thirties*, and *New York Jew*—although, contrary to this second title, it would be misleading to see this phenomenon in ethnic terms. Counterposed to Kazin's recollections, but interesting in their own right, are the memoirs of one of the most important intellectuals who journeyed from left to right—Sidney Hook, *Out of Step*; Alan Wald, *The New York Intellectuals*; and Diggins, *Up from Communism*, are particularly good in tracing the complex trajectory of this current, although regarding Selig Perlman one should consult David Brody, "Selig Perlman," in *Dictionary of American Biography*; A. L. Owen, ed., *Selig Perlman's Lectures on Capitalism and Socialism*. Useful on the background of the post-Marxist political trajectory is Lasch, *The Agony of the American Left*. For a more general intellectual history, see Pells, *The Liberal Mind in a Conservative Age*. Some of the key issues are discussed and debated in Waxman, ed., *The End of Ideology Debate*. An informative and stimulating polemic focused on some of the more conservative figures can be found in Peter Steinfels, *The Neoconservatives*; a scholarly celebration is offered in G. H. Nash, *The Conservative Intellectual Movement in America since 1945*.

9.   Bell, *The Coming of Post-industrial Society*, 40, 55.

10. Perlman, *A Theory of the Labor Movement*, vii, viii, 4–6.

11. Rostow, *Stages of Economic Growth*, 158.

12. Burnham, *The Machiavellians*, 162, 247, 253, 254, 346.

13. Dewey, *The Living Thoughts of Thomas Jefferson*, 27.

14. Joseph A. Schumpeter, *Capitalism, Socialism and Democracy*, 253, 264.

15. Burnham, *The Machiavellians*, 236, 254, 270; Burnham, *The Managerial Revolution*, x.

16. Mayo, *An Introduction to Democratic Theory*, 270, 271, 286, 287.

17. Dahl, *A Preface to Democratic Theory*, 131, 132, 133.

18. See, for example, Rostow, *The United States in the World Arena*, 503–15; Bell, *The End of Ideology*, 74, 90–91, 404–5.

19. Dewey, "Democracy and Educational Administration," in *Intelligence in the Modern World*, 401; Macpherson, *Democratic Theory*, 173.

20. Bachrach, *The Theory of Democratic Elitism*, 93–94, 7, 8. These and related issues are discussed and debated in greater detail in the various contributions to Green, ed., *Democracy*, as well as Etzioni-Halevy, ed., *Classes and Elites in Democracy and Democratization*.

21. Dewey, "Democracy and Educational Administration," 401–3. Also relevant is discussion of Dewey's perspectives in Westbrook, *John Dewey and American Democracy*, 429–62.

22. Laski, *Introduction to Politics*, 14, 16, 31, 33, 72.

23. For documentation on the democratic nature of Marx's political thought, see Hunt, *The Political Ideas of Marx and Engels*. On Lenin's, see N. Harding, *Lenin's Political Thought*, and my own *Lenin and the Revolutionary Party*, as well as Lenin, *Revolution, Democracy, Socialism*.

24. Novack, *Democracy and Revolution*, 238, 239, 240.

25. Ibid., 237.

26. Rueschemeyer, E. Stephens, and J. Stephens, *Capitalist Development and Democracy*, 43, 47; Roper, *The History of Democracy*, 2; Ishay, *The History of Human Rights*, 9.

27. Regarding the debate on the extent to which democracy is possible in such economically underdeveloped areas as late twentieth-century Latin America, see Wiarda, "Can Democracy Be Exported?"; O'Donnell, "The United States, Latin America, Democracy"; Braun, "The Human Rights Question in U.S.-Latin American Relations"; Crahan, "Human Rights and U.S. Foreign Policy"; Di Palma, "Comment: Democracy, Human Rights, and the U.S. Role in Latin America"; Torres-Rivas, "Comment: Constraints on Policies regarding Human Rights and Democracy"—all in Middlebrook and Rico, eds., *The United States and Latin America in the 1980s*, 325–480. Also see Malloy and Seligson, eds. *Authoritarians and Democrats*, particularly two essays by Seligson: "Democratization in Latin America" and "Development, Democratization and Decay."

28. Laski, *Introduction to Politics*, 28.

29. Novack, *Democracy and Revolution*, 242.

30. This section draws from Le Blanc, *Leon Trotsky*, 78–83.

31. Trotsky, *History of the Russian Revolution*, vol. 1, 5–6.

32. T. Harding, "Dependency, Nationalism and the State in Latin America," 4; Trotsky, *Permanent Revolution and Results and Prospects*, 131. Also relevant are Chilcote and Johnson, eds., *Theories of Development: Mode of Production or Dependency?*; Chilcote and Edelstein, *Latin America: Capitalist and Socialist Perspectives of Development and Underdevelopment*.

33. Löwy, *The Politics of Combined and Uneven Development*, 40, 43; Deutscher, "Trotsky in Our Time," *Marxism in Our Time*, 36. An essential source is Day and Gaido, eds., *Witnesses to Permanent Revolution*. Also see Nadezhda Krupskaya's discussion of the evolution of Lenin's thinking in 1915–16 regarding the linkage of democratic and socialist revolutions in Krupskaya, *Reminiscences of Lenin*, 328–30. Shanin, ed., *Late Marx and the Russian Road*, documents Marx himself inclining toward a "permanentist" approach in analyzing revolutionary possibilities in late nineteenth-century Russia. In their March 1850 "Address of the Central Committee to the Communist League" (which concludes with the declaration that the workers' "battle cry must be: The Permanent Revolution"), Marx and Engels lay out the basic perspective, but key elements can also be traced in their *Communist Manifesto*—see Marx, *Political Writings*, vol. 1, 86–87, 98, 319–30. In *Karl Marx and Friedrich Engels*, Bolshevik archivist and historian David Riazanov notes the 1850 circulars happened to be "precisely" what "Lenin, who knew them by heart, used to delight in quoting" (100).

34. Trotsky, *1905*, 49; Trotsky, *Permanent Revolution*, 132.

35. Trotsky, *On the Paris Commune*, 24; Trotsky, *Permanent Revolution*, 69, 70, 72.

36. Trotsky, *On the Paris Commune*, 13.

37. Ibid., 25, 26. The same points can be found in Trotsky's more widely read *Results and Prospects*, published in *Permanent Revolution and Results and Prospects*.

38. Trotsky, *Permanent Revolution*, 133, 278–79.

INDEX

ABOUT
HAYMARKET BOOKS

Haymarket Books is a radical, independent, nonprofit book publisher based in Chicago.

Our mission is to publish books that contribute to struggles for social and economic justice. We strive to make our books a vibrant and organic part of social movements and the education and development of a critical, engaged, international left.

We take inspiration and courage from our namesakes, the Haymarket martyrs, who gave their lives fighting for a better world. Their 1886 struggle for the eight-hour day—which gave us May Day, the international workers' holiday—reminds workers around the world that ordinary people can organize and struggle for their own liberation. These struggles continue today across the globe—struggles against oppression, exploitation, poverty, and war.

Since our founding in 2001, Haymarket Books has published more than five hundred titles. Radically independent, we seek to drive a wedge into the risk-averse world of corporate book publishing. Our authors include Noam Chomsky, Arundhati Roy, Rebecca Solnit, Angela Davis, Howard Zinn, Amy Goodman, Wallace Shawn, Mike Davis, Winona LaDuke, Ilan Pappé, Richard Wolff, Dave Zirin, Keeanga-Yamahtta Taylor, Nick Turse, Dahr Jamail, David Barsamian, Elizabeth Laird, Amira Hass, Mark Steel, Avi Lewis, Naomi Klein, and Neil Davidson. We are also the trade publishers of the acclaimed Historical Materialism Book Series and of Dispatch Books.

ALSO AVAILABLE FROM HAYMARKET BOOKS

IN CELEBRATION OF THE CENTENARY OF THE RUSSIAN REVOLUTION

1905
Leon Trotsky

Alexander Shlyapnikov, 1885–1937
Barbara C. Allen

Alexandra Kollontai: A Biography
Cathy Porter

*All Power to the Soviets: Lenin
1914–1917 (Vol. 2)*
Tony Cliff

The Bolsheviks Come to Power
Alexander Rabinowitch

*Building the Party: Lenin
1893–1914 (Vol. 1)*
Tony Cliff

Clara Zetkin: Selected Writings
Clara Zetkin, edited by Philip
S. Foner, Foreword by Angela
Y. Davis and Rosalyn Baxandall

*Eyewitnesses to the Russian
Revolution*
Edited by Todd Chretien

History of the Russian Revolution
Leon Trotsky

Lenin and the Revolutionary Party
Paul Le Blanc

Lenin Rediscovered
Lars T. Lih

Lenin's Moscow
Alfred Rosmer,
Translated by Ian Birchall

Lenin's Political Thought
Neil Harding

*Leon Trotsky and the Organizational
Principles of the Revolutionary Party*
Dianne Feeley, Paul Le Blanc,
and Thomas Twiss, introduction
by George Breitman

*Leon Trotsky:
An Illustrated Introduction*
Tariq Ali, illustrated by Phil
Evans

Lessons of October
Leon Trotsky

The Life and Death of Leon Trotsky
Natalia Sedova and Victor Serge

*The October Revolution in Prospect
and Retrospect*
John E. Marot

*October Song: Bolshevik Triumph,
Communist Tragedy, 1917–1924*
Paul Le Blanc

*Red Petrograd: Revolution in the
Factories, 1917–1918*
S. A. Smith